INTERNATIONAL LAW ISSUES IN THE SOUTH PACIFIC

International Law Issues in the South Pacific

Edited by

GEOFF LEANE and BARBARA VON TIGERSTROM
University of Canterbury, New Zealand

Routledge
Taylor & Francis Group
LONDON AND NEW YORK

First published 2005 by Ashgate Publishing

Reissued 2018 by Routledge
2 Park Square, Milton Park, Abingdon, Oxon OX14 4RN
711 Third Avenue, New York, NY 10017, USA

Routledge is an imprint of the Taylor & Francis Group, an informa business

A Library of Congress record exists under LC control number: 2005013245

ISBN 13: 978-0-815-38979-8 (hbk)
ISBN 13: 978-1-351-15548-9 (ebk)

Contents

List of Contributors

Michael Barutciski, BA (McGill), LLB (Montreal), LLM (Osgoode), Doctorate in Law (Paris). Assistant Professor, International Studies Programme, Glendon College, York University.

Neil Boister, BA, LLB, LLM (Natal), PhD (Nottingham). Senior Lecturer, School of Law, University of Canterbury.

Alex Conte, LLB (Canterbury), LLM (Hons) (Victoria University of Wellington). Senior Lecturer, School of Law, University of Canterbury.

Scott Davidson, MA (Cambridge). Pro-Vice-Chancellor and Dean, School of Law, University of Canterbury.

Geoff Leane, BEc (Hons) (Adelaide), LLB, LLM (British Columbia), LLM (Harvard). Senior Lecturer, School of Law, University of Canterbury.

Michelle Rogan-Finnemore, BSc (Hons) (Pittsburgh), LLB (Canterbury). Centre Manager, Gateway Antarctica, University of Canterbury.

Barbara von Tigerstrom, BA (Alberta), MA (Toronto), LLB (Toronto), PhD (Cambridge). Senior Lecturer, School of Law, University of Canterbury.

List of Abbreviations

ACP	African, Caribbean and Pacific
AFP	Australian Federal Police
AG	Attorney General
AGO	Australian Greenhouse Office
AIJ	Activities Implemented Jointly
AOSIS	Alliance of Small Island States
APCs	Asia Pacific Consultations
APEC	Asian Pacific Economic Cooperation
APG-ML	Asia Pacific Group on Money Laundering
ASEAN	Association of South East Asian States
AT	Antarctic Treaty
ATCM	Antarctic Treaty Consultative Meeting
ATS	Antarctic Treaty System
Austrac	Australian Transaction Report and Analysis Centre
CBD	Convention on Biological Diversity
CCAMLR	Convention for the Conservation of Antarctic Marine Living Resources
CDM	Clean Development Mechanism
CER	Closer Economic Relations Australia/New Zealand Trade Agreement
CHM	Common Heritage of Mankind
CLAGS	Combined Law Agency Groups
COMNAP	Council of Managers of National Antarctic Programmes
COMSEC	Commonwealth Secretariat
COPs	Conferences of the Parties
CRAMRA	Convention for the Regulation of Antarctic Mineral Resource Activity
CSCAP	Council for Security Cooperation in the Asia Pacific
CTD	Council on Trade and Development
DDA	Doha Development Agenda
DPOS	Domestic Policy Option Statement
DSU	Dispute Settlement Understanding (Understanding on Rules and Procedures Governing the Settlement of Disputes)
EBA	Everything But Arms
EC	European Communities
EEZ	Exclusive Economic Zone
EITs	Economies in Transition
EPA	Economic Partnership Agreement
EXCOM	Executive Committee (UNHCR)
FADTC	Foreign Affairs, Defence and Trade Committee

FATF	Financial Action Task Force (OECD)
FFA	Forum Fisheries Agency
FIU	Financial Intelligence Unit
FLNKS	Kanak Socialist National Liberation Front
FON	Freedom of Navigation
FORUM	Pacific Islands Forum
Forumsec	Forum Secretariat
FRSC	Forum Regional Security Committee
FICs	Forum Island Countries
GAM	Aceh Liberation Front
GATS	General Agreement on Trade in Services
GATT	General Agreement on Tariffs and Trade
GDP	Gross Domestic Product
GHGs	Greenhouse Gases
GSP	Generalized System of Preferences
GSTP	Generalized System of Trade Preferences
IAEA	International Atomic Energy Agency
ICJ	International Court of Justice
IGY	International Geophysical Year
IMB	International Maritime Bureau
IMDG	International Maritime Dangerous Goods
IMO	International Maritime Organization
INF	Irradiated Nuclear Fuel
IP	Information Paper
IPCC	Intergovernmental Panel on Climate Change
IPR/IP	Intellectual Property Rights/Intellectual Property
ISA	International Seabed Authority
IUU	Illegal, Unreported and Unregulated
IWC	International Whaling Convention
JI	Joint Implementation
JUSCANZ	Japan, US, Canada, Australia and New Zealand
LDC	Least Developed Country
LECP	Law Enforcement Cooperation Program
Lomé IV	Fourth ACP-EEC Convention of Lomé
MFN	Most Favoured Nation
MLAT	Mutual Legal Assistance Treaty
MOU	Memorandum of Understanding
MRET	Mandatory Renewable Energy Targets
MSG	Melanesian Spearhead Group
Mt CO2	Million tonnes of Carbon Dioxide
NEECS	National Energy Efficiency and Conservation Strategy
NGA	Negotiated Greenhouse Agreement
NGO	Non-governmental Organization
NGRS	National Greenhouse Response Strategy
NGS	National Greenhouse Strategy
NZP	New Zealand Police

OCO	Oceania Customs Organisation
ODA	Official Development Assistance
ODCCP	Office for Drugs Control and Crime Prevention (UN)
OECD	Organisation for Economic Co-operation and Development
OFC	Offshore Financial Centre
PACER	Pacific Agreement on Closer Economic Relations
PACRIM	Pacific Rim Immigration Intelligence Officer's Conference
PACTRA	Agreement on Trade and Commercial Relations between the Government of Australia and the Government of Papua New Guinea
PICs	Pacific Island Countries
PICCAP	Pacific Island Climate Change Assistance Program
PICTA	Pacific Island Countries Trade Agreement
PIDC	Pacific Immigration Directors Conference
PILOM	Pacific Islands Law Officers Meeting
PNG	Papua New Guinea
PSI	Proliferation Security Initiative
PSSA	Particularly Sensitive Sea Areas
RMA	Resource Management Act
RTA	Regional Trade Agreement
SCAR	Scientific Committee for Antarctic Research
SCM	Subsidies and Countervailing Measures
SDT	Special and Differential Treatment
SIDS	Small Island Developing States
SIS	Small Island States
SLOC	Sea Lines of Communication
SNEC	Safety Navigation and Environment Committee
SOLAS	Safety of Life at Sea
SPARTECA	South Pacific Regional Trade and Economic Cooperation Agreement
SPCPC	South Pacific Chief of Police Conference
SPREP	South Pacific Regional Environmental Programme
SUA	Suppression of Unlawful Act (Against the Safety of Navigation)
SUAPROT	Protocol for the Suppression of Unlawful Acts Against the Safety of Fixed Platforms Located on the Continental Shelf
TBT	Technical Barriers to Trade
TRIPS	Trade-Related Aspects of Intellectual Property Rights
UDHR	Universal Declaration of Human Rights
UN	United Nations
UNCLOS	United Nations Convention on the Law of the Sea
UNESCAP	United Nations Economic and Social Commission for Asia and the Pacific
UNFCCC	UN Framework Convention on Climate Change
UNHCR	United Nations High Commissioner for Refugees
UNODC	UN Office on Drugs and Crime
UNSC	United Nations Security Council

WMD	Weapons of Mass Destruction
WP	Working Paper
WTO	World Trade Organization

Map of the South Pacific Region

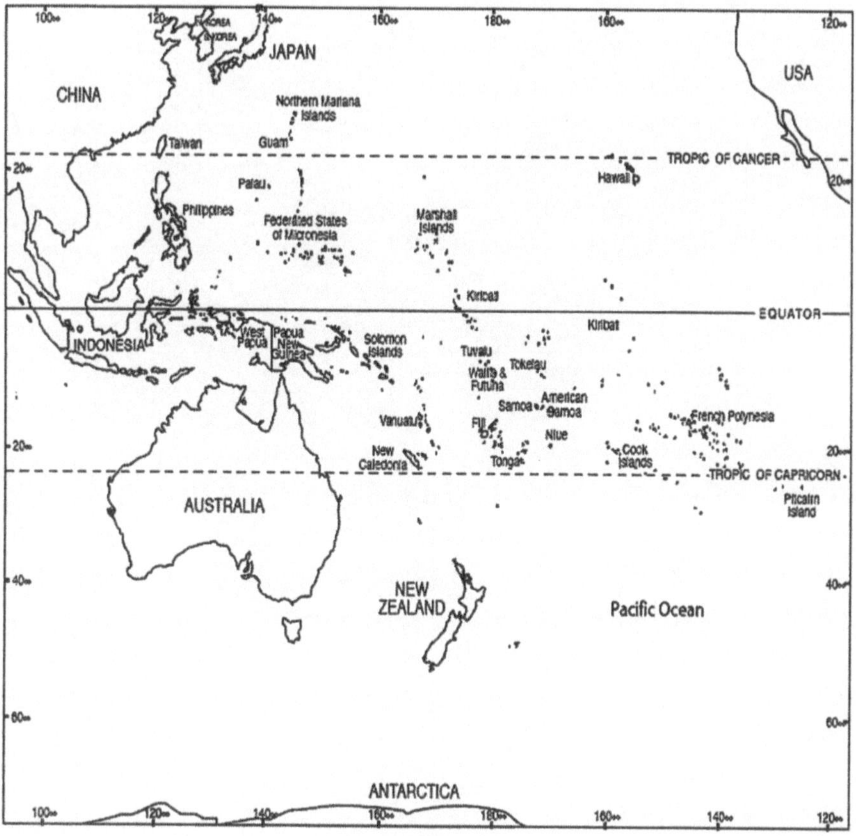

Source: Geography Department, University of Canterbury

Introduction

Geoff Leane and Barbara von Tigerstrom*

The South Pacific is a distinctive and fascinating region that too often escapes the attention of the global community. This book seeks to inform on some of the international legal issues and challenges facing the South Pacific and its varying subject matter reflects the diversity of those issues and challenges. The authors collectively constitute the International Law Group at the University of Canterbury School of Law in Christchurch, New Zealand. Their respective interests and expertise converged to produce this first part of an ongoing engagement with a region that represents, in microcosm, many of the contemporary issues and challenges that confront international law and international lawyers everywhere.

One of the first issues facing those with an interest in this region is how the 'region' itself should be defined. A variety of terms – Pacific, South Pacific, Asia Pacific, Oceania – are often used in different contexts. The Pacific Islands Forum provides some structure, and this grouping of sixteen countries[1] is the core focus of many of the chapters in this volume. However, for some purposes, it is useful and even necessary to look beyond its boundaries to the larger Asia-Pacific region (as in Scott Davidson's chapter on freedom of navigation) or to the unique area of Antarctica and the Southern Ocean on its southern edge (as in Michelle Rogan-Finnemore's chapter on bioprospecting). There are also subgroups within the Forum membership, such as the Forum Island Countries (or Pacific Island Countries), referring to the Forum members except Australia and New Zealand; the Small Island States, including the smallest Forum members;[2] and the Melanesian Spearhead Group.[3]

The various groupings reflect differences in size, ethnicity and common or historical ties and hint at the considerable diversity within the region. If we look at matters of culture, ethnicity, geography, demographics or socio-economic indicators in the region, the diversity is such as to render unrealistic any temptation to simplify consideration of these countries as a collective. For example, Australia and New Zealand are developed states whilst the island countries are either developing or least developed countries. Australia has a land mass of some 7.7 million square km and a population of some 19 million of which 90 per cent is of European extraction; the Cook Islands occupies only 240 square km with a

---

* The editors would like to acknowledge the assistance of Danie Benkman (LLB student, University of Canterbury) in compiling the index.

[1] Australia, Cook Islands, Federated States of Micronesia, Fiji, Kiribati, Nauru, New Zealand, Niue, Palau, Papua New Guinea, Republic of the Marshall Islands, Samoa, Solomon Islands, Tonga, Tuvalu and Vanuatu.

[2] Cook Islands, Kiribati, Nauru, Niue, Republic of the Marshall Islands and Tuvalu.

[3] Fiji, Papua New Guinea, Solomon Islands and Vanuatu.

population of around 16,000 which is 94 per cent Polynesian; Fiji has a land mass of 18,272 square km with a population of around 800,000 which is a little more than half ethnic Fijian but around 40 per cent Indian.

The region includes diverse ethnic groups whose origins are Polynesian, Melanesian and Micronesian, though ethnicity is not fixed. Some island populations have been denuded by emigration. In the case of Cook Islanders four live in New Zealand for every one remaining in the Cook Islands,[4] whilst in the 1970s Niue began to accept immigrants from other Pacific islands because 80 per cent of its own people had emigrated to New Zealand.[5] Today some 92 per cent of Niueans live in Australia or New Zealand.[6] Of the world's two million Polynesians only 14 per cent live in the independent Polynesian nations (Cook Islands, Niue, Tonga and Tuvalu); the rest live in the United States, Australia and New Zealand.[7] Those emigrant populations have been a critical source of income through remittances. Patterns of migration between the islands have always been a feature of Pacific history and were further complicated by the arrival of metropolitan European powers in the sixteenth century when Spain first settled Guam, later followed by the British, French and Americans. Asian migration also followed later, for example, in Indian migration to Fiji and Chinese migration throughout the region.

The political units of the island countries also demonstrate a fascinating diversity, perhaps more than any equivalent population in the world. They include a kingdom (Tonga), a state in which only chiefs may stand for election (Samoa), a republic with different electorates for different ethnic groups (Fiji) and the world's smallest republic (Nauru). By and large democracy has prospered in the form of regular elections, respect for democratic processes and conformity with constitutions. In only one case (Fiji) has power not devolved to a government elected by majority vote. Generally the Pacific island states have rated highly in respect of political and civil rights, particularly for a region of less developed states.[8] Relations between them are relatively harmonious, perhaps in significant part because they share no land borders. A risk, however, is that in light of the very small populations and (often) a lack of institutional checks and balances, leaders may have irresistible opportunities to run countries as personal fiefdoms and political and bureaucratic elites may wield unhealthy measures of power.[9] All of the island states save Tonga have at some time been colonies, and colonial influence remains strong in many, for example, in the widely adopted Westminster system of government. Independent national governments became the norm in the second half of the twentieth century and most adopted the constitutional arrangements of their former colonizers. However, the region still contains

---

[4] Ron Crocombe, *The South Pacific* (2001) 54.

[5] Ibid 64.

[6] Ibid 66.

[7] Ibid 66-7.

[8] Ibid 482, footnote 7.

[9] See, e.g. Asian Development Bank, *Responding to the Priorities of the Poor: A Pacific Strategy for the Asian Development Bank 2005–2009* (2004) 94 (examples include Nauru, Solomon Islands and Marshall Islands); Crocombe, above n 4, ch. 19.

overseas territories of the United States[10] and France[11] and a non-self-governing territory of New Zealand (Tokelau), as well as countries in free association with New Zealand[12] or the United States.[13] Economic and political ties with former colonial powers in the form of development assistance, trade and other forms of cooperation remain important. The South Pacific receives more international aid per capita than any other region. However, that introduces yet another aspect of vulnerability as aid levels have been declining and average real income per capita is virtually unchanged over the past decade.[14] Australia is the largest aid donor but is being increasingly challenged by East Asian countries and Japan in particular.

The region's resources are diverse and unevenly distributed. Papua New Guinea, for example, is blessed with mineral wealth, forests, agricultural and fish resources and a substantial domestic market of almost five million people, though it is constrained by poor infrastructure and political instability. Fiji enjoys a relatively diversified economy (including tourism, gold mining and sugar) and work force with a population of some 800,000 but is constrained by ethnic and communal tensions and the threat of loss of preferential market access to Europe. Some of the smaller islands are dependent on narrow resource bases which limit their opportunities for diversification. Generally speaking most observers see the region as having under-performed economically given its high level of aid and relatively plentiful natural resources.[15] Economic indicators vary widely; for example, in terms of US$ Gross National Income per capita, Solomon Islands ($580) and Kiribati ($960) lagged well behind Fiji ($2130) and Palau ($6820).[16] Some countries have high levels of poverty despite having relatively plentiful natural resources, some have moderate resources but higher levels of social development, while others have a very small resource base and hence are extremely vulnerable.[17]

Although the smallest islands and those most limited in resources are most at risk in many respects, vulnerability is a quality shared to some degree by all of the island countries in the region. They manifest that vulnerability in a variety of contexts ranging from the physical environment to international markets. They face multiple risks, including volatile markets, resource depletion, crime, political instability and racial tensions, from both internal (for example, very small populations and limited resources) and external (for example, crime and globalization) sources. These vulnerabilities raise the question of whether some of

---

[10] American Samoa, Guam and Commonwealth of the Northern Mariana Islands.

[11] French Polynesia, New Caledonia and Wallis and Futuna. French Polynesia and New Caledonia are now 'overseas countries' of France with greater autonomy.

[12] Cook Islands and Niue. Samoa has a Treaty of Friendship with New Zealand.

[13] Federated States of Micronesia, Palau and Republic of the Marshall Islands.

[14] Crocombe, above n 4, 390.

[15] See, e.g. Asian Development Bank, *Responding to the Priorities of the Poor*, above n 9, ch. 3.

[16] Ibid 41 (Table A3) (2002 data).

[17] Ibid 19. The first group is said to include Papua New Guinea, Solomon Islands and Vanuatu, the second group Cook Islands, Fiji, Federated States of Micronesia, Samoa, Tonga, and the third Kiribati, Republic of the Marshall Islands, Nauru and Tuvalu.

these states are indeed viable, at least in the sense of being functioning and functional states in the modern international order of sovereign, independent states. Whilst all except the Cook Islands and Niue (which are in free association with New Zealand), are members of the United Nations, at least some might be characterized as 'quasi-states, brought into existence by external forces, and shored up by international and bilateral support'.[18] They are cloaked with the mantle of sovereignty but lack the necessary capacities to practise it, and indeed in some cases political independence may not have been either desired or desirable.

One way of dealing with vulnerability and recurring questions about the viability of small island states is to move toward regional integration. Regional institutions in this part of the world are relatively undeveloped compared to most other regions. The Pacific Islands Forum, recently described by its Secretary-General as the 'peak Pacific regional political body',[19] has a Secretariat, holds annual meetings of heads of government and provides a forum for cooperation and dialogue on a range of issues. In the larger Asia Pacific region, Asia Pacific Economic Cooperation (APEC) has an important, though limited, role.[20] Generally regionalist impulses are restricted to institutional linkages, cooperative networks in matters of trade, culture, religion and so forth, but not significant political integration in the sense of compromises of sovereignty to a collective entity such as, say, the European Union. Certainly compared to Europe or even the less developed regional regimes of Africa or the Americas, these regional organizations represent fairly tentative steps toward formalized regional integration. However, as will be seen in a number of the following chapters, pressures for greater integration and cooperation are increasingly felt in the region, for example in trade or security. As this book goes to press, a draft 'Pacific Plan for Strengthening Regional Cooperation and Integration' has been released for public comment.[21]

But regionalist currents are hampered by some commonality of internal problems, for example, endemic corruption, incompetent governance, excessive bureaucracy, racism, political instability, widespread unemployment and, perhaps most importantly, resistance within the island countries themselves to any erosion of a sovereignty only recently attained. More recent crises have included administrative decay and conflict in the Solomon Islands, constitutional crises in Vanuatu and Fiji, ethnic strife in Fiji, class struggle in Tonga, threats of national disintegration in Papua New Guinea, massive emigration from the Cook Islands and Niue, and the tenuous viability of countries like Tuvalu. As much as these

---

[18] A.V. Hughes, *A Different Kind of Voice: Development and Dependence in the Pacific Islands* (Asian Development Bank (Office of Pacific Operations) 1998) 13.

[19] Greg Urwin, 'Preventing Conflict in the Pacific: What Role for the Pacific Islands Forum' (Keynote Address at the Conference on 'Securing a Peaceful Pacific: Preventing and Resolving Conflict', University of Canterbury, 15 October 2004).

[20] Australia, New Zealand and Papua New Guinea are among the 21 'member economies' of APEC.

[21] Pacific Islands Forum Secretariat, 'The Pacific Plan for Strengthening Regional Cooperation and Integration: Working Draft' (2005) New Zealand Ministry of Foreign Affairs and Trade <http://www.mfat.govt.nz/foreign/regions/pacific/pifsec/pacificplan.html> at 22 February 2005.

create challenges for internal governance, they also present obstacles to effective cooperation.

Another impetus to regionalism derives from the desire for greater influence in the international community. In some contexts, the island countries can wield influence disproportionate to their size – although the political units of the South Pacific are the smallest in the world, the fourteen island states of the Pacific Islands Forum, representing seven million people, collectively assert more voting power in some fora than the 3.5 billion people of China, India, Japan and the USA together! However, their economic and political influence are in other important respects severely limited by their small size and remoteness, giving an added incentive for regional integration.

These questions are not directly addressed in the chapters here in, for example, a review of alternative models of regionalism which might redress asymmetries of viability both in the region and globally, or in a comprehensive review of the cooperative arrangements which reflect intra-regional relationships. That would constitute another project which will receive much attention in the coming years.[22] Rather the relationships within and beyond the region are revealed in the context of (mostly) external challenges such as international crime and security issues, the challenges presented by global warming and refugee issues, and difficult resource and geographical challenges to trade. Those regional relationships also reveal the gravitational force and influence asserted by the regional hegemon, Australia, and to a lesser extent New Zealand, both Western liberal democracies geographically located in a diverse region of small island developing states. But as in the wider global order the United States exerts great influence, not just directly in its 'area of influence' but more generally in maritime issues, security issues, trade and the inter-governmental 'management' of external issues such as crime.

The international community is well aware of the region's challenges and also of the fluctuating strategic significance of the region and its component states. The various island countries of the South Pacific are presently in a process of realigning their relations with external powers as the strategic importance of the individual countries is constantly re-evaluated and exploited (by all sides). The region, like much of the global order, appears to be in a period of transition as it moves from a post-colonial, post-Cold War period to a yet-to-be-written future of considerable uncertainty and risk. The island states share serious difficulties in adapting to external forces such as globalization, the need to 'fit' into the global order as functional sovereign states and the need to resist some of the more malevolent forces of that global order, for example, international crime and terrorism.

This collection does not attempt to present a comprehensive overview of the issues facing the Pacific region. Indeed, those with local knowledge will notice the

[22] For example, the University of Canterbury School of Law is sponsoring a post-doctoral study of possible models of pooled sovereignty which might serve to empower Pacific Island states in a framework of supra-national regional governance without fatally compromising local aspirations (estimated completion late 2007).

absence of some critically important issues, such as fisheries and regional peace building efforts, from the list of topics covered. Rather these chapters explore a wide variety of issues in international law and seek to relate them to the particular context of the region. In that sense they might be characterized as a range of mostly external global forces to which South Pacific countries are responding, either voluntarily or under pressure from either or both of regional and global powers. Such tensions between authentic local voluntariness and external pressures are clearly at play in most of these chapters.

In the first chapter Michael Barutciski considers the dilemma posed by mass refugee flows, wherein the tension is perhaps best symbolized by Australia's treatment of the Tampa boat people and their subsequent relocation to Nauru. The so-called 'Pacific solution' of offering financial inducements to a third state to accept the refugees can arguably be seen as a pragmatic compromise between advocates of open borders and those who would impose only minimal legal obligations on states in relation to the protection of asylum seekers. It nonetheless poses difficult moral and political issues concerning regional cooperation.

In Chapter 2 Neil Boister considers the issue of transnational crime in the South Pacific and the efforts of Pacific Forum countries to suppress such threats within a framework of international obligations. He argues that the participation of small island states in this global regime is not necessarily benign as local consent is not always authentic and the legitimacy of the regulatory regime is thereby threatened. There is a threat to the sovereignty of reluctant states that may need to be addressed by some kind of empowered regional organization which more effectively represents their interests.

On a parallel topic Alex Conte looks to the implications of international terrorism in the South Pacific in Chapter 3. Whilst the exposure of island states to terrorism, however defined, has been minimal and its immediate relevance therefore questionable it is another example of heightened global concerns manifesting themselves as local issues. As a specific example of transnational crime the risks are as much about island states being used as unwitting conduits for terrorists aiming at third states as they are about the islands themselves representing terrorist targets.

Chapter 4 looks to wider stage as Scott Davidson reviews the law of the sea and freedom of navigation in the Asia Pacific region. The tension between principles of closed seas and of seas being open to all nations appears to be re-emerging and has important implications for island states such as those of the South Pacific, as well as generally. That tension has produced a somewhat unstable relationship between security conscious coastal states and those seeking maximum freedom of navigation for trade, resource exploitation and naval mobility.

Climate change and the Kyoto Protocol, the subject of Geoff Leane's Chapter 5, goes more directly to the vulnerability of small island states in the South Pacific. Their contributions to climate change through greenhouse gas emissions are miniscule yet they are perhaps the most vulnerable of all states to climate change impacts on weather patterns and rising sea levels. As with transnational crime and international terrorism they are forced to react to aspects of globalization which are not of their making and which are largely beyond their control. The policy responses of the regional powers, Australia and New Zealand, reflect the wider international order and give little cause for comfort.

Antarctica typically presents its own peculiar issues in Michelle Rogan-Finnemore's chapter on bioprospecting in Antarctica and the Southern Ocean. As a continent with no permanent population and no widely recognized sovereign it presents unique jurisdictional problems in any attempt at regulating activities there. Bioprospecting is an emerging issue which challenges those states that participate in the Antarctic Treaty System as well as the international community whose interests are less well defined. Australia and New Zealand are claimant states with direct interests but must, like other participating states, seek consensus solutions which will protect the integrity of the continent whilst meeting the legitimate scientific and increasingly commercial interests of the international community.

Finally, in Chapter 7 Barbara von Tigerstrom deals with the challenges of development and international trade in the island states of the South Pacific. Not only is vulnerability an underlying theme but here the question of viability is most directly addressed. In a climate of free trade many of these states simply lack both sizable domestic markets and the necessary efficiencies for an export base to sustain a viable economy. They rely largely on aid, remittances and privileged access to foreign markets, all of which are in some degree uncertain and in some cases presently threatened. The extent to which international trading arrangements adequately respond to the difficulties faced by these countries is questionable, and again questions about the most effective forms of regional cooperation are raised.

It will be apparent to even the casual reader that the outline of a bigger picture emerges from these chapters. As in the wider global order there is a fundamental question that goes to the relevance of international legal rules and principles to less (and least) developed states which lack the resources and infrastructures to fully participate in that order yet are increasingly being pressured to do so. Those pressures are evident here with respect to mass refugee flows, transnational crime, terrorism, law of the sea and trade. The participation of at least the small island states of the South Pacific is sometimes little more than symbolic as they respond to, and sometimes exploit, the pressures from local and global powers. Indeed in many cases the island states have not assented to the various instruments – for example, few have ratified the two main refugee treaties[23] and there has been a mixed degree of consent to the various counter-terrorism instruments.[24]

As a final observation it is probably fair to say that regional issues have been significantly under-researched – models of regional governance, for example, or mitigation options for climate change – but this book represents a contribution toward considering the impacts of international law frameworks as (mostly) external forces requiring local responses. It highlights the growing importance of the interface between these small regional states and the global order which exerts an increasingly powerful gravitational force upon them.

---

[23] See the chapter by Michael Barutciski.

[24] See the chapter by Alex Conte.

Chapter 1

Mass Refugee Flows and Burden-sharing in the South Pacific

Michael Barutciski

Introduction

Commentaries on refugee law are often divided between two polarized views: refugee advocates who tend to present maximalist positions on the entitlements enjoyed by asylum seekers and border control proponents who tend to minimize the protection obligations imposed on States. The problem surfaces when the politics of the situation marginalize the law. For example, in response to recent political troubles in Haiti and concerns about an exodus of migrants toward the coast of Florida, the President of the United States declared that '[US officials] will turn back any [Haitian] refugee that attempts to reach our shore, and that message needs to be very clear as well to the Haitian people'.[1] The fact that US officials were in fact not returning boat people without a screening process indicates the priorities in the public message preoccupying the President's speechwriter: national political leaders have to appear tough on border control and may even be unaware of the actual legal protection accorded to migrants by those implementing official policy.[2] Political leaders are not the only actors using refugee policy to score public opinion points: the response of non-governmental organizations (NGOs) to the President's declaration is equally troubling. Most refugee advocates went on to condemn the supposed policy as a violation of international law,[3] even though they must be aware that the US Supreme Court has already established that their interpretation is not correct in terms of the law as it is applied in the US.[4]

[1] Human Rights Watch, 'US: Don't Turn Away Haitian Refugees' (Press Release, 26 February 2004).

[2] See 'Haitians flee to US in boats', CNN, 27 February 2004 <http://www.cnn.com/2004/US/South/02/26/haiti.refugees/index.html> at 8 March 2005 and Rachel L Swarns, 'Advocates for Immigrants Scorn Bush Policy on Haitian Refugees', The New York Times, 27 February 2004, A13.

[3] See, e.g. Human Rights Watch, 'Haiti: US Return of Asylum Seekers Is Illegal' (Press Release, 2 March 2004); US Committee for Refugees and Immigrants, 'President Bush Finally Speaks the Truth about America's Unlawful Treatment of Haitian Refugees' (Press Release, 26 February 2004); Amnesty International, 'Haiti: Refugees and asylum seekers are not part of the conflict' (27 February 2004).

[4] Sale v Haitian Centers Council, 113 S Ct 2549 (1993).

Legal arguments can serve for political purposes even when one knows that they will not stand up in court. The example illustrates how, in different ways, two opposing actors can both position themselves in a manner that marginalizes the law. This kind of politics concerning refugee issues is prevalent throughout the world, including the South Pacific, and it is unfortunately not the basis for a genuine debate on the legal situation of asylum seekers.

The following analysis of refugee policy in the South Pacific emphasizes a positivist approach to certain legal dilemmas created by mass refugee flows. While the public presentation of refugee policy is often used by various actors with wide-ranging political agendas, judicial bodies play a particularly important role in terms of judging the validity of legal arguments. With their decisions that constrain or justify refugee protection policies, courts have developed enough jurisprudence to allow debates on the subject to be framed within certain parameters. This chapter seeks to contribute to the debate surrounding mass refugee flows and burden-sharing in a region of the world that has been forced to confront difficult problems related to boat people.

International law should reflect the actual political conditions found in international society if it is to be relevant to policymakers. While it may be understandable that humanitarian and migration issues tend to attract activist approaches to the role of law, a certain amount of realism is necessary in order to respond to refugee situations in a viable manner. To the extent that it deals with the entry of aliens, refugee law is clearly part of immigration law. The affirmation from advocacy circles that 'refugee law is not immigration law'[5] and that it is actually part of human rights law may be useful in underlining the sensitivity required when dealing with foreigners who claim to flee persecution. In some ways, it may be true that all areas of law can be affected by human rights. However, the suggestion that these fleeing foreigners have special immigration entitlements or that they may trump existing immigration laws[6] does not reflect accurately the current relationship between international law and municipal law. This is a key observation in terms of the problems addressed in this chapter.

By focusing on the dramatic situation of mass refugee flows, the chapter examines the problems of burden-sharing from the perspective of international law. The dynamics mentioned above are illustrated in a particularly effective manner by examples concerning the South Pacific. Indeed, this region is characterized by at least two striking features: it includes a significant number of States not bound by

---

[5] James C Hathaway, 'Refugee Law is Not Immigration Law' (2002) World Refugee Survey 38. See also Amnesty International, 'Refugee Protection is Human Rights Protection' (Amnesty International Statement to the Ministerial Meeting of States Parties to the 1951 Refugee Convention and/or its 1967 Protocol, 1 December 2001).

[6] See, e.g. Refugee Appeal No. 72668/01 (5 April 2002) in which the New Zealand Refugee Status Appeals Authority states that 'refugee status trumps all immigration control and immigration policy' [39].

the 1951 Convention relating to the Status of Refugees,[7] as well as a hegemonic power attempting to coordinate bilateral responses to boat people.

The regional incident that has attracted the most attention in terms of boat people is undoubtedly the Tampa affair. About two weeks before the US was the object of terrorist attacks in 2001, the Australian authorities assisted a Norwegian flagged container ship, the MV Tampa, in rescuing 433 people aboard an Indonesian registered vessel that was sinking in the Indian Ocean. The desperate rescuees were of Iraqi, Afghan and Pakistani origin, and they threatened to commit suicide if they were transported to Indonesia. Contrary to orders from the Australian authorities, the Tampa attempted to enter Australian territorial waters near Christmas Island because the ship's captain was afraid that loss of life was imminent. The ship was boarded by 45 Australian Special Air Service troops who took over control. Federal Court litigation began on 31 August 2001 when a Melbourne-based solicitor filed applications on behalf of the boat people who wanted to seek refugee status in Australia. As the Australian government announced that intergovernmental agreements were reached to transfer the rescuees to Nauru and New Zealand for processing of their refugee claims, the parties to the litigation agreed to allow the courts to resolve certain legal issues. The rescuees were temporarily transferred to an Australian troop ship with medical facilities.

On 11 September 2001, a judge of the Federal Court of Australia ruled that the expulsion of the asylum seekers aboard the Tampa was illegal and that they should be allowed to land on Australian territory in order to apply for protection visas.[8] On 18 September 2001, the full Federal Court of Australia overturned this ruling in a majority decision.[9] The boat people were then sent to Nauru and New Zealand for processing. Over the following weeks, new legislation was enacted in order to validate the government's actions relating to the Tampa affair and to facilitate similar responses in the future. The so-called 'Pacific Solution' adopted by the Australian government was being proposed as a general response to the problem of boat people in the region.

The distinctive features of refugee protection in the South Pacific, and particularly Australia's 'Pacific Solution', have attracted attention from policymakers and criticisms from refugee advocates around the world. In some ways, the region may be at the forefront of some key developments in international refugee law.

Who is a refugee?

As States in the South Pacific have not adopted a regional instrument with a distinct refugee definition, the main international refugee definition applied in the

---

[7] Opened for signature 28 July 1951, 189 UNTS 150 (entered into force 22 April 1954) ('Refugee Convention').

[8] Vadarlis v Ruddock [2001] FCA 1297.

[9] Ruddock v Vadarlis [2001] FCA 1329.

region comes from two complementary treaties approved by the UN General Assembly.

South Pacific States bound by the 1951 Refugee Convention and the 1967 Protocol relating to the Status of Refugees[10] have accepted the following refugee definition:

> For the purposes of the present Convention, the term 'refugee' shall apply to any person who … owing to a well-founded fear of being persecuted for reasons of race, religion, nationality, membership of a particular social group or political opinion, is outside the country of his nationality and is unable or, owing to such fear, is unwilling to avail himself of the protection of that country; or who, not having a nationality and being outside the country of his former habitual residence as a result of such events, is unable or, owing to such fear, is unwilling to return to it.

According to the Office of the United Nations High Commissioner for Refugees (UNHCR), the above definition is declaratory and not constitutive of refugee status. In other words, a 'refugee' is any person who meets the Convention definition regardless of whether there has been a formal recognition of refugee status by the host State. Indeed, formal recognition of refugee status is not included as one of the conditions of the definition. The logic of UNHCR's argument is the following: when a State grants refugee status, it only 'recognizes' a condition that already existed prior to the State's administrative determination.[11] As a result, a State that mistreats a refugee claimant prior to a decision on the claim runs the risk of violating Convention obligations if the claimant is effectively a refugee.

While the declaratory nature of the Convention definition has generally not posed problems in case law, some doubts have been raised by the MV Tampa affair in 2001 concerning the rescue of 433 boat people near Christmas Island. In its decision on the Australian government's seizure of the Norwegian-owned vessel carrying the asylum seekers, the full Federal Court of Australia refers to a constitutive dimension of the refugee definition:

> The question whether all or any of the rescuees are refugees has not been determined … nothing done by the Executive on the face of it amounts to a breach of Australia's obligations in respect of non-refoulement under the Refugee Convention.[12]

The reasoning of the majority opinion seems to suggest that asylum seekers do not benefit from the Refugee Convention's guarantees unless they are recognized by the competent Australian authorities. Although this interpretation contributes in making the international refugee protection treaty regime somewhat incoherent, it apparently influences political decision-making and is found occasionally in doctrinal sources.[13]

---

[10] Opened for signature 31 January 1967, 606 UNTS 267 (entered into force 4 October 1967).

[11] UNHCR, Handbook on Procedures and Criteria for Determining Refugee Status (1979) [28].

[12] Ruddock v Vadarlis [2001] FCA 1329, [203] (French J). See also [126] (Beaumont J).

[13] See, e.g. Julius Grey, Immigration Law in Canada (1982) 120.

The bulk of administrative and judicial decisions on refugees in the region concern the interpretation of the various elements of the above definition. Yet the Refugee Convention and its Protocol do not include provisions relating to status determination procedures, thereby leaving this key aspect of refugee protection largely to the discretion of host States. This is supported by article 1(3) of the Declaration on Territorial Asylum: 'It shall rest with the State granting asylum to evaluate the grounds for the grant of asylum'.[14] Given the human rights-related context surrounding refugee protection, it is safe to assume that this discretionary power does not justify arbitrary government decisions.

The above norms apply to States bound by the Convention definition. However, the South Pacific stands out because of the high number of States that are not party to the Convention or its Protocol. The list of non-party States from the region is long: Cook Islands, Kiribati, Micronesia, Nauru, Niue, Palau, Marshall Islands, Tonga and Vanuatu. We could add several significant non-party States if we extend the region to include neighbouring Asia-Pacific countries: Indonesia, Malaysia and Singapore.[15] It appears that the 'Asian values' specificity so prominent in human rights debates[16] also plays an important role in the region's refugee protection policies. The actual role it plays, however, is far from clear: some of the above listed States have an arguably stronger record of refugee reception than many States bound by the Refugee Convention. To a large extent, it is the political and moral constraints found in each society that provide refugees with actual protection.

Another international refugee definition affecting the region that deserves mention is that found in UNHCR's Statute. It is almost identical to the definition found in the Refugee Convention,[17] even though it solely concerns the protection mandate entrusted to UNHCR by the UN General Assembly. The implications of this distinct definition will be explored below.

In a region where a significant number of States are not party to the Refugee Convention and have not implemented domestic legislation on refugees,[18] it is sometimes not easy to answer a simple legal question such as 'who is a refugee?'. This underlines the limited role played by international law in resolving forced migration problems.

---

[14] GA Res 2312 (XXII), 22 GAOR Supp (No 16), 81, UN Doc A/6716 (1967).

[15] Brunei, Thailand and Vietnam are also not bound by the Refugee Convention.

[16] See, e.g. Bilahari Kausikan, 'Asia's Different Standard' (1993) 92 Foreign Policy 24; Aryeh Neier, 'Asia's Unacceptable Standard' (1993) 92 Foreign Policy 42; Joanne R Bauer and Daniel A Bell (eds), The East Asian Challenge for Human Rights (1999).

[17] Statute of the United Nations High Commissioner for Refugees, GA Res 428 (V), 5 UN GAOR Supp (No 20) 46, UN Doc A/1775 (1950) ('Statute') [6].

[18] The following South Pacific States do not have refugee-specific legislation: Cook Islands, Fiji, Kiribati, Micronesia, Nauru, Niue, Palau, Papua New Guinea, Marshall Islands, Samoa, Solomon Islands, Tonga, Tuvalu and Vanuatu.

What protection is guaranteed to a refugee?

Refugee definitions in themselves can be meaningless; it is the corresponding entitlements that give them significance. This section explores the key protection guarantee afforded to refugees by international law.

Refugee advocates often cite article 14(1) of the Universal Declaration of Human Rights (UDHR)[19] to suggest that refugees enjoy a right to asylum: 'Everyone has the right to seek and to enjoy in other countries asylum from persecution'. This provision is well known in advocacy circles and it exerts a considerable amount of influence on protection policies.

However, courts rely generally on binding legal instruments when making decisions and the UDHR was adopted in 1948 as a non-binding instrument. While many rights found in the UDHR were eventually codified in human rights treaties, article 14 was not. In fact, there was an international conference on asylum in the 1970s that was convened in order to adopt a draft Convention on Territorial Asylum.[20] It failed miserably and there have been no further attempts to draft a universal treaty concerning asylum.

The suggestion that the norm found in article 14 is now part of customary international law is also unlikely to be accepted by courts. Practice over the last decades clearly shows that States capable of preventing refugee arrivals generally adopt interdiction policies when they perceive themselves to be threatened by asylum seekers. Regardless of the humanitarian language used by governments to describe their refugee policies in a positive light, this is the harsh reality of the world in which we live. It indicates that evidence is lacking of a general practice accepted as law in relation to an absolute 'right to asylum'.

While courts may use soft law instruments such as the UDHR to interpret existing legal rules, the binding international protection standards granted to a refugee are formulated explicitly in the Refugee Convention. This key instrument is composed largely of socio-economic entitlements that provide a refugee with minimum protection so that he or she can survive in a host State until a durable solution is found. Yet it is the non-refoulement provision found in article 33(1) that constitutes the most basic form of protection afforded to a refugee:

> No Contracting State shall expel or return ('refouler') a refugee in any manner whatsoever to the frontiers of territories where his life or freedom would be threatened on account of his race, religion, nationality, membership of a particular social group or political opinion.

This is as close as the Refugee Convention gets to addressing the issue of territorial asylum. It should be emphasized that the Convention does not oblige States to

---

[19] GA Res 217A (III), UN Doc A/810, 71 (1948).

[20] See Atle Grahl-Madsen, Territorial Asylum (1980) and François Leduc, 'L'asile territorial – Conférence des Nations Unies' (1977) 23 Annuaire français de droit international 221.

provide asylum to a person who satisfies its refugee definition;[21] it simply prohibits refoulement to dangerous territories. In other words, the most basic form of protection found in the Convention, non-refoulement, can be offered in the country of first asylum or in any third country capable of providing refuge. As stated by the full Federal Court of Australia in the Tampa case:

> International law imposes no obligation upon the coastal State to resettle those rescued in the coastal State's territory. This accords with the principles of the Refugee Convention. By Article 33, a person who has established refugee status may not be expelled to a territory where his life and freedom would be threatened for a Convention reason. Again, there is no obligation on the coastal State to resettle in its own territory.[22]

To further complicate the legal situation, the moment at which non-refoulement applies has been the object of considerable debate. For example, one of the grandfathers of international refugee law, Atle Grahl-Madsen, has written that non-refoulement does not apply if the persecuted individual does not actually cross the border of the host State.[23] In some ways, the interpretation in the United States is even stricter: the Supreme Court has established in the Haitian case that the Coast Guard can physically prevent the arrival of boat people on US territorial waters without violating the non-refoulement principle.[24]

As seen from the above quotes, the majority of the full Federal Court of Australia considers that asylum seekers cannot be sent back to a dangerous territory if they are recognized as refugees by the competent authorities. Given that an interdiction operation by Australian forces in international waters can prevent boat people from claiming refugee status in Australia, the court's reasoning arguably makes it possible for the government to return an intercepted boat to a dangerous territory. If such an interpretation is correct, it would represent a considerable step backward in terms of regional protection standards.

In recent years UNHCR's position on this issue appears to be the opposite extreme. In the face of restrictive governmental actions relating to border control and interdiction policies, the UN refugee agency has recently endorsed a paper promoting a rather progressive interpretation of non-refoulement:

---

[21] See, e.g. the declaration by one of the US representatives at the Conference: 'Those who drafted the Convention recognized that governments were not prepared to commit themselves to grant asylum, even to bona fide refugees … In short, as I understood Article 33, and as I believe all members of the Committee understood Article 33, it amounted to this: a State would not be obliged to admit any refugee. But a State could not seize a refugee in its territory and hand him over to his oppressors.' Affidavit of Louis Henkin, 15 December 1992, reproduced in Harold Hongju Koh, 'Reflections on Refoulement and Haitian Centers Council' (1994) 35 Harvard International Law Journal 45.

[22] Ruddock v Vadarlis [2001] FCA 1329, [126] (Beaumont J).

[23] Atle Grahl-Madsen, The Status of Refugees in International Law (1972) vol 2, 94. See also Neremiah Robinson, Convention relating to the Status of Refugees: A Commentary (1953) 163.

[24] Sale v Haitian Centers Council, 113 S Ct 2549 (1993).

> Non-refoulement is a principle of customary international law … The principle of non-refoulement embodied in Article 33 encompasses any measure attributable to the State which could have the effect of returning an asylum seeker or refugee to the frontiers of territories where his or her life or freedom would be threatened, or where he or she is at risk of persecution, including interception, rejection at the frontier or indirect refoulement.[25]

While the principle of non-refoulement may indeed be part of customary international law and consequently bind South Pacific States that are not party to the Refugee Convention, its content is far from clear. The debate on this issue will not be resolved in the near future.

In terms of interpreting the content of the non-refoulement principle, the Declaration on Territorial Asylum provides some guidance in its paragraph 3(1): 'No person … shall be subjected to measures such as rejection at the frontier or, if he has already entered the territory in which he seeks asylum, expulsion or compulsory return to any State where he may be subjected to persecution'. This constitutes a progressive interpretation when considered in light of the consequences of the influential Australian and US court decisions on boat people.

When assessing the practicality and feasibility of burden-sharing mechanisms, it is important to address whether an asylum seeker can choose a country of refuge (or engage in 'forum shopping' as it is called by critics). Indeed, the whole notion of emergency burden-sharing is generally premised on the possibility of transferring refugees to third countries. This implies difficult questions concerning refugee relocations in situations where consent by the affected person may not be forthcoming. At present, there do not appear to be any binding legal rules that suggest a refugee cannot be relocated involuntarily, as long as the principle of non-refoulement is respected. In other words, international law protects refugees from persecution, but it does not allow them necessarily to choose the State where protection will be granted. Furthermore, it appears that the transfer of refugees to other countries without the refugees' consent is not illegal, even if the country of relocation is not party to the Refugee Convention.[26] The issue in terms of international refugee law is whether the refugees will be indirectly refouled (or sent to a dangerous territory).

Yet a practical problem that has contributed in undermining recent burden-sharing proposals is that international human rights organizations are uncomfortable with the idea that a refugee may not always have a choice regarding the territory on which she or he is provided refuge. Until humanitarian actors are willing to accept this limitation on protection options for the asylum seeker, there is limited hope for effective burden-sharing mechanisms in emergency situations. These opposing views reflect the tensions associated with the Tampa affair and similar incidents in the South Pacific.

---

[25] 'Cambridge Roundtable Summary Conclusions – The principle of Non-Refoulement' in Erika Feller, Volker Türk and Frances Nicholson (eds), Refugee Protection in International Law (2003) 179.

[26] Contra Jean-Pierre L Fonteyne, 'All Adrift in a Sea of Illegitimacy: An International Law Perspective on the Tampa Affair' (2001) 12 Public Law Review 249, 251.

Asylum seekers at sea raise specific protection problems that need to be highlighted. Article 98 of the Law of the Sea Convention 'requires the master of a ship flying its flag, in so far as he can do so without serious danger to the ship, the crew or the passengers ... to render assistance to any person found at sea in danger of being lost'.[27] The issue is particularly problematic in the case of asylum seekers because it involves the disembarkation of rescuees who do not want to return to their home State. Yet article 98 does not mention the issue of disembarkation of the rescuees. Neither does the Refugee Convention contain any obligation on this issue. The result is that there is legal controversy over the ultimate responsibility for the fate of people rescued at sea.[28]

As an example of the practical consequences of this legal uncertainty, during the 1970s south-east Asian States denied that they had responsibility to allow disembarkation of Indochinese boat people. The coastal States allowed boat people to disembark only after seeking resettlement commitments from other States. Proposed solutions to this problem will be explored below.

What is a mass flow?

As seen above, the Refugee Convention uses the singular form in its refugee definition and its non-refoulement provision. There is no reference to the specific treatment of groups of refugees in either the Convention or its Protocol. This contrasts with, for example, the Convention Governing the Specific Aspects of Refugee Problems in Africa which refers frequently to 'refugees' in addressing situations that imply group movements.[29]

While the concept of 'mass flow' is not used or defined in any of the above mentioned treaties, it is used in numerous soft law instruments. For example, the Declaration on Territorial Asylum refers to 'a mass influx of persons' in its paragraph 3(2). It does not, however, define the term. Likewise, the concept is found in several conclusions adopted by UNHCR's executive committee (EXCOM) (for example, Conclusion No. 22 on the protection of asylum seekers in situations of large-scale influx[30]) and General Assembly Resolution 58/169 of 22 December 2003 on human rights and mass exoduses. Yet these soft law instruments provide no definition.

The closest example we have of States identifying some of the elements that characterize 'mass flows' is found in EXCOM's Conclusion No. 100 on

---

[27] United Nations Convention on the Law of the Sea, opened for signature 10 December 1982, 1833 UNTS 3 (entered into force 16 November 1994).

[28] See, e.g. Fonteyne, above n 26, 249.

[29] Opened for signature 10 September 1969, 1001 UNTS 45, art 2, 3, 5 (entered into force 20 June 1974).

[30] EXCOM, Protection of Asylum Seekers in Situations of Large-Scale Influx (No. 22 (XXXIII) – 1981) ('Conclusion No. 22').

international cooperation and burden and responsibility sharing in mass influx situations.[31] Its paragraph (a) specifies

> that mass influx is a phenomenon that has not been defined, but that, for the purposes of this conclusion, mass influx situations may, inter alia, have some or all of the following characteristics: (i) considerable numbers of people arriving over an international border; (ii) a rapid rate of arrival; (iii) inadequate absorption or response capacity in host States, particularly during the emergency; (iv) individual asylum procedures, where they exist, which are unable to deal with the assessment of such large numbers.

Governments seem to have a certain amount of discretion in characterizing a group of refugees as constituting a mass flow. As we shall see below, this has crucial consequences in terms of protection obligations.

Does non-refoulement apply to mass flows?

There are a wide variety of opinions concerning the issue of whether the non-refoulement principle applies in mass flow situations. Even though the issue was not as contentious at the time of the drafting of the Refugee Convention, refugee advocates have managed to promote higher protection standards so that this question has actually become one of the more controversial debates in international refugee law today.

The position adopted by UNHCR is summed up in a recent policy paper: 'The principle of non-refoulement applies in situations of mass influx'.[32] Although this paper is based on a relatively lengthy study of non-refoulement, [33] unfortunately the study does not really address thoroughly the various arguments in the debate. Nevertheless, the view that non-refoulement applies in mass flow situations is supported by most non-governmental human rights groups working on refugee issues and it is shared by many academics.[34]

Several soft law instruments adopted by States lend support to this view. EXCOM's first conclusion on the protection of asylum seekers in situations of large-scale influx set a high standard that continues to influence official policy statements by UNHCR. In the section entitled 'Admission and non-refoulement' of Conclusion No. 22, EXCOM expressed support for the concept of first asylum by stating that non-refoulement is to be interpreted as including non-rejection at the border in cases of mass influx:

---

[31] EXCOM, Conclusion on International Cooperation and Burden and Responsibility Sharing in Mass Influx Situations (No. 100 (LV) – 2004) ('Conclusion No. 100').

[32] 'Cambridge Roundtable Summary Conclusions', above n 25.

[33] Sir Elihu Lauterpacht and Daniel Bethlehem, 'The scope and content of the principle of non-refoulement' in Erika Feller, Volker Türk and Frances Nicholson (eds), Refugee Protection in International Law (2003) 89.

[34] See, e.g. Fonteyne, above n 26, 251.

1. In situations of large-scale influx, asylum seekers should be admitted to the State in which they first seek refuge and if that State is unable to admit them on a durable basis, it should always admit them at least on a temporary basis and provide them with protection according to the principles set out below. They should be admitted without any discrimination as to race, religion, political opinion, nationality, country of origin or physical incapacity.
2. In all cases the fundamental principle of non-refoulement including non-rejection at the frontier must be scrupulously observed.[35]

In Conclusion No. 23 on problems related to the rescue of asylum seekers in distress at sea, EXCOM explicitly extended the interpretation to boat people: 'In cases of large-scale influx, asylum seekers rescued at sea should always be admitted, at least on a temporary basis'.[36] It should be noted that both Australia and the United States have been members of EXCOM since its creation in 1958 and that its conclusions are adopted by consensus. Although these instruments are not legally-binding in the sense of immediately enforceable binding commitments, they represent authoritative interpretations that are adopted as political recommendations.

The various EXCOM conclusions on boat people adopted in the 1980s refer to the South China Sea and relate to asylum seekers fleeing from the Indochinese peninsula.[37] Given that the influential western liberal democracies which dominate EXCOM debates were not the coastal States directly impacted by the principle of disembarkation at the next port of call, this begs the question as to whether they intended these high standards to apply to themselves as well as the poorer Asia-Pacific coastal States. We will return to this theme later in the chapter after exploring the actual legal position of the Australian and US governments in court cases.

The preceding comments highlight the importance of distinguishing hard law from soft law, and possibly law from politics. Turning to the text of the Refugee Convention, the answer to the question posed in this section becomes less clear. We have already seen how the refugee definition and the non-refoulement principle found in the Convention are both drafted in the singular form (i.e. 'a refugee').

Recourse to the preparatory work of a treaty is generally accepted as a supplementary means of interpretation.[38] Interestingly, the Convention's *travaux préparatoires* indicate that the issue of mass flows preoccupied many of the State representatives during the Conference of Plenipotentiaries on the Status of Refugees and Stateless Person, convened in Geneva in July 1951.[39] The declarations by government delegations are revealing in terms of the commitments

[35] Above n 30, [II(A)].

[36] EXCOM, Conclusion on Problems Related to the Rescue of Asylum Seekers in Distress at Sea (No. 23 (XXXIII) – 1981) [3].

[37] The point is emphasized in Tara Magner, 'A Less than "Pacific" Solution for Asylum Seekers in Australia' (2004) 16 International Journal of Refugee Law 53, 67, 70.

[38] Vienna Convention on the Law of Treaties, opened for signature 23 May 1969, 1155 UNTS 331 (entered into force 27 January 1980).

[39] Conference of Plenipotentiaries on the Status of Refugees and Stateless Persons, Summary Record of the Sixteenth Meeting (held at the Palais des Nations, Geneva, on Wednesday, 11 July 1951, at 3 pm), UN Doc A/CONF.2/SR.16 (1951).

accepted by the States participating in the drafting process. For example, the Swiss representative declared that 'States were not compelled to allow large groups of persons claiming refugee status to cross its frontiers'. The Dutch representative shared this concern and hinted at possible solutions: 'the Netherlands was somewhat diffident about assuming unconditional obligations so far as mass influxes of refugees were concerned, unless international collaboration was sufficiently organized to deal with such a situation'. The link with security concerns was made explicitly by the Italian representative who declared that 'a State could not commit itself not to expel or return large groups of refugees who presented themselves on its territory, and who might endanger public security'.[40]

In fact, during the negotiations on the drafting of the non-refoulement provision (which took place on 11 July 1951, the Convention was signed on the 28th), discussions focused largely on the link between mass flows and destabilization. The *travaux préparatoires* of the Convention show that the signing of this instrument was actually conditional on the understanding that it did not impose any obligations in cases of mass flows.[41] This was noted by the president of the conference on 25 July, allowing the representatives to move on to other issues and eventually sign the Convention three days later. As stated by one of the US representatives at the 1951 Conference: 'Some delegates did express the concern that the right of non-refoulement should not become a vehicle for requiring the admission of massive numbers of migrants ... By expressing a caveat about mass migrations, the delegates were confirming that the right of non-refoulement attached to individual refugees and not to groups'.[42]

A number of doctrinal sources recognize that the non-refoulement principle can be the object of exceptions in mass flow situations.[43] At the very least, we must acknowledge that non-refoulement as expressed in treaty law has been left deliberately imprecise in certain situations. Indeed, the Refugee Convention does

---

[40] Ibid.

[41] Baron van Boetzelaer (Netherlands): '[T]he Netherlands Government attached very great importance to the scope of the provision now contained in article 33. The Netherlands could not accept any legal obligations in respect of large groups of refugees seeking access to its territory. At the first reading the representatives of Belgium, the Federal Republic of Germany, Italy, the Netherlands and Sweden had supported the Swiss interpretation. From conversations he had since had with other representatives, he had gathered that the general consensus of opinion was in favour of the Swiss interpretation. In order to dispel any possible ambiguity and to reassure his Government, he wished to have it placed on record that the Conference was in agreement with the interpretation that the possibility of mass migrations across frontiers or of attempted mass migrations was not covered by article 33.' Conference of Plenipotentiaries on the Status of Refugees and Stateless Persons, Summary Record of the Thirty-fifth Meeting (held at the Palais des Nations, Geneva, on Wednesday, 25 July 1951, at 2.30 pm), UN Doc A/CONF.2/SR.35 (1951).

[42] Affidavit of Louis Henkin, 15 December 1992, reproduced in Koh, above n 21, 45-7.

[43] Grahl-Madsen, Territorial Asylum, above n 20, 42; Patricia Hyndman, 'Asylum and Non-Refoulement – Are these Obligations owed to Refugees under International Law?' (1982) 57 Philippine Law Journal 68; David A Martin, 'Large Scale Migrations of Asylum Seekers' (1982) 76 American Journal of International Law 598.

not contain provisions addressing specifically mass flow situations. This omission suggests that the drafters did not want State reactions to mass inflows to be regulated by international treaty obligations. The lack of precision in the treaty text allows political leaders increased flexibility when dealing with concrete problems related to large refugee movements so that they do not find themselves hampered by unworkable international principles.

Even though refugee advocates will argue that the normative framework has evolved since the drafting of the main refugee protection instrument over a half-century ago, it is far from evident that courts will follow such reasoning to the extent that it is intended to have non-refoulement cover mass flow situations. The restrictive judicial interpretations that have limited the scope of non-refoulement in Australia and the US suggest that a legal strategy based on including mass flows within its sphere of protection is unlikely to win in a court setting. For example, the losing party in the Haitian boat people case never suggested that the government had to admit a large-scale influx on US territory; it simply wanted to prevent the refugees intercepted on the high seas from being sent directly to Haiti.[44] It lost on this minimalist point.

The main example of State practice that confirms the above analysis is found in the treatment of asylum seekers from the former Yugoslavia in Europe during the 1990s. The divergence between the European application of temporary protection measures in relation to these asylum seekers and the Refugee Convention's specific rights regime has been noted by many commentators.[45] As the difference in protection standards was justified largely in exceptional terms resulting from an alleged 'mass inflow', the position of some European States suggests implicitly that they consider the Convention does not apply in situations of mass influx. Although this has not been declared formally by the European Union, it is likely the only way that the various temporary protection policies in the 1990s concerning forced migrants from the former Yugoslavia can be defended on legal grounds.

To the extent that UNHCR approved the ad hoc European temporary protection schemes and accepted that the Convention's rights regime would not apply in this particular case,[46] it is awkward for the UN agency now to insist that the Refugee Convention applies in mass flow situations. Why did it not make this position clear in response to European policies in the 1990s? This problem of different standards applying to different host States is explored below.

The above discussion shows that the drafters of the Refugee Convention did not intend its key protection guarantee, non-refoulement, to apply to mass flows. However, refugee advocates contend that the norms have evolved along with the

---

[44] 'Respondents have never claimed that the Attorney General is obliged to admit a mass Haitian migration across our frontiers or borders, only that Article 33 and § 243(h) [of the 1980 Refugee Act] bar the Attorney General from returning all arriving ships to Haiti.' Koh, above n 21, 55.

[45] See, e.g. Michael Barutciski, 'The Reinforcement of Non-Admission Policies and the Subversion of UNHCR' (1996) 8 International Journal of Refugee Law 49.

[46] UNHCR, Note on International Protection, UN Doc A/AC.96/830 (1994).

development of human rights law over the last few decades. As courts have not dealt directly with this question, there is consequently a certain amount of legal uncertainty over this problem.

How does national security affect State obligations?

It should be noted that in neither the Tampa nor the Haitian case did any party invoke a threat to national security, yet the courts rendered relatively restrictive decisions. It is safe to assume that courts would not be any less restrictive if a threat to national security were actually invoked. Although it involves an individual and not a refugee group, the case of Ahmed Zaoui in New Zealand illustrates the point: he was recognized as a refugee by the country's Refugee Status Appeals Authority,[47] yet the government detained him for two years because it alleges that he has terrorist connections. The country's newly created Supreme Court is still examining the case.

The inclusion in the Refugee Convention of article 9 authorizing provisional measures in cases involving national security is an example of the pragmatic dimension of the principles codified in international law. Article 9 allows the following exceptions:

> Nothing in this Convention shall prevent a Contracting State, in time of war or other grave and exceptional circumstances, from taking provisionally measures which it considers to be essential to the national security in the case of a particular person, pending a determination by the Contracting State that that person is in fact a refugee and that the continuance of such measures is necessary in his case in the interests of national security.

As traditionally conceived, refugee protection principles do not contradict legitimate State interests. It has also become increasingly clear in recent years that courts in liberal democracies are ready to severely restrict rights and liberties when national security is at stake.

The above comments help explain the inclusion of an exception to non-refoulement based on national security reasons in paragraph 2 of the Refugee Convention's article 33:

> The benefit of the present provision may not, however, be claimed by a refugee whom there are reasonable grounds for regarding as a danger to the security of the country in which he is, or who, having been convicted by a final judgment of a particularly serious crime, constitutes a danger to the community of that country.

Although the provision refers to a threat posed by individuals, the destabilization context created by a mass influx suggests that individuals represent a threat due to their membership of a larger group. Any other interpretation would oblige a host

---

[47] Refugee Appeal No 704540/03 (1 August 2003). See also Zaoui v Attorney-General, High Court (Auckland), CIV-2003-404-5872 (19 December 2003).

State to insist that the Refugee Convention's non-refoulement guarantee does not apply to mass flows. The latter interpretation was apparently favoured by the drafters.[48]

The UN General Assembly helps to clarify this issue in its Declaration on Territorial Asylum. Paragraph 3(1) of this non-binding instrument stipulates that a person seeking asylum shall be protected against 'rejection at the frontier or, if he has already entered the territory in which he seeks asylum, expulsion or compulsory return to any State where he may be subjected to persecution'. This provision is followed by an exception in paragraph 3(2) that refers explicitly to security and mass flows: 'Exception may be made to the foregoing principle only for overriding reasons of national security or in order to safeguard the population, as in the case of a mass influx of persons'.

It is interesting to note that UNHCR, as an agency created by the General Assembly, rejects the idea that non-refoulement can be restrained in situations of mass inflows and destabilization. Even after an independent evaluation that was commissioned by the agency and that dealt with the consequences of this problem,[49] the UN refugee agency considers that a State has to admit (at least temporarily) all refugees who present themselves at the border, regardless of whether they are part of a larger group that may destabilize the country. With such absolutist legal opinions, UNHCR exposes itself to harsh criticisms.[50] It also distances itself from its mandate which is to cooperate with UN member States to protect refugees.[51] The agency is not necessarily supposed to be a non-governmental type of watchdog on refugee policy,[52] despite the various suggestions that it assume

[48] 'Mr Theodoli (Italy) … personally felt that a State could not commit itself not to expel or return large groups of refugees who presented themselves on its territory, and who might endanger public security. The Italian delegation would therefore reserve its position on the article, unless some satisfactory explanation was forthcoming.' Conference of Plenipotentiaries on the Status of Refugees and Stateless Persons, Summary Record of the Sixteenth Meeting (held at the Palais des Nations, Geneva, on Wednesday, 11 July 1951, at 3 pm), UN Doc A/CONF.2/SR.16 (1951).

[49] Astri Suhrke et al., The Kosovo Refugee Crisis: An independent evaluation of UNHCR's emergency preparedness and response, UN Doc EPAU/2000/001 (2000).

[50] See, e.g. Guy S Goodwin-Gill, 'The Kosovo Refugee Crisis: An Independent Evaluation of UNHCR's Emergency Preparedness and Response' (2000) 16 Relief and Rehabilitation Network Newsletter 33-4: '[The performance of UNHCR] on first asylum strongly implies that staff initially responsible for protection in the region, and possibly also in Headquarters, are unfamiliar with basic principles. If … UNHCR seriously considers that first asylum should be considered as an absolute and unconditional legal obligation consistent with the 1951 Refugee Convention, then there is something wrong with its perception of international law … [F]irst asylum is a fine ideal but it does not reflect general international law or the requirements of the 1951 Convention/1967 Protocol … [UNHCR] seems to be confused as to its basic legal standing and as to the international law which it is supposed to apply.'

[51] See, e.g. Statute, above n 17, [1], [8], [10].

[52] Adrienne Millbank, 'The Problem with the 1951 Refugee Convention', Parliamentary Library of Australia, Research Paper No 5 (5 September 2000).

something akin to such a role.[53] To the extent that it must follow policy directives from the General Assembly[54] and that it depends on voluntary governmental contributions,[55] the UN refugee agency does not have an appropriate mandate for a watchdog role typically assumed by NGOs.[56]

It is worth emphasizing the uncompromising nature of the position taken by UNHCR and many NGOs on this issue.[57] According to these refugee advocates, States must open their borders to any migrant who claims to be a victim of human rights violations even if there exists a serious fear of destabilization provoked by a massive influx. This proposition does not, however, reflect an interstate consensus. Ironically, it is partly because of this kind of advocacy that western governments seek to contain refugee flows in less affluent regions of the world and to prevent people from poor countries to seek asylum in rich countries.

Indeed, the suggestion that refugees may have an unconditional right to first asylum clashes with some of the most basic premises of legal systems in the South Pacific. As pointed out by Judge French of the Federal Court of Australia:

> The power to determine who may come into Australia is so central to its sovereignty that it is not to be supposed that the Government of the nation would lack under the power conferred upon it directly by the Constitution, the ability to prevent people not part of the Australian community, from entering.[58]

Yet it is rather astonishing that Australia, as a member of UNHCR's executive committee, participated in the adoption of international norms (along with other OECD member States) that actually embrace the unrealistic standard criticized above.

---

[53] See e.g. Saul Takahashi, 'Recourse to Human Rights Treaty Bodies for Monitoring the Refugee Convention' (2002) 20 Netherlands Quarterly of Human Rights 53 and Volker Türk, 'UNHCR's supervisory responsibility', New Issues in Refugee Research, UNHCR Working Paper No 67 (October 2002).

[54] Statute, above n 17, [3].

[55] Statute, above n 17, [20].

[56] For a discussion on UNHCR's mandate, see Michael Barutciski, 'A Critical View of UNHCR's Mandate Dilemmas' (2002) 14 International Journal of Refugee Law 365.

[57] See, e.g. European Council on Refugees and Exiles, 'The Kosovo Refugee Crisis. ECRE's Observations on the independent evaluation of UNHCR's emergency preparedness and response' (Press Release, February 2000); Human Rights Watch, 'Macedonia must keep border open to refugees' (Press Release, 1 April 1999); Amnesty International, 'Former Yugoslav Republic of Macedonia: The Protection of Kosovo Albanian Refugees' (Press Release, 1 May 1999).

[58] Ruddock v Vadarlis [2001] FCA 1329, [193] (French J). See also the remarks by Judge Beaumont ([125]): 'It follows, in my view, that the occupants [of the MV Tampa] had no legal right at common law enforceable in a court to enter Australia. It must follow, in my view, that no foundation existed for the grant of a common law prerogative writ of habeas corpus compelling their entry into Australia ... there is nothing in any of the authorities to contradict the principle that an alien has no common law right to enter Australia. This aspect is beyond argument. For this reason alone, I would allow the appeal.'

As we have seen, EXCOM had already concluded in 1981 that it should call for asylum in the country of first arrival and that this principle applied to mass arrivals as well as individual asylum seekers.[59] It later further concluded that asylum must be unconditional.[60] More recently, EXCOM (including New Zealand as a new member) has confirmed its position on unconditional first asylum in the preamble of Conclusion No. 100.[61]

This leads to the following question: would these EXCOM members insist on having these norms apply to themselves? We know from the Tampa affair and subsequent government policies that Australia does not consider itself bound by such high standards. Likewise, US policy in relation to Haitian and Cuban boat people does not conform to these standards. So why do these States participate in the promulgation of norms that they do not intend to respect if faced with destabilizing mass flows?

While soft law contributes to the evolution of international law, the introduction of a wide range of norms that vary in terms of their legal nature exposes the practice of international law to a type of criticism that is evoked commonly by developing States: a selective use of norms. In other words, it allows powerful States to pick and choose among the norms that are the most convenient for their political goals and their relative ability to impose their political positions on the international scene. After all, if a State does not agree with the particular application of certain norms, it can always resort to a formalist positivist approach generally favoured by courts. We return to power politics in terms of securing international support and legitimacy.

In relation to the particular problem regarding refugees addressed in this chapter, the apparently 'progressive' use of soft norms may actually reinforce the double standards that are implicit in refugee flow containment strategies adopted by affluent States. From a containment perspective, it is entirely consistent to insist on an absolute right of unconditional first asylum, without a complementary commitment to burden sharing. The last point about a lack of commitment is explored in the next section.

It has been noted that the closure of Australian territorial waters on national security grounds may be difficult to justify in the specific case of the Tampa.[62] However, the wider picture might be more complex. At stake are numerous intangible security issues. From a governmental viewpoint, the proliferation of sea-based people smuggling sends a message that Australia is a soft target and an

---

[59] EXCOM, Conclusion No. 22, above n 30.

[60] See, e.g. EXCOM, Conclusion on International Protection (No. 85 (XLIX) 1998).

[61] EXCOM notes 'that persons who arrive as part of a mass influx seeking international refugee protection should always receive it, at least on a temporary basis'. The wording in this important conclusion may suggest a slight shift in tone to a more pragmatic approach to the extent that this provision is now only found in the preamble. Conclusion No. 100, above n 31.

[62] Donald R Rothwell, 'The Law of the Sea and the MV Tampa Incident: Reconciling Maritime Principles with Coastal State Sovereignty' (2002) Public Law Review 118, 122; Cecilia Bailliet, 'The Tampa Case and its Impact on Burden Sharing' (2003) 25 Human Rights Quarterly 741, 750.

attractive destination. Even though the 433 asylum seekers aboard the Tampa may not have directly threatened Australia's security, it was argued by the government that allowing such breaches of the country's maritime boundaries sends a dangerous message and demonstrates Australia's limited capacity to control its borders. After the peak period of 1998–2001 in which the government claims that over 10,000 boat people were smuggled to Australia, there have been only a few boats attempting to reach the Australian mainland.[63] The policies developed in the wake of the Tampa affair are undoubtedly responsible for this development. It is interesting to note that New Zealand also adopted emergency legislation during the early phases of the peak period when public concern was raised about the (far-fetched) possibility that boat people could approach the North Island.[64]

Is there an obligation to share the burden?

The refoulement of refugees to dangerous territories is clearly not an acceptable solution to the problems addressed in this chapter. The arguments presented in the preceding sections are intended to underline the limitations concerning international legal obligations, precisely in order to encourage a genuine debate regarding political solutions and commitments. This section explores one of the key ideas mentioned in the Refugee Convention's preamble: the promotion of international cooperation to alleviate the burden on vulnerable host States. The present analysis suggests that a realist approach offers better chances to implement such a form of international cooperation.

The first point to underline is that there is no binding obligation regarding burden-sharing in the 46 articles found in the Refugee Convention. In fact, international law presently imposes no obligations on States other than the ones that are confronted directly with refugee movements. The unfairness resulting from 'accidents of geography' has inspired detailed proposals from academics and advocates who are interested in introducing authentic burden-sharing mechanisms in international refugee policy.[65] The idea is to conceive an international system in which the State confronted with the refugee flow is not the only one bound by legal obligations. In the current context, it is unlikely that this proposition will be met with a favourable response from States that would have to assume new duties.

Ironically, it may be partly because human rights activists insist that first asylum always be granted unconditionally that it is difficult to impose an

[63] Department of Immigration and Multicultural and Indigenous Affairs, Fact sheet no 74: Unauthorised Arrivals by Air and Sea (6 October 2004).

[64] Immigration Amendment Act (No 2) 1999. See also John Armstrong, 'Orion to scan seas for boat people', New Zealand Herald, 17 June 1999, A3; Greg Ansley, 'Trade in people ruthless', New Zealand Herald, 17 June 1999, A15; Editorial, 'Unwelcome by boat', New Zealand Herald, 17 June 1999, A16.

[65] See, e.g. James C Hathaway and R Alexander Neve, 'Making International Refugee Law Relevant Again: A proposal for Collectivized and Solution-Oriented Protection' (1997) 10 Harvard Human Rights Journal 116.

obligation on other States to share the burden of refugee protection. Why should another State commit itself to admit refugees onto its territory if the first State of arrival is obliged to provide unconditional asylum? Numerous intergovernmental negotiations have demonstrated that it is easier for States to shift the burden and avoid any responsibility.

To some extent, this is an example of counterproductive advocacy in the sense that the existence of a (non-binding) standard of unconditional asylum encourages UNHCR not to prepare serious contingency plans for alternative protection measures in case borders are closed.[66] Until recently, its strategy, like that of many NGOs, has been generally to pressure host States into admitting the refugees.

As States and international bodies are increasingly making the link between security and refugee flows in order to restrict admission to asylum seekers, it is necessary to ensure that any reference to the accepted exceptions in the Refugee Convention is done in order to promote burden-sharing and not to defend refoulement. How can this be achieved within the legal framework described above? From a realist perspective, successful burden-sharing initiatives must be based on a combination of principles and diplomacy.

According to article 35 of the Refugee Convention, States have an obligation to cooperate with UNHCR. As the UN agency is mandated to protect refugees regardless of whether a frontline State claims an exception to protection obligations, this suggests a duty to engage in contingency planning for burden-sharing in situations where a host country is too vulnerable to accept a mass influx. The forms of possible sharing relate to the costs of the operational response and provision of territorial asylum in safe countries.

Unfortunately, this has not been the practice of UNHCR to date. If the UN refugee agency were to be persuaded to engage seriously in contingency planning, then this would represent a significant shift in international attempts to implement burden-sharing mechanisms. In this regard, EXCOM Conclusion No. 100 includes several new ideas and provisions that have not been adopted in soft law instruments in the past.

In order to understand the significance of this conclusion, it is important to remember that UNHCR several years ago defended its lack of contingency planning in its response to criticisms:

> [T]he evaluation suggests that UNHCR should have given more and earlier attention to the probability that the refugees would not be admitted to a potential country of asylum, and that alternative protection strategies should have been explored. UNHCR is concerned that contingency planning which assumes that States will not comply with their responsibilities to receive and host new arrivals, particularly in mass influx situations, runs the risk of becoming a self-fulfilling prophecy. At a time when the commitment of States to the institution of asylum appears to be in decline, that risk is real and dangerous.[67]

---

[66] Suhrke et al., above n 49.
[67] Ibid, Appendix D.

The logic to this defence is akin to suggesting that there is no need for a lifeboat aboard a ship because it would undermine the passengers' confidence in the seaworthiness of the ship. Implicitly contradicting UNHCR's views, EXCOM has noted in Conclusion No. 100 the importance of emergency preparedness and response strategies in anticipation of situations likely to lead to a mass influx.[68] EXCOM further notes that UNHCR should convene consultations as early on in a crisis as possible in order to explore refugee protection mechanisms in the spirit of international solidarity involving arrangements among States, regional and international organizations, as well as financial institutions.[69] The fact that EXCOM has requested UNHCR to report regularly on developments regarding burden-sharing in mass flow situations certainly represents a positive step forward.[70]

Given the lack of legally-binding commitments regarding burden-sharing, the political and diplomatic factors that encourage cooperation by regional actors are essential. Here again the South Pacific, along with the Asia-Pacific region more generally, stands out because it includes various States that have managed to cooperate during certain refugee crises over the last few decades. In order to promote burden-sharing, it is necessary to explore the political, moral, institutional and financial factors that made this cooperation possible.

What can we learn from governmental policies?

The above legal analysis helps to understand governmental policies relating to mass refugee flows and burden-sharing in the region. Governments are willing to protect refugees, but only if the measures conform to their immigration concerns and objectives.

Although burden-sharing could theoretically be conceived in different ways, practice shows that it depends generally on the existence of resettlement programmes. Through careful diplomatic initiatives, it is possible to secure a temporary form of initial protection for refugees during mass influxes. However, this initial protection is dependent on assurances that the burden of settling the refugees will be shared with other States. Notwithstanding the language and recommendation in several EXCOM conclusions, practice demonstrates clearly that first asylum is offered only conditionally. The reaction of coastal States to the outflow of Vietnamese boat people during the 1970s and 1980s illustrates this point particularly well. States such as Malaysia, Indonesia, Thailand and the Philippines were willing to grant first asylum, but only after resettlement countries provided quotas for resettlement places.[71] If we want international law to be

---

[68] Above n 31, [(e)].

[69] Ibid, [(g)]-[(h)].

[70] Ibid [(o)].

[71] This 'unwritten arrangement' is described in Sten A Bronee, 'The History of the Comprehensive Plan of Action' (1993) 5 International Journal of Refugee Law 534. See also Astri Suhrke, 'Indochinese Refugees: The Law and Politics of First Asylum' (1983) 467 The Annals of the American Academy of Political and Social Science 102. For a critical

realistic and not simply to indicate aspirations, it may be better to acknowledge this important feature of past burden-sharing schemes, rather than promote standards that do not reflect actual State practice.

To the extent that burden-sharing depends on resettlement, it should be noted that the South Pacific includes two influential States that are recognized by UNHCR as being among the most important refugee resettlement countries in the world: Australia and New Zealand.[72] In recent years, Australia has been resettling between 7,000 and 12,000 people per year for humanitarian reasons, whereas New Zealand has an annual humanitarian resettlement quota of 750 places.[73] During the Tampa crisis, 131 boat people were handed from the Australian authorities to New Zealand for processing and were eventually included in the annual quota.

Despite these significant resettlement programmes, both Australia and New Zealand deal with only a few hundred spontaneous asylum claims per year by individuals who arrive at international airports.[74] This type of uninvited migrant claiming refugee status presents considerably more complicated policy problems than the selection of refugees in overseas camps. While the latter reflects the discretionary powers of an immigration country, the former represents in some ways a failure of border control measures. The picture is relatively clear: States are willing to protect refugees as long as they preserve the impression of controlling their frontiers and the numbers seeking protection are relatively low.

Australia's concerns are worth underlining in order to understand its proposed regional solution to the problems associated with refugee flows. The government believes that the country is facing a serious challenge to its immigration programme due to the increases in the number of illegal migrants entering its territory. The concern relates specifically to people arriving by sea with the help of people-smuggling rackets that have been targeting Australia. Given the country's vast coastline and proximity to south-east Asia, the government is worried that the country's strong economy attracts economic migrants using asylum procedures in order to gain entry. The following comment illustrates the perception motivating governmental policies: 'Australia is the blatant target of

---

assessment, see James C Hathaway, 'Labelling the Boat People: The Failure of the Human Rights Mandate of the Comprehensive Plan of Action for Indochinese Refugees' (1993) 15 Human Rights Quarterly 686.

[72] See, e.g. UNHCR, Resettlement Statistics 2002 (June 2003) which places Australia in 3rd place overall (behind the US and Canada) and New Zealand in 6th place (behind Sweden and Norway).

[73] Department of Immigration and Multicultural and Indigenous Affairs, Fact sheet no 60: Australia's Refugee and Humanitarian Program (20 January 2004). See also the New Zealand Immigration Service (NZIS) website: <www.immigration.govt.nz>.

[74] Department of Immigration and Multicultural and Indigenous Affairs, Fact sheet no 61: Seeking Asylum within Australia (12 November 2003). The figures in Australia have dropped considerably in recent years. Refugee statistics for New Zealand are posted on the NZIS website, ibid.

smugglers who take thousands of dollars to transport human cargoes onto its northern coast'.[75]

In terms of asylum seekers rescued at sea, we have already seen that there is no clear legal obligation to allow boats to enter Australian territorial waters in order to disembark rescuees who intend to seek asylum.[76] A solution needs to explore cooperation between flag States, coastal States and resettlement States. As the port-of-call State is not obliged to accept rescuees for resettlement, practice has been for such States to accept rescuees for disembarkation after obtaining assurances for resettlement from the flag State.[77]

The Australian government's approach to the problems mentioned above is to intercept and detain boat people on offshore territories for processing. To a certain extent, the government's position resembles US initiatives in the Caribbean: the general idea in relation to the interception of Haitian and Cuban boat people is that disembarkation at a transit camp with no specific guarantee of resettlement in the US will discourage asylum seekers from making dangerous sea voyages to the US mainland.

One of the main features of Australia's 'Pacific Solution' is that it involves the use of the Australian Navy to prevent boat people from landing on mainland Australia. The boat people are then transferred to detention centres on offshore Australian territories which have been excised from the country's migration zone where regular immigration rules are in application.[78] Detention centres for such transfers have also been set up on Nauru and Manus Island (Papua New Guinea).[79] As Australia's immigration laws do not apply in these detention centres, the government has assigned Australian officials to apply UNHCR's procedures for determining the legal status of the asylum seekers instead of the domestic procedures.[80] The need for a credible screening process is one of the lessons from the Indochinese boat people crisis of the 1970s and 1980s. The unwritten arrangement involving conditional first asylum was problematic in that resettlement was basically assured for the Indochinese migrants who were rescued and disembarked: this encouraged abuse by some people who were not fleeing persecution.[81]

---

[75] Ryszard Piotrowicz, 'The Case of MV Tampa: State and Refugee Rights Collide at Sea' (2001) 76 Australian Law Journal 12, 13.

[76] Fonteyne, above n 26, 250.

[77] Piotrowicz, above n 75, 16.

[78] The Christmas and Cocos Islands, as well as Ashmore Reef have been excised from the migration zone.

[79] Papua New Guinea was an Australian colony until 1975 and Nauru's foreign relations were handled by Australia until 1975. The territorial application clause found in art 40 of the Refugee Convention was used by Australia to cover Nauru until 1975 (date of receipt of the notification: 22 January 1954).

[80] See, e.g. Graham Thom, 'Human Rights, Refugees and the MV Tampa Crisis' (2002) 13 Public Law Review 110, 110.

[81] For an analysis from a refugee advocate who acknowledges that the arrangement was intended to address the alleged abuse, see Arthur C Helton, 'Refugee Determination under the Comprehensive Plan of Action' (1993) 5 International Journal of Refuge Law 544, 556-7. While the first refugee treaties of the 1920s did not involve screening procedures for the

Unsurprisingly, the controversial 'Pacific Solution' has attracted mixed political reactions: some lawyers morally oppose the government's offloading of asylum claimants on poor and remote territories,[82] while others justify the measures because of the perception that the country has to defend its vast borders in the face of unauthorized boat people arrivals.[83] It is worth emphasizing that courts should generally limit their judgments to the positive law and leave political assessments to the appropriate bodies, even if they may disapprove of the harsh nature of executive actions against boat people. This is one of the basic messages from the full Federal Court of Australia in the Tampa case:

> The steps taken in relation to the MV Tampa which had the purpose and effect of preventing the rescuees from entering the migration zone and arranging for their departure from Australian territorial waters were within the scope of executive power. The finding does not involve a judgment about any policy informing the exercise of that power. That is a matter which has been and continues to be debated in public and indeed international forums. Through that debate and the parliamentary process the Ministers involved can be held accountable for their actions.[84]

The complicated political and moral issues around the 'Pacific Solution' are not explored in this chapter.[85]

In terms of the key international legal obligations, to date there are no reports suggesting that the intercepted boat people have been returned to dangerous countries. Indeed, Australia's assistance with the disembarkation and the determination procedures, along with its financial contributions demonstrate its acceptance of some obligations to facilitate resettlement.

As New Zealand is geographically situated further from refugee-producing areas, it has not been confronted directly with the problems associated with boat people. Government policy is undoubtedly influenced by this favourable context. Yet actions have been taken to protect the country from such eventualities. Indeed, the government has recently conducted interdepartmental exercises to explore various scenarios involving boat people. It is not clear what contingency plans it has prepared in the unlikely case that boat people were to approach New Zealand's

---

designated beneficiaries (eg fleeing Russians and Armenians), by the end of the Second World War it was deemed necessary to have the newly created International Refugee Organization apply what were probably the first individualized determination procedures in public international law. See, e.g. Denis Alland, 'Les organisations internationals et les réfugiés' in René-Jean Dupuy (ed.), Manuel sur les organisations internationals (1998) 496.

[82] For receiving the Tampa asylum seekers, Australia promised Nauru A$10 million worth of fuel, A$3 million for new generators, cancellation of A$1 million worth of hospital bills run by Nauruans in Australia, refurbishment of the small island's sports oval, as well as sporting and educational scholarships for Nauruans to go to Australia.

[83] For an example of a refugee advocate who believes the measures are justified, see Carlos Scott Lopez, 'Australian Immigration Policy at the Centenary: The Quest for Control' (2003) 18 Georgetown Immigration Law Journal 1, 54.

[84] Ruddock v Vadarlis [2001] FCA 1329, [204] (French J).

[85] For a useful and critical discussion on these issues, see OXFAM, Adrift in the Pacific: The implications of Australia's Pacific Refugee Solution (February 2002).

territorial waters,[86] although mass detention in the remote Rangipo desert prison has been discussed in the past.

The above analysis suggests that the regional 'Pacific Solution' to the problem of boat people is politically awkward. However, to the extent that its main promoter, Australia, has seen a dramatic drop in the number of boat people attempting to enter its territorial waters, the approach has been at least partly successful from a border control perspective. This is undoubtedly why several European states have expressed an interest in exploring a similar concept: the establishment of safe areas for refugee processing on the periphery of Europe. As with US attempts to create a similar regional approach in the Caribbean, the combination of interception and offshore processing appears to be limited to an ad hoc response for emergency situations. Australia has taken this approach as far as it has been implemented to date and its experiences indicate that the diplomatic constraints are considerable. The lessons from its experiences will undoubtedly be used by other actors who are interested in pursuing this approach as a generalized policy response to boat people.

Conclusion

States have indicated formally that they intend to protect refugees by adopting the Refugee Convention and its Protocol, along with various soft law instruments. However, the protection commitments are not unconditional. Not only are they placed within the larger context of immigration control, but they are mitigated by discretionary powers concerning security.

Although notions of sovereignty have evolved over recent years, our international system continues to be dominated by the key concept of State sovereignty. This is particularly evident in the area of transnational migration controls. To date States have not even consented to a binding system that grants territorial asylum to individuals who actually meet the legal requirements of the refugee definition in the Refugee Convention. The non-refoulement guarantee that forms the backbone of the international refugee protection system simply prohibits States from sending refugee claimants to dangerous territories where they may fear persecution. In other words, the refugee can be sent to a third country where there is no fear of persecution or risk of being transferred to another dangerous country. From a refugee protection standpoint, this is clearly far from ideal. Yet it is important to underline that this legal situation reflects the actual political commitments that State representatives are willing to assume on the international stage.

Given the context of limited international legal obligations described in this chapter, the struggle for the free movement of people across national borders should not be waged on the back of asylum seekers. This is a particularly vulnerable group of foreigners who risk suffering disproportionately from any xenophobia in host societies. Genuine refugees cannot afford survival strategies based on wishful thinking because they are de facto stateless. Neither should they

[86] 'Personnel take part in migrant ship exercise', New Zealand Herald, 8 October 2003.

be encouraged to do so by well-intentioned human rights advocates. The tone of the decision rendered by the US Supreme Court regarding Haitian boat people intercepted by the Coast Guard deserves to be emphasized in order to avoid misguided legal strategies in the future:

> The drafters of the Convention ... may not have contemplated that any nation would gather fleeing refugees and return them to the one country they had desperately sought to escape; such actions may even violate the spirit of Article 33; but a treaty cannot impose uncontemplated extraterritorial obligations on those who ratify it through no more than its general humanitarian intent.[87]

Advocates for open borders should focus their political activism on easing border restrictions between liberal democratic States for this more accurately reflects the positive developments concerning sovereignty and migration in recent years. Indeed, national borders and community membership in some of the affluent parts of the world have been transformed to such an extent that notions of citizenship and nationality are no longer what they used to be in the post-Second World War period. However, it is less evident that this development characterizes exchanges between countries with widely varying cultures and economic performance. Intercontinental migration that involves significant cross-cultural differences continues to be dominated by the key concept of State sovereignty.

The above reflections are crucial to understanding the legal and political dimensions of refugee burden-sharing. Whether it is conceived as an emergency mechanism intended to save refugees from an overburdened host State or as a pre-planned 'insurance' scheme meant to provide a multilateral response to future refugee flows, the issue of burden-sharing has been debated considerably in recent years. Yet despite repeated attempts to establish norms that can be translated into practice, burden-sharing has never been more than an ad hoc and discretionary feature of the current system. Even though thousands of persons displaced by the conflicts in Bougainville and the Solomon Islands have contributed to instability in local host communities, their plight has not attracted the kind of attention that mobilizes third countries to share the burden by providing asylum. Likewise, protection for the thousands of people who have fled Indonesian-ruled West Papua has been limited to refuge in Papua New Guinea and assistance from international organizations.

Acknowledging the circumstances under which refugees can raise regional security concerns helps policymakers respond more effectively in order to manage the problem. Managing refugee movements is, after all, a primary objective of international refugee law. It is not, as suggested by some refugee law scholars, simply to protect refugees. If such were the case, unconditional protection guarantees relating to asylum would have found their way in treaty law. The drafters of the Refugee Convention were clearly preoccupied by other dimensions as well. It is this balancing act that makes refugee law a complicated field.

---

[87] Sale v Haitian Centers Council, 113 S Ct 2549 (1993).

At the beginning of the twenty-first century, refugee protection is an area of international law and policy in which it is often difficult to have a frank debate. This is due largely to the symbolic importance for the key actors to project certain images of themselves when dealing with refugee law. States such as New Zealand and Australia are rightly proud of their contribution to international refugee protection through resettlement programmes, and their governments make good use of this record for public relations purposes. At the same time, domestic political circumstances often dictate the need to appear tough on border control, as was demonstrated by the Tampa affair.[88]

The analysis in this chapter does not encourage potential host States to prevent admission of mass influxes on their territory because that would likely increase tensions in border areas. Temporary admission with assurances of burden-sharing from third States appears to be the only acceptable policy response. It is this form of international solidarity that the chapter seeks to promote. Recognizing the conditionality of admission in such situations simply acknowledges actual State practice, as demonstrated by an examination of the South Pacific, as well as the Asia-Pacific region more generally. This is the realist response to burden-sharing in mass refugee flow situations. It proposes that being upfront about the actual protection obligations assumed by States in terms of binding law is more useful for policymakers than pretending that States will meet vaguely-defined high standards in soft law instruments which may jeopardize national security. The objective is not to avoid any State responsibility in terms of refugee protection, but rather to articulate the commitments in a politically acceptable manner. A genuine debate on this issue must first acknowledge the complicated interplay between law and politics in the field of international refugee protection, as wall as the contrasting interests and agendas that limit what is possible in terms of policy formulation.

---

[88] See, e.g. William Maley, 'Security, people smuggling, and Australia's refugees' (2001) 55 Australian Journal of International Affairs 351 and Mark Beeson, 'Issues in Australian Foreign Policy' (2002) 48 Australian Journal of Politics and History 226, 231-2.

Chapter 2

Regional Cooperation in the Suppression of Transnational Crime in the South Pacific

Neil Boister*

Introduction

The Honiara Declaration on Law Enforcement Cooperation, adopted by the Pacific Islands Forum (hereinafter the Forum) in 1992, initiated a significant regional effort to suppress transnational crime in the South Pacific.[1] This chapter sketches the development of this regional response. It first examines why the Forum has identified certain activities as threats to the region. It then examines how the Forum has attempted to suppress these threats using a regional approach within a framework of international obligations. Finally it examines how effective this process is in getting domestic laws updated and implemented in Forum members. It does so with the further aim of making some general observations about the process of transferring penal norms from the developed to the developing world through regional systems.

The Forum provides a good case study of this process because it consists mainly of poor developing countries (the Pacific Island Countries or PICs) which have been identified as source and transit zones of transnational criminal activity into developed states (Australia, New Zealand and other states outside the region). The transfer of penal policies and associated legal norms from the developed to the developing world is not new; consider, for example, the impact of colonial penal

---

* Versions of this piece were presented at the ANZSIL Conference, Australian National University, 18–20 June 2004, and the SLS Conference, University of Sheffield, 13–16 September 2004. I am grateful to Professor Lawrence Kalinoe, UPNG, for his comments on a draft of this chapter.

[1] The South Pacific may be defined as either region or sub-region. The Forum members are: Australia, Cook Islands, Federated States of Micronesia, Fiji, Kiribati, Nauru, New Zealand, Niue, Palau, Papua New Guinea, Republic of the Marshall Islands, Samoa, Solomon Islands, Tonga, Tuvalu, Vanuatu. The Forum has observer status at the UN. The Forum's 'dialogue partners', states or organizations with significant interests in the region, are: Canada, the PRC, the EU, France, Indonesia, Japan, Republic of Korea, Malaysia, the Philippines, the UK and the US.

codes. In the post-colonial period, however, this process has continued through international law. Transfer usually follows a simple pattern.[2] Developed states initiate formal diplomatic contact with developing states in order to transfer crime control measures. This contact leads to a diplomatic conference and the adoption of a multilateral treaty. Developed states are the active law givers[3] and developing states are largely passive 'law-takers' in this process; they may play a role in the negotiation and adoption of these treaties but the content and enforcement of these treaties is largely in the hands of developed states.

In association with this macro-level process a range of meso- and micro-level contacts occur between law enforcement middle managers and operational officers where the bulk of the actual 'technology transfer' takes place. The technology involves more than laws, it involves policy, practical know-how, administrative arrangements and institutions.[4] Informal contacts set the development of a treaty under way and develop domestic law and practice; the adoption of the treaty provides a formal obligation upon which law enforcement officials from developed states can rely when enthusiasm for cooperation ebbs. The essence of this model is that not only policy is transferred, legal norms are transferred, and not only political pressure is exerted to ensure transfer, international legal obligations are relied upon to ensure transfer. Regional organizations play an intermediate role in developing regional norms and policies to meet global concerns through adapting global models to regional conditions, and serving as conduits for the transfer of these norms and policies. The goal of the process is to harmonize the practice of all states with regard to the definition, punishment and processing of transnational crimes.[5]

The motivation for this transfer is rhetorically the interest of the international community in the internal welfare of its members. This rhetoric conceals concerns about developing states being used as springboards for transnational crimes directed at and harmful or at least potentially harmful to the interests of developed states. Examining the motivation for transfer more closely, if transnational crime is conceptualized as a 'global public bad', and the international and national laws suppressing this crime as a 'global public good',[6] the question is: who benefits from this good? To be a global public good, transnational criminal law must serve the interests of a broad spectrum of states and of a broad socio-economic spectrum

---

[2] These ideas are more fully explored in Neil Boister, 'Transnational Penal Norm Transfer: The Transfer of Civil Forfeiture from the United States to South Africa as a Case in Point' (2003) 16 *South African Journal of Criminal Justice* 271.

[3] See Susan Silbey, '1886 Presidential Address: "Let Them Eat Cake": Globalization, Postmodern Colonialism, and the Possibilities of Justice' (1997) 31 *Law and Society Review* 207, 221.

[4] See David Dolowitz and David Marsh, 'Who Learns From Whom? A Review of the Policy Transfer Literature' (1996) 44 *Political Studies* 343, 344.

[5] See generally Mireille Delmas-Marty, *Global Law: A Triple Challenge* (2003) 81.

[6] See generally Inge Kaul, Isabelle Grunberg and Marc Stern, 'Defining Global Public Goods' in Kaul, Grunberg and Stern (eds), *Global Public Goods: International Cooperation in the 21st Century* (1999) 2ff.

within those states.[7] The development of transnational criminal law is a matter of concern because it is clearly the product of developed states designed to protect their interests. Developing states may not choose to suppress this conduct without pressure from developed states. Having given in to this pressure, they will usually have no alternative but to seek lessons from abroad on how to suppress this conduct because of their impoverishment.[8] In doing so they must ignore the fact that the developed states' policies and practices frequently arise in inefficient, costly, inhumane and discriminatory justice systems.[9]

The danger is that, in general terms, a unidirectional dispersal of norms from certain developed states to the rest of the international community becomes a process of the globalization of laws through their spatial distribution, rather than the universalization of laws through the development of shared meaning.[10] To put this into context, for developed states interested in the South Pacific the key issue is claimed to be effectiveness. But this issue conceals two questions: first, whether there is a genuine consensus to suppress transnational crime in the South Pacific at a national level through the agency of a regional organization, and second, whether these norms will be understood and internalized as obligatory social rules by the inhabitants of the countries to whom they are applied because they recognize these norms as legitimate expressions of authority.[11] Effectiveness cannot be divorced from issues of legitimacy both at a national and personal level.

Transnational crime in the South Pacific

The Forum responds: the Honiara Declaration

There is a plethora of organizations engaged in crime control in the South Pacific. Many cover a broader jurisdiction of which the South Pacific is only a part;[12] others are more specifically focused on the South Pacific.[13] The Forum is the pre-eminent intergovernmental institution working only in the South Pacific. In 1992, responding to an initiative of the Pacific Islands Law Officers' Meeting (PILOM), the Forum identified the need for strengthening regional cooperation in the law

---

[7] Ibid 10-12.

[8] See Tim Newburn, 'Atlantic Crossings: "Policy Transfer" and Crime Control in the USA and Britain' (2002) 4 *Punishment and Society* 165, 170.

[9] Ibid 166.

[10] Delmas-Marty, above n 6, 2.

[11] On the difference see Herbert Hart, *The Concept of Law* (2nd ed, 1994) 56ff.

[12] For example, the Manila Process, Asia Pacific Consultations (APCs), Regional Ministerial Conferences, the Association of South East Asian States (ASEAN), Asian Pacific Economic Cooperation (APEC), Council for Security Cooperation in the Asia Pacific (CSCAP), Pacific Rim Immigration Intelligence Officer's Conference (PACRIM), the Pacific Immigration Directors Conference (PIDC), and the Oceania Customs Organisation (OCO).

[13] For example, the South Pacific Chief of Police Conference (SPCPC) and the Pacific Islands Law Officers Meeting (PILOM).

enforcement field and agreed to a declaration on law enforcement cooperation. Forum leaders set out the rationale for the Honiara Declaration[14] in its opening paragraphs:

1. … An adverse law enforcement environment could threaten the sovereignty, security and economic integrity of Forum members and jeopardize economic and social development. The threats to the stability of the region were complex and sophisticated, and the potential impact of transnational crime was a matter of increasing concern to regional states and enforcement agencies. The Forum agreed that there was a need for a more comprehensive, integrated and collaborative approach to counter these threats.

2. The Forum considered that law enforcement cooperation should therefore remain an important focus for the region. The scale of criminal activity affecting the region could expand. Forum leaders noted that the balance in economic and social development, the primary goal of all the countries of the region, could not be achieved without the assurance of safety and security. Early action to strengthen the existing framework to tackle potential law enforcement problems should therefore be taken.

The Declaration prioritizes certain law enforcement areas:

3. The Forum noted that certain areas of law enforcement had emerged as particularly important to members. These included necessary legislation on extradition, proceeds of crime (assets forfeiture), mutual criminal assistance, and other aspects of economic crime. In addition, further legislation might be necessary in some areas concerning drug issues.

The Declaration is a regional response to policy makers' perceptions of the growth of transnational economic and drug offences in the South Pacific.[15] Its stated goal is effective law enforcement to suppress these activities through the implementation and use of national legislative measures in the key areas of extradition, mutual legal assistance and money laundering/asset forfeiture.

The justification for this action is the threat presented by transnational crime to the safety and security of Forum members. In 1992, the threat of transnational crime in the South Pacific appeared largely potential; the Declaration states that 'the scale of criminal activity affecting the region could expand'. By 2001,

---

[14] *Declaration by the South Pacific Forum on Law Enforcement Cooperation*, Annex to the *Forum Communiqué*, Twenty-Third Pacific Islands Forum, Honiara, Solomon Islands, 8–9 July 1992 ('Honiara Declaration'); all Forum communiqués were available at The Pacific Islands Forum Secretariat <http://www.forumsec.org.fj/> at 26 January 2005.

[15] A concern repeated over the years by key figures. See, for example, the statement of then Forum Secretary General Noel Levi to the 2001 PILOM Meeting, 22 October 2001, *Press Statement 8101*, The Pacific Islands Forum <http://www.forumsec.org.fj/news/2001/Oct04.htm> at 29 December 2003.

however, the Forum felt able to state that there was 'clear evidence of serious transnational crime moving into the region and posing serious threats to the sovereignty, security and economic integrity of forum members'.[16] These threats included money laundering, terrorist recruitment, identity fraud, West African fraud, people smuggling, issuing passports of convenience, engaging in electronic crimes, small arms trafficking, illegally trading in endangered wildlife, drug trafficking and organized crime.[17] It is worth examining some of these threats more closely.

Money laundering

Prior to the adoption of the Honiara Declaration in 1992, the Forum Secretariat (Forumsec) engaged in a 'Law Enforcement Needs Assessment Study', which identified the South Pacific as a risk area for money laundering activities.[18] Twelve years later, the image of PICs as money laundering centres is pervasive, and it appears to be borne out by the evidence.[19] The opportunity for laundering arose when PICs, relying on foreign legal and commercial skills, began to develop lucrative businesses as Offshore Financial Centres (OFCs) through removing exchange controls, deregulating currency movement, imposing strict bank secrecy legislation and allowing anonymous shareholding.[20] The Cook Islands High Court, for example, confirmed memorably that the purpose of the Cook Islands' haven law was to make it as difficult as possible for creditors to exercise their rights.[21] The incentive to launderers was provided by more restrictive practices elsewhere,[22] the incentive to PICs by the opportunity to acquire alternative sources of revenue.[23] Since the mid-1990s a large number of financial institutions have been registered

---

[16] *Forum Communiqué*, Thirty-Second Pacific Islands Forum, Republic of Nauru, 16–18 August 2001, [38].

[17] *Forum Communiqué*, Thirty-Fourth Pacific Islands Forum, Auckland, New Zealand, 14–16 August 2003, [21]-[25]. See generally, on the criminal threats facing the Pacific, Andreas Schloenhardt, 'Transnational Crime and Island State Security in the South Pacific' in Eric Shibuya and Jim Rolfe (eds), *Security in Oceania in the 21st Century* (2003) 171; UNODC, *Profile on the Pacific Islands* (2003), UNODC Regional Center Thailand <http://www.unodc.un.or.th/material/document/2004/Regional%20Profile%20Pacific%20Island.pdf> at 20 December 2004.

[18] Honiara Declaration, above n 14, [10].

[19] Anthony Van Fossen, 'Money Laundering, Global Financial Instability, and Tax Havens in the Pacific Islands' (2003) 15(2) *Contemporary Pacific* 237, 239-41; Schloenhardt, above n 17, 178-83; UNODC, above n 17, 18.

[20] Van Fossen, above n 19, 362-7; Anselm Herman, 'Money Laundering and the Law in the Republics of Fiji and Vanuatu: A Critical Analysis' (1999) 3 *Journal of South Pacific Law* 17, 18.

[21] High Court of the Cook Islands Civil Division, Plain No 208/94, 6 November 1995, Judgment on Appeal 20 Dec 1995, cited by Ron Crocombe, *The South Pacific* (2001) 364-5.

[22] Herman, above n 20, 21.

[23] Australian Senate Foreign Affairs, Defence and Trade Committee Report, *A Pacific Engaged: Australia's Relations with Papua New Guinea and the Island States of the South West Pacific* (2003) 177, Parliament of Australia, <http://www.aph.gov.au/senate/Committee/fadt_ctte/png/report/C07.pdf> at 7 October 2004.

in OFCs across the Pacific.[24] The discovery in 1995 that the Bank of New York had laundered billions for the Russian Mafia through banks in Nauru resulted in large US banks unilaterally suspending dealing with banks in Nauru, Palau, Vanuatu and Niue.[25] In 1998, the Financial Action Task Force (FATF) claimed that Vanuatu's legislation provided favourable conditions for an increase in money laundering.[26] In 2000, FATF blacklisted as non-cooperative the Cook Islands, Marshall Islands, Niue and Nauru, opening them to counter-measures including heightened security by banks dealing with financial transactions originating from these jurisdictions.[27] The Cook Islands responded by enacting legislation and joining the Asia Pacific Group on Money Laundering (APG-ML), but FATF was unconvinced and the blacklisting is still being maintained.[28] In 2001, FATF recommended sanctions against Nauru[29] and in 2004 complained that Nauru licenced 400 offshore shell banks with no physical presence and maintained excessive bank secrecy provisions.[30] The APG-ML reports a number of cases of money laundering through Vanuatu,[31] but Vanuatu and the Marshall Islands have avoided a similar fate through legislative reform. Ironically, both the pressure to liberalize finance markets and deregulate exchange control regulations and the effort to control money laundering has emanated largely from developed states.[32] Local and global financial stability is said to be at stake,[33] but laundering's potential to cause harm in PICs is difficult to assess. It is said to be able to corrupt weakly regulated local institutions, destabilize legitimate economic activity and discourage development.[34]

Drug trafficking

The location of PICs between Asia and markets in North America, Australia and New Zealand makes them potential way stations for trans-Pacific smuggling. A desire to attract tourists and investors, small police forces, and outdated laws all suggest increased vulnerability. The pattern of drug seizures suggests transit rather than the import or export of drugs. In 1996, nearly a million dollars worth of

[24] Australian Bureau of Criminal Intelligence, *Australian Illicit Drug Report 1998–1999* (2000) 115.

[25] Van Fossen, above n 19, 244-8.

[26] Van Fossen, above n 19, 240.

[27] FATF, *Annual Review of Non-Cooperative Countries or Territories* (2004) (*Annual Review 2004*) 1.

[28] In 2004 the Cook Islands still had 1200 companies registered and no relevant information about them, but only 16 offshore banks: see ibid 8.

[29] FATF, *Review to Identify Non-Cooperative Countries or Territories* (2001).

[30] FATF, *Annual Review 2004*, above n 27, 12.

[31] Herman, above n 20, 21.

[32] Herman, above n 20, 22.

[33] Van Fossen, above n 19, 268.

[34] Pierre-Laurant Chatain, 'The World Bank's Role in the Fight Against Money Laundering and Terrorist Financing' (2004) 6 *International Law Forum* 190, 190-91.

cocaine was found in a shipment of Tongan yams bound for Auckland.[35] In 2000, police in Suva seized 350kg of heroin used as a stockpile to supply Australia, New Zealand and Canada.[36] In 2001, 90kg of cocaine was seized transiting New Caledonia, and 100kg of cocaine was seized in Tonga.[37] In 2002, 74kg of methamphetamine was found on a ship in Singapore headed for Fiji and Australia and Hawaiian police broke-up a syndicate that smuggled cocaine and methamphetamine to the US mainland, Tonga, Fiji, Australia and New Zealand, while in 2003, almost 2.5kg of pseudoephedrine, a key ingredient in amphetamines, was found in scuba tanks shipped to Brisbane from Fiji.[38] In 2004, police shut down a large methamphetamine laboratory near Suva apparently intended to supply the market in Thailand, New Zealand and Australia.[39] They found 5kg of methamphetamines and nearly a tonne of precursor chemicals with an estimated street value once refined of $522 million. The Fijian Police Commissioner stated:

> This is a frightening example of transnational organised crime elements using Fiji as a staging ground for their illegal activities. Increasingly we are seeing these elements coming to Fiji and joining up with local organised criminal groups.[40]

A Chinese Malaysian conspiracy allegedly ran the drug factory and bribed a local official to cooperate. In September 2004, 120kg of cocaine was found on a beach in Vanuatu, the largest amount ever discovered in that country.[41] These are not small amounts by any standard.

Summing up the situation, the Australian Federal Police (AFP) warns that the region has been targeted to move drugs and that drug trafficking is a good indicator of the rise in transnational criminal activity.[42] Cooperation is offered as the only solution. Superintendent Larry Reid, acting national manager of the New Zealand Police (NZP), concludes: 'No single country can deal with the problem on its own'.[43] But there are leading players in the cooperative effort. After the raid on the methamphetamine laboratory in Suva in 2004, the Australian Minister for Justice and Customs, Senator Chris Ellison said:

> The success of this operation sends a crystal-clear message to organised drug syndicates that the combined efforts of international law enforcement agencies will ensure that transnational crime will not be allowed to gain a foothold in the region …

---

[35] Crocombe, *The South Pacific*, above n 21, 370.

[36] Elizabeth Feizkhah, 'Ice: From Gang to Bust', *Time Asia Magazine*, 21 June 2004, Time Online <http://www.time.com/time/asia/magazine/article/0,13673,501040628-655460,00.html> at 28 February 2005.

[37] Australian Senate Foreign Affairs, Defence and Trade Committee Report, above n 23, 194.

[38] Feizkhah, above n 36.

[39] David Fickling, 'Police Bust Fiji Drug Factory', *The Guardian Weekly*, 18–24 June 2004, 5.

[40] Ibid.

[41] 'Record Cocaine Haul in Vanuatu', *Port Villa Presse*, 10 September 2004 <http://www.news.vu/en/news/national/record-cocaine-haul-in-va.shtml> at 28 February 2005.

[42] Australian Senate Foreign Affairs, Defence and Trade Committee Report, above n 23, 195.

[43] Feizkhah, above n 36. See Schloenhardt, n17, 183, for similar sentiments.

> Australia has been providing funding and other forms of assistance, such as training, in the Pacific region to ensure that countries in the South Pacific cannot be exploited by drug traffickers and manufacturers, particularly against the backdrop of a world wide growth in amphetamine supply and demand ... The best way to stop drugs harming Australians is for our law enforcement and border protection agencies to work closely with our international partners to attack the illicit drug trade offshore.[44]

Drug trafficking in the region is largely directed at supplying illicit markets elsewhere and has been planned and financed from elsewhere. The authors of a United Nations Office of Drugs and Crime (UNODC) discussion report note that '[t]here is little evidence of a local presence in the Pacific Islands controlling the transhipments; rather most cases reveal criminal syndicates operating from outside the Pacific'.[45] Other than cannabis cultivation for markets within the region, drug production in the region is not significant.[46] The use of drugs in PICs is less easy to quantify. There is extensive use of cannabis in many PICs (Papua New Guinea and Micronesia report the highest prevalence in the world), and in Palau, for example, police ignore public consumption. Consumption of more potent drugs has taken root in Palau and Guam and appears to be increasing in Samoa but it is not a regional epidemic.[47]

Arms smuggling

The proliferation of small arms has had a negative impact on recent regional security threats in the islands, such as the civil wars on Bougainville and in the Solomons, and incidents of violence in Vanuatu, Fiji, the Solomon Islands and Papua New Guinea (PNG).[48] There have been, for example, informal reports of weapons smuggling from Bougainville to the Solomon Islands. The April 2003

---

[44] Quoted in *Massive Drug Bust in Fiji*, 10 June 2004, Findlaw Australia <http://www.findlaw.com.au/news/default.asp?task=read&id=20505&site=CN> at 14 July, 2004.

[45] UNODC, above n 17, 10.

[46] Crocombe, *The South Pacific*, above n 21, 85. This leads Shibuya to suggest that the major supply of drugs originates within the region – Eric Shibuya, 'Oceania's Post 9/11 Security Concerns: Common Causes, Uncommon Approaches' (2003) 2(7) *Asia-Pacific Center for Security Studies* 1, 2, <http//:www.apcss.org/Research/research_publications.html> at 20 December 2004. However, although it records cannabis production in the region, the UNODC reports that none of the islands is considered a major global producer of any kind of drug. See UNODC, above n 17, 8.

[47] Transform Aqorau, *The Pacific: Maintaining the rule of law and regional cooperation* (Unpublished paper presented to the Twenty Second PILOM Meeting, Melbourne, Australia, 20–22 October 2003) 3; Crocombe, *The South Pacific*, above n 21, 86; Mac Marshall, 'Alcohol and Drug Abuse' in Brij V Lal and Kate Fortune (eds), *The Pacific Islands: An Encyclopaedia* (2000) 448. An outbreak of heroin abuse in Palau occurred in 1985–86, but is no longer considered a problem. See UNODC, above n 17, 9-10.

[48] Aqorau above n 47, 5, citing Pacific Islands Forum Secretariat, *Small Arms Control*, PIFS (03) FRSC 11 Session 1, Paper prepared for the Forum Regional Security Committee Meeting, 18–20 June 2003 (2003).

Report Small Arms in the Pacific[49] details the proliferation of arms trading in the Pacific but points to the removal of weapons from police and military armouries as the biggest source of supply. The negative effect has not been felt directly by surrounding developed states. For example, there appears to be little arms trafficking from PNG into Australia.[50]

Terrorism[51]

The Bali Bombings of 12 October 2002 and terrorist activities in the Southern Philippines have raised fears of transnational terrorism in the region.[52] The AFP cites the potential for the South Pacific to serve as an operational base for terrorism because of porous borders, inadequate law enforcement capacity, isolated islands and the presence of 'soft Western targets'.[53] As a concrete example, PNG is concerned about possible terrorist threats to Australian and American interests in PNG through terrorist incursions from Irian Jaya (West Papua), the Indonesian part of New Guinea.[54] The issuing of passports of convenience by Forum members is viewed as a potential risk from the point of view of terrorist activity.[55] At the local level, internal political struggles within PICs have seen the actual perpetration of terrorist acts.[56]

Corruption

Hughes speaks of 'corruption on a relatively wide scale' in PICs[57] and in 2003 Transparency International identified corruption as a major threat to PICs.[58] The evidence suggests that corruption is endemic in the governments of many PICs, official positions are used to attract foreign economic patronage, and official measures to suppress this corruption are ineffective.[59] Crocombe reports corruption

---

[49] Philip Alpers and Conor Twyford, 'Small Arms in The Pacific', *Small Arms Survey Occasional Paper no. 8*, March 2003 <http://www.smallarmssurvey.org/OPs/OP08Pacifics.pdf> at 27 January 2004.

[50] Australian Senate Foreign Affairs, Defence and Trade Committee Report, above n 23, 182-4.

[51] On terrorism in the Pacific see Alex Conte in this volume.

[52] Aqorau, above n 47, 5.

[53] Australian Senate Foreign Affairs, Defence and Trade Committee Report, above n 23, 194, citing *Committee Hansard*, 27 March 2003, 354, 358 (AFP).

[54] Australian Senate Foreign Affairs, Defence and Trade Committee Report, above n 23, 194.

[55] Aqorau, above n 47, 6.

[56] See the 'Pacific Islands Security: Old Challenges, New Threats', *Report on the Pacific Islands Political Science Association (PIPSA) Conference, University of the Sunshine Coast, 4–6 December 2002*, 3.

[57] Robert Hughes, 'Corruption' in Anita Jowitt and Tess Newton-Cain (eds), *Passage of Change – Law, Society and Governance in the Pacific* (2003) 35, 36.

[58] *The Kooralbyn Declaration*, Transparency International, <http://www.transparency.org.au/documents/Kooralbyn_Declaration.pdf > at 4 August 2003.

[59] Crocombe, *The South Pacific*, above n 21, 513-15.

in the timber industry, conflicts of business interests, broad small scale corruption, the elimination of government opponents, corruption disguised as tradition and affirmative action, the involvement of whole governments, and the purchase of elections and electors.[60] Some of this activity is transnational in nature, some purely internal. Sometimes the potential is devastating. For example, in 1996 the Vanuatu Ombudsman exposed a financial scam that involved the Prime Minister and Minister of Finance and that had the potential to bankrupt the country.[61] Possible reasons for the proliferation of corruption include the vulnerability of officials and the cultural irrelevance of Western institutions.[62]

Human trafficking and people smuggling

The region is being used as a transit zone for both human trafficking and people smuggling, and identity document fraud compounds the problem.[63] New Zealand is a destination country for trafficking of women from South East Asia for sexual commercial purposes, while Australia is a destination country for women trafficked for commercial sexual exploitation and for people smuggling.[64] However, PICs are themselves the destination for illegal migrants from outside and within the region.[65]

Organized and other crimes

Organized crime appears to be more common in some areas than in others. For example, there is evidence that Asian organized crime has moved into Micronesia.[66] Organized crime groups diversify. Thus identity fraud has been

[60] Ibid 520-41.

[61] Herman, above n 20, 21. Ombudsman Marie-Noelle Ferrieux-Patterson denounced the diversion of funds meant for cyclone victim aid, the issuing of false passports and the misappropriation of monies from pension funds – *The World Guide 2001–2002* (2001) 563.

[62] Hughes, above n 57, 46.

[63] Schloenhardt, above n 17, 174. At 175 Schloenhardt notes the use of fraudulent travel documents from Naura, Tonga and the sale by the Marshall Islands of 1000s of passports. See also Shibuya, above n 46, 3.

[64] See *New Zealand*, Human Trafficking.org <http://.www.humantrafficking.org/countries/eap/new_zealand/index.html> at 22 October 2004, and *Australia*, Human Trafficking.org <http://www.humantrafficking.org/countries/eap/australia/index.html> at 22 October 2004. Schloenhardt, above n 17, 176-7, notes reports of transiting migrants through PNG and New Caledonia. These activities have lead Australia to leasing out island state territory for quarantine and processing services – see the statement of the then Secretary General of the Forum Noel Levi to the 2001 PILOM Meeting, 22 October 2001, *Press Statement 8101*, Pacific Islands Forum, <http://www.forumsec.org.fj/news/2001/Oct04.htm> at 29 December 2003.

[65] Schloenhardt, above n 17, 177. The UNODC, above n 17, 24, notes concerns about Fiji becoming a centre for child-sex tourism.

[66] Crocombe, *The South Pacific*, above n 21, 569.

linked to other transnational crimes such as human trafficking, terrorism[67] and the illegal trade in endangered species.[68] The syndicate exposed by Fiji's 2000 heroin seizure was, for further example, also involved in people smuggling and credit card fraud.

Evaluating threats

These threats to external and local interests cannot be individually assessed here. Nevertheless, they have been used to support the process of development of a regional response to transnational crime. The necessity for such a response is, however, buttressed by a number of further motivating factors.

Much reliance is placed on the impact of globalization. At the 2002 Meeting of the Forum in Suva, the Forum endorsed the Nasonini Declaration, which reiterated the commitment made in the Honiara Declaration to act collectively to meet security challenges including the adverse effects of globalization such as transnational crimes.[69] In the rhetoric of the UN criminal justice agencies, transnational crime is a risk run by all.[70] All states are vulnerable because national borders are more porous, there are fewer trade restrictions and finance and telecommunications systems are global.[71] With respect to the South Pacific, Aqorau notes:

> Developments in communications technology suggest that the types of threats and violence facing the region are changing, and could rapidly alter the ability of many Pacific island governments to cope with this shifting dynamic.[72]

However, the hypothesis that criminal activity inevitably follows interconnectedness depends in part on illustrating that the region is interconnected, which is difficult considering its poor infrastructure. A sceptic might argue that what we are witnessing is a global moral panic that constructs transnational crime as a 'folk-devil' deserving of the most serious response, a panic shaped by

---

67 Aqorau, above n 47, 7, citing Pacific Islands Forum Secretariat, *Identity Fraud: PIFS (03) FRSC.6 Session 1*, Paper prepared for the Forum Regional Security Committee Meeting, 18–20 June 2003 (2003).

68 Aqorau, above n 47, 7, citing Pacific Islands Forum Secretariat, *Illegal Trade in Endangered Species*, PIFS (03) FRSC.10, Session 1, Paper prepared for the Forum Regional Security Committee Meeting, 18–20 June 2003 (2003).

69 *Nasonini Declaration on Regional Security*, [1], Annex 1 to the *Forum Communiqué*, Thirty-Third Pacific Islands Forum, Suva, Fiji Islands, 15–17 August, 2002 ('Nasonini Declaration').

70 See, for example, the *Discussion Guide to the Eleventh United Nations Congress on Crime Prevention and Criminal Justice*, UN Doc. A/Conf.203/PM.1.

71 Ibid [9].

72 See Transform Aqorau, *Current Developments on Forum Initiatives to Combat Transnational and Organised Crime: the 2003 Extradition Act* (Unpublished Paper presented to the 2003 Fiji Attorney-General's Conference, Outrigger Hotel, Sigatoka, 14–16 November 2003) 4; Schloenhardt, above n 17, 172.

politicians, the media, the police and the courts rather than entirely by the criminals themselves.[73] Whatever the case, it does seem likely that the global and regional dimensions of crime are not necessarily identical, and that given that PICs are at the global periphery, arguments about the penetration of the region by transnational crime must be buttressed by something other than just 'globalization'.

A more compelling argument for a regional response is the link made between external threats and the manifest internal problems of PICs. Threats to sovereignty and stability, such as land disputes, economic disparities, ethnic tensions, and failures of governance and the rule of law,[74] encourage penetration of the region by transnational crime. The Forum acknowledged this in the 2000 Biketawa Declaration by linking good governance and security.[75] In particular, relative immunity from law enforcement makes developing states attractive bases for criminals to use for provision of illicit goods and services to areas where the risks are higher. Governments may prove unwilling or unable to suppress these activities.[76] In the most severe cases the spectre of a 'failed state' looms.[77] If transnational crime appears to be a contributing factor to potential failure, it justifies pressure from developed states for action against transnational crime. The reverse is also true; failed states may provide safe harbour for transnational crime which will also justify intervention. Crocombe notes that Australia's interest in the 'arc of instability' in the South Pacific grew from the position where it refused to get involved in the Solomons to its wholesale support for intervention, not because of a deep-seated humanitarianism but because of the potential a failed state provided for transnational crime directed at Australia.[78] A problem with this rationalization is that some PICs may not have been established in any meaningful sense as sovereigns in the first instance, which makes demanding that they suppress transnational crime inapt, and portends the likelihood of continued direct suppression by developed states from the colonial into the post-colonial era.

A unique regional factor that compounds the opportunity for transnational crime is the size of the region and the fact that most PICs are completely surrounded by international waters through which private individuals can travel

---

[73] Stanley Cohen, *Folk Devils and Moral Panics: The Creation of Mods and Rockers* (1972) 9.

[74] Aqorau, above n 72, 3. Schloenhardt, above n 17, 172, points out the absence of diversification in island state economies makes them more vulnerable to transnational crime.

[75] *Biketawa Declaration*, Attachment 1 to the *Forum Communiqué*, Thirty-First Pacific Islands Forum, Tarawa, Kiribati, 27–30 October 2000.

[76] Phil Williams and Ernestor Savona, 'Problems and Dangers Posed by Organized Transnational Crime in the Various Regions of the World' in Phil Williams and Ernestor Savona (eds), *The United Nations and Transnational Crime* (1996) 1, 38.

[77] The Australian Strategic Policy Institute Report, *Beyond Bali, ASPI's Strategic Assessment 2002*, November 2002, 28, identified an arc of island states as failing neighbours that could provide potential havens for terrorist groups.

[78] Ron Crocombe, 'The Pacific Plan Among Larger and Smaller Regional Approaches' (Plenary Paper presented at the Conference on Securing a Peaceful Pacific: Preventing and Resolving Conflict in the Pacific, University of Canterbury, Christchurch, New Zealand, 15–17 October 2004).

unimpeded by government regulation until they enter territorial waters.[79] The situation of the region between more developed areas makes this free movement very attractive to smugglers. Kiribati, for example, has an Exclusive Economic Zone (EEZ) the size of the continental US and one Australian sponsored patrol boat to patrol it.[80]

Finally, compulsion for change within the region emanates directly from the vulnerability of developed states outside the region. In early 2004 New Zealand Prime Minister Helen Clark urged PICs to comply with rules aimed at cutting the flow of funds to terrorists and ensuring the security of imports into the US, pointing out: 'All countries face economic risks if they fail to comply with these measures'.[81] These views were echoed by the new Forum Secretary General, Greg Urwin, who noted that Forum members would have to meet new shipping and aviation security requirements or lose markets and tourists and increase the costs of imports.[82] Not surprisingly, the Forum took up this call for compliance at the 2004 Meeting, recognizing the serious risks to the region's trade and tourism of non-compliance.[83] The irony is obvious: developed states tell PICs that they must protect their sovereignty from transnational criminals by enacting new laws when succumbing to such pressure derogates from that sovereignty.

The adoption of the Honiara Declaration by the Forum does not validate the threat of transnational crime; it simply confirms that Forum leaders are receptive to argument that transnational crime is such a threat. Moreover, there is a participation gap in the process of threat-assessment: the leaders of PICs are marginalized when it comes to the establishment of a threat because they receive the threat as a given. What is missing is information. In the light of the difficulties of evaluating risks, it is critical to undertake further research about transnational criminal activities in the region. This will be difficult, given that information about all criminal activities in the region is poor.[84] The appointment of a Law Enforcement Statistics Officer in the Forumsec to input data and produce statistical analyses is a first step.[85] But it is necessary that more is known about the local and external impact of all crime including transnational crime, in order to give regional policymakers rather than law enforcement officials enough information to shape an appropriate response and to expose inappropriate responses. When Europe began to evolve its third pillar of regional cooperation around justice and home affairs, it

---

[79] On freedom of navigation in the Pacific see the chapter by Scott Davidson in this volume.

[80] Shibuya, above n 46, 2.

[81] Tracy Watkins, 'Pacific States Told to Target Security', *The Press* (Christchurch) 15 April 2004, A6.

[82] *Forum Monthly Review*, May 2004, Pacific Islands Forum < http://www.forumsec.org.fj/> at 23 October 2004.

[83] *Forum Communiqué*, Thirty-Fifth Pacific Islands Forum, Apia, Samoa, 3–10 August 2004, [28].

[84] Tess Newton, 'Policing in the South Pacific Region', *University of the South Pacific Occasional Papers Series*, Occasional Paper no. 1, 10.

[85] The LESO as she is known, is responsible for a regional events calendar, a regional illicit drugs database, and the development of other databases: *Pacific Islands Forum Annual Report*, 2001–2002 (2002) 22.

set up independent regional organs to analyse criminal activity in Europe.[86] The establishment of such organs in the South Pacific would be useful to answer a host of questions: how much local participation is there in transnational crime and is it really mainly a foreign intrusion? What are the peculiar features of the different markets for illicit goods? Are there purely South Pacific regional crimes that have no external analogue?

The measures in the Honiara Declaration and subsequent Forum declarations

Introduction

The Honiara Declaration calls for a range of procedural and substantive measures, which have been supplemented by subsequent Forum declarations. These measures are set out below in the order in which the Forum introduced them, and an attempt has been made to sketch the international legal context of the particular measure.

Law enforcement cooperation

Paragraph 3 of the Honiara Declaration makes it clear that rather than duplicate existing regional bodies working in law enforcement, the Forumsec would seek through the Forum Regional Security Committee (FRSC) to serve as a contact point for specialist agencies and to provide advice to Forum leaders on law enforcement issues. Article 9 of the 1988 UN Drug Trafficking Convention[87] provides a multilateral legal basis for such direct contact to exchange information and analysis and also makes provision for cooperation in law enforcement training.

Mutual assistance in criminal matters

Paragraph 7 of the Honiara Declaration states:

> The Forum recognized that the establishment of a framework for mutual assistance in criminal matters between themselves would enhance cooperation between their courts, prosecution authorities and law enforcement agencies.

The purpose of paragraph 7 is to urge Forum members to adopt measures to assist one another in the identification of persons, search and seizure, and the taking of testimony. The most important international legal frameworks for mutual assistance include article 7 of the 1988 UN Drug Trafficking Convention, the 1990

---

[86] In Lisbon, the European Monitoring Centre on Drugs and Drug Addiction (EMCDDA) was established in terms of Council Regulation 1302/93 in order to gather and analyse reliable data on the full range of drug problems and the control strategies being developed in Europe.
[87] *1988 United Nations Convention Against Illicit Traffic in Narcotic Drugs and Psychotropic Substances*, Vienna, 20 December 1988, 185 UNTS 453 (entered into force 11 November 1990).

UN Model Treaty on Mutual Assistance[88] and the 1986 Commonwealth Scheme for Mutual Legal Assistance.[89] These treaties provide part of the framework to enhance cooperation between judicial and law enforcement authorities, while bilateral relations, such as the diplomatic note exchanged by New Zealand and Fiji for mutual assistance in criminal matters allowing video link evidence of witnesses,[90] provides another part. Ultimately, however, new legislation will be required to make legal assistance possible.

Money laundering, asset forfeiture and banking regulation

Paragraph 7 of the Honiara Declaration continues:

> The Forum recognized that large profits from organized crime provide both an incentive to criminal activity together with capital to develop criminal organizations large enough to operate on an international scale. The Forum accepted the need to strengthen national and international legal provisions to enable the proceeds of and instrumentalities of crime to be traced, frozen and seized and acknowledged the need to regulate banking and other financial services to reduce the possible manipulation of these services to 'launder' the proceeds of crime.

The implicit purpose of this part of paragraph 7 is to suppress money laundering, although there is no direct call for its criminalization. Paragraph 7 does call explicitly for provision for the freezing and seizing of criminal proceeds and instrumentalities. This involves locating the proceeds, engaging in forfeiture and enforcing confiscation orders, even if they are made in other states. Paragraph 7 also acknowledges the necessity of regulating the banking and finance industries to prevent their misuse, which involves inter alia the removal of bank secrecy laws. The 1988 Drug Trafficking Convention provides the basic legal framework. Article 3 of the Convention criminalizes drug money laundering.[91] Article 5's anti-money laundering regime obliges states parties to adopt an asset forfeiture regime that inter alia removes bank secrecy and makes it possible to request mutual assistance for asset forfeiture. FATF's Forty Recommendations[92] expand this money laundering regime to an all-crime regime,[93] and provide for stronger regulatory mechanisms. The updated Forty Recommendations add eight Special Recommendations directed at suppressing the funding of terrorism. Paragraph 10 of the Honiara Declaration urges Forum members to adopt and implement these

---

[88] GA Res 45/117, UN GAOR 45th Sess., Supp. No. 49A, 215.

[89] *Scheme Relating to Mutual Assistance in Criminal Matters within the Commonwealth*, Commonwealth Secretariat, London, LMN (86) 13 (as updated).

[90] See Kevueli Tunidau, 'Current Situation and Countermeasures Against Money Laundering' *UNAFEI Resource Material Series* no. 58, December 2001, Tokyo, 399, 400, 409 <http://unafei.or.jp/pdf/58-29.pdf> at 5 October 2004.

[91] Article 3(1)(b) and article 3(1)(c)(i).

[92] FATF, *The Forty Recommendations*, <http://www1.oecd.org/fatf/40Recs_en.htm> at 10 December 2004.

[93] Recommendation 1 refers to 'all serious crimes'.

recommendations as a priority. The direction provided in the Honiara Declaration was supplemented at the 2000 Forum meeting,[94] which endorsed the establishment of domestic Financial Intelligence Units (FIUs). At the 2002 Forum meeting[95] a regional FIU was mooted. The Egmont Group, an informal gathering of the FIU's of 84 different states named after the venue of the first meeting, has adopted a Revised Statement of Purpose that sets out the definitions and functions of FIUs.[96]

Extradition

Paragraph 9 of the Honiara Declaration provides:

> The Forum recognized that while most members have Extradition Acts which reflect the pre-1986 text of the London Scheme for the Rendition of Fugitive Offenders, there was still a need to review extradition arrangements within the region. The Forum agreed that members should review their extradition arrangements and, if required, take steps to introduce and bring into force legislation based on the United Nations Model Treaty on Extradition or on the current London Scheme for the Rendition of Fugitive Offenders within the Commonwealth.

Relaxing the requirements for extradition in new legislation appears to be the aim of paragraph 9 of the Honiara Declaration. This relaxation is driven by the notion that as apolitical transnational crime has increased the risk of the political misuse of extradition has diminished. The 1990 UN Model Treaty on Extradition[97] and the updated London Scheme for Extradition within the Commonwealth[98] provide the international legal framework with regard to extradition. These instruments are designed to smooth the process by reducing the conditions for a valid extradition, such as the prima facie case requirement insisted upon in some common law states, and by restricting the inappropriate use of bars to extradition, such as the political offence and nationality exceptions. Bilateral extradition treaties provide the normal platform for extradition. Bilateral treaties between Forum members[99] and between

---

94 *Forum Communiqué*, Thirty-First Pacific Islands Forum, Tarawa, Republic of Kiribati, 27–30 October 2000.

95 *Forum Communiqué*, Thirty-Third Pacific Islands Forum, Suva, Fiji Islands, 15–17 August, 2002.

96 *Statement of Purpose of the Egmont Group of Financial Intelligence Units*, Guernsey, 23 June 2004, Egmont Group <www.egmontgroup.org./statement_of_purpose.pdf> at 8 December 2004.

97 GA Res 45/116, 14 December 1990.

98 *Scheme Relating to Rendition of Fugitive Offenders within the Commonwealth*, London, 1966, as updated at Kingston, Jamaica, 2002, Commonwealth Secretariat, <http://www.thecommonwealth.org/shared_asp_files/uploadedfiles/%7B56F55E5D-1882-4421-9CC1-71634DF17331%7D_London_Scheme.pdf> at 9 December 2004.

99 For example, the *Agreement on Extradition between the Government of New Zealand and the Government of the Republic of Fiji*, 21 March 1992, annexed to *The Extradition, Republic of Fiji Order, 1992*, New Zealand.

a Forum member and an external state[100] do exist. However, they are rare. Tunidau complains, for example, that there are too many accessible countries with which Fiji has no extradition relations.[101] Domestic legislation that does not depend upon such a treaty or makes it possible to back warrants issued in other states may provide a suitable substitute.

Drugs offences

Paragraph 13 of the Honiara Declaration prioritizes the ratification and implementation of the 1988 Drug Trafficking Convention, which introduces a range of new drug related offences. The 2002 Forum meeting[102] reiterated this call. The 2003 Forum meeting[103] singled out Amphetamine Type abuse as a problem requiring raised awareness and increased cooperation.

Environmental offences

Paragraph 15 of the Honiara Declaration singles out the importance of suppression of breaches of environmental laws such as waste dumping,[104] driftnet fishing,[105] oil spills and other pollution emergencies,[106] and wildlife smuggling to the region.[107]

---

[100] For example, the *Federated States of Micronesia – United States Extradition Treaty of 1986, Compact of Free Association and Agreement on Extradition and Mutual Assistance and Cooperation in Law Enforcement Matters* (entered into force 3 November 1986).

[101] Above n 90, 408.

[102] *Forum Communiqué*, Thirty-Third Pacific Islands Forum, Suva, Fiji Islands, 15–17 August 2002.

[103] *Forum Communiqué*, Thirty-Fourth Pacific Islands Forum, Auckland, New Zealand, 14–16 August 2003.

[104] In contravention of the *Basel Convention on the Control of Transboundary Movement of Hazardous Wastes and other Wastes and their Disposal*, opened for signature 22 March 1989, 1637 UNTS 71 (entered into force 5 May 1992). See also the *Protocol for the Prevention of the Pollution of the South Pacific Region by Dumping*, opened for signature 25 November 1986, 26 ILM 65 (entered into force 18 August 1980).

[105] There are various regional agreements in this regard. For example, the *South Pacific Forum Fisheries Agency Convention*, opened for signature 10 July 1979, 1979 ATS 16 (entered into force 9 August 1979), provides for cooperation in surveillance and enforcement under article 5(2)(c).

[106] See the *International Convention on the Prevention of Pollution from Ships, 1973, as modified by the Protocol of 1978 relating thereto*, opened for signature 2 November 1973, 12 ILM 1319, 17 ILM 546 (entered into force 2 October 1983) ('MARPOL 73/78').

[107] In contravention of the *1973 Washington Convention on International Trade in Endangered Species of Fauna and Flora*, opened for signature 3 March 1973, 12 ILM 1085 (entered into force 1 July 1975) ('CITES').

Terrorism

Paragraph 16 of the Honiara Declaration provides:

> The Forum recognized terrorism as a threat to the political and economic security of the region, and noted the various international conventions in the field. It identified areas of possible cooperation amongst Forum governments, particularly in intelligence gathering, training of personnel and joint exercises in dealing with serious incidents.

The terrorism conventions have multiplied since 1992,[108] adding to many of the areas of possible cooperation tentatively identified by the Declaration and making some of them mandatory. The 2002 Forum meeting noted the threat offered post 9/11 and held the Honiara Declaration up as a 'firm foundation for action'[109] to address new and heightened threats. Forum leaders underlined their commitment to implement anti-terrorist measures such as UN SC Resolution 1373[110] and the FATF Special Recommendations,[111] including associated reporting requirements.

Maritime surveillance

Paragraph 17 of the Honiara Declaration notes the Forum Fisheries Agency's (FFA) increased capacity to engage in maritime surveillance to assist Forum members in managing their fisheries resources and enforcing their sovereignty. The UN Convention on the Law of the Sea and more specifically the 1995 UN Fish Stocks Agreement[112] sets out the coastal state's rights over fisheries. At a regional level article 5 of the 1979 South Pacific Forum Fisheries Agency Convention[113] made possible the agreement of the 1992 Niue Treaty on Cooperation in Fisheries Surveillance and Law Enforcement in the South Pacific Region,[114] which provides under articles 6 and 7 for general cooperation among the parties in enforcement of their fisheries law. It allows for the exchange of information on foreign fisheries licensing, on the location of foreign fishing vessels and on law enforcement and surveillance.[115] It also provides a legal basis for bilateral agreements that allow Parties to use each other's physical enforcement platforms to arrest foreign fishing

---

[108] See the chapter by Alex Conte in this volume.

[109] *Forum Communiqué*, Thirty-Third Pacific Islands Forum, Suva, Fiji Islands, 15–17 August, 2002, [4].

[110] SC Res 1373 (2001), 28 September 2001.

[111] FATF, *The Forty Recommendations*, above n 92.

[112] *Agreement for the Implementation of the Provisions of the United Nations Convention on the Law of the Sea of 10 December 1982 Relating to the Conservation and Management of Straddling Fish Stocks and Highly Migratory Fish Stocks*, opened for signature 4 December 1995, 2167 UNTS 3 (entered into force 11 December 2001).

[113] Above n 101.

[114] Done at Honiara 9 July 1992 (entered into force 20 May 1993), Internet Guide to International Fisheries Law <http://www.oceanlaw.net/texts/niue.htm> at 10 December 2004.

[115] Article 5(1).

vessels in each other's waters and to appear in each other's courts to prosecute for violations that occurred in another state's waters.[116]

Taxation

Paragraph 18 of the Honiara Declaration notes the importance of taxation issues for the development of the economies of the region and suggests further study to identify the specific needs of Forum members. It is unclear whether cooperation in the pursuit of transnational tax evaders is contemplated. Bilateral double taxation conventions provide elements of the international legal framework in this respect.

Prison administration

Paragraph 19 of the Honiara Declaration notes the failure of other bodies promoting cooperation in the region to address adequately the special circumstances of island countries with small prison populations, and endorses a meeting of the heads of regional prison services. The UN Standard Minimum Rules for the Treatment of Prisoners provide elements of the international legal framework here.[117]

Indigenous issues

Paragraph 20 of the Honiara Declaration provides:

> The Forum agreed on the importance of indigenous issues in its member countries. It was stressed that an understanding of indigenous issues, in particular a knowledge of customary laws, was essential to the development and security of the region.

The point being made by the Declaration is that security in the region is impossible without taking indigenous issues into consideration, but what bearing they have on the suppression of transnational crime is left unexplained. The international legal framework in this regard is provided for by the general human rights conventions and those instruments dealing specifically with indigenous people's rights.[118]

Human trafficking

The Honiara Declaration is silent on human trafficking, which was only identified as a threat to the region at the 1999 Forum meeting.[119] The 2000 FRSC Meeting

---

[116] Articles 6-9.

[117] Adopted by the UN Congress on the Prevention of Crime and the Treatment of Offenders, held at Geneva in 1955, and approved by the ECOSOC Res 663 C (XXIV) of 31 July 1957 and 2076 (LXII) of 13 May 1977.

[118] For example, the *UN's Draft Declaration of the Rights of Indigenous Peoples*, 34 ILM 541.

[119] *Forum Communiqué*, Thirtieth Pacific Islands Forum, Koror, Republic of Palau, 3–5 October 1999.

asked the Oceania Customs Organisation (OCO) and the Pacific Immigration Directors Conference (PIDC) to develop a regional perspective on migrant smuggling.[120] The PIDC has also engaged in further discussion on information exchange and regional collaboration in developing migration and passport services. The recent attention to the issue by the Forum parallels the current international emphasis on human trafficking that culminated with the adoption in 2000 of the Protocol to Prevent, Suppress and Punish Trafficking in Persons, Especially Women and Children,[121] which criminalizes this activity in article 5.

Regional security

Paragraph 1 of the 2002 Nasonini Declaration on regional security targets for collective response 'unlawful challenges to nationality and independence' in addition to transnational crime.[122] The link between transnational crime and such challenges is unexplained. The Forum also reiterated the commitment to good governance as a key strategy to address conflict and tension in the region.

Small arms proliferation

The Honiara Declaration does not mention the proliferation of small arms. This is not surprising as it has little external impact, but the 2003 Forum meeting[123] noted poor control of small arms is an integral part of regional insecurity. It is regulated by the Firearms Protocol,[124] and supported by the United Nations Programme of Action to Prevent, Combat and Eradicate the Illicit Trade in Small Arms and Light Weapons in All its Aspects.[125]

Identity fraud

The 2003 Forum[126] also added identity fraud to the list of activities considered by the Forum to be of concern and the Forumsec was directed to explore the

---

[120] See Andreas Schloenhardt, *Migrant Smuggling: Illegal Migration and Organised Crime in Australia and the Asia Pacific Region* (2003) 374.

[121] Supplementing the *UN Convention on Transnational Organised Crime*, opened for signature 14 December 2000, GA Res 55/25, UN GAOR, 55th sess, Supp No 49, 44, UN Doc A/45/49 (Vol I) (2001) (entered into force 29 September 2003).

[122] Above n 69.

[123] *Forum Communiqué*, Thirty-Fourth Pacific Islands Forum, Auckland, New Zealand, 14–16 August 2003.

[124] *Protocol Against the Illicit Manufacturing of and Trafficking in Firearms, Their Parts, Components and Ammunition, Supplementing the United Nations Convention against Transnational Organized Crime*, UN GA Res. 55/25, 15 November 2000, annex to UN Doc A/55/383.

[125] UN Doc. A/Conf. 192/15 (New York: UN Department for Disarmament Affairs, 2001).

[126] *Forum Communiqué*, Thirty-Fourth Pacific Islands Forum, Auckland, New Zealand, 14–16 August 2003.

possibility of Forum members joining the Identity Fraud Register project run by the Australian Crimes Commission.

Corruption

The raising of the issue of good governance in the 2000 Biketawa Declaration, followed by the adoption of the Forum Principles of Good Leadership at the 2003 Forum meeting, led to the 2004 Forum inviting Forum members to consider signing and ratifying the 2003 UN Convention against Corruption[127] in order to strengthen good governance.[128]

Taking appropriate measures

Through the Honiara Declaration and subsequent statements the Forum has adopted a series of measures against transnational crime. The order in which these provisions emerged illustrates that Forum concerns have tracked global concerns. This reactive, incremental process is typical of the development of transnational criminal law. A product of their time, the actions prioritized by the Forum do not specifically include suppression of the full gamut of activities involved in the global criminal economy. Even activities identified as a threat to the region, such as weapons proliferation, smuggling of illegal migrants and corruption, are not specifically subject to control measures. The priority appears to have been to smooth criminal justice processes between different jurisdictions through reducing barriers to all forms of legal assistance including extradition, rather than establish an exhaustive regional criminal law suppressing all possible substantive crimes. This smoothing of interstate criminal procedure has been singled out from the early 1980s as important to the international community as a whole. Only towards the end of the list do the local concerns – fisheries surveillance, prisons, and indigenous issues – begin to emerge, included, it appears, as ineffectual after-thoughts. As a whole, the measures themselves are so broadly worded that it is fairly clear that the Forum's aim is regional harmonization of domestic law through some form of functional equivalence rather than uniformity. They serve as signposts to relevant international treaties and as invitations for detailed legal change though consultation with technical experts.

The legal status of these measures is uncertain. The Forum is the leading intergovernmental organization in the South Pacific in a de facto sense only because it has no treaty basis.[129] Thus participation in a declaration generates no treaty-derived obligation. Indeed, from an international perspective the Forum's

---

[127] *United Nations Convention against Corruption*, opened for signature 9 December 2003, GA Res 58/4, 43 ILM 37 (not in force).

[128] *Forum Communiqué*, Thirty-Fifth Pacific Islands Forum, Apia, Samoa, 3–10 August 2004, [29].

[129] Richard Herr, 'South Pacific Forum' in Brij V Lal and Kate Fortune (eds), *The Pacific Islands: An Encyclopaedia* (2000) 329 notes the lack of a foundation treaty but points out its regional importance and the fact that it operates as an IGO.

objective existence in abstract from its members is debateable. This confusion is mirrored in the Honiara Declaration: sometimes it is the Forum that speaks, sometimes it is the Forum leaders who speak. It is probably most appropriate to consider the Forum as generating state practice of the individual member states. This practice may serve as the basis for emerging regional norms of customary international law given that the statements are couched in normative terms, have been supported by subsequent reiterations of this commitment and have been followed in some instances by formal legislative change and increased cooperation on criminal matters among Forum members. However, the aspirational nature of many of the statements and the poor record of implementation in some cases weakens the case for a customary basis, which has not yet been made out. In result, as a matter of positive law it appears that Forum members are not obliged to adopt the measures recommended. The Declaration depends on multilateral suppression conventions and on bilateral conventions to establish legal obligations that generate implementation.

Legal responses in Forum members

Introduction

This section examines the steps taken by Forum members to respond to the Forum's recommendations. The Honiara Declaration highlights two general issues about implementation: first, the need for Forum members to engage in legislative change; and second, the critical lack of resources to meet the region's emerging needs in law enforcement and the necessity for assistance from the region's international partners to meet these needs.[130] However, before examining legislative modernization, it is apt to examine treaty adherence by Forum members as the Honiara Declaration anticipates that the Forum members should also sign up to the appropriate multilateral suppression conventions and establish the appropriate bilateral relations in order to facilitate such modernization. The function of these multilateral conventions and how they relate to domestic law reform is set out by the UNODC:

> Multilateral conventions form bridges between legal systems and represent a kind of *acquis communitaire* of the international community. They allow the states that are parties to those treaties to deal with challenges posed by transnational organized crime and international terrorism. Modalities of inter-State cooperation in criminal matters that have traditionally been the subject of bilateral agreement are increasingly becoming enshrined in international legal instruments such as the International Convention for the Suppression of Terrorist Bombings (General Assembly resolution 52/164, annex) and the International Convention for the Suppression of the Financing of Terrorism. Matters of extradition, legal assistance, investigative assistance, collection of evidence (hearing of witnesses and the carrying out of searches, for example), transfer of sentenced persons, transfer of documents and penal proceedings,

[130] Above n 14, [6] and [5].

> seizure and forfeiture of illicit proceeds of crime, as well as the recognition of foreign penal judgements, are issues that can be addressed in such multilateral instruments. In that context, the United Nations Office on Drugs and Crime has, in cooperation with the International Institute of Higher Studies in the Criminal Sciences, been working on model laws to reflect the provisions of international instruments, as well as the revision and updating of manuals on extradition and legal assistance. Furthermore, guidelines on technical assistance are being prepared in order to facilitate international cooperation by strengthening the capacity of national law enforcement agencies to respond promptly to requests for assistance from other states.[131]

The international community is concerned about adherence to these conventions.[132] In this regard, the record of ratification or accession of Forum members to the 1988 Drug Trafficking Convention,[133] perhaps the central treaty in the system of transnational criminal law, is revealing. Although the treaty came into force in 1990 and currently has 169 states parties, of the 16 Forum members only Australia, the Federated States of Micronesia, Fiji, New Zealand and Tonga are currently parties. The participation of PICs in the '*acquis communitaire*' is poor. Initial responses to the much newer 2000 UN Transnational Organized Crime Convention[134] and its protocols on human trafficking,[135] migrants[136] and firearms[137] has been slow,[138] as has the response to the 2003 UN Corruption Convention.[139] The vacuum in international legal obligation with respect to the suppression of transnational crime in the South Pacific contrasts nicely with the general alarm projected by powerful developed states about transnational crime in the region. For example, the US State Department's International Narcotic Control Strategy Report 2003[140] lists as 'countries monitored' Fiji, Marshall Islands, Micronesia,

---

[131] Above n 70, [57].

[132] Above n 70, [14].

[133] Above, n 87.

[134] The *UN Convention on Transnational Organized Crime*, opened for signature 14 December 2000, GA Res 55/25, UN GAOR, 55th sess, Supp No 49, 44, UN Doc A/45/49 (Vol I) (2001) (entered into force 29 September 2003) ('TOC Convention').

[135] Above n 121.

[136] *Protocol Against the Smuggling of Migrants by Land, Sea or Air, Supplementing the United Nations Convention against Transnational Organized Crime*, opened for signature 14 December 2000, GA Res 55/25, UN GAOR, 55th sess, Supp No 49, 65, UN Doc A/45/49 (Vol I) (2001) (entered into force 28 January 2004) ('Migrants Protocol').

[137] *Protocol Against the Illicit Manufacturing and Trafficking in Firearms, their Parts, Components and Ammunition, Supplementing the United Nations Convention against Transnational Organized Crime*, opened for signature 31 May 2001, GA Res 55/255 (not in force).

[138] Australia is a party to the TOC Convention and the Migrants Protocol but has only signed the other instruments; the Cook Islands is a party to the TOC Convention; Fiji is a party to the TOC Convention; the FSM is a party to the TOC Convention; Nauru has signed the TOC Convention and its protocols; New Zealand is party to the TOC Convention and its protocols and has signed the Corruption Convention; and Tonga is party to the TOC Convention.

[139] See n 127.

[140] Bureau for International Narcotics and Law Enforcement Affairs, March 2004.

New Zealand, Niue, PNG, the Solomon Islands and Tonga; as 'countries of concern' the Cook Islands, Palau, Samoa, and Vanuatu; and as a 'major money laundering' countries Australia and Nauru. More serious is the FATF's listing of the Cook Islands and Nauru among the six Non-Cooperative Countries and Territories not meeting international money laundering standards.[141] Yet despite this external pressure to take steps against transnational crime, unlike developing states in other regions, PICs have not even made the formal commitment to suppression conventions. One reason may be disinterest because of the perceived absence of local impact coupled with weak legal and political infrastructures. They may simply not have the money to engage. It is significant that most PICs are unable to attend the negotiations of these treaties. For example, only Australia, New Zealand and PNG attended the 1988 Diplomatic Conference that adopted the Drug Trafficking Convention.[142] There may also be internal reasons for not becoming party, such as jurisdictional conflicts between different law enforcement arms. Nonetheless, pressure for adherence is mounting[143] and appears to be bearing some fruit.[144]

The Honiara Declaration is essentially about promoting legislative reform and the body of this section examines the steps taken by Forum members in response to the Forum's recommendations. Our interest here is not Australia and New Zealand, which claim to have in place the full range of legislation to implement the Honiara Declaration,[145] but the PIC members of the Forum, and the laws that they have enacted in response to regional declarations.[146] In order to provide some sense of what laws have been made, I have provided an Appendix which, using the same subject break-down as is used below, provides a fairly comprehensive list of pertinent legislation together with the year it came into force. Finally, while the upgrade of legislation is the key concern it is not the only concern, and the section also examines changes in law enforcement policy and practice in the various subject areas.

<http://www.state.gov/g/inl/rls/nrcrpt/2003/vol2/html/29919.htm> at 23 October 2004.

[141] FATF, *Annual Review 2004*, above n 27, 1.

[142] *United Nations Conference for the Adoption of a Convention against Illicit Traffic in Narcotic Drugs and Psychotropic Substances, Official Records, Volume I* (New York, 1994) UN Doc E/CONF 82/16, UN Publication Sales No E 94 XI 5, 197.

[143] Australian Senate Foreign Affairs, Defence and Trade Committee Report, above n 23, 192.

[144] For example, since 2003 Palau has ratified almost all of the extant anti-terrorism conventions.

[145] Australian Senate Foreign Affairs, Defence and Trade Committee Report, above n 23, 191.

[146] For a record of legislation enacted in response to the Forum's declarations see *Australian Parliamentary Debates, House of Representatives, Official Hansard* no. 10 of 2004, 30440, Parliament of Australia, <http://parlinfoweb.aph.gov.au/piweb/view_document.aspx?ID=913369&TABLE=HANSARDR> at 14 October 2004. In addition, see the Forumsec Survey on the Implementation of the Legislative Priorities of the Honiara Declaration on Law Enforcement Cooperation, 13 October 2004.

Law enforcement cooperation

Although there appears to be no specific record of legislative change with regard to law enforcement cooperation as a general enterprise, there has been extensive national participation in regional law enforcement activities. At the diplomatic level, the lead organization is the FRSC, an annual meeting of Forum member representatives to review priorities, institutional linkages and resource needs. Significantly, it is preceded by a 'pre-meeting' of law enforcement officials convened by the Forumsec's Law Enforcement Liaison Officer. Other important regional policing and customs meetings addressing current issues and developments in transnational crime and law enforcement include the Pacific Islands Law Officers Meeting (PILOM), the South Pacific Chiefs of Police Conference (SPCPC),[147] OCO and the Australasian and South West Pacific Commissioners Conference. The Forum works closely with these organizations and brings national law enforcement officers together for updates on matters such as border control.[148] In addition to the Law Enforcement Liaison Officer, the Forumsec's Suva-based Political, International and Legal Affairs Division has a Legal Advisor, an Anti-Money Laundering Consultant, Law Enforcement Training Coordinating Advisor and Law Enforcement Statistics Officer. The Forum also cooperates with intergovernmental law enforcement organizations. For example, the Forum cooperated with the UN Office for Drug Control and Crime Prevention (now UNODC) to implement the South Pacific Police – Customs Law Enforcement Project from 1995–1998.[149]

The Forum has also made an effort to establish a training programme for law enforcement personnel to address shortcomings in police training, such as the skills necessary to investigate money laundering.[150] The Forumsec's Law Enforcement Training Coordinator, on secondment from the AFP, is responsible for coordinating all Pacific law enforcement training.[151] Following the 2003 Forum Australia, New Zealand and Fiji announced the establishment of the Pacific Regional Policing Initiative, to be based in Suva, and to be implemented over five years. Australia committed itself to spending A$17 million over three years to strengthen regional police forces and New Zealand added a further NZ$2.5 million. The intention was to support law enforcement efforts in the region through the establishment of a 'virtual police academy' to coordinate and deliver a standardized training to over 900 officers across the Pacific. The PRPI is also intended to strengthen regional policing strategies and foster regional networking

[147] It includes all Pacific island states including non-Forum states. The AFP provides travel funds for this meeting.

[148] See the Honiara Declaration, above n 14, [11], [12], and the *Pacific Islands Forum Annual Report*, 2002–2003 (2002) 20.

[149] *ODCCP Statement at the FSC Meeting*, Port Vila, Vanuatu, 12–14 July 2000, see UN Office for Drugs and Crime, <http://www.unodc.un.or.th/factsheet/nontraditional.htm> at 21 October 2004.

[150] Herman, above n 20, 32.

[151] Australian Senate Foreign Affairs, Defence and Trade Committee Report, above n 23, 196.

and the pooling of regional resources. The 2004 Forum called for a focus on forensics analysis and capability, provision of equipment and appropriate training for staff, and maritime and border patrol and surveillance capability.[152]

At an operational level new regional arrangements have been developed. One of the concrete results of the Honiara Declaration has been the formation under the guidance of the AFP and NZP of Combined Law Agency Groups (CLAGS) in Kiribati, Samoa, the Cook Islands, Fiji, the Solomon Islands and Vanuatu. CLAGS draw together officers from the customs, police, coastguard, immigration, and so forth to exchange information and coordinate activities. The principal law enforcement agencies in the region are the police forces and customs organizations of Fiji, PNG, Solomon Islands and Samoa. Joint operations with developed state agencies take place. For example, a 2001 anti-drug operation in Suva involved 20 agents from the Fiji Royal Police Force, the AFP, the Royal Canadian Mounted Police, the US Drug Enforcement Administration and the NZP.[153] The AFP and NZP also played key roles in the 2004 Fijian drug 'bust', backing up Fiji's police. Australian state police also work with island police.[154] The nine-nation mission to restore order to Solomon Islands is considered to be a model of what close cooperation can achieve.[155] However, the most influential operational organization in the region is the AFP. Since the early 1980s, the AFP has posted liaison officers to a number of PICs.[156] The AFP now operates a Law Enforcement Cooperation Program (LECP) in the region to improve cooperation and capacity and to provide for intelligence gathering on transnational organized crime groups threatening Australia's regional interests. From 2002, the AFP through LECP has established Transnational Crime Units in Fiji, Samoa, Tonga, Vanuatu and PNG and plans to establish a unit in the Solomon Islands in 2005.[157] Cooperation from the host PIC is not always forthcoming. In 2004, Vanuatu's new administration decided to expel two AFP members, a move criticized by Australia as breaking pledges by PICs to cooperate in fighting transnational crime.[158] The latest regional development with operational implications is the Pacific Transnational Crime Coordination Centre which opened in Suva on 15 June 2004 as part of an AFP and SPCPC plan to

---

[152] *Forum Communiqué*, Thirty-Fifth Pacific Islands Forum, Apia, Samoa, 3–10 August 2004, [27].

[153] Tunidau, above n 90, 401.

[154] Australian Senate Foreign Affairs, Defence and Trade Committee Report, above n 23, 196.

[155] See also ibid, 205.

[156] In 2003 there were officers in PNG (Port Moresby), the Solomons (Honiara), Vanuatu (Port Vila) and Fiji (Suva). The Fiji office is responsible for all island states to the east of Fiji, while the AFP Region Coordinator Pacific Islands retain responsibility for Micronesia and the French territories: Australian Senate Foreign Affairs, Defence and Trade Committee Report, above n 23, 195.

[157] *AFP Media Release*, 15 June 2004, Australian Federal Police <http://www.afp.gov.au/afp/page/Media/2004/1506suva.htm> at 1 October 2004.

[158] Gratien Tiona, 'AFP – The Doors Remain Open', 16 September 2004, *Port Villa Presse* <http://www.news.vu/en/news/diplomacy/afp-the-doors-remain-open.shtml> at 28 January 2004.

combat transnational crime in the region.[159] The PTCCC is intended to become the hub of a Pacific Transnational Crime Unit Network that will manage and coordinate law enforcement intelligence provided by the network of national law enforcement agencies.[160] Although the Forum did not initiate this development, it welcomed the establishment of the PTCCC.[161] As should by now be apparent, Australia and New Zealand also provide extensive technical support for law enforcement. Australia has trained prosecutors and will provide judicial training in the region.[162] NZAID provides direct police and customs support in some cases and has recently established a Pacific Security Fund to provide training and advice to border control services.

Mutual assistance in criminal matters

Mutual assistance depends on states having legislation that allows the articulation of their criminal procedures with the criminal procedures of other states. Most Forum members have enacted such legislation. The members without new legislation are Nauru, PNG (legislation is before parliament) and Samoa. Drafting assistance, such as that supplied by Forumsec to the Cook Islands to enable adoption of the Mutual Assistance in Criminal Matters Act 2003, has been essential to enable some PICs to meet the recommendations of the Honiara Declaration.

Fiji's Mutual Assistance in Criminal Matters Act, 1997, is a relatively early response to the Honiara Declaration.[163] Requests from foreign states are directed to Fiji's Attorney General (AG) who has the authority to decide whether assistance will be given. If the decision is positive, she forwards the request to the Commissioner of Police or Director of Public Prosecutions depending on whether investigation or judicial action is requested. The Act makes it possible to request assistance from other states. Kiribati's Mutual Assistance in Criminal Matters Act 2003 is among the very latest legislation. It regulates the full gamut of assistance given by or requested by Kiribati to or from other states.[164] The AG determines the conditions under which assistance will be granted, which might include payment of any expenses incurred by Kiribati.[165] An unusual ground of refusal at the AG's discretion is if 'the provision of assistance would impose an excessive burden on the resources of' Kiribati.[166] The Act also makes provision for requests by Kiribati for forfeiture orders, pecuniary penalties and restraining orders to be enforced in a foreign country, and allows for the registration and enforcement of similar foreign

---

[159] See above n 157.

[160] The inaugural team leader is Inspector A Banmatakaui of the Vanuatu Police Force.

[161] *Forum Communiqué*, Thirty-Fifth Pacific Islands Forum, Apia, Samoa, 3–10 August 2004, [27].

[162] Australian Senate Foreign Affairs, Defence and Trade Committee Report, above n 23, 192.

[163] See generally Tunidau, above n 90, 399, 400, 409.

[164] In terms of sections 2 and 4.

[165] Section 9.

[166] Section 11(g).

orders.[167] An interesting feature of the Act is that it allows a defendant to request the court to certify the AG to ask a foreign state for evidence or witnesses to come to Kiribati if it is 'necessary for the proceedings'.[168] This addresses the criticism that legal assistance usually only serves the prosecution.[169] In making this decision the court can take into account inter alia the risk of unfair prejudice to the defendant if the material were not available[170] and whether the foreign state is likely to grant the request.[171] It is unclear what would happen if the foreign state refused the request after the court determined that a risk of injustice exists. Although the Act preserves the right of cross-examination of a witness from whom evidence was taken abroad, it makes it clear that if that person has to be brought to Kiribati, the defendant may have to pay if the cross-examination of the witness was trivial, unnecessary or irrelevant.[172] Resources are an issue, but this legislation is as sophisticated as any.

The extent to which the new mutual assistance legislation has actually been used is unknown. Vanuatu's Financial Services Commissioner is reported as stating that Vanuatu receives many requests for assistance by foreign investigators and that '[w]e provide assistance where we can, but there's a difference between fishing for information and specifics'.[173] A problem is the absence of bi-lateral mutual legal assistance treaties (MLATs) between Forum members. In 2003, Australia did not have an MLAT with any PIC.[174] MLATs are unnecessary when relying on the Commonwealth Scheme Relating to Mutual Assistance because it allows mutual assistance through enabling complementary domestic legislation for those Forum members that are Commonwealth members. Domestic legislation like Kiribati's Mutual Assistance in Criminal Matters Act 2003 assumes that assistance can be requested and provided without a bilateral treaty between the parties, but there would be no obligation to provide it.

Money laundering, asset forfeiture and banking regulation

Preventing money laundering and pursuing the proceeds of crime are the main thrusts of the Honiara Declaration and all Forum members have engaged in some activity in the field. Provision for asset forfeiture seems to have fared better than the criminalization of money laundering, while financial regulation remains a difficult area. PICs are not members of FATF, but Australia, the Cook Islands, Fiji, the Marshall Islands, New Zealand, Niue, Palau, Samoa and Vanuatu are all members of the APG-ML, the purpose of which is to facilitate the adoption and

[167] Section 41 and Part 7 generally.
[168] Section 50. This is possible in Fiji but under the *Proceeds of Crime Act 1998*.
[169] See Neil Boister, 'Human Rights Protections in the Suppression Conventions' (2002) 2 *Human Rights Law Review* 199, 200.
[170] Section 51(4)(e).
[171] Section 51(4)(a).
[172] Section 59(2).
[173] See Herman, above n 20, 21.
[174] Australian Senate Foreign Affairs, Defence and Trade Committee Report, above n 23, 193.

implementation of the FATF recommendations, taking into account regional and country factors.[175] Kiribati, Nauru, PNG, the Cook Islands and Tonga have observer status in the APG-ML. Cooperation does not appear, however, to have had as much effect as direct pressure from FATF. For example, blacklisted by FATF in 2000, Niue was de-listed in 2002 after reforming its laws.[176] Technical assistance to facilitate change has been provided by the IMF, the UN, the Commonwealth Secretariat (Comsec), the Forumsec laundering consultant and the NZP. Legislative development, such as the FSM Money Laundering and Proceeds of Crime Act of 2000, has been funded by Forumsec, which also provides for money laundering training needs assessment.[177]

Some Forum members had enacted legislation prior to 1992 but it had limitations. In 1989, Vanuatu enacted the Serious Offences (Confiscation of Proceeds) Act, 1989, but, an established OFC, it lacked the political will to meet the 1988 Drug Trafficking Convention's obligation to remove bank secrecy,[178] the application of this removal to requests by other states for mutual assistance[179] and the duty to cooperate in investigation into the movement of the proceeds of crime.[180] The Basle Committee and FATF's preventative measures such as 'know your customer' rules were equally difficult to accept. Much of the legislation enacted after 1992 was based on Commonwealth models. Fiji's Proceeds of Crime Act, 1997, is a good example.[181] It criminalizes money laundering,[182] but the Fijian offence is harsher than the 1988 Drug Trafficking Convention because it only requires objective fault[183] while the Convention requires subjective fault.[184] In line with the FATF Recommendations the offence is an 'all crimes laundering offence' in that the predicate offence can be of any kind and can occur within or outside of Fiji, the only requirement being that if it had occurred in Fiji it would have been considered 'serious' because it carries a minimum maximum penalty of one year imprisonment.[185] The Act targets the proceeds of serious offences by permitting courts to grant forfeiture and confiscation orders, and together with the Mutual Assistance in Criminal Matters Act, 1997, provides for such orders issued in another state to be given effect in Fiji.[186] The Act's conviction-based value confiscation

---

[175] See Asia Pacific Group on Money Laundering <http://www.apgml.org/content/index.jsp> at 23 October 2004. Forumsec cooperates with the APG-ML through the Coordinating Office for the Participating Countries Anti-Money Laundering Initiative.

[176] FATF, *Annual Review 2004*, above n 27, 15.

[177] See Pacific Islands Forum <http://www.forumsec.org/fj/division/PILAD/Pilad.htm> at 4 October 2004.

[178] Article 5(3).

[179] Article 7(5).

[180] Article 9(1)(b)(ii).

[181] Herman, above n 20, generally.

[182] Section 69(2).

[183] Section 69(3).

[184] Article 3(1)(b)(i).

[185] Section 3.

[186] Tunidau, above n 90, 400.

system[187] may be considered to be of limited value by those who favour civil forfeiture not dependant upon conviction. Although the Act does give authorities extensive powers to lift the corporate veil, to freeze, seize, monitor, disclose and keep records, and obliges banks to report suspicious transactions, it has limitations.[188] For example, the definition of a bank[189] does not cover lawyers who operate in sole partnership, accounting firms, foreign exchange agencies, travel agencies, second hand car dealers and other handlers of finance. The more recent Kiribati Proceeds of Crime Act no. 8 of 2003, includes a range of innovations. It defines 'financial institution' broadly, listing 31 different forms of conduct including acting as a friendly society and money and currency changing and 'any other business prescribed by the minister'.[190] 'Cash dealers' are also subject to the Act and again the definition is broad. Provision is made for the establishment of an FIU within the Kiribati Police.[191] However, the Act protects innocent and perhaps less than innocent third parties by requiring a court making a forfeiture order to take into account 'any right or interest of a third party' and 'any hardship that is reasonably to be expected to be caused to any person by the operation of the order'.[192]

Legislative development with regard to banking regulation has been difficult. FATF pressure resulted in Niue's Financial Transactions Reporting Act 2000, which requires suspicious transaction reporting, the establishment of an FIU and some degree of customer identification. The International Banking Repeal Act 2002 eliminated Niue's offshore banks. The Cook Islands, also blacklisted by FATF, enacted the Financial Supervisory Commission Act 2003, the Banking Act 2003 and the Financial Transactions Reporting Act 2003, to provide for increased regulation of finance and banking regimes, with explicit provisions preventing the establishment of shell banks by requiring 'physical presence'. The latter Act provides for reporting requirements and requires financial institutions to retain information for 6 years in a form that allows the Cook Island's FIU to readily reconstruct a transaction.[193] The Act also empowers the FIU to enter the premises of financial institutions to ensure compliance[194] and specifically overrides the secrecy provisions in other legislation.[195] By 2004, as a result of the 2003 legislation aimed at eliminating shell banks within one year through re-licensing, 9 out of 16 offshore banks had applied for licences.[196] Other PICs have been slower to respond. After Nauru was subject to FATF blacklisting for failing inter alia to provide for customer identification and suspicious transaction reporting,[197] it

[187] Section 20(1).
[188] Tunidau, above n 90, 402.
[189] Section 63.
[190] Section 3(1).
[191] Section 16-20.
[192] Section 26(4).
[193] Section 6.
[194] Section 30.
[195] Sections 35 and 36.
[196] FATF, *Annual Review 2004*, above n 27, 8.
[197] Ibid 12.

enacted the Anti-Money Laundering Act of 2001 which provided for such measures, and again under pressure amended the Act to apply to the offshore banking sector. However, FATF was still concerned about the licensing and supervision of the offshore sector. In 2003 Nauru enacted the Corporation (Amendment) Act of 2003 and the Anti-Money Laundering Act of 2003, laws intended to abolish offshore shell banks and prohibit the granting of new licences. Nauru has indicated that it has since revoked the licences of all remaining offshore banks, but FATF has maintained its blacklisting to pressure Nauru to ensure that previously licenced offshore banks are no longer conducting banking activity and are no longer in existence.

Large-scale currency transaction reporting to FIUs in Forum members is a relatively recent development. The Australian Transaction Report and Analysis Centre (Austrac), the Cook Islands Financial Intelligence Unit, the Marshall Islands Domestic Financial Intelligence Unit, New Zealand Police Financial Intelligence Unit, and the Vanuatu Financial Intelligence Unit are all members of the Egmont Group. Aqorau notes that success stories, like the progress made by the Fiji FIU, are invariably the result of individual enthusiasm rather than national design.[198] Austrac is the senior partner here, and the Pacific islands are a priority area for its international work. In terms of the Australian Suppression of the Financing of Terrorism Act 2002, the Director of Austrac has the power to enter into a memorandum of understanding (MOU) with foreign FIUs to facilitate the exchange of financial intelligence but by 2003 it only had an MOU with Vanuatu, although it was working towards signing MOUs with the Cook Islands and the Marshall Islands.[199] The Eminent Persons' Group Review of the Forum suggests the establishment of a regional FIU,[200] and Australia or New Zealand have been mooted as possible locations.[201]

There is evidence of rapid legislative modernization, but the extent to which these new powers have actually been used is uncertain. As we have seen, there have been some concrete results in regulating the banking sector. However, PICs face capacity problems in implementing regional and international directives. Aqorau suggests that Palau, which has had the necessary legislation since 2001, exemplifies these problems. He cites a March 2003 report from an APG-ML Mutual Evaluation which noted that Palau's authorities

> lack [the] resources and financial intelligence to gauge the extent of money laundering resulting from international cross border crimes. It noted Palau's lack of devoted resources and training, the absence of implementing regulations or comprehensive guidance for financial institutions, the absence of an onsite inspection plan, and weaknesses in existing legislation. Although the Bureau of Public Safety and the Office of the Attorney General are currently responsible for enforcing anti-

---

198 Above n 47, 12.

199 Australian Senate Foreign Affairs, Defence and Trade Committee Report, above n 23, 198.

200 The Report is available at New Zealand Ministry of Foreign Affairs and Trade <http://www.mfat.govt.nz/foreign/regions/pacific/pif03/pifreviewdocs/wayforward.html> at 4 October 2004.

201 Tunidau, above n 90, 402.

> money laundering provisions, no funds have been budgeted for this purpose. Thus far there have been no investigations or prosecutions conducted under the anti-money laundering laws.[202]

Moreover, FATF reports indicate the unwillingness of certain PICs to cooperate with law enforcement agencies and international organizations in the suppression of money laundering,[203] and the enactment of new legislation may not change this recalcitrance.

Extradition

Although new extradition laws have been enacted in many Forum members since 1992, some PICs, such as Nauru and PNG, have not updated their laws. After the adoption of the Honiara Declaration, the Forum developed a Model Extradition Law which was tabled at the 1999 PILOM Meeting. The Model Law's purpose is to bring the domestic law of Forum members into line with the Commonwealth's London Scheme for the Rendition of Fugitive Offenders and the UN Model Treaty on Extradition. The Forumsec has also funded new legislation.[204]

Some Forum members engaged in legislative modernization earlier than others. A recent example of legislative reform by a PIC is Fiji's Extradition Act 2003.[205] Although the new Act takes into account the Fiji Bill of Rights and Freedoms,[206] the impact of the UN Model Treaty is patent and illustrates the global tendency towards streamlining extradition. Although the Act still requires offences to carry at least a maximum sentence of one year or more before extradition is allowed (rather than 6 months, which is the recent trend), it allows extradition where the offence carries the death penalty, which may fall foul of Fiji's Bill of Rights and Freedoms.[207] The Act expands the category of extraditable offences to include fiscal and revenue offences,[208] although Aqorau complains that the Act does not make offences against the exploitation of natural resources extraditable despite their serious economic consequences for PICs.[209] He gives the specific example of violation of fisheries laws, where imprisonment is not usually an option thus precluding extradition. The Act removes the political offence exception which raises questions about the vulnerability to extradition of fugitive militants back to

---

[202] Above n 47, 11, citing PACNEWS, 'Money Laundering', *Palau Horizon*, Thursday 24 July 2003.

[203] FATF, *Review to Identify Non-Cooperative Countries or Territories*, above n 29 and FATF, *Annual Review 2004*, above n 27.

[204] For example, the FSM's *Transnational Extradition and Transfer of Convicted Persons Act of 2000 and Interstate Extradition Act of 2000.*

[205] See generally Tunidau, above n 90, 400; Aqorau, above n 72, 3.

[206] *The Fiji Constitution Amendment Act, 1997*, chapter 4.

[207] Section 22.

[208] Section 3(4).

[209] See above n 72, 6.

Pacific hotspots such as the Solomons[210] and PNG. It also abandons the prima facie case requirement for extradition and provides for extradition to requesting Forum members on the backing of warrants issued in those countries.[211] Kiribati's Extradition Act no. 17 of 2003 shows the influence of the Forum's Model Law. Terrorist offences are extraditable and they are expansively defined.[212] Although the prima facie proof requirement has been abandoned, the nationality exception has not.[213] Following a now common approach, the Act permits surrender of fugitives to different states on different bases. Extradition to Commonwealth states other than PICs[214] requires only an authenticated record of the case.[215] The Act provides for extradition to other states on the basis of a treaty or comity, but extradition to Forum members is on a backing of warrants procedure.[216] An unusual reason for refusing surrender that only applies to Forum members is that the 'the prison conditions in the requesting country are not substantially equivalent to the minimum standards for imprisonment in Kiribati',[217] a violation of the rigid rule of non-inquiry into the criminal justice systems of requesting states.[218] Provision is made for Kiribati to establish jurisdiction to prosecute where it refuses to extradite on humanitarian grounds (including poor prison conditions) or because of the nationality exception, as well as provision to surrender for trial only on condition the person is returned to serve their sentence.[219]

The existence of a new cut-down extradition process is only the first step, however; it has to be used properly. Tunidau notes about the Fiji experience:

> Our experience with the extradition cases in the past decade or so has shown that it requires a level of expertise not only in the ability to compare offences in two different countries but also in the ability to work with the Extradition Act and a bilateral treaty.[220]

He records a spate of extradition requests by and to Fiji made under the old legislation for offences that included drug and arms smuggling.[221] Yet it is difficult to gauge how many extradition requests have been made by and to Forum members; what little material there is suggests that this legislation is not heavily used. For example, although Australia can conduct extradition under the

---

[210] See Aqorau, above n 72, 8, discussing the presence of Malaita Eagle Force members (Solomon Island militants) in Fiji.
[211] Part 4.
[212] Section 4.
[213] Section 19(2)(a).
[214] Part 3.
[215] Section 24.
[216] Part 4.
[217] Section 36(2).
[218] For a recent example of the rule see *Decision on the extradition of Ricardo Miguel Cavallo* (2003) 47 ILM 888, 902.
[219] Section 59.
[220] Tunidau, above n 90, 408.
[221] Ibid.

Extradition (Commonwealth countries) Regulations with the Cook Islands, Kiribati, Nauru, PNG, Samoa, the Solomon Islands, Tonga, Tuvalu and Vanuatu and under separate non-treaty regulations with Fiji and the Marshall Islands, few actual requests are made. To 2003, Australia had made one request to PNG for four people involved in drug trafficking and PNG had made no successful extradition request to Australia.[222]

Drugs offences

While the impact of more than a century of drug treaty adherence is evident in the legislative record of Forum members, it is remarkable that even post the 1988 Drug Trafficking Convention and the 1992 Honiara Declaration, nine of the fifteen Forum PICs appear to have either outdated or no specialist drug legislation.[223] Experience provided a strong motivation for legal change. For example, the Fiji Dangerous Drugs Act 1938, which reflects its provenance in treaties from 1925[224] and 1931,[225] does not meet the obligations contained in the 1988 Drug Trafficking Convention, which lays out a comprehensive penal regime concerned with suppressing every form of involvement in the illicit traffic. The main offender following the 2000 seizure of 350kg of heroin in Fiji received the existing maximum penalty of eight years' imprisonment for trafficking whereas in Australia he would have received life.[226] Surveillance of the Fijian methamphetamine operation went on for 14 months before it was closed down in 2004 because Fiji's law did not prohibit methamphetamine's precursors. The Illicit Drugs Control Act 2004, which came into force on 9 July 2004, designed to bring Fijian Law up to date with a broader range of offences carrying harsher penalties (it increased the maximum sentence for trafficking to life imprisonment and a million dollar fine), was not ready to put before Parliament until the day of the raid. It appeared that the Chinese conspirators would be prosecuted in Hong Kong rather than in Fiji because of the low maximum sentence available. PNG is also considering new laws, as the maximum penalty under its Dangerous Drugs Act is two years.

The 2000 Forum meeting noted shortcomings in the national drug legislation within the region, and as a result a joint working group of Forum members and the SPCPC and the OCO produced the 'Canberra Framework', the basis for draft

---

[222] Australian Senate Foreign Affairs, Defence and Trade Committee Report, above n 23, 193. In 2001, PNG applied for the extradition of Jimmy Maladina for the infamous National Provident Fund fraud but he returned voluntarily from Brisbane to face charges in 2002.

[223] The Cook Islands, FSM, Fiji, Kiribati, Nauru, PNG, Samoa, Tonga, and Tuvalu.

[224] *International Opium Convention*, signed at Geneva on 19 February 1925, 81 LNTS 317 (entered into force September 1923).

[225] *Convention for Limiting the Manufacture and Regulating the Distribution of Narcotic Drugs*, signed at Geneva on 13 July 1931, 139 LNTS 301 (entered into force 9 July 1933).

[226] Australian Senate Foreign Affairs, Defence and Trade Committee Report, above n 23, 192 (submission by the AFP – see *Committee Hansard*, 27 March 2003, 361). This contrasted starkly with the three month mandatory prison sentence any drug offence including possession, struck down by the courts in 2001 as a breach of the *1997 Bill of Rights*. See the UNODC, above n 17, 33.

model drug legislation.[227] The 2002 Forum meeting endorsed the resulting Illicit Drug Control Bill and encouraged all Forum PICs to examine the possibility of enacting the legislation in its entirety.[228] The working group has also been providing in-country support to law enforcement officers and prosecutors on implementation of the new law. Apart from their input into the Bill, New Zealand and Australian law enforcement agencies have provided technical assistance and training for Pacific island law enforcement agencies.[229] Yet there appears to have been little resulting legislative change.

Effort has also been put into regional drug law enforcement. The 1992–1997 South Pacific Police-Customs Drug Enforcement Project was aimed at improving drug enforcement capabilities of regional law enforcement agencies.[230] In 1999, the UN ODCCP and Forumsec held a Drug Control Master Plan Workshop in Suva, while in 2001, the SPCPC mooted the establishment of a database for drug seizures and requested members to provide details of seizures to the Law Enforcement Liaison officer at the Forumsec.[231] The 2003 Forum encouraged law enforcement agencies to undertake drug awareness campaigns for officers.[232] An area of concern is the general absence of facilities for rehabilitation of drug offenders in the region.[233]

Environmental offences

General regional coordination of the environment is provided by the South Pacific Regional Environment Programme, a stand alone body dating back to 1982, while the South Pacific Applied Geoscience Commission also deals with environmental and resource management issues. The Forum does respond to specific environmental abuses. For example, with regard to wildlife smuggling, the 2003

---

[227] See generally the *Statement by H.E. Mr A. Naidu, Permanent Representative of Fiji to the United Nations on behalf of the Pacific Islands Forum Group at the General Debate of the Third Committee on Item 100 (Crime Prevention and Criminal Justice) and Item 101 (International Drug Control)*, 2 October 2022, United Nations Headquarters, 2, United Nations <http://www.un.int/nauru/pifstatement.o3pdf > at 6 October 2004. UNODC Model laws were used as a template. See the UNODC, above n 17, 33.

[228] *Forum Communiqué*, Thirty-Third Pacific Islands Forum, Suva, Fiji Islands, 15–17 August, 2002, [22].

[229] *NZ Country Report to the UN Commission on Narcotic Drugs, 46th Session, 2003*, National Drug Policy <http://www.ndp.govt.nz/publications/NZCtyRpt03B.pdf> at 8 December 2004.

[230] See Pacific Islands Forum <http://www.forumsec.org/fj/division/PILAD/Pilad.htm> at 4 October 2004.

[231] See UNODC <http://www.unodc.un.or.th/factsheet/nontraditional.htm> at 21 October 2004, and Resolution 7, *Resolutions of the Thirtieth SPCP Conference 2001*, South Pacific Chiefs of Police Conference <http://www.spcpc.org/resolutions_2001.htm> at 4 October 2004.

[232] *Forum Communiqué*, Thirty-Fourth Pacific Islands Forum, Auckland, New Zealand, 14–16 August 2003, [23].

[233] See UNODC, above n 17, 36-7. It recommends preventative rather than rehabilitative responses because of the general shortage of resources.

Forum urged Forum members to provide information on the trade in endangered species and whether or not they are signatories to the CITES convention.[234] Protection of marine resources is the main area of environmental concern involving penal measures and is discussed below under maritime surveillance.

Terrorism

Prior to 9/11, many PICs did not have legislation dealing with terrorism.[235] The 2001 SPCPC meeting highlighted this inadequacy and urged new legislation to ban proscribed terrorist groups, freeze and forfeit terrorist assets and extradite terrorists.[236] After the adoption of the 2002 Nasonini Declaration the Forum agreed that in 2003 an expert working group on terrorism composed of representatives from Forum members and regional law enforcement agencies would develop a regional framework to address terrorism by, in particular, the provision of model legislation.[237] Once the draft legislation was complete in-country visits would take place by legal drafters to adapt the model legislation to local conditions. A framework for compliance with UN SC Resolution 1373 was produced. The unrealistic target date for updating legislation was the end of 2003. However, new laws have been passed in the Marshall Islands and Samoa. In Samoa, for example, the Prevention and Suppression of Terrorism Act 2002 provides for fast track extradition for foreign nationals accused of the commission of a wide range of terrorist and terrorist financing offences. Samoa is also preparing legislation to enable its OFC to comply with a range of post-9/11 international obligations concerning money laundering, terrorism, financing of terrorism and transnational crime. In other PICs there has been debate about the necessity of these draconian laws and who is going to pay for them.[238] Steps have been taken to increase regional law enforcement cooperation on terrorism. In 2003 the Micronesian Presidents agreed to greater information sharing on anti-terrorist measures.[239] A regional security strategy was discussed at a Pacific Round Table on Terrorism held in Wellington from 10–12 May 2004. The 2004 Forum called for enhanced cooperation on counter-terrorism, including the establishment of a network of

---

[234] *Forum Communiqué*, Thirty-Fourth Pacific Islands Forum, Auckland, New Zealand, 14–16 August 2003, [22].

[235] Australian Senate Foreign Affairs, Defence and Trade Committee Report, above n 23, 191.

[236] Resolution 2; see above n 231. The Forumsec also sent a report to the Chair of the UN Committee on Counter Terrorism highlighting ongoing regional counter terrorist activities – *Pacific Islands Forum Annual Report*, 2001–2002 (2002) 20.

[237] Composed of representatives from Australia, Fiji, Kiribati, Marshall Islands, New Zealand, PNG, Samoa, and Vanuatu, as well as two representatives from the OCO, PIDC, SPCPC and PILOM. See *Expert Working Group to Address Pacific Terrorism Issues*, 21 February 2003, Pacific News, <http://www.hellopacificnews.com/news/general/news/2003/02/21/c.hml> at 4 October 2004.

[238] See the chapter by Alex Conte in this volume.

[239] 'Joint Communiqué of the Third Micronesian President's Summit', *Hello Pacific*, 19 August 2003 <http://www.hellopacific.com/news/general/news/2003/08/19/19regmeeting.html> at 4 October 2004.

central contact points and a counter-terrorism working group in advance of the 2005 meeting of the FRSC.[240] It called for further work on extradition and mutual legal assistance, and raised the possibility of a regional counter-terrorism contingency planning exercise.[241]

Maritime surveillance

Maritime surveillance applies to the policing of territorial waters and EEZs for all transnational crimes, but the most effort has been put into fisheries surveillance. The FFA is the key regional agency with an interest in the enforcement of Forum members' national fisheries laws in their EEZs. The legal basis for regulation of fisheries is the Minimum Terms and Conditions for harmonizing foreign fishing vessels' access to fisheries. The FFA has in place a vessel monitoring system, but it was noted at the 2004 Forum meeting that members continue to licence vessels that are not in compliance with this system.[242] National laws, such as Fiji's Fisheries Act 1942 (as amended), makes provision for a range of offences, for extension of jurisdiction to include the EEZ, and for powers to board, search and seize. But penalties are low. The master, owner or charterer of a foreign registered vessel convicted of fishing without a licence in Fiji's waters may be subject to a maximum fine of F$100,000 (US$60,800),[243] which compares unfavourably with the maximum NZ$250,000 (US$181,110) available for the same offence in New Zealand.[244] The actual practice of surveillance appears sporadic. Although patrol boats sponsored by Australia are in operation through the region their under-use has been questioned, and the Australian Senate has recommended maritime surveillance operations using air patrols, satellite surveillance, and coast-watchers.[245] I am not aware of any Forum member that has used the provisions of the Niue Treaty on Regional Fisheries Cooperation and Enforcement to reach agreement with their neighbours to allow their patrol boats to arrest any foreign fishing vessels. At a strategic level, the expansion of a more wide-ranging surveillance policy may be facilitated by the Pacific Islands Regional Ocean Policy and the Pacific Islands Regional Ocean Forum – Integrated Strategic Action framework to be included for consideration in the Pacific Plan.[246]

---

[240] *Forum Communiqué*, Thirty-Fifth Pacific Islands Forum, Apia, Samoa, 3–10 August 2004, [28].
[241] Ibid.
[242] Ibid [14].
[243] Section 10(3).
[244] Section 113(1) read with section 252(3) of the *New Zealand Fisheries Act 1996*.
[245] Australian Senate Foreign Affairs, Defence and Trade Committee Report, above n 23, 205.
[246] *Forum Communiqué*, Thirty-Fifth Pacific Islands Forum, Apia, Samoa, 3–10 August 2004, [14].

Taxation

The Forum takes an interest in taxation through its development of economic cooperation and an open market in the region. The 2002 Forum Economic Action Plan[247] notes the international dialogue on taxation proposed by the IMF, OECD and World Bank, and asked Forumsec to advance Forum members' interests in this regard. However, there appears to have been no attempt to harmonize tax offences other than the harmonization indirectly achieved through adopting money laundering legislation criminalizing the laundering of the proceeds of tax offences, and drugs legislation with excise offence implications. The Australian Customs Service has had regional input through the OCO to provide technical assistance and training to PICs while Japan provides training on tax-collection regimes. Forum members belong to the Pacific Association of Tax Administrators.

Prison administration

Since 1998 an annual Regional Heads of Prisons Meeting has been held, which discusses matters of concern, shares information and ideas, and develops mutual assistance and cooperation on corrections-related matters, among Pacific states generally. Despite the concern expressed in the Honiara Declaration there does not appear to have been any formal study undertaken of the problems prison administrators face on small islands. Given that pursuit of transnational criminals will add a new dimension to the prison population of PICs with the incarceration of individuals who may continue to manage transnational criminality from jail, this seems short-sighted.

Indigenous issues

No effort appears to have been made to integrate a greater understanding of indigenous issues and particularly customary laws into formal legal changes made to address transnational crime. Certainly no new legislation that I have seen acknowledges in any way the importance of indigenous issues or laws; the new laws are analogues of the laws of developed states. Indigenous issues are important in explaining the causes of crime and in the actual practice of law enforcement, but what does a court do when requested to confiscate communally held land under asset forfeiture legislation?

Human trafficking[248]

The legislative development in this area in New Zealand and Australia is advanced, but in the PICs there is a legislative vacuum. To facilitate change, Forumsec has developed model legislation to address people smuggling, human trafficking,

---

247 See Pacific Islands Forum <http://www.forumsec.org.fj/docs/FEMM/2002/Action%2520Plan.pdf> at 11 November 2004.

248 See the chapter by Michael Barutciski in this volume.

refugee determination and associated issues. Fiji's Immigration Bill introduced in 2002 imposes serious penalties for failure to provide adequate information,[249] for people smuggling[250] and for harbouring a deportee.[251] Multilateral cooperation on these matters takes place through the Asia-Pacific Consultation (APC) on Refugees, Displaced Persons and Migrants; the Regional Ministerial Conference on People Smuggling, Trafficking in Persons and Related Transnational Crime; and the Pacific Immigration Directors Conference (PIDC). National law enforcement agencies cooperate on human trafficking, people smuggling, and refugee determination, and exchange information and analysis on these matters.[252] But they operate in a sensitive social context, and there have been complaints that PIC police have harassed ethnic minorities during operations aimed at removing illegal immigrants.[253] The most significant national agency operating in the region is the Australian Department of Immigration and Multicultural and Indigenous Affairs. It provides law enforcement training and expert assistance for law reform,[254] and negotiates MOUs to facilitate cooperation in immigration control and border issues.[255] Unsurprisingly, Australia has been a major provider of technical assistance. In 2003, the Australian Government announced an A$20 million package to combat trafficking in persons.

Regional security

Since 2000 the Forum Foreign Affairs Ministers Meeting has been trying to develop proposals for Forum leaders to respond to political instability that has plagued PICs such as the Solomon Islands and Fiji.[256] The Forumsec has commissioned national security studies in individual PICs to help focus attention on the security situation in these countries.[257] The main regional operational initiative has been the Regional Assistance Mission to the Solomon Islands, which required legislation in participating states.[258] The Forumsec has observer status on the

---

[249] F$20,000 or 5 years' imprisonment.

[250] F$75,000 or 20 years' imprisonment.

[251] F$100,000 fine or 7 years.

[252] *Forum Communiqué*, Thirty-Fourth Pacific Islands Forum, Auckland, New Zealand, 14–16 August 2003. Forum states are participants in Customs Asia Pacific Enforcement Reporting System, which has two regional support centres in Australia and New Zealand.

[253] See Newton, above n 84, 12 referring to allegations made by the Fiji Chinese community, reported in the *Fiji Times* 5 April 1999.

[254] Australian Senate Foreign Affairs, Defence and Trade Committee Report, above n 23, 200.

[255] Ibid.

[256] Australian Senate Foreign Affairs, Defence and Trade Committee Report, above n 23, 192.

[257] 2001: Fiji, PNG, Solomon Islands, Kiribati; 2002: Kiribati, Nauru, Samoa, Tonga; 2003: Cook Islands, Niue, Tuvalu; and 2004: FSM, Palau, Marshall Islands. See the *Pacific Islands Forum Annual Report*, 2002–2003 (2003) 21.

[258] See generally, Derek McDougall, 'Intervention in the Solomon Islands' (2004) 93 *The Round Table* 213-223. In a further regional intervention, in terms of the *Joint Agreement on Enhanced Cooperation Between Australia and Papua New Guinea*, Port Moresby, signed 30

Council for Security Cooperation in the Asia Pacific, an NGO of government and private security analysts working on Asia-Pacific security matters.

Small arms proliferation

A specific problem for regional security is the proliferation of small arms. The 2003 Report on Small Arms in the Pacific[259] discusses the lack of adequate legislation covering small arms in the Pacific and the inadequate enforcement of existing laws, and identifies legislative variation as a problem because it creates holes exploited by traffickers.[260] The need for new laws was recognized in 1999 when Forum Leaders agreed to the development of a draft legal framework for weapons control, and in 2000, the SPCPC produced a draft Legal Framework for a Common Approach to Weapons Control. It was taken up by the FRSC and the Forumsec produced a Model Illicit Weapons Control Bill, aimed at providing a proper regulatory framework for controlling small arms,[261] and based on the principle that the possession and use of firearms, ammunition, and other related materials is a privilege conditional on the overriding need to ensure public safety. The model law is designed to improve public safety by imposing strict controls on the importation, possession and use of firearms, ammunition, other related materials and prohibited weapons.[262] No legislative modernization has occurred thus far.

Identity fraud

Legislative change in this area has not been a priority. The 2003 Forum meeting directed the Forumsec to coordinate the formation of a working group to explore the viability for Forum PICs to join and participate in the Identity Fraud Register project.[263]

Corruption

Stocktaking undertaken by the Forum reveals that implementation of the Forum Eight Principles of Accountability is far from complete. However, legislative reform has occurred. For example, the Cook Islands Crimes Amendment Act 2003 creates new offences and widens powers in relation to the corrupt use of official information, conspiring to defeat justice and corrupting juries and witnesses.

June 2004, [2004] ATS 24 (in force 13 August 2004), AFP officers began patrolling the streets of PNG in December 2004.

[259] Alpers and Twyford, above n 49.

[260] Above n 49, xvi-xvii.

[261] See Aqorau, above n 47, 9.

[262] *Forum Communiqué*, Thirty-Fourth Pacific Islands Forum, Auckland, New Zealand, 14–16 August 2003.

[263] Ibid. The first meeting of the group took place at the Australian Crime Commission, Canberra from 5–8 April 2004.

However, the major legislative reform required by the UN Corruption Convention is still to be undertaken.

Ensuring implementation

The implementation of the Honiara Declaration has been a source of concern to the Forum. In 1997, Forum Secretary General Noel Levi stated that '[p]rogress in this area would assist in establishing a regional legislative framework to combat transnational crime'.[264] The 2001 Forum meeting expressed 'serious concerns that, despite the provision of legal drafting assistance, progress in implementing the legislative priorities of the Honiara Declaration had been disappointingly slow'.[265] It ordered the Forumsec to undertake a 'stock-take' of members' progress. At the 2001 PILOM meeting Noel Levi commented: 'If we are failing in our commitments under the Honiara Declaration, what does that say to our commitment to the principles of cooperation, peace and stability that underpin the Declaration?'[266] The 2002 Forum meeting noted that 'while some progress had been made in the implementation of the Honiara Declaration, further urgent action was required of some member states'.[267] A commitment was made to full legislative implementation of the Declaration by 2003.[268] The 2003 Nasonini Declaration called again for a legislative stock-take, in order to explain why implementation has been slow.[269] Noel Levi noted that at this point only five Forum members had enacted most of the legislation, and he termed much of the existing legislation 'archaic'.[270] Yet the 2004 Forum meeting once again 'urged members who had not yet done so to enact and implement existing model legislative provisions'.[271] The new statutes enacted in the last four years provide evidence that the Forum's efforts have borne fruit. However, some members that have had drafts prepared for them by consultants supported by the Forumsec have yet to legislate, and implementation is incomplete.[272] There are a number of possible explanations for the difficulties PICs have had in responding to the Honiara Declaration, all of which bear further investigation.

---

[264] See Herman, above n 20, 31.

[265] *Forum Communiqué*, Thirty-Second Pacific Islands Forum, Republic of Nauru, 16–18 August 2001, [38].

[266] Statement of the then Secretary General of the Forum Noel Levi to the 2001 Pacific Islands Law Officers Meeting, 22 October 2001, *Press Statement 8101*, Pacific Islands Forum <http://www.forumsec.org.fj/news/2001/Oct04.htm> at 29 December 2003.

[267] *Forum Communiqué*, Thirty-Third Pacific Islands Forum, Suva, Fiji Islands, 15–17 August, 2002, [7].

[268] Ibid [8].

[269] Above n 262.

[270] Radio Australia News, 1 October 2003, Australian Broadcasting Corporation <http://www.abc.net.au/ra/newstories/RANewsStories_957745.htm> at 29 December 2003.

[271] *Forum Communiqué*, Thirty-Fifth Pacific Islands Forum, Apia, Samoa, 3–10 August 2004, [27].

[272] Transform Aqorau, *Implementation of the Honiara Declaration: National Case Study (Draft)*, 2004, 2 (paper on file with the author).

PICs confront a problem of legislative modernization in all areas of law. Newton notes strikingly that 'law reform is not a high priority in most South Pacific jurisdictions, largely due to a lack of available resources'.[273] In criminal justice systems where small numbers of poorly resourced officials[274] still apply colonial era laws, struggle to report cases and update official collections of legislation,[275] enacting and enforcing transnational criminal laws is not going to proceed as smoothly as others might hope. The fact that it has happened at all is because of outside intervention. Only this intervention has overcome the natural response of PICs to prioritize pressing viability issues rather than lawmaking. PICs are almost completely dependant on technical assistance in respect of the legislative response necessary to meet obligations under suppression conventions. The 1998 FRSC Action Plan provided for legal drafting assistance to implement the Declaration. In response, the Forumsec supplies frameworks, model legislation, technical expertise, funds and the necessary impetus to help Forum members to draft and vet the necessary laws. Developed states, heavy funders of the Forumsec,[276] also provide direct assistance. Some PICs may simply have to wait for help. For example, reform of Tuvalu's drug trafficking legislation depends on the finalization of the regional model drug trafficking law and the provision of assistance to implement it. Others may use this as an excuse for inaction. For example, Vanuatu, in turn, has decided to wait to bring the Vanuatu Convention against Illicit Traffic in Narcotic Drugs and Psychotropic Substances Ratification Act No. 27 of 2001 into force until it had 'confirmation that other Pacific countries have enacted the Model law on Illicit Drug Control prepared with the assistance of the Forum Secretariat'. However, the Forumsec is unable to intervene until it is formally requested to do so by the Forum member.[277]

A more formal regional system where members are obliged to bring laws into operation by a specified date and regional organs have greater powers of intervention might overcome such problems. It must be observed, however, that technical assistance is a necessary but not sufficient condition of modernization. Many of these laws struggle through the technical stages of development or are held up in Parliament itself, which suggests that there are other reasons preventing change. Some of these involve the negotiation process and the nature of the organs and individuals involved. Disjuncture between regional declarations negotiated by diplomats and the implementation of these measures by criminal justice officials

---

[273] Tess Newton, 'Sources of Criminal Law in the South Pacific', *University of the South Pacific Occasional Papers Series*, Occasional Paper no. 6, 5.

[274] Australian Senate Foreign Affairs, Defence and Trade Committee Report, above n 23, 192.

[275] Newton, above n 273, 19.

[276] In 2001 PILAD's internal budget (member's contributions) was F$421,000 and it spent F$502,000 while its extra budget (the list of external funders of the Forum for all purposes is Australia, New Zealand, Japan, the EU, France, Portugal, the UNDP, ESCAP, Canada, Taiwan, the UK and US) was F$2,600,000 and it spent F$1,403,000. In 2002 PILAD's internal budget was F$475,000 and it spent F$508,000 while its extra budget was F$4,204,000 and it spent F$2,184000. *Pacific Islands Forum Annual Report*, 2001–2002 (2002) 24 and *Pacific Islands Forum Annual Report*, 2002–2003 (2003) 27.

[277] See Aqorau, above n 272, 4.

can be a problem, which can be compounded by turf wars, poor communication and poor coordination.[278] The use of foreign consultants may be perceived as intrusive and disempowering. Finally, resistance to legal change in PICs may arise through fear or economic benefit to officials and policymakers. Conflicting interests are most obvious around the regulation of OFCs. Formal legal obligations do pose a risk to the 'grey' economies of PICs. Designed to suppress the activities of transnational criminals involved with drugs and small arms, the new laws become equally available against petty traffickers and smugglers of all kinds, tax evaders and participants in the unregulated economy, which brings into prospect a more general resistance to compliance.[279]

These are just some possible explanations for the generally slow pace of legislative modernization under Forumsec tutelage. The further problem is explaining why, when new laws have been enacted, the evidence suggests that implementation of these laws by the law enforcement authorities of PICs is poor. To be fair, these laws may be having an unknowable deterrent effect. Many are new so there may have been little opportunity to use them. Having said that, modelled as they are on the laws of highly developed criminal justice systems and containing a plethora of complex and obscure rules, implementation costs are high and sometimes prohibitive in PICs, so they may not be applied. A significant problem for implementation of these new laws is poor law enforcement capacity. The AFP cites a lack of resources, poor education, inadequate recruitment, poor wages, poor conditions of service, inadequate financial management practices, ineffective leadership, inadequate basic policing skills, stagnant demographics, donor fatigue, inadequate communications and infrastructure, and geographic remoteness as factors compounding this incapacity.[280] Although police to population ratios are significantly lower in the islands than they are in Australia or New Zealand, this may indicate inefficiency and present more of a problem than a solution, particularly when these forces become directly involved in politics.[281] Corruption is a problem for capacity, and although it is low, indications are that it is penetrating police organizations and the potential for direct police involvement in transnational crime should not be ignored.

The solution may be greater provision of resources. However, critics question whether this will help, pointing to the futility of using more resources to shore up developed state policing models that are inappropriate to the social situations in the region.[282] Others suggest that the sharing and enhancing of existing capacity is possible through a cooperative multi-agency approach.[283]

---

[278] Aqorau, above n 272, 3.

[279] Berta Hernandez, 'RIP to IRP – Money laundering and drug trafficking controls score a knockout victory over bank secrecy' (1993) 18 *North Carolina Journal of International Law and Commercial Regulation* 235, 293-5.

[280] Australian Senate Foreign Affairs, Defence and Trade Committee Report, above n 23, 194-5, citing *Committee Hansard*, 27 March 2003, 358 (AFP).

[281] Newton, above n 84, 5-6.

[282] Newton, above n 84, 13-14.

[283] Aqorau, above n 47, 12.

Developed states are obviously cognisant of the problems of capacity. Much of the progress that has been made in modernizing PIC's law enforcement practices can be attributed to technical support from developed states[284] and the Forumsec has become involved in the facilitation of this technical support. But the AFP questions the utility of regional meetings and conferences and of training in Australia and New Zealand when local conditions demand in-country training and 'back to basics' in recruitment and training.[285] A standing regional police to make up for problems of local operational incapacity has been rejected.[286] But it appears unnecessary if that incapacity, at least in respect of transnational crime, is already being met by the AFP and NZP through liaison officers and the PTCCC.

Lastly, we do not know whether, if the new laws are enacted, and problems of implementation are overcome, they will actually work. The South Pacific has only got the examples of developed states to rely upon, and the effectiveness of these laws is highly contentious.[287] Moreover, little provision appears to have been made for actually monitoring the effectiveness of this legislation in suppression of transnational crime. Steps need to be taken at the regional level to ensure that empirical research is done on how the application of individual measures actually impacts on the harm threatened so that these measures can be adjusted appropriately.

Towards a regional transnational criminal law regime in the South Pacific

The South Pacific as a spatial and social entity

It is trite to say that the difficulties of sovereignty, differences in criminal laws and different experiences of crime present enormous obstacles to the development of a regional transnational criminal law regime in the South Pacific. However, borrowing from the literature on globalization,[288] it seems that there are at least two fundamental aspects to any process of regionalizing identification of and response to crime. The first is the objective fact of interconnectedness: the region is in some sense, because of communications, economic and social links, geography and, in certain cases, ethnicity, one place. The International Association of Criminal Law takes this view when it notes that 'regionalisation' equates to 'developing methods of international collaboration linking at least three independent states belonging to

---

[284] For example, Japan has played a significant role in providing technical support, expertise, training and funding to facilitate the combating of crime in the Pacific. See Tunidau, above n 90, 399.

[285] Australian Senate Foreign Affairs, Defence and Trade Committee Report, above n 23, 194-5, citing *Committee Hansard*, 27 March 2003, 358 (AFP).

[286] The Australian Senate Foreign Affairs, Defence and Trade Committee rejected this option – see above n 23, 205.

[287] Consider the war on drugs.

[288] Roland Robertson, *Globalization* (1992) 8.

a clearly specified geographical entity'.[289] This interconnectedness facilitates all human activity including criminal and legal activity. The extent to which the South Pacific is a region in this sense is questionable; it occupies an identifiable geographical space but communications are poor, trade and social contact difficult.[290] It may look more like a region from without than from within. In addition, however, a region exists because the people within it subjectively consider it to be a single place. It is not clear to what extent the peoples of the South Pacific consider themselves as belonging to one place. The region is not socially well integrated;[291] PICs have stronger connections within Micronesia, Melanesia and Polynesia, and individually with New Zealand and Australia, than with states in the South Pacific region as a whole. This makes regional cooperation difficult, and means that responses arise through the agency of the two regional powers. Whether their motivations are selfish, or altruistic, it appears as though the region is partially a construct imposed by these and other developed states in order to police the transnational criminals operating in PICs. Paradoxically, the region is, at least in part, being assembled by foreign criminals and foreign law enforcement agents.

An exercise in hegemony?

Transnational criminal law is a rationalist intrusion based on the suppression of harm into a world of economic globalization driven by desire for goods both licit and illicit.[292] As the Australian Attorney General's Department put it in a report on the criminal environment in the South Pacific, 'there is a need to reconcile two seemingly contradictory aims: trade liberalisation and the effective control of transnational criminal activities'.[293] The 'invisible hand' of the market seeks to supply both licit and illicit demands, but the licit market cannot 'supply' suppression of the illicit market, so the state must. Because PICs are unable to supply this good, developed states do so out of self-interest. Given that, as Hughes puts it, 'much of the agenda of the small island states is written elsewhere',[294] the development of a regional transnational criminal law in the South Pacific is open to the criticism that it is an exercise in hegemony, and not the dispersal of a global public good.

The Honiara Declaration and its antecedents implicitly claim legitimacy because they are a projection of the global rule of law through international law. But international law is not always considered to be the universalist project that it claims to be. Critics condemn it as an instrumental tool for advancing the interests

---

289 *La Revue Internationale de Droit Pénal* (1994) 21.

290 See, for example, the travails of Air Pacific and the Pacific Forum Line, set up to link PICs, and despite considerable foreign subsidization, considered failures – Crocombe, *The South Pacific*, above n 21, 606ff.

291 Crocombe, *The South Pacific*, above n 21, 591ff, is critical of the notion that there is a South Pacific region.

292 On these two views of globalization see Silbey, above n 3.

293 Australian Senate Foreign Affairs, Defence and Trade Committee Report, above n 23, 190, citing submission 34, 1 (Attorney-General's Department).

294 Hughes, above n 57, 47.

of particular peoples, nations and regions at the expense of others.[295] Delmas-Marty warns that:

> … hegemony is imposed overtly, in the form of what can be called imperial law, or covertly, either through the apparent consent of countries to which dominant legal systems are exported like simple merchandise, or through the appearance of legal no man's lands, where the law of the market reigns.[296]

In her view hegemony encourages a total war without mercy against transnational crime.[297] The specific danger is over-criminalization. She suggests that one response is to assert a criminal justice policy that avoids sole reliance on penalization and uses other sanctions and administrative measures to achieve its goals; another is to impose 'a strict definition of concepts such as terrorism or money laundering, which are too often criminalized for purely political reasons'.[298] Suspicious of a free market in suppression which exports foreign laws to states, she supports a moral trade, and considers that this requires a global criminal law enforceable against everyone, including the most powerful economic or political actors. She believes that the ethical basis of such a law will lead to a supranational conception that aims to protect all humanity.[299]

Given that transnational criminal law is largely instrumental to the needs of developed states concerned about extraterritorial crime, it is difficult to conceive how it can provide a supra-national, universal, ethical criminal law in the sense that Delmas Marty suggests and still remain popular with developed states. To suggest an example, if a PIC that has large scale local usage of cannabis wished to adopt new drug legislation in order to meet its obligations under article 3(2) of the 1988 Drug Trafficking Convention to suppress simple possession by either a) allowing for non-prosecution of possession and diversion, or b) construing possession in a limited way to the same effect, it seems likely that this PIC would be subject to a great deal of international pressure to mend its ways. Silbey is less sanguine about the possibilities of establishing universal human values in this context:

> … I am concerned about the consequences of marketing specific legal devices as if they were one of those dresses that fit all sizes. I am worried about how local justice can be achieved within a supposedly universal, all purpose, one size fits all law.[300]

She believes that there is no likelihood of pluralism; the globalization of Western laws, including by implication transnational criminal laws, is purely instrumental to Western purposes and will not be appropriated or reconstructed by the locals

---

[295] Makua Wa Matua, 'Critical Race Theory and International Law: The View of an Insider-Outsider' (2001) 45 *Villanova Law Review* 841.
[296] Above n 5, 3.
[297] Mireille Delmas-Marty, 'Criminal Law as Ethics of Globalisation' [2004] *Humanitäres Völkerrecht-Informationsschriften* 4, 4.
[298] Ibid 5.
[299] Ibid.
[300] Above n 3, 222.

themselves.[301] It is unclear precisely how much space for appropriation and adaptation to meet local needs island leaders have when they take these laws. However, it is notable that the regional concerns, such as indigenous issues, added to the end of the Honiara Declaration's catalogue, have since been neglected in the process of legislative modernization.

Why then, do island leaders accept the need for these laws? Ikenberry and Kupchan argue that local elites adopt the hegemon's norms principally because of material incentives, but also because the hegemon changes their substantive beliefs.[302] This socialization is achieved through a combination of technical assistance and advice from policy advisors and pressure groups. The leaders may 'agree' for strategic purposes such as gaining legitimacy in the eyes of international society; however, such 'agreement' is unlikely to result in suppression. Even if the recent legislative reforms mean that island leaders are now convinced that transnational crime does threaten their societies, this may not achieve real change if that acceptance is not shared generally. The populace may be hostile because of over-criminalization and draconian police powers,[303] or they may not consider these laws a priority given their other problems. These views may alter under the impact of media concern and the activities of civil society concerned about, for example, trafficked women and drug-induced harm. Nevertheless, the top-down nature of the modernizing program that is transnational penal norm transfer means that even if elite compliance is achieved, it may not generate the kind of social compliance necessary to effectively suppress these forms of behaviour.

Effectiveness

The absence of such social compliance means that developed states have limited options when it comes to pursuing the effective suppression of extraterritorial crime in the South Pacific. The current option appears to be to use technical assistance to modernize laws and effect surrogate policing through local law enforcement. However, even if these criminal activities also have a negative local impact, this kind of intervention is unlikely to generate popular support for suppression of these offences, and foreign 'supervision' of local policing will generate hostility. An alternative approach would be to wait until these criminal activities begin to have such a negative local impact – through, for example, increased hard drug use – that local populations seek external help. Aside from its ethical problems, this impact may not occur, and even if it does locals may not

---

301 Above n 3, 223.

302 John Ikenberry and Charles Kupchan, 'Socialization and Hegemonic Power' (1990) 44 *International Organization* 283, 285ff.

303 For a case study of such a response see Sappho Xenakis, *The International versus Domestic Pressures on the Development of Organised Crime Policy: The Case of Greece* (Paper presented at the 2nd ECPR Conference, 18–21 September 2003, Marburg), European Consortium for Political Research <http://www.essex.ac.uk/ecpr/events/generalconference/papers/19/10/xenakis> at 15 January 2004.

seek help to suppress activities that do not have a local effect, but do have consequences abroad. A more appropriate option, which does not prioritize the global aspects of transnational crime at the expense of ignoring its local aspects,[304] may be to develop and support laws and law enforcement mechanisms that are versatile enough to be used to suppress both local and transnational criminal activities. Money laundering laws that can be and importantly are used against the laundering of the proceeds of fisheries fraud, or corruption laws that can be and again are used against corrupt local politicians as well as transnational corruption, are likely to engender more local support than laws and enforcement perceived solely to be in the interests of developed states. This approach can be adopted through the negotiation of regional crime control conventions that adequately meet local as well as external concerns, after regional crime control institutions have engaged in adequate empirical research to identify these concerns.

The next steps

The members of the South Pacific Forum are under pressure to regionalize. Some of this pressure comes from outside the region. The European Union, for example, is driving regionalization by linking it to the grant of development aid under the Cotonou Agreement.[305] Some pressure comes from within the region. The Review of the Forum by the Forum Eminent Person's Group in 2003–2004 resulted in the Auckland Declaration, produced by the Forum Leaders Special Retreat in Auckland on 6 April 2004. It proposed a Pacific Plan that 'would create stronger and deeper links between sovereign countries of the region and identify the sectors where the region could gain the most from sharing resources of governance and aligning policies'.[306] The 2004 Forum reiterated that the Pacific Plan was to be the main instrument for the promotion of a new Pacific vision.[307] The desired outcome appears to be efficiency, to discard the more time consuming aspects of the 'Pacific Way'[308] that prevent adaptation to modern conditions. Security from transnational crime is one of a number of forces driving regionalization.[309] Constructed as a

[304] See generally Richard Hobbs, 'Going Down the Glocal: The Local Context of Organised Crime' (1998) 37 *The Howard Journal of Criminal Justice* 407-422.

[305] *Partnership agreement between the members of the African, Caribbean and Pacific Group of States of the one part, and the European Community and its Member States, of the other part*, signed 23 June 2000 [2000] OJ L 317/3 (entered into force 1 April 2003). See Malakai Koloamatangi, 'EU, Cotonou and EPAs: the view from the Pacific Islands' (2003) 200 *The Courier ACP-EU* 14.

[306] *Auckland Declaration*, Pacific Island Forum Leaders Special Retreat, Auckland 6 April 2004, [1], Pacific Islands Forum <http://www.forumsec.org.fj/docs/Gen_Docs/Auckland_Declaration.pdf> at 14 December 2004.

[307] *Forum Communiqué*, Thirty-Fifth Pacific Islands Forum, Apia, Samoa, 3–10 August 2004, [3].

[308] See generally Crocombe, 'The Pacific Plan', above n 78, 159.

[309] The Eminent Person's Group Report consider that 'processes for meeting international legal demands' and 'regional law enforcement aimed at transnational crime' are areas that would benefit from greater shared effort. See above n 200.

problem of the integrity of these PICs as sovereign entities,[310] it provides a powerful, if overstated, rationalization for some attenuation of their sovereignty.

However, this shift to greater regionalization is likely to be resisted because it is being imposed on the Pacific by developed states that see it as the best way of managing the region. Moreover, greater regionalization points to tighter legal regulation, which may also be resisted; as Crocombe points out, the Forum has thus far 'successfully kept the lawyers at bay'.[311] On the positive side, a stronger independent regional organization may provide some compensation for loss of sovereignty if it offers PICs a greater opportunity to exercise a new regional sovereignty. In responding to transnational crime, for example, the region may have more control over choosing what to consider criminal, to respond with appropriate legal measures and to adjust this response according to the efficacy of these measures, than an individual state responding to outside pressure. Regionalization may also provide a greater opportunity to counterbalance the negative effects of the suppression of transnational crime by guaranteeing due process in inter-state cooperation on investigation, the gathering of evidence and the transfer of suspects.[312] We can only speculate at this stage about what form greater regional cooperation in the suppression of transnational crime might take, if it occurs at all. While it is likely to go beyond the Honiara Declaration's soft-law, it is unlikely to take the form of supra-national criminal law; even within the EU the regulation of criminal matters is still dealt largely through international treaty.[313] A possible next step for Forum members is to provide either for a regional treaty to suppress a range of transnational crimes or for separate regional treaties focusing on specific crimes.

---

[310] See, e.g. Schloenhardt, above n 17, 191; Shibuya, above n 46, 2, 4.

[311] Crocombe, 'The Pacific Plan', above n 78.

[312] Delmas-Marty, above n 6, vi. This has happened elsewhere: in the European legal space, criminal law cooperation was made palatable by regional human rights cooperation. See Geert Cortsens and Jean Pradel, *European Criminal Law* (2002) generally. It is notable that the Forum has raised human rights as a more recent concern. See the Eminent Person's Group Report, above n 200. The 2000 Biketawa Declaration explicitly links the effective suppression of transnational crime with respect for individual human rights. See generally Steve Peers, *EU Justice and Home Affairs Law* (2000) 15-30, 48-62.

[313] See Peers, above n 312.

Appendix

Mutual assistance in criminal matters

Australia

Mutual Assistance in Criminal Matters Act 1987 (1987)
Foreign Evidence Act 1994 (1994)

Cook Islands

Mutual Assistance in Criminal Matters Act No. 9 of 2003 (2003)

Federated States of Micronesia

FSM Foreign Evidence Act of 2000 (not yet in force)
FSM Mutual Assistance in Criminal Matters Act of 2000 (2001)

Fiji

Mutual Assistance in Criminal Matters Act 1997 (1998)
Mutual Assistance in Criminal Matters Amendment Bill under discussion

Kiribati

Mutual Assistance in Criminal Matters Act 2003 (2003)
Evidence Act 2003 (2003)

New Zealand

Mutual Assistance in Criminal Matters Act 1992 as amended in 1998 (1992; 1999).

Niue

Mutual Assistance in Criminal Matters Act 1998 (1998)

Palau

Mutual Assistance in Criminal Matters Act 2001 (2001)
Foreign Evidence Act of 2001 (2001)

Republic of the Marshall Islands

Mutual Assistance in Criminal Matters Act, 2002 (2002)
Foreign Evidence Act 2002 (2002)

Solomon Islands

Mutual Assistance in Criminal Matters Act 2002 (2002)

Tonga

Foreign Evidence Act 2000 (2000)
Mutual Assistance in Criminal Matters Act 2000 (2000)

Tuvalu

Mutual Assistance in Criminal Matters Bill drafted but further assistance requested from Forumsec

Vanuatu

Mutual Assistance in Criminal Matters Act No. 14 of 2002 (2003)

Money laundering, asset forfeiture and banking regulation

Australia

Proceeds of Crime Act 2002 (2003)
Division 400 Criminal Code Act 1995 (2003)

Cook Islands

Financial Transactions Reporting Act No. 10 of 2003 (2003)
Financial Supervisory Commission Act No. 11 of 2003 (2003)
International Companies Amendment Act No. 5 of 2003 (2003)
Banking (substantive Act of 57) No. 7 of 2003 (2003)
Crimes Amendment Act No. 6 of 2003 (2003)
Criminal Procedure Amendment Act 2003 (2003)
Proceeds of Crime Act No. 12 of 2003 (2003)

Federated States of Micronesia

FSM Money Laundering and Proceeds of Crime Act of 2000 (2001)
FSM Cooperation in Law Enforcement Act of 2001 (not yet submitted to Congress)

Fiji

Part V of the Proceeds of Crime Act 1997 (1998)
Proceeds of Crime Act 1998 (1998)

Kiribati

Proceeds of Crime Act 2003 (2003)
Kiribati draft bill on money laundering

Nauru

Anti-Money Laundering Act, 28 August 2001
Anti-Money Laundering Act 2003
Anti-Money Laundering (Amendment) Act 2004
Draft Proceeds of Crime Act Banking (Amendment) Act 2004

New Zealand

Proceeds of Crime Act 1991 (1992)
Crimes Act 1961 (1995)
Misuse of Drugs Amendment Act 1998 (1999)

Niue

Proceeds of Crime Act 1998 (1998)
Financial Transaction Reporting Act 2000

Palau

Money Laundering and Proceeds of Crime Act of 2001 (2001)
Financial Institutions Act of 2001 (2001)

Papua New Guinea

Draft Bill on Proceeds of Crime, 2003

Republic of the Marshall Islands

Banking (Amendment) Act 2000 (2000)
Banking (Amendment) Act 2002 (2002)
Banking (Amendment) Act, 2003
Proceeds of Crime Act, 2002 (2002)

Samoa

Money Laundering Prevention Act 2000 (2000)
Money Laundering Prevention Amendment Act 2000 (2000)

Solomon Islands

Money Laundering and Proceeds of Crime Act 2002 (2002)

Tonga

Money Laundering and Proceeds of Crime Act 2000 (2000)

Tuvalu

Proceeds of Crime Bill drafted but further assistance requested from the Forumsec

Vanuatu

The Serious Offences (Confiscation of Proceeds) Act 1989
Proceeds of Crime Act No. 13 of 2002 (2003)
Financial Transactions Reporting Act No. 33 of 2000 (2000)
International Banking Act No. 4 of 2002

Extradition

Australia

Extradition Act 1988 (1988)

Cook Islands

Extradition Act No. 8 of 2003 (2003)

Federated States of Micronesia

FSM Trans-national Extradition and Transfer of Convicted Persons Act of 2000 (legislation introduced but not yet passed)
FSM Interstate Extradition Act of 2000 (legislation introduced but not yet passed)

Fiji

Extradition Act 2003 (not in force)

Kiribati

Extradition Act 2003 (2003)

New Zealand

Extradition Act 1999 (1999)

Niue

Extradition Act 1998 (1998)

Palau

Extradition and Transfer Act of 2001 (signed by President but not clear if necessary regulations promulgated)

Republic of the Marshall Islands

Trans-national Extradition and Transfer of Convicted Persons Act, 2003

Papua New Guinea

Extradition Act 1975 (1975)

Samoa

Extradition Act 1974 (1975)
Extradition Amendment Act 1994
Prevention and Suppression of Terrorism Act 2002

Solomon Islands

Extradition Act 1987 (1987)

Tonga

Extradition Act 1993 (1994)

Tuvalu

Extradition Bill has passed first reading

Vanuatu

Extradition Act No. 16 of 2002 (2003)

Drug offences

Australia

Commonwealth Crimes (Traffic in Narcotic Drugs and Psychotropic Substances) Act 1990 (1990)
Commonwealth Customs Act 1901 (1901)
Commonwealth Customs (Prohibited Import) Regulations 1956
Commonwealth Customs (Prohibited Export) Legislation 1958 (1958)
Commonwealth Narcotic Drugs Act 1967 (1968)
Commonwealth Psychotropic Substance Act 1976 (1976)
National Drug Strategy (for treatment and rehabilitation)
ACT Poisons and Drugs Act 1978 (1978)
ACT Drugs of Dependence Act 1989 (1989)
ACT Drugs of Dependence Regulations 1993 (1993)
NSW Drug Misuse and Trafficking Act 1985 (1985)
NSW Poisons and Therapeutic Goods Act 1966 (1966)
NT Poisons and Dangerous Drugs Act 1983 (1983)
Misuse of Drugs Act NT 1990 (1990)
QLD Health Act 1937 (1937)
QLD Health (Drugs and Poisons) Regulations 1966 (1966)
QLD Health (Drugs and Poisons Regulations 1996 (1996)
QLD Drugs Misuse Act 1986 (1986)
QLD Health Regulation 1966 (1966)
QLD Health Regulation 1996 (1996)
SA Controlled Substances Act 1984 (1984)
Tasmania Poisons Act 1971 (1971)
Victorian Drugs, Poisons and Controlled Substances Act 1981 (1981)
Victorian Alcoholics and Drug Dependent Persons Act 1986 (1986)
WA Poisons Act 1964 (1964)
WA Poisons Amendment Act 1995 (1995)
WA Misuse of Drugs Act 1981 (1981)

Cook Islands

Misuse of Drugs Bill under consideration (not yet in force)

Federated States of Micronesia

Controlled Substances Act, 11 FSMC section 1101 ff (1982)
FSM Controlled Substances Act 2000 (pending)

Fiji

Dangerous Drugs Act 1938, as amended (1938)
Dangerous Drugs Decree 1990 (1990)

Customs Act 1968 (1968)
Pharmacy and Poisons Act 1938 (1938)
Dangerous Drugs (Amendment) Decree 1991 (not in force)
Illicit Drug Control Act (2004)

Kiribati

Dangerous Drugs Ordinance 1977 (1977)
Pharmacy and Poisons Ordinance
Evidence Act 2003 (2003)

New Zealand

Misuse of Drugs Act 1975 (1977)
Misuse of Drugs Amendment Act 1998 (1999)
Crimes Act 1961 as amended in 1996 (1962; 1996)
Proceeds of Crime Act 1991 (1991)
Financial Transactions Reporting Act 1996 (1996)
Sentencing Act 2002 (2002)
Alcoholism and Drug Addiction Act 1966 (1969)
Mutual Assistance in Criminal Matters Act 1992 as amended in 1998 (1993; 1999)
Evidence Act 1908 (1908)

Niue

Misuse of Drugs Act 1998 (1998)

Palau

Controlled Substances Act, Chapters 30-33 of Title 34 of the Palau National Code

Papua New Guinea

Customs Act 1951 (1951)
Poisons and Dangerous Substances Act 1952 (1952)
Dangerous Drugs Act 1952 (1955)
Drugs Act Ch 229 (1955)
Pharmacy Act Ch. 94 (1955)
Dangerous Drugs (Extension of Definition) Act 1968 (1968)
Dangerous Drugs (Possession) Act 1970 (1970)
Public Health Act 1974 (1974)
Criminal Code Ch. 262 (1975)
Customs (Prohibited Imports) Regulation

National Narcotics Control Board Act 1992 (1992)
Medicines and Cosmetics Act of 1999 (not yet in force)

Republic of the Marshall Islands

Narcotic Drugs (Prohibition and Control Act) 1987 as amended (1987; 1992; 2002)

Samoa

Narcotics Act 1967 (1967)
Food and Drugs Act 1967 (1967)
Pharmacy Act 1976 (1976)
Customs Act 1977 (1977)
Maritime Zones Act 1999 (1999)

Tonga

Regional model legislation currently being vetted by Crown Law Office

Vanuatu

Dangerous Drugs Regulation (Amendment) Act 1984 (original Act 1939)
Convention against Illicit Traffic in Narcotic Drugs and Psychotropic Substances Ratification Act No. 27 of 2001 (?)
The Serious Offences (Confiscation of Proceeds) Act 1989 (1990)

Terrorism

Australia

Crimes (Aviation) Act 1991
Crimes (Ships and Fixed Platforms) Act 1992
Nuclear Non-Proliferation (Safeguards) Act 1987 (in force 1987)
Crimes (Hostages) Act 1989 (in force 1990)
Crimes (Internationally Protected Persons) Act 1976 (in force 1977)
Criminal Code Amendments (Suppression of Terrorists Bombings) Act 2002 (in force 2002)
Suppression of the Financing of Terrorism Act 2002 (in force 2002)

Republic of the Marshall Islands

Counter-Terrorism Act, 2002 (2002)

Fiji

Penal and Criminal Procedure Codes
Civil Aviation (Security) Act 1994

Nauru

Combating Financing Terrorism Bill in process

Palau

Draft Omnibus Counter-Terrorism Bill introduced in 2003 but still awaiting further legislative action

Samoa

The Prevention and Suppression of Terrorism Act 2002 (2002)

Maritime surveillance

Australia

Border Protection Legislation Amendment Act 1999 which implements Article 17 of the 1988 Drug Trafficking Convention (in force 1999)

Federated States of Micronesia

FSM Controlled Substances Act of 2000 (pending)

New Zealand

Misuse of Drugs Act 1975 (1977)
Customs and Excise Act 1996 (1996)
Mutual Assistance in Criminal Matters Act 1992 as amended in 1998 (1993; 1999)

Samoa

Maritime Zone Act 1999

Human trafficking

Australia

Border Protection Legislation Amendment Act 1999 (1999)
Crimes (Child Sex Tourism) Amendment Act 1994 (1994)

Criminal Code Amendment (Slavery and Sexual Servitude) Act 1999 (1999)
Migration Act 1958, Amendment 1999 (Cth), Division 12 (1999)
Crimes Legislation Amendment Act (Act No. 141 of 2002) (2002)
Human Rights (Sexual Conduct) Act 1994 (1994)

Cook Islands

The Entry, Residence and Departure Act 1971–72

Fiji

Immigration Act 2004 (before Parliament)
Passport Act 2002 (2002)

New Zealand

The Crimes Act 1961, Amendment of 1995 (1995)
The Children, Young Persons and their Families Act 1989 (1989)
Immigration Act 1987 (1987)
Prostitution Reform Act 2003 (2003)

Palau

Draft People Smuggling and People Trafficking Act, 2003, awaiting approval by Congress

Small arms proliferation

Australia

Mutual Assistance in Criminal Matters Act 1987 (in force 1987)
Proceeds of Crime Act 2002 (in force 2003)
Extradition Act 1988 (in force 1988)

Cook Islands

Crimes Act 1969
The CI Arms Ordinance Act 1954

Vanuatu

Penal Code Amendment Bill 2003
United Nations Convention against Transnational Organised Crime Ratification Bill 2003

Chapter 3

International Terrorism and the South Pacific

Alex Conte

Introduction

International terrorism is not a new phenomenon. Indeed, the origin of the word *terrorism* dates back to the French Revolution of 1788 as the label used by the establishment to describe the conduct of revolutionaries.[1] Likewise, terrorism has been a subject of concern with the United Nations since the 1960s, following a series of aircraft hijackings.[2] Notwithstanding the long-held attention of the international community upon terrorism, the subject deserves special attention within this book for several reasons. Terrorism has, some would argue, entered a new phase over recent decades (and as evident in the terrorist attacks of 11 September 2001): an age where trans-national activity has intensified and been made easier, and where technology and the media can be taken advantage of by terrorist entities to further the impact of terrorist conduct and the delivery of messages or fear-inducing images.[3]

Perhaps more importantly, the issue of terrorism is one that has not been responded to in meaningful terms by all Pacific Island countries, many failing to perceive a need for action in the absence of any immediate threat of terrorist conduct within their borders. This brings into play interesting issues concerning the aim of international counter-terrorism and the interface between international, regional and national security. The focus of this chapter, then, is upon the relevance of counter-terrorism to the South Pacific. Against that background, this chapter aims to consider firstly whether counter-terrorism is relevant to the South Pacific. Irrespective of the answer to that question, regard will also be had to the international anti-terrorist obligations of States within the South Pacific. Finally, an examination of the South Pacific response to those obligations will be undertaken.

In undertaking that examination, this chapter will focus its attention upon the South Pacific region, rather than the Pacific at large or the Asia-Pacific region. For

---

[1] French Ambassador to Fiji, His Excellency Berg, 'Terrorism: The New International Challenge' (Paper presented at the public workshop *How Should Fiji Respond to the Threat of Terrorism?*, Suva, Fiji, 17 July 2004, copy on file with author).

[2] Discussed further below.

[3] Berg, above n 1.

the purpose of this chapter, then, the countries upon which it will focus are those that are members of the Pacific Islands Forum, with particular attention paid to New Zealand.[4] It should be noted at this point that one could approach this topic by also addressing the influence of Australia as a 'driving force' behind counter-terrorism in the South Pacific. While it would be fair to do so, this chapter focuses instead on the question of international law and United Nations influences upon counter-terrorism in the region and the relevance of the topic (and responses to it) by the South Pacific in general.

How is counter-terrorism relevant to the South Pacific?

Other than the bombing by French military agents of the *Rainbow Warrior* in New Zealand in 1985, the South Pacific has not been subject to, or had to deal directly with, international terrorism. As such, many public submissions on counter-terrorist legislation within the region have questioned the need for action against international terrorism.[5] Similar views have been expressed by some leaders within the Pacific, seeing the region as an unlikely target of terrorism, such that counter-terrorism should be low on the list of the region's many priorities.[6] The question is valid, although a little simplistic, and the answer partly depends on the definition of terrorism being used. A legal reason for the pursuit of counter-terrorism in the South Pacific is that such action is an obligation at international law for most Pacific Forum members. This is not the same thing as a needs-based explanation for that pursuit. Three particularly important matters do, however, point to the relevance of counter-terrorism to the South Pacific. Before addressing each of those issues, it is important to have regard to the definition of terrorism.

What is terrorism?

In considering international counter-terrorism and its relevance to the South Pacific region, it must be acknowledged that there are problems associated with the definition of the term. The United Nations Terrorism Prevention Branch describes

---

[4] Australia, Cook Islands, Federated States of Micronesia, Fiji, Kiribati, Nauru, New Zealand (incorporating the non-self governing territory of Tokelau), Niue, Palau, Papua New Guinea, Republic of the Marshall Islands, Samoa, Solomon Islands, Tonga, Tuvalu, Vanuatu. This excludes French Polynesian States and American Samoa, being States that are governed by laws of France and the United States respectively.

[5] This was a common theme, for example, in the submissions made to the New Zealand Foreign Affairs, Defence and Trade Committee on the Terrorism Suppression Bill (as redrafted and contained within the Committee's interim report: Foreign Affairs, Defence and Trade Committee, *Interim Report on the Terrorism (Bombings and Financing) Bill*, 8 November 2001).

[6] Greg Urwin, 'The Need for Anti-Terrorism Legislation in Fiji' (Paper presented at the public workshop *How Should Fiji Respond to the Threat of Terrorism?*, Suva, Fiji, 17 July 2004, copy on file with author), [7].

terrorism as a unique form of crime. Terrorist acts, it says, often contain elements of warfare, politics and propaganda. It continues, stating that '[f]or security reasons and due to lack of popular support, terrorist organisations are usually small, making detection and infiltration difficult. Although the goals of terrorists are sometimes shared by wider constituencies, their methods are generally abhorred'.[7]

The inability of the international community to achieve consensus on a global definition of terrorism is one of the major obstacles facing the fight against terrorism. The Executive Director of the International Policy Institute for Counter-Terrorism, Boaz Ganor, has emphasized the point, saying that UN Security Council Resolutions can only have an effective impact once all States agree upon what type of acts constitute terrorism.[8] Despite this, there is still no definition of the term to which all States subscribe.

Generally speaking, the twelve international treaties on counter-terrorism[9] deal with specific forms of terrorist conduct and are therefore precise in nature and not of general application. Furthermore, they are not a solution in themselves, since treaties are only binding upon States parties.[10] Nor does the United Nations Charter contain a definition of the term. The Rome Statute of the International Criminal Court does not include terrorism as one of the international crimes within the Court's jurisdiction.[11] Perhaps most surprising is the fact that Security Council Resolution 1373, which imposes various obligations concerning counter-terrorism, does not define the term.[12]

---

[7] United Nations Office for Drug Control and Crime Prevention, 'UN Action Against Terrorism', <http://www.odccp.org/terrorism.html> at 19 June 2002.

[8] Boaz Ganor, 'Security Council Resolution 1269: What it Leaves Out', 25 October 1999, web site of the International Policy Institute for Counter-Terrorism, <http://www.ict.org.il/articles/articledet.cfm?articleid=93> at 1 June 2002.

[9] To be discussed further in this chapter.

[10] *Pacta tertii nec nocent nec prosunt.*

[11] Statute of the International Criminal Court, opened for signature 17 July 1998, 2187 UNTS 90 (entered into force 1 July 2002). The Court has within its jurisdiction the 'most serious international crimes', according to its preamble. It was proposed, within the draft Statute, to include terrorism within the Court's jurisdiction, but the failure of States to agree upon a definition of the term resulted in the crime being removed from the scope of the Court's jurisdiction and subject matter of the constitutive treaty. There are arguments, however, that terrorist acts fall within the jurisdiction of the Court as constituting crimes against humanity, as crimes under article 7 of the Rome Statute.

[12] Having said this, the lack of definition was most likely due to the fact (as will be seen through subsequent discussions) that there is a lack of consensus on just what amounts to terrorism. In a desire to issue a forceful, and at the same time early, resolution in the wake of September 11 it is likely that the Council saw use of the term, without definition, as the only viable option in the short term. The problem with this approach is that it has left the question of defining the term with individual member States, leading to inconsistent definitions and, arguably, a weak rather than forceful resolution.

Attempts to define terrorism

Attempts to define the term have been made since before the establishment of the United Nations. The Draft League of Nations Convention for the Prevention and Punishment of Terrorism was to provide that terrorism comprised:

> All criminal acts directed against a State and intended or calculated to create a state of terror in the minds of particular persons or a group of persons or the general public.[13]

This provision was never adopted due to dissent over the definition.

There have been suggestions that terrorism be defined as the peacetime equivalent of war crimes. In a report to the UN Crime Branch, Schmidt proposed taking the already agreed upon definition of war crimes (comprising deliberate attacks on civilians, hostage taking and the killing of prisoners) and extending it to peacetime.[14] Terrorism would then be simply defined as the 'peacetime equivalents of war crimes'. Again, however, this did not gain acceptance. Schmidt appears to have been more successful in gaining acceptance of a more complex definition of terrorism, as identified by the UN Office for Drug Control and Crime Prevention (ODCCP):

> An anxiety-inspiring method of repeated violent action, employed by a (semi-) clandestine individual, group or state actors, for idiosyncratic, criminal or political reasons, whereby – in contrast to assassination – the direct targets of violence are not the main targets. The immediate human victims of violence are generally chosen randomly (targets of opportunity) or selectively (representative or symbolic targets) from a target population, and serve as message generators. Threat and violence-based communication processes between terrorist (organisation), (imperilled) victims, and main targets are used to manipulate the main target (audience(s)), turning it into a target of terror, a target of demands, or a target of attention, depending on what intimidation, coercion, or propaganda is primarily sought.[15]

What might be observed is that the common threads throughout this, and various other, definitions are as follows: firstly, that the *physical* targets of a terrorist act are not the *intended* targets (the target against whom a message is being sent, usually a government or international organization); next, that the purpose of the threat or violence is to intimidate and create a situation of fear or terror (hence the term *terror*ism); and, finally, that this is intended to persuade or dissuade the primary target to do or abstain from doing something, in pursuit of some ideological reason(s).

---

[13] Geneva Convention for the Prevention and Punishment of Terrorism (Draft, 1937).

[14] This definition was put to the United Nations Crime Branch by Alexander Schmidt in 1992: see the web site of the United Nations Office for Drug Control and Crime Prevention, 'Definitions of Terrorism', <http://www.odccp.org/terrorism_definitions.html> at 19 June 2002.

[15] Ibid.

Why a lack of consensus?

The sticking point, it seems, is not so much with the technical wording of what physical conduct amounts to a terrorist act (what might be seen as an objective definition). The problem appears to lie with the purpose of the conduct (incorporating subjective elements). For instance, does a bombing carried out by a rebel group, which is directed towards the destabilization of oppressive authorities (the Pol Pot Regime, for example), amount to a terrorist act or an act of 'freedom fighters'? The point to make is that this is not just a cliché. To give two very striking examples, the United States' list of the most wanted terrorists[16] once featured Yasser Arafat and Nelson Mandela (both of whom were subsequently awarded the Nobel Peace Prize); clearly evidence that this is a highly political and controversial issue. An observation made by a journalist on this point encapsulates the issue very nicely, when he noted that 'terrorists are those who use violence against the side that is using the word'.[17]

A number of States argue that a subjective analysis and definition of such conduct (by examining the purpose of the conduct) should therefore be made. The United Nations ODCCP reports that Arab States such as Libya, Syria and Iran have all campaigned for a definition that excludes acts of 'freedom fighters' from the international definition of terrorism by employing the argument that a justified goal may be pursued by any available means.[18]

While it must be acknowledged that these positions are firmly held by a number of States, it should also be pointed out that the majority of States adhere to an objective definition of terrorism (one which does not take into account the motives of the conduct). In 1994, the UN General Assembly adopted the Declaration on Measures to Eliminate International Terrorism.[19] The Declaration was based on the notion of peace and security and the principle of refraining from the threat or use of force in international relations.[20] It pronounced that terrorism constitutes a grave violation of the purpose and principles of the United Nations.[21] While it did not purport to define 'terrorism', it did say that criminal acts intended or calculated to provoke a state of terror in the general public for political purposes are in any circumstances unjustifiable:

---

[16] This is maintained by the United States Federal Bureau of Investigation and may be accessed by internet: <http://www.fbi.gov/mostwant/terrorists/fugitives.htm>.

[17] The Observer, 30 September 2001, quote contained within *Submissions of the Indonesian Human Rights Committee to the Foreign Affairs, Defence and Trade Committee on the Terrorism (Bombings and Finance) Suppression Bill*, TERRO/88, Parliamentary Library, Wellington.

[18] Above n 11.

[19] Declaration on Measures to Eliminate International Terrorism, adopted under GA Res 60, 49 UN GAOR (84th plen mtg), UN Doc A/Res/49/60 (1994).

[20] Ibid, as is evident through its preamble.

[21] Ibid [2].

> The States Members of the United Nations solemnly reaffirm their unequivocal condemnation of *all* acts, methods and practices of terrorism, as criminal and unjustifiable, *wherever and by whomever committed*, including those which jeopardize the friendly relations among States and peoples and threaten the territorial integrity and security of States.[22] [emphasis added]

Of even greater value in this respect, according to the Executive Director of the International Policy Institute for Counter-Terrorism, is the Security Council's Resolution 1269.[23] While the Resolution also fails to define terrorism, it does clearly take an objective approach to the question of terrorist conduct, stating that the Security Council:

> 1. *Unequivocally condemns* all acts, methods and practices of terrorism as criminal and unjustifiable, *regardless of their motivation*, in all their forms and manifestations, wherever and by whomever committed, in particular those which would threaten international peace and security; [...] [emphasis added]

The concept of terrorism

One further matter warrants consideration before leaving the issue of definition. The word 'terrorism', particularly in the vocabulary of the media since September 11, has come to be used as a description of a significantly wide range of violent conduct. Little regard is paid in use of the word to the three common threads identified above (differential targets; terror-inducing conduct; to influence a government or organization for ideological ends). It has become all too common, in the observation of the author, for events with some level of 'fear-factor' to be sensationalized as terrorist acts. Care must be taken when considering and assessing situations and how they might impact upon the topic. Civil conflicts where there is no differential targeting should be treated as civil conflicts, not as acts of terrorism. Criminal acts should likewise be dealt with in the context of normal criminal practice and procedure.

This opens the door to an even more fundamental question: *why talk about terrorism at all?* And if one doesn't need to talk about the term, then what need is there for a specific response on the part of Pacific Forum members? An act of 'terrorism', after all, will comprise a series of acts which, in and of themselves, constitute various criminal offences. To take an example, a bombing of an Embassy will likely involve the unlawful possession of explosives, the wilful destruction of property and the wilful injury to or killing of persons. Each element is a criminal offence in most jurisdictions and, as such, is capable of being dealt with by the relevant municipal jurisdiction. In submissions before the New Zealand Foreign Affairs, Defence and Trade Committee on the Counter-Terrorism Bill, for example, Professor Matthew Palmer argued that there are no good policy grounds

---

[22] Ibid [1].

[23] SC Res 1269, 54 UN SCOR (4053rd mtg), UN Doc S/Res/1269 (1999).

to justify a separate, parallel regime of counter-terrorism law.[24] Having regard to the composite nature of terrorist conduct, there is some merit to that argument.

The need to establish a separate regime must also be questioned having regard to the frequency and material effects of terrorist conduct. The annual publication of the United States Department of State, *Patterns of Global Terrorism*, has tracked the following patterns: 208 acts of international terrorism took place in 2003, up slightly from the 198 attacks in 2002, but down from the 355 attacks in 2001; with a corresponding death toll of 625 persons in 2003, 725 in 2002 and 3636 killed and injured in 2001.[25] In the twenty years up to September 11, the incidents of terrorist conduct fluctuated, without any discernable pattern, from the high 200s to the high 600s.[26] While one can never undervalue the loss of human life, it must be acknowledged that there are many more causes of death resulting in higher death tolls than as a result of terrorist conduct. If that is the case, then why add to the extant law?

The answer seems to lie in a combination of factors, not all of which are unique to terrorism, but which cumulatively appear to have been seen by States as calling for a different treatment of the subject matter. The common thread in each factor, or at least in the way each factor can be perceived, is the political interests of States. At least the following factors are relevant to the move by the international community towards treating terrorism as a unique form of crime deserving special attention.[27] The most apparent is the fear-inducing nature of terrorist conduct and the attention this brings to terrorist events through the media and public alike. This in turn adversely affects the credibility of national executive administrations in the eyes of the domestic public, and also the credibility of the United Nations as an institution established to maintain international peace and security in the eyes of the international community. The more severe the terrorist act, the greater the terror induced, to the extent that the public may in fact be paralysed in a real sense, affecting their freedom of movement and association, and enjoyment of life.[28] That again serves to adversely impact upon national and

---

[24] New Zealand, *Counter-Terrorism Bill. Government Bill. Commentary*, as reported from the Foreign Affairs, Defence and Trade Committee (2003) 2. See also Matthew Palmer, 'Counter-Terrorism Law' (2002) *New Zealand Law Journal* 456.

[25] United States Department of State, *Patterns of Global Terrorism 2001*, May 2002, *Patterns of Global Terrorism 2002*, April 2003, *Patterns of Global Terrorism 2003*, April 2004 (Revised 22 June 2004).

[26] The 2001 Report, in reviewing patterns over a twenty-year period from 1981, also identifies that the least number of terrorist attacks, at 274, was recorded in 1998, with the highest number of incidents in 1987 at 666 attacks: ibid.

[27] These are views posited in an attempt to illustrate *some* of the reasons that terrorism has been treated differently by the international community and constituting policy reasons (whether sound or not) for a separate or parallel counter-terrorism regime.

[28] As explicitly recognized within GA Res 164, 54 UN GAOR (83rd plen mtg), UN Doc A/Res/54/164 (2000). The Resolution is very similar to its three predecessors: GA Res 185, 49 UN GAOR (94th plen mtg), UN Doc A/Res/49/185 (1994); GA Res 186, 50 UN GAOR (99th plen mtg), UN Doc A/Res/50/186 (1995); and GA Res 133, 52 UN GAOR (70th plen mtg), UN Doc A/Res/52/133 (1998). Its contents were similarly reaffirmed within

international 'executive' credibility. As will be seen through the discussion of international documents on terrorism that follows, terrorism is therefore viewed as being a crime of 'international concern' (using the wording of the Rome Statute on the International Criminal Court). Terrorism was, as already indicated, proposed to be included within the jurisdiction of the International Criminal Court, to stand beside genocide, war crimes and crimes against humanity.[29]

A further issue of concern to States is the transnational nature of terrorist offending. Whether through Embassy bombings on foreign soil or direct attacks within the territory of a State (such as the September 11 attacks and the Madrid rail bombing), national interest and national security are affected. Through an international framework on counter-terrorism, those interests can arguably be better protected through the ability to secure the extradition of perpetrators of such attacks[30] and cut off the means by which terrorist organizations operate.[31]

A final and individual self-interest of States is that of combating revolutionary or secessionist terrorism, that is, terrorism occurring solely within a State and aimed at destabilizing or overthrowing the established government of the State, or conduct aimed at 'breaking away' from the State. The established government has, in those circumstances, a very real and pressing desire to eradicate terrorism.[32] The international community, in seeking to maintain the integrity of statehood and the stability of regions, also has a vested interest. Examples include the Basque Fatherland and Liberty movement in Spain,[33] the Kurdistan Workers' Party in Turkey[34] and the Liberation Tigers of Tamil Eelam in Sri Lanka.[35] Recent examples within the South Pacific will be discussed below. It should be noted that the classification of some such entities as terrorist organizations is disputed on the basis that these are freedom-fighting or liberation movements, again illustrating the complex nature of defining terrorism and terrorist entities.

---

subsequent resolutions of the General Assembly: GA Res 160, 56 UN GAOR (88th plen mtg), UN Doc A/Res/56/160 (2002); and GA Res 174, 58 UN GAOR (77th plen mtg), UN Doc A/Res/58/174 (2004).

[29] Above n 11.

[30] This being a common feature of the counter-terrorist conventions: see below.

[31] Whether by obliging States to prevent the use of their territories for training facilities or suppressing access to funds, explosives and the like.

[32] By way of example, India's Prevention of Terrorism Act 2002 describes a terrorist act as one including conduct by a person 'with intent to threaten the unity, integrity, security or sovereignty of India' (section 3(1)(a) of the Act).

[33] See Appendix A 'Background Information on Designated Foreign Terrorist Organizations' in Russel Howard and Reid Sawyer (eds), *Terrorism and Counterterrorism. Understanding the New Security Environment (Revised and Updated)* (2003) 507.

[34] Ibid 514.

[35] Ibid 516.

Terrorism and the South Pacific

As intimated, there are three particularly important matters that point to the relevance of counter-terrorism to the South Pacific, beyond the application of international obligations upon particular States. The first is that the region has, depending upon what definition of terrorism is employed, experienced terrorist, or at least secessionist or revolutionary, acts. Secondly, regard should be had to the vulnerability of the region. Finally, and most importantly in the view of the author, the role of the region should be seen as contributing to a wider, international, framework on counter-terrorism.

Terrorist acts in the South Pacific

Having said that the *Rainbow Warrior* bombing was the only incident of international terrorism within the South Pacific, it should be recognized that this statement is dependent (as just mentioned) upon what definition of terrorism is adopted. Certainly, it is the only *international* terrorist act occurring within the Pacific. On 10 July 1985, French military agents Mafart and Prieur bombed and sank the Greenpeace flag-ship the *Rainbow Warrior* in the Auckland harbour port, resulting in the death of a Greenpeace activist on board the vessel. The bombing took place just days before the *Rainbow Warrior* was to undertake a protest voyage to the French nuclear test site at Moruroa Atoll.[36]

Simpson, however, points to various *internal* acts of terrorism within the Pacific.[37] In New Caledonia in the 1980s, the Kanak Socialist National Liberation Front (FLNKS) was denounced as a separatist terrorist movement.[38] It subsequently formed part of the coalition government in 2001 and is now the main opposition party in New Caledonia.[39] The Fiji coups of 1987 and 2000 have likewise been classified as terrorist events,[40] although they might more properly be categorized as internal civil conflicts.[41] The 'civil conflict' in the Solomon Islands during 2000, in contrast, has been said to include terrorist conduct on the part of both main factions, the Malaita Eagles Force and the Isatabu Freedom Movement.[42]

---

[36] Greenpeace, 'The Bombing of the Warrior', <http://archive.greenpeace.org/comms/rw/pkbomb.html> at 16 September 2004.

[37] Stanley Simpson, 'A Brief History of Terrorism in the South Pacific' (Paper presented at the public workshop *How Should Fiji Respond to the Threat of Terrorism?*, Suva, Fiji, 17 July 2004, copy on file with author).

[38] Ibid.

[39] Electionworld.org, 'Elections in New Caledonia', <http://www.electionworld.org/newcaledonia.htm> at 16 September 2004.

[40] Simpson, above n 37.

[41] See the discussion above concerning the misuse of the term 'terrorism' in the absence of differential targeting and fear-inducing conduct.

[42] Simpson, above n 37.

The risk of terrorism in the South Pacific

There is a common view that the likelihood of terrorist acts being perpetrated within the Pacific is remote, such that counter-terrorism should remain at the low end of priorities for the region. While this risk assessment might well be correct, there are various factors that count in favour of a more proactive approach, from even a purely self-serving perspective. As evident from the foregoing discussion, the South Pacific has been subject to terrorist incidents in the past, however defined. Regard should also be had to the possibility and consequences of a direct attack. Of particular relevance to a number of Pacific Island countries, as nations reliant upon the export of commodities such as dairy, meat and fruit,[43] is the biosecurity of those countries. This is a matter dealt with primarily under the domestic legislation of each State including, for example, the Biosecurity Act 1993 in New Zealand. Bioterrorism might, as will be discussed in the examination of the international counter-terrorism framework, fall within the global definition of terrorism under article 2(1)(c) of the Draft Comprehensive Convention on International Terrorism.[44] New Zealand recently took steps towards including bioterrorism as an offence under its domestic law, effected through the Counter-Terrorism Act 2003.[45]

Despite its geographical isolation, the reality of the contemporary world is that globalization has dissolved distances that might have once protected the Pacific Islands. Transport and communications systems, access to the internet, and more efficient means of moving people and money mean that it is easier for the world to interact with the Pacific.[46] Individuals thought to be connected with al-Qaeda have been reported to have been present in New Zealand, Australia and Fiji.[47] Pacific Forum Secretary General, Greg Urwin, adds that while terrorists may not seek to attack citizens and institutions of Pacific countries, the region might prove to be a tempting target, either for an attack like the one in Bali in October 2002, or as a base or staging point from which terrorist cells might undertake

---

[43] By way of example, Statistics New Zealand identifies exports for the years ended June 2001, 2002 and 2003 to be as follows: milk powder, butter and cheese at $5790 million (2001), $5891 million (2002) and $4679 million (2003); meat and edible offal at $4182 million (2001), $4429 million (2002) and $4112 million (2003); logs, wood and wood article at $2192 million (2001), $2378 million (2002) and $2386 million (2003); fish, crustaceans and molluscs at $1374 million (2001), $1402 million (2002) and $1032 million (2003); and fruit at $1045 million (2001), $1159 million (2002) and $1032 million (2003): see Statistics New Zealand online information 'Quick Facts – Economy', <http://www.stats.govt.nz/domino/external/ web/nzstories.nsf/htmldocs/Quick+Facts+Economy> at 17 September 2004.

[44] On that subject, however, see (as a starting point) Richard Hoffman, 'Preparing for a Bioterrorist Attack: Legal and Administrative Strategies', 9(2) (2003) *Emerging Infectious Diseases* 241.

[45] Section 6 of the Act amended the Crimes Act 1961 to include new sections 298A and 298B, making it an offence to contaminate food, crops, water or other products.

[46] Urwin, above n 6, [8].

[47] Ibid [9]. Anecdotal reports are that one of the September 11 hijackers spent a considerable time living in Fiji up until six months prior to the World Trade Centre attacks.

planning for an attack elsewhere.[48] The New Zealand Security Intelligence Service recently reported, for example, that Islamic extremists with links to international terrorist organizations are likely to be operating in New Zealand:

> From the Service's own investigations we assess that there are individuals in or from New Zealand who support Islamic extremist causes. The Service views these developments, most of which have come to attention within 2003/04, with considerable concern. They indicate attempts to use New Zealand as a safe haven from which activities of security concern elsewhere can be facilitated and/or the involvement of people from New Zealand in such activities.[49]

Supporting an international framework on counter-terrorism

The most important point to make is a relatively simple one, although the consequences of it are wide-ranging. The international conventions and protocols, reinforced by customary law and resolutions of the General Assembly, and added to by Security Council resolutions, create an *international* framework for counter-terrorism. A considerable measure of their effectiveness lies in the universal adoption and implementation of the obligations under that framework in order to prevent *any* State being either targeted by terrorists or used by them as a base of operations (whether that be the establishment of physical training camps or the laundering of money to fund activities of terrorist organizations).

Following the train bombing in Madrid on 11 March 2004, in which nearly 200 people were killed, Spain's Ambassador to the United Nations (who also chairs the Security Council Counter-Terrorism Committee) criticized unnamed nations for a 'lack of effort' in countering terrorism.[50] The point was also later made by the US Ambassador to the United Nations, John Danworth:

> [The Counter-Terrorism Committee] must never forget that so long as a few states are not acting quickly enough to raise their capacity to fight terrorism or are not meeting their international counterterrorism obligations, all of us remain vulnerable.[51]

The question is no longer simply one of domestic or regional security in order to prevent attacks from occurring within a State's own borders and, in doing so, assessing the risks of such attacks and the appropriate measures in response. Although those assessments and corresponding national security interests remain, effective counter-terrorism requires (to achieve international security and in light of the manner in which terrorists and terrorist organizations operate) that all States

---

[48] Ibid [10].

[49] New Zealand Security Intelligence Service, *Report to the House of Representatives for the year ended 30 June 2004*, presented to the House of Representatives pursuant to section 4J of the New Zealand Security Intelligence Service Act 1969, 11.

[50] United Nations Foundation, 'Spanish Diplomat Blames Nations for "Lack of Effort" on Terrorism', <http://www.unwire.org/UNWire> at 12 March 2004.

[51] United Nations Foundation, 'Counterterrorism Cooperation Improving, Security Council Told', <http://www.unwire.org/UNWire> at 20 July 2004.

prevent and preclude terrorist conduct and preparations. A high level of threat posed to a State might cause that State to impose measures *above* those required by the international framework, but the reverse does not apply. Even if it is accepted that the South Pacific does not bear any substantial risk of being the subject of a terrorist attack, its role in combating international terrorism through the implementation of anti-terrorism obligations is equal to that of all other States.

All of these various points are reiterated on the website of the New Zealand Security Intelligence Service, equally applicable to other Pacific Island countries:

> The terrorist threat to New Zealand is low, but it cannot be discounted. The country learned at the time of the Rainbow Warrior bombing that relative geographic isolation, in itself, is no guarantee of immunity. The events in the United States on 11 September 2001 confirmed that terrorism is an international phenomenon and terrorists consider the world their stage when they look for a way to advance their cause.
>
> There are individuals and groups in New Zealand with links to overseas organisations that are committed to acts of terrorism, violence and intimidation. Some have developed local structures that are dedicated to the support of their overseas parent bodies. There are also isolated extremists in New Zealand who advocate using violence to impress on others their own political, ethnic or religious viewpoint.
>
> But the threat of terrorism could come equally from beyond New Zealand. Modern transport and communication have effectively made the world a smaller place. Events such as a visit by an overseas dignitary, or a major international gathering may be seen by off-shore terrorists as providing the opportunity to do something spectacular to capture world wide publicity, or to otherwise further their cause.
>
> There is also the risk that individuals or groups may use New Zealand as a safe haven from which to plan or facilitate terrorist acts elsewhere.[52]

Indeed, New Zealand appears to see its role in supporting counter-terrorism within the South Pacific as an important one.[53] It has assessed that, due to an inadequate capacity by some Pacific Island countries for border control and for the control of passports and travel documents, the potential exists for these inadequacies to be exploited by terrorist groups.[54] In its reports to the Security Council Counter-Terrorism Committee, New Zealand has said that it is helping to manage these risks and to provide additional assistance to Pacific Island countries.[55]

The international framework on counter-terrorism

It has been posited that one of the primary reasons for the South Pacific to fully embrace counter-terrorism is the need for it to support and contribute to the

[52] New Zealand Security Intelligence Service website, *Protecting New Zealand from Terrorism*, <http://www.nzsis.govt.nz/work/work.html> at 16 November 2004.

[53] See New Zealand's first report to the Security Council Counter-Terrorism Committee, *Report to the Counter-Terrorism Committee pursuant to paragraph 6 of Security Council resolution 1373 (2001) of 28 September 2001, New Zealand*, 2 January 2002, S/2001/1269, 5.

[54] Ibid.

[55] Ibid.

international anti-terrorist framework. Two issues arise from that position. What *is* the international framework on counter-terrorism? How have the Pacific Forum members *responded* to that framework?

The phenomenon of terrorism became an international concern in the 1960s, with a series of aircraft hijackings hitting the headlines. When the 1972 Munich Olympic Games were disrupted by the kidnapping of Israeli athletes by a Palestinian group, the then Secretary-General of the UN, Kurt Waldheim, asked that the issue be placed on the General Assembly's agenda. In the heated debate that followed, the Assembly assigned the issue to its Sixth (Legal) Committee, which subsequently proposed several conventions on terrorism. There are now twelve conventions and protocols on terrorism, all of which have entered into force.[56] In addition to those instruments, a draft Comprehensive Convention on the Elimination of International Terrorism has been under consideration, since 2000.[57] Both the General Assembly and Security Council have also been active in adopting resolutions on the subject.

The international anti-terrorism treaties

Of the twelve international conventions on terrorism, one starts (in chronological order) with the Convention on Offences and Certain Other Acts Committed on Board Aircraft (the Tokyo Convention).[58] The Convention applies to acts affecting in-flight safety. It authorizes the aircraft commander to impose reasonable measures, including restraint, on any person he or she believes has committed or is about to commit an act affecting in-flight safety, when necessary to protect the safety of the aircraft. It also requires contracting States to take custody of offenders and to return control of the aircraft to the lawful commander. The second and third

[56] A situation that had not existed at the time of the September 11 terrorist attacks, as discussed below in the context of SC Res 1373, 56 UN SCOR (4385th mtg), UN Doc S/Res/1373 (2001).

[57] Almost one year prior to the September 11 attacks, India had proposed that there be a comprehensive convention against terrorism: the draft Comprehensive Convention on the Elimination of International Terrorism, as contained in the *Report of the Ad Hoc Committee Established under resolution 51/210*, 57 UN GAOR (57th mtg), UN Doc A/57/37 (2002). The draft convention was referred to the Ad Hoc Committee Established by General Assembly Resolution 51/210 (which had been established by the General Assembly in 1996 to work on conventions for the suppression of terrorist bombings and financing of terrorist operations and, thereafter, to address means of developing a comprehensive legal framework dealing with international terrorism): GA Res 210, 51 UN GAOR (88th plen mtg), UN Doc A/Res/51/210 (1996), [9]. As yet, the draft has not been finalized and is likely to be some time away, if it is ever to become a reality. Due to the lack of unanimity on various issues, and the range of issues involved, the Committee has concluded that finalizing a comprehensive international treaty on terrorism will depend primarily on agreement as to whom would be entitled to exclusion from the treaty's scope, and on what grounds. Otherwise, the majority of the 27 articles of the Draft Convention have been preliminarily agreed upon by the Committee.

[58] Opened for signature 14 September 1963, 704 UNTS 219 (entered into force 4 December 1969).

conventions are also concerned with air safety. The Convention for the Suppression of Unlawful Seizure of Aircraft (the Hague Convention),[59] makes it an offence for any person on board an aircraft in flight to 'unlawfully, by force or threat thereof, or any other form of intimidation, seize or exercise control of that aircraft' or to attempt to do so. It requires parties to the Convention to make hijackings punishable by severe penalties. It requires parties that have custody of offenders to either extradite the offender or submit the case for prosecution and also requires parties to assist each other in connection with criminal proceedings brought under the Convention. The Convention for the Suppression of Unlawful Acts Against the Safety of Civil Aviation (the Montreal Convention)[60] makes it an offence for any person unlawfully and intentionally to perform an act of violence against a person on board an aircraft in flight, if that act is likely to endanger the safety of that aircraft; to place an explosive device on an aircraft; and to attempt such acts or be an accomplice of a person who performs or attempts to perform such acts. As for the Hague Convention, it requires parties to make offences punishable by severe penalties and again requires parties that have custody of offenders to either extradite the offender or submit the case for prosecution.

In 1973, the Convention on the Prevention and Punishment of Crimes against International Protected Persons, including Diplomatic Agents (the Protected Persons Convention) was adopted.[61] Internationally protected persons are defined as a Head of State, a Minister for Foreign Affairs, a representative or official of a State or of an international organization who is entitled to special protection from attack under international law (these people being popular terrorist targets). The Convention requires each State party to criminalize and make punishable by appropriate penalties which take into account their grave nature, the intentional murder, kidnapping, or other attack upon the person or liberty of an internationally protected person, a violent attack upon the official premises, the private accommodations, or the means of transport of such person; a threat or attempt to commit such an attack; and an act constituting participation as an accomplice. Also within the theme of protecting persons, the International Convention against the Taking of Hostages (the Hostages Convention)[62] states that 'any person who seizes or detains and threatens to kill, to injure, or to continue to detain another person in order to compel a … State, an international intergovernmental organization, a natural or juridical person, or a group of persons, to do or abstain from doing any act as an explicit or implicit condition for the release of the hostage' commits the offence of taking of hostages within the meaning of this Convention.

[59] Opened for signature 16 December 1970, 860 UNTS 105 (entered into force 14 October 1971).

[60] Opened for signature 23 September 1971, 974 UNTS 177 (entered into force 26 January 1073).

[61] Opened for signature 14 December 1973, 1035 UNTS 167 (entered into force 20 February 1977).

[62] Opened for signature 18 December 1979, 1316 UNTS 205 (entered into force 3 June 1983).

Next in time is the Convention on the Physical Protection of Nuclear Material (the Nuclear Materials Convention).[63] This criminalizes the unlawful possession, use or transfer of nuclear material, the theft of nuclear material, and threats to use nuclear material (to cause death or serious injury to any person or substantial property damage).

The Protocol on the Suppression of Unlawful Acts of Violence at Airports Serving International Civil Aviation 1988 (the Montreal Protocol) was a further addition to air-safety-related counter-terrorist conventions.[64] The Protocol extends the provisions of the Montreal Convention of 1971 to encompass terrorist acts at airports servicing international civil aviation.

The Convention for the Suppression of Unlawful Acts Against the Safety of Maritime Navigation (the Rome Convention) was adopted in 1988.[65] Here, the treaty establishes a legal regime applicable to international maritime navigation that is similar to the regimes established concerning international aviation. More specifically, it makes it an offence for a person unlawfully and intentionally to seize or exercise control over a ship by force, threat, or intimidation; to perform an act of violence against a person on board a ship if that act is likely to endanger the safe navigation of the ship; to place a destructive device or substance aboard a ship; and other acts against the safety of ships. An optional protocol to this Convention, the Protocol for the Suppression of Unlawful Acts Against the Safety of Fixed Platforms Located on the Continental Shelf (the Rome Protocol) was also adopted in 1988,[66] at the same time as its parent Convention. Again by way of extension, the Protocol establishes a legal regime applicable to fixed platforms on the continental shelf (similar to the regimes established with regard to international aviation).

Last in the list of conventions relating to air safety, and within the jurisdiction of the Secretary-General of the International Civil Aviation Organization, is the Convention on the Marking of Plastic Explosives for the Purpose of Identification (the Plastic Explosives Convention).[67] This is designed to control and limit the used of unmarked and undetectable plastic explosives (negotiated in the aftermath of the 1988 Pan Am 103 bombing). Parties are obligated in their respective territories to ensure effective control over 'unmarked' plastic explosive, that is, those that do not contain one of the detection agents described in the Technical Annex to the treaty. Each party must, among other things: take necessary and effective measures to prohibit and prevent the manufacture of unmarked plastic explosives; prevent the movement of unmarked plastic explosives into or out of its territory; ensure that all stocks of such unmarked explosives not held by the military or police are destroyed or consumed,

---

[63] Opened for signature 3 March 1980, 1456 UNTS 124 (entered into force 8 February 1987).

[64] Opened for signature 24 February 1988, ICAO Doc 9518 (entered into force 6 August 1989).

[65] Opened for signature 10 March 1988, 1678 UNTS 221 (entered into force 1 March 1992).

[66] Opened for signature 10 March 1988, 1678 UNTS 304 (entered into force 1 March 1992).

[67] Opened for signature 1 March 1991, ICAO Doc 9571 (entered into force 21 June 1998).

marked, or rendered permanently ineffective within three years; take necessary measures to ensure that unmarked plastic explosives held by the military or police are destroyed or consumed, marked, or rendered permanently ineffective within fifteen years; and ensure the destruction, as soon as possible, of any unmarked explosives manufactured after the date of entry into force of the Convention for that State.

More recent in time is the International Convention for the Suppression of Terrorist Bombing (the Suppression of Bombing Convention).[68] As the name suggests, this creates a regime of universal jurisdiction over the unlawful and intentional use of explosives and other lethal devices in, into, or against various public places with intent to kill or cause serious bodily injury, or with intent to cause extensive destruction in a public place. Finally, there is the International Convention for the Suppression of the Financing of Terrorism (the Suppression of Financing Convention).[69] Of the 12 conventions, this is the most controversial. It requires parties to take steps to prevent and counteract the financing of terrorists, whether direct or indirect, through groups claiming to have charitable, social or cultural goals or which also engage in such illicit activities as drug trafficking or gun running. It commits States to hold those who finance terrorism criminally, civilly or administratively liable for such acts and provides for the identification, freezing and seizure of funds allocated for terrorist activities, as well as for the sharing of the forfeited funds with other States on a case-by-case basis. Bank secrecy will no longer be justification for refusing to cooperate under the treaty.

In summary, then, the twelve anti-terrorism conventions are directed at the protection of potential terrorist targets or at the means through which terrorist organizations operate and do three main things: they criminalize certain conduct, they provide for the prosecution or extradition of perpetrators of such criminal acts, and they impose obligations upon States to suppress the conduct in question. Three potential target groups exist within the twelve conventions: civil aviation (the Tokyo, Hague and Montreal Conventions and the Montreal Protocol); persons (the Protected Persons Convention and the Hostages Convention); and operations at sea (the Rome Convention and Rome Protocol). Four means through which terrorist acts might be executed or facilitated are the subject matter of the remaining four conventions: the Plastic Explosives and Nuclear Materials Conventions and the Suppression of Bombing and Suppression of Financing Conventions.

Utility of the international conventions

The number and scope of these conventions might, at first instance, seem impressive and comprehensive. They have, however, various limitations. To begin with, they only apply to States parties to the conventions. Even then, the conventions themselves are of limited application because of the very precise subject matter of each treaty. The conventions are not of general application but,

---

[68] Opened for signature 12 January 1998, 2149 UNTS 286 (entered into force 23 May 2001).
[69] Opened for signature 10 January 2000, 2179 UNTS 232 (entered into force 10 April 1992).

rather, relate to specific situations in which terrorist acts might have effect, whether on board aircraft, in airports or on maritime platforms.

The only treaty with the potential to impact a wider audience and scope of activity is the International Convention for the Suppression of the Financing of Terrorism. Firstly, the convention mirrors a good number of the suppression of financing obligations contained in Resolution 1373. As a resolution binding upon all members of the United Nations,[70] this has had a significant impact upon the status of the convention. Prior to September 11, 2001, there were just four States parties to the convention and, accordingly, the convention was not in force. Since then, and largely in response to UN Security Council Resolution 1373 and the work of the Counter-Terrorism Committee, almost 120 States have becomes parties to the convention, which has now come into force.[71]

The other reason the Suppression of Financing Convention is of greater relevance is the fact that, in prohibiting the financing of terrorist entities or operations, it defines (for those purposes) what type of acts one may not finance:

> Any other act intended to cause death or serious bodily injury to a civilian, or to any other person not taking an active part in the hostilities in a situation of armed conflict, when the purpose of such act, by its nature or context, is to intimidate a population, or to compel a government or an international organization to do or to abstain from doing any act.

The Convention does therefore have some potentially wider application and is useful for States in determining the type of conduct they are to prohibit.

United Nations action

Beyond the work of the Sixth (Legal) Committee of the General Assembly in working towards the various counter-terrorism conventions discussed, both the General Assembly and Security Council have been working in concert on the issue of counter-terrorism.

In December 1994, the UN General Assembly adopted the Declaration on Measures to Eliminate International Terrorism.[72] The Declaration was based on the notion of peace and security and the principle of refraining from the threat or use of force in international relations.[73] It pronounced that terrorism constitutes a grave

---

[70] By application of article 25 of the Charter of the United Nations.

[71] The convention came into force on 10 April 2002, above n 69. There are now 132 signatories and 117 parties: see <http://untreaty.un.org/ENGLISH/Status/Chapter_xviii/treaty11.asp> at 12 December 2004.

[72] Above n 19. The Declaration has been restated and adopted in subsequent resolutions of the General Assembly, with the contents being much the same: see UNGA Resolutions A/RES/50/53 of 11 December 1995; A/RES/51/210 of 17 December 1996; A/RES/52/165 of 19 January 1998; A/RES/54/110 of 2 February 2000; A/RES/55/158 of 30 January 2001; A/RES/56/88 of 24 January 2002; A/RES/57/27 OF 15 January 2003; and A/RES/58/81 of 8 January 2004.

[73] Ibid, as is evident through its Preamble.

violation of the purpose and principles of the United Nations.[74] While it did not purport to define 'terrorism', it did say that criminal acts intended or calculated to provoke a state of terror in the general public for political purposes are in any circumstances unjustifiable.[75] The Declaration urged all States to consider, as a matter of priority, becoming party to the conventions on terrorism adopted up to that time.[76] It called on States to refrain from organizing, instigating, assisting or participating in terrorist acts, and from acquiescing in or encouraging activities within their territories directed towards the commission of such acts.[77]

In particular, States were directed that, in order to fulfil this obligation, they must refrain from facilitating terrorist activities. Paragraph 5(a) of the 1994 Declaration appears to indicate that a State must be proactive in doing so, obliging States to take appropriate practical measures to ensure that their territory is not used for terrorist installations or training camps, or for the preparation or organization of terrorist acts. Paragraph 5(b) then refers to the obligation to apprehend and prosecute or extradite perpetrators of terrorist acts.

The practical observation to make is that, although compelling and strongly worded, this is a declaration of the General Assembly and therefore does not have the same weight as a convention, nor does it have signatories that are bound by its content. Indeed, article 10 of the UN Charter specifically provides that resolutions and declarations of the United Nations General Assembly are recommendatory only.

More significant, however, are the resolutions of the Security Council, which do place binding obligations upon member States of the United Nations.[78] On the day after the September 11 attacks, the United Nations Security Council (UNSC) adopted Resolution 1368, through which it unequivocally condemned the terrorist attacks and expressed that it regarded them as a threat to international peace and security.[79] It called on all States to urgently work together to bring to justice the perpetrators, organizers and sponsors of the terrorist attacks.[80] Security Council Resolution 1373 was later adopted, through which the UNSC determined that all States were to prevent and suppress the financing of terrorist acts, including the criminalization of such financing and the freezing of funds and financial assets.[81] Described as one of the most strongly worded resolutions in the history of the Security Council,[82] it also

---

[74] Ibid [2].

[75] Ibid [1].

[76] Ibid [6].

[77] Ibid [4].

[78] If made under Chapter VII of the Charter of the United Nations and couched in mandatory language (see later discussion on this point: Charter of the United Nations, art 25.

[79] SC Res 1368, 56 UN SCOR (4370th mtg), UN Doc S/Res/1368 (2001).

[80] Ibid [3].

[81] SC Res 1373, 56 UN SCOR (4385th mtg), UN Doc S/Res/1373 (2001).

[82] Richard Rowe, 'Key Developments: Year of International Law in Review' (Paper presented at the 10th Annual Meeting of the Australian and New Zealand Society of International Law, *New Challenges and New States: What Role for International Law?*, Australian National University, Canberra, Australia, 15 June 2002). Richard Rowe at that time worked in the International Organisations and Legal Division of the Australian Department of Foreign Affairs and Trade. He was the Australian representative and Vice-

requires countries to cooperate on extradition matters and the sharing of information about terrorist networks.[83]

As a decision made under Chapter VII of the United Nations Charter, compliance with Resolution 1373 is mandatory for UN members, imposing certain obligations upon those members.[84] Those obligations can be viewed in two parts. The first is the imposition of specific counter-terrorist obligations, as follows:

> *Acting* under Chapter VII of the Charter of the United Nations,
>
> 1. *Decides* that all States shall:
> (a) Prevent and suppress the financing of terrorist acts;
> (b) Criminalize the wilful provision or collection, by any means, directly or indirectly, of funds by their nationals or in their territories with the intention that the funds should be used, or in the knowledge that they are to be used, in order to carry out terrorist acts;
> (c) Freeze without delay funds and other financial assets or economic resources of persons who commit, or attempt to commit, terrorist acts or participate in or facilitate the commission of terrorist acts; of entities owned or controlled directly or indirectly by such persons; and of persons and entities acting on behalf of, or at the direction of such persons and entities, including funds derived or generated from property owned or controlled directly or indirectly by such persons and associated persons and entities;
> (d) Prohibit their nationals or any persons and entities within their territories from making any funds, financial assets or economic resources or financial or other related services available, directly or indirectly, for the benefit of persons who commit or attempt to commit or facilitate or participate in the commission of terrorist acts, of entities owned or controlled, directly or indirectly, by such persons and of persons and entities acting on behalf of or at the direction of such persons;
>
> 2. *Decides also* that all States shall:
> (a) Refrain from providing any form of support, active or passive, to entities or persons involved in terrorist acts, including by suppressing recruitment of members of terrorist groups and eliminating the supply of weapons to terrorists;
> (b) Take the necessary steps to prevent the commission of terrorist acts, including by provision of early warning to other States by exchange of information;
> (c) Deny safe haven to those who finance, plan, support, or commit terrorist acts, or provide safe havens;
> (d) Prevent those who finance, plan, facilitate or commit terrorist acts from using their respective territories for those purposes against other States or their citizens;
> (e) Ensure that any person who participates in the financing, planning, preparation or perpetration of terrorist acts or in supporting terrorist acts is brought to justice and ensure that, in addition to any other measures against them, such terrorist acts are established as serious criminal offences in domestic laws and

---

Chairman of the Ad Hoc Committee Established by General Assembly Resolution 51/210 during its Sixth Session, which followed the September 11 attacks.

[83] Above n 81, [3].

[84] Article 25 of the Charter of the United Nations.

regulations and that the punishment duly reflects the seriousness of such terrorist acts;

(f) Afford one another the greatest measure of assistance in connection with criminal investigations or criminal proceedings relating to the financing or support of terrorist acts, including assistance in obtaining evidence in their possession necessary for the proceedings;

(g) Prevent the movement of terrorists or terrorist groups by effective border controls and controls on issuance of identity papers and travel documents, and through measures for preventing counterfeiting, forgery or fraudulent use of identity papers and travel documents;

[...].

This set of obligations expands upon and significantly strengthens the Council's earlier Resolution 1269 of 1999.[85] While Resolution 1269 considered steps to be taken by States to suppress terrorism, deny safe haven to terrorists and cooperate with others in the bringing to justice perpetrators of terrorist conduct, the language of this earlier Resolution is weaker for two principal reasons. First, paragraphs 1 and 2 of Resolution 1373 are considerably more specific in the steps to be taken in countering terrorism. Second, the instructive words of the more recent Resolution provides that 'all States *shall*', whereas the earlier Resolution used a less forceful provision *calling upon* States to take *appropriate steps* to achieve the stated objectives. In short, then, Resolution 1373 takes a considerable step forward in the imposition of counter-terrorism obligations upon members of the United Nations.

The second obligation is a more general requirement to enter into what might be described as a reporting and monitoring dialogue between States and a special committee of the Security Council established under the Resolution, the Counter-Terrorism Committee. Paragraph 6 of the Resolution provides as follows:

6. *Decides* to establish, in accordance with rule 28 of its provisional rules of procedure, a Committee of the Security Council, consisting of all the members of the Council, to monitor implementation of this resolution, with the assistance of appropriate expertise, and *calls upon* all States to report to the Committee, no later than 90 days from the date of adoption of this resolution and thereafter according to a timetable to be proposed by the Committee, on the steps they have taken to implement this resolution;

Since Resolutions 1368 and 1373, there have been further resolutions of the Security Council dealing with the issue of international terrorism.[86] Recognizing

---

[85] Above n 23.

[86] Interestingly, though, the only resolution of the United Nations Security Council prior to September 11 and dealing with terrorism in the international context, rather than relating to and restricted to specific events, is SC Res 1189, 53 UN SCOR (3915th mtg), UN Doc S/Res/1189 (1998). Although the resolution was adopted in response to the 1998 bombings in Nairobi, Kenya and Tanzania, it called upon all States 'to adopt, in accordance with international law and as a matter of priority, effective and practical measures for security cooperation, for the prevention of such acts of terrorism, and for the prosecution and punishment of their perpetrators', [5].

the considerable burden upon States in the domestic implementation process following their party status to the twelve international conventions and in complying with Resolution 1373, the Council tasked the Counter-Terrorism Committee with exploring ways in which States could be assisted.[87] Resolutions 1452 and 1455 concerned themselves specifically with the Taliban and al-Qaida.[88]

Response of the South Pacific to the international framework on counter-terrorism

The response of States within the South Pacific to the international framework just described can be characterized, in the main, as being positive. However, the response of some Pacific Island countries (together with their party status to the UN Charter and the anti-terrorism treaties) creates disparate sets of obligations and legal frameworks within the region. The influence of Asia-Pacific Economic Cooperation Organization and the Organisation for Economic Cooperation and Development (OECD) should also be noted.

Party status to the UN Charter and anti-terrorism treaties

Of the sixteen members of the Pacific Forum, the Cook Islands and Niue are not members of the United Nations and, consequently, are not bound by the provisions of United Nations Security Council Resolution 1373.[89] The binding and substantive obligations contained within paragraphs 1 and 2 of the Resolution (set out earlier) do not therefore apply to those countries, although they have both reported to the Security Council Counter-Terrorism Committee under the procedures established through paragraph 6 of the Resolution.[90]

In terms of the anti-terrorism conventions identified, only Australia, New Zealand and the Marshall Islands are party to all twelve anti-terrorism conventions, and Palau to all but one.[91] At the other end of the scale, Kiribati, Niue and Tuvalu are not party to any of the treaties and the Cook Islands is only party to the

---

[87] SC Res 1377, 56 UN SCOR (4413th mtg), UN Doc S/Res/1377 (2001).

[88] SC Res 1452, 57 UN SCOR (4678th mtg), UN Doc S/Res/1452 (2002), and SC Res 1455, 58 UN SCOR (4686th mtg), UN Doc S/Res/1455 (2003).

[89] Since article 25 of the Charter of the United Nations restricts the need to comply with decisions of the Security Council to members of the organization.

[90] Cook Islands Government, *Report to the United Nations Security Council Counter-Terrorism Committee on counterterrorism activities in the Cook Islands*, 27 December 2001, S/2001/1324 (first report), *Supplementary Report to the United Nations Security Council Counter-Terrorism Committee on counterterrorism activities in the Cook Islands*, 31 May 2002, S/2002/1445 (second report), and *Addendum to Supplementary Report to the United Nations Security Council Counter-Terrorism Committee on counterterrorism activities in the Cook Islands*, 16 September 2003, S/2003/1445/ADD.1 (third report). Niue Government, *Report to the Counter-Terrorism Committee of the United Nations Security Council on resolution 1373 (2001)*, 24 December 2001, S/2001/7 (sole report).

[91] Palau is not a party to the Nuclear Materials Convention.

Suppression of Financing Convention. Fiji, the Solomon Islands and Tuvalu are party to a selection of the treaties relating to civil aviation, most likely reflecting the importance of international tourism to those countries.[92] The final four (Micronesia, Nauru, Papua New Guinea and Samoa) have had a mixed response to the twelve conventions, but are all party to the Suppression of Financing Convention.[93]

Against that background, it is difficult to base international obligations as *the* reason to treat counter-terrorism as relevant to the South Pacific. Indeed, even if all South Pacific States were party to all treaties, there can always be a disparity between party status and the effective implementation of treaty obligations, irrespective of the subject matter. What can be said is that suppression of financing obligations apply to all countries but Niue, since the obligations contained within Resolution 1373 are binding upon all countries but the Cook Islands and Niue, and since the Cook Islands is a party to the Suppression of Financing Convention.

It is also relevant to note that at the thirty-third Pacific Islands Forum in Fiji, Forum Leaders adopted the Nasonini Declaration on Regional Security.[94] The Declaration underlined the commitment of Forum Leaders to the implementation of internationally agreed anti-terrorism measures, with express reference to Resolution 1373, and tasked the Forum Regional Security Committee to review the regional implementation of the Resolution.[95]

Asia-Pacific Economic Cooperation Organization

APEC, made up of 21 'Member Economies',[96] includes three members of the Pacific Forum (Australia, New Zealand and Papua New Guinea) and is predominantly concerned with trade and economic issues. In the wake of the September 11 attacks in 2001 APEC leaders adopted the *Shanghai Counter-*

---

[92] Fiji is party to all four aviation-related conventions (being the Tokyo, Hague and Montreal Conventions and the Montreal Protocol). The Solomon Islands is party to the Tokyo and Montreal Conventions only. Vanuatu is party to all but the Montreal Protocol.

[93] Micronesia is a party to four of the twelve conventions, excluding the Tokyo and Hague Conventions on civil aviation, the two conventions on the protection of persons (the Protected Persons and Hostages Conventions), the Rome Protocol on the safety of maritime platforms, and the Plastics and Nuclear Materials Conventions. Nauru is party to the three civil aviation conventions (but not to the Montreal Protocol), and party to the Suppression of Financing Convention. Papua New Guinea is party to eight conventions, excluding the two maritime conventions and the Plastics and Nuclear Materials Conventions. Samoa is not party to the two protection of persons conventions, nor to the Rome Protocol on maritime platforms, nor the Suppression of Bombings and Nuclear Materials Conventions.

[94] *Forum Communiqué*, Thirty-Third Pacific Islands Forum, Suva, Fiji Islands, 15–17 August 2002, Annex 1, 'Nasonini Declaration on Regional Security'.

[95] Ibid [5] and [9].

[96] Being Australia; Brunei Darussalam; Canada; Chile; People's Republic of China; Hong Kong, China; Indonesia; Japan; Republic of Korea; Malaysia; Mexico; New Zealand; Papua New Guinea; Peru; The Republic of the Philippines; The Russian Federation; Singapore; Chinese Taipei; Thailand; United States of America; Viet Nam.

Terrorism Statement on 21 October 2001.[97] As well as condemning the September 11 attacks, the Leaders characterized terrorism as a direct challenge to APEC's vision of free, open and prosperous economies.[98] Pledging to implement Security Council Resolution 1373, the Statement expressed a commitment to prevent and suppress all forms of terrorism, called for increased cooperation and for the early signing of the anti-terrorism conventions, and identified various practical measures through which Member Economies could cooperate to enhance counter-terrorism.[99] The Shanghai Statement, and the principles within it, were reaffirmed in the APEC Leaders' statements of 2002, 2003, and 2004.[100]

The 2002 Statement on Fighting Terrorism was particularly detailed in setting out ways through which secure trade could be achieved, with focus upon protecting cargo, ships, international aviation, people in transit, and upon cyber security and halting terrorist financing. It established a Counter-Terrorism Task Force, with the mandate to implement and assist with achieving the measures identified (labelled 'STAR', Secure Trade in the APEC Region). By requiring Member Economies to each submit a Counter-Terrorism Action Plan,[101] working with various international organizations,[102] and expanding APEC's extant 'Finance Ministers' Process' to include a focus on the suppression of terrorist financing, the Task Force reports that Member Economies have significantly strengthened counter-terrorist measures.[103]

Of the three countries that are members of both the Pacific Forum and APEC, both Australia and New Zealand have since become party to all conventions,[104]

---

[97] Asia-Pacific Economic Cooperation, 'APEC Leaders' Statement on Counter-Terrorism', Shanghai, People's Republic of China, 21 October 2001, available online at <http://www.apec.org/apec/leaders_declarations/2001/statement_on_counter-terrorism.html>.

[98] Ibid [1 and 2].

[99] Ibid [6].

[100] Asia-Pacific Economic Cooperation, 'APEC Leaders' Statement on Fighting Terrorism and Promoting Growth', Los Cabos, Mexico, 20 October 2002. Asia-Pacific Economic Cooperation, 'APEC Leaders' 2003 Declaration "Bangkok Declaration on Partnership for the Future"', *2. Enhancing Human Security*, Bangkok, Thailand, 21 October 2003. Asia-Pacific Economic Cooperation, 'APEC Leaders' 2004 Santiago Declaration "One Community, Our Future"', *Enhancing Human Security – Underpinning Economic Growth*, Santiago de Chile, 21 November 2004.

[101] All Member Economies have done so, New Zealand being the most recent to submit a (revised) Action Plan in October 2004. The Action Plans are available on APEC's website at URL <http://www.apec.org/apec/apec_groups/som_special_task_groups/counter_terrorism/counter_terrorism_action_plans.html>.

[102] Including the International Monetary Fund, World Bank, Asia Development Bank, United Nations Counter-Terrorism Committee, Inter-American Committee Against Terrorism and the Association of Southeast Asian Nations (ASEAN).

[103] APEC Counter Terrorism Task Force, 'Counter Terrorism', <http://www.apec.org/apec/apec_groups/som_special_task_groups/counter_terrorism.html> at 7 December 2004.

[104] At 11 September 2001, Australia was party to nine of the twelve conventions (excluding the Plastic Explosives Convention and the Suppression of Bombing and Suppression of Financing Conventions) and New Zealand was party to eight conventions (being those that Australia was not party to, as well as the Nuclear Materials Convention).

while Papua New Guinea has yet to become party to the two maritime conventions and the Plastic Explosives and Nuclear Materials Conventions.

Work of the OECD Financial Action Task Force

The Financial Action Task Force (FATF), a specialist group of the OECD, has been particularly active on the question of money laundering and the suppression of the financing of terrorism. Although only Australia and New Zealand, of the sixteen Pacific Forum members, are members of the OECD, the organization has active relationships with numerous other countries through its Centre for Co-Operation with Non-Members. More importantly, the Nasonini Declaration on Regional Security, as well as committing to implementation of Resolution 1373, saw Pacific Forum Leaders commit to implementation of the FATF Special Recommendations.[105]

Alongside its Forty Recommendations on Combating Money Laundering, the FATF added Eight Special Recommendations on Terrorist Financing.[106] These recommended ratification of the Suppression of Financing Convention and implementation of Resolution 1373, including the criminalizing of financing of terrorist entities, the freezing and confiscating of terrorist assets and the reporting of suspicious transactions related to terrorism.[107] The Special Recommendations also call for international cooperation and for measures to be taken to ensure that alternative remittance, wire transfers and non-profit organizations cannot be used or manipulated by terrorist entities.[108] The Task Force provided guidance on implementing the Special Recommendations,[109] along with a self-assessment questionnaire[110] for States to complete and submit to the agency, as well as guidance for financial institutions.[111]

The international response to this exercise has, according to the FATF, been generally positive, with over 100 non-FATF members undertaking the self-assessment and cooperating with the agency. Regrettably, however, the FATF has identified the Cook Islands, the Marshall Islands and Niue as non-cooperative

---

105 Above n 108, [5 and 9].

106 The latter recommendations were adopted 31 October 2001.

107 Recommendations I to IV inclusive. In the case of New Zealand, these matters are addressed within the Terrorism Suppression Act 2002: sections 8, 9 and 10 prohibiting the financing of terrorism, dealing with terrorist property, and making property or financial or related services available; sections 43 to 47 establish procedures and rules for the reporting of suspicious transactions, lying alongside similar anti-money laundering provisions in the Financial Transactions Reporting Act 1996; and sections 55 to 61 provide mechanisms for the forfeiture of terrorist assets.

108 Recommendations V to VIII.

109 Financial Action Task Force, *Annual Report 2002–2003*, 7-8. See also Financial Action Task Force, *Combating the Abuse of Non-Profit Organisations*, 11 October 2002.

110 Financial Action Task Force, *Self-Assessment Questionnaire: FATF Special Recommendations on Terrorist Financing*, 31 January 2002.

111 Financial Action Task Force, *Guidance for Financial Institutions in Detecting Terrorist Financing*, 24 April 2002.

countries in its work on money laundering, seen as inherent in the fight against the financing of terrorism (although it has also identified that progress has been made by those States).[112] Countermeasures by OECD members were recommended against Nauru, the FATF considering that inadequate progress had been made by that State.[113]

Reporting to the Counter-Terrorism Committee

As noted, all members of the Pacific Islands Forum, including non-members of the United Nations, have reported to the Security Council Committee under Resolution 1373. By way of example, New Zealand has identified in its reports to the Committee the following features of its domestic legislative framework as measures by which it has implemented the two binding paragraphs, paragraphs 1 and 2, of Resolution 1373:

- *Para 1(a): prevent and suppress the financing of terrorist acts.* Paragraph 1(a), which requires the prevention and suppression of the financing of terrorist acts, is a general provision, expanded upon by the subparagraphs that follow it. In addition to those more specific requirements, New Zealand identified the fact that the Reserve Bank of New Zealand took steps to notify financial institutions of these requirements and prohibitions.[114] Also, funding for security and counter-terrorism has been boosted, with the Minister for Foreign Affairs and Trade identifying the post-September 11 environment as requiring this.[115]
- *Para 1(b): criminalize the provision of funds for terrorist acts.* In compliance with this provision of Resolution 1373, the Terrorism Suppression Act 2002 (the Act) creates offence of the financing of terrorism.[116]
- *Para 1(c): freeze funds and assets of terrorist entities.* The freezing of assets is said to be given effect through various provisions of the Act.[117] New Zealand has described the establishment of various stages in achieving this

[112] OECD, 'Financial Action Task Force on Money Laundering, 2000–2001 Report Released', <http://www.oecd.org/document/57/0,2340,en_2649_201185_1900665_1_1_1_1,00.html> at 9 December 2004 (concerning the Cook Islands). See also Financial Action Task Force, *Annual Review of Non-Cooperative Countries or Territories* (2003) 1 (concerning the Marshall Islands and Niue).
[113] Ibid. See also Financial Action Task Force, *Annual Review of Non-Cooperative Countries or Territories* (2003) 11-12.
[114] See New Zealand's first report to the Counter-Terrorism Committee, above n 145, 6.
[115] The New Zealand Budget for 2003 provided an additional $5.9 million for 2004 and $1.9 million in future years: Hon Phil Goff, 'Funding boost for security, counter-terrorism and emergency responses', Beehive Press Release 12 May 2003, <http://www.behive.govt.nz/PrintDocumentcfm?DocumentID=16723> at 17 Mat 2003.
[116] Section 8 of the Terrorism Suppression Act 2002. See New Zealand's first report to the Counter-Terrorism Committee, ibid 6-7, which also refers to the defining provisions of the Act (sections 4 and 5) and the extraterritorial jurisdiction attached to the offences (sections 14, 15, 17 and 18).
[117] See New Zealand's first report to the Counter-Terrorism Committee, above n 145, 7-9.

obligation.[118] The first stage is to identify the assets to be frozen, through sections 20 to 42 of the Act, which provide a process by which individuals or groups may be designated as terrorist or associated entities. Next, obligations are imposed upon financial institutions to report suspicions of the holding or control of property belonging to or controlled by such entities (sections 43 to 47). Third, section 9 of the Act prohibits dealing with property belonging to terrorist entities. Finally, sections 55 to 61 establish procedures through which terrorist assets can be forfeited.

- *Para 1(d): prohibit the provision of financial or related services to terrorist entities.* Responding to paragraph 1(d) of the Resolution, section 10 makes it unlawful to make property, or financial or related services available to terrorist or associated entities (subject to the express permission of the Prime Minister under section 11).
- *Para 2(a): suppress support to terrorists and eliminate supply of weapons.* In compliance with paragraph 2(a), the Terrorism Suppression Act prohibits the recruitment of persons into terrorist groups, under section 12, and participation in terrorist groups (section 13). New Zealand reported that existing law would see New Zealand comply with the requirement to work towards the elimination of the supply of weapons to terrorists, pointing to the Customs Prohibition Order 1996,[119] the Arms Act 1983,[120] the Crimes Act 1961 (prohibiting the unlawful possession of an offensive weapon),[121] the New Zealand Nuclear Weapons Free Zone, Disarmament and Arms Control Act 1987,[122] and the Chemical Weapons (Prohibition) Act 1966,[123] together with its intended ratification of the Firearms Protocol to the United Nations Convention against Transnational Organized Crime.[124] New Zealand also reported that it would become party to the Plastic Explosives and Nuclear Materials conventions, which would see it create offences under the Terrorism Suppression Act, as required by the treaties and create corresponding offences.[125] This was ultimately done through sections 13B, 13C and 13D of the latter Act.
- *Para 2(b): prevent the commission of terrorist acts.* Additional to the above matters, New Zealand identified measures through which the New Zealand police and intelligence community can investigate groups or organizations of interest.[126] Under the Counter-Terrorism Act, this has seen the creation of authority to obtain interception warrants, warrants to attach tracking devices to

---

[118] As explained within New Zealand's report to the United Nations 1267 Committee, *Response of New Zealand to the Security Council Committee under Security Council resolution 1455 (2003)*, 17 April 2003, 4-7.

[119] Made under the Customs and Excise Act 1996.

[120] See New Zealand's second report to the Counter-Terrorism Committee, *Supplementary report providing additional information on the measures taken by New Zealand to implement the provisions of Security Council resolution 1373 (2001)*, S/2002/795, 19 July 2002, 6.

[121] Ibid.

[122] Ibid.

[123] Ibid.

[124] Not yet in force. See New Zealand's first report, above n 145, 11. See, also, New Zealand's report to the United Nations 1267 Committee, above n 153, 8-9.

[125] See New Zealand's second report, above n 155, 6.

[126] See New Zealand's first report, above n 145, 11.

persons or things, deterrence through more severe penalties, and requiring a computer owner or user to provide information to access data subject to security codes and the like.

- *Para 2(c): deny safe haven.* Sections 7, 73 and 75 of the Immigration Act 1987 (already extant at the time of the adoption of Resolution 1373) were identified by New Zealand as satisfying the requirement to deny safe haven to terrorists.[127]
- *Para 2(d): prevent the use of State territory by terrorists.* The extraterritorial nature of the offences created under the Terrorism Suppression Act, together with extant party liability provisions under the Crimes Act 1961, were identified as further measures to prevent terrorists acting from New Zealand territory against other States or citizens.[128] The further creation of offences of harbouring or concealing terrorists was relied on (offences under 13A of the Terrorism Suppression Act).
- *Para 2(e): ensure prosecution and severe punishment.* As discussed later in this chapter, the various offences created under the Terrorism Suppression Act carry severe penalties.[129]
- *Para 2(f): assist in criminal investigations and prosecutions.* New Zealand again reported that current law permitted New Zealand to comply with this paragraph, referring to the Mutual Assistance in Criminal Matters Act 1992 and the Extradition Act 1999.[130]
- *Para 2(g): effective border controls to prevent the movement of terrorists.* The Passports Act 1992 and Immigration Act 1987 were identified by New Zealand as means through which compliance with paragraph 2(g) of the Resolution could be achieved.[131]

The impact of international counter-terrorism upon executive decision making

One further issue arises from Security Council Resolutions 1373 and 1456, and the impact these resolutions have had upon the decisions of States to enter into treaty relations.[132] Adopted in January 2003, Resolution 1456 calls upon the Counter-Terrorism Committee to intensify its efforts to promote the implementation of Resolution 1373.[133] It also contains the following provisions:

> The Security Council therefore calls for the following steps to be taken:
>
> 1. All States must take urgent action to prevent and suppress all active and passive support to terrorism, and in particular comply fully with all relevant resolutions of the Security Council, in particular resolutions 1373 (2001), 1390 (2002) and 1455 (2003);

---

[127] See New Zealand's first report, above n 145, 11-12.
[128] Ibid 12.
[129] See New Zealand's first report to the Counter-Terrorism Committee, above n 145, 13-14.
[130] Ibid 14.
[131] Ibid 14-15.
[132] SC Res 1456, 58 UN SCOR (4688th mtg), UN Doc S/Res/1456 (2003).
[133] Ibid [4].

2. The Security Council calls upon States to:

(a) become a party, as a matter of urgency, to all relevant international conventions and protocols relating to terrorism, in particular the 1999 international convention for the suppression of the financing of terrorism and to support all international initiatives taken to that aim, and to make full use of the sources of assistance and guidance which are now becoming available;

(b) assist each other, to the maximum extent possible, in the prevention, investigation, prosecution and punishment of acts of terrorism, wherever they occur;

(c) cooperate closely to implement fully the sanctions against terrorists and their associates, in particular Al-Qaeda and the Taliban and their associates, as reflected in resolutions 1267 (1999), 1390 (2002) and 1455 (2003), to take urgent actions to deny them access to the financial resources they need to carry out their actions, and to cooperate fully with the Monitoring Group established pursuant to resolution 1363 (2001);

[...].

The content of paragraph 1 and paragraphs 2(b) and 2(c), by themselves, do not cause any particular concern. Indeed, they are entirely consistent with earlier resolutions of the Council. It is paragraph 2(a), building upon paragraph 3(d) of Resolution 1373, that raises some issues about the proper role of the Security Council. By calling upon States to become party to all counter-terrorist conventions and protocols, is the Council over-stepping its function and impinging upon State sovereignty?

This is an interesting constitutional question that warrants at least some consideration. On the one hand, member States of the United Nations have to some degree surrendered their sovereignty by becoming a party to the United Nations Charter, to the extent that they have agreed to be bound by decisions of the Security Council.[134] At the same time, however, it could hardly have been intended by those becoming party to the Charter to grant the Security Council the authority to direct members in their treaty-making decision processes. A considerable number of States have complex constitutional rules concerning the executive's treaty-making power which must be complied with before a State can ratify or accede to a treaty. Is the Security Council, by issuing the directions contained in paragraph 3(f) of Resolution 1373 and paragraph 2(a) of Resolution 1456, able to override such domestic constitutional safeguards?

Answering that question appears to lie in one further enquiry: whether any such resolution is indeed binding within the terms of article 25 of the Charter. To avoid an unnecessary examination of this issue (for the purpose of this chapter), it is sufficient to say that it is clear at law that, since paragraph 2 is exhortatory in its nature, it does not impose a legal duty upon States to become signatories to the various international counter-terrorism conventions.[135]

---

[134] Article 25 of the Charter of the United Nations.

[135] For further discussion on this issue, see Alex Conte, *Security in the 21st Century. The United Nations, Afghanistan and Iraq* (Ashgate Publishing Ltd, 2005), 26-8.

Notwithstanding this conclusion at law, it is interesting to note that the resolutions, combined with the interactive dialogue between States and the Counter-Terrorism Committee have resulted in a number of States becoming party to treaties that they might not otherwise have signed or ratified. In the case of South Pacific States, this appears to be a particularly relevant issue. A striking example can be seen in the case of New Zealand's legislative action since 9/11. At the date of adoption of Resolution 1373, New Zealand was not party to the Suppression of Bombing and Suppression of Financing Conventions, nor to the Plastic Explosives or Nuclear Materials Conventions. It became party to the first two conventions once the Terrorism Suppression Act 2002 was enacted.[136] Given the subject matter of those two conventions, there is nothing overly surprising about this. In respect of the Plastic Explosives and Nuclear Materials Conventions, however, the influence of the Security Council's resolutions and Counter-Terrorism Committee are evident.

As treaties that were subject to ratification or accession, New Zealand Parliamentary Standing Order 384 applied,[137] so that the four conventions had to be referred to the Foreign Affairs, Defence and Trade Committee (FADTC)[138] with a National Interest Analysis[139] and then presented to the House.[140] The National Interest Analyses (NIAs), which are contained within the respective international treaty examination reports of the Committee, identify New Zealand's desire to become party to the conventions as being based upon its support of efforts to strengthen the rule of law at the international level[141] and support for an effective and well-supported network of multilateral legal instruments to combat terrorism.[142] In the case of the Plastic Explosives and Nuclear Materials Conventions,

---

136 As confirmed in New Zealand's third report to the Counter-Terrorism Committee, see *New Zealand Response to the Questions and Comments of the Security Council Counter-Terrorism Committee Contained in the Chairman's Letter of 30 May 2003*, S/2003/860, 5 September 2003, 6-7. New Zealand acceded to the International Convention for the Suppression of Terrorist Bombing on 4 November 2002: as recorded by the United Nations in its record on *Multilateral Treaties Deposited with the Secretary-General*, as at 12 October 2004 at <http://untreaty.un.org/ENGLISH/Status/Chapter_xviii/treaty9.asp>. The International Convention for the Suppression of the Financing of Terrorism was signed by New Zealand on 7 September 2000 but not ratified until 4 November 2002: as recorded by the United Nations, <http://untreaty.un.org/ENGLISH/Status/Chapter_xviii/treaty11.asp>.

137 See Parliamentary Standing Order 384, [1].

138 Ibid [3].

139 Ibid [2].

140 Ibid [1].

141 New Zealand Ministry of Foreign Affairs and Trade, *National Interest Analysis, International Convention for the Suppression of Terrorist Bombings*, [2], and *National Interest Analysis, International Convention for the Suppression of the Financing of Terrorism*, [2].

142 New Zealand Ministry of Foreign Affairs and Trade, *National Interest Analysis, International Convention for the Suppression of Terrorist Bombings*, [2], *National Interest Analysis, International Convention for the Suppression of the Financing of Terrorism*, [2], and *National Interest Analysis, Convention on the Marking of Plastic Explosives for the*

the NIAs noted that New Zealand neither manufactures explosives domestically, nor engages in the transportation of nuclear material.[143] Notwithstanding this, the Analyses pointed to the change in the post-September 11 international context and the call by the Security Council for UN members to become party to all anti-terrorism conventions[144] as sound bases for New Zealand becoming a party to the conventions.[145]

Conclusion

International terrorism has been identified by both the UN General Assembly and Security Council as one of the most serious threats to international peace and security. The terrorist attacks of September 11, 2001, ultimately prompted the intervention in Afghanistan. They also shook the United Nations into concerted action in the fight to eradicate terrorism. Due to a lack of international consensus on the meaning of the term terrorism, however, that action has failed to produce a comprehensive convention on the subject. Despite the considerable work of the Security Council Counter-Terrorism Committee and the Ad Hoc Committee Established under General Assembly Resolution 51/210, the international law on counter-terrorism is mainly based upon twelve very specific conventions that do not have general application and are limited in their binding nature to States parties to those treaties. Given the divergence of party status within Pacific Island countries, this is particularly problematic when considering counter-terrorism in the Pacific. Having said this, the Suppression of Financing Convention does have potentially wider application in its description of conduct that may not be financed. Its effect, either through party status to the Convention or the application of its provisions under Security Council Resolution 1373, is binding on all Pacific Island countries, save Niue.

Both the General Assembly and Security Council have issued numerous resolutions on the topic of counter-terrorism. Although not binding, the General Assembly has built on various guiding principles and expectations in its declarations on measures to eliminate international terrorism. The Security Council established a Counter-Terrorism Committee very soon after the terrorist attacks of September 11, 2001, with the role of liaising with UN members on the implementation of Resolution 1373 and the twelve counter-terrorism conventions,

---

Purpose of Detection, [2], and *National Interest Analysis, Convention on the Physical Protection of Nuclear Materials*, [2].

143 New Zealand Ministry of Foreign Affairs and Trade, *National Interest Analysis, Convention on the Marking of Plastic Explosives for the Purpose of Detection*, [2], and *National Interest Analysis, Convention on the Physical Protection of Nuclear Materials*, [4].

144 Resolution 1373, above n 33, [3(d)].

145 New Zealand Ministry of Foreign Affairs and Trade, *National Interest Analysis, Convention on the Marking of Plastic Explosives for the Purpose of Detection*, [2], and *National Interest Analysis, Convention on the Physical Protection of Nuclear Materials*, [5 and 7].

as well as to provide means by which States could be assisted in doing so. The Committee has seen reports lodged by all Pacific Island countries, even those not members of the United Nations.

The Council has imposed various specific obligations upon States under Resolutions 1373 and 1456. It has been posited, however, that the requirement to become a party to each of the treaties on terrorism remains the sole privilege of State executives and is not a binding provision of Resolution 1456. Notwithstanding that conclusion, it has been observed that the post-September 11 environment, combined with these Resolutions and the work of the Counter-Terrorism Committee, have contributed to States such as New Zealand becoming party to anti-terrorism treaties that might not actually have a great deal of relevance, if any, to those States.

The interface between international, regional and national security is one that is particularly interesting when relating international counter-terrorism to the South Pacific. Although the risk of terrorist attacks within the South Pacific might be assessed as remote, various good reasons exist for Pacific Island countries to act against the threat of international terrorism. Although the region has been fortunate not to be exposed to any considerable history of terrorism, the consequences of a bioterrorist attack could be devastating upon the agricultural and tourist industries. The nature of modern communications and travel, and the lack of infrastructure within some countries, makes the Pacific a potential target for the preparation and planning of terrorist attacks. The OECD Financial Action Task Force has expressed particular concern about the vulnerability of some Pacific countries to being used for the laundering of money and financing of terrorist activities. Both the Task Force and APEC have been active in attempting to redress this vulnerability. Ultimately, if one accepts the position advocated by the current Chair of the Counter-Terrorism Committee, the relevance of counter-terrorism lies not just in national and regional security but also in the establishment and maintenance of an effective international framework.

Chapter 4

The Law of the Sea and Freedom of Navigation in Asia Pacific

Scott Davidson

Introduction

Freedom of navigation is more than a slogan; it represents the essence of a policy which is concerned with the facilitation of maritime trade, the effective disposition of naval forces and the encouragement of hydrographic and marine scientific research. Although it seemed that the seventeenth century debate between Grotius in his *Mare Liberum* (1609) and Selden's *Mare Clausum* (1635) had been resolved in favour of the former, more recent events appear to be displacing Grotius' argument that the seas should be open to all nations and could not be reduced to the sovereignty of any single state. While this principle can be clearly discerned in article 89 of the United Nations Convention on the Law of the Sea 1982,[1] it seems that in recent decades Selden's doctrine of the closed sea has been gaining ascendancy. While a number of states seek to extend their jurisdictional competences ever further seaward, the maritime powers, particularly the United States of America, are concerned to ensure that these developments do not hinder their strategic, commercial and scientific goals in the world's oceans. Given the geography of Asia Pacific, the seaward creep of coastal state jurisdiction has the potential to produce profound consequences for the maintenance and development of seaborne trade and naval mobility. Furthermore, freedom of navigation in Asia Pacific is subject to considerable insecurity through the activities of pirates and maritime robbers who, through their acts of violence and depredation, threaten the often tenuous sea lines of communication in the region.

Before examining the issues affecting freedom of navigation in Asia Pacific, it is perhaps appropriate in a book which is concerned primarily with the South Pacific to say something about the region as a whole. *The Oxford English Dictionary* defines a region as 'an area of land, or division of the earth's surface having definable boundaries or characteristics'. It might be added to this that, in

---

[1] *UN Convention on the Law of the Sea*, opened for signature 10 December 1982, 1833 UNTS 3 (entered into force 16 November 1994) ('UNCLOS'). The full text of the Convention is available at (1982) 21 ILM 1245 and UN Division for Ocean Affairs and Law of the Sea <http://www.un.org/Depts/los/convention_agreements/texts/unclos/closindx.htm>. Art 89 provides: 'No State may validly purport to subject any part of the high seas to its sovereignty'.

geopolitical terms, a region is an area of the earth's surface containing states whose geographical contiguity creates certain political imperatives. In these terms, the Asia Pacific can be more or less defined as an identifiable geographical area with reasonably precise boundaries and shared, if not identical, political imperatives. Certainly, a number of cognate political and economic objectives have been identified by the United Nations Economic and Social Commission for Asia and the Pacific (UNESCAP) and Asia Pacific Economic Cooperation (APEC). At the Track I (governmental) and Track II (mixed governmental and non-governmental) levels the Western Naval Symposium and the Association of Southeast Asian Nations' (ASEAN) Council for Security and Cooperation in Asia Pacific (CSCAP) treat Asia Pacific as a geopolitical whole.

While the narrower geopolitical issues affecting the South Pacific and Southeast Asia differ considerably, in a wider sense, developments in the law of the sea and their impact on freedom of navigation for both commercial and military purposes possess a high level of homogeneity. As we shall see below, the maximization of the right to freedom of navigation which is so important for trade, resource exploitation, scientific developments and naval mobility are in many instances juxtaposed with coastal state security in its widest sense. It is doubtful that an appropriate equilibrium has yet been achieved, but whether a predictable regime which is acceptable to regional and extra-regional states is emerging from the current variety of state practice is also questionable.

Development of maritime zones

Prior to the middle of the twentieth century the limited number of maritime zones meant that the description and content of the right to freedom of navigation was relatively straightforward.[2] Beyond the three mile territorial sea lay the high seas in which the civil or military vessels of all states could navigate and engage in related activities unimpeded.[3] There were certain potential limitations on this right, but these were reserved to the residual public policing function of naval vessels in cases of slave trading and piracy and in the exercise of the right of hot pursuit.[4] From the mid-1970s onward, however, the zonal divisions of the oceans became a much more complex matter, and one which was to have, and still has, a profound impact on the exercise of navigational rights. One of the first major developments

[2] This much is evidenced by the fact that only two of the four Geneva Conventions of 1958, the Geneva Convention on the Territorial Sea and the Geneva Convention on the High Seas were primarily concerned with navigational rights. The lacunae in the regulation of navigation in international straits, for example, were regulated by customary international law.

[3] The width of the territorial sea was set at three miles by customary international law. The Geneva Convention on the Territorial Sea 1958 did not contain any reference to the actual width of the territorial sea, since no agreement could be reached on this by the negotiating states at Geneva. See R R Churchill and A V Lowe, *The Law of the Sea* (3rd ed, 1999) 77-81.

[4] The right of hot pursuit permits the public vessels of a coastal state to pursue and arrest on the high seas foreign vessels which have violated the laws of the coastal state. For the conditions under which this might be effected see art 111 UNCLOS.

to occur was the emergence of the 200 nautical mile exclusive economic zone (EEZ).[5] Although the *raison d'etre* of this zone is to allow coastal states to manage and exploit their resources in a sustainable manner, states also enjoy jurisdiction to protect and preserve the marine environment.[6] These jurisdictional capacities raise questions about the extent to which coastal states may interfere with navigational rights to achieve this end. The hybrid nature of the EEZ – a mixture of coastal state jurisdiction and reserved high seas freedoms – has also raised questions about the legitimacy of naval activities in this area.[7]

A further development which occurred during the 1970s and 1980s was the extension in the width of the territorial sea from three to a maximum of twelve miles.[8] This expansion of coastal state sovereignty was not accompanied by any resolution of the question of the limits of the right of innocent passage thus providing further potential for disputes between naval powers and coastal states.[9] In addition, the extension in the width of the territorial sea meant that certain straits became 'zone locked' and thus emerged as 'choke points' potentially restricting the passage of foreign warships.[10] Finally, the emergence of the archipelagic state had the effect of further reducing the area which was formerly high seas by permitting states able to claim this status to enclose large areas of water within straight baselines and subjecting it to their sovereignty.[11]

While most of these developments took place in customary international law and parallel to the United Nations Conference on the Law of the Sea (UNCLOS III, 1973 to 1982), they were incorporated into the architecture of the United Nations Convention on the Law of the Sea (UNCLOS) which was adopted in 1982. Although the Convention had been negotiated as a 'package deal' the administration of US President Ronald Reagan, contrary to the spirit in which UNCLOS had been negotiated, called for its adoption by vote.[12] Although the

---

[5] On the development of the EEZ see David Attard, *The Exclusive Economic Zone in International Law* (1987) 1-42.

[6] See Part V UNCLOS, particularly art 56.

[7] See below.

[8] Art 3 UNCLOS. Churchill and Lowe, above n 3, 80, remark that 'the twelve-mile limit is now firmly established in international law …'. They also argue that 'the time may soon come … when customary international law moves beyond the Law of the Sea Convention and regards twelve miles not merely as the maximum, but as the minimum, mandatory limit for the territorial sea'.

[9] See below.

[10] John Noer and David Gregory, *Chokepoints: Maritime Economic Concerns in Southeast Asia* (1996). On the development of the law relating to straits in general see José A de Yturriaga, *Straits Used for International Navigation* (1990) 21-56.

[11] On the development of the archipelagic state concept see Muhammad Munawwar, *Ocean States: Archipelagic Regimes in the Law of the Sea* (1995).

[12] On the negotiating method used at UNCLOS III see Edward Miles, *Global Oceans Politics: The Decision Process at the Third United Nations Conference on the Law of the Sea 1973–1982* (1997); James Sebenius, *Negotiating the Law of the Sea* (1984). See also the series of articles by Bernard Oxman and John Stephenson on UNCLOS III published by the *American Journal of International Law* which appear at (1974) 68 *American Journal of International Law* 1; (1975) 69 *American Journal of International Law* 1; (1977) 71

Convention was adopted, the US, which had profound ideological objections to Part XI UNCLOS on the regime for deep seabed mining, remained aloof and refused to sign; a position which still obtains today despite a subsequent agreement to modify Part XI.[13] The failure of the US to accede to UNCLOS (the Convention has now been in force since 1997) cannot be dismissed lightly since that state is today the world's preeminent naval power with global commercial and strategic interests. Furthermore, it is committed as a matter national policy to maximizing freedom of navigation through its Freedom of Navigation (FON) Program.[14] As Rear Admiral Joseph C Strasser put it in his foreword to the first edition of Roach and Smith's *United States Responses to Excessive Maritime Claims*:

> The national security and international commerce of the United States depend upon the freedoms of navigation and overflight on or over the seas. The Freedom of Navigation Program is designed to further the vital need to protect maritime rights by minimizing efforts of other States to reduce global mobility through the assertion of maritime claims that do not conform to the careful balance of interests reflected in the 1982 United Nations Convention on the Law of the Sea.[15]

While the US FON Program is designed to apply worldwide, there are clear challenges to it in the Asia Pacific region where much of the ocean space has now been incorporated into maritime zones in which coastal states purport to exercise greater or lesser degrees of control over certain navigational activities. This chapter will examine the state practice of a number of Southeast Asian and South Pacific states with a view to assessing the extent to which it impinges upon freedom of navigation, and to reflect on whether there can be any resolution of the 'grey areas' which currently afflict this area of the law of the sea in its current state of development.

American Journal of International Law 247; (1978) 72 *American Journal of International Law* 57; (1979) 73 *American Journal of International Law* 1; (1980) 74 *American Journal of International Law* 1; (1985) 75 *American Journal of International Law* 211 and (1982) 76 *American Journal of International Law* 1.

[13] *Agreement on the Implementation of Part XI of the Law of the Sea Convention of 10 December 1982*, opened for signature 28 July 1994 (1994) 33 ILM 1309 (entered into force provisionally 16 November 1994; definitively 28 July 1996). See Annick de Marffy-Mantuano, 'The Procedural Framework of the Agreement Implementing the 1982 United Nations Convention on the Law of the Sea' (1995) 89 *American Journal of International Law* 814.

[14] The Freedom of Navigation (FON) Program was introduced during the Carter Administration in 1979. The purpose of the FON Program is to maintain navigational freedoms for US naval forces by challenging what the US perceives to be maritime claims in excess of those permitted by extant international law. See 1979 *Digest of US Practice in International Law* 997-8.

[15] J Ashley Roach and Robert W Smith, *United States Responses to Excessive Maritime Claims* (2nd ed, 1996) x.

The Asia Pacific context

The Pacific Ocean is the largest of the world's five oceans. It has a surface area of approximately 156 million square kilometres and occupies about 28 per cent of the world's total surface. The South Pacific Ocean is divided from the North Pacific Ocean by the Equator and is characterized geographically by the presence of a multitude of coral atolls which are either low lying or which fringe mountainous, volcanic islands. The larger coastal states are Australia, New Zealand, Papua New Guinea and the west coast states of Latin America – Chile and Peru. Economically, the South Pacific is of prime importance to its coastal states. It provides the main source of economic sustenance for what are characterized by the United Nations as small island developing states (SIDS), while for regional and extra-regional states it provides access to rich fisheries and a relatively cheap medium for seaborne transport from both North to South and East to West. The main security threats in the South Pacific are not military in character, but relate primarily to issues of human security.[16] These include maritime boundary disputes, fishery disputes between regional and extra-regional states, illegal fishing and pollution, trafficking in drugs, humans and small arms and, more recently, the seaborne transit of ultra-hazardous waste, especially the product of spent nuclear fuel reprocessing.[17]

The maritime configuration of Southeast Asia differs from that of the South Pacific. It is characterized by a high land to sea ratio in which states are densely packed in what is essentially an archipelagic formation with a significant number of enclosed and semi-enclosed seas. The region is connected by a number of straits, some of which are heavily used by civil and military vessels. The Malacca, Lombok, Sunda, Philip and Singapore Straits, for example, are some of the most heavily used straits in the world and form the major sea lines of communication (SLOC) between Southeast Asia and the Pacific.[18] Some of the largest ports on the globe are also located in this region and their security and access has become of even greater significance in the post-September 11 world. Because of the close proximity of the states in this sub-region, there are a number of significant maritime boundary disputes, some of which are a cause of major friction between contesting states.[19] This friction arises not only because of jurisdictional uncertainty in respect of foreign fishing vessels, but because of contested territorial sovereignty, especially in the South China Sea where, despite the adoption of a Code of Conduct to reduce tensions, title to the Spratly Islands is still sharply

---

[16] Sam Bateman, 'The Functions of Navies in the Southwest Pacific and Southeast Asia' in Hugh Smith and Anthony Bergin (eds), *Naval Power in the Pacific: Toward the Year 2000* (1993) 129.

[17] Stanley Weeks, 'Existing Maritime Cooperation Arrangements in the Asia-Pacific Region' in Sam Bateman (ed), *Maritime Cooperation in the Asia-Pacific Region: Current Situation and Prospects* (1999) 1.

[18] Ibid.

[19] For a description of past and current disputes see Jonathan I Charney and Lewis M Alexander (eds), *International Maritime Boundaries* (1993), vol I, 905-1184; vol II, 1195-1474 and vol III, 2295-2368.

contested.[20] There are, however, other activities which hinder freedom of navigation in this region. Southeast Asia is commonly regarded as one of the major 'piracy' hotspots of the world. The word piracy is placed in inverted commas, because what is often colloquially referred to as piracy is nothing of the sort. As will be seen below, piracy *iure gentium* can only occur on the high seas while much of what is referred to as piracy in Southeast Asia is in fact simply criminal activity which takes place in maritime areas under the jurisdiction of coastal states.[21] The possibility of maritime terrorism is also something which needs to be taken into account when considering freedom of navigation in Southeast Asia. While to date there has been minimal interference with shipping by the major terrorist/liberation groups in the region – Abu Sayyef in Malaysia and Jamia Islamia and the Aceh Liberation Front (GAM) in Indonesia – none the less the potential for a major terrorist strike against commercial or military shipping remains a strong possibility, especially in a post-9/11 world.[22]

Freedom of navigation in Asia Pacific: general issues

As noted above, the law of the sea affecting freedom of navigation in the Asia Pacific region has undergone a profound realignment in the last thirty to forty years. The United Nations Convention on the Law of the Sea 1982 (UNCLOS) has increased the potential of coastal states to limit freedom of navigation in areas which were previously characterized as high seas. This potential is further enhanced by the number of so-called 'grey areas' in the law of the sea which can be exploited by states either to minimize or maximize navigational rights.[23] Furthermore, rather than contributing to a stable maritime environment, the differing interpretations of UNCLOS have the capacity to create instability in inter-state relations affecting maritime areas. Similarly, progress towards an agreed, common understanding of the relevant provisions of UNCLOS, which has been promoted by certain Track II bodies, is capable of enhancing stability and promoting confidence in maritime relations between regional states.[24]

---

[20] The adoption of a Code of Conduct for the South China Sea might mitigate some of the more extreme aspects of the claims by the contesting states, especially China and Vietnam. See the *Declaration on the Conduct of Parties in the South China Sea*, done in Phnom Penh, Cambodia on 4 November 2002. Text available at <http://www.asean.or.id/13163.htm> at 10 March 2005.

[21] See below.

[22] Scott Davidson, 'International Law and the Suppression of Maritime Violence' in Richard Burchill, Justin Morris and Nigel White (eds), *International Conflict and Security Law* (forthcoming 2005).

[23] Erik Jaap Molenaar, 'Navigational Rights and Freedoms: Grey Areas and Scope for Regional Agreement' in Bateman, above n 17, 97.

[24] The Maritime Cooperation Working Group of the Council for Security and Cooperation in Asia Pacific (CSCAP) has done a significant amount of work in this area. See in particular *CSCAP Memorandum No 6: The Practice of the Law of the Sea in the Asia Pacific* (2002). CSCAP reports to the ASEAN Regional Forum (ARF).

The grey areas in the law of the sea exist largely for one of two reasons: first, since UNCLOS was negotiated as a package deal the Convention embodies a significant amount of compromise.[25] The negotiating states were prepared to trade off their interests in one area of the law of the sea in order to gain advantage elsewhere. In some cases, no agreement could be reached at all and therefore in certain areas UNCLOS represents an agreement to disagree with the relevant provisions designed to have a certain constructive ambiguity. Constructive ambiguity can, of course, turn to destructive ambiguity when confronted with actual circumstances. One area where this issue is particularly acute is the question of the innocent passage of warships in the territorial sea of certain coastal states. The lack of certainty in this area can have the effect of heightening tension if the demands of the coastal state are ignored, as will be demonstrated below. The second reason for the emergence of grey areas is the poor and imprecise drafting of certain provisions of UNCLOS which creates ambiguities. This raises more or less traditional questions of treaty interpretation relating to the ordinary meaning of the words and the intentions of the drafters. Again, given the process which was used to negotiate UNCLOS, the *travaux préparatoires* (preparatory works) are often of little assistance in divining the actual intentions of the parties. An example of this which will be addressed below is the precise content of the right of transit passage in straits used for international navigation, but there are a number of other examples of the use of opaque language and imprecise terminology.

In addition to the so-called grey areas in the law of the sea, there are two further ways in which freedom of navigation in Asia Pacific may be affected by the law of the sea: first, in cases where excessive maritime zones are claimed and, second, by states claiming an excess of jurisdiction within declared zones. Often excessive jurisdictional and zonal claims will be married to create even more objectionable limitations to freedom of navigation. Claims to excessive maritime zones are a world-wide phenomenon with a number of states using methods for delimiting their maritime areas which are not entirely consonant with the applicable law. Sometimes this is because the law lacks clarity, but often it is because the letter of the law is leaned upon rather too heavily or simply ignored. The use of straight baselines is a good – and important – example of this. As will be seen below the wrongful use of straight baselines can have the effect of projecting maritime zones significantly seaward, so that, for example, the outer limit of a state's EEZ might be extended from 200 miles to 250 miles from the coast. Furthermore, the wrongful use of archipelagic baselines can result in the enclosure of thousands of additional square miles of ocean. The second issue is that of coastal states claiming an excess of jurisdiction in certain maritime zones, again most especially the EEZ. As this chapter will show there is a tension between the high seas right of freedom of navigation and the obligation on the coastal state to protect and preserve the marine environment.

---

[25] See the literature cited above at n 12.

The use and abuse of straight baselines

The use of straight baselines in measuring maritime zones (outside closing lines for bays) has been controversial since they first made their appearance in the *Anglo-Norwegian Fisheries* case in 1947.[26] In that case the International Court of Justice (ICJ) declared that Norway was entitled to use a straight baseline system rather than the low water mark for measuring the outer limit of its territorial sea because of the deeply indented nature of the Norwegian coast, because it was fringed by a barrier known as the *skjaergaard* and because of Norway's economic dependence on fisheries. The Court placed limits on the use of baselines but these were restricted to the injunction that they should not depart from the general direction of the coastline and that economic factors should be proven by demonstrable long use. The judgment of the ICJ was adopted by the International Law Commission and codified in article 7 of the Geneva Convention on the Territorial Sea 1958. This provision was subsequently transformed unamended into UNCLOS.

While Article 5 UNCLOS thus adopts the conventional approach that the normal baseline from which the outer limits of a state's maritime zones are measured is the low water mark, Article 7 provides that straight baselines may be used 'in localities where the coastline is deeply indented and cut into, or if there is a fringe of islands along the coast in its immediate vicinity'. Article 7(3) further provides that 'the drawing of straight baselines must not depart to any appreciable extent from the general direction of the coast, and the sea areas lying within the lines must be sufficiently closely linked to the land domain to be subject to the regime of internal waters'. The relevance of a coastal state's economic interests in drawing straight baselines is also retained in Article 7(5). While the constituent elements of Article 7 appear to be self-explanatory, they do, in fact, raise a number of critical questions. It seems that what the drafters of this provision had in mind was a coastline like that of Norway: jagged, precipitous and bounded almost entirely by the outlying *skjaergaard* or a territory in which the land and maritime domain were closely interlinked, if not inseparable. While the words of article 7 are capable of conveying this idea of geographical complexity, they are also capable of other meaning. How, for example, does one gauge what is 'deeply indented'? What does 'a fringe of islands' mean? If straight baselines must 'not depart to any appreciable extent from the general direction of the coast', just how significant must any departure be before it violates the provision? These are unresolved issues which some states have been able to exploit for their own advantage.[27]

---

[26] *Fisheries (United Kingdom v Norway)* [1951] ICJ Rep 116.

[27] The USA, however, has attempted to clarify the position under its FON Program. Roach and Smith, above n 15, 62-3 state that there must be at least three indentations which are in close proximity to each other and that 'the depth of penetration of each deep indentation from the proposed straight baseline enclosing the indentation at its entrance to the sea is, as a rule, greater than half the length of that baseline segment'. In the case of islands, Roach and Smith argue that they must mask at least 50 per cent of the mainland coastline.

Straight baselines are used for the measurement of maritime zones by a number of states in Asia Pacific. These include Australia, Cambodia, China, South Korea and Vietnam. Each of these has been criticized as exceeding the requirements imposed by UNCLOS, but those used by Vietnam and Cambodia have caused particular concern and have elicited protest from the USA.[28] Both these states have drawn their baselines from islands which are minimal in number and, in some cases, more than 50 miles offshore. Since the water enclosed by the baselines became internal waters over which states exercise unrestricted sovereignty, the use of straight baselines by these states had the potential to transform high seas through which there was general freedom of navigation into a maritime zone in which there are limited navigational rights. Furthermore, since the other maritime zones are calculated from the baselines, Vietnam and Cambodia's territorial seas have been projected significantly seaward, with the effect that in some places the outer limits of the territorial sea is 62 miles from the actual coastline.[29] There is certainly no satisfaction of the requirement that the use of straight baselines be predicated on the intimate relationship between the sea and the land domain of the coastal state. Although the water enclosed on the landward side of straight baselines has the characteristics of internal waters over which states are entitled to exercise full sovereignty, article 8 provides that where such waters had not previously been considered as such prior to their enclosure by straight baselines, the right of innocent passage continues to obtain. While this might be regarded as a satisfactory conclusion in the case of merchant vessels, the position is different for warships. The innocent passage of warships is a contentious issue in Asia Pacific with some states claiming that, unlike merchant vessels, warships have no right of innocent passage within the territorial sea.[30] This argument would apply *a fortiori* to internal waters newly enclosed by straight baselines. If one examines the situation in the case of Vietnam which prohibits the passage of warships through its territorial sea without its prior permission, then unnecessarily large areas of the South China Sea are closed to the passage of foreign warships.[31]

Straight baselines can also be used to enclose bays, historic bays and historic waters, as well as atolls and islands having fringing reefs. While the closing line for bays is normally 24 nautical miles, there is no limit on the length of closing lines for historic bays.[32] The effect of this can be that where a state uses straight baselines to enclose large areas of water as internal waters, it once again has the potential to impede navigation. Unlike the use of straight baselines on highly indented coastlines or those fringed with islands, a straight baseline which is used to enclose an historic bay or historic waters is not subject to the proviso in article 8 UNCLOS which retains the right of innocent passage for vessels in the newly enclosed waters. This means that not only might warships be excluded from the zone by the coastal state, but so too might merchant vessels.

---

[28] Roach and Smith, above n 15, 102-103.

[29] Ibid.

[30] See below.

[31] Roach and Smith, above, n 15, 267.

[32] Art 10(6) UNCLOS. See Gayl Westerman, *The Juridical Bay* (1987) 176-8.

UNCLOS does not provide a definition of historic bays, but in the *Tunisia-Libya Continental Shelf Case*[33] the ICJ stated that there was no single legal regime for historic bays and that each case must to be proved on its merits. A 1962 UN study suggested that in order to prove that a bay is 'historic' a state must show that it has claimed the bay as internal waters for a considerable period of time and that it has exercised authority over it during the period in question.[34] It also suggested that such a bay must be so closely linked to the land domain as to be indistinguishable from it. This differs somewhat from the *Digest of US Practice in International Law* which provides that in order to establish a claim to historic waters (a concept which might be wider than that of an historic bay) a state must demonstrate its open, effective, long-term and continuous exercise of authority of the water in question coupled with the acquiescence by other states in the exercise of that authority.[35] Roach and Smith's 'Blue Book' goes on to say that the USA has taken the position 'that an actual showing of acquiescence by foreign states in such a claim is required, as opposed to a mere absence of opposition'.[36]

In the Asia Pacific region there have been few claims of historic bays or waters. Vietnam and Cambodia entered into an agreement in 1982 which claimed part of the Gulf of Thailand as historic waters.[37] The bases of the joint claim were the special geographical conditions of the states and the importance and significance of the waters to each country's national defence and economy. The claim was rejected by the USA on the grounds that these were not valid criteria under international law as that state understands it; that there was no evidence that Vietnam and Cambodia had effectively exercised their authority in the waters in question and that the claim was of too short a duration to be effective.[38] In addition to its claim to part of the Gulf of Thailand, Vietnam also claimed that the Gulf of Tonkin constituted an historic bay. Again, the US suggested that the international legal criteria were not met, but in addition to this, the Gulf was also bordered by China which had not itself claimed the bay as historic and had, in fact, contested Vietnam's boundary with it in the Gulf of Tonkin.[39] Similarly, the claim by Australia that Anxious, Encounter, Lacepede and Rivoli Bays in South Australia are historic bays has been rejected by the USA also on the grounds that they did not fulfil the criteria required by international law.[40]

One area where the use of baselines is provided for in UNCLOS but which seems to have caused few practical problems in Asia Pacific is the case of reefs.[41]

---

[33] *Continental Shelf (Tunisia/Libyan Arab Jamahiriya)* [1982] ICJ Rep 1.

[34] UN Secretariat, 'Juridical regime of historic waters including historic bays', *ILC Yearbook* (1962) vol 2, 1.

[35] *1973 Digest of US Practice in International Law* (1974) 244-5.

[36] Roach and Smith, above n 15, 31.

[37] Ibid 39-40.

[38] Ibid.

[39] Ibid 52-3.

[40] Ibid 35-8.

[41] On reefs generally see P B Beazley, 'Reefs and the 1982 Convention on the Law of the Sea' (1991) 6 *International Journal of Marine and Coastal Law* 281. As Churchill and Lowe, above n 3, 56 observe, the drawing of straight baselines by a number of archipelagic

Article 6 provides that 'in the case of islands situated on atolls or of islands having fringing reefs, the baseline for measuring the breadth of the territorial sea is the seaward low-water line of the reef ...'. The rationale for the adoption of this provision was to protect submerged reefs from environmental damage. As can be seen, however, article 6 only permits reefs which are above water at low tide to form the baseline for other maritime zones. Because of this, there is little to differentiate reefs, whether fringing or otherwise, from drying rocks which have their own regime within UNCLOS. None the less reefs may be designated particularly sensitive sea areas (PSSA) by the International Maritime Organization (IMO) and therefore be subject to special navigational rules.[42] The IMO defines a PSSA as 'an area that needs special protection through action by IMO because of its significance for recognized ecological, socio-economic or scientific reasons, and which may be vulnerable to damage by international shipping activities'.[43] Designation of a maritime area as a PSSA gives coastal states the opportunity to adopt additional protective measures to combat the particular risks associated with international shipping in the area. The only PSSA in the Asia Pacific region to date is Australia's Great Barrier Reef. Here, Australia has introduced a compulsory pilotage system along the Reef's inner shipping route for vessels over 70 metres in length.[44] This would normally be regarded as an impermissible restriction on navigation, but the fact that the Reef is an IMO-approved PSSA remedies this.

Archipelagic states

One of the major potential limitations on freedom of navigation in Asia Pacific has arisen from the emergence of the archipelagic state. Article 46 defines an archipelago as 'a group of islands, including parts of islands, interconnecting waters and other natural features which are so closely interrelated that such islands,

states, including Fiji, Kiribati, Nauru, Cook Islands, Tokelau, Tonga and Tuvalu, has obviated the need to apply art 6 UNCLOS.

42 Guidelines for the designation of special areas under the *International Convention for the Prevention of Pollution from Ships 1973 as Modified by the Protocol of 1978 Relating Thereto*, opened for signature 17 February 1978, 1340 UNTS 61 (entered into force 20 October 1983) and guidelines for the identification and Designation of particularly sensitive sea areas are contained in IMO Resolution A.927(22), 29 November 2001. Roach and Smith comment (at page 459) that 'the concept of [PSSAs] has raised considerable concern because of its potential for upsetting the navigation/environment balance contained in [UNCLOS]'.

43 Resolution A.927(22), 29 November 2001, Annex II, [1.2].

44 Australian Maritime Safety Authority, 'Great Barrier Reef Marine Park Authority – Major Issues', <http://www.amsa.gov.au/About_AMSA/Corporate_information/AMSA_speeches/Shipping_In_The_Asia-Pacific_Conference/Great_Barrier_Reef_Marine_Park_Authority.asp> at 10 March 2005. Peter Ottesen, Stephen Sparkes and Colin Trinder, 'Shipping Threats and Protection of the Great Barrier Reef Marine Park: The Role of the Particularly Sensitive Sea Area Concept (1994) 9 *International Journal of Marine and Coastal Law* 507.

waters and other natural features form an intrinsic geographical, economic and political entity, or which historically have been regarded as such' and an archipelagic state as 'a state which is constituted wholly by one or more archipelagos'. Such a state may draw straight baselines joining the outermost points of the outermost islands and drying rocks of the archipelago, but the main island must be included within the straight baselines and the land (including fringing reefs and atolls[45]) to water ratio must fall within 1:1 to 9:1. The length of straight baselines must not exceed 100 miles, except that up to 3 per cent of the total number of baselines may exceed that length up to a maximum length of 125 miles. The baselines themselves must not depart to any appreciable extent from the general configuration of the archipelago, nor must they be used in such a way as to cut off the high seas, EEZ or the territorial sea of another state. All other maritime zones are drawn from these straight baselines, thus projecting state jurisdiction to maritime areas previously thought of as high seas. Furthermore, the creation by UNCLOS of a new maritime regime – archipelagic waters – has further imposed limitations on navigational rights.

Eight regional states now claim archipelagic state status,[46] and while there appears to be little controversy over these claims, nonetheless the Philippines, rather than claiming the waters enclosed by its straight baselines as archipelagic waters, defines them in its constitution as internal waters with the effect that other states have no navigational rights within the area enclosed by the Philippines' straight baselines.[47] This position is contrary to Article 52 which gives the vessels of third states the right of innocent passage through archipelagic waters. Under article 53 archipelagic states may designate sea lanes and air routes suitable for the continuous and expeditious passage of ships and aircraft through and above archipelagic waters and its adjacent territorial sea. Ships and aircraft using such sea lanes are said to be exercising the right of archipelagic sea lanes passage. In the exercise of this right vessels and aircraft must navigate 'in the normal mode solely for the purpose of continuous, expeditious and unobstructed transit between one part of the high seas or an EEZ and another part of the high seas or an EEZ'. There is some dispute over what constitutes the normal mode of transit for the purposes of these UNCLOS provisions. The naval powers assert that this includes the navigation under water by submarines, formation steaming by surface warships to facilitate their operational security and the launching and recovery of military aircraft from vessels. Roach and Smith argue that 'the provisions regarding the

---

[45] It is not indicated whether the fringing reefs and atolls must be above water at low tide, but to be consistent with arts 6 and 8 UNCLOS it is assumed that this must be so.

[46] These are Fiji, Indonesia, Kiribati, Papua New Guinea, the Philippines, the Solomon Islands, Tuvalu and Vanuatu.

[47] Art 1 of the *Constitution of the Republic of the Philippines* reads, 'The national territory comprises the Philippine archipelago, with all the islands and waters embraced therein, and all other territories over which the Philippines has sovereignty or jurisdiction, consisting of its terrestrial, fluvial and aerial domains, including its territorial sea, the seabed, the subsoil, the insular shelves, and other submarine areas. The waters around, between, and connecting the islands of the archipelago, regardless of their breadth and dimensions, form part of the internal waters of the Philippines.'

width of archipelagic sea lanes were specifically designed to accommodate defensive formations and navigation practices normally used in open waters' thus suggesting that function gives rise to form.[48] It is, however, difficult to square this with the right of innocent passage which exists in other parts of archipelagic waters. Even allowing for the fact that the Philippines requires prior permission for the passage of warships through its territorial sea and archipelagic waters,[49] it would seem that formation steaming could be regarded as a hostile rather than a defensive act and thus inconsistent with the requirements of innocent passage both under customary international law and article 19 UNCLOS.

There is continuing disagreement between the maritime powers and the archipelagic states over the appropriate locations and regimes for archipelagic sea lanes passage. Indonesia and the Philippines restrict the passage of foreign warships and aircraft as well as potentially polluting vessels through designated sea lanes. Indonesia has declared three sea lanes through the Sunda, Lombok and Ombai-Wetar Straits running north-south, but the United States insists that an east-west sea lane through the Java and Banda Seas is a more appropriate route for navigation.[50] As noted above, this causes difficulties where navigation in archipelagic waters outside of an archipelagic sea lane is under the regime of innocent passage. In order to comply with article 19 UNCLOS there must be no overt threat to the coastal state, so according to the Philippines, weapons and radar systems must be deactivated, submarines must navigate on the surface and show their flag, and vessels carrying aircraft can neither launch nor receive them. Indonesia has provided a short east-west sealane in its waters adjacent to Singapore but that is considered insufficient by the United States.[51]

Straits

There are about forty-five international straits in Southeast Asia, over twenty of which are of major strategic importance.[52] The most significant are the Straits of Malacca and Singapore, Luzon, Formosa, Torres, Sunda, Lombok, and Obai-Wetar in Indonesia, and San Bernardino, Surigao and Balut in the Philippines. If the Malacca/Singapore Straits were to be closed the principal link between the Indian and the South Pacific Oceans would be either the Sunda Strait to the South China Sea or the Lombok Strait to the Sulawesi Sea. The alternative route for shipping with tonnage greater than 200,000 gross registered tonnes and drafts too deep for the Malacca-Singapore Straits, would be through the Lombok-Makassar Straits and

[48] Roach and Smith, above n 15, 378.

[49] Ibid 267.

[50] The Nippon Foundation Library, 'Threats to Sealane Safety and Security', <http://nippon.zaidan.info/seikabutsu/2001/00800/contents/00007.htm> at 10 March 2005.

[51] Ibid.

[52] The Nippon Foundation Library, 'Asian Sealane Security', <http://nippon.zaidan.info/seikabutsu/2001/00800/contents/00006.htm> at 10 March 2005.

the Sulawesi Sea south of Mindanao, through the Surigao Strait and on through eastern Philippine waters.[53]

The question of straits and their associated navigational rights were a matter of some controversy during the UNCLOS III negotiations. The main complicating issue was that with the extension of the territorial sea regime from three to a maximum of twelve nautical miles a number of straits would have become zone locked by the bordering states' territorial seas. In order to avoid this, a new navigational regime of transit passage was negotiated. Transit passage applies when the straits in question connect one part of the high seas or an EEZ to another part of the high seas or EEZ.[54] In such straits the ships and aircraft of all nations (including military ships and aircraft) enjoy the right of unimpeded passage solely for the purpose of continuous and expeditious transit. Such transit must be in the 'normal mode'.[55]

There is some disagreement over the precise legal status of transit passage with the USA claiming that it has become a right under customary international law and other states asserting that the right is only available to those states which are party to UNCLOS.[56] Given that the USA is not party to UNCLOS the clear implication here is that it should not be entitled to the more liberal regime of transit passage, but should be restricted to the customary law right of non-suspensable innocent passage in straits used for international navigation.[57] As noted above, transit passage, like archipelagic sea lanes passage, exists solely for the expeditious passage of vessels in their normal modes from one part of the EEZ or high seas to another. Like archipelagic sea lane passage, there is no general agreement on what constitutes the normal mode of passage. Again, the USA, the UK and Australia take a consistent position on this and maintain that it permits submarines to navigate underwater; for surface vessels to steam in formation for security purposes and the launching and recovery of aircraft where this is consistent with sound navigational practices.[58] It is reasonably plain that these requirements are designed to maximize the efficacy of naval operations, but coastal states might well perceive them as threats to their national security. The USA would respond that in exercising transit passage rights it is meticulous in observing the requirements that its vessels and aircraft proceed without delay; that it must refrain from the threat or the use of force against the sovereignty, territorial integrity or political independence of nations bordering the strait; and must otherwise refrain from any activities other than those incidental to their normal modes of continuous and expeditious passage.[59] This issue, however, remains unresolved and the possibilities of inter-state tension which might result from this are apparent.

---

[53] Ibid.
[54] Art 37 UNCLOS.
[55] Art 39(1)(c) UNCLOS.
[56] Roach and Smith, above n 15, 24-6.
[57] *Corfu Channel Case (Albania v United Kingdom)* [1949] ICJ Rep 4.
[58] Roach and Smith, above n 15, 282-4.
[59] Ibid.

Innocent passage in the territorial sea

If the extent of the newly created rights of archipelagic sea lane passage and transit passage in international straits is controversial, the same remains true of the question of whether warships have the right of innocent passage in the territorial sea of coastal states.[60] Section 3 UNCLOS is entitled 'Innocent Passage in the Territorial Sea' and Subsection A is headed 'Rules Applicable to All Ships'. Article 17 UNCLOS further provides that 'the ships of all states ... enjoy the right of innocent passage through the territorial sea'. From this and from the alleged existence of a prior rule of customary international law which allowed warships the right of innocent passage, the naval powers argue that it is self-evident that warships have a right of innocent passage in the territorial seas of other states which they are allowed to exercise without interference. In particular the naval powers assert that they are not required to give prior notification or request prior permission for their warships to exercise the right. This, however, is not the view of a number of regional states who argue that warships have no right of innocent passage because such passage represents a threat to their national security.[61] Cambodia, China, Indonesia, South Korea, the Philippines and Vietnam all require prior permission before a foreign warship can enter their territorial waters.[62]

The effect of this disagreement over the true meaning, extent and application of the rights of archipelagic sea lane passage, transit passage and innocent passage contributes to maritime insecurity in the Asia Pacific region.[63] While there has been no incident similar to the Black Sea bumping incident between American and Soviet naval vessels during the Cold War,[64] this does not mean that the situation is free from all risk. In 2001 a squadron of three Australian warships entered Chinese territorial waters without prior permission. Beijing protested to Canberra over this incursion, but the matter remained unresolved with Australia stating that the protest was 'a fairly standard diplomatic procedure'.[65] Given that this incident occurred during a period of heightened international tension between the USA and China over the downing of an American aircraft by Chinese warplanes, it seems clear that the Australian naval incursion was designed to test China's response. While it would seem desirable for regional states to come to some agreement over the nature of the precise content of the various rights of passage, it is apparent that this is unlikely to happen. Attempts to secure agreement on the content of these indeterminate rights have generally served to illustrate the distance by which states

---

[60] F David Froman, 'Uncharted Waters: Non-innocent Passage of Warships in the Territorial Sea' (1984) 21 *San Diego Law Review* 625.

[61] Roach and Smith, above n 15, 251-70.

[62] Ibid, Table 10, 266-7.

[63] *CSCAP Memorandum No 6: The Practice of the Law of the Sea in the Asia Pacific* (December 2002) 1.

[64] John W Rolph, 'Freedom of Navigation and the Black Sea Bumping Incident: How "Innocent" Must Innocent Passage Be?' (1992) 135 *Military Law Review* 137.

[65] Sam Blay, 'Australia's Warships and Innocent Passage' (2001) 75 *Australian Law Journal* 660.

are separated on this matter.[66] In the absence of any agreement therefore, it is clear that there must be some form of confidence building measures which contribute towards regional maritime stability.

The EEZ

The effects of the EEZ regime in Asia Pacific

As noted above, one of the major developments in the law of the sea during the 1970s was the emergence of the EEZ. In the Asia Pacific region this development alone has led to the enclosure of massive areas of maritime territory. With the use of straight baselines and the declaration of archipelagic state status by Indonesia, the Philippines and a significant majority of the South Pacific island states, there has been a considerable projection seaward of coastal state jurisdiction. In the region some states, such as Singapore, have effectively been zone-locked, that is, fully enclosed by the EEZs of neighbouring states, and in the South Pacific, the ocean is now almost fully enclosed by interlocking EEZs leaving very few areas which can truly be described as high seas. One of the salient features of the South Pacific is that the EEZs of the archipelagic small island states are exponentially larger than the land territories on which they are based. As Anthony Bergin points out, 'virtually all the resources and economic uses in this vast area of more than 30 million square kilometres … (11.5 million square miles …) are under the control of island states'.[67] Bergin goes on to give some examples of this phenomenon. Kiribati, for example, has a land area of 690 km^2 (266 ml^2) but controls a sea area of 3.5 million km^2 (1.4 million ml^2).[68] While this clearly has significant consequences for marine resource management and protection of the marine environment, it also has the potential to affect navigational rights since there is some disagreement between states as to the extent to which coastal states are able to place limits on freedom of navigation within the EEZ. As Rose has pointed out, 'the EEZ is a modern arena in which the ancient clash between *mare clausum* and *mare liberum* continues to play itself out'.[69] This much is evident in current state practice with states such as China placing clear restrictions on the ability of other states to engage in military or intelligence gathering activities within its EEZ.[70] While

[66] An attempt to secure agreement on a uniform interpretation of the right of innocent passage as it relates to warships as the Maritime Cooperation Working Group of CSCAP in Vancouver in December 2001 foundered because of significant differences of opinion. The best that could be achieved was an agreement to disagree which was not ultimately recorded in *CSCAP Memorandum No 6*, above n 63.

[67] Anthony Bergin, 'New Developments in the Law of the Sea' in H Smith and A Bergin (eds), *Naval Power in the Pacific* (1993) 67.

[68] Ibid.

[69] Stephen A Rose, 'Naval Activity in the EEZ – Troubled Waters Ahead?' (1990) 39 *Naval Law Review* 67.

[70] See the dispute between the US and China over the voyage of US vessel *Dowdich* within China's EEZ in September 2002. China claimed that the *Dowdich* was a naval intelligence

South Pacific states have so far not placed restrictions on navigational rights within their EEZs, this does not mean that at some future stage this might not happen. A situation could easily be envisaged where these states, who have already expressed concerns over the transport of reprocessed nuclear waste through their region, might legislate to curb transit of vessels carrying such materials through their individual EEZs.[71] As will be seen below, the New Zealand Green Party has already sponsored a bill which would curtail the navigational rights of vessels carrying nuclear waste through New Zealands's EEZ and while this initiative has not been successful, it gives a lead to regional states who might wish to limit such activities. For the major naval states therefore, the nightmare scenario is an Asia Pacific region in which naval manoeuvres, weapons practice and the transport of certain sensitive cargos are essentially prohibited. The question, of course, is whether UNCLOS is capable of leading to such a result.

The EEZ regime in UNCLOS

Part V UNCLOS contains the major part of the legal regime governing the EEZ. Like other parts of UNCLOS it was negotiated as part of the package deal and therefore represents a compromise in terms of the competing interests of coastal and other states. While this approach might have had the virtue of allowing textual agreement at UNCLOS, it has undoubtedly stored up future conflict in terms of the true extent of navigational rights in this particular maritime area. Attard has argued that the 'delicate, intricate and sometimes ambiguous mechanism' that is the legal regime governing the EEZ will have to be clarified by actual state practice over the years.[72] In essence, the issue is which of the prevailing views will succeed: that which sees the EEZ as a modified form of high seas regime or that which sees it as primarily subject to coastal state jurisdiction: the age old tension between *mare liberum* and *mare clausum*.

While article 55 makes clear that the EEZ is a specific regime in which the competing rights of states are balanced, the content of article 56 gives an indication that the primary *raison d'etre* of the EEZ is resource related. Article 56 provides:

> 1. In the [EEZ], the coastal State has:
>
> (a) sovereign rights for the purpose of exploring and exploiting, conserving and managing the natural resources, whether living or non-living, of the waters superjacent to the sea-bed and of the sea-bed and its subsoil, and with regard to other activities for the exonomic exploitation and exploration of the zone, such as the production of energy from the water, currents and winds;

---

vessel which required prior permission to enter China's EEZ. See Li Heng, 'What's US Vessel up to in Chinese Waters?', *People's Daily Online*, 30 September 2002, <http://english.people.com.cn/200209/29/eng20020929_104144.shtml> at 10 March 2005.

[71] The South Pacific Forum has already expressed concern over nuclear fuel shipments though its participating states' waters. See Pacific Islands Forum, 'Forum Concerned about Nuclear Waste Shipment' (Press Statement 1499, 2 March 1999).

[72] Attard, above n 5, 66.

(b) jurisdiction as provided for in the relevant provision of this Conventon with regard to:
   (i) the establishment and use of artificial islands, installations and structures;
   (ii) marine scientific research;
   (iii) the protection and preservation of the marine environment;
(c) other rights and duties provided for in this Convention.

From this it is apparent that coastal states have two types of right in the EEZ: sovereign rights which are directly resource related, and jurisdictional rights which are intimately concerned with the exploration, exploitation and protection of resources. The name EEZ is thus derived from its function which is to allow coastal states to explore, exploit and protect resources having *economic* value. It would not therefore seem legitimate for a coastal state to restrict navigational rights unless such rights interfered with its ability to explore, exploit or protect its resources. This delicate balance of rights and duties is alluded to in article 56(2) which provides that:

> In exercising its rights and performing its duties under this Convention in the [EEZ], the coastal State shall have due regard to the rights and duties of other States and shall act in a manner compatible with the provisions of this Convention.

In order to make explicit and further reinforce the balancing of rights and duties between coastal and other states in the EEZ, article 58 provides:

> 1. In the [EEZ] all States ... enjoy, subject to the relevant provisions of this Convention, the freedoms referred to in article 87 of navigation and overflight and of the laying of submarine cables and pipelines, and other internationally lawful uses of the sea related to these freedoms, such as those associated with the operation of ships, aircraft and submarine cables and pipelines, and compatible with the other provisions of the Convention.

The reference to article 87 is particularly crucial to the naval powers who regard it as guaranteeing their ability to conduct military manoeuvres in the EEZs of other states. It will be recalled that article 87, which is regarded as a codification of customary international law, provides that 'the high seas are open to all States' and further that it comprises, *inter alia*, 'freedom of navigation'. The arguable pre-eminence of freedom of navigation is also further underpinned by article 86 which provides that while the provision, which describes the extent of the high seas, does not apply to the EEZ, none the less, 'this article does not entail any abridgement of the freedoms enjoyed by all states in the [EEZ] in accordance with article 87'. As in article 56, however, the freedom of navigation on the high seas must be exercised 'with due regard for the interests of other states in their exercise of the freedom of the high seas'.[73]

---

[73] Art 87(2) UNCLOS.

Balancing rights in the EEZ

The balancing of coastal and non-coastal states' rights in the EEZ is a fertile area for potential dispute. As Song points out, the right of states to conduct military activities in the EEZ of other states was not greatly discussed at UNCLOS III.[74] Upon the signing of UNCLOS, however, Brazil, Cape Verde and Uruguay made declarations to the effect that the Convention did not permit other states to carry out naval manoeuvres or weapons tests in another state's EEZ without that state's prior permission.[75] These declarations elicited strong protest from both Italy[76] and, most pertinently, the USA which consistently maintains that all aspects of military operations on the high seas are preserved by the provisions of UNCLOS.[77] Thus the conduct of naval manoeuvres, weapons testing, the launching and landing of aircraft and other military devices, military surveys and the collecting of intelligence are all regarded as traditional uses of the high sea.

On the other hand, some coastal states such as China argue that the conduct of military activities in the EEZ has the potential to hamper resource exploitation. Say, for example, that the Royal Australian Navy wished to conduct military exercises in China's EEZ which conflicted with the activities of a Chinese fishing vessel. Which state would have the better right to engage in its chosen activity? The coastal state would doubtless assert the 'due regard' provision, especially since it has 'sovereign rights' over the exploitation of resources, while the naval power would most likely assert its high seas freedoms. There is probably no absolute solution to this conundrum since much will depend on the policy adopted by the states in question. The position of the maritime powers on this matter is well known as, equally, is the position of other states in the region, such as China. In general terms, however, the state practice of the South Pacific states on such matters is not clear. The experience of a number of these states in the era of nuclear testing might suggest that they would favour stronger controls over the naval activities of the maritime powers in their region. If this were to occur, then the maritime powers would find their room for manoeuvre much reduced.

Regulating military activities in the EEZ

It can hardly be said that the EEZ regime regarding military activities is satisfactory. In their efforts to secure agreement at UNCLOS III the negotiators have created considerable uncertainty and this uncertainty could easily lead to insecurity if this is not reduced by confidence and security building measures

[74] Yann-huei Song, 'The PRC's Peacetime Military Activities in Taiwan's EEZ: A Question of Legality' (2001) 16 *International Journal of Marine and Coastal Law* 625, 635.
[75] UN Division for Ocean Affairs and the Law of the Sea, *United Nations Convention on the Law of the Sea: Declarations Made upon Signature, Ratification, Accession or Succession or Anytime Thereafter*, <http://www.un.org/Depts/los/convention_agreements/convention_declarations.htm> at 10 March 2005.
[76] Ibid.
[77] Roach and Smith, above n 15, 409-14.

among regional states. This much has been foreseen by commentators such as Rose[78] and Boczek[79] who have both recognized the potential of the current regime to lead to international conflict. Where such conflict does arise, as in the *USS Dowdich* case referred to above, article 59 provides for a means of resolution between contesting states. This provides:

> In cases where this Convention does not attribute rights or jurisdiction to the coastal State or to other States within the [EEZ], and a conflict arises between the interests of the coastal State and any other State or States, the conflict should be resolved on the basis of equity and in the light of all the relevant circumstances, taking into account the respective importance of the interests involved to the parties as well as to the international community as a whole.

While article 59 might be regarded as supplementary to the obligation found in article 33 of the UN Charter which requires states to resolve their disputes in a peaceful manner, it is a clear obligation underpinned by the requirement of *pacta sunt servanda.*[80] Thus any action taken by regional states which would lead to a potential military conflict would have to be resolved by way of article 59. As Song indicated, the difficulty with the provision is that 'in the absence of compulsory judicial settlement of disputes concerning military activities in the EEZ, it is very difficult to render an authoritative legal interpretation whenever a dispute arises' and that these matters will only be resolved authoritatively when they are adjudicated by the International Court of Justice or the International Tribunal for the Law of the Sea.[81]

Transportation of hazardous materials through the EEZ

In addition to the disagreement over the extent of the navigational rights of military vessels in the EEZ, there is also potential disagreement over the transportation of hazardous materials through this zone. In the Asia Pacific this has been highlighted most recently by the protests elicited by the transportation of reprocessed nuclear waste from the United Kingdom and France to Japan. The voyages of the armed merchant vessels *Pacific Pintail* and *Pacific Teal* have caused concern on a number of levels.[82] There is some anxiety that in a post 9/11 world such vessels might become targets for terrorists, while for those with environmental concerns the possibility of catastrophic damage to the sea, its ecosystems and human kind which might be brought about by their sinking is a serious concern. Although the voyage details of the nuclear waste vessels is generally kept secret to frustrate those who

---

[78] Rose, above n 69.

[79] Boleslaw Adam Boczek, 'Peacetime Military Activities in the Exclusive Economic Zones of Third Countries' (1989) 19 *Ocean Development and International Law* 452.

[80] *Vienna Convention on the Law of Treaties*, opened for signature 23 May 1969, 1155 UNTS 331 (entered into force 27 January 1980) art 26.

[81] Song, above n 74, 637.

[82] Grant Hewison, 'Return Shipments of Nuclear Material from Europe to Japan' in Bateman, above n 17, 145.

might have designs on hijacking or seriously damaging them, the New Zealand government has requested that they not pass through New Zealand's EEZ.[83] Furthermore, in 2001 the New Zealand Green Party introduced a bill which would have extended the application of New Zealand's anti-nuclear legislation to its EEZ.[84] This would have had the effect of prohibiting vessels carrying nuclear waste from entering New Zealand's EEZ. The justification for this legislation advanced by the Green Party was that it would be consistent with New Zealand's jurisdictional rights to protect the maritime environment and ecosystems of the EEZ. The advice given to the New Zealand Government on this Bill was that it would be contrary to international law as an unjustifiable interference with freedom of navigation.[85] There is little doubt that if New Zealand had proceeded with this legislation it would have elicited protests from a number of maritime states including the UK, France, Japan and the USA contrary to international law.

The issue of whether or not restrictions can be placed on the transit through the EEZ of vessels carrying nuclear waste cannot be resolved simply by examining the current legal regime pertinent to that maritime area, but must be analysed in the light of the various international institutional arrangements which are in existence and which govern the transportation of irradiated materials. These include regulatory arrangements put in place by both the International Atomic Energy Agency (IAEA) and the International Maritime Organization (IMO).[86] Before examining these arrangements, however, it is necessary to consider the relevant provisions of UNCLOS which might have an effect upon the regional transportation of highly active reprocessed nuclear materials.

As noted in the discussion above, while article 56(1)(b)(iii) gives coastal states jurisdiction to protect and preserve the marine environment, this is balanced by article 58 which preserves the high seas right of freedom of navigation which is provided for in article 87. In both cases the rights of the coastal states and states seeking to exercise the right of freedom of navigation in the EEZ is balanced by the need for each to have due regard for the rights of the other. Again, the lack of clarity inherent in this arrangement allows both groups of states to argue on a continuum from absolute freedom of navigation to complete exclusion of vessels carrying certain cargos from the EEZ. Furthermore, in the event of a dispute over such matters, article 59 requires states to resolve their conflict 'on the basis of equity and in the light of all other circumstances, taking into account the respective

---

[83] Ibid 150-51.

[84] The relevant legislation is the *New Zealand Nuclear Free Zone, Disarmament, and Arms Control Act 1987*. The *New Zealand Nuclear Free Zone Extension Bill*, which received a second reading, was sent to the Select Committee on Foreign Affairs, Disarmament and Trade for consideration in 2001. It was returned to Parliament in 2002 and was rejected on 29 June 2002.

[85] For the Green Party's arguments that the Bill was consistent with international law see *New Zealand Nuclear Free Zone Extension Bill*, Parliamentary Network for Nuclear Disarmament, <http://wildrooster.com/~pnndorg/nz_nfz_ext_debate.htm> at 10 March 2005.

[86] See A Suzette V Suarez, 'Post-September 11 Security Challenges to the Legal Regime of the Maritime Carriage of Nuclear and Radioactive Materials' (2003) 18 *International Journal of Marine and Coastal Law* 423.

importance of the interests involved to the parties as well as to the international community as a whole'. Bearing in mind this imprecise legal framework, what arguments can be adduced that could justify limitations on the freedom of navigation of vessels carrying nuclear waste? It is suggested that the primary argument would be based on article 56(1)(b)(i) giving coastal states jurisdiction to protect and preserve the marine environment. Given both the predictable and unpredictable consequences of the introduction of toxic radioactive waste into the marine environment and hence the food chain, it might be argued that prudence dictates action which would prevent such occurrences. The counter-argument would be that the generation of nuclear power is a legitimate activity, as is the reprocessing and storing of spent irradiated fuel. Furthermore, the transportation of nuclear or other inherently dangerous or noxious substances is explicitly recognized by article 23 UNCLOS. Article 23 provides:

> Foreign nuclear-powered ships and ships carrying nuclear or other inherently dangerous or noxious substances shall, when exercising the right of innocent passage through the territorial sea, carry documents and observe special precautionary measures established for such ships by international agreements.

If therefore UNCLOS sanctions the transport of nuclear waste through the territorial sea subject only to certain formalities, then, *a fortiori*, the carrying of such materials through the EEZ where states have only jurisdictional rights and not sovereignty is clearly permissible, subject to similar special precautionary measures established by international agreements where these are in force. Indeed, the very existence of such international agreements governing these activities would tend to suggest that the transport of nuclear waste around the world is clearly envisaged as a lawful, and hence permissible, activity.

Both the IAEA and IMO working individually and in tandem have produced a series of arrangements designed to ensure the safe transportation of nuclear materials.[87] In 1961 the IAEA adopted a recommendatory instrument entitled the Regulations for the Safe Transport of Radioactive Materials. These Regulations were subsequently incorporated into the IMO's International Maritime Dangerous Goods (IMDG) Code which was finally made legally binding by its incorporation into the International Convention for the Safety of Life at Sea (SOLAS) in 2002. The IMDG Code is subject to biannual revision and lays down standards for, among other things, documentation, containment standards, stowage and dealing with contamination. Under SOLAS the IMO also determines the appropriate seaworthiness standards for vessels. In the case of vessels carrying radioactive materials Chapter VII of SOLAS incorporates the Irradiated Nuclear Fuel (INF) Code devised by the IAEA. This code determines the protection standards, including the specifications of containment, for all vessels carrying irradiated material, including highly active waste. While there has been some criticism of the

[87] The IAEA and IMO have worked together on these issues since 10 April 1962 when they signed a Cooperation Agreement. See *Cooperation Agreement between IAEA and IMO*, 10 April 1962, IAEA/INFCIRC/20/Add.1.

IAEA/IMO standards,[88] it is none the less apparent that the regulatory framework for the carriage of irradiated materials is an accepted aspect of international maritime commerce. While it might be desirable in the interests of prudence to prohibit the worldwide transport of highly active nuclear waste, it would seem that international law has not yet reached this stage and that in the absence of such a prohibition it is not possible to argue that states have jurisdiction to exclude vessels carrying such waste from their EEZs.

Piracy, armed robbery at sea, maritime terrorism and maritime interdiction of weapons of mass destruction

As noted above, various forms of maritime violence also have the capacity to interfere with freedom of navigation by affecting the security of SLOC. While piracy, and more particularly armed robbery at sea, have been the bane of seafarers and ship and cargo owners in the region for many years, particularly in the waters around Indonesia and the Philippines, in more recent years terrorist activities have become a real threat to navigational security. Furthermore, in the post-9/11 world in which the transport by sea of weapons of mass destruction (WMD), their precursors and delivery systems by non-state actors has become a matter of concern, the US sponsored Proliferation Security Initiative (PSI) has introduced a further mechanism for interfering with navigational freedom.

The nature of the maritime environment in Asia Pacific creates particular challenges for coastal states in the prevention and control of violence at sea. Among the particular factors which make it difficult for regional navies and maritime law enforcement agencies to combat the various species of maritime violence are the archipelagic nature of many of the region's states; the close geographical proximity of many states in Southeast Asia; the large ocean spaces of the South Pacific; territorial and boundary disputes leading to a lack of certainty in jurisdiction; the lack of confidence in political relations between a number of regional states; the absolute or relative poverty of maritime policing resources in certain states, particularly in the South Pacific; and the lack of political will or capacity in some regional states. Taken as a whole, these factors contribute to an exceedingly complex matrix which has to be managed through a combination of unilateral, bilateral and multilateral measures.

Piracy

There is very little true piracy in the modern world since most acts which are described as piracy are, in fact, simply criminal acts within the ports, harbours, internal waters or territorial seas of states.[89] As such, these acts fall squarely within the jurisdiction of the coastal state. The main problems here tend not to be those of

[88] See Hewison, above n 82, 156-61.

[89] Scott Davidson, 'Dangerous Waters: Combating Maritime Piracy in Asia' (2000) 9 *Asian Yearbook of International Law* 3.

legal uncertainty, but of detection and apprehension. Very often, those who commit crimes in the coastal waters of regional states are able to flee and hide among the many islands or flee to the coastal waters of neighbouring states, raising the same sorts of problems created by fugitive offenders on land.

Traditional piracy or piracy *jure gentium* is defined by article 101 of UNCLOS as:

> (a) Any illegal acts of violence or detention, or any act of depredation, committed for private ends by the crew or the passengers of a private ship or a private aircraft, and directed:
> (i) on the high seas, against another ship or aircraft, or against persons or property on board such ship or aircraft;
> (ii) against a ship, aircraft, person or property in a place outside the jurisdiction of any State;
> (b) any act of voluntary participation in the operation of a ship or of an aircraft with knowledge of facts making it a pirate ship or aircraft;
> (c) any act of inciting or of intentionally facilitating an act described in subparagraph (a) or (b).

It is noticeable that the definition of piracy in UNCLOS is restrictive as to both the types of act and the *locus* in which those acts take place. The essential requirements of piracy under international law, as opposed to any behaviour which might be classified as such under the domestic law of various states,[90] are that there must be acts of violence, detention or depredation; those acts must be illegal; they must be undertaken for private ends; they must be done by the crew or passengers of a private ship or aircraft; they must be committed on the high seas or in a place outside the jurisdiction of any State; and they must be directed against another ship or aircraft, or persons or property on board a ship or aircraft.

Without analysing each of these requirements in detail, it is apparent that piracy must take place beyond the jurisdiction of states on the high seas, including the EEZ,[91] or on *terra nullius* that is, territory which is not subject to the sovereignty of any state.[92] Furthermore, the relevant illegal acts must be committed by private individuals for private ends.[93] The 'two vessel' requirement also means that a ship upon which a mutiny takes place or which is hijacked by members of the crew or passengers will not be piracy under article 101 of UNCLOS. These two factors appear to have been relevant in the case of the *Santa Maria* where a Portuguese cruise ship was reported to have been captured by pirates in the

---

[90] The laws of a number of states have definitions of piracy which include activities taking place within their coastal waters. These definitions are for the purposes of domestic law alone and do not affect the definition of piracy at international law. See Barry H Dubner, *The Law of International Sea Piracy* (1980).

[91] By virtue of art 58(2) UNCLOS.

[92] Whether this refers to a question of contested and unresolved sovereignty such as the case of the Spratly Islands is a moot point. See Davidson, 'Dangerous Waters', above n 89, 15-17.

[93] On the problems associated with this see Samuel Pyeatt Menefee, 'The Case of the Castle John, or Greenbeard the Pirate?: Environmentalism, Piracy and the Development of International Law' (1993) 24 *California Western International Law Journal* 2.

Caribbean.[94] The Portuguese government issued a request for assistance from the British, Dutch and US navies which began searching for the vessel. Upon further investigation by the State Department, however, it was found that the *Santa Maria* had been boarded by a Captain Henrique Galvao while the ship was in port and had been hijacked on the high seas by Galvao and his men to make a political point prior to elections which were to be held in Portugal. In consequence of this, it was clear that the action was not piracy since it had not been undertaken for private ends, and the US refused to intervene further.[95] In the *Castle John* case,[96] however, certain action by Greenpeace to prevent alleged environmental damage by the dumping of titanium dioxide in the North Sea was held by the Belgian *Cour de Cassation* to be piracy within the meaning of article 15 of the Geneva Convention on the High Seas, since, despite the political colour of the acts in question, they were done for 'personal ends'.

It was also the absence of the two vessel requirement and possibly the existence of a political motivation which prevented the hijacking of the Italian-registered cruise ship *Achille Lauro* in the Mediterranean and the killing of the American hostage, Leon Klinghoffer, by Palestininan terrorists from being classified as piracy *jure gentium.*[97] The four hijackers were eventually apprehended, tried by the Italian courts and convicted of murder. Although the US issued warrants for their arrest on the grounds, *inter alia*, of piracy under 18 USC subsection 1651, it is clear that their actions did not constitute piracy under international law. The hijackers' actions were politically motivated and there was no satisfaction of the two vessel/aircraft requirement. The response of the international community to the lacuna in international law exposed by the *Achille Lauro* affair was to negotiate and adopt the Convention for the Suppression of Unlawful Acts Against the Safety of Navigation 1988 (SUA).[98]

---

[94] Whiteman, *Digest of United States Practice in International Law* (1983), vol 4, 665-7; Dubner, above n 90, 146-9 and Leslie C Green, 'The Santa Maria: Rebels or Pirates?' (1961) 37 *British Yearbook of International Law* 496.

[95] It can also be observed that this incident did not satisfy the 'two vessel' requirement of art 15 of the *Geneva Convention on the High Seas 1958*, opened for signature 29 April 1958, 450 UNTS 11 (entered into force 30 September 1962), whose terms were incorporated without amendment as art 100 UNCLOS. Galvao and his insurgents eventually put into the Brazilian port of Recife and were granted political asylum.

[96] *Castle John and Nederlandse Stichting Sirius v NV Marjlo and NV Parfin* (1986) 77 *International Law Reports* 537.

[97] David Freestone, 'The Convention for the Suppression of Unlawful Acts Against the Safety of Navigation' (1988) 3 *International Journal of Estuarine and Coastal Law* 305; Malvina Halberstam, 'Terrorism on the High Sea: The Achille Lauro, Piracy and the IMO Convention on Maritime Safety' (1988) 82 *American Journal of International Law* 269.

[98] Opened for signature 10 March 1988, 1678 UNTS 222 (entered into force 1 March 1992) ('SUA'); also known as the 'Rome Convention'. On SUA see below.

Armed robbery against ships

As noted above, most acts which are referred to colloquially as piracy are simply crimes under the domestic law of the states in whose coastal waters they take place. A review of most acts of 'piracy' reported to the Piracy Reporting Centre of the International Maritime Bureau (IMB) or to the IMO fall within this category.[99] The IMO makes clear the distinction between piracy proper and armed robbery against ships in its *Draft Code of Practice for the Investigation of Crimes of Piracy and Armed Robbery against Ships.*[100] Under the Code of Practice, 'piracy means unlawful acts as defined by article 101 (UNCLOS)'[101] while 'armed robbery against ships' means:[102]

> Any unlawful act of violence or detention or any act of depredation, or threat thereof, other than an act of 'piracy', directed against a ship or against persons or property on board such ship, within a State's jurisdiction over such offences.

It will be noted that while this definition bears similarity to the definition of piracy in article 101, it omits the two vessel requirement and says nothing about the private motive of such unlawful acts. The main requirement is that the acts be unlawful, presumably under the law of the coastal state. The IMB definition does not make a distinction between piracy and armed robbery, but since it is for statistical purposes alone, this has little significance from a legal point of view.[103] It is interesting, however, that the IMB definition of piracy and armed robbery includes inchoate crimes, as well as those crimes which have been consummated. The definition provides that piracy and armed robbery is:[104]

> An act of boarding or attempting to board any ship with the intent to commit theft or any other crime and with the intent or capability to use force in furtherance of that act.

It will be noted that the *locus* of the offence appears to be irrelevant under the IMB definition, and this is confirmed by a perusal of the many incidents contained in that organization's annual reports.

Both the IMO and IMB definitions are also capable of comprehending crimes which extend beyond the notions of theft or armed robbery. In its 2001 report the IMB noted that a new trend in 'piracy' had emerged in the northern parts of the Malacca Straits in the waters off the Indonesian province of Aceh, where pirates had started to kidnap the crew members of ships for the purposes of holding

---

[99] The IMB is a branch of the International Chamber of Commerce which established its Piracy Reporting Centre in Kuala Lumpur in 1992 in response to the increasing number of armed attacks against ships and their crews. International Chamber of Commerce Commercial Crime Services, *IMB Piracy Reporting Centre* <www.icc-ccs.org/prc/overview.php> at 18 March 2005.

[100] MSC/Circ.984, 20 December 2000.

[101] Ibid [2.1].

[102] Ibid [2.2].

[103] *IMB Report 2001* (2001) 3.

[104] Ibid.

them for ransom.[105] As the IMB report observed, this trend was previously confined to Somali waters, but in the context of kidnap and ransom off Aceh, it seems that a political element was involved with the Free Aceh Movement being held responsible for these activities by the Indonesian Government.[106] Given the existence of such a political element, it seems that kidnap and ransom to finance secessionist activities could very well fall into the next category of violent activity at sea: terrorism.

Terrorism

States have argued for decades about the legal meaning of terrorism and the need for a comprehensive instrument to deal with the issue.[107] As yet, however, there is no international legal instrument which provides a comprehensive definition of terrorism. There are a number of instruments which clearly deal with the phenomenon or aspects of it, but they singularly fail to define it.[108] The United Nations General Assembly has, however, indicated what it believes the nature of terrorism to be in a number of resolutions. In General Assembly Resolution 51/210 which is entitled *Measures to Eliminate International Terrorism* it stated that it:

> 1. Strongly condemns all acts, methods, and practices of terrorism as criminal and unjustifiable, wherever and by whomsoever committed;
> 2. Reiterates that criminal acts intended or calculated to provoke a state of terror in the general public, a group of persons or particular persons for political purposes are in any circumstance unjustifiable, whatever the considerations of a political, philosophical, ideological, racial, ethnic, religious or other nature that may be invoked to justify them.[109]

In short, it might be said that terrorism, in a colloquial sense, is politically motivated violence which is perpetrated against both military and civilian targets by non-state actors. Whatever the motivation for terrorism, it is clear that the use of violence will constitute a crime under the criminal law of all states.

While maritime terrorism remains relatively insignificant in comparison to piracy and armed robbery against ships in the Asia Pacific region, analysts agree that it is a phenomenon which is likely to become increasingly common as terrorist groups realize the potential for exerting pressure on target states which this form of

---

[105] Ibid 17.

[106] Ibid.

[107] Laqueur states that between 1936 and 1981 no less than 109 different definitions of terrorism were advanced in a variety of forums. See Walter Laqueur, 'Reflections on Terrorism' (1986) 65 *Foreign Affairs* 86. See also the chapter by Alex Conte in this volume.

[108] See the conventions discussed in the chapter by Alex Conte at footnotes 58-69 and accompanying text.

[109] GA Res 51/210 (1996).

terrorism will afford them.[110] The Sri Lankan Tamil Tigers and Filipino Abu Sayyef secessionists have undertaken a number of maritime terrorist attacks and have engaged in piratical activity to fund their operations.[111] The Al Quaeda network also signalled its terrorist intentions with an attack upon the *USS Cole* in Yemen in 2000.[112] The chaos which maritime terrorism could create should not be underestimated. Not only could it cause a significant loss of life, but it could also threaten important SLOC and cause massive environmental damage, particularly in the multiplicity of narrow straits in the South East Asia region or the sensitive ecosystems of the South Pacific.[113] If a very large oil tanker of 250,000 tonnes or greater were sunk in the Malacca Straits, for example, the major oil route to the Far East would be blocked and significant global economic and security consequences would ensue. The Free Aceh Movement (GAM), which is seeking autonomy from Indonesia, has indicated in the past that it would be prepared to disrupt shipping in the Malacca Straits in order to further its cause.[114]

It was, in fact, an earlier terrorist incident which gave rise to the drafting and adoption in 1988 of possibly the most important legal instrument designed to fight criminal activity at sea, regardless of location. Following the hijacking of the *Achille Lauro* in 1985 the IMO sponsored Convention for the Suppression of Unlawful Acts Against the Safety of Maritime Navigation and its associated Protocol for the Suppression of Unlawful Acts Against the Safety of Fixed Platforms Located on the Continental Shelf was adopted.[115] The main purpose of this Convention is to deal with the jurisdictional issues arising from criminal offences perpetrated on vessels and their personnel and to facilitate the prosecution or extradition of offenders involved in such offences.

Although SUA was adopted under the auspices of the IMO largely to deal with the threat of terrorism against ships, the convention has considerably wider scope than this and covers a range of criminal activity, including armed robbery and piracy, directed at ships and fixed continental shelf platforms. Under article 3

---

[110] For a recent response to this assumption see the Council for Security Cooperation in the Asia-Pacific Maritime Cooperation Working Group, *Statement Against Maritime Terrorism* (19 February 2002, Seoul, Republic of Korea).

[111] William Joseph Ackerman, 'Transnational Crime and Terrorism and its Effects on the Maritime Industry' (2003) 13 *Port Technology International* 223; Rohan Gunaratna, 'Trends in Maritime Terrorism – The Sri Lankan case', *Lanka OutLook*, Autumn 1998, Spotlight on Sri Lanka <http://www.is.lk/is/spot/sp0316/clip8.html> at 10 March 2005.

[112] For an account of the facts and US responses see Raphaeil Perle and Ronald O'Rourke, *CRS Report to Congress: Terrorist Attack on USS Cole*, 30 January 2001, Findlaw <http://news.findlaw.com/cnn/docs/crs/coleterrattck13001.pdf> at 10 March 2005.

[113] See Stanley B Weeks, 'Sea Lines of Communication (SLOC) Security and Access' (Policy Paper 33, University of California Institute on Global Conflict and Cooperation, 1998).

[114] 'Gam says it controls ship lanes', *Nation*, 4 September 2001. On 25 August 2001, the coal transporter *Ocean Silver* was hijacked by members of GAM who were armed with guns and grenade launchers. The hijackers released six crew members, but held another six hostage and demanded a ransom for their release. *IMB Report 2001*, above n 103, 36.

[115] For documents detailing the *Achille Lauro* incident see (1985) 24 *International Legal Materials* 1509. See also Freestone and Halberstam, above n 97.

SUA specifies as offences a number of acts against shipping, including the seizure or destruction of ships and the endangering of safe navigation by the use of violence against any person on a ship or by damaging a ship, its cargo or equipment, including its navigational facilities. States are required to make the offences identified by the convention punishable under their laws[116] and establish jurisdiction over offences committed on or against their ships or in their territory or by their nationals.[117] States may also assert jurisdiction over offences committed by stateless persons habitually resident within their territory, offences where their nationals are victims and offences aimed at compelling a state to do or abstain from doing some act.[118] The offences identified in the Convention are deemed to be included as extraditable offences in extradition treaties between states parties,[119] and a state party in whose territory an alleged offender is found is either obliged to extradite him to a requesting state party or to prosecute him.[120] In order to ensure that this latter is possible, states parties are required to ensure that the appropriate jurisdictional arrangements are in place to allow prosecution to take place.[121]

One of the noticeable features of SUA is its territorial application. By article 4 the convention applies to ships which are navigating, scheduled to navigate into, through or from waters beyond the outer limit of the territorial sea of a single state or the lateral limits of its territorial sea with adjacent states. This means that an offence committed in contemplation of a vessel making an international voyage, or in the course of making an international voyage beyond the territorial sea of the state will be subject to the jurisdiction of any of the convention states into whose hands the perpetrator of an offence might fall. A problem with which SUA does not grapple, however, is that of whether an individual might still claim the political offence exception in cases of politically motivated terrorism. The convention is silent on this matter, so it must be assumed that this remains a distinct possibility and could be used to undermine the effectiveness of the instrument.[122]

While it is recognized that there is a broad array of practical issues affecting the control of violence at sea, none the less, the existence of a soundly based and

---

[116] Art 5 SUA.

[117] Art 6(1) SUA.

[118] Art 6(2) SUA.

[119] Art 11 SUA.

[120] Art 10 SUA.

[121] Art 6(4) SUA.

[122] A diplomatic conference is to be held under the auspices of the IMO in 2005 to adopt changes made to SUA and *Protocol for the Suppression of Unlawful Acts Against the Safety of Fixed Platforms Located on the Continental Shelf*, opened for signature 10 March 1988, 1678 UNTS 304 (entered into force 1 March 1992) ('SUAPROT') to make them more responsive in dealing with maritime terrorism. A range of new offences is likely to be added to art 3 and art 8 will provide for the boarding of vessels suspected of being involved in terrorist activities. See the *Report of the Legal Committee (LEG)*, 89th session, 25–29 October 2004, IMO <http://www.imo.org/Newsroom/mainframe.asp?topic_id=280&doc_id=3662> at 22 November 2004.

predictable legal framework for combating such violence is a prerequisite for effective action. A sound legal basis for taking measures against armed robbers, pirates and terrorists might also be seen as a confidence building measure since it must be underpinned by strong levels of cooperation. Indeed, cooperation is central to the provisions of UNCLOS on piracy where all states are duty bound to cooperate in the suppression of piracy,[123] and in SUA where cooperation is identified as a primary means of preventing violence against ships and their personnel. Article 12 of SUA states that states parties must afford each other the greatest measure of assistance in connection with criminal proceedings brought in respect of the convention offences in article 3. Article 13 of SUA further provides:

> 1. States Parties shall cooperate in the prevention of the offences set forth in Article 3, particularly by:
> (a) taking all practicable measures to prevent preparations in their respective territories for the commission of those offences within or outside their territories;
> (b) exchanging information in accordance with their national law, and co-ordinating administrative and other measures taken as appropriate to prevent the commission of offences set forth in Article 3.

While SUA is potentially one of the most potent weapons in the legal armoury of states, it has not attracted a significant number of ratifications from states in the Asia Pacific region, despite calls upon these states to do so from the UN and the shipping industry.[124] As the UN Secretary-General has noted in his 1998 Report on Oceans and the Law of the Sea, SUA 'provides another more useful vehicle for prosecution than the nineteenth century piracy statutes'.[125] More recently, the UN General Assembly has urged states to ratify SUA to help combat violence at sea. In Resolution 56/12 entitled *Oceans and Law of the Sea*[126] the General Assembly urged states to become parties to SUA and SUAPROT and to ensure its effective implementation through the adoption of legislation aimed at ensuring that there is a proper framework for responses to incidents of armed robbery at sea.

At the industry level, the Safe Navigation and Environment Committee (SNEC) of the Asian Shipowners Forum at its meeting in November 2001 observed:

---

[123] Art 100 UNCLOS.

[124] IMO, *Summary of Status of Conventions as at 30 October 2004* <http://www.imo.org/HOME.html> at 22 November 2004. For details of ratifications see IMO, *Status of Complete Listings of Conventions* <http://www.imo.org/includes/blastDataOnly.asp/data_id%3D10614/status.xls> at 22 November 2004. The Convention entered into force 1 March 1992. States in the Asia Pacific region which are parties to SUA and SUAPROT are Australia, China, India, Japan, Marshall Islands, New Zealand, Russian Federation, Samoa, Tonga, USA, Vietnam and Vanuatu.

[125] UN Doc A/53/456 (1998) [151].

[126] UN Doc A/RES/56/12 (2001).

> Following the recent terrorists attacks on the United States, the SNEC expressed concerns that cargo ships could become easy targets of pirates or hijackers who may be linked to terrorist groups. In this respect, the SNEC was of the view that governments should be encouraged to ratify the 1988 Convention for the Suppression of Unlawful Acts Against the Safety of Maritime Navigation (Rome Convention as it is commonly called) and to implement its provisions in their national legislation as soon as possible. The Convention should provide a very useful tool for governments to combat acts of piracy and armed robbery against ships.[127]

In the light of these calls to ratify SUA, it would seem that a concerted effort to secure ratification and implementation of SUA in Asia Pacific would be a significant step forward in combating violence at sea in the region.

IMO recommendations

In June 1999 the Maritime Safety Committee of the IMO issued a circular entitled *Recommendations to Governments for preventing and suppressing piracy and armed robbery against ships*,[128] in which the IMO suggested that states should develop action plans for dealing with piracy, as well as establishing the necessary infrastructure and operational arrangements for the purposes of preventing and suppressing piracy and armed robbery against ships.[129] On the question of jurisdiction, the IMO recommended that states take such measures as may be necessary to establish their jurisdiction over the offences of piracy and armed robbery at sea, including adjustment of their legislation to enable them to apprehend and prosecute persons committing such offences.[130] While the IMO did not recommend ratification of SUA, none the less, this would go a long way to meeting the issues raised in its *Recommendations*. As a further adjunct to the assumption of state jurisdiction over the offences of piracy and armed robbery against ships, however, the IMO stated that a person apprehended outside the territorial sea of any state for committing these crimes should be prosecuted under the laws of the investigating state by mutual agreement with other substantially interested states, including the flag state or states within whose jurisdiction an offence occurs.[131] While the potential expansion of the jurisdictional bases which

---

[127] Press Release, 2 November 2001.

[128] MSC/Circ.622/Rev.1 (1999).

[129] Ibid [4]. At an international conference involving fifteen regional States which took place in Tokyo in March 2000 the IMO and a number of ship-owners and their associations issued the *Tokyo Declaration* and a *Model Action Plan* which closely follows the IMO *Recommendations*. These relate primarily to reporting structures and the development of effective communications between the various law enforcement agencies of regional States. The conference *communiqué* noted, however, that anti-piracy activities 'including potential cooperation can only be done subject to relevant international treaties, each Participating Administration's domestic legislation as well as its availability of adequate resources to sustain these activities'.

[130] Above n 128, [17].

[131] Ibid [16].

the IMO has recommended is welcome, the history of the ratification of SUA does not suggest that rapid implementation is likely to occur.

A further initiative suggested by IMO is the adoption of a *Regional Agreement on Cooperation in Preventing and Suppressing Acts of Piracy and Armed Robbery against Ships.*[132] The agreement, which remains in draft form, stresses the need for international cooperation in suppressing piracy and armed robbery at sea. While it reiterates the right and obligation of states to take measures to suppress piracy and armed robbery in its own waters, it none the less also recognizes that jurisdictional boundaries inhibit effective action against fugitive offenders. The draft regional agreement therefore sets out a process for cooperation which would allow the vessels of one state to pursue offenders into the national waters of another state. Such pursuit would only be permitted where a law enforcement liaison officer is embarked on the law enforcement vessel of the other state and gives his or her permission for pursuit into national waters.[133] This form of devolved state authorization which would allow a foreign state to engage in law enforcement activities appears to be some way from becoming a reality, but it does not preclude other forms of bilateral cooperation in the interim.

The Proliferation Security Initiative

In the post 9/11 period one of the policies that has been developed which is likely to have a significant impact on freedom of navigation is the Proliferation Security Initiative (PSI). This policy, which was announced by US President George W Bush in Poland on 31 May 2003 represents an attempt to stop trafficking in weapons of mass destruction (WMD). The policy permits national authorities of reciprocating states to stop and search ships and aircraft carrying suspect cargo and to seize illegal weapons or missile technologies. In essence, the fifteen states[134] who are now participants in the PSI commit themselves to board suspicious vessels flying their own flags; to consent to the boarding and search of their vessels by other states who are members of the PSI; to stop and search suspicious vessels in their territorial seas and their contiguous zones; to require suspicious aircraft in their airspace to land for inspection; to carry out rigorous inspections at their ports and airfields and not to transport WMD to or from states of concern. The PSI is not a legal instrument, but rather an understanding among the fifteen participating states that by acting in this reciprocal way they are simply applying existing rules of international law. As Byers says, '... much of the PSI involves nothing more than the consistent and rigorous application of existing rights under national and international law'.[135] Despite this observation, however, it should be noted that the

[132] Ibid, Appendix 5.
[133] Ibid, art 5.
[134] Australia, Canada, France, Germany, Italy, Japan, the Netherlands, Norway, Poland, Portugal, Russia, Singapore, Spain, the UK and the US.
[135] Michael Byers, 'Policing the High Seas: The Proliferation Security Initiative' (2004) 98 *American Journal of International Law* 526, 528.

US has signed a bilateral agreement with Liberia in which both states grant each other reciprocal rights to board suspect vessels flying their respective flags on the high seas. Because this agreement applies to all areas of high seas, its potential sphere of application is considerable. Liberia is second only to Panama in terms of tonnage under its flag, so this brings a considerable amount of shipping within the purview of the agreement. If the US were to reach similar agreements with other flag of convenience states, it would have search rights to nearly ninety five per cent of world shipping. While in terms of most of the PSI members this would be underpinned by a degree of reciprocity, in terms of Liberia and Panama, which do not have navies, the right of stop and search on the high seas is likely to consist of one-way traffic.

Conclusion

The nature of the maritime environment and the geopolitical realities of Asia Pacific make it a crucible for the development of the law of the sea. The pressures created by the lack of precision in the drafting of UNCLOS are more likely to be tested to their limit in this region than in any other part of the world. In addition to this the regional incidence maritime violence (piracy, armed robbery at sea and terrorism) and the respective counter-measures designed to deal with it add a new dimension to limitations on freedom of navigation and the security of maritime trade. While attempts have been and continue to be made to resolve some of the more pressing issues through a variety of mechanisms, it is apparent that the tensions between the perceived need of certain coastal states to extend their jurisdictional competences ever further seaward and the resistance by the maritime powers to the extension of coastal state power create a climate of uncertainty and insecurity. Although it can be argued that the claim and counter-claim of coastal states and maritime powers by way of testing the acceptability or otherwise of their demands is simply part of the usual international intercourse which results in the organic development of the law, none the less it would be short-sighted to fail to recognize that not taking action to resolve these issues in a more structured way could result in conflict. As the tenth anniversary of the entry into force of UNCLOS looms, it becomes even more apparent that the Convention was not an end in itself, but only a beginning. There is still much work to be done if the law of the sea is to be a suitable vehicle not only for maintaining freedom of navigation but for building security and confidence in the maritime areas of the Asia Pacific region.

Chapter 5

Climate Change in Oceania: Responses to the Kyoto Protocol

Geoff Leane

Introduction

Climate change issues are of great importance in the Pacific region given the particular vulnerability of its small island developing states. They are in an invidious position having not experienced the development cycle of industrialized states that is the motivating force behind greenhouse gas emissions, yet are among the most vulnerable likely victims of global warming due to their particular geographies and fragile economies. They are juxtaposed with two industrialized states – Australia and New Zealand – whose responses to the challenge of climate change might generously be described as ambiguous. The region is really a microcosm of the international order in this at least, and the Kyoto Protocol assumes great symbolic as well as practical importance as its aspirations and limitations are magnified by the peculiarities of the region and its disparate actors.

This chapter will first give a broad outline of the structure, status and limitations of the Kyoto Protocol to the United Nations Framework Convention on Climate Change (UNFCCC).[1] The discussion will then move to a review of policy responses in the region, concentrating on Pacific Forum states of the South Pacific and in particular Australia and New Zealand, the two industrialized states in the region.

The Kyoto Protocol

Background

An international response to climate change concerns began with the establishment of an Intergovernmental Panel on Climate Change (IPCC) in 1988 as a joint initiative of the World Meteorological Organization and the United Nations

[1] *United Nations Framework Convention on Climate Change*, opened for signature 9 May 1992, 1771 UNTS 107 (entered into force 21 March 1994) ('UNFCCC'); *Kyoto Protocol to the United Nations Framework Convention on Climate Change*, opened for signature 11 December 1997, (1998) 37 ILM 22 (entered into force 16 February 2005) ('Kyoto Protocol').

Environment Program. It warned of possible threats and the need for an institutional response, which in 1992 took the form of the UNFCCC at the Rio 'Earth Summit'.[2] The Convention was signed by 155 states, and was the first international environmental agreement to be negotiated by almost all of the international community. The ambition of the Convention (article 2) was to stabilize so-called greenhouse gases (GHGs) 'at a level that would prevent dangerous anthropogenic interference with the climate system'. This objective was further articulated in five principles (article 3), including those of intergenerational equity, the precautionary principle and the need to take account of the special circumstances of developing countries through an emerging principle of 'common but differentiated responsibility' in international environmental law. States made commitments to mitigate climate change (article 4) but the means of implementation were left substantially to states' discretion, though they might include not only abatement of emissions but also enhancement of greenhouse 'sinks' (human-induced land-use change and forestry activities) and possible trading in emission reduction units.

The Kyoto Protocol to the UNFCCC allows parties to choose their preferred mix of regulation through 'command and control' measures and economic instruments which lean toward market-based responses. The former tend to be more democratic, transparent and enabling of accountability, though often expensive and inefficient. They may also be less encouraging of innovation compared to economic instruments, which tend to foster technological development as emitters try to reduce compliance costs. Economic instruments may in theory at least be more flexible, and although public participation is limited in the formative stages it may come into play later as consumers exercise product choices. In New Zealand, for example, economic instruments include carbon charges and the creation of a market in tradable emission permits. It should be noted, however, that the so-called economic instruments are still, at least in their formative stages, regulatory creations of government and may continue to require a regulatory and administrative support framework. Whilst economic instruments may be more cost effective it is not always possible to demonstrate this.[3]

In light of the relative resources available to different states and their incommensurate contributions to present elevated levels of GHGs, parties were assigned different levels of commitments in pursuit of the goals of the Convention 'in accordance with their common but differentiated responsibilities and respective

---

[2] For a more comprehensive history see Daniel Bodansky, 'The History of the Global Climate Change Regime' in Urs Luterbacher and Detlef Sprinz (eds), *International Relations and Global Climate Change* (2001) 23, 40. The threats included an increase in global mean surface temperatures of 1.4-5.8 degrees Centigrade, rising sea levels (9-88 cm by 2100), flooding of low-lying coastal areas, changing rainfall patterns resulting in floods and droughts, and a more variable climate generally with increased threats of extreme weather events: UNFCCC, *A Guide to the Climate Change Convention and its Kyoto Protocol* (2002) 5.

[3] See, e.g. Klaus Bosselmann, Jenny Fuller and Jim Salinger, *Climate Change in New Zealand: Scientific and Legal Assessments* (2002) 79: a 1994 OECD survey indicated that in 90 per cent of cases validating data on the incentive impacts of economic instruments was inconclusive or unavailable.

capabilities' (article 3(1) of the UNFCCC). In particular, developed (OECD) states and those with economies 'in transition' (EITs) – for example, Hungary, Bulgaria, Belarus, the Czech Republic and the Russian Federation – were grouped in Annex I to the Convention. Those states were originally required to reduce their GHG emissions[4] to 1990 levels by the year 2000, though in fact over the 1990s the OECD states from Annex I actually increased emissions by 6.6 per cent whilst emissions from the EITs declined by more than 40 per cent.[5] OECD states from Annex I are also listed in Annex II, and thereby assigned responsibility for providing financial resources (via the UN Global Environment Facility) to assist developing states and for providing environmentally friendly technologies to both developing states and EITs.

The original framework was to be developed in annual Conferences of the Parties (COPs), the supreme decision-making body of the Convention, beginning in 1995. COP-1 produced the 'Berlin Mandate' to pursue more ambitious commitments via some new legal instrument, eventually realized in the Kyoto Protocol at COP-3 in December 1997. Although the scientific evidence for global warming is still controversial, the context for an institutional response includes the IPCC findings in 2001 that confirm 'an increasing body of observations giv[ing] a collective picture of a warming world' with 'new and stronger evidence that most of the warming observed over the last 50 years is attributable to human activities'.[6]

Not only did the Kyoto Protocol demand stronger measures on GHG emissions but it also established some innovative mechanisms by which goals might be realized. With respect to emissions, most developed states must reduce their emissions, in varying degrees below 1990 levels, over a five year average in the 'first commitment period' 2008–2012. The collective commitment of the developed states is to a reduction of at least five percent below 1990 levels, although much greater reductions are expected to be necessary in the future. As to mechanisms for achieving their targets, states have a range of policy instruments available to them. Conventional methods might include, for example, carbon taxes, energy efficiency measures and modified agricultural practices. More innovative and largely market-oriented measures were included at the behest of the so-called 'umbrella group' of countries,[7] namely the so-called 'JUSCANZ' group comprising Japan, the United States, Canada, Australia and New Zealand plus Russia and Norway. Among such measures were the inclusion of GHGs other than carbon dioxide, reductions achieved through clean technology investment in developing countries, establishment of an emissions trading market for the purchase of 'credits' from states which have reduced emissions by more than their stipulated target, and carbon credits for contributions to carbon 'sinks', usually by growing

---

[4] For six stipulated gases: carbon dioxide, methane, nitrous oxide, hydrofluorocarbons, perfluoroarbons, sulphur hexafluoride.

[5] UNFCCC, *Guide to the Climate Change Convention*, above n 2, 11.

[6] *Third Assessment Report of the IPCC*, quoted in UNFCCC, Guide to the Climate Change Convention, above n 2, 5.

[7] See, e.g. Frank Loy, 'On a collision course? Two potential environmental conflicts between the U.S. and Canada' (2002) 28 Canada-United States Law Journal 11.

trees. Carbon sinks are based on the theory that the process of photosynthesis sequesters atmospheric carbon and stores it in living tissue. The importance of these carbon sinks is attested to by the claim that global deforestation between 1850 and 1990 accounts for one third or more of carbon dioxide emissions – reforestation can substantially redress that loss.[8] Ironically, having successfully lobbied for the inclusion of these mechanisms two of the most GHG-intensive states, the United States (which originally agreed to a 7 per cent reduction on 1990 levels) and Australia (one of the few states which negotiated an actual increase – of 8 per cent – on 1990 levels), declined to ratify the Protocol (see discussion below).

Joint Implementation (JI) is another market-oriented policy option whereby a government or private entity in an Annex I state invests in an emission-reducing project in another Annex I state, claiming credit for the resulting 'emission reduction units' against its own target. Its most obvious application would be in EIT states where there is more likely to be scope for low cost abatement projects. With respect to developed states implementing such projects in less-developed states provision is made for a 'Clean Development Mechanism' (CDM) which again allows the Annex I state to use the 'certified emission reductions' to help meet its own targets. It was agreed at COP-6 in Bonn that CDMs may include afforestation and reforestation projects, though an Annex I country may only claim an amount equal to one percent of its base year emissions. In effect the implementing country is utilizing comparative advantage *vis a vis* the host country as in trade generally. However, as an aspect of the more general discord on North-South issues, including climate change but also relating to many other issues such as poverty, debt and trade, CDMs too become controversial and sensitive. They may, for example, be seen as exploitation of vulnerable developing states or as a breach of equitable principles in relation to the historical responsibility of developed states for global warming generally. On the other hand the CDM program, commenced in 2000, is expected to generate investment in developing countries.

The Kyoto Protocol was itself incomplete and further Conferences of the Parties continued, notably at COP-7 in 2001 with the package known as the Marrakesh Accords which finalized implementation rules for the Protocol. There are broadly five elements to the program. First are the commitments to legally binding emission targets in relation to 1990 baseline emissions; states so committed are listed in Annex B to the Protocol. For example, Canada and Japan must reduce by 6 per cent, Russia and New Zealand must maintain 1990 levels, the European Union must collectively reduce by 8 per cent but can re-distribute its quota between member states.

Secondly, parties may pursue these binding commitments by a variety of means. They have a wide range of domestic policy options at their disposal to

---

[8] J Ford-Robertson, J Maclaren and S Wakelin, 'The Role of Carbon Sequestration as a Response Strategy to Global Warming, with a Particular Focus on New Zealand' in Alexander Gillespie and William Burns (eds) *Climate Change in the South Pacific: Impacts and Responses in Australia, New Zealand, and Small Island States* (2000) 189, 189.

reduce emissions – for example, through enhanced energy efficiency, carbon taxes, sustainable agriculture – but also to absorb emissions in so-called 'carbon sinks', for example by planting trees. Their inclusion in the subsequent COP-6 2001 Bonn Accord resulted from intense pressure from the Umbrella Group of countries. The European Union unsuccessfully resisted, and the practice has been criticized for including 'business as usual' reforestation, for justifying the dubious practice of substituting new, fast-growing, managed forests for old-growth native forest, and for providing states with the opportunity to actually increase emissions.[9] Other policy options already mentioned include JI, CDMs and emissions trading.

Thirdly, the Protocol seeks to minimize impacts on developing countries. Those impacts may be manifest in different ways, including flooding of small island states as a result of rising sea levels, droughts, floods and so on due to more extreme and variable weather events, and constraints on urgent development needs in least developed states. Annex I parties are committed to minimizing such impacts, including the creation of an 'adaptation fund' to be administered by the Global Environment Facility, which is the financial agent of the Convention and Protocol.

Fourthly, information needs – clearly vital to the integrity of the Protocol – are to be met by various accounting, reporting and review procedures such as a national registry for GHG transactions, submission of an annual inventory and review by expert review teams. That information provides the basis for the final element – compliance. This regime is comprised of a Compliance Committee which is in turn constituted by 'facilitative' and 'enforcement' branches. The former provides advice and assistance toward compliance, and makes decisions on the basis of a three-quarters majority. The latter is empowered to impose consequences on errant parties, and its decisions require not only a three-quarters majority but also a majority of both Annex I and non-Annex I parties. Annex I Parties are given one hundred days to remedy any shortfall in compliance, failing which they must carry it into the next commitment period along with a 30 percent penalty.

Although global warming is usually characterized as an 'environmental' problem given its material impacts on our physical environment its genesis is of course in 'development' issues: population growth, land use, materialism, patterns of energy consumption, technological innovations and so on. They are outcomes of growing affluence in developed economies but also of growth aspirations in developing states. Ambitions to regulate – or more crudely to manipulate – development in light of global warming issues, indeed of environmental issues generally, must address the quandary of how to deal with developed versus less developed states given their wildly disparate historic contributions to the problems and their respective resource constraints in attempting to address them. For example, the developed states have contributed ten times more than the developing

---

[9] For a more detailed critique of the practice see, e.g. Dayna Scott, 'Looking for Loopholes' (Fall, 2001) 27 *Alternatives Journal* 22. Thus (at 24) it was estimated that concessions to the Umbrella Group would mean that emissions from industrialized nations could be allowed to increase by 7 per cent above 1990 levels rather than the overall 5 per cent reduction by 2010 mandated by the Kyoto Protocol.

states in the recent buildup of greenhouse gases, including 84 per cent of emissions since 1800.[10] Thus there is an inevitable mix of elements of both retributive justice (in assigning responsibility to those who cause the problem, though manipulable empirical data make this difficult) and distributive justice (in shifting costs and benefits between interdependent parties).[11] As well as these essentially intra-generational issues there are further ethical issues of inter-generational equity. We visit these problems (and solutions) on future generations, or alternatively we are asking present generations to pay the price for the indulgences of past generations in order to benefit future generations.

In any event it is likely that the impacts of climate change will fall disproportionately on developing states with marginal agricultural sectors reflecting small scale and low technology. They lack both capital resources and redundancies in their production systems that would support adaptive responses to relatively sudden changes.[12] Developed industrial states will in all probability prove more resilient. Thus, say some, why should less developed states be expected to do anything, and in any event what can they possibly do? In the South Pacific these issues echo loudly with the wealthy industrialized states of Australia and New Zealand being responsible both for disproportionate contributions to the problem and for measures to mitigate it. The small island states in turn are likely to be disproportionately and perhaps even catastrophically affected and lack the resources and potential adaptive strategies to mitigate. The ethical question is arguably fairly straightforward and most acutely observed in the stance taken by the United States as the only major developed state to repudiate the Kyoto Protocol. The question is this: that even if the United States considers that the dangers of global warming pose an acceptable level of risk, does it then have the right to impose dangerous threats on the most vulnerable states given that effective global action on what other states have judged to be dangerous threats is all but impossible without US co-operation?[13] Of course the US is free to make that judgement in respect of its own nationals, but what if any right does it have to effectively impose it on the overwhelming majority of dissenting states who must endure the United States' disproportionate contribution to the threat? Unsurprisingly the US decision not to ratify the Protocol drew sharp criticism from other states,[14] though some observers are more sympathetic to the US position and sceptical of the motives and policy positions of Kyoto states, especially the

[10] D Brown, 'The U.S. Performance in Achieving Its 1992 Earth Summit Global Warming Commitments' (2002) *Environmental Law Reporter* 10741, 10762.

[11] See, e.g. M Paterson, 'Principles of Justice the Context of Global Climate Change' in Luterbacher and Sprinz, above n 2, 121.

[12] See, e.g. Urs Luterbacher and Detlef Sprinz, 'Global Climate Change in the Context of Interactions Between Society and Environment' in Luterbacher and Sprinz, above n 2, 1, 6.

[13] See, e.g. Brown, above n 10, 10757.

[14] See, e.g. Steven Freeland, 'The Kyoto Protocol: An Agreement Without A Future?' (2001) 24 *University of New South Wales Law Journal* 532, 538, citing (at note 21) condemnation by the European Parliament ('appalling and provocative'), Japanese lawmakers ('shocking'), China ('irresponsible') and the U.N. Secretary General ('unfortunate').

member states of the European 'bubble'.[15] These questions become more acute in the South Pacific where the asymmetry between contribution to the problem, likelihood of serious local consequences and leverage in global policy is most pronounced.

Status of the Protocol

In order to enter into force article 25(1) stipulated that at least 55 states must ratify the Protocol (in whatever form), a requirement that has now been met.[16] As well, however, those ratifying states must include sufficient Annex I parties to account for at least 55 per cent of 1990 carbon dioxide emissions from the Annex I group. That requirement was finally satisfied in 2004 with ratification by Russia. The Protocol will now enter into force on 16 February 2005.

By November 2004, 129 states had given notice of ratification. They represent some 61.6 per cent of total Annex I party emissions.[17] Given the withdrawal of the United States in March 2001, representing some 36 per cent of Annex I party emissions of carbon dioxide in 1990, the next best hope – indeed the only hope – for the Protocol coming into force was the accession of the Russian Federation, accounting for some 17 per cent of the relevant emissions.[18] That was by no means certain; after initially signalling its intent to ratify Russia appeared to reverse its position. Suggested reasons for the Russian delay are varied. One argument runs that the post-1990 Russian economy has shrunk so significantly that it will be in a position to sell substantial carbon credits under the Protocol, but that with the withdrawal of the United States (which would likely have been the major buyer) those credits will have considerably less value than was first thought. A contrary argument runs that the Russian economy needs to recover to (or better) Soviet-era levels and that the Protocol will inhibit that ambition. The argument is qualified by the observation that Russia can utilize presently unrealized production efficiencies. Its emissions per unit of Gross Domestic Product (GDP) are double those of the U.S. and at least four times those of Western European countries, so that it could theoretically double its GDP without increasing emissions by realizing comparable efficiencies.[19] Ironically Russia's assent to the Protocol will probably have a negative effect on the environment, at least in the short term. The substantial carbon credits which Russia will bring to the international carbon trading market will tend to lower the price of these 'permits to emit' and discourage the implementation of higher cost abatement measures by those who

---

15 For example, Bruce Yandle and Stuart Buck, 'Bootleggers, Baptists, and the Global Warming Battle' (2002) 26 *Harvard Environmental Law Review* 177.

16 In May 2002 with the accession of Iceland.

17 UNFCCC, *Kyoto Protocol: Status of Ratification* (2004) <http://unfcc.int/essential_background/kyoto_protocol/statuts_of_ratification/items/2613.php> at 2 December 2004.

18 UNFCCC, *Guide to the Climate Change Convention*, above n 2, 39.

19 Michael Grubb, 'Jumping to Conclusions on Kyoto', *The Moscow Times* (Moscow), 9 January 2004, 8 <http://www.themoscowtimes.com/stories/2004/01/09/006.html> at 20 February 2004.

purchase them.[20] Yet another argument holds that Russia has been indulging in 'brinksmanship' in search of either concessions or of a *quid pro quo* in the form of, for example, European support for its entry into the World Trade Organization (which was in fact announced at the same time).[21]

Meanwhile the United States position has been to rely on voluntary and market forces rather than government regulation.[22] Rather than seeking to achieve an actual reduction in emissions the goalposts have been moved to reducing 'greenhouse gas intensity', that is to say, the ratio of emissions to Gross National Product. Some estimates are that this would allow an actual increase in carbon dioxide emissions of as high as 43 percent above 1990 levels even if targets and voluntary reductions were realized.[23] In any event this emissions intensity focus in reality amounts to 'business as usual' since its successes derive from efficiency gains which were already taking place.[24] It is in effect a plan to do nothing.[25] For this among other reasons the US has been said to be in violation of its commitments under the UNFCCC[26] and the Kyoto Protocol, to both of which it is a signatory. On the other hand the Bush administration has taken the unusual step of formally opposing the Protocol.[27]

The Russian and United States positions raise interesting questions under the Vienna Convention on the Law of Treaties. Had Russia not acceded to the Protocol and thus brought it into force then signatories would have been placed in a difficult position. From a legal perspective obligations prior to coming into force are covered under article 18 of the Vienna Convention on the Law of Treaties, namely the obligation not to defeat the object and purpose of a treaty prior to its entry into force. States which have indicated consent to be bound are obliged to 'refrain from acts which would defeat the object and purpose' pending entry into force 'provided that such entry into force is not unduly delayed'.[28] The meaning of the provision is unclear – for example, the extent of the obligation – and there is a dearth of

---

[20] See, e.g. Bjart Holstmark and Knut Alfsen 'Implementation of the Kyoto Protocol without Russian Participation' (Discussion Paper No. 376, April 2004, Statistics Norway, Research Department, copy on file with author).

[21] Peter Baker, 'Russia Backs Kyoto to Get on Path to Join WTO', *The Washington Post* (Washington), 22 May 2004, A15 <http://www.washingtonpost.com/wp-dyn/articles/A46416-2004May21.html> at 15 December 2004.

[22] See, e.g. Christopher Joyner, 'Burning International Bridges, Fuelling Global Discontent: The United States and Rejection of the Kyoto Protocol' (2002) 33 Victoria University of Wellington Law Review 27, 46.

[23] Ibid 69.

[24] Brown, above n 10, 10758.

[25] Loy, above n 7, 15.

[26] Brown, above n 10, 10757.

[27] Jutta Brunnee, 'The United States and International Environmental Law: Living with an Elephant' (2004) 15 *European Journal of International Law* 617, 645 (citing The White House, 'Text of a Letter from the President to Senators Hagel, Helms, Craig and Roberts', 13 March 2001).

[28] *Vienna Convention on the Law of Treaties*, opened for signature 23 May 1969, 1155 UNTS 331 (entered into force 27 January 1980), art 18(b).

practice on its application but it is likely to mean that not all acts which would be prohibited after coming into force must be avoided. Rather a state must refrain from acts which actually invalidate the purpose of the treaty, for example, destroying objects whose return is the subject of the treaty.[29]

With regard to the Protocol the implication is that a ratifying state could legally do almost anything (or nothing) in respect of its omissions so long as it did not make compliance impossible in the first commitment period. That is similarly the case with those states which still have not ratified, particularly the United States and Australia. They are parties to the UNFCCC and signatories to the Protocol though they have not ratified it. Thus whilst not legally bound to meet the emission targets of the Protocol they are nonetheless required under international law to refrain from actions which would make the discharge of Kyoto obligations impossible. [30] In practice that permits considerable latitude – what level of greenhouse gas emissions would be sufficient to render impossible adherence to treaty obligations given, for example, uncertainty with respect to future technological innovations, economic cycles, policy alternatives, and so on? In any event the United States has expressly disavowed the Kyoto Protocol and so is presumably not restricted even by the article 18 language. Both countries claim to have adopted voluntary programs (discussed below). As well state and local authorities have in many cases adopted climate change initiatives that in practice may come to have a cumulative impact notwithstanding inaction by central governments in both countries.

But now that entry into force of the Protocol is finally assured it means that thirty industrialized countries will be legally bound to meet their respective quantitative emission targets. Important climate change institutions will now take their place in the regime – the international carbon trading market for buying and selling emission credits, the Clean Development Mechanism for encouraging investment in developing-country projects, and the Adaptation Fund for assistance to developing countries in dealing with impacts of climate change. At the time of writing only four industrialized countries have not yet ratified the Protocol – the United States and Australia, together accounting for more than a third of industrialized state emissions, and Liechtenstein and Monaco.

Limitations of the Protocol

The efficacy of the Protocol is compromised in a variety of ways. There is no pretence that it will 'solve' the climate change problem. Even with implementation some 75 per cent of global emissions are not covered; it will probably only reduce global emissions by around 1 per cent by the end of the first commitment period, whilst the best available science suggests that global emissions need to be reduced by some 60 per cent by the end of the century merely to stabilize them at 1990 levels, though those levels are themselves some 25 per cent higher that pre-

[29] See, e.g. Anthony Aust, *Modern Treaty Law and Practice* (2000) 93-5.
[30] Ibid.

industrial levels.[31] Similarly, even full implementation of the Protocol is projected to reduce warming by only one twentieth of one degree centrigrade, and to have only a minimal effect on sea levels.[32] Thus, many of the predicted impacts of climate change are most likely to occur regardless of present international policy responses. With some justification one veteran of the climate change regime describes its history as a 'sort of elegantly choreographed evasion'.[33]

The underlying reasons for the limited ambitions of the Protocol are of course many and complex but might be crudely summarized by the observation that greenhouse gas emissions go to the very core of modern economic activity. Curtailing them presents real but unknowable challenges both to the affluent, materialist cultures of developed states and to the growth ambitions of developing states. Both the sources and impacts are truly global. They are not amenable to the more straightforward amelioration of, for example, substances that deplete the ozone layer – the subject of the Montreal Protocol on the Protection of the Ozone Layer. In that case the sources of the ozone depleting substances were limited in number and readily identifiable, and substitute products were available.

The ongoing refusal of the United States to ratify the Protocol presents an insurmountable barrier to even the modest aspirations of the first commitment period. As noted above, the United States contributed some 36 per cent of Annex I party emissions of carbon dioxide in 1990, more than double the next largest emitter (the Russian Federation) and half as much again as fifteen European Union states combined.[34] It initially agreed to reduce those 1990 levels by 7 per cent, but over the 1990s its GHG emissions increased by some 13 per cent and continue to grow.[35] It would now have to reduce emissions by close to one third to meet its Kyoto target. It has taken some steps in regard to its ratification of the UNFCCC – for example, its reporting responsibilities, its research commitments and (arguably) its minimum obligations to provide finance to developing nations, but has failed to comply with its emission reduction responsibilities under the UNFCCC[36] or to ratify the Kyoto Protocol. Its reasons for not ratifying seemingly boil down to some combination of the lack of binding commitments for the developing world, scientific uncertainty as to the quantum and timing of climate change and (unsubstantiated) fears of the economic cost of policy responses. The first and last of these issues motivated the 1997 U.S. Senate vote (95-0) to resist any Kyoto agreement that did not include targets for developing countries or which threatened significant damage to the U.S. economy. Domestic political resistance flows from

[31] IPCC, *First Assessment Report* (1990), Overview <http://www.ipcc.ch/pub/reports.htm> at 15 December 2004.
[32] See William Burns, 'The Impact of Climate Change on Pacific Island Developing Countries in the 21st Century' in Gillespie and Burns, above n 8, 233, 249.
[33] Hon. Simon Upton (then New Zealand Minister for the Environment), 'Risks Surrounding the Kyoto Protocol' in The New Zealand Institute of International Affairs, *Seminar Papers: Climate Change: Implementing the Kyoto Protocol* (1999) 1, 13.
[34] Joyner, above n 22, 39.
[35] Brown, above n 10, 10751.
[36] Ibid 10768.

both the Democratic Party (fearing a threat to its labour base) and the Republican Party (fearing a threat to its corporate base).[37] Present prospects for U.S. ratification of the Kyoto Protocol appear bleak.[38]

The absence of binding commitments on developing countries, at least for the time being, is obviously a serious constraint on the efficacy of measures to address climate change. Under the Kyoto Protocol they effectively face no limits on their greenhouse gas emissions, notwithstanding that many are significant contributors (in absolute terms though not per capita) – for example, in terms of quantum of emissions China ranked second in 1998, India sixth, South Korea eighth, South Africa eleventh and Mexico twelfth.[39] By way of illustration, in 1999 the industrialized countries contributed some 51 per cent of total world carbon emissions, which share is expected to drop to around 41 per cent by 2020 if emissions are not controlled.[40]

Finally, the present Kyoto regime does not incorporate greenhouse gas emissions from international flights and shipping, though there is pressure from Europe to reduce these emissions in the second commitment period from 2012. It is expected that they will be debated at COP-10 at Buenos Aires in December 2004. They have been conservatively estimated at 3.5 per cent and 1.8 per cent respectively of global emissions of greenhouse gases, though environmental groups claim that these numbers may actually double if indirect effects are included.[41] Of concern is the expected growth in world transport demand – perhaps as much as 55 per cent over the period 1995–2020.[42]

So the Kyoto Protocol is at best a hesitant first step, and any significant efforts to address climate change must be deferred until at least the second commitment period. Developing states will have to be included in binding commitments and the United States must be persuaded to participate, though present indications are that its emissions are likely to be so high as to make any meaningful reduction unlikely in the near term. But the symbolism of the present ambitions of the Protocol is nonetheless signficant, most particularly in the willingness of the developed states to set at least a modest example and to acknowledge at least in principle the notion of common but differentiated responsibility. Policy responses in the Pacific region ought to be considered in that context, though as we shall see they offer no more cause for optimism than does the wider international response.

---

[37] Ibid 10749.

[38] For a more sympathetic reading of the U.S. response to Kyoto see, e.g. Yandle and Buck, above n 15.

[39] Senator The Hon. Nick Minchin 'Responding to Climate Change: Providing a Policy Framework for a Competitive Australia' (2001) 24 *University of New South Wales Law Journal* 550, 553.

[40] Yandle and Buck, above n 15, 183.

[41] Maarten Messiaen, 'New Take-Off Proposed for Kyoto' *Inter Press Service News Agency*, 29 November 2004 <http://www.ipsnews.net/africa/interna.asp?idnews=26458> at 15 December 2004.

[42] Ibid.

Regional responses

That wider global order is reflected immediately in the disparate array of states which constitute the South Pacific region. They vary radically in degrees of industrialization, geography, climate, natural resources, patterns of energy use, sources of GHGs, and so on. The most obvious demarcation is between the various small, developing island states and the larger developed states of Australia and New Zealand. Australia might reasonably be characterized as the major regional power, with New Zealand in closer geographical and cultural proximity to the small island states, of which Fiji would be the largest in demographic and economic terms. In the context of climate change Australia and New Zealand are, in per capita terms, major contributors to greenhouse gas emissions whilst the small island states contribute only negligible emissions but are extremely vulnerable to climate change impacts. One might then simplistically characterize the former as perpetrators of climate change and the latter as victims. Certainly remedial measures would be expected from the high-polluting, resource-rich developed states and assistance with mitigation measures might be expected for the developing states. The parallels between the region and the wider international order are again obvious and the notion of common but differentiated responsibility apposite.

In looking to the policy responses of regional states the most striking contradiction is the presence of Australia as one of only two regional states (along with Tonga) not to ratify the Protocol, again seeming to mirror the wider context in its mimicry of the United States. It has implemented a 'voluntary' program aimed at realizing its Kyoto target of an 8 per cent increase of emissions over 1990 levels. New Zealand has ratified and is implementing policies which will maintain emissions at 1990 levels, though it expects to make a small economic gain as a result. The small island developing states are not required to meet any emission targets – their concerns are with mitigating the impacts of climate change.

Australia

Background

Australia accepts the IPCC's conclusions on climate science 'as the most authoritative available'[43] and accepts 'the reality that climate change is occurring'.[44]

---

[43] Hon. Dr. David Kemp MP (Australian Federal Minister for the Environment and Heritage), 'Australia's Approach to Climate Change' (Opening Address at the Beyond Kyoto: Economic Impacts and Alternative Mitigation Strategies Conference, Institute of Public Affairs, Melbourne, 28 February 2003), Department of the Environment and Heritage <http://www.deh.gov.au/minister/env/2003/sp28feb03.html> at 15 December 2004.

[44] Ibid.

From an ecological perspective the impacts of global warming on Australia are difficult to predict[45] but are expected to include impacts on vulnerable ecosystems in the arid and semi-arid areas of the south-west and inland, alpine systems and coral reefs. Climate variation is expected to include increases in the intensity of heavy rains and tropical cyclones with associated risks to human life, property and infrastructures. Water supply and agricultural production will be vulnerable, particularly in the south-west and inland regions.

Australia contributes just over 1 per cent of total greenhouse emissions but its per capita emissions are among the world's highest[46] and notwithstanding its relatively small population it is one of the top twelve emitters.[47] Under a 'business as usual' scenario Australia's emissions would be expected to grow by around 26 per cent over 1990–2010, with energy sector emissions expected to grow by 40 per cent.[48]

From an economic perspective Australia claims to be peculiarly vulnerable to greenhouse gas reduction measures in having an energy-intensive economy and in having an international competitive advantage in low cost energy from huge reserves of coal and gas.[49] For example, by offering cheap electricity from low cost coal Australian governments were able to induce energy-intensive users like the aluminium industry to locate in Australia in the early 1980s. Australia lacks extensive hydro resources and has followed a policy of not developing nuclear power, though it does have great potential for renewable energy sources such as solar and wind power.

The policy implications of a coal-dependent economy are significant for Australia. The production and use of coal accounts directly for some 38 per cent of Australia's total greenhouse gas emissions – compared to 31 per cent from all other energy sources and 31 per cent from other activities such as agriculture.[50] In terms of carbon dioxide emitted per unit of energy provided, coal is almost twice as intensive as natural gas and one and a half times as intensive as petroleum products.[51] As well, coal extraction releases large amounts of methane, which is considerably more potent a greenhouse gas than is carbon dioxide. Not surprisingly, in light of this dependence on coal, critics say that the coal industry has exerted an

---

[45] See, e.g. Australian Government, *Living with climate change: An overview of potential climate change impacts on Australia* (2002), Australian Greenhouse Office <www.greenhouse.gov.au/science/impacts/overview/index.html> at 3 February 2004.

[46] Australian Government, *National Greenhouse Strategy*, Executive Summary, vii <www.greenhouse.gov.au/pubs/ngs/ngs.html> at 15 December 2004. See also Clive Hamilton, 'Climate Change Policies in Australia' in Gillespie and Burns, above n 8, 51, 63.

[47] Hon. Dr. David Kemp MP (Australian Federal Minister for the Environment and Heritage), 'Australia's Domestic Climate Change Approach' (Speech to COP-9, Milan, 9 December 2003) <http://www.deh.gov.au/minister/env/2003/sp09dec03.html> at 15 December 2004.

[48] Australian Government, *National Greenhouse Strategy*, above n 46, vii.

[49] Kemp, 'Australia's Approach to Climate Change', above n 43. These policy positions have been strongly criticized elsewhere – see, e.g. Hamilton, above n 46 and W. Hare, *Australia and Kyoto: In or Out?* (2001) 24 University of New South Wales Law Journal 556.

[50] Hugh Saddler, 'Australia and Greenhouse Gas Emissions' (2002–2003) 51 *Dissent* 51.

[51] Ibid.

extraordinary influence on policy responses to Kyoto – for example, in pressuring the government in 1995 to abandon a carbon tax in return for voluntary agreements under the Greenhouse Challenge program, and even then only requiring 'no regrets' actions which would be at least cost-neutral.[52] Similarly in 2000 the government was effectively dissuaded from a domestic emissions trading scheme which would have placed a cost on excessive greenhouse gas emissions,[53] and work on an international emissions trading scheme was abandoned in 2004.

In addition to its reliance on low-cost fossil fuels, other specific factors influencing Australia's ability to reduce greenhouse gas emissions include a relatively high economic growth rate, a wide range of climatic zones, relatively high population growth, very long distances between urban centres and land use patterns which are still undergoing significant change.[54] However, the economic model used to justify Australia's claim to a peculiar vulnerability in pursuing emission reductions came under widespread criticism for *inter alia* its bias toward business interests.[55]

A further complication for Australia arises from its constitutional arrangements. As a federal state it is governed under a division of powers framework between the central federal government and the various state and territorial governments (as are, for example, the United States and Canada but not, for example, New Zealand or the United Kingdom). In the Australian case certain specified powers are assigned to the Commonwealth Parliament with legislative powers over the remainder left to the legislative authority of the states. Various areas in which governments would need to regulate in respect of climate change policy lie with the states; examples include energy and land clearing.[56] Under the National Greenhouse Strategy (see below) the policy adopted has been one of cooperation between the Commonwealth, State, Territory and Local governments. Representatives of each level of government are responsible for managing the program's principles, guidelines, goals and measures, and are in turn responsible to the Council of Australian Governments.[57] The Agreement does not, however, create legally binding obligations and there is no guarantee of its effective implementation by the states – only political pressure can be applied. Should it choose to the Commonwealth could introduce its own legislation to implement its obligations under the UNFCCC and (if it ratifies) the Kyoto Protocol. Such legislation would likely be a valid exercise of the Commonwealth external affairs power (s 51 (xxix) of the *Australian Constitution 1900*). That power has been interpreted to include federal legislative competence in matters that are of

---

[52] Ibid 51-2.
[53] Ibid 53.
[54] Australian Government, *Tracking to the Kyoto Target* (2004) 3 <http://www.greenhouse.gov.au/projections/tracking/pubs/tracking2004.pdf> at 16 December 2004.
[55] Hare, above n 49, 558.
[56] Laura Horn, 'The Kyoto Protocol: Australia's Commitment and Compliance' (2001) 24 *University of New South Wales Law Journal* 583, 584-5.
[57] Ibid.

inherently international concern as well as legislation pursuant to an international treaty or convention.[58] Either, and certainly a combination of both would seem sufficient to ground the authority of the federal government to legislate in respect of the Kyoto Protocol should it choose to ratify. However, actions by the various state governments are also important, and New South Wales in particular has been pro-active in adopting more forceful regulatory strategies than has the federal Howard government.[59] But as with environmental law generally, the policy choice has been to favour a model of cooperative federalism.[60]

Australia ratified the UNFCCC in 1992 and signed the Kyoto Protocol in 1998, but has declined to ratify the Protocol. Its stated reason is the Protocol's lack of application of binding targets to developing countries with the associated threat of loss of jobs and investment to developed countries. The claim is that Australia will become less competitive and the resulting 'carbon leakage' (as GHG industry moves to developing states) would undermine the Protocol itself.[61] Generally with respect to climate change negotiations Australia has been characterized as being 'at best, a reluctant partner and, at worst, a country whose engagement is little more than a naked defence of its coal and aluminium industries'.[62] With respect to developing countries and the dangers of their pursuing the emissions intensive growth path of developed countries, Australia (like the United States) has adopted a hard line in demanding, if not targets and binding commitments then possibly some kind of incentive structures.[63] It has, however, undertaken to meet its Kyoto target.[64] Its commitment under the Protocol was to limit greenhouse emissions to 108 per cent of 1990 levels over the period 2008–2012. The only other states allowed to actually increase emissions were Norway (by 1 per cent) and Iceland (by 10 per cent).

Policy responses

A sectoral analysis of greenhouse gas emissions (1996 data) showed the (non-transport) Energy sector to be the largest contributor at 55 per cent, followed by Agricultural production (excluding land clearing) at 20 per cent, the Transport sector at 17 per cent, Waste at 4 per cent and Industrial Processes at 2 per cent.[65]

The recent policy discourse within which Australia has responded to climate change issues has been characterized as 'ecological modernisation', that is to say

---

[58] James Crawford 'The Constitution and the Environment' (1991) 13 *Sydney Law Review* 11.

[59] R Taplin and X Yu, 'Climate Change Policy Formulation in Australia: 1995–1998' in Gillespie and Burns, above n 8, 95, 105-107.

[60] Robert Hughes, Geoffrey Leane and Andrew Clarke, *Australian Legal Institutions: Principles, Structures and Organisation* (2nd ed, 2003) 112.

[61] Kemp, 'Australia's Approach to Climate Change', above n 43.

[62] Hare, above n 49.

[63] Kemp, 'Australia's Approach to Climate Change', above n 43.

[64] Ibid.

[65] Australian Government, *National Greenhouse Strategy*, above n 46, ix.

the assumption that environmental issues can be accommodated within, or internalized in, existing political, economic and social institutions.[66] That 'shallow ecology' approach goes back to the Brundtland Report assumption that there is no necessary contradiction between economic growth and environmental imperatives – indeed that the former is necessary to finance the latter. Environmental policy more generally has historically been caught up in the tensions of Australia's federalist system of government; control of the environment was traditionally a responsibility of the states but became controversial in the 1980s as the federal government asserted its foreign affairs power in certain environmental conflicts. Nonetheless the requirement for harmonization of federal and state legislation presents itself in respect of Kyoto measures as in other areas; for example, in legislation to give legal recognition to carbon sequestration rights in pursuit of an emissions trading scheme.[67] A number of 'carbon trades' have already been contracted, for example, between Japanese interests and Australian forestry interests.[68]

At the same time the federal government was attempting to articulate a national strategy on Ecologically Sustainable Development.[69] During the early 1990s the federal government sponsored working groups whose aim was to suggest appropriate policy responses on Ecologically Sustainable Development generally and on the Greenhouse issue. A variety of (but not all) stakeholders participated and reached a surprising degree of consensus within the 'ecological modernisation' paradigm, that is to say by utilizing existing institutional and social structures.[70] One of the outputs was the National Greenhouse Response Strategy (NGRS), though it apparently did not ultimately reflect the original consensus of the working group participants and was in fact disowned by them.[71] This preliminary work motivated Australia to confidently sign the UNFCCC in December 1992 – indeed it was the eighth state to do so.

The NGRS was criticized for lacking new measures, lacking firm commitments and for relying on ad hoc government processes and commercial decisions – in other words for simply maintaining the status quo.[72] The imposition of a carbon tax was considered but rejected after strong opposition from industry. A program of voluntary emission reductions was adopted, but with an explicit commitment to 'the business objectives of development and growth' and with no penalty for withdrawal.[73] By 1995 the program was arguably an 'abject failure' and

[66] Harriet Bulkeley, 'The Formation of Australian Climate Change Policy: 1985–1995' in Gillespie and Burns, above n 8, 33, 35.

[67] For more detail see, e.g. David Jones, 'The Kyoto Protocol, Carbon Sinks and Integrated Environmental Regulation: an Australian Perspective' (2002) 19(2) *Environment and Planning Law Journal* 109, 122-9.

[68] Ibid 125.

[69] Bulkeley, above n 66, 35.

[70] Ibid 40-42.

[71] Ibid.

[72] Ibid 45.

[73] Ibid 47. For a summary critique of the NGRS see also Taplin and Yu, above n 59, 96-7.

offered little prospect of reconciling economic and environmental values.[74] The NGRS was further developed in 1995 with the addition of Greenhouse 21C, a program which sought to bring together all relevant actors in responding to the Berlin COP in 1995.

One outcome of Greenhouse 21C was the establishment of the Greenhouse Challenge program which was to facilitate cooperative partnerships between government and industry. The program was voluntary, and only required the pursuit of 'no regrets' actions. It survived a change in government in 1996. The results have included active participation by the aluminium industry (which consumes 19 per cent of all electricity sold in Australia) and the electricity generation industry, but not the coal industry.[75] There have, however, been some recent signs of coal industry cooperation, for example in the establishment of the COAL21 action plan with the federal government (with a particular emphasis on carbon sequestration, which involves capturing carbon dioxide and burying it underground).

It was in this context that Australia approached the Kyoto Protocol with less confidence than the 1992 UNFCCC. The Australian government's approach leading up to the 1997 Kyoto Conference was to argue for 'differentiation', that is to say an approach that states should suffer equally in pursuing greenhouse gas emission reductions and that therefore they should be subject to different targets depending on relative economic costs. Thus it was argued that Australia was heavily dependent on fossil fuels for domestic energy and for export revenue – therein lay its international competitive advantage – and was therefore deserving of more lenient targets. That position was strongly criticized by many Australian economists, who suggested that the government's economic models on impacts, costs and benefits were misleading and further that the model chosen was substantially financed by the fossil fuel industry.[76]

There appeared to be a number of glaring contradictions in the government's 'differentiation' policy response to Kyoto.[77] The model it presented in international forums assumed that there were no 'no regrets' reductions (that is, costless energy savings measures) available whereas its domestic strategy depended largely on the existence of just such options.[78] For example, the Greenhouse Challenge program requires only that 'no regrets' actions be pursued; if these are in fact available then the model Australia presented internationally must exaggerate the cost of emission reduction programs. If they are not available then the domestic program must be a

[74] Bulkeley, above n 66, 49.

[75] Saddler, above n 50, 52.

[76] Hamilton, above n 46, 54-8. These accusations received some support in a report by the Commonwealth Ombudsman (at 58). See also Mark Diesendorf, 'A Critique of the Australian Government's Greenhouse Policies' in Gillespie and Burns, above n 8, 79.

[77] These arguments are largely drawn from Hamilton, above n 46, 63-6.

[78] Hamilton, above n 46, 57.

farce.[79] In fact there is compelling evidence that Australia is a relatively energy-inefficient user and therefore has potential for significant efficiency gains.[80]

The policy ran contrary to long-established 'polluter pays' principles – as perhaps the highest per-capita polluter in the world Australia was demanding permission to actually continue to increase emissions to a degree second only to Iceland. That would make it even more difficult for Australia to conform to what will presumably be a much stricter post-Kyoto regime. Because it anticipated relatively high population growth as a consequence of its immigration policies – a policy choice presumably driven by economic benefits – Australia argued for per capita targets, notwithstanding the implications that such a policy would have for the emissions of those developing countries (with high population growth) that Australia wanted included in the Kyoto targets.

In the event Australia 'won' concessions at Kyoto which went considerably further than merely easing its allegedly unfair reduction burden; rather it would in all likelihood actually result in surplus emission savings which under the projected Kyoto emissions trading system it could sell to other signatory states, thus effecting a wealth transfer from other developed countries to the country with perhaps the highest per capita emissions in the world![81] One critic summarizes this outcome as 'the outstanding anomaly from Kyoto', achieved by threats to withdraw if it was not granted.[82]

As well as being permitted to actually increase its emissions by 8 per cent it was also permitted to include emissions from land clearing in its total, thus inflating the 1990 base level. The so-called 'Australia' clause allowed countries with net positive land-use emissions, that is to say where there was actually a net loss of forest 'sinks' with their associated capacity to absorb greenhouse gases, to include those positive emissions in the 1990 base year calculation. The effect is to increase the base year number and, for a country like Australia which was one of only three allowed to actually increase emissions, to allow a larger increase in 2008–2012. Australia was the only country to qualify for this concession as all other industrialized countries were experiencing a net growth in forests and therefore negative land-use emissions. It has been estimated that Australia thereby effectively obtained an increase of something like 19 per cent in its 1990 emissions – which in turn it can grow by another 8 per cent in the first adjustment period – worth some $10 billion.[83] As these emissions appear to be declining without intervention it may be that the target of 8 per cent increase can be achieved without policies to reduce emissions in the energy sector.[84] Indeed it has been estimated that the 'Australia' clause will allow it to increase fossil fuel and related emissions

79 Saddler, above n 75.
80 Hamilton, above n 46, 70.
81 Ibid 72-4.
82 Ibid 76; also Hare, above n 49, 560.
83 D Victor, *The Collapse of the Kyoto Protocol and the Struggle to Slow Global Warming* (2001) 63.
84 Diesendorf, above n 76, 79.

by some 22-33 per cent during the first commitment period.[85] For example, between 1990 and 2002 Australia's total net emissions were said to have grown by 1.3 per cent,[86] but this number includes a fall of more than 75 per cent in the Land Use category. Without that category total net emissions would have shown an increase of more than 23 per cent.[87] Put another way, the reduction in Land Use emissions from 1990 accounted for some 31 per cent of the overall decline in emissions per dollar of Gross Domestic Product[88] – such is the impact of the 'Australia' clause. The irony of Australia still refusing to ratify the Protocol becomes still sharper.

As to further policy initiatives, the conservative Howard Government, elected in 1996, had implemented a number of new greenhouse initiatives in 1996–1997. One was the Activities Implemented Jointly (AIJ) program, which sought to implement the UNFCCC option of joint emission reduction projects between developed and developing states, though no government funding was provided and little activity has ensued.[89] The Prime Minister's Greenhouse Package was introduced in the lead up to Kyoto in 1997, including such measures as a Renewable Energy Innovations Investment Fund, fuel efficiency goals, energy efficiency codes and labelling requirements, and a program to establish carbon 'sinks'. The package was, however, seen as disappointing by many commentators.[90] Although there are indications of significant interest by industry in reducing emissions – for example, by signing on to the Greenhouse Challenge program – such undertakings are only voluntary and only some 17 per cent of projected reductions were direct consequences of the program, the balance being likely to have occurred in any event.[91] In 1998 the government established the Australian Greenhouse Office (AGO) under the environment portfolio to co-ordinate greenhouse policy, issue discussion papers and deliver federal government programs. It was the first such institution of its kind in the world.

The National Greenhouse Strategy (NGS), which superseded the NGRS and included the above initiatives, is meant to provide a strategic framework within which to realize Australia's Kyoto ambitions. In terms of emission reduction programs a major initiative has been the Mandatory Renewable Energy Targets (MRET) scheme, aimed at utilizing Australia's solar, wind, water and biomass resources. Its original target was a 2 per cent uptake of renewable energy by 2010 (versus a goal of 15 per cent by 2010 proposed by the European Union), although this was later converted to an absolute target.[92] Since 2001 large wholesale

[85] Jones, above n 67, 116.

[86] Australian Government, 'Analysis of Recent Trends and Greenhouse Indicators 1990 to 2002' (2004) Australian Greenhouse Office, National Greenhouse Gas Inventory <www.greenhouse.gov.au/inventory2002/trends/index.html> at 11 May 2004.

[87] Ibid.

[88] Ibid.

[89] Taplin and Yu, above n 59, 101.

[90] Ibid 104.

[91] Ibid 107-108.

[92] Of 9500 GigaWatt/hour, which of course is a static target which would represent a proportionately smaller achievement in the event of energy demand increasing: see Sarojini

purchasers of electricity have been required to obtain legislated amounts of their electricity from such renewable sources as wind farms and hydro-electric power; the prescribed levels increase gradually over a ten year period with penalties for non-compliance.[93] An innovatory aspect is the legislative creation of a renewable energy market in tradeable certificates, that is to say, the commercialization of renewable energy technologies. There are also grants-related programs to encourage the development of commercial renewable energy and alternative fuels.

Further programs include the Greenhouse Gas Abatement Program, which targets large-scale, cost-effective projects in various sectors, and a joint government-industry International Greenhouse Partnerships Office to facilitate Joint Implementation and Clean Development Mechanism projects in other countries. Other programs seek, for example, improved fuel efficiency in motor vehicles (a non-binding target of 15 per cent improvement by 2010), enhanced greenhouse sinks (a trebling of the plantation estate by 2020), and greenhouse best practice in waste and industrial processes. As in New Zealand, however, there seems to be a conspicuous absence of ambitious strategies for the agricultural sector. Local government participation is facilitated through a Cities for Climate Change Protection Program under the International Council for Local Environmental Initiatives. Monitoring strategies include an enhanced National Greenhouse Gas Inventory and National Carbon Accounting System, along with ongoing investment in climate science (for example, the role of Antarctica and the Southern Ocean in the climate system). Trade in emission permits has been estimated to be worth up to A$12 billion per annum, although the present government is unwilling to implement a domestic emissions trading system until it ratifies the Kyoto Protocol, the Protocol has entered into force (which it now has) and an international trading regime is in place.[94]

Finally, the Australian government has entered into a number of bilateral partnerships or collaborations on climate change – partners include the United States, the European Union, Japan, China and New Zealand. Projects typically relate to climate change science, including accounting and monitoring strategies, energy innovations and, in the case of China, capacity building. The New Zealand partnership includes common interest areas such as agriculture (particularly methane emissions from livestock) and the particular challenges faced by Pacific Island neighbours.

Conclusions

Given Australia's reliance on cheap fossil fuels for its industrial and export base it will be necessary to develop technologies for cleaning up fossil fuel emissions; promising possibilities are thought to lie with coal gasification and sequestration of

---

Krishnapillai, 'Bad Neighbour Policy – Australia, Kyoto, and the Pacific' (August–September 2002) *Arena* 14, 14.

[93] Jones, above n 67, 122.

[94] Ibid 119, 121.

carbon dioxide in underground strata and aquifers. In the longer term there is the prospect of a hydrogen economy whereby improved technology may offer the prospect of extracting molecular hydrogen from various common elements (such as water) to power a future energy system rather than relying on fossil fuels. Nonetheless Australia's ability to meet its 108 per cent target in the first commitment period is almost entirely dependent on a dramatic decrease in emissions due to land-use changes, that is to say mostly from a decrease in the removal of forest cover and to a lesser extent from reforestation.[95] It will be recalled that the net positive emissions from land-use change were the subject of the so-called 'Australia' clause which enable that country, and only that country, to inflate its 1990 emissions and thereby benefit from a less demanding target in the first commitment period since it was permitted to increase that high level to 108 per cent. So those land-use changes not only served to provide a more amenable target but also serve as the means to achieve it; that is to say, the very generous emissions target was effectively a consequence of undesirable land-use practices, whilst the reversal of those practices will allow Australia to meet its target using sink credits rather than actually reducing emissions! Its past poor practices effectively allow it to evade the pain of authentic emission reductions.

In general, Australia's climate change strategy eschews tax and regulation strategies in favour of voluntary, co-operative schemes with industry using 'cost-effective technology' that does not threaten economic growth. This last imperative, together with international competitiveness, appears to be the primary motivation behind its greenhouse strategy. But for reasons discussed above both its international and domestic policy responses to the Kyoto Protocol appear to be incoherent.[96]

The pattern of emissions since 1990 is not particularly encouraging. By 1995 net greenhouse gas emissions (including the Land Use sector) had risen 6 per cent over 1990 levels, including an 8 per cent rise for the Energy sector (which accounted for more than half of all emissions), and a separate government study suggested even higher increases in the energy sector of 11 per cent in 1995–1996 with possible increases of 40 per cent by 2010.[97] In 2000 greenhouse gas emissions stood at 105 per cent of 1990 levels and, based on existing policies, were projected to reach 111 per cent by 2010[98] according to the government's own data. That emissions might yet exceed the already generous 108 per cent target, notwithstanding the artificial inflation of the base year emissions resulting from the 'Australia' clause, must give rise to a certain cynicism. Business-as-usual emissions, that is to say without Kyoto policy measures, were projected to be 123

---

[95] Australian Government, *Tracking to the Kyoto Target*, above n 54, 4-5.

[96] See, e.g. Saddler, above n 50, Bulkeley, above n 66, Hamilton, above n 46, Diesendorf, above n 76, Taplin and Yu, above n 59.

[97] Taplin and Yu, above n 59.

[98] Kemp, 'Australia's Approach to Climate Change', above n 43. This figure was revised in 2004 with new data suggesting that the Kyoto target of 108 per cent was achievable (see Australian Government, *Tracking to the Kyoto Target*, above, n 54) though it is probably still too soon to tell.

per cent of 1990 levels over the first commitment period.[99] Emissions for 2020 are projected to be 126 per cent over 1990 levels, mainly due to growth in the energy sector.[100]

The latest available greenhouse gas inventory data submitted for the period 1990–2002 demonstrates the pattern of emissions – they declined to their lowest post-1990 levels in 1992, rose over the intervening years to their highest point in 1998, then declined for the next few years to 2001 and finally increased again by 1.5 per cent in 2002.[101] Again the sectoral data are more revealing; for example, over 1990–2002 Energy sector emissions (the largest contributor) rose by 30 per cent and Agriculture by 11 per cent, but growth in all sectors was outweighed by a 76 per cent fall in the Land Use, Land Use Change and Forestry sector due to a significant reduction in the area of forest conversion. In terms of emissions intensity over 1990–2002 there was a 12.5 per cent reduction in emissions per capita and a 31 per cent reduction in emissions per dollar of Gross Domestic Product. The latter was due to a variety of factors, including higher growth in the services sector as compared to manufacturing, and the substantial reduction in the Land Use, Land Use Change and Forestry sector. Over the period to 2020 emissions per real dollar of Gross Domestic Product are expected to fall to 52 per cent of 1990 levels.[102] But of course 'per unit' measures of emissions are misleading as the critical measure in terms of climate change is the absolute level of emissions, and that level continues to grow in Australia.

Australia's Kyoto policies have not gone unnoticed by the vulnerable island states of the South Pacific: they were described as 'self-serving' by the Cook Islands Prime Minister, and were impliedly criticized by a call for greater emission reductions by the South Pacific Forum meeting of leaders in 1997.[103]

The post-Kyoto image from Australia then is of one of the world's wealthiest nations, producing one of the highest per capita levels of greenhouse emissions in the world, with an excellent environmental 'history' backed by first rate science, extracting extraordinary self-serving concessions at Kyoto and then refusing to ratify the Protocol. It had ironically been viewed as a repository of world-class climate change science since the early 1970s,[104] and had been 'an exemplary international environmental citizen', a position from which the greenhouse policy response represents a 'radical departure'.[105] Of the four developed states still

[99] Australian Government, *Tracking to the Kyoto Target*, above n 54, 2.

[100] Hon. Dr. David Kemp MP (Australian Federal Minister for the Environment and Heritage), 'Australia Moves Closer to Kyoto Target' (Press Release, 18 September 2003) Department of Environment and Heritage <http://www.deh.gov.au/minister/env/2003/mr18sep03.html> 16 December 2004.

[101] Australian Government, 'Analysis of Recent Trends and Greenhouse Indicators 1990 to 2002', above n 86.

[102] Australian Government, *Tracking to the Kyoto Target*, above n 54.

[103] Taplin and Yu, above n 59, 113.

[104] Reid Basher, 'The Impacts of Climate Change on New Zealand' in Gillespie and Burns, above n 8, 121, 137.

[105] X Yu and R Taplin, 'The Australian Position at the Kyoto Conference' in Gillespie and Burns, above n 8, 113.

declining to ratify the Protocol – at the time of writing the United States, Australia, Liechtenstein and Monaco – two of them number among the worst polluters, are among the few richest countries in the world, were successful in extracting major concessions from other negotiating parties, and yet still refuse to enter into binding commitments. Those who see the United States as something of a rogue state in the climate change regime might see Australia similarly mirrored in the South Pacific. Only its relatively small size prevents it from seriously eroding the practical effect of the Kyoto Protocol, though it doubtless undermines the Protocol's symbolic importance both internationally and regionally.

New Zealand

Background

New Zealand contributes only 0.2 per cent of total Annex I state emissions, although on the basis of 'all greenhouse gas' emissions it is the fourth highest per-capita emitter.[106] It occupies an interesting space, geographically and politically, between on the one hand a large, regionally dominant Australia with high greenhouse emissions and an ongoing resistance to compulsory Kyoto reductions, and on the other hand the highly vulnerable small island states of the South Pacific.[107] As the other industrialized 'European' society in the region, and with a high degree of economic interdependence with Australia, it tends to co-ordinate policy with Australia including with respect to climate change. On the other hand it strongly identifies with the Pacific island states, and as well has constitutional responsibility for the islands of Tokelau.

Unusually for a first-world country, the New Zealand economy is significantly dependent on primary production, wherein lies its comparative advantage in the world community. It therefore relies on an equable and stable climate to maintain this advantage and the prosperity it brings. The corollary is that New Zealand's agricultural sector produces an unusually large (for a developed nation) proportion of its greenhouse gas emissions – a little over 49 per cent in 2002.[108] In terms of climate change impacts New Zealand, a mid-latitude country, is likely less vulnerable than either the hot and dry expanses of Australia or the low lying atolls of the Pacific. It is likely to experience reduced snowpack and a shorter snow season, together with shrinkage of glaciers but generally (as compared to Australia) its '... cooler, wetter, mid-latitude location may lead to some benefit

---

106 Alexander Gillespie, 'Defending the Irresponsible: A Reply to Chapman and Gray' (1998) 2 *New Zealand Journal of Environmental Law* 233, 247.

107 Basher, above n 104, 136.

108 New Zealand Government, *Report on revised projections for the Kyoto Protocol – first commitment period 30 April 2004* (2004) New Zealand Climate Change Office <http://www.climatechange.govt.nz/resources/reports/revised-projections-kyoto-/index.html> at 19 October 2004.

through the ready availability of suitable crops and likely increases in agricultural production'.[109] This optimistic view is not, however, shared by all.[110]

New Zealand is one of the few developed countries which expects to make a small net economic gain from the first Kyoto commitment period, mainly due to the carbon sink credits it will receive from reforestation.[111] As compared to 'business as usual', a small decline in Gross Domestic Product (0.08-0.26 per cent) is predicted to be offset by a gain in income from international sales of sink credits for an overall increase in Gross National Product of 0.05-0.52 per cent.[112]

New Zealand's obligation under the Kyoto Protocol is to maintain emissions at 1990 levels over the first commitment period, notwithstanding that it is the fourth highest per capita emitter on an 'all greenhouse gas' basis.[113] That was a very successful outcome, at least for New Zealand, after negotiations conducted as 'self-interested hard-ball from beginning to end'.[114] A peculiarity of New Zealand emissions is the concentration of methane, a particularly potent heat-trapping gas. This concentration is a consequence of the relatively small population of humans as compared to ruminants (such as cattle and sheep). At the time of the Kyoto meeting methane accounted for some 45 per cent of New Zealand's total greenhouse gas emissions, and represented some ten times the average global per capita rate for methane emissions.[115] Fortuitously for New Zealand, its emissions of non-carbon dioxide greenhouse gases (particularly methane and nitrous oxide) actually fell over the period 1990–1996 due to extraneous variables such as lower prices for beef and sheep meat, although the trend was partially reversed in the mid-1990s.[116] Another problematic policy issue for New Zealand has been the transport sector (accounting for some 40-45 per cent of carbon dioxide emissions) which is characterized by a high and growing level of car ownership (second only

---

[109] IPCC Working Group II, *Summary for Policymakers: The Regional Impacts of Climate Change: An Assessment of Vulnerability* (November 1997) [6.4] (reproduced in Gillespie and Burns, above n 8, Appendix IV).

[110] See, e.g. Ken Piddington, 'A commentary on the Minister's Chatham House Speech of 14 June' in New Zealand Institute of International Affairs, above n 33, 1-2.

[111] New Zealand Government, *National Interest Analysis: Kyoto Protocol to the UN Framework Convention on Climate Change* (13 February 2002) 5, New Zealand Climate Change Office <http://www.climatechange.govt.nz/resources/consultation/round1/national-interest-analysis.pdf> at 17 December 2004.

[112] New Zealand Climate Change Program, Climate Change Working Paper: Assessment of Economic Modelling (November 2001) New Zealand Climate Change Office <www.climatechange.govt.nz/resources/economic/index.html> at 20 October 2004.

[113] Alexander Gillespie, 'New Zealand and the Climate Change Debate: 1995–1998' in Gillespie and Burns, above n 8, 165.

[114] The Hon. Simon Upton (Kyoto negotiator and then Minister for the Environment), quoted in Gillespie, 'Defending the Irresponsible', above n 106, 248.

[115] Gillespie, 'New Zealand and the Climate Change Debate', above n 113, 179.

[116] Gillespie, 'Defending the Irresponsible', above n 106, 242-4.

to the United States at 69 vehicles per 100 population),[117] an aging car fleet and the absence of emission controls on vehicles.[118]

Policy Responses

The New Zealand Climate Change Program was initiated in 1988 by a Labour government to consider what national response might be required of New Zealand. In 1990 the Labour government, and then successive National governments, adopted climate change policies and greenhouse gas reduction targets. This pre-Kyoto program initially envisaged a 20 per cent reduction in GHGs by 2005 by the soon-to-be defeated Labour government and similarly by the Opposition National Party (though with a target date five years earlier, that is by 2000).[119] By 1992, with a forecast growth in emissions between 1990–2000, the aim of 20 per cent reduction was abandoned by the governing National Party, and in 1993 its policy was changed to one of stabilization of net carbon dioxide emissions at 1990 levels by 2000,[120] still a decade earlier than the later first commitment period from Kyoto. The recent history of New Zealand energy efficiency was particularly poor: between 1973 and 1987 its intensity of energy use (energy used per unit of Gross Domestic Product) grew by more than 30 per cent in contrast to a 20 per cent overall reduction for OECD states.[121] There was therefore arguably scope for significant emission reductions on the demand side through efficiency measures as well as supply side options such as wind power. More recently, carbon dioxide emissions actually grew by one third over the period 1990–2002.[122]

As a general context for policy responses to the Kyoto Protocol it should be noted that in the mid-1980s New Zealand undertook a major re-structuring of its economy, characterized principally by a down-sizing of government and an embrace of market mechanisms as opposed to a regulatory state. It was a self-imposed regime of neo-liberal economics reflecting the so-called Washington consensus. Initially introduced by a Labour government and followed by all subsequent governments, these economic reforms have exerted a powerful gravitational pull on government policy and are reflected in an ongoing move away from a regulatory state and toward a more market-driven economy. There is an aversion to either increasing the cost of emission-producing processes and uses to

117 Ibid 245.

118 Gillespie, 'New Zealand and the Climate Change Debate', above n 113, 183.

119 For a detailed (and critical) review of New Zealand climate change policy in the early 1990s see Kirsty Hamilton, 'New Zealand Climate Change Policy Between 1990 and 1996: A Greenpeace Perspective' in Gillespie and Burns, above n 8, 143.

120 Ibid 153-5.

121 Ibid 148.

122 New Zealand Climate Change Office *New Zealand's Greenhouse Gas Inventory 1990–2002: Executive Summary* (April 2004) New Zealand Climate Change Office <www.climatechange.govt.nz/resources/reports/nir-apr04/html> at 27 July 2004.

reflect environmental and 'Kyoto' externalities through, for example, taxation policies, or to subsidizing alternative processes and uses.

The relationship between Kyoto measures (in the framework of international legal obligations) and the domestic regime for regulating the environment requires an understanding of the New Zealand *Resource Management Act 1991* (RMA). The RMA was a consolidating statute, replacing or amending over 50 statutes, and was heavily influenced by the 1987 Brundtland Report and its emphasis on sustainable development and integrated resource management.[123] It adopted a principled and comprehensive approach to sustainable development which was considered innovative at the time and which earned it a reputation as one of the more advanced environmental statutes in the world. Control of greenhouse gas emissions falls within the ambit of the Act (under s.15(1)(c) and s.2), particularly in the sense that both pursue the priority of sustainability. Climate change policies might arguably have been more completely incorporated into the existing mechanisms of the RMA, primarily through the use of resource consents for emitters and the development of appropriate plans by regional authorities, but also including carbon tax and carbon trading mechanisms. However, that has not been the policy choice of governments to date.[124] One of the virtues of a regulatory framework – an enhanced degree of public participation – is thereby lost in the embrace of economic instruments, although contrary arguments might be made for economic instruments in terms of least-cost responses, flexibility, technological innovation and lower transaction costs.[125] In the event the Domestic Policy Option Statement (DPOS) supported the use of stand-alone economic instruments with the RMA consigned to a complementary role. In 2004 the RMA was amended to remove the ability of regional councils to directly control greenhouse gas emissions through resource consents and regional plans, the government's desire being to address emissions through national policies.

But in terms of policy in the mid-1990s two principles came to drive the climate change response in New Zealand.[126] The first was one of minimal interference with markets: for example, a market-oriented approach to research by various non-government agencies was introduced in 1992 by the (conservative) National government,[127] with few resources available for government agencies. As an aside, an interesting feature of the New Zealand climate change regime is said to be the voluntary networking of scientists from various specialty areas – climate scientists, agricultural scientists, hydrologists, coastal specialists, environmental managers, industry experts and social and medical researchers. This rather ad hoc

[123] For a more detailed account of Kyoto policies in the context of the RMA see Bosselmann, Fuller and Salinger, above n 3, 83-102.

[124] Ibid 88-98. The authors are critical of that choice (at 102-109), and argue that risks such as inconsistency between regional plans could be overcome by issuing a National Policy Statement.

[125] See, e.g. ibid 98-102.

[126] Gillespie, 'New Zealand and the Climate Change Debate', above n 113, 169-179.

[127] For example, Hamilton, above n 119, 149-152.

model is said to be both efficient and effective in the absence of substantial state funding.[128]

The second principle required 'least economic cost' policies, which in practice translated as an emphasis on carbon sequestration in forests rather than lower emissions at source. This latter policy is known as a 'net approach' (as opposed to the 'gross approach' of emission reductions), and in 1994 it was proposed that such sequestration constitute 80 per cent (lowered to 60 per cent in 1997) of the proposed climate change response.[129]

New Zealand's negotiating stance at Kyoto was, like that of Australia, controversial in demanding the inclusion of carbon sinks in emission accounting and in seeking commitments from developing countries.[130] As was the case with Australia and other sink supporters,[131] this promotion of carbon sinks as a policy option resulted in criticism from other Kyoto states – not only on grounds of narrow self-interest but also because there were still many scientific uncertainties surrounding their operation, because of methodological problems in accounting for them and because the carbon would eventually be released. In fact New Zealand may be well placed to allow large increases in greenhouse gas emissions on the basis of credits it will receive for carbon sinks, much of which will flow from 'business as usual' forestry.[132] In terms of reductions in carbon dioxide emissions through sinks the average for Annex I countries (according to 1997 estimates) was 8 per cent but for New Zealand was 81 per cent, the highest of any Annex I country.[133] It was in that context that one commentator characterized New Zealand's approach as 'parochial self-interest, combined with sleight of hand'.[134]

The post-Kyoto policy response of the ruling National Government took the form of the DPOS, the primary objective of which was to pursue 'least cost' measures, which in turn were judged to be the use of economic instruments which would reach to all rather than merely large emitters via pricing mechanisms. The relevant instruments were taken to be environmental taxes and a domestic emissions trading system. The domestic trading system would interface with the international system, requiring emitters to hold certificates sufficient to cover their greenhouse gas emissions; they could sell any surplus or purchase more in the event of falling short.[135] Other policy objectives within the DPOS included maintaining international credibility, equity with respect to impacts, practicality and durability over time, and flexibility.

---

[128] Basher, above n 104, 139 (though no evidence is offered).

[129] Ibid.

[130] Hamilton, above n 119, 143.

[131] For example, Canada, Norway, Iceland, the United States and the Russian Federation.

[132] Bosselmann, Fuller and Salinger, above n 3, 121.

[133] Gillespie, 'Defending the Irresponsible', above n 106, 235.

[134] 'Kyoto' (1997) 3 *ECO Newsletter* 2 (quoted in Gillespie, 'Defending the Irresponsible', above n 106, 234).

[135] For a more detailed analysis of the emissions market see, e.g. Paul Radich, 'Kyoto and the Emissions Trading Market' (2001) *New Zealand Law Journal* 463; Paul Radich, 'The Emissions Market' (2002) *New Zealand Law Journal* 14.

A Labour government was elected in 1999 and proceeded with a consultation process and a Preferred Policy Package in 2002. Its stated 'overall climate change goal is that New Zealand should have made significant greenhouse gas reductions on business-as-usual and be set towards a permanent downward path for gross emissions by 2012'.[136] The policy response was again dominated by non-regulatory, market-based options, mostly aimed at modest emission reductions which would be swamped in importance by the sink credits which New Zealand had aggressively (and controversially) promoted as a member of the JUSCANZ group. An overview of projections[137] for the first commitment period (2008–2012) illustrates the point.

Total GHG base year (1990) emissions were 61.64 million tonnes of carbon dioxide-equivalent (Mt CO2-equivalent), so the commitment for 2008–2012 is for an aggregate 308 Mt CO2-equivalent for the five years. Best estimates for 'business-as-usual', that is to say in the absence of Kyoto policies, are for 399 Mt CO2-equivalent, an increase of 30 per cent. By 2002 total emissions had already grown by 21.6 per cent, including large increases for methane from dairy cows (up 65 per cent), transport (up 61 per cent) and electricity generation (up 58 per cent, with growth in electricity production coming from thermal rather than hydro generation).[138] Existing Kyoto policies are estimated to reduce that business-as-usual total to 360 Mt CO2-equivalent, still an increase of 17 per cent over the base year. But sink credits for the same period are projected at 95 CO2-equivalent, thus generating an emissions 'credit'. In other words, emissions will actually increase significantly over 1990 levels, but will be more than compensated for by reforestation – hence New Zealand's aggressive advocacy of carbon sinks and a 'net' emissions approach.

On a sectoral basis, Agriculture is the largest source of greenhouse gas emissions with 49 per cent of total emissions, and on a business-as-usual basis was expected to grow by 26 per cent above 1990 in the first commitment period.[139] There was a growth of 15.5 per cent to 2002. Agriculture is at present largely exempt from Kyoto measures though emissions in this sector are expected to ease somewhat due to land use changes such as forestry, tenure reviews, conversion to lifestyle blocks and intensive horticulture. The Energy (including transportation) sector contributed 43 per cent of total emissions, with a projected business-as-usual growth of 43 per cent above 1990 levels by the first commitment period.[140] There was a 35 per cent increase in emissions from this sector to 2002. Note that the domestic transport sector accounted for some 45 per cent of carbon dioxide

---

[136] New Zealand Climate Change Office, Q&A on GHG Inventory and New Zealand's net position <www.climatechange.govt.nz/resources/info-sheets/qa-inventory-net-position.html> at 27 July 2004.

[137] New Zealand Government, *Report on revised projections for the Kyoto Protocol*, above n 108.

[138] New Zealand Climate Change Office, Q&A, above n 136.

[139] New Zealand Government, *Report on revised projections for the Kyoto Protocol*, above n 108.

[140] Ibid.

emissions but has not been subject to any explicit policy response other than a general expression of concern for its environmental impacts.[141]

The Industrial Processes sector contributes only 5 per cent of total emissions, with business-as-usual estimates of 29 per cent growth above 1990 levels in the first commitment period.[142] Emissions in this sector increased by 20.5 per cent over 1990–2002. The Waste sector contributed some 3 per cent of total emissions in 2002 through landfill disposal and waste water.[143] Business-as-usual projections for the first commitment period are not currently available, but emissions had actually fallen by 17.7 per cent in 2002.

There are a range of programs through which actual reductions in emissions, as compared to 'business as usual', are expected to be achieved.[144] That is to say, these are reductions which would not have occurred but for the various government policies either presently in place or planned. Firstly, the National Energy Efficiency and Conservation Strategy (NEECS) seeks to improve energy efficiency by some 20 per cent and to increase energy supplies from renewable energy sources. The expected impact over the first commitment period is 5 Mt CO2-equivalent. Secondly, the New Zealand Waste Strategy aspires to 'moving towards zero waste by 2010' through reductions in waste together with re-use, recycling and recovery economic incentives for a total abatement of 6 Mt CO2-equivalent. Thirdly, a Project to Reduce Emissions program provides incentives for projects which will reduce emissions below 'business as usual' during the first commitment period. Incentives take the form of emission units which are awarded to projects which would not otherwise be economically viable. The units will be internationally tradable when the Protocol comes into force. The value of the units will be determined by the future international market, leaving current tenderers to make their own value estimates, though some assistance is available from the emerging European Union Emissions Trading Scheme. Estimates are for savings of some 8-12 Mt CO2-equivalent. Some four million emission units have been awarded to date, with another six million to be available from late 2004. Fourth, Local Government Initiatives will take the form of a three year program, beginning in 2004, called 'Communities for Climate Protection'. It is based on the 'Cities for Climate Protection' program that has proven successful internationally in reducing emissions both from local councils and their constituent communities through energy efficiency, waste reduction, sustainable transportation and other locally oriented initiatives. It is expected to realize some 0.6 Mt CO2-equivalent. Fifth, there is a Small to Medium Enterprises and Business Opportunities policy aimed at encouraging smaller businesses to reduce emissions and their exposure to emissions charges. They are expected to generate some 3 Mt CO2-equivalent in emissions abatement. Finally, the government plans to introduce price based measures, including an emissions charge on fossil fuels and industrial process

[141] Bosselmann, Fuller and Salinger, above n 3, 74.
[142] Ibid.
[143] Ibid.
[144] See generally New Zealand Government, *Report on revised projections for the Kyoto Protocol*, above n 108.

emissions from 2007. The charge will approximate the international emissions price with a cap of NZ$25 per tonne of CO2-equivalent – at NZ$15 per tonne the charges are expected to generate some 11 Mt CO2-equivalent. Enterprises whose viability is then particularly at risk may voluntarily pursue international best practice in return for carbon charge exemptions under a program of Negotiated Greenhouse Agreements (NGAs). Note that agriculture is not subject to the charge, but in return is required to enter into a Memorandum of Understanding to implement an agricultural research strategy to reduce methane and nitrous oxide gases.

Other policy strategies relate to transport, waste, climate change research and public awareness. The various policies are to be differentially applied to four economic groups: those whose competitiveness is most at risk, general energy users including businesses, institutions and households, on-farm agriculture and 'others' for whom policy responses are difficult (for example, due to lack of abatement options and/or measurement difficulties).

As required by the Kyoto Protocol the government formulated a National Energy Efficiency and Conservation Strategy (NEECS) and passed the Energy Efficiency and Conservation Act 2000 to promote energy efficiency, conservation and renewable energy sources, though without a specific regulatory framework. The NEECS aims to achieve a 20 per cent improvement in energy efficiency by 2012 together with a substantial increase in renewable energy sources.

Thus Kyoto policies in New Zealand have as yet barely targeted the energy sector (just a commitment to efficiency), the transport sector (environmental impacts merely noted) and the agriculture sector (a commitment to more research).[145] The reluctance to implement meaningful policy measures in the agricultural sector is perhaps the most significant policy anomaly, as government (that is to say taxpayers) are to bear the Kyoto costs of the sector's non-carbon dioxide emissions. The obvious reasons are the difficulty of reducing these emissions and the importance of the sector to the New Zealand economy, though in the long term some practical measures must be implemented. There is now a Pastoral Greenhouse Gas Research Strategy which seeks to develop abatement technologies which will lower ruminant methane and nitrous oxide emissions by at least 20 per cent at the end of the first commitment period.[146]

In any event, overwhelming the policies for actual emission reductions are the anticipated sink credits from Landuse Change and Forestry. The best estimate of carbon sequestration from sinks is 95 Mt CO2-equivalent, largely due to high levels of planting in the mid-1990s – over the period 1992–2002 planted forests were taking over farmed land at an average rate of 40 000 ha per year, but planting rates declined to some 15 000 ha per year in 2003.[147] The government's forecast

---

[145] Ibid.

[146] Mark Leslie and Peter O'Hara, 'A Pastoral Greenhouse Gas Research Strategy' (October 2003) New Zealand Ministry of Agriculture and Forestry <http://www.maf.govt.nz/mafnet/rural-nz/sustainable-resource-use/climate/pastoral-greenhouse-gas-strategy/index.htm> at 22 October 2004.

[147] New Zealand Government, *Report on revised projections for the Kyoto Protocol*, above n 108.

planting rates are for 30 000 ha per annum. As the plantings from the 1990s mature in the mid-2020s a future government will in fact face net liabilities from Kyoto forests, at least for a period of 2 to 5 years. Carbon sequestration from these forest sinks increased by 17.7 per cent over the period 1990–2002.

The government has proposed a Forest Industry Framework Agreement to promote and co-ordinate climate change policy for the sector, and has set aside funding for new initiatives contingent on the signing of a Memorandum of Understanding. As well, and in light of the importance of forestry to New Zealand's ability to meet its Kyoto commitments, the government has felt it necessary to issue a 'clarification' to the industry on the management of the benefits and liabilities which will accrue under Kyoto rules for sink credits.[148] In short, the government has decided to retain all sink credits and to assume any associated liabilities, at least for the first commitment period. Those liabilities arise because credits claimed for 'Kyoto' forests (those planted since 1990) create contingent liabilities in the future when the same forests are harvested or otherwise degraded. Replacement emission units will have to be purchased on the international market and may be more expensive if and when the price of carbon credits increases over time. Should these liabilities be devolved to private individuals and companies they would not only face these possible capital losses but other ongoing obligations, such as insurance of some kind to ensure their ability to discharge the liabilities and the costs of monitoring and verification of carbon data. However, there is a Permanent Forest Sink Initiative which aims to enable landowners, particularly those with largely marginal land, to establish permanent forests which cannot be harvested until after 35 years have elapsed and then on a 'continuous canopy basis'.[149] Rights (in the form of tradable Kyoto emission units) and obligations (regarding costs and replacement of units in the event of forest loss) will be the subject of contracts between landowners and the Crown, and will include an insurance requirement to guarantee landowner liabilities in the event of accidental or deliberate loss of forest.

New Zealand has also entered into Climate Change Partnerships with Australia and the United States. The NZ-US partnership began in July 2003 and, at the time of writing, included 32 projects in such priority areas as climate change science, greenhouse gas accounting in forestry and agriculture, climate change research in Antarctica and cooperation with developing countries.[150] The Australia-New Zealand Bilateral Climate Change Partnership announced a number of projects in December 2003, including climate monitoring and prediction in the

---

[148] New Zealand Government, *Clarification on sink credits* (2004) New Zealand Climate Change Office <www.climatechange.govt.nz/sectors/forestry/sink-credits.html> at 27 July 2004.

[149] New Zealand Government, *Questions and answers on the Permanent Forest Sink Initiative* (2004) New Zealand Climate Change Office <www.climatechange.govt.nz/resources/info-sheets/qa-forest-sink-intiative.html> at 27 August 2004.

[150] Hon. Pete Hodgson, 'NZ-U.S. consolidate partnership on climate change' (Press Release, 16 July 2004) New Zealand Government <http://www.beehive.govt.nz/PrintDocument.cfm?DocumentID=20342> at 27 July 2004.

South-West Pacific Region, facilitation of local government engagement on climate change issues, common energy efficiency regulatory requirements and further research into climate variability and predictability. There is a fairly high degree of collaboration between New Zealand and Australia, for example within the scientific establishment but also within economic, environmental and foreign policies although clearly their respective policy responses to climate change differ. For example, in November 2004 seven new partnership projects under the Bilateral Climate Change Partnership were announced in such areas as methane emissions from livestock and nitrous oxide from agriculture, adaptation strategies with developed countries, extension of a joint end-use energy efficiency scheme to Fiji and improved climate observations for Pacific Island Countries.[151]

Conclusions

In summary, New Zealand's policy response to the Kyoto Protocol might reasonably be described as disappointing. It is one of only four states (excluding two Economies in Transition) to have negotiated for itself a no-reduction position from 1990 base levels of GHGs. It was a vigorous promoter of self-serving JUSCANZ initiatives on carbon sinks and the various 'flexible' policy options which allows it to avoid any significant pain of actual emission reductions by utilizing forest sinks. Indeed it is likely to make an economic gain from its Kyoto measures. In that sense it could not be said to have exercised leadership in the difficult task of persuading the international community to make the hard decisions which will surely be necessary to make any substantial impact on global warming.

Small Island States

The Alliance of Small Island States[152] (AOSIS) emerged as an independent grouping at the fourth round of negotiations leading to the UNFCCC. The Pacific Island Countries (PICs) fall within a general category of Small Island Developing States (SIDS). Many of the South Pacific states belong to a regional grouping known as the Pacific Forum – the fourteen members are Australia, the Cook Islands, the Federated States of Micronesia, Fiji, Kiribati, Nauru, New Zealand, Niue, Palau, Papua New Guinea, Republic of the Marshall Islands, Samoa, Solomon Islands, Tonga, Tuvalu and Vanuatu. Among the Forum's objectives is the 'sustainable management of its resources', along with other objectives such as

[151] Hon. Pete Hodgson, 'Joint Australia, New Zealand action on climate change' (Press Release, 4 November 2004) New Zealand Government <http://www.beehive.govt.nz/PrintDocument.cfm?DocumentID=21393> at 20 December 2004.

[152] Defined by the UN as being of less than 10 000 square km in land area and with less than 500 000 inhabitants. The group includes states from the Atlantic, Indian and Pacific Oceans, the Caribbean, the Mediterranean (Cyprus, Malta) and the South China Sea (Singapore).

economic prosperity and good governance.[153] But generally their vulnerability to climate change is the most pressing environmental issue they presently face, particularly with respect to rising sea levels and their impacts on coastal environments, bleaching of coral reefs and unpredictable changes in productivity in marine ecosystems.[154] Coastal populations are under particular threat: in Fiji, for example, half of the population live within sixty kilometres of the coast and 90 percent of villages are located on the coast.[155] Their economies are similarly threatened as the major sectors – fishing, tourism and agriculture – will all be affected by climate change.[156] Further implications follow with respect to destabilizing effects on the social and political orders of what are already in many cases only marginally viable states.

Generally, they lack the resource and infrastructures for a significant scientific establishment, with monitoring often supported by Australia and New Zealand. They are generally characterized by small, weak and dependent economies and will be largely dependent on other states to manage climate change impacts. Given that any solutions will depend on negotiations between major states, through the Kyoto Protocol or otherwise, then climate change will remain an external issue for Pacific Island states notwithstanding that they are likely to be its first victims.[157] The reluctance of their most important neighbour, Australia, to ratify the Protocol suggests the weak degree of influence these states exert even in their own region. Indeed all of the so-called JUSCANZ 'Kyoto-hostile' states – Japan, the United States, Canada, Australia and New Zealand – are Pacific Rim states and seemingly impervious to the likely plight of the small and largely fragmented Pacific Island states.

They are indeed particularly vulnerable to climate change impacts.[158] It has been predicted that over the period 2000–2100 the global mean sea level will rise 0.09-0.88m.[159] The particular threat to SIDS has been recognized by the international community – for example, in the discussions of the UNFCCC and the UN Global Conference for the Sustainable Development of Small Island

---

[153] See, e.g. Pacific Islands Forum, *Special Leaders' Retreat: The Auckland Declaration* (2004) <www.forumsec.org.fj> at 6 April 2004.

[154] Laurence Cordonnery, 'Environmental Law Issues in the South Pacific and the Quest for Sustainable Development and Good Governance' in Anita Jowitt and Tess Newton (eds), *Passage of Change: Law, Society and Governance in the Pacific* (2003) 233, 234.

[155] Ashleigh Lezard et al, *Climate Change in the Pacific* (2003) 3 World Wildlife Federation <http://www.wwfpacific.org.fj/climate_change/CC%20Booklet%20(lite).pdf> at 20 December 2004.

[156] Ibid.

[157] Cordonnery, above n 154.

[158] For a more complete assessment see, e.g. Burns, above n 32, 233.

[159] J T Houghton et al (eds), *IPCC, Climate Change 2001: The Scientific Basis* (2001) 16, cited in Alexander Gillespie, 'Small Island States in the face of climatic change: the end of the line in international environmental responsibility' (2004) 22 UCLA *Journal of Environmental Law and Policy* 107, 110. Other estimates vary – for example, an IPCC projection of 0.15-0.95m, with a best estimate of 0.49m by 2100 (quoted in Burns, above n 32, 235).

Developing States.[160] In many cases SIDS rise only a few metres above sea level and are therefore at risk for significant land loss – examples include the Marshall Islands, Tuvalu, Kiribati, Tonga and Vanuatu.[161] Kiribati, for example, could lose 12.5 per cent of its land mass from a one metre rise in sea levels, and in fact has already seen two of its uninhabited islands disappear under rising sea levels.[162] Other impacts such as coastal erosion, dislocation of population and costs of adaptation will be common to other affected countries though usually with less severity.[163] Those impacts would be further exacerbated by any increase in violent weather events. Amelioration measures are likely beyond the economic capabilities of these states – for example, effective sea walls in the Marshall Islands are estimated to cost US$100 million in a country with a gross domestic product of only US$80 million.[164]

Notwithstanding the uncertainty surrounding likely impacts of global warming, vulnerability assessments for the Pacific Island states suggest that they are highly vulnerable to climate change and sea levels, that they have considerable natural resilience which is impaired by human pressures, that they themselves make only insignificant contributions to global environmental changes, and that they have a low capacity to respond to change.[165] This vulnerability is acknowledged in the preamble to the UNFCCC, 'recognizing ... that low-lying and other small island countries ... are particularly vulnerable to the adverse effects of climate change', in Principle 2 that '... those that are particularly vulnerable to the adverse effects of climate change ... should be given full consideration', in (article 4) Commitment Four that 'the developed country Parties ... shall ... assist the developing country Parties that are particularly vulnerable to the adverse effects of climate change in meeting costs of adaptation to those adverse effects' and in (article 4) Commitment Eight that 'the Parties shall give full consideration to ... [necessary] actions ... including [those] ... related to funding, insurance and the transfer of technology ... especially on ... (a) small island states; (b) countries with low-lying coastal areas'. The South Pacific SIDS have, through the Pacific Forum, similarly called for 'urgent action to reduce greenhouse emissions and for further commitments in the future by all major emitters'.[166]

All of the Pacific Forum states except Australia and Tonga have ratified (or acceded to) the Kyoto Protocol, and three of them – the Cook Islands, Niue and Nauru – have added a Declaration that article 3 of the Protocol (stipulating an overall 5 per cent reduction of 1990 emissions by Annex I countries over the first commitment period) is 'inadequate to prevent dangerous anthropocentric

---

[160] Gillespie, above n 159, 112-13.
[161] Ibid.
[162] Burns, above n 32, 235.
[163] For a more complete treatment of likely effects on SIDS, see Gillespie, above n 159.
[164] Burns, above n 32, 236.
[165] John Hay, 'Climate Change in the Pacific: Science-based Information and Understanding' in Gillespie and Burns, above n 8, 269, 285.
[166] *Forum Communiqué*, Thirty Third Pacific Islands Forum, Fiji, August 2002, [24]-[25] (quoted in Gillespie, above n 159, 120).

interference with the climate system'.[167] As developing (or in some cases least developed) countries they are not required to meet any specific emission reduction targets under the Kyoto Protocol.

An interesting problem for the future may be that of environmental refugees from states such as Tuvalu. Its total land size is only 26 square km, its highest point is only 4-5m above sea level and its population only 11 000.[168] It has already requested that Australia and New Zealand take some of its people as the islands become less habitable; New Zealand has agreed to plan a thirty year immigration program but Australia has declined. As well Tuvalu is threatening to file a lawsuit with the International Court of Justice against the United States and Australia over the refusal of those countries, respectively the largest emitter of greenhouse gases and the biggest per capita emitter of greenhouse gases, to ratify the Kyoto Protocol.[169] In that context the response of New Zealand and particularly Australia must be a considerable disappointment to the Pacific Forum states.[170] More generally, there is also a question as to whether there might be a claim in state responsibility for the impacts of climate change on vulnerable states.[171]

Regional cooperation has, however, offset some of the disadvantages of under-developed island states. They coordinate climate change policy through the Alliance of Small Island States (AOSIS), whose priorities are understandably in tension with industrialized states including Australia and New Zealand, neither of whom were required to actually reduce emissions below 1990 levels. Actual climate change efforts are financed by the Global Environment Facility (a joint program of the World Bank and UN Development Programme) under the Pacific Island Climate Change Assistance Program (PICCAP), to which Australia is a significant contributor.[172] More generally there is a South Pacific Regional Environment Programme (SPREP), supported by Australia and New Zealand, that monitors regional environmental issues such as marine pollution and biodiversity as well as climate change.[173] In addition there are government agencies – for

---

[167] UNFCCC, *Kyoto Protocol: Status of Ratification*, above n 17.

[168] 'Tiny country struggles to keep its head above water' (November 2003) 15 *Global Environmental Change* 5.

[169] Kalinga Seneviratne, *Tuvalu Steps Up Threat to Sue Australia*, U.S. (2002) Pacific Islands Report <www.tuvaluislands.com/news/archives/2002/2002-09-10.htm> at 18 August 2004.

[170] This was most clearly demonstrated at the 1997 South Pacific Forum, where this disappointment drew an aggressive response from Australian Prime Minister Howard: see Basher, above n 104, 138. See also ibid.

[171] See, e.g. Phillip Barton, 'State Responsibility and Climate Change: Could Canada be Liable to Small Island States?' (2002) 11 *Dalhousie Journal of Legal Studies* 65.

[172] In 2003 Australia substantially increased its contribution to the GEF to $68 million for the third replenishment period, some 40 per cent of which was targeted at climate change projects including the PICCAP. See Kemp, 'Australia's Approach to Climate Change', above n 43.

[173] Note a more sceptical view of such programs as being tainted by 'ecocolonialism' and 'scientific neocolonialism'; see, e.g. Michael Edwards 'Parochialism and Empowerment:

example, in New Zealand the Climate Change Office and the National Institute of Water and Atmospheric Research – which participate in various climate change initiatives in the Pacific, including the Global Climate Observing System which monitors climate on a global scale.

Under the Kytoto Protocol's Clean Development Mechanisms program for Annex I states to facilitate emission reductions in non-Annex I states there would seem to be opportunity for Australia and New Zealand to offset their relatively high domestic costs of emission reduction with low-cost projects in the neighbouring South Pacific, for example in energy and land use. Australia has undertaken a number of emission reduction projects in the South Pacific and Indonesia,[174] but New Zealand has not yet taken any formal initiatives.

Summary and Conclusions

The Kyoto Protocol is a significantly limited instrument for addressing the threat of climate change. It will come into force in 2005 with Russia's ratification, and may reasonably be expected to meet its modest ambition of a 5 per cent reduction in greenhouse gas emissions in the first commitment period. Its major limitations are three-fold: the absence of the United States as the most prolific emitter, the lack of binding commitments for developing states such as China, and the modesty of its ambitions given the necessary reduction in emissions to even stabilize greenhouse gas concentrations. Each is a reflection of the realpolitik of the international order, wherein the trade-off between economic growth and the unknown net impacts of emission reduction measures lead to an unenthusiastic response from many states. Nowhere was this clearer than largely market-oriented concessions granted to the JUSCANZ group, of whom two states (the United States and Australia) still refused to ratify the Protocol. One thing seems likely though: if the developed states (including the United States) fail to meet even the modest aspirations of the first commitment period then it seems unlikely that developing states will embrace any future regime which requires legally binding commitments to reduce their own emissions.

The limitations of the Protocol have particular significance for Pacific Island states. They are especially vulnerable both in terms of geography and of economics. They will most likely be disproportionately affected by climate change notwithstanding that their contribution to the problem is negligible. Similarly they lack (individually at least) any political influence sufficient to sway powerful states, and are unable to exert significant influence even in their own Pacific region in respect of Australia in particular.

It must be particularly galling to the Pacific Island states that one of the Pacific Forum members – Australia – is one of the highest per capita emitters of

---

Responding to Ecocolonialism and Globalisation in the SouthWest Pacific' in Gillespie and Burns, above n 8, 251.

[174] See, e.g. Peter Alsop, 'Joint Implementation: A Survey of Principles and Practical Issues' in Gillespie and Burns, above n 8, 209, 226-8.

greenhouse gases and was able to plead a 'special case' and negotiate one of the most favourable state regimes for emission targets and abatement practices, yet still refuses to ratify. As a party to the original Framework Convention on Climate Change it has undertaken voluntary measures but in spite of its being permitted an 8 per cent increase in emissions (the most favourable of any major developed state) it appears unlikely to meet even that target.

Similarly New Zealand, the other significant regional power and major per capita emitter, was a member of the reluctant group of JUSCANZ states and was successful in negotiating a 'no-reduction' emissions position. Although it is unusually dependent on agriculture and must deal with the difficult issue of methane emissions from livestock, it is one of the few states which may actually realize an economic gain from the first commitment period. Its reluctance to accept a reduction on 1990 emission levels, its reliance on carbon sinks rather than actual emissions, its reluctance to make hard choices (for example, in agriculture) and its promotion of developing country commitments all point to its being one of the 'Kyoto-reluctant' states. New Zealand may compare favourably to Australia and the United States but that is damning with faint praise.

Neither Australia nor New Zealand appear willing to exercise leadership in the region, at least in this, and the small island states are unable to bring meaningful pressure to bear. In that sense the region might bc seen as a microcosm of the broader international order both in terms of power relations and in the efficacy of the Protocol. Notwithstanding that the Kyoto Protocol is finally coming into force, it may well be defined not by its achievements but by its limitations. Its first and most vulnerable victims may well be the small Pacific island states, whilst at least one of their affluent neighbours might be characterized as one of the 'villains' of what may prove to be a fatally compromised regime.

'Melanesian Spearhead Group' (MSG): Papua New Guinea, Solomon Islands, Vanuatu and Fiji. The MSG was formed in the late 1980s primarily as a political group, but more recently evolved into the 'Pacific islands' first serious experiment in freeing-up trade and investment among themselves'.[171] The agreement provides for duty-free trade in a range of goods between the MSG member states. Although this does not account for a significant proportion of members' trade and some consider the agreement to be a failure,[172] it represents an important experiment in trade liberalization for the region.[173]

The FICs have enjoyed preferential market access in Australia, New Zealand and other trading partners under several trade agreements. The South Pacific Regional Trade and Economic Cooperation Agreement (SPARTECA),[174] in force since 1981, provides for non-reciprocal duty free access to New Zealand and Australian markets for products from FICs. Under this agreement, almost all exports from these countries enter New Zealand and Australia duty free and without quantitative restrictions.[175] As members of the African, Caribbean and Pacific (ACP) group, many of the FICs have been eligible for preferential market access in the EU under the Lomé Conventions,[176] now succeeded by the Cotonou Agreement[177] (to be discussed below). Under the Compacts of Free Association with the United States, most products from the Marshall Islands, the Federated States of Micronesia and Palau may be imported duty free into the United States.[178] As developing and least-developed countries, FICs have also been beneficiaries of the Generalized System of Preferences and preference arrangements of various countries.

---

[171] Hughes, above n 12, 30. Fiji was not an original member but joined in 1996 following the establishment of the trade agreement: Crocombe, above n 23, 597.

[172] Jane Kelsey, *Big Brothers Behaving Badly: The Implications for the Pacific Islands of the Pacific Agreement on Closer Economic Relations (PACER)* (Interim Report, 2004) Action, Research and Education Network of Aotearoa <http://www.arena.org.nz/bigbully.pdf> at 15 December 2004, 12. See also World Bank, *Embarking on a Global Voyage: Trade Liberalization and Complementary Reforms in the Pacific*, Report No. 24417-EAP (2002), 12-13.

[173] Hughes, above n 12, 30.

[174] *South Pacific Regional Trade and Economic Cooperation Agreement*, opened for signature 14 July 1980, [1982] ATS 31 (entered into force 1 January 1981) ('SPARTECA'), as amended. As between Papua New Guinea and Australia, PACTRA rather than SPARTECA applies: *Exchange of Notes constituting an Agreement on the continued application of the Agreement on Trade and Commercial Relations between Australia and Papua New Guinea of 6 November 1976*, signed 17 February 1982 and 17 March 1982, [1982] ATS 6 (entered into force 17 March 1982).

[175] World Bank, above n 172, 28.

[176] Most recently *Fourth ACP-EEC Convention of Lomé*, opened for signature 15 December 1989 (1990) 29 ILM 783.

[177] *Partnership Agreement Between the Members of the African, Caribbean and Pacific Group of States of the one part, and the European Community and its Member States, of the other part*, signed 23 June 2000 [2000] OJ L 317/3 (entered into force 1 April 2003) ('Cotonou Agreement').

[178] *Compact of Free Association*, 48 USC §§ 1901, 1931 (2003).

These non-reciprocal arrangements – both unilateral preferences and more stable agreements providing for preferential treatment – are illustrative of the pre-Uruguay Round approach to trade and development. As described above, this approach, reflected in the Enabling Clause and Part IV of the GATT, focused on non-reciprocal trade preferences for developing countries as a means of encouraging export-led growth. The subsequent shift toward reciprocal commitments and the full integration of developing countries into the world trading regime has more recently begun to make itself felt in the region. At the same time, tariff preferences have diminished in value and importance as their margins are eroded by liberalization. In addition, recent developments reflect renewed concern about compliance with WTO disciplines on RTAs. Rules governing RTAs have been contained in the GATT since its inception, but have taken on greater importance as the number and significance of RTAs increases and more effective dispute settlement (post-Uruguay Round) makes them more vulnerable to challenge by third countries.

Preferential treatment among parties to an RTA would, in principle, violate the obligation of MFN treatment in the GATT, which requires equally favourable treatment to be given to the like products of all parties. However, in recognition of the potential benefits of RTAs, article XXIV of the GATT allows them to coexist with the multilateral regime provided they meet certain conditions. The first main condition is that upon the formation of a customs union or free trade area, the barriers to trade for third countries (i.e. those that are not part of the customs union or free trade area) must not be higher than before its formation.[179] This is known as the 'external trade' requirement. The second main condition, known as the 'internal trade' requirement, is that duties and other restrictions on 'substantially all trade' among the parties to the RTA must be eliminated.[180] The meaning of 'substantially all trade' has not been precisely defined, but coverage of a comprehensive range of sectors and a substantial proportion of trade is likely required. In summary, then, in order for an RTA's parties to be protected from allegations of MFN violations under the GATT, the RTA must comprehensively eliminate trade barriers among its parties and not result in higher barriers for third parties.

---

[179] GATT art XXIV:5. In the case of a customs union, the rule is that duties and other regulations must not 'on the whole' be higher than their 'general incidence' prior to its formation: art XXIV:5(a). For free trade areas, the rule is stated in more absolute terms: art XXIV:5(b). Greater flexibility is afforded to customs unions because a customs union will have common external tariffs and other restrictions (as well as liberalising trade within the union, as in a free trade area), and achieving this consistency means that some members of the union may have higher external barriers following the formation of the union. This is permitted provided that the overall level of barriers for the customs union as a whole will not be greater.

[180] GATT art XXIV:8. A similar but somewhat more relaxed internal trade requirement is found in the GATS, which allows liberalization of trade in services among parties to an RTA if the agreement has 'substantial sectoral coverage' and provides for 'the absence or elimination of substantially all discrimination … between or among the parties' in the covered sectors: GATS art V:1. A footnote to this article states that 'substantial sectoral coverage' is 'understood in terms of number of sectors, volume of trade affected and modes of supply' and that 'agreements should not provide for the *a priori* exclusion of any mode of supply'.

All RTAs are to be notified to the WTO. The Committee on Regional Trade Agreements is responsible for supervising their consistency with GATT article XXIV. In practice, the supervision process has not had much effect, but there is also the possibility of RTAs being challenged in dispute settlement proceedings. This has been important in the context of the EU's arrangements with the ACP countries, under the Lomé and now Cotonou agreements. These agreements do not fit the GATT definition of an RTA because they do not provide for elimination of restrictions on substantially all trade; rather they (like SPARTECA within the Pacific region) provide for preferential access to EU markets, but not reciprocal or necessarily comprehensive liberalization. They were also supplemented by protocols to provide market access for certain key commodities, like bananas and sugar. Regional trade agreements among developing country parties are covered by the Enabling Clause[181] and therefore need not comply with the GATT article XXIV requirements. For example, the MSG trade agreement was notified to the WTO under the Enabling Clause, not GATT article XXIV.[182] However, this does not apply in the case of an RTA that includes both developed and developing country parties. Historically these have been granted waivers by the GATT contracting parties and, more recently, by the WTO members. However, the most recent waiver for the Cotonou Agreement, granted in 2001, will only last until 31 December 2007.[183] Moreover, these waivers have not protected certain aspects of the scheme from challenges by other WTO members who are excluded from their benefits. A long and complex dispute over the EU scheme for bananas pitted the EU and the ACP countries receiving preferential market access, on the one hand, against other developing countries excluded from preferences, backed by the United States (whose multinationals have substantial interests in non-ACP banana production), on the other. Following a series of decisions finding that the EU was in violation of its WTO obligations, the EU was forced to modify its bananas regime and to seek a further waiver for a transitional period.[184] Although these developments directly affected the African and Caribbean ACP countries, it also had wider implications. More recently, the EU's sugar regime, one part of which involves preferential arrangements for ACP sugar, has been successfully challenged in the WTO, with important implications for ACP countries and in particular Fiji, as a major Pacific island producer of sugar.[185] As we saw above, the

[181] Above n 49, [2(c)].

[182] *Melanesian Spearhead Group Trade Agreement*, WTO Doc WT/COMTD/N/9 (1999) (Notification from Papua New Guinea).

[183] *European Communities – The ACP-EU Partnership Agreement*, WTO Doc WT/MIN(01)/15 (2001) (Decision of 14 November 2001).

[184] *European Communities – Transitional Regime for the EC Autonomous Tariff Rate Quotas on Imports of Bananas*, WTO Doc WT/MIN(01)/16 (2001) (Decision of 14 November 2001).

[185] *European Communities – Export Subsidies on Sugar*, WTO Doc WT/DS265/R (2004) (Report of the Panel). The complaint was brought by Australia, Brazil and Thailand. Fiji and other ACP countries were third parties. The EC has announced that it will appeal this decision.

EU's scheme of unilateral GSP preferences was also challenged in respect of its differentiation between subcategories of developing countries.[186]

These disputes have showed that WTO members are willing to challenge preferential arrangements from which they are excluded, and the more effective procedures for dispute resolution put in place in the Uruguay Round mean that these challenges have more 'teeth' than previously. The Bananas dispute had resulted in $200 million worth of trade sanctions by the US against the EU,[187] providing a sharp incentive to the EU to ensure the WTO-compatibility of its preferential trade arrangements for ACP countries. This environment, combined with the shift in thinking about trade and development, away from non-reciprocal preferences toward full integration of developing countries on a reciprocal basis, has led to major changes in trade arrangements involving developing countries. The South Pacific is no exception to this trend.

A new generation of agreements has recently been concluded that have the potential to significantly change the trading environment for FICs. The EU-ACP relationship is now governed by the Cotonou Agreement, which replaces the Lomé Conventions and is intended to establish new WTO-compliant arrangements. Existing preferences under the Lomé regime will remain in place during a transitional period, ending in 2007.[188] During this period, new 'Economic Partnership Agreements' (EPAs) will be negotiated between the EU and regional groupings of ACP countries. Unlike previous arrangements, these will be reciprocal free trade agreements to liberalize trade in both directions. The Pacific ACP group includes all of the FICs, even those that were not previously party to the Lomé Conventions.[189]

Within the region, the Pacific Island Countries Trade Agreement (PICTA),[190] concluded in 2001, provides for the gradual establishment of a free trade area among the FICs. It is open only to FICs, not to Australia or New Zealand. The Cook Islands, Fiji, Kiribati, Nauru, Niue, Papua New Guinea, Samoa, Solomon Islands and Tonga are presently parties to PICTA,[191] and the agreement came into force in April 2003. This agreement is often referred to as a 'stepping stone'

---

186 *European Communities – Conditions for the Granting of Tariff Preferences to Developing Countries*, WTO Doc WT/DS246/AB/R, AB-2004-1 (2004) (Report of the Appellate Body).

187 'Dispute Settlement Update: Bananas; US-EC Steel' (2001) 43(5) *Bridges Weekly Trade News Digest*, <http://www.ictsd.org/weekly/01-12-20/story2.htm> at 29 December 2004.

188 The WTO waiver, above n 184, is designed to cover this transitional period.

189 Note that this doesn't necessarily mean all of these countries need be party to the eventual EPA. As in other regions, there are questions about the extent to which all members of the regional group will share the same interests in the EPA negotiations. Members that are LDCs will continue to benefit from unilateral preferences under the EBA scheme (see above n 90) and may consider that they have little more to gain from an EPA.

190 *Pacific Islands Countries Trade Agreement*, opened for signature 18 August 2001 (entered into force 13 April 2003) ('PICTA').

191 Vanuatu has passed ratification legislation for PICTA but this legislation was not yet commenced at the time of writing: *Pacific Island Countries Trade Agreement (PICTA) Act* (Vanuatu) No. 6 of 2003.

toward the liberalization and integration of FICs. A separate agreement including Australia and New Zealand was negotiated alongside PICTA. The Pacific Agreement on Closer Economic Relations (PACER)[192] is a framework agreement providing for trade negotiations in the region. The current parties to PICTA, along with Australia and New Zealand, are also parties to PACER. [193] The latter agreement has been in force since October 2002. It does not itself establish a free trade area but sets out obligations to negotiate in certain circumstances: the parties will enter into negotiations for reciprocal free trade arrangements within eight years of the agreement coming into force or earlier as agreed,[194] and if any of the FIC parties, or the parties to PICTA jointly, enter into negotiations for a free trade agreement with a non-Forum country, they will undertake consultations with Australia and New Zealand 'with a view to the commencement of free trade arrangements'. [195] The most likely trigger for this obligation to consult with Australia and New Zealand is the negotiations with the EU under Cotonou. Therefore, although an eventual Cotonou EPA itself may not have a large impact on FICs, given the relatively low volume of their imports from Europe,[196] the EPA negotiations will have important implications. For the Compact countries (Federated States of Micronesia, Republic of the Marshall Islands and Palau), a similar obligation to provide equally favourable treatment to the United States is triggered when any of them agrees to lower its barriers to another developed country.[197] The FICs are now in a position of interlocking obligations, such that once the first free trade agreement including a developed country party is negotiated, obligations to other developed country trading partners will be triggered.

The conclusion of PACER and PICTA and the evolution of the FICs' relationship with the EU under the Cotonou Agreement represent significant changes for the region. The next section will take a closer look at these changes within the global context and at the extent to which they respond to the needs and concerns of SIDS as articulated in the multilateral context.

Special and differential treatment in regional trade agreements

As noted above, participation in RTAs is attractive from the point of view of developing countries because these may offer more stable and secure preferences than the unilateral preference arrangements of developed countries. They also promise deeper integration among a smaller group of trading partners who might

---

[192] *Pacific Agreement on Closer Economic Relations*, opened for signature 18 August 2001, [2004] ATS 10 (entered into force 3 October 2002) ('PACER').

[193] Again, Vanuatu has passed ratification legislation but this legislation was not yet commenced at the time of writing: *Pacific Agreement on Closer Economic Relations (PACER) Act* (Vanuatu) No. 5 of 2003.

[194] PACER art 5.

[195] Ibid art 6 (3), 6(4).

[196] Wadan Narsey, 'PICTA, PACER and EPAs: Where are We Going? Tales of Fags, Booze and Rugby' (Working Paper No. 6/2004, Pacific Institute of Advanced Studies in Development and Governance, Employment and Labour Market Studies Program, 2004) 16.

[197] See World Bank, above n 172, 23.

be expected to be more understanding of one another's particular needs. If one accepts the prevailing wisdom that liberalization by developing countries is beneficial for their development but requires a period of adjustment, RTAs represent an important opportunity to move toward liberalization in a gradual way – a view that is reflected in the 'stepping stone' approach to PACER and PICTA. For SIDS, in particular, RTAs may provide ways of overcoming some of their inherent disadvantages. The formation of a larger market by establishing a free trade area among a number of small states potentially allows greater economies of scale, competition and attractiveness to investors. Regional integration may also make it easier for small states to be heard on the international scene, pooling their resources and political influence in negotiations with other trading partners. In theory, at least, regional integration sounds like a promising strategy for SIDS, particularly if the multilateral regime seems unresponsive to their needs. The present reality is somewhat more complex, however.

A primary concern is the extent to which regional arrangements allow for SDT and for differentiation among developing country members in order to provide treatment appropriate to each party's needs. PACER and the Cotonou Agreement both include a commitment to SDT in the eventual RTAs to be negotiated under these agreements. Any trade agreement negotiated under PACER is to 'recognise the differences in development status of the Parties by the inclusion of appropriate measures providing for special and differential treatment of developing countries'.[198] The Cotonou Agreement in several places reaffirms the parties' commitment to SDT[199] and provides that negotiations for the EPAs 'shall take account of the level of development and the socio-economic impact of trade measures on ACP countries'.[200]

Special and differential treatment in RTAs can manifest itself in different ways. First, the division of the Forum members' trade agreements into PICTA and PACER, rather than moving directly to a single free trade area including all Forum members, in effect provides differentiated treatment to the FICs as a group. The FICs that are parties to PICTA will liberalize trade among themselves first before including Australia and New Zealand. Most imports into FICs are from Australia and New Zealand, and the amount of trade among the FICs is relatively small.[201] This means that the impact on FICs will be modest at first, increasing gradually as trade barriers are reduced among them and then more rapidly when Australia and New Zealand join the group. A built-in transition period is thus provided for, during which FICs can adjust to the loss of tariff revenue and increased competition with their domestic products. The next step is a free trade area including Australia and New Zealand, which will have a larger impact. Then, once free trade within the whole region is established, the stated goal is to move toward

[198] PACER art 7(c).
[199] Cotonou Agreement arts 34(4), 35(3).
[200] Ibid art 37(7).
[201] World Bank, above n 172, 8 (trade among the PICTA countries amounts to only 4 per cent of their total trade).

full integration with the global trading regime.[202] Similarly, the Cotonou Agreement between the ACP countries and the EU contemplates that groups of ACP countries will move toward regional integration as a first step, then that these will enter into agreements with the EU, and finally that they will achieve full integration with the global economy.[203] This 'stepping stone' approach could be described as analogous to the adjustment model of SDT in the WTO, allowing longer transitional periods to developing countries for the adjustment that will be necessary to cope with trade liberalization. Full integration into the global economy is the eventual goal, but is to take place gradually for these states in recognition of their more limited capacity for adjustment.

PACER, the Cotonou Agreement and the Compacts of Free Association also provide for assistance to be granted by the developed country parties. Article 11 of PACER provides that a programme of work for financial and technical assistance, including trade facilitation and promotion, capacity building and structural adjustment, will be developed. It states that the parties recognize the need for 'significant additional resources' for this programme of work and that it 'shall be supported by an adequate level of funding' by Australia and New Zealand and other interested donors. A programme of trade facilitation is also provided for (in article 9 and Annex I). These provisions are reminiscent of technical assistance SDT in the WTO agreements, and similarly reflect an obligation of parties who are in a position to offer assistance to help developing country parties implement their obligations and obtain greater benefit from trade liberalization. In addition, the Cotonou Agreement and Compacts of Free Association contain more general provisions on development and financial assistance. In these agreements, trade liberalization is one part of a larger framework for economic cooperation. Although PACER has similar goals – to promote sustainable development and eliminate poverty in the region – it deals only with trade as a presumed driver of development, leaving other forms of development assistance to separate ad hoc arrangements.

The regional agreements therefore contemplate SDT for FICs as a group by setting out a framework for gradual integration, establishing the principle of SDT for the trade agreements to be negotiated, and providing for various types and amounts of assistance by developed country trading partners. The existing agreements also contain another layer of differentiation in the form of special provisions for LDC and SIS parties. The SIS (Small Island States), it will be recalled, are the smallest of this group of small states, and include the Cook Islands, Kiribati, Nauru, Niue, Republic of the Marshall Islands and Tuvalu. Two of these, Kiribati and Tuvalu, are also LDCs, as are Samoa, Solomon Islands and Vanuatu. This means that of the nine FICs that are parties to PACER and PICTA, six are

---

202 PACER art 3(2).

203 Cotonou Agreement arts 1, 34(1). These state that the objective of the agreement and its economic and trade cooperation framework is the 'gradual integration of ACP [countries] into the world economy'. The APEC Bogor Goals also reflect a two-stage strategy, in this instance providing for liberalization among developed countries first, followed by developing countries.

either SIS or LDC parties (or both); of the fourteen FICs that are parties to the Cotonou Agreement and part of the Pacific Group of ACP states, nine belong to the SIS and/or LDC categories. As noted above, there is evidence to suggest that the very smallest states (which would include the Pacific SIS) face particularly intense, and to some extent insurmountable, challenges in international trade.[204] In principle, then, special treatment for these countries is justified.

All three of these agreements contain provisions allowing special treatment for LDC and SIS parties. PICTA provides that in the establishment of the free trade area, 'Least Developed Countries and Small Island States may be integrated in accordance with different structures and by different time frames than other Parties'.[205] They have a different schedule of reduced import duties which allows higher rates.[206] The LDC and SIS parties must be represented and their particular constraints considered in the context of rules of origin,[207] and they are permitted to maintain higher tariffs to protect developing industries for a longer period.[208] PACER also provides, in language identical to PICTA, that LDC and SIS parties may be integrated by different structures and time frames.[209] Article 7(d) explicitly allows SDT for LDC and SIS parties as an exception to the requirement that any new trade arrangement between FICs and Australia and New Zealand must not discriminate between FIC parties. Trade facilitation is to be designed to take account of the 'special needs and resource and capacity constraints of Least Developed Countries and Small Island States'.[210] The Cotonou Agreement provides for special treatment for least-developed, landlocked and island ACP states.[211] Differentiation is among the fundamental principles of the agreement and the 'vulnerability of landlocked and island countries shall be taken into account'.[212] Article 35(3) specifically states that this vulnerability is to be taken into account in economic and trade cooperation.

Differentiation between developing countries is therefore established as a guiding principle of these framework agreements, in addition to SDT for developing country parties generally. The full extent of special treatment to be provided will only be apparent in the RTAs that are to be negotiated within the framework: an eventual Forum-wide free trade agreement under PACER and the EPA between the EU and Pacific ACP states. However, both agreements explicitly contemplate differentiation and PACER specifically provides for SDT for LDC and SIS parties to a free trade agreement. This is in contrast to the multilateral regime, which, as we have seen, has resisted recognizing any subcategories of developing countries other than LDCs.

---

[204] See, e.g. Winters and Martins, above n 33, 376.
[205] PICTA art 3(1).
[206] Narsey, above n 196, 3.
[207] PICTA arts 5(3), 5(6)(m).
[208] Ibid art 14(3).
[209] PACER art 3(6).
[210] Ibid art 9(4).
[211] Cotonou Agreement arts 85-90.
[212] Ibid art 2.

Two main questions arise from this. First, is the differentiated treatment contemplated by these agreements in compliance with the WTO rules on RTAs? PACER and the Cotonou Agreement are not themselves RTAs, but they provide for the negotiation of RTAs that are intended, by the terms of both agreements, to be WTO-compliant.[213] Second, assuming that the current approach with its two layers of differentiation is permissible, is it likely to be beneficial for FICs, including for the smallest among them?

As explained above, the GATT provisions require an RTA to eliminate restrictions on substantially all trade among the parties. This has been thought to mean that agreements that only partially liberalize trade – in particular that provide for non-reciprocal liberalization – may not meet this condition. Arrangements like the Lomé Conventions between developed and developing country parties, where the developing country parties did not eliminate their trade barriers, were vulnerable to challenge for this reason. It would seem that differentiation among developing countries, such that some of them – here SIS parties – might have lesser obligations, might run into the same difficulties.[214] The lack of clarity on this point and the implications for RTAs involving developing countries have placed this question on the agenda for WTO negotiations. The Doha Ministerial Declaration contains an agreement to negotiate to clarify and improve the disciplines applying to RTAs, and these negotiations are to 'take into account the developmental aspects of regional trade agreements'.[215] The particular issue of SDT and differentiated obligations in RTAs has been raised as part of these negotiations. The ACP group has submitted a paper drawing attention to the fact that the existing rules on RTAs do not provide for SDT in 'North-South RTAs', despite the fact that SDT is 'a key principle and integral part of the legal architecture of WTO', and proposing that 'appropriate flexibility shall be provided for developing countries in meeting the "substantially all trade" requirement in respect of trade and product coverage' and to allow certain protective non-tariff measures for developing countries.[216] This could provide the necessary flexibility for RTAs not only to provide SDT for developing countries generally, but also to differentiate between subcategories of developing countries as may be appropriate in each particular region. The present rules would only constrain certain kinds of SDT and differentiation, since asymmetrical obligations of technical assistance, for example, would not run afoul of the GATT rules. The potential constraint is nevertheless important. This is therefore another aspect of the current WTO negotiations that will be significant for SIDS. If differentiation and SDT are not

---

[213] PACER art 2(2)(e); Cotonou Agreement arts 34(4), 36(1), 37(7).

[214] Note, however, that this probably only applies to Cotonou EPAs and an RTA negotiated under PACER, but not to PICTA, since PICTA is an RTA among developing countries only and therefore covered by the Enabling Clause rather than GATT art XXIV.

[215] Doha Declaration, above n 81, [29].

[216] *Developmental Aspects of Regional Trade Agreements and Special and Differential Treatment in WTO Rules: GATT 1994 Article XXIV and the Enabling Clause*, WTO Doc TN/RL/W/155 (2004) [7], [11] (Communication by the Mission of Botswana on Behalf of the ACP Group of States).

permitted in RTAs, this will work to undermine whatever progress may be made on these issues in the multilateral regime.

The next question, then, involves the extent to which the emerging framework of RTAs involving FICs has the potential to adequately address their particular needs. Views on this point are mixed, although there appear to be some common concerns. Some of the differences of opinion reflect uncertainty about the likely impact of changes in trade policy on Pacific island populations and economies. They also reflect different judgements about what counts as a benefit. For example, the effect of RTAs in 'locking in' domestic trade and economic policy reforms is seen by some as a benefit, by others as a harm. Similarly, trade creation following the creation of a regional free trade area – that is, displacement of local production by imports from another producer from within the free trade area – can be seen as either a harm or a benefit, depending on one's perspective. It has a negative impact on the local producers who lose their market share, but a positive impact on the other producers and on overall efficiency.

Given these differences in perspective and the inherent uncertainty involved in predicting outcomes in a complex system, we are unlikely to reach any definitive conclusions on the likely impact of the current framework. Divergent views have led commentators to offer directly conflicting advice as to the best course of action for FICs.[217] However, it is significant that some common points seem to emerge from the debate. Numerous commentators have questioned the benefits of the 'stepping stone' approach to economic integration of small developing countries like the FICs. In theory, a gradual, step-by-step process of integration seems like a good idea for these countries: it allows them to adjust more slowly to the policy changes that are required and their impacts. This seems consistent with the rationale supporting longer transitional periods as a form of SDT for developing countries in the multilateral system. However, moving toward full integration through a series of progressively larger RTAs presents some specific problems.

First, it is suggested that a trade agreement among only the FICs would result in more trade diversion than trade creation. That is, it is more likely that imports from outside the free trade area will be displaced by imports from within the area (trade diversion), rather than domestic production being displaced by imports from within the area (trade creation). Although in either scenario there are winners and losers, trade diversion is seen as negative overall: it results in the importing country losing tariff revenue (because tariff-attracting imports from outside the free trade area are displaced by tariff-free imports from within the area) and a higher cost, less efficient product gaining market share (because the tariff-free import can be higher priced and still compete with external tariff-attracting imports which would otherwise have an advantage). The government loses and a less efficient outcome results.

[217] For example, Kelsey, above n 172, 34-6, sets out various alternative 'escape routes' from PACER (primarily ways to avoid triggering the obligation to negotiation an RTA under PACER), while Narsey, above n 196, 18-19, suggests that it may be preferable for PICs to pro-actively trigger PACER and negotiate an RTA with Australia and New Zealand simultaneously with the EU-Pacific ACP EPA.

Compounding this problem is the fact that those industries within the region that successfully grow and capture market shares within the free trade area will not necessarily succeed when the next steps toward integration are eventually taken. A producer that is able to be competitive within the region while it is still protected from external imports often will not remain competitive on a larger or global stage once external barriers are lowered. Therefore, the effort and resources that are invested in these producers during the first phase of limited integration may ultimately be wasted and even greater adjustment required in the long run.[218] In the case of RTAs among small developing countries particularly, it is thought unlikely that integration will be sufficient to overcome the disadvantages of small economic size and make industries competitive. Finally, where a free trade area is established among developing countries, there is a tendency for this to increase income disparities between those countries, with the richest members becoming richer and those least well-off being further disadvantaged. Clearly this could damage rather than promote regional cooperation and solidarity.

There seems to be a degree of consensus supporting these concerns, which are based on experiences with the MSG trade agreement and other regional agreements among developing countries as well as economic modelling.[219] If correct, they predict that the gradual approach to integration, although it appears to be a logical response to the particular circumstances and needs of FICs, will not in fact be beneficial for them. The proposed remedy then depends on whether commentators view the ultimate goal of integration as desirable for these states or not: either they should attempt to halt the 'stepping-stone' process before it goes any further,[220] or move more quickly toward integration with developed country trading partners and/or broader liberalization on an MFN basis in the multilateral system.[221] However, both of these courses of action seem unlikely, and it appears that pursuing the stepping stone approach may be another example of the broader tendency for less desirable forms of differential treatment to be favoured because they are politically more feasible.[222]

As for differentiated treatment of SIS within RTAs, the extent to which this is likely to be beneficial depends on the specific forms of SDT that are adopted. PICTA and PACER provide for 'different structures and time frames' for integration of LDC and SIS parties. Longer transition periods for these countries may well be appropriate given their dependence on a limited range of revenue

---

[218] Another concern is that this will increase resistance to further liberalization because the producers that are successful within the region have a vested interest in ensuring they are not exposed to global competition. See, e.g. World Bank, above n 172, 12.

[219] See World Bank, above n 172, 7-14, 22; Nathan Associates Inc., 'Regional Approaches to Integrating Small Economies into the World Trade System' (Research Paper, Submitted to USAID, 2002), 7-10; Gutiérrez, above n 30, 211-13; Kelsey, above n 172, 25; Narsey, above n 196, 7-9.

[220] Kelsey, above n 172, 41, advising FICs to avoid negotiating with the EU or otherwise triggering PACER, freeze accessions to the WTO and consider withdrawing from PICTA and PACER.

[221] See, e.g. Narsey, above n 196, 18; World Bank, above n 172, 30.

[222] See above n 160.

sources and more limited capacity. Under PICTA they are allowed to maintain higher import tariffs (in general and for the protection of developing industries) and this may be contemplated under PACER and Cotonou as well. Reducing developing countries' liberalization commitments to allow them to maintain protectionist policies has fallen out of fashion as a general rule; however, the appropriateness of this strategy in the particular case of very small developing countries may need to be reassessed. There is evidence that very small island countries will find it difficult or impossible to compete in a free trade environment,[223] so the usual prescription of liberalization for developing countries may not apply. Certainly technical assistance and other means of dealing with the limited capacity of these countries on a long term or even permanent basis would seem to be appropriate forms of SDT.

Conclusion

The difficulties facing small states like the FICs in international trade are finally beginning to receive some sustained attention in the WTO with the Doha Declaration work programme on small economies. However, at the same time, changes in the trade regime seem to be exacerbating some of these difficulties: tariff reductions are eroding margins of preference for developing countries that helped them to compete in foreign markets, pressures toward reciprocal liberalization mean sharp declines in tariff revenues upon which many small developing states rely for income, and many countries are increasingly unsympathetic to the use of protective measures to help domestic industries compete in home or export markets. These changes are affecting WTO Members and non-Members alike, directly and indirectly, so there is no way of opting out of the changing global regime and small states are extremely limited in their capacity to influence the regime to reflect their interests.

Requests for special treatment for SIDS and other small, vulnerable economies challenge the prevailing wisdom in trade and development that expects developing countries to be able to diversify their economies, exploit areas of comparative advantage and work toward competitiveness in free regional and global trade. Although differences of opinion remain, there is widespread agreement that for small states and especially SIDS, it is difficult – perhaps even impossible – to be competitive in a free trade environment: 'there may be some very small economies that face such great absolute disadvantages that exporting at world prices is either impossible or generates factor incomes that are too low to subsist. In the limit free trade could mean no trade for these countries'.[224] Although these countries are urged to diversify their economies to decrease their vulnerability and dependence, diversification further exacerbates the lack of economies of scale, so there may be a trade-off between diversification, on the one hand, and efficiency and competitiveness, on the other. There are also obstacles to

---

[223] See, e.g. Winters and Martins, above n 33.

[224] Winters and Martins, above n 33, 348.

developing new industries. For example, it has been suggested that SIDS take advantage of new communications technologies that make remoteness less of a disadvantage by exploiting niches in internet-based service industries, and some have begun to do so.[225] However, they have faced opposition by other states[226] and difficulties with regulatory capacity which are also typical of small states.

Although the situation is by no means hopeless, it seems clear that the challenges facing SIDS must be taken seriously and that they do, in fact, reflect inherent disadvantages that are not likely to disappear if their governments would only 'try harder'. Of course the 'right policies' will mitigate some disadvantages and increase opportunities (if we could only agree on what the right policies are). Many analysts believe, however, that long-term, even permanent, assistance and support will be required – unpopular as this view may be. In particular, assistance with supply capacity and regulatory capacity will be required to enable small states to take advantage of trade opportunities.[227] In addition, countries dependent on tariff revenue will need both immediate and long-term support to deal with the fiscal impact of the loss of revenue from liberalization.[228] Since tariff reductions will result in savings for developed country trading partners, this could be seen as merely reversing the flow of revenue from developing to developed countries.

In addition, a good case has been made for some forms of special treatment in trade rules, for example exemptions from some commitments that are costly and of little or no benefit to the implementing country itself,[229] extended transition periods and assistance with compliance. More controversial are exemptions or reduced commitments that allow SIDS to subsidize or protect their producers – although these are attractive to many countries they are considered ultimately to be counterproductive, because they will impair the competitiveness of those producers even further in the long run.[230] There is also urgent need for attention to systemic issues that impose particular burdens on small developing states, notably accessions to the WTO, limitations of dispute settlement in the WTO for small economies and costs of participation.

In respect of both assistance and deviations from trade rules, the cost to the rest of the world will be relatively very small. The tiny share of world trade represented by small developing states means that any distortion from SDT will be

---

[225] See, for example, Government of the Republic of Vanuatu, *Vanuatu's Internet Free Trade Zone* <http://www.vanuatugovernment.gov.vu/cyberspace.html> at 15 December 2004.

[226] For example the attempts by the United States to prohibit internet gambling that resulted in the dispute with Antigua and Barbuda: see above n 154.

[227] See, for example, Ransford Smith, 'Size matters' (2004) 3 *World Trade Review* 441, 445; Dominique Njinku, 'Uniform treatment for Africa in the DDA' (2004) 3 *World Trade Review* 433, 439.

[228] Although these revenue losses may be partly replaced by other sources such as sales taxes (World Bank, above n 172, 34ff), implementing these may be problematic (ibid 45ff; Kelsey, above n 172, 25).

[229] Mattoo and Subramanian, above n 156, 403. Examples they give include intellectual property protection under TRIPS and customs valuation requirements.

[230] Ibid, 403-404; Winters and Martins, above n 33, 376.

minimal, as is the relative cost of assistance.[231] It does not seem that it would be difficult for developed states to agree to many of the demands. However, as we saw above, several commentators have noted that responses to requests for special treatment do not necessarily reflect whether they would be effective and cost-efficient. There is a tendency, for various political reasons, to reject more desirable solutions in favour of less desirable ones. Recent negotiations have also shown a significant degree of resistance to the full range of proposals for accommodating the needs of SIDS.[232]

What does all of this mean for the FICs? We see all of these issues reflected in the experience of these countries in their global and regional contexts. Trade liberalization, through multilateral WTO commitments or gradually expanding regional arrangements, deprive FICs of an important form of revenue as they reduce their tariffs, and expose their producers to greater competition in domestic and export markets. Trade preferences that have been important for some of the island economies[233] are being eroded or subjected to legal challenges by other developing states. The WTO accessions process has been a significant barrier for Pacific island countries like Vanuatu and Samoa, which have faced what many perceive to be unreasonable demands from other WTO members. The regional environment has undergone a radical shift from nonreciprocal preferential arrangements (under SPARTECA and the Lomé Conventions) toward reciprocal trade liberalization as developed country trading partners seek to satisfy WTO disciplines on regional agreements. The new generation of regional agreements are significant in that they recognize the need for special treatment of the smallest developing countries as well as SDT for developing countries generally. This is an important example of differentiation, corresponding to a distinction drawn in economic studies between 'countries that will have the most extreme difficulty competing in the global market' and those that may stand a better chance at competing, with external assistance.[234] It was also seen that the 'stepping stone' approach to regional trade liberalization, however appealing in theory, may represent an example of countries accepting a less desirable solution to the challenges they face.

Many of the changes that would benefit the small island developing states of the Pacific must take place on the global stage where they have limited ability to influence events. However, they can participate in worldwide partnerships of SIDS and small economies which have been reasonably effective in raising the profile of these issues in the UN and the WTO. In addition, there are some strategies that

---

231 See, e.g. Winters and Martins, above n 33, 378.

232 See the draft document for the January 2005 UN meeting on SIDS, which shows that the EU has sought to delete or significantly amend virtually every point under the heading 'Trade: globalization and trade liberalization' and the United States has suggested deleting the whole section: *Draft strategy for the further implementation of the Programme of Action for the Sustainable Development of Small Island Developing States*, [65]-[67], UN Doc A/CONF.207/L.1 (2004).

233 Hughes, above n 12, 72.

234 Grynberg, 'Towards Doha-lite', above n 1, 428-9.

could be undertaken within the region itself which could help the FICs to deal with the daunting challenges of the international trading system. Although regional economic integration in the 'stepping stone' model is problematic, other forms of regional cooperation are more promising.[235] For example, proposals to share the burden of administrative requirements (such as trade remedies investigations) among groups of small states could be explored within the Forum or other regional frameworks. Efforts to increase supply capacity will likely be most effective with some external support, but important cooperative initiatives could be undertaken among the FICs. Australia and New Zealand arguably have an important responsibility to support the island countries in these efforts, not least because they will be the major beneficiaries of trade liberalization by FICs (through savings on tariffs by their exporters, who supply the largest proportion of goods to the islands). They also have an opportunity to show some leadership at the global level in responding to the concerns of SIDS.

[235] See Andrew S Downes, 'The trade environment and small countries' (2004) 3 *World Trade Review* 416, 420; Njinku, above n 227, 437-8.

Index

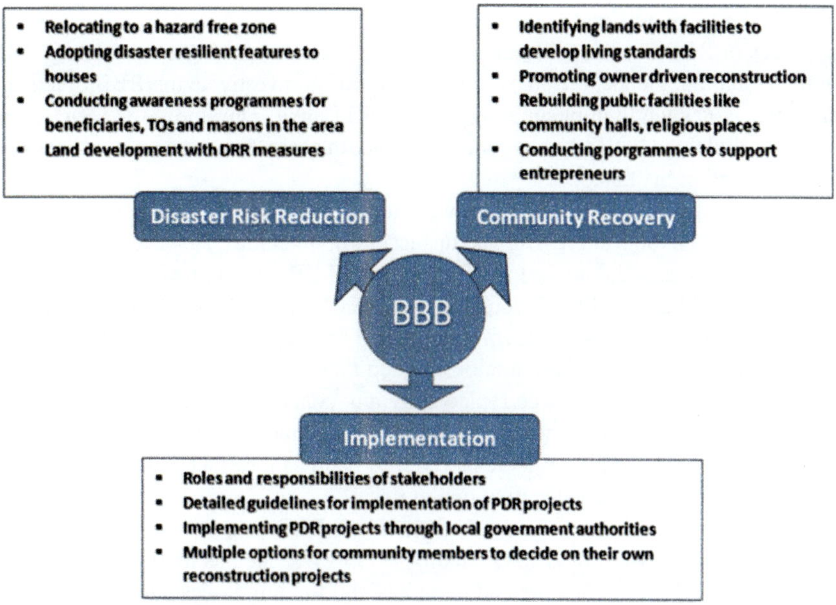

Fig. 2 BBB practices in Sri Lanka

while both Case 2 and Case 3 are owner-driven projects. Therefore, Case 2 and Case 3 had allowed more community participation in reconstruction activities which was appreciated by the community. Options given to the beneficiaries in the above-mentioned guideline had allowed them to make decisions considering their own social and cultural expectations.

According to the empirical findings of the case studies, local government authorities and NBRO work together in implementing PDR projects. Therefore, necessity of a separate authority or organization has not occurred during the implementation of PDR projects.

The above findings on BBB practices related to key areas of BBB are illustrated in the following Fig. 2.

6 Conclusions

This research signifies the implementation of Build Back Better (BBB) concept in Post-Disaster Reconstruction (PDR) projects in Sri Lanka. BBB concept was introduced to Sri Lanka after the Tsunami 2004. BBB aims to enhance the effectiveness of disaster recovery activities in future disasters expressing the best practices that stakeholders should follow in the recovery stage after a disaster. Disaster Risk Reduction, community recovery and implementation are three key components of BBB that were identified after reviewing the concept. However, there was a necessity to identify the practices of BBB used in Sri Lankan context in order to assess the success of BBB implementation. Hence, the study was carried out to investigate the BBB practices and their issues while implementing them in Sri Lanka. The study was focused on landslide and flood PDR projects conducted since they are the most common disasters that occurred in Sri Lanka.

Accordingly, many BBB practices were identified under three key areas of BBB which resulted in both successful and unsuccessful outcomes. However, the disaster affected community did not see any importance of BBB to improve their lifestyles. They believed that their lives before disasters were better compared to new lifestyles in PDR projects. Majority of the community had lost their properties and livelihoods due to disasters. Affected communities argued that the value of lost properties and lives during disasters cannot be replaced by any concept. However, some of them agreed that building houses with resilient features reduces the risk of experiencing another disaster in the future. It was a relief to them as they had lived with the fear of disasters in the previous location due to risk.

According to research findings, implementing BBB practices identified in this research helped to overcome some challenges in PDR such as minimizing corruption, non-availability of labours and materials and funding issues. However, proper practising of implementation guidelines that have been designed based upon BBB is required to attain successful PDR. Even though good practices have been identified in Sri Lankan context, neglecting responsibilities of stakeholders has become the barrier to assuring the achievements of BBB in PDR.

According to research findings, BBB is a concept of reconstruction that can be adopted for the development of PDR in Sri Lanka. This concept plays a major role in creating disaster resilient communities in the world. Thus, BBB is not a concept limited to improving disaster resilience. The concept of BBB is to improve the state of affected communities to a less vulnerable state prior to a forthcoming disaster. After a disaster, lifestyles of communities are greatly changed. Therefore, PDR activities must support people to adapt to changes in a better way. Community recovery practices identified in BBB concept help to develop social and economic conditions of a community.

Accordingly, implementation of BBB in PDR activities can be recommended for the development of the community in Sri Lanka. Using funds for implementation of BBB can be considered as an investment for development in the country which should be considered by the Sri Lankan government. Sustainability of reconstructions is another achievement of BBB as it reduces the risk of disasters.

References

1. Benson C, Twigg J, Myers M (2001) NGO initiatives in risk reduction: an overview. Disasters 25(3):199–215
2. Bilau AA, Witt E, Lill I (2018) Practice framework for the management of post-disaster housing reconstruction programmes. Sustainability. https://doi.org/10.3390/su10113929
3. Chang Y, Wilknson S, Brunsdon D, Seville E, Potangaroa R (2011) An integrated approach: managing resources for post disaster reconstruction. *Disasters* 739–765
4. Clinton WJ (2006) Key propositions for building back better. Office of the UN Secretary-General's Special Envoy for Tsunami Recovery
5. Creswell JW (2014) Research design, 4th edn. SAGE, London
6. Davidson CH, Johnson C, Lizarralde G, Dikmen NS (2007) Truths and myths about community participation in post-disaster housing projects. Habitat Int 100–115
7. De LL (2011) Post-disaster reconstruction strategy: opportunity or opportunism? University of Auckland
8. Ekanayaka EM, Vijekumara PA, Rathanajith BA (2018) An evaluation of locational distribution of Individually Resetted Sites (IRS). In: 9th annual NBRO symposium. NBRO, Colombo, SL, pp 323–331
9. Fan L (2013) Disaster as opportunity? Building back better in Aceh, Myanmar and Haiti. Overseas Development Institute, London, UK
10. Gillham B (2005) The research interview. Continuum, London
11. Ginige K, Amaratunga D, Haigh R (2009) Developing capacities for disaster risk reduction in the built environment: capacity analysis in Sri Lanka. Int J Strateg Property Manage 287–303
12. Hidayat B, Egbu C (2010) A literature review of the role of project management in post-disaster reconstruction. In: 26th annual ARCOM conference. Association of Researchers in Construction Management, UK, pp 1269–1278
13. Ismail D, Majid T, Roosli R, Samah HN (2014) A review on post-disaster reconstruction project: issues and challenges faced by International Non-Governmental Organisations (INGOs). In: Engineering challenges towards better life and humanity. University teknologi MARA, Shah Alam, p 72
14. Johns Hopkins Bloomberg School of Public Health, International Federation of Red Cross and Red Crescent Societies (2007) Disaster definitions. In Public Health Guide in Emergencies. IRFC, Geneva, Switzerland, pp 24–39
15. Jones TL (2006) Mind the gap! Post-disaster reconstruction and the transition from humanitarian relief. RICS, London, UK
16. Kennedy J, Ashmore J, Babisiter E, Kelman I (2008) The meaning of build back better: evidence from post-Tsunami Aceh and Sri Lanka. J Contingencies Crisis Manage 16(1):24–36
17. Lyons M (2009) Building back better: the large-scale impact of small-scale approaches to reconstruction. World Dev 37(2):385–398. https://doi.org/10.1016/j.worlddev.2008.01.006
18. Maly E (2018) Building back better with people centered housing recovery. Int J Disaster Risk Reduc 84–93
19. Mannakara S (2014) A framework for building back better during post-disaster reconstruction and recovery
20. Mannakkara S, Wilkinson S (2013) Build back better principles for post disaster structural improvements. Struct Surv 31(4):314–327. https://doi.org/10.1108/SS-12-2012-0044
21. Ministry of National Policies and Economic Affairs, Ministry of Disaster Management (2017) The post-disaster recovery pan for the follds and landslides
22. National Building Research Organisation (2015) Hazard resilient housing construction manual. NBRO, Colombo, SL
23. National Building Research Organisation (2017) Implementation framework for the resettlement of landslide and flood victims. Author
24. Perera BS, Kariyawasam SS, Vijekumara PA (2018) An evaluation of socio-economic sustainability of the disaster resttlement housing projects in Sri Lanka. In: 9th annual NBRO symposium. NBRO, Colombo, SL, pp 332–340

25. Rathnasiri PH, Wijegunarathne EE (2015) An evaluation of landslide risk assessment process of construction activities in landslide prone areas. In: NBRO symposium for innovations for resilient environment. NBRO
26. Sathyendrakajan N, Karunasena G, Wedikkara C (2012) Exploring capacity of construction industry post disaster housing reconstruction. Built Environ 11(1):2–6
27. Schilderman T (2010) Putting people at the centre of reconstruction. In: Lyons M, Schilderman T, Boano C (eds) Building back better: delivering people-centred housing reconstruction. Practical Action Publishing Ltd., Warwickshire, UK, pp 7–38
28. Shaw R (2006) Indian ocean Tsunami and aftermath. Disaster Prev Manag 15(1):5–20
29. Shaw R, Goda K (2004) From disaster to sustainable civil society: the Kobe experience. Disasters 28(1):16–40
30. Silva JD (2010) Key considerations in post-disaster reconstruction. Practical Action Publishing, Warwickshire, UK
31. Siriwardana JD (2018) Effect of land use pattern on land instability and slope failures in tea cultivated terrain in the central highlands of Sri Lanka. In: 9th annual NBRO symposium proceedings. NBRO, Colombo, SL, pp 277–282
32. Sri Lanka Red Cross Society (2017, May 26) Severe rain affects over half million people in Sri Lanka. Retrieved from relief web http://reliefweb.int/report/sri-lanka/severe-rain-affects-over-half-million-people-sri-lanka-many-areas-flooded-updated-
33. Srimulyani E, Inayatillah (2015) Women empowerment in Aceh: community self reliance group on women. Maret 1(1):1–14
34. Thurairajah N, Amaratunga D, Haigh R (2008) Post disaster reconstruction as an opportunity for development: women's perspective. In: CIB W89 international conference on building education and research (BEAR), 11–15th February 2008. Sri Lanka, pp 1106–1115
35. UVijekumara PA (2015a) A review on donor driven housing constructions in post disaster reconstruction projects—a case study on Kegalle resttlement programme, Sri Lanka. In: Investing in disaster risk reduction for resillience. NBRO, pp 234–241
36. United Nations Office for Disaster Risk Reduction (2015) Sendai framework for disaster risk reduction 2015–2030. UNISDR, Sendai. Retrieved Dec 10, 2018, from United Nations Office for Disaster Risk Reduction: https://www.unisdr.org/we/coordinate/sendai-framework
37. Vijekumara PA, Ekanayaka EM, Anuradha D, Rathnajith BA (2018) An assessment on knowledge transfer in post disaster housing construction. In: 9th annual NBRO symposium. NBRO, Colombo, SL, pp 314–322
38. Wai S (2015) Vulnerability assessment, stakeholder assessment, community assessment and strategy formulation: a case study of the humanitarian response to cyclone Nargis in Myanmar
39. Wardak ZS, Coffey V, Trigunarsyah B (2012) Rebuilding housing after a disaster: factors for failure. In: Proceedings of 8th annual international conference of the international institute for infrastructure, renewal and reconstruction (IIIRR). Kumamoto University, Kumamoto, Japan, pp 292–300
40. Yi H, Yang J (2014) Research trends of post disaster reconstruction: the past and the future. Habitat Int 21–29
41. Yin RK (2009) Case study research—desing and methods. SAGE, Califonia

Disaster Affected People's Vulnerability Assessment Through Addressing Padma River Bank Erosion

Md. Awual Baksh, Sharmin Akter, Md. Shahidullah Pramanik, and Farzana Bobi

Abstract Rajshahi, a divisional city of Bangladesh, is located on the bank of the Padma River. Peoples living in the riverbank areas face different types of natural hazards like floods, riverbank erosion, and draught. For the immediate years, riverbank erosion causes severe damages to the Char people who lived beside the city. So, this study focuses on identifying the erosion affected peoples' vulnerability during flood and riverbank erosion. Both qualitative and quantitative methods were followed during the study. To identify the vulnerable condition of the people's several variables like damages of the resources, economic crisis, unemployment problem, food crisis, various diseases, and social problems were measured. The results show that riverbank erosion causes huge losses of land, houses, crops, and other assets of the residents every year. Besides they suffer from a short time severe food crisis, diseases, and unemployment problems as well. They get only a limited amount of help from the government and non-governmental organizations. They mainly get helps from relatives and kin-members. It is supposed government assistance does not often reach the vulnerable and affected groups due to the insincerity and dishonesty of the responsible authorities. As a result, during the disaster, they resettled themselves in the city either on the embankment or here and there. They also face various problems and City Corporation also failed to handle the problem properly. So, the researcher suggests some specific actions to prevent the rapid river erosion incident along with some other recommendations to reduce the vulnerability of the affected peoples.

Keywords Riverbank erosion · Vulnerability reduction · Adaptation · Qualitative and quantitative research

---

Md. A. Baksh
Plan Plus Limited, Dhaka, Bangladesh

S. Akter (✉)
Department of Urban and Regional Planning (URP), RUET, Rajshahi, Bangladesh

Md. S. Pramanik
German Development Cooperation (GIZ), Rajshahi, Bangladesh

F. Bobi
Dhaka North City Corporation (DNCC), Dhaka, Bangladesh

C. Ghosh and S. Kolathayar (eds.), *A System Engineering Approach to Disaster Resilience*, Lecture Notes in Civil Engineering 205, https://doi.org/10.1007/978-981-16-7397-9_4

1 Introduction

1.1 Background of the Study

Riverbank erosion is an environmental calamity in Bangladesh that is more frequent and devastating in comparison with other kinds of natural inversion in Bangladesh. Day by day environmental refugees are increasing due to riverbank erosion at the riverside areas of Bangladesh [13]. Some of the researchers claim that climate change, geographic location, and geomorphologic conditions are more likely responsible for the increasing number of riverbank erosion events [25]. Millions of affected peoples lost their croplands, homesteads, farmlands, and more other valuable things due to riverbank erosion. And the most alarming issue is that around 5 of total floodplains is directly affected by riverbank erosion in Bangladesh. The situation mostly goes worsens during the monsoon season because of gradual migration of channel shifting of the river and high volume of water with a higher flow rate. Unpredictable shifting behavior not only affects the floodplain populations but also cause great damage to urban infrastructure and hampers urban growth [4, 12, 17]

In Bangladesh, different types of impact of riverbank erosion can be seen among the affected peoples. Some of the major impacts are social, economic, environmental, political, and health impacts [19]. Resulted multidimensional problems also create many problems for the affected peoples with the changing economic, sociopolitical, cultural adaptation strategies and that happens at the selected study area of this study.

To solve the raised problems regarding the adaptation strategies of the affected peoples at first, we must know the context and aspect of the vulnerability of any area. But, there is always lácking proper study and initiative to explore the extent and context of the vulnerability of the affected area and community. Even the aspect of adaptation strategies and mechanisms to survive in society is always remain unknown to us. And the reason behind this is being at the "*Char*" (Tracks of land surrounded by water) area that is located at far away from the city area. So, this research was conducted on one of the wards of Rajshahi City Corporation (RCC, Ward-29). Based on the field study, this research identified different types of vulnerability in the study area (Fig. 1).

1.2 Objectives of the Study

The goal of the study is to analyze the vulnerable situation and take different kinds of adaptation strategies for the river erosion affected people in the Dharampur community (RCC, Ward-29) during the erosion and post erosion period. The specific objectives are below:

- To find out the nature of the vulnerability of erosion affected citizens in the study area.

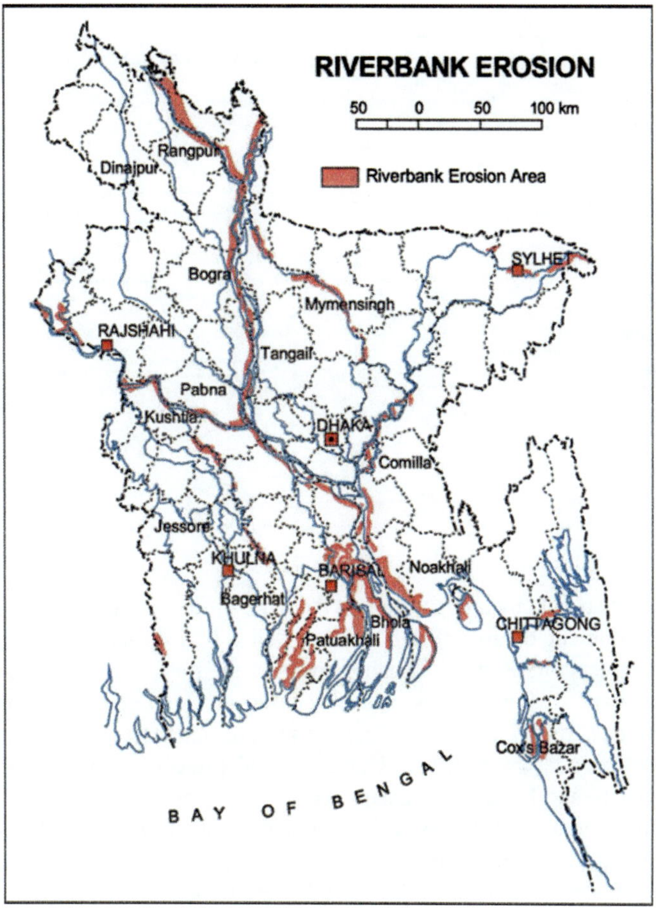

Fig. 1 Vulnerable areas of river bank erosion in Bangladesh

- To examine the impact of erosion on the livelihood and social aspects of the affected people.

2 Literature Review

Bangladesh is known as the land of rivers and about 230 rivers across the country. Most of the cities are located beside the river. Thus, the effect of riverbank erosion on the city is very much. Every year erosion affected people who gathered or resettled themselves into the city during the time of flood and post-flood period. Table 1 will show the riverbank erosion affected cities of Bangladesh:

Table 1 The riverbank erosion scenario of Bangladesh

S. No	River	No. of breaking points	Breaking area (m)	Affected cities
1	BrahmaputaraJamuna	43	162,544	Sirajganj, Kurigram, Jamalpur, Gaibandha
2	Ganges-Padma	26	94,433	Rajshahi (Godagari, Sardah, Nobinagara, Bulanpur)
3	Meghna	8	67,044	Chandpur
4	Teesta	8	34,854	Rangpur
7	Surma	23	13,224	Sylhet
8	Kushiara	17	11,003	Sunamganj, Jakirganj, Fenchuganj, Sherpur

Source Islam, 1985

Rajshahi is an old city and situated on the bank of the Padma River. Bangladesh Water Development Board (BWDB) was started a project named "Rajshahi City Protection Project" to protect Rajshahi City from the flood and erosion created by the Padma River. This project is mainly focused on flood control, drainage, and protects the city from river erosion. The duration of this project was 3 years (from 2004 to 2006). Under this project, 17 km river bank protects the wall, 19 regulatory sluices, 7 groins, and 1 spar were constructed. This project demarcated 1715 hectares of the drainage area and 6868 hectares of flood control area (Source: BWDB).

Vulnerability accesses the socio-economic and environmental conditions. These include the location of homes, structure and type of housing workplaces. And both of these are strongly related to different types of factors like household income, availability or cost of building materials, legal and social limitations on land use and the location and variety of livelihood activates. In the years 1988 and 1998, in Bangladesh, two subversive floods took place. During these floods, more than 65 of the country's geographic area got inundated. The impacts of those floods and riverbank erosion on society and economies were so severe that it took a longer time duration to back the affected people at a normal life and to minimize the losses. An analysis of crop damage to wet seasons shows that annually 3.7 of crop production often gets at damage-prone annually (averaged over 37 years).

In the case of vulnerability assessment, The Inter-governmental Panel on Climate Change [7] presented vulnerability as a function that considers the character, climate variation rate, magnitude toward which a system is exposed. Vulnerability also includes both internal and external dimensions like exposer to climate (external), sensitivity, adaptive capacity (internal) [10]. Some researchers also focused on realizing both biophysical and socioeconomic processes simultaneously [2].

Disruptions of communication and losing of crops reduce the availability of food, which results in an increasing food crisis and increases the price of local foods. The resulted situation creates a hardship for the poor in terms of food availability and provisions. To solve the raised problems in case of any disaster, a sustainable adaptation strategy is must require. Adaptation strategies for climate change include different types of adaptation strategies at the socioeconomic system, transportation system, and environmental systems as well. But in the case of developing countries like Bangladesh, most of the time context of vulnerability often exceeds the capacity of the community or countries. And so, the goal of the adaptation strategies must be increasing the capacity along with reducing the extent of vulnerability.

As a most efficient way of assessing system current adaptation strategies for disaster management, the IPCC technical guidelines proposed a process, "seven steps adaptation development strategy" [6]. The steps pointed to some specific issues like defining the objectives, specifying the important climatic impacts, identifying adaptation strategies, revealing constraints and examining alternative strategies, evaluating tradeoffs, and recommending some other adaptation measures [6]. Historically, women and men in natural disasters like drought, flood, and riverbank erosion have evolved their strategies, coping mechanisms to protect their assets, to increase livelihood security, to protect their families. In most cases, these methods are no scientific and these are experience-based strategies. Some of these are preserving dry foods so that they can support their families during the flood. Some of them preserve seeds for post-flood cultivation processes [16, 29].

As the main cause of riverbank erosion is flooding, the idea of controlling floods and minimizing the losses started after the devastating floods that took place in 1954 and 1955. Bangladesh Water Development Board (BWDB) was formed as the first legal institution to control floods, making embankment, incentives to minimize the losses of life and assets, and post-flood activities that is the current flood management planning and executing committee. After the flood in 1954 and 1955, another devastating flood of 1988 and 1998 took place. After that, flood action plan (FAP) and a series of mitigation plans and programs are taken [27].

Vulnerability and loss of property of riverside slum areas are common at riverbank erosion. To overcome these problems, national level institutional arrangement, safeguard policy statement (SPS), income and livelihood restoration program (ILRP), resettlement program have already taken [5]. But, in the study area there has a weak evidence of proper implication of these rules.

Although different types of plan and policies have already taken by BWDB, Char areas in Rashahi specially Dharampur and Char Khidirpur areas face devastating riverbank erosion in almost every year. The amount of property and other thing losses is also significant. A study on riverbank erosion on Gaibandha and Sirajganj district by Unnayan Onneshan, (2012) showed that, along with socio-economic loss and property damage, affected people faces different types of health issues. And the displacement causes a great experience to the affected peoples. But, it is a matter of concern that still now a little or no number of studies are available regarding riverbank erosion at the selected study area. In case of the selected study area, as the area is far away from the city corporation area, and basically a char area, so the area always lacks of adequate research and attention of the city authority.

3 Background of the Study Area

Dharampur community is selected in this study area, which is situated in Rajshahi City Corporation. The area was selected as the study area after systematic field reconnaissance, verbal interview survey, expert opinion survey, and key informant survey. The total area is about 3.5 square km. The population size of this community is 3500. Another 1500 people came here to resettle themselves after riverbank erosion which vanishes everything from their village named "Char Khidirpur". The Padma River is across between Dharampur and Char Khidirpur. For the geographical location, flood occurs here every year. The duration of flood is generally 15 days to two months from last August to mid of October. The causes of floods are heavy rainfall and the Farakka barrage. There is only one embankment (Rajshahi City Protection Embankment) which is located beside the city, while the other side of the river has no embankment. As a result, riverbank erosion highly affects the embankment during and post-flood period. During the time of flood and post-flood period, the affected people made their alternate shelter in Dharampur. Most of them were built their houses on the embankment. Housing pattern: Most of the houses are made of tin, hay, and bamboo; some houses are made of brick, but the roof is made of tin. Most of the affected people losing their job become unemployed. They become day labor to feed themselves and their family. Dharampur area has the local market for marketing necessary materials, primary and high school, Madrasha, and five Jumma Mosques. Though the area is located in the city, all the facilities do not reach the resettled people. The GO and NGO activities are not enough for the erosion affected people (Fig. 2).

4 Methodology

In this study, a mixed-method research approach was adopted. The approach utilizes both qualitative and quantitative research methods. For a quantitative approach, a self-developed questionnaire survey was used for data collection. About 301 people have been selected for the questionnaire survey. The respondents of the Dharampur community (RCC, W-29) were selected by random sampling. All respondents were selected from sex, religion, and no discretion was used in collecting information from the respondents. For the qualitative method, a verbal interview, key informant survey were used. So, all of the necessary data and information were collected from primary and secondary sources. The structured questionnaire survey is used to clearly understand the following issues:

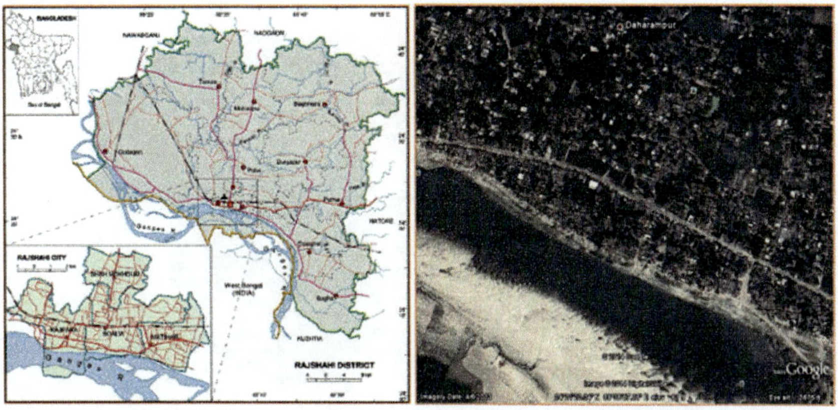

Fig. 2 Rajshahi district and city corporation area. The satellite view of the study area (Dharampur, RCC, W-29)

- Vincible people's socio-economic and socio-demographic status.
- Flood and riverbank erosion rapidity.
- Economic loss causes due to riverbank erosion.
- Human responses to riverbank erosion behavior.
- Social capital status after resettlement in the city.
- Issues of adaptation and vulnerability imposition.
- Policy intervention toward vulnerability, and adaptation.

This study is more concerned with people's vulnerability and human reaction to hazard (how affected people adapt to riverbank erosion) rather than the physical disposition of erosion. In this sense, this study has adopted "multi-method" research techniques.

In this research, data collected through a structured questionnaire survey by random sampling and has been analyzed in terms of the frequency distribution. Besides, necessary graphical representations have been used to represent data. These activities have been conducted by using SPSS and MS Excel used for some cases. The other qualitative data gathered from case studies are analyzed by hand and those have been represented in descriptive mode. For qualitative data, observed phenomena were also emphasized with the collected questionnaire survey data, verbal interview, and key informant survey data.

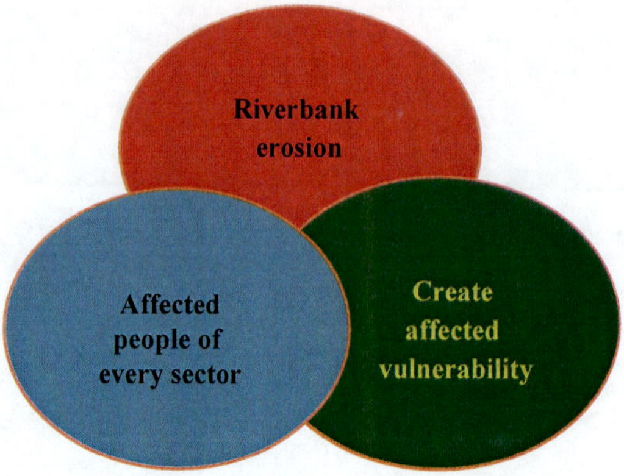

5 Data Analysis and Result

In this study, each respondent was considered as a unit of analysis. The representative of the household (HH) has been preferred to interview while judge as a respondent. A total of 301 households were interviewed where 38.9 male and 61.1 female respondents. In the beginning, demographic and socioeconomic information had been collected from each respondent including their age, sex, gender, education level, occupation, and so on. This information provided facts that helped the researcher to reach the point.

5.1 Effect on the Livelihood of the Respondents After Riverbank Erosion

Flood and riverbank erosion brought to the riverine people a lot of problems. They are highly affected by this natural phenomenon more or less annually. Every year they lost their house, habitat, crops, agricultural land, pet animals, and trees. Also, they face to change their regular work, and they have to divert themselves to other professions which they didn't want.

Duration of resettlement of the respondents after riverbank erosion. The duration of resettlement mainly depends on the severity of the disaster. The percentage distribution of respondent's resettlement duration after riverbank erosion. A large portion (51.5) of the total respondents is resettled in the city very recently due to seasonal flood and riverbank erosion as well as riverbed destruction, *i.e.,* 12 months ago. 20.9 of them have resettled themselves in the last five years. Along with the 8 of the respondents are living here for the last 20 years after their resettlement in the city (Fig. 3).

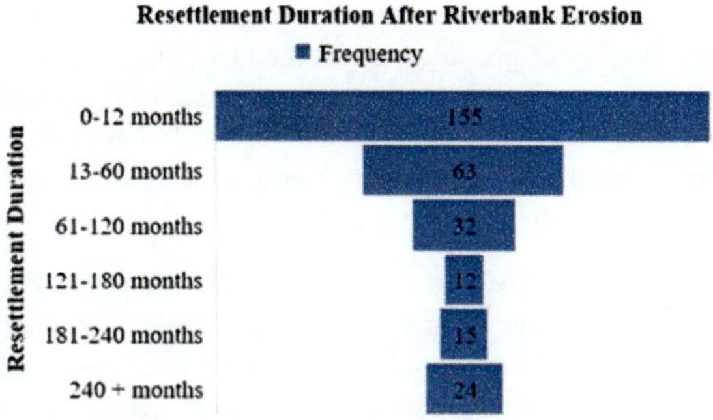

Fig. 3 Resettlement duration of the respondents

Major Losses/damages faced by the respondents after riverbank erosion. Apart from the damage and loss of dwelling, many other types of resources always face losses and damages due to riverbank erosion. Some of the common resource losses are crop damage, loss of land, animals, trees. All of the losses have a great impact on the changing livelihood pattern of the residents. Some of them decide to change their occupation. That is not all, the whole things create a great problem for the educational system of the area. From the analysis, it has been observed that 83.72 of the total respondents are lost their crops (either paddy or vegetable crops). About 99.67 of the total respondents are lost their habitat and dwellings; 98.01 lost their land; 83.72 lost their pet animals (including cattle, poultries) which were their secondary income source also. About 74.75 lost their trees, small vegetable gardens, etc. Occupational change occurs to 51.49 of the total respondents (Table 2).

Dwelling damage of the respondents by riverbank erosion. Dwelling loss and damage are one of the most common and severe losses of the affected peoples due to riverbank erosion. From the data collected from the respondents, it has been observed that about 52.8 of the total respondents are lost their dwelling due to flood and riverbank erosion, and 25.9 lost 2 times. 20.6 of them is lost for the first time, while 0.7 of the total respondents are lost their dwelling more than 3 times. So, the results show that the affected people rarely come back to the affected areas after they lose their dwellings twice at the riverbank erosion incidents.

Table 2 Distribution of problem/loss/damage faced by the respondents after riverbank erosion

	Crop loss (%)	Dwelling damage (%)	Land loss	Animal loss	Tree loss	Children's study problem	Occupational change
Yes	83.72	99.67	98.01	83.72	74.75	85.05	51.49
No	16.28	0.33	1.99	16.28	25.25	14.95	48.51
	100	100	100	100	100	100	100

Source Field Survey

Housing loss of the respondents by riverbank erosion. Previously, we have found the number of people who lost their dwelling and also found the frequency of losing their houses. In this section, what number of houses they frequently loss was found. Around 71.4 of the total respondents lost 1–3 houses, while 28.2 lost their 4–7 houses, and only 0.3 of respondents lost more than 8 houses by riverbank erosion. So, the majority of the affected people losses 1–3 houses frequently.

Losses of cattle's and poultry of the respondents by riverbank erosion. The livelihood of the peoples in the Char area mainly depends on agricultural activities, having cattle's and poultries, small scale business activities. So, the loss of these activities means a great loss toward their livelihood sustainability (Figs. 4 and 5).

In case of loss of cattle's, 59.8 of the total respondents lost 1–5 cattle, while 8.3 lost their 6–10 cattle, and only 0.3 of respondents lost more than 15 cattle by riverbank erosion. About 30.6 of respondents didn't have any cattle during the disaster period. In the case of loss of poultry, about 40.2 of the total respondents lost 1 to 10 poultry, while 12.3 lost 11–20 p, and only 0.3 of respondents lost more than 50 poultry by riverbank erosion. About 46.2 of respondents didn't have any poultry during the disaster period.

Fig. 4 Parentages of dwelling damage of the respondents

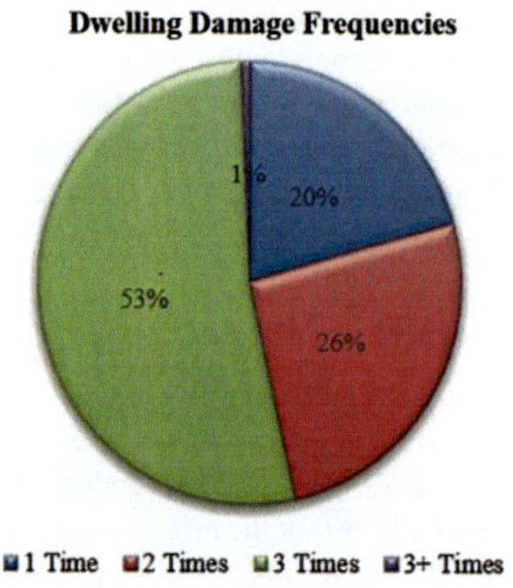

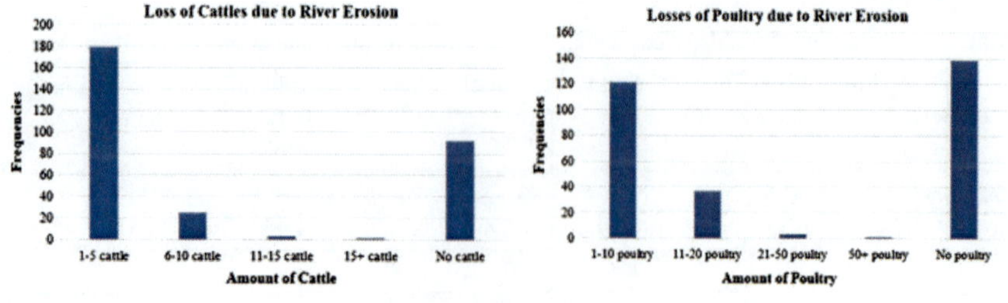

Fig. 5 Loss of cattle's and poultry due to riverbank erosion

Table 3 Percentage distribution of pre-and post-riverbank erosion land status of the respondents

Land area (in decimal unit)	Agriculture		Non-agricultural		Dwelling ground	
	Pre (%)	Post (%)	Pre (%)	Post (%)	Pre (%)	Post (%)
0	10.29	89.04	79.4	97.01	5.32	23.92
1–99	32.23	5.98	19.27	2.99	93.69	76.08
100–330	43.85	4.65	1.33	0	0.99	0
331–660	10.96	0.33	0	0	0	0
661–1650	2.67	0	0	0	0	0

Source Field Survey

Distribution of other losses of the respondents by riverbank erosion ***Loss of trees***. About 36.2 of the total respondents lost 1–5 trees, while 10.3 lost 6–10 trees, and only 0.3 of respondents lost more than 20 trees by riverbank erosion. About 46.2 of respondents didn't have lost any tree during the disaster period.

Loss of ponds: From the interview, it has been noticed that the percentage of pond damage is null, *i.e.*, any of the respondents haven't pond. They were fishing from the river directly.

Loss of Boats: About 85.4 of respondents didn't have any boat during the disaster period, while 14.3 of the respondents had 1 boat which they sold after riverbank erosion to overcome some of their misery.

Loss of Business: Only 0.66 of the total respondents had other small businesses as their secondary income source which damage at the period of river erosion.

5.2 *Before and After Riverbank Erosion Land Status*

After flood and riverbank erosion, most of the respondents lost their habitat and agricultural and non-agricultural lands. About 89.04 of the total respondents lost their cultivable land, 97.01 lost their non-cultivable land, and 23.92 lost their dwelling ground. Only respondents (10.96) have land for cultivation. Moreover, a huge change in the land status at agricultural, non-agricultural, and dwelling change has occurred due to the erosion (Table 3).

5.3 *Before and After Riverbank Erosion Dwelling Status*

About 14.3 of respondents were lost their house. 79.1 have smaller and only 6.6 has a larger house than the pre-riverbank erosion period. After riverbank erosion, 14.62 of total respondents lost their house, while all the respondents have their own

Table 4 Percentage distribution of pre-and post-riverbank erosion effect on the dwelling structure

	Wall			Floor			Roof	
	Pre (%)	Post (%)		Pre (%)	Post (%)		Pre (%)	Post (%)
No house	0.00	14.62	No house	0.00	14.62	No house	0.00	14.62
Bamboo	86.05	63.46	Katcha	99.67	81.72	Bamboo	68.77	30.56
Tin shed	1.66	7.31	Semi-pucca	0.33	1.99	Tin shed	31.23	54.15
Mud wall	12.29	14.61	Pucca	0.00	1.66	Pucca	0.00	0.67

Source Field Survey

house before erosion. The rest of the respondents built their houses after resettlement. Table 4 shows that after resettlement the respondents built their house with better equipment. The percentage of using tin very much increased in all cases. A very low percentage of respondents (about 0.67) made their roofs with concrete.

5.4 Occupational Change After Riverbank Erosion

A significant amount of occupational change occurs among the respondents after flood and riverbank erosion. After losing the cultivable land about 15.9 of farmers lost their profession, and they chose the alternate profession. So, the percentage of day labor, a rickshaw puller, and unemployed increased. Before riverbank erosion and flood, major occupations among the respondents were farmer, homemaker, and day labor. After flood and riverbank erosion, people mainly switched to small businesses, day labor, three-wheeler/van driver etc. Besides, the unemployment situation among the respondents increased from 1.7 to 4 (Fig. 6).

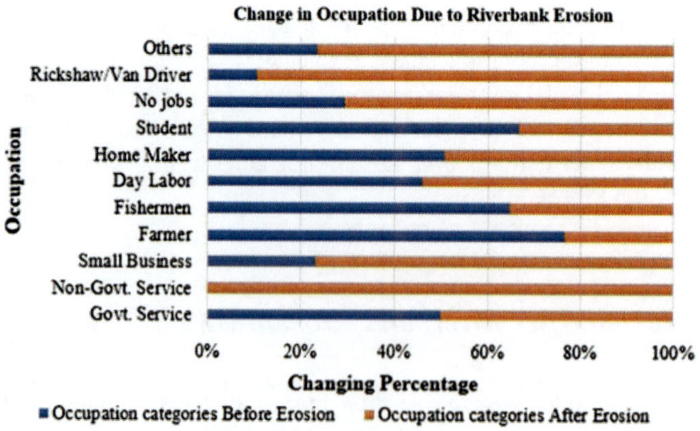

Fig. 6 Occupation change due to riverbank erosion

5.5 Resettlement Problems After Riverbank Erosion

The riverine people not only faced problems during the time of flood and riverbank erosion it continues for many years after resettlement. They become a victim of various resettlement problems in the city after riverbank erosion. Among these, first of all is the place of alternative shelter of the respondents in the city. Most of the people haven't relatives or own house so they have to resettle themselves either on the river embankment or in the disaster shelter after riverbank erosion. In this case, most of the respondents (76.4) resettle into their own home, 14.3 to another house, and 6.6 to relative's house; 2 resettle themselves on the embankment of the river.

Pre- and post-erosion drinking water sources and sanitation status of the respondents. During the flood and riverbank erosion, problems with drinking water and sanitation facilities increase at a rapid rate. At a normal time, people mainly use tube well and river water for drinking, taking bath, and other purposes. But, most of the respondents (95.7) drink tube-well water after riverbank erosion for safety purposes. In some cases, they also use community water supply tap (3) for getting pure drinking water. In the case of sanitation facilities, around 85 of the respondents get the facilities of using Pucca toilets after riverbank erosion. After that, around 8 of the respondents get the facilities of using semi-Pucca toilets. The rest of the respondents (7) use the Katcha toilet as well.

The situation of other basic facilities. About 83 of the total respondents confirmed the waste management problem. About 61.5 of respondents haven't the electricity supply facilities due to their inability. About 87.4 of the total respondents confirmed the health service problem. People also face communication problems due to riverbank erosion. In the study area, 65.1 is covered by pitch road followed by herring-bone bond (HBB) road 20.9 and 14 soil road (Fig. 7).

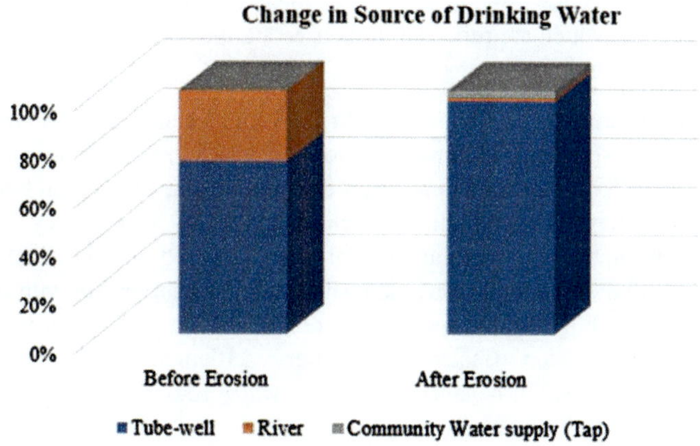

Fig. 7 Change in source of drinking water of the respondents

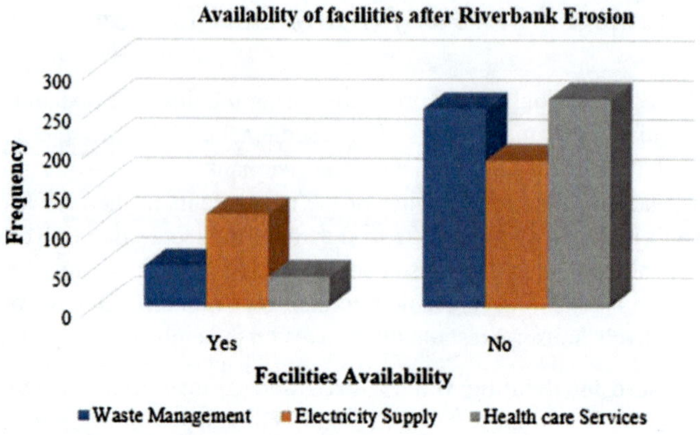

Fig. 8 Facilities availability after Riverbank Erosion

Educational institution. A positive response to educational opportunities to the respondent, in this case, has been shown. The area has schools, Madrasah, colleges, and universities. So, the respondents have a better chance to educate their children than the pre-riverbank erosion period (Fig. 8).

5.6 *Social Capital Status in the City After Riverbank Erosion*

Natural disaster(s) caused heavy damage to the victim people both financially, mentally, and socially. First of all, victims lost their habitat, financial way of living. Secondly, they are depressed and deprived mentally, and lastly, they are detached from their previous relatives/neighbors. In the meantime, they also face poverty due to insufficient aids which are reflected in their economic and social deprivation and their vulnerability to different types of crisis events.

Communication and social behavior with the other relatives/neighbors. About 82.4 of the total respondents communicate to their relatives after riverbank erosion, while the rest 17.6 of the respondents didn't communicate. The reason behind this is resettlement. They resettled in different places in the city area, so they are unable to contact each other at the regular interval after the flood and riverbank erosion period. About 95.3 of the total respondents have a good relationship with their new neighbor(s). According to the respondent's social behavior of the new neighbor(s) with the riverbank erosion affected people after resettlement in the city was good (78.1), and 6 was very well behaved with them, while 15.9 said that they were not effortlessly welcome by their new neighbor(s). Facilitate commitment of the new neighbor(s) to the resettled people is just over 50 (51.8) which indicates that the affected people have faced various problems during the time of resettlement in the city (Fig. 9).

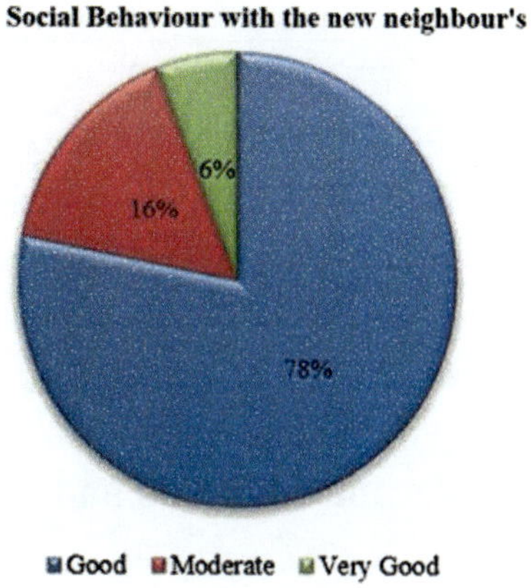

Fig. 9 Neighborhoods behavior at resettled areas

Environmental safety and women's safety after resettlement. After resettlement, one of the major issues of concern is the safety and security at the resettled area. 75.7 of respondents state that their women are secured in the city after resettlement. About 79.4 of the total respondents have concurred that the city environment is better than their "char" environment.

Job opportunity in the city area. About 79.4 of the total respondents have concurred that they had better job opportunities than their "char" environment. Due to the lack of adequate job opportunities, some of the resettled people often allied with the illegal job(s) after resettlement in the city, while they were not associated with these before resettlement. The reasons behind this are their poverty, insufficient job opportunities, low income, and inadequate aids from different organizations to overcome the crisis conditions they had.

5.7 *Aid from Different Organization After Riverbank Erosion*

About 3.32 of the total respondents obtained government aids and only 0.99 obtained aids from different NGOs, while no aids from the local or other side have been reported. As they didn't get any type of help or support from the GO or NGO, they have to sell their cattle and household utensils, ornaments to manage their livelihood in the critical situation of flood and riverbank erosion. Sometimes they took a loan from the "Local Somitee" or the NGO or the bank with the burden of high interest which also cause misery to them. According to the statement of respondents, about 15.94 of the total respondents took a loan from the Somitee and 3.65 from the bank) (Table 5).

Table 5 Aids/supports from different organizations to the respondents after resettlement in the city

Help status	Government		Local		NGO		Somitee		Bank loan		Other	
	Freq.	%	Freq.	%	Freq.	%	Freq.	%	Freq.	%	Freq.	%
Yes	10	3.32	0	0	3	0.99	48	15.94	11	3.65	0	0
No	291	96.68	301	100	298	99.01	253	84.05	290	96.34	301	100
Total	301	100	301	100	301	100	301	100	301	100	301	100

Source Field Survey

6 Recommendation and Conclusion

Based on our preceding evidence, it is reflected from our survey data that most of the villagers belong to the agricultural community, and severe riverbank erosion has already dislocated from the original settlement of this community. Being displaced, the respondents have taken accommodation in the new place, *i.e.,* Dharampur. They adopted traditional techniques for their survival during the serious situation of riverbank erosion. While exploring a brief history of the study area, a clear view of the local adaptation strategies was found. During and after a disaster or at the time of resettlement, the villagers mainly get help from the relatives and kin-members.

Whenever they come back to their previous residence, also then they get help from the relatives and kin-members for rebuilding and repairing their houses. During riverbank erosion, most of the villagers of the study area become fully shelter-less. And so, a quick response, recovery, and help are must require at that critical moment.

The study reveals that peoples having good savings can somehow manage the resettlement and food crisis dure the disaster, but poor peoples need social help and economic assistance to cope up with that situation. And sometimes they get helps only from relatives, they don't get any help or assistance from the government or NGO's in the emergency situation. Government assistance and NGO's help either reach them quite later or not. For example, during interviews, we found that a few families received rice and clothes from government (3.32%) and NGOs (0.99%) but no aids from the local sector(s). The percentage of aids is quite insufficient for their survival. The scenario is quite the same for the local organizations and Ward Council. In that case, the villagers suspect that dishonesty and insincerity are the main reason that's why government support does not often reach properly to them.

During the disaster, they resettled themselves in the city either on the embankment or here and there. So, that time population increased in the city. They also face various problems and City Corporation also failed to handle the problem properly. The goal of this research was to mitigate these problems and finding some solutions to overcome from riverbank erosion resettlement crisis in the city area. Several recommendations are suggested by the researcher to mitigate this riverbank erosion and resettlement problem in the city area.

6.1 Recommendation

This research has been conducted to focus on the socio-demographic, socio-economic, environmental conditions, and resettlement problems of the victims in the city after riverbank erosion.

To overcome these circumstances, the followings are recommended: Rehabilitate the embankment dwellers; giving priority to women and children who are the most vulnerable group.

- All of the governmental departments must have a clear idea and understanding regarding the impacts of climate change on their sector.
- The central government needs to decentralized development policy to plan for appropriate adaptation and mitigation strategies of disaster risk and vulnerability. National level activities need to be distributed to the local level. Provision of effective information along with different training and awareness-raising should take place.
- Only relief and aids cannot change the vulnerable situation of flood-affected people. The basic changes in socio-economic factors should be an effective strategy in removing vulnerabilities.
- Need to improve the transport communication system and an effective surveillance system.
- Sensitization/mass awareness-raising (for both public and policymakers) on natural disasters and management should be undertaken by both government and NGOs.
- The government should arrange seminars, symposiums to increase the participation of rural people in disaster issues and management.
- It needs to create a large scope of job opportunities based on confined planning to reduce vulnerabilities during flood and riverbank erosion.
- Awareness about the diseases during disaster time should be done on regular basis.
- New projects and policies should be developed to protect the infrastructures and permanent settlement for affected peoples.
- Construction of embankments using updated methods and technology to protect communities from the riverbank side to reduce the risks of erosion should be emphasized. Involving communities for routine management and maintenance of embankments will create a sense of ownership among the community peoples.
- Loan without or at very low interest from the government banks of Bangladesh should be provided to the disaster affected people.
- Local government needs to special care with the affected people during and post-disaster periods.
- Provide health and education facilities to the embankment dwellers. First-aid to the wounded and post-flood and riverbank erosion should be provided.
- Provide employment and increase the income-generating capacity of the women beside the men through training in skill development.

- Stop the threat of forcible eviction. Without proper measures of resettlement and rehabilitation, it will only increase human misery.
- The arrangement of alternate shelters for the affected people, possibly also for cattle and security of other properties should be built by the government.
- Community capacity building is very much solicited, and for this training should be arranged on disaster preparedness involving local government along with community people. This will enhance the capacity of the local community in risk mitigation and assessment.

References

1. Adams GR, Schvaneveldt JD (1991) Understanding research methods, 2nd ed. Longman, New York (1991)
2. Adger WN (2006) Vulnerability. www.gsdrc.org/go/display&typedocument7id=3922
3. Alam J (1986) Erosion at 283 places. Holiday 22(5):5
4. Amin ATMN (1991) Settlement strategy for riverbank erosion displaces in Bangladesh: a human resource development approach. In Elahi KM, Ahmed KS, Mafizuddin M (eds) Riverbank erosion, flood, and population displacement in Bangladesh. REIS, JU, Dhaka
5. BWDB (1989) Pre-feasibility study for flood control in Bangladesh, vol 2. Bangladesh Water Development Board, GOB
6. Carter TR, Parry ML, Harasawa H, Nishioka S (1994) Intergovernmental panel on climate change technical guidelines for assessing climate change impacts and adaptation. University College London and Center for Global Environmental Research, London
7. Climate Change, 2000(a) (2002) Climate change and agriculture in Bangladesh: ministry of environment and forests
8. Environment and GIS Support Project for Water Sector Planning (EGIS), Riverine Chars in Bangladesh, The University Press Limited (2000)
9. FAP 21/22, Bank protection and river training (AFPM) pilot project, Final Report, Annex 7, Flood Action Plan 21/22 (1993) Fifth Five Year Plan 1997–2002, Planning Commission, Ministry of Planning, GOB (1998)
10. Füssel HM, Klein RJT (2006) Climate change vulnerability assessments: an evolution of conceptual thinking. Clim Change 75:301–329
11. Hossain MZ (1991) Dispalcees of riverbank erosion in urban squatter settlements in Sirajganj: the process of impoverishment. REIS-JU, Dhaka
12. Islam MA (1995) Environment land use and natural hazards in Bangladesh. The University of Dhaka
13. Islam MF, Rashid AMNB (2011) Riverbank erosion displacees in Bangladesh: need for institutional response and policy intervention. Bangladesh J Bioethics 2(2):4–19
14. Islam MZA (2000) Socio-economic loss of the riverbank erosion displaces in riverine Bangladesh: a case of precarious habitat. In: A paper submitted for publication in the forthcoming issue of Journal of the Institute of Bangladesh (Bangladesh), vol XIII
15. Karim AHMZ (1988) Managing poverty: the applicability of Grameen Bank model for the Muslim minority community around the world. In: A paper presented at the Islamic Economic Development Conference at the University Sains Malaysia, December 1988
16. Little PDM, Stone PT, Mogues A, Castro P, Negatu W (2004) "Churning" on the margins: how the poor respond to drought in South Wollo, Ethiopia
17. Mamun MZ, Amin ATMN (1999) Densification, The University Press Limited, Dhaka
18. McCracken G (1989) Interpretive consumer research. In: Elizabeth C (ed). Association for Consumer Research, Hirschman, Provo, UT, pp 168–183

19. Mondal T, Tripathy B (2020) Riverbank Erosion and Environmental degradation. Int J Res 7(7) (2020). E-ISSN 2348-6848
20. Nasreen M (2012) Women in disaster: an analysis of the division of labor and survival strategies in a disaster. Academic Publishers Above ground biomass, Dhaka. Agric Ecosyst Environ 158: 216–224
21. Nasreen M (2004) Disaster research: exploring sociological approach to disaster in Bangladesh. Bangladesh e-J Sociol 2
22. Oliver-smith (1982) Here there is life: the social and cultural dynamics of successful resistance to resettlement in post-disaster Peru 49:85–104
23. Punch K (1998) Introduction to social research: quantitative and qualitative approaches. Sage, London
24. Rahman A (1986) Impact of riverbank erosion: survival strategies of displaces. ADAB NEWS 13(4)
25. Shajahan A, Reja MY (2012) Riverbank erosion and sustainable planning guidelines for Bangladesh with emphasis on Padma River. J Habitat Eng Design 4(2):145–156. ISSN 2186-6503
26. Silverman EK (2001) In the field: the Iatmul continuing work in mead's research sites. http://www.mead2001.org/iatmul.html
27. Smit B (2006) Adaptation, adaptive capacity, and vulnerability. Glob Environ Chang 16:282–292
28. Tashakkori A, Teddlie C (2003) Handbook of mixed methods in social & behavioral research. Sage, Thousand Oaks
29. Verhagen J, Bhatt M (2002) Community-based disaster risk mitigation: a case study in the semi-arid areas of Gujarat presented at ADB conference on water and poverty, Dhaka, Bangladesh

An Investigative Study on Material and Its Performance of Intermediate Disaster Relief Shelters

Divyatanu Dev and Shanta Pragyan Dash

Abstract Intermediate disaster relief shelters play a significant role after any disaster as it is an integral part of disaster response and recovery which helps to provide security and safety for the people who have left or lost their accommodation due to the disaster. These shelters not only provide accommodation but also help them to overcome the trauma of the disaster initiating the process of rehabilitation. In the past review of literature, case studies and reports related to the design of disaster relief shelters it has been found that due to the lack of adequate consideration related to climatic conditions, locally available materials, unskilled labour, cost constraints and other socio-cultural issues and construction delays resulted in its poor performance contributing to an unacceptable standard of living for the victims. The paper aims to explore the types of intermediate relief shelters with respect to various materials available through literature and case studies addressing the key factors affecting the environmental, economic, technical and socio-cultural criteria affecting the provision and performance of such shelters. The outcome of the paper is to propose strategic recommendations for addressing the major key aspects to be taken into consideration during the decision-making and design processes of such shelters for the effective and better performance of these shelters.

Keywords Intermediate disaster relief shelters · Decision-making · Design processes · Rehabilitation

1 Introduction

Disasters in any form continue to be devising recurring phenomena for the entire world [1]. The world disaster report of 2007 states that the number of disasters deported in the year 1997 to 2006 has increased drastically by 60% as compared during the phase 1987 to 1996 [2]. Since the Indian continent is highly vulnerable to

D. Dev (✉) · S. P. Dash
Manipal School of Architecture and Planning, Manipal, Karnataka, India

S. P. Dash
e-mail: shanta.dash@manipal.edu

C. Ghosh and S. Kolathayar (eds.), *A System Engineering Approach to Disaster Resilience*, Lecture Notes in Civil Engineering 205, https://doi.org/10.1007/978-981-16-7397-9_5

disasters. Around 25 states of India are vulnerable to search for disasters. 56% of the total land area of the country is vulnerable to see snake activities [3]. Apart from the loss of life, the destruction of the house due to such disasters are the most important and critical concern after the disaster [4]. A disaster victim's shelter rehabilitation process is complex. The survivors' main challenge after the post-disaster is to meet the basic shelter needs of government and humanitarian agencies [5]. Disaster relief shelters are considered important for defence, security, climate control and resistance to disease and ill health. Such shelters are used mainly by people relocated from their original location and rehabilitated from permanent dwellings [6, 7]. Most examples of such shelters are plastic sheets, public community centres, places of worship, sporting venues, private rentals used as immediate shelters for disaster relief. Search filtering may be needed for a duration of several months or even years after the disaster [8]. Therefore, such shelters entail various planning and design aspects such as location, user needs and aspirations [9].

Some crucial concerns need to be addressed to achieve a successful outcome for the shelter needs of the victims of the disaster [10]. One of the main concerns is recognizing the shelter's specific need for the victims involved, what are the expected and actual time frame to fulfil their needs, what resources are accessible and are needed, the building process skills and local awareness and the degree of participation and influence of local communities during the construction process [3, 11]. Besides design, various NGOs, local authorities, politicians and volunteers who are the main stakeholders in the disaster process also need complementary support [12]. Although the facilities of such shelters are commonly accepted for immediate response and recovery from disasters such as earthquakes and tsunami, floods, it is not evident which shelter type is best suited under what circumstances in actual practice [13]. Because of this, many times such shelters prove ineffective in some cases hampered by unfit climate, local set-ups, costs, overcrowding and delays [14]. In addition to material visibility, local skilled labour is equally essential for building such shelters. In some cases, such rehabilitation shelters are of no value for potential storage and reuse [15].

In the paper's first phase, the authors address why intermediate disaster relief shelters are required during the disaster phase and what are the factors that influence these shelters performance during post-disaster scenarios. The second phase of the paper reviews the factors influencing the design decision of Disaster Shelters (environmental, economic, technical, socio-cultural) and investigates the different types of intermediate disaster relief shelters based on materials. The paper's last part suggests recommendations for consideration during the decision-making and design processes of disaster-resistant shelters for effective and better performance during disaster and post-disaster scenarios to increase their efficiency and performance.

1.1 Why is There a Need for Intermediate Semi-permanent Shelters?

Since disaster is natural or manmade in any form, it not only damages the dwellings of people but also has a severe impact on interacting aspects that shape human settlements such as human activities, the structure of socio-cultural and political-economic settlements, topography, geology and natural resources that define human settlement of a particular area [10]. To empower the victim during emergency rescue and relief, encouraging semi-permanent shelters is crucial to allowing them to engage in such collective processes to resolve the disaster's impact [11]. In this step, if the victim's shelter needs are properly addressed, the rehabilitation process of permanent dwellings can be enriched by integrating the above-mentioned factors [16]. Poor intermediate shelters typically trigger short-term settlement pressure [17]. It also needs a better understanding of the differences between emergency shelters immediately after the disaster and semi-permanent shelters in the first three months after the disaster, a crucial aspect of relief and recovery [18]. Emergency shelters usually provide immediate protection against heat, wind, rain, human life and the climate as simple shelters. Being a simplified view, but complex dynamics are observable over time [19]. Emergency shelters were found to be inadequate in terms of intermediate length before long-term construction of permanent houses as temporary relief [20]. Besides, there is less international aid funding and other programs to meet the tragedy-impacted people, relatively limited in numbers that do not resolve the immediate needs of the victims adequately [21]. In that case, immediately-motivated victims begin to create their emergency shelters with shared community support and their social network to overcome the disaster faster [22]. Often after a week, the group needs transfers to intermediate semi-permanent shelters allocated to families with inadequate and low-quality shelters [18, 23]. In the past, the victims gathered CGI boards, timber, etc. from the debris after the 1993 Marathwada earthquake to quickly create the shade for immediate use even before the government reacted in the form of organized relief shelters that came up later. Similarly, in Kutch Earthquake 2001, people have preferred building their immediate relief shelters on their clothes rather than heading to the tense black polypropylene sheets. The government's external response took over a week to reach the communities affected [24]. Likewise, in terms of their quality appropriateness and living conditions for victims, the inadequacies of temporary shelters after the 2004 Indian Ocean Tsunami were reported [10]. Therefore, considering all these considerations, it is necessary to note that the community victims themselves can manage immediate shelter response before organizations with piles of materials are reached. Along with this, understanding external humanitarian processes is necessary to focus on the immediate semi-permanent frameworks allowed by the community victims themselves.

2 Literature Review

2.1 Review of the Factors Influencing the Design Decision of Disaster Shelters

A comprehensive literature review of available documentation and research papers on Disaster Shelters was conducted to understand how these shelters were designed in the past to adapt to the types of disasters and with the disaster's environmental economic, technological and social context [15]. Transitional Shelter Guidance [18], Collective Centre Guidelines (Camp Co-ordination/Camp Management, 2010), describes the various types of shelters, where-as other guidelines are briefly identified in general papers such as "Strategic Planning for Post-Disaster Temporary Housing" [25] and "Guidelines to Improve Sustainability and Cultural Integration of Temporary Housing Units" [26], among others; others were written in government documents such as the Evacuation and Shelter Guidance [15], among others; and lastly, other guidelines can be taken from the Humanitarian Charter and the Minimum Standards in Humanitarian Response (The Sphere Project, 2011), among others [3, 2]. Factors relevant to the design such as the performance of shelters in consultation with the players concerned, government, private and other disaster recovery stakeholders, were summarized below in terms of addressing their environmental, economic, technical and socio-cultural needs.

I. **Environmental factors:**

a. ***Climate patterns*** are considered a critical factor influencing seasonal changes in possible disaster locations. People with different contexts and locations in different temperature regions will find different shelter types more suitable and comfortable based on their built environment [20]. Design elements such as high ceilings and verandas can cause shelters to cool down in hot weather, minimize air gaps, or provide a lobby area that can keep shelters warmer in cold weather [14]. Temporary and progressive shelters must be built to make the winter. Different climatic considerations require different shelter arrangements. Victims should have enough fuel and stoves in mattresses and beds in extremely cold temperatures, with sufficient clothes and blankets. Hot, dry and hot humid climatic ventilation plays an important part, as does the Sunshade [27]. In hot weather, a good drainage system is strongly recommended. The shelter should also consider potential temperature drops in open areas such as high altitude areas, deserts, etc. during the night.

b. ***Maintaining water and air hygiene*** is important to protect victims, personal and environmental hygiene. The shelter should address sufficient, often complex and expensive, sanitation, water supply and hygiene facilities [7]. Camp Co-ordination/Camp Management (2010), The Sphere Project (2011) has set standards for preserving health hygiene by introducing washing programs for people to wash their clothes and serve them with the best use of water for the disposal of human faeces, managing mosquitoes and diseases and maintaining a proper drainage system. Improving victim nutrition also finds appropriate storage facilities equally essential for treatment, hygiene and fitness [18].

c. ***Recycling, upgrading and disposal of disassembled shelter:*** As per International Mitigation Organizations 2012, disaster-resistant shelter material should be easy to recycle, reuse and relocate after the shelter is dismantled [28]. A shelter is described as recycled if it can be partially or fully replicated. However, if economic viability can be robust and appropriate in different climatic environments, it is environmentally friendly [15]. Therefore, it was highly advised that the shelters disaster consists of products recycled, upgraded and reused rather than disposed of after use [22]. Low-income families may also use these shelters as leisure camps or any other uses where permanent settlement is not desirable.

II. Economic factors:

a. ***Shelter types:*** The economic factor is a critical role in restoring and adapting to disasters [8]. Hence, shelter costs are often considered a significant element in ensuring affordable design [5]. The different materials used to build the shelters have already been addressed in the paper to be used for a temporary period [26]. The redesign and improvisation of the shelter are cheaper than moving face-to-face from temporary shelters to permanent constructions [18]. The practice of comparing the different types of shelters between host and affected populations is equally relevant in shelter design [14].

b. ***Durability and lifespan:*** Because designing and preparing disaster-resistant shelters with their expected lifespan and minimum quality and location requirements are equally relevant, the design process needs to consider its durability and the amount of money spent on it to maintain it for a long time [17]. In some cases, investing money in temporary shelters to permanent shelters is better to give them permanent residence if the contexts permit [28].

c. ***Victims' livelihood:*** In most situations where long-term relocation scenarios are apparent, victim assistance is required [29]. Help groups will help victims and locals make money by helping them start new business ventures after supplying the initial shelters [22]. For example, after the Great Eastern Japan earthquake, the victims started selling "Tamaki" or friendship bands made up of fishing nets along with some additional things like slippers, keychains, fabric back made by womenfolk. After such a catastrophe, it is important to raise the socio-economic status of the victims impacted by such activities to cope with the psychological rehabilitation of these victims [30].

III. Technical factors:

a. ***Ease of installation and dismantling:*** Selecting material for installation and dismantling is very important since it is lightweight and is available in modules [8]. If this design is complex, it may take more time and expertise to build it, resulting in potential delays [19]. A major feature of these shelters is that they can be rapidly built within a timeline to encourage fast recovery after a disaster [18].

b. ***Insulation properties:*** Any material chosen for disaster shelter should not only be inexpensive, locally accessible but should also avoid pollution of any kind without creating any harmful emissions, ideally it should be recyclable sustainable material to be easy to produce and create with its lightweight [31]. For example, prefabricated wood panels are flexible in size making horizontal and vertical transport simple and convenient with limited components. It was also decided that the shelter should be constructed with noise-insulating, weather-insulating and temperature-insulating materials to withstand the various climatic impacts and the built environment's surrounding effects [32].

c. ***Hazard performance:*** The shelter system should be built to protect its occupants from hazards including Storms earthquakes and other diseases. In such situations, structures made of bamboo framed ok timber are highly resistant to the fatality caused by the disaster by resisting the light structure compared to the masonry structures [2]. Contrary to this, areas are more vulnerable to extreme thunderstorms and high-speed winds. Therefore, it is important to have a system that takes into account areas vulnerable to flooding and high winds to withstand climatic pressure [21].

d. ***Psychological and physical effects:*** According to research, the victims who have lost their homes are experiencing serious stress issues [33]. Losing a house not only causes psychological stress, but also post-traumatic stress disorder that causes long-term detrimental effects on the survivor. Therefore, consumer attitudes and attitudes towards various types of shelters have often been important in terms of their effect on post-traumatic stress levels. Designers need to include develop features to reduce the stress effect of those impacted when constructing these disaster-resistant shelters [4].

IV. Socio-cultural factors:

a. ***Cultural differences:*** The shelter design has experienced a considerable difference, its orientation-style design element specifics among different countries, regions and even ethnic groups [17]. Therefore, it is important to adapt to local culture and community lifestyle to provide appropriate shelter solutions. It should represent the requirements and needs of users of traditional values family sizes, cultural practices, family, architectural styles religion and other relevant cultural aspects [18].

b. ***Security and dignity:*** Shelter design should not only be built based on a basic physical framework but should also make users feel socially integrated and provide them with space to live in a more dignified manner, taking into account security aspects [1]. The designs should recognize the integrity of privacy protection as well as the flexibility to promote the design so that users can change or alternate the design by inserting partitions in shelters according to the family sizes and specifications of the victim [4].

c. ***Social connectivity:*** In the early stages of disaster recovery, social interaction and communication are vital factors for the victims to be part of the recovery disease that happens during this time and to minimize the effect by allowing them to think about needs such as potential locations and needs

[32]. Communication should be improved in terms of social networks, television, radio, telephone, internet services, by organizing stakeholder training workshops [29].

2.2 Types of Intermediate Disaster Relief Shelters

a. ***Tarpaulin shelters:*** Tarpaulins tents procurement and distribution are the immediate first-phase disaster response initiatives (Fig. 1). Tents were always the commonly used relief shelters that were emergency shelters often found as a post-earthquake response in Western countries like Italy, Turkey, Mexico. They are not climate-friendly, however and offer limited security with very high costs. There are also many logistical challenges in vulnerable areas where tents with sufficient amounts are stored. Another major challenge is transporting these tents to areas affected by disasters. While these tents can be built in these areas, occupancy rates are very low as they are placed far from the victims' homestead plots.
b. ***Prefab concrete Shelters:*** Prefabricated shelters are another form of intermediate shelters available as the second choice during the disaster (Fig. 2). The selection of these shelters is based on the assumptions that they can be constructed and provided rapidly, as being a prototype would fit the families of the victims affected as it will be difficult for the communities affected to do so on their own voluntarily because of the disaster trauma. However, the rapid experience of these shelters indicates that there are very poor acceptability and efficiency in terms of climate consideration and functionality of the shelters, for example after the earthquake in Bam, Iran (2003), where these shelters were given but only a few people with smaller families moved into it as they preferred to remain only in their gardens and yards. Also, the distribution costs were very high compared to other relief shelters so people tend to build their permanent residence with indigenous materials in almost half the cost of the shelters as

Fig. 1 Tarpaulin shelter. *Source* Canvas relief shelter disaster tent

Fig. 2 Pre-fab concrete shelter. *Source* Emergency shelter design IN Habitat

seen in the Tsunami case in India despite the government spending around. $15 million per 10,000 interim shelters on Andaman Nicobar Islands for families affected.

These two types of shelters have not only failed to meet the standard donor requirements for the unit distribution and financial accounting but have also failed to represent the social-cultural and livelihood-related activities and needs of the victims' families. The rapid delivery and construction of these shelters were also considered. Rarely were distribution aspects considered because of complicated relations to the social structure of the household affected. This has contributed to the government and non-governmental organizations having increasing unrealistic expectations of the society impacted by a catastrophe that they have failed to meet. Owing to the exorbitant costs and the slow completion of such facilities during the pandemic, the result was adversely affected.

c. ***Steel Shelters:*** Steel as a Building material is being widely used because it withstands tension and is effective in dissipating earthquake tremors (Fig. 3). Steel elements can also be reused in the structural framework or formwork. But

Fig. 3 Steel shelter. *Source* Deep blue ningbo smart house

Fig. 4 Clay brick shelter. *Source* Alternative Africa, mass housing

the most challenging factor while using steel is its weight. The raw materials used for the manufacture of steel are again nonrenewable resources and also indulge a huge amount of labour for its construction. Along with this also the technical knowledge is required to join the elements without which the structure might tend to collapse. Post the Haiti Earthquake in 2010, simple Steel frames were provided as temporary shelter constructions which ensured protection, privacy and more space. Up to 2000, light Gauge Steel Shelters were built which were more resistant to hurricanes and heavy rains which have been designed to resist wind up to 120 to 240 miles per hour wind speed.

d. ***Clay bricks shelters:*** Clay bricks are another sustainable material that has been used for the construction of temporary Shelters in India during earthquakes. The material is easily available in and around the locality it is economic to procure the material for quick construction (Fig. 4). Since masonry is strong in compression but very weak in tension hence during the earthquake shake a significant number of deaths have occurred around the world because of this masonry houses construction. One of the major challenges of using this material is its drying process which takes a lot of energy and duration. During the post floods of August 2007 which hits the states of Uttar Pradesh and Bihar, small transitional houses incorporating brick plinths with a tiled bamboo roof were proposed which could have been more sturdy and safe than the kutcha houses made of thatch and mud.

e. ***Confined masonry shelters:*** Confined masonry is another type of earthquake material for construction during a disaster (Fig. 5). After the earthquake in Quetta in 1935, some innovations were made in the construction of Rehabilitation structures. Bricks are being good in compression but cannot withstand tension effectively whereas Steel as a material is good in tension. The bricks were laid in an interlocking pattern where the interlock gaps were filled with steel. This style of construction was adopted by the IIT Gandhinagar campus. The site is located in seismic zone III in compliance with the Indian seismic code. Student homes and staff quarters are suitable for the use of confined masonry technology

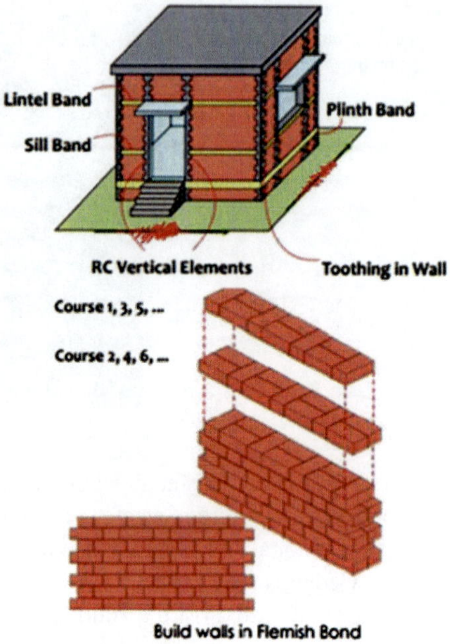

Fig. 5 Confined masonry shelter. *Source* Gujarat state disaster management authority

in buildings, small spaces (in contrast to academic facilities) and a large number of walls (wall density). Preliminary estimates suggested that the use of confined masonry technology would save 10 to 15% on alternative construction of RC frames.

f. ***Composite shipping pallets:*** Shipping crates used to transport items like fruits, vegetables, etc. may be used in shelter construction. Softwood, hardwood, plastic, cardboard, aluminium and composites are some of the materials that make pallets (Fig. 6). They are 100% reusable as shipping pallets and eco-friendly though easy to assemble and dismantle. The holes/gaps in these crates'

Fig. 6 Composite shipping pallets. *Source* In HABITAT

Fig. 7 Corten steel shipping containers. *Source* J K Technologies Private Limited

design help dissipate forces through it without letting it affect the structure. However, it cannot endure environmental conditions like rain or storm. This solution is only possible for earthquakes. This shelter cannot be used as a permanent shelter for material wood as it can attract insects. The holes/gaps in these crates' design can cause privacy issues. Originally built as temporary accommodation for Baltic War refugees in the 1990s, the accessible, robust shelter helps families to rebuild a house. Pallets of uniform size render it a perfect construction material. When supplies arrive from all over the world, shipping pallets can be erected to render partitions, ceilings and floors for those supplies. By coating these structures in local finishing materials, a quality shelter can be built that will last long enough for families to construct permanent housing.

g. ***Corten steel shipping containers:*** Recently, this material has seen its usage increasing due to its potential to be reused (Fig. 7). The material can be shipped and is weather resistant. Every unit houses up to four individuals, consists of recycled materials and can be assembled on-site with simple tools. And because units can be mounted on solid ground or float on six inflatable pontoons, they are extremely flexible for various circumstances. Shipping container units apply to a variety of impact areas, from a large-scale catastrophe involving high numbers of displaced persons, such as during Hurricane Katrina, to fewer displaced persons. This is due to shipping container housing choices inherent modularity and arrangement flexibility. This form of shelter choice can become a permanent solution for the poor.

h. ***Cardboard Shelters:*** Cardboard and other alternative materials reveal many possibilities beyond those most frequently used in the construction of temporary emergency buildings, such as canvas-covered steel-frame tents (Fig. 7). Cardboard tubes enable quick assembly and disassembly of partition units in a gymnasium or even freestanding structures, without needing professional work, which is a key factor in emergencies. Apart from the above-mentioned structures built by Ar. Shigeru Ban, cardboard can play an important role in furniture design such as beds, seats and storage facilities that can be supplied to pre-cut sheets and with instructions for folding and assembly.

Fig. 8 Cardboard shelters. *Courtesy* Paper log house Kobe. Takanobu Sakuma

i. ***Rubber Shelters:*** Rubber can be recycled and used, among other items to make bricks (Fig. 8). In comparison to conventional bricks, rubber recycled bricks are simple to build and occupy immediately. Their low density is the most important advantage, resulting in very light blocks. The shelters designed with this technology can also remain in post-emergency times due to the high material strength compared to water-proof materials more commonly used for the construction of emergencies.
j. ***Bamboo Shelters:*** Bamboo is a highly flexible, bending and compressive fibre. It's the availability and rapid growth in most parts of the world is another valuable asset (particularly in hot climates). Bamboo is perfect for temporary structures like concrete frames, but also walls and roofs (Fig. 10). It offers the added advantages of fast mounting and permanent housing prospects when building emergency shelters. However, bamboo needs to be considered a construction material that has a good life and excellent mechanical characteristics, that chemical treatment is required before being used in construction to prevent rotting and infestations of insects. Another major challenge for constructing bamboos is the need to protect the components from rain and sunlight very well (Fig. 9).
k. ***3D printed recycled materials:*** Despite its comparatively high cost, 3D printing has spread over the years, proving to be a possibility for emergency shelter construction. For example, the Netherlands company DUS Architects developed a completely mobile 3D printer ("Kamer Maker") capable of printing whole rooms out of recycled materials (Fig. 11). In an emergency, however, 3D printers may be of specific use when printing tiny connecting components. The design of joints to enhance installation and the assembly of sections of various materials can be of great benefit.
l. ***Crates Sandbag Shelters:*** Used in many Ar. Shigeru Ban emergency shelters, sandbag-filled crates will serve as a shallow foundation for building structure (Fig. 12). Whenever possible, the crates can be used to protect from weather other building materials and prevent wetting. Using crates makes more sense when used to carry materials to the site. In such instances, all resources must

Assessment of Socio-economic Impact of Urban Flooding in Hyderabad Due to Climate Change

Md. Abdul Jabbar Sharief and Bharadwaj Vangipuram

Abstract Cities are urbanising at a rapid rate to accommodate the inflow of population who come for better opportunities and life. According to the United Nations Development Programme, about half of the world's population lives in cities and is estimated that by 2050 three quarters will live in cities. In countries like India, the centralisation of opportunities and quality of life in cities had started the trend of people migrating to cities. There are many factors that contribute to the flooding of Indian cities. Human intervention has only amplified the situation. People most prone to be affected by flooding in cities are people living near river basins, catchment areas of lakes and encroachments over water bodies. Maintenance of the system of stormwater drains also plays a huge role in determining the areas that are inundated in a city. Considering the vast scope of the study, Hyderabad, the capital city of Telangana which faced the wrath of unseasonal rains resulting in flooding of the Musi river and inundation of few areas in October 2020. This city has been considered for the study of the socio-economic impacts of urban flooding. Data on rainfall from literature review of various papers have concluded that average unseasonal rainfall has been increasing over the years since 1905. Considering this uptrend of rainfall, using Representative Concentration Path (RCP) future rainfall data is predicted till the year 2100 using literature review. The study of socio-economic factors includes the per capita income of people, the extent of disruption of economic activity, supply chain disruption and the possibility of people being pushed into poverty again. Analysing these factors will help future policymaking and mitigation efforts which will help in reduction of damages caused by urban flooding.

Keywords Urban flooding · Migration · Global climate model · Representative concentration path · Policymaking · Mitigation

---

Md. A. J. Sharief (✉)
Chegg India, Hyderabad, India

B. Vangipuram
Empire Builders, Chennai, India

C. Ghosh and S. Kolathayar (eds.), *A System Engineering Approach to Disaster Resilience*, Lecture Notes in Civil Engineering 205, https://doi.org/10.1007/978-981-16-7397-9_10

1 Introduction

1.1 Background

South Asia has always been susceptible to flooding during monsoon and unseasonal rains. The frequency of flooding has tripled and the corresponding economic and loss of human lives have increased by more than five-fold in the last three decades [1]. Moreover, Indian cities, which have been struggling to endure with ailing infrastructure, are not able to cope up with increasing urbanisation. There is an uptrend of rural population migrating to cities for better opportunities and quality of life. Indian cities are densely populated and migrating populations from rural areas are causing stress on city's infrastructure. The reverse trend of people migrating from city to villages is insignificant, thus causing cities unable to handle the migrating population [2].

Flooding is a phenomenon where there is an interruption to the natural flow of water or immense rainfall which the existing stormwater drains cannot control. The rapid urbanisation of Indian cities has led to both obstructions of the natural flow and water flow into existing stormwater drains that are immense that it is unable to handle. The increasing urbanisation of Indian cities has escalated the flood peaks from 1.6 to eight times and flood volume up to six times. This increases the economic losses and human causalities [3].

1.2 Flooding in Indian Cities

Indian cities have been facing the fury of floods which can be attributed to various reasons. Enumerating the floods in Hyderabad in 2000, Ahmedabad in 2001, Delhi 2002 and 2003, Chennai in 2004, Mumbai in 2005, Surat in 2006, Kolkata in 2007, Jamshedpur in 2008, Delhi in 2009, Guwahati and Delhi in 2010, Srinagar in 2014, Chennai in 2015, Gurugram in 2016, Hyderabad in 2020. Furthermore, a series of floods affected the entire states of Kerala, Karnataka and Gujarat in 2018 and 2019 respectively. Analysing the causes for the floods in urban areas, the causes can be categorised into river floods, flash floods (generally caused by the failure of reservoir or dam on the upstream side), poor stormwater drain infrastructure, encroachments over natural catchment areas.

Urban flooding in India is a persistent problem due to which there are predicaments in terms of economic losses and vulnerability to communities living in flood-prone areas. The economic losses due to urban flooding in India account for the range of 1.1$ billion to 5$ billion a year [3]. The losses do not account for the impact of these floods on informal settlements like slums which reside in flood-prone areas and small businesses in these localities which are subjected to the vulnerability of shutting down their respective business.

1.3 Impact of Climate Change and Urbanisation on Flooding

The haphazard growth of a city can lead to improper city planning leading to blocking the natural flow of water and irregular water management infrastructure. This exponential growth along with climate change has caused havoc in Indian cities in the form of floods.

The study was conducted in Hyderabad, the capital city of Telangana. The impact of climate change on rainfall and urbanisation during the period of flood along with corresponding economic damages caused during the years 1908, 2000, 2008, 2020 are enumerated in Table 1 and Fig. 1. Although the amount of rainfall in 1908 was more than in the other years, the economic damages caused in recent years have been increasing with each flood. The urbanisation of the city has been rapidly increasing over years resulting in mounting economic losses.

Table 1 Urban flood events in Hyderabad [4–6]

Rainfall event	28/29th February 1908	23/24 August 2000	8/9/10 August 2008	13/14 October 2020
Rainfall magnitude	430 mm	240 mm	237 mm	241 mm
Loss property	₹ 10 Million	₹ 10.35 Million	₹ 4.9 Million	₹ 6.7 Billion
Loss of life	1500	26	39	36

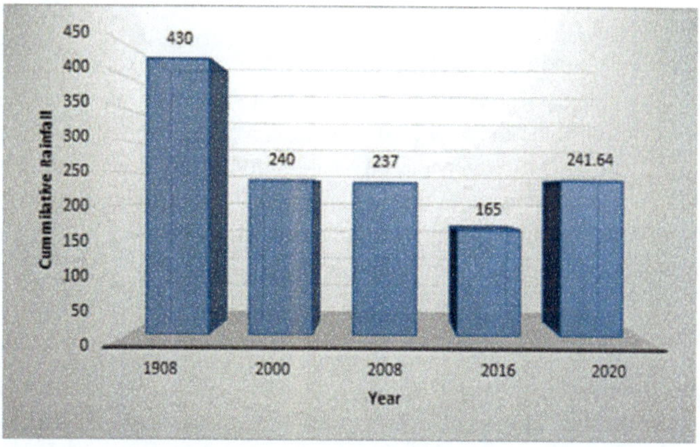

Fig. 1 The cumulative rainfall of years 1908, 2000, 2008,2016 and 2020 are compared for their magnitude (Compiled from Indian Meteorological Department)

2 Methodology

The study aims at analysing the socio-economic impacts of urban flooding in Indian cities for which Hyderabad city was chosen as the study area. The study was conducted in three phases which are outlined below:

1. Rainfall data of 120 years of Hyderabad city was collected which would help in analysing the frequency of flooding and intensity of rainfall for corresponding floods. Literature review based on Representative Concentration Path which could predict the intensity of rainfall for coming 100 years.
2. Using the available data on Hyderabad city, ArcGIS was used to represent the areas and water bodies that cause flooding in nearby areas. A survey was conducted in areas that were inundated during the 2020 Hyderabad floods. The areas to be surveyed were chosen based on different types of urban flooding, which will widen the perspective on urban flooding' effects.
3. The survey involved interviewing people affected during the floods and collecting parameters such as income range, damage caused, compensation, government schemes usage among many to identify the effects of urban floods. Data collected in the survey is used to analyse the socio-economic impacts of flooding in Hyderabad city. The generalised impact of urban flooding for other cities is discussed based on collected parameters during the survey.

2.1 Study Area

The study has been conducted in Hyderabad city, which is capital of Telangana state in India. Hyderabad city was chosen for the current study as it has faced flooding in recent years as highlighted in the previous section. Musi, a tributary of river Krishna flows through the city. Moreover, the city has many artificial water bodies such as Hussain Sagar and natural water bodies which make it easy for the study to generalise the impact of urban flooding to other Indian cities which have a similar case of river flowing through the city and natural water bodies (Fig. 2).

2.2 Climate Change and Rainfall

Analysing the rainfall data of Hyderabad for the last 120 years reveals that the recurrence of intense rainfall has increased in the last four decades. The normal annual rainfall as given by Indian Meteorological Department for Hyderabad is 845.6 mm and in last four decades, the cumulative rainfall in Hyderabad has exceeded 1000 mm several times. From Fig. 3, it can be observed that intensity of rainfall has been increasing during the last few decades. Since the last 120 years, Hyderabad has recorded its highest rainfall of 1331.37 mm in 2020.

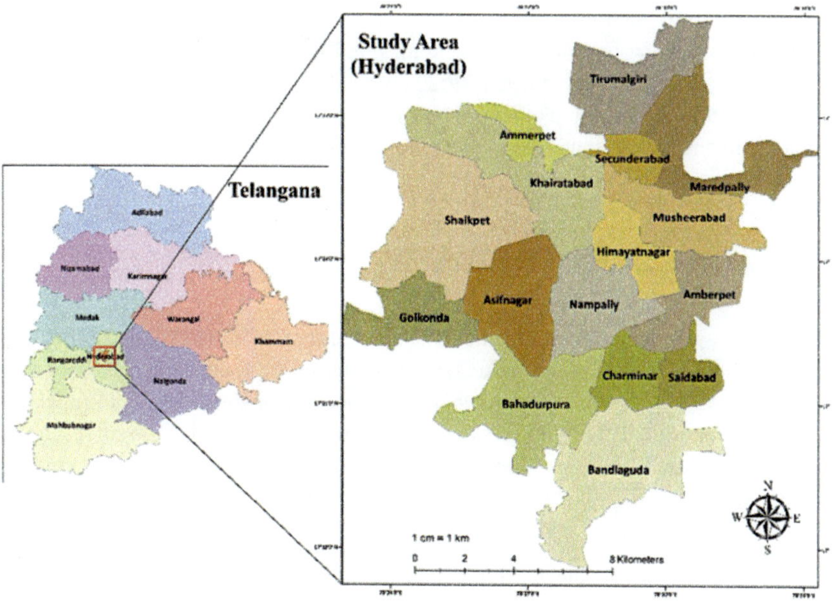

Fig. 2 The representation of Hyderabad in Telangana and zones in Hyderabad using ArcGIS

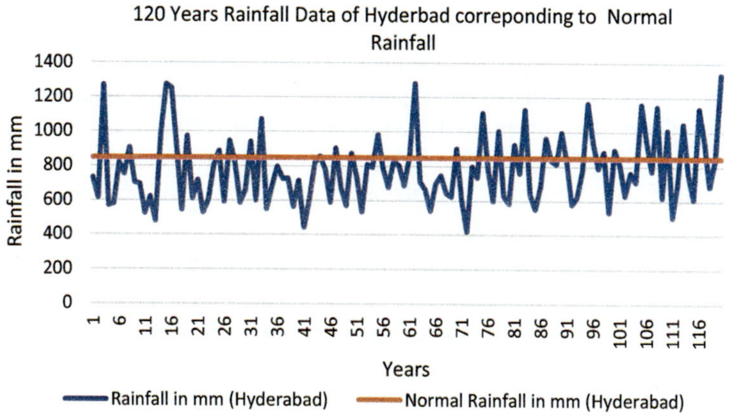

Fig. 3. 120 years cumulative rainfall data of Hyderabad compared with normal rainfall (Compiled from IMD)

Considering both the scenarios of Representative Concentration Pathways of 6.0 and 8.5. The models analysed for historic rainfall and calculated rainfall with RCP 6.0 and 8.5, RCP 8.5 was accurate with its peak rainfall in the year 2083. The RCP 6.0 overestimates the rainfall intensity as observed when compared with historic rainfall of Hyderabad [5].

As observed from Table 2, the intensity of daily rainfall will increase till 2084–2093 and reduce in consequent years. With rainfall intensity and urbanisation, the economic damage that was caused in 2020 Hyderabad floods was about ₹ 6.7 billion. The increasing rainfall intensity along with rapid urbanisation tends to cause more damages in terms of human lives and economic loss.

2.3 Survey and Data Collection

A survey was conducted for assessment of socio-economic impact of the 2020 floods in Hyderabad. The survey was divided into two phases, first, one aimed at evaluating the parameters for residential houses and second one was to assess the impact of floods on economic activity in the same area. Primarily, to conduct the survey, areas were chosen based on the source and type of flooding. As mentioned in previous section that urban flooding is caused by various reasons. Based on various types, areas were chosen for survey (Fig. 4).

- Moosarambagh was selected for survey owing to the fact that the flooding was caused by Musi river which passes through the area. Musi experienced a maximum flood level of about 9 feet during the floods in that area. This led to inundation of areas near the Musi river.
- Chandrayangutta was one of the most affected floods in Hyderabad. Primarily, the area was flooded due to breach and overflow of water from nearby Gurram Cherruvu Lake and improper functioning of stormwater drains.
- Yakuthpura was flooded due to multiple reasons. The nearby Balapur lake was breached and Musi was flooded due to release of water from Himayat Sagar. The area is low lying which resulted in inundation of the area by about 9 feet.
- Kavadiguda was flooded due to water mismanagement. The improper functioning of stormwater drains led to stagnation of water in the area. Although the area was flooded, the intensity of flooding was mild when compared to other areas of the present study.

The survey included the income of an individual or family, losses due to floods, financial aid provided by government, utilisation of government schemes and real estate after flooding. The economic activity survey included gross income of the business, loss due to floods, capital required to restart the business, extent of supply chain disruption.

3 Result and Discussion

The data collected during the survey enable the study to analyse the income groups which were vulnerable to urban flooding. People from each area were interviewed for the details, around 100 people were interviewed in each area during the survey (Table 3; Fig. 5).

Table 2 Maximum daily rainfall intensity in Hyderabad predicted using RCP 8.5 [5]

	2017–2027	2028–2038	2039–2049	2050–2060	2061–2071	2072–2082	2084–2093	2094–2100
RCP 8.5	150 mm	120–130 mm	190–200 mm	140–150 mm	280–290 mm	300–310 mm	540–550 mm	250–260 mm

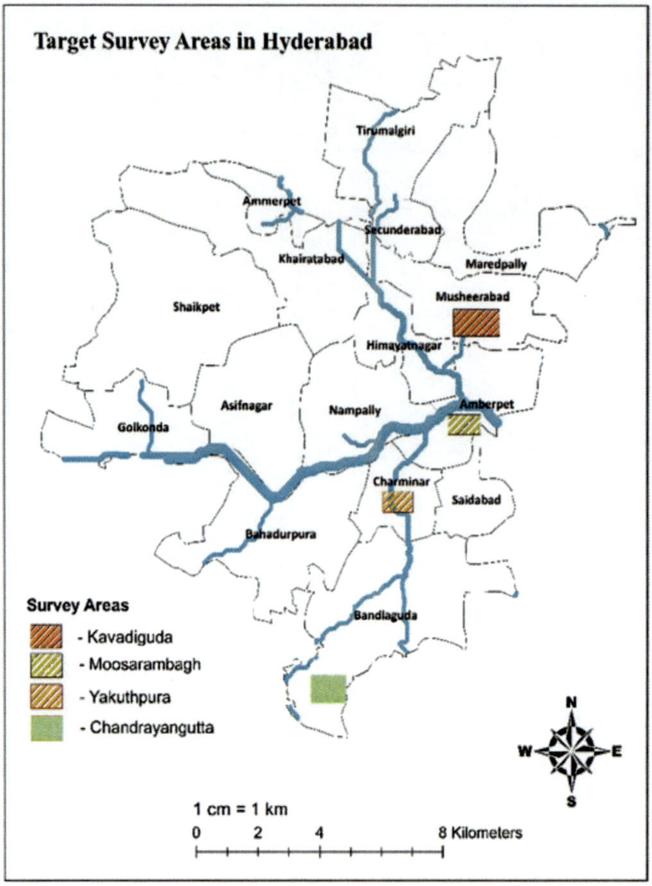

Fig. 4 Surveyed area along with water bodies near the corresponding areas

Residential houses with more than one storey were mostly damaged on the first storey and higher storeys were unaffected. But vehicles owned by higher storey people were damaged or washed away by the floods. The damages mentioned in Table 4 does not account for vehicular damages but only accounts for property, valuables damaged partly or fully by the flooding. The astonishing data on real estate in the areas which were flooded did not drop due to flooding but flourished with the same prices for rental and sale.

The shops in the areas were also affected by the flooding. The shops are mostly small-scale neighbourhood retail shops and repair shops. Apart from this the areas also had other retail activity which was generally community/neighbourhood shops such as ironing shops, small-scale fast-food joints. Most of the shops were on the ground floor of buildings which led to complete inundation in all the areas except Kavadiguda. Kavadiguda experienced waterlogging, thus shops were not completely damaged (Fig. 6).

Table 3 Survey data collected from residential houses in listed areas

Area	Kavadiguda	Moosarambagh	Yakuthpura	Chandrayangutta
Income range of individual /business				
Below poverty line	0	120	20	4
Poor	40	10	45	78
low-income Group	57	30	20	40
Medium income group	31	7	15	3
Higher medium income group	27	2	0	0
Total	155	179	100	125

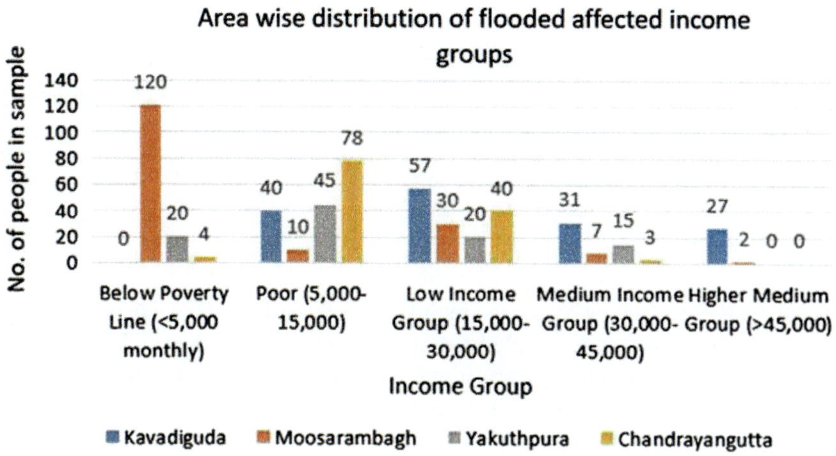

Fig. 5 Income ranges of people affected by floods in areas where survey was conducted

Table 4 Loss due floods in surveyed areas for residential houses

Range of loss/damage	<one lakh	1.5–2 lakhs	No loss
No. of people	300	200	201

The shops which are the economic activity in the flooded areas which were surveyed were completely inundated which resulted in damaging the stock in the shops. During the floods, the shops which were functional were not able to access essential commodities such as milk and vegetables among many. The supply chain during the period of flooding was completely disrupted leading to a shortage of essential commodities. The loss incurred by the shops in the areas were in the range of 2.5–3 lakh rupees. More than the damage caused, owners of the shops were facing trouble in restarting their business as they were short of capital.

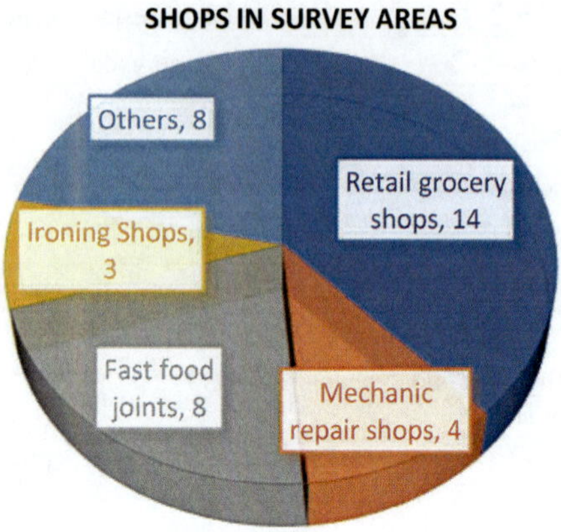

Fig. 6 Various types of shops in flooded areas which were surveyed

The capital for restarting business has become a hurdle for local shop owners. Due to flooding, the business has slowed down which has resulted in a few shops shutting down.

4 Conclusions

The analysis of the survey conducted in flood-affected areas of Hyderabad indicated that a set of income range people were affected more than other income ranges. The poor and low-income group sections are more affected by the flooding than other income ranges of the corresponding flood surveyed areas. The damage or loss that were incurred during the flooding caused substantial stress in those income groups. The financial aid provided by the government for loss incurred during flood is insufficient to suffice the loss caused by it.

Those income groups are vulnerable to being pushed back into poverty. During the last two decades, India has successfully helped millions alleviate poverty. The poverty was alleviated by opportunities in terms of business opportunities or jobs, but urban flooding has become a hurdle in creating more opportunities. These floods have caused damage pushing the progress of few people back by few decades.

The present study was limited to Hyderabad for conducting socio-economic impact of urban flooding due to vast scope of the study. Many Indian cities are vulnerable to flooding which are resulting in massive economic losses and pushes people into poverty. It is predicted that will have 20 metropolitan cities by the end of the next decade. Climate change and urbanisation will have an impact on flooding in cities resulting in hindering the development and upliftment of people.

The present study highlighted the vulnerable sections of people who will be affected by floods. Mitigation measures must be planned by authorities to avoid loss of property and human life. If measures are not taken to curb the damages future rainfalls will have repercussions in terms of poverty, opportunity and functioning of businesses. Water management in cities must be strengthened in order to avoid future inundations. This will partly ensure sustainable cities & communities, no poverty and climate change goals are achieved as set by United Nations Development Program.

Acknowledgements The authors gratefully acknowledge the reviewers for their constructive comments and feedback which made the study more efficient. We are grateful for Indian Meteorological Department for the open source data on rainfall and corresponding distribution of rainfall in Hyderabad. We would also like to thank B. Sai Kiran and K. Sai Teja for helping us in conducting the survey during these difficult times.

References

1. Dutta D, Babel MS, Gupta AS (2004) An assessment of socio-economic impacts of floods in large coastal areas, Asia Pacific Network for Global Change Research, Asia Institute of Technology
2. Bhaskaran RP (2011) From the village to the city: the changing dynamics of migration in contemporary India. The Ind J Labour Econom 54(3)
3. Baghel A (2016) Causes of urban flooding in India: study of Mumbai in 2006 and Chennai in 2015. In: International Conference on Disaster and Risk Management: AGORA, pp 1–27
4. Ahmed Z, Rao RM, Reddy KRM. Raj YE Urban flooding—case study of Hyderabad. Glob J. Eng. Des. Technol. 2(4):63–66
5. Vemula S, Raju KS, Sai VS, Santhosh KA (2019) Urban floods in Hyderabad, India, under present and future rainfall scenarios: a case study. Nat Hazards 95:637–655
6. Somasekar M (2020) Hyderabad floods highlight the need for a disaster mitigation and climate resilience plan. Mongabay Series: Floods Drought

Application of ArcGIS and HEC-RAS in Assessing Sedimentation in Godavari River Reach

S. Kiran, Anwesna Poudyal, Samer Pradhan, and Monalisha Gautom

Abstract Assessment of sediment load is paramount in understanding the process of erosion and deposition in rivers. Excess sedimentation is hazardous as it reduces the carrying capacity of the river and destabilizes the channel banks. In this study, the transport model in Hydrologic Engineering Centre's River Analysis System (HEC-RAS) is coupled with quasi-unsteady flow series to quantify the sediment discharge and assess erosion and deposition at each cross section along the Godavari River reach. The topography of the river reach is extracted and digitized using HEC-GeoRAS tool in ArcGIS. To accurately reproduce the natural hydraulic behaviour in the river reach, the cross-sectional lines are positioned at optimal spacing and approximately perpendicular to the direction of river flow. The Manning's roughness coefficient (n) is calibrated using one-dimensional unsteady flow model in HEC-RAS. The unsteady model computes the hydraulic properties and provides simultaneous solutions for discharge and stage at each computational time step for all cross sections. The sediment continuity equation is solved for non-equilibrium sediment transport over the control volume along with the hydraulic sorting and armouring. Results from the simulated models are compared and calibrated against observed field measurements. Weighted coefficient of determination (ωr^2), Nash–Sutcliffe efficiency (E), modified Nash–Sutcliffe efficiency (E_1) and Modified index of agreement (d_1) are used to provide an objective assessment about the closeness between the simulated and observed values. Among the transport models in HEC-RAS, the Wilcock-Crowe model provides more accurate estimates of sediment discharge and deposition and erosion at each cross section along river reach.

Keywords Sediment transport · Godavari river · ArcGIS · HEC-RAS · Wilcock-crowe

S. Kiran (✉) · A. Poudyal · S. Pradhan · M. Gautom
Sikkim Manipal Institute of Technology, Majhitar, Sikkim, India
e-mail: kiran.sriram@smit.smu.edu.in

C. Ghosh and S. Kolathayar (eds.), *A System Engineering Approach to Disaster Resilience*, Lecture Notes in Civil Engineering 205, https://doi.org/10.1007/978-981-16-7397-9_11

1 Introduction

Influx of excess sediment impacts erosion and aggradation in dynamic rivers and modifies the channel characteristics altering the river's morphology. Extreme climatic conditions, nature of topography, land use pattern and terrain slope are few among the several natural factors that enhance the rate of sediment yield in a river. Unsustainable farming techniques and inadequate watershed management have also contributed to an increase in the influx of sediment load. Excess sedimentation is hazardous as it reduces the carrying capacity of the river and destabilizes the channel banks. Assessment of sediment load in rivers is paramount in understanding the process of erosion and deposition. It will also provide vital information required in planning, designing and managing water resource systems.

Godavari River originates in the Western Ghats and flows eastwards across the Deccan plateau into Bay of Bengal. The study reach extends from Peruru to Polavaram which is approximately 268 km in distance. Width of the channel in the study reach varies from 700 m at its narrowest to 3000 m at its widest sections. Due to its high erosion rate, which differs from one part of the basin to another, Godavari River is characterized by excessive sediment discharge. Almost 95% of the sediment load in Godavari River is predominantly monsoonal or transported during the wet season [1].

Several studies have been carried out to simulate the sediment transport process in natural flows. The hydraulic characteristics of the channel are emulated in the model through Manning's roughness coefficient. Stability of finite difference scheme is influenced by the weighting factor and computational time step during calibration of Manning's roughness coefficient [2]. Though sediment transport is unsteady, most formulae have limited applicability and can be used only to evaluate the transport capacity in steady uniform flows. To overcome this limitation, one-dimensional sediment transport algorithms adopted the quasi-unsteady approach. A comparison between the unsteady and quasi-unsteady sediment transport models indicated that the unsteady model made no significant improvement in accuracy over the quasi-unsteady model [3]. The quasi-unsteady transport model provided approximate results for erosion and deposition in meandering channels, assuming equilibrium between the volumetric sediment discharge and transport capacity [4]. However, it is unlikely and unrealistic to assume the flux in the system to be in equilibrium as the process of sediment transport is often complex and imbalanced. For a credible model assessment, the combination of different efficiency measures should be consistent. The sensitivity in each efficiency criteria has to be considered before application. The over and under predictions are to be reflected along with other attributes of transport, providing a more comprehensive evaluation of model results [5].

With the advancement in technology, simulation of sediment transport using sophisticated algorithms has enabled robust modelling and prediction of the sediment dynamics in river systems. For this process, several modelling packages like FLUENT, CFX, PHOENIX, FLUIVAL, MIKE 21, CCHE2D, CCHE1D and HEC-RAS are used. In this study, the hybrid one-dimensional HEC-RAS (version 5.0.7) model developed by Hydrologic Engineering Centre of the US Army Corps of Engineers is considered [6]. Among the four river analysis components in HEC-RAS, the unsteady flow condition is used in calibrating Manning's roughness coefficient and the quasi-unsteady sediment transport model is used in determining the sediment discharge in the river reach.

2 Methodology

2.1 Geometry

The geometric data which includes the river path, cross section, flow lines and bank stations are extracted from the digital elevation model (DEM) having a spatial resolution of 1- arc second. DEM is obtained from the satellite images of Shuttle Radar Topography Mission (SRTM) by the U.S. Geological Survey (USGS). The reach of Godavari River between Perur and Polavaram (refer Fig. 1 and Table 1) is digitized in ArcGIS.

To accurately depict the hydraulic conditions in the river reach, the cross-sectional lines are approximately perpendicular to the direction of flow. The optimum spacing

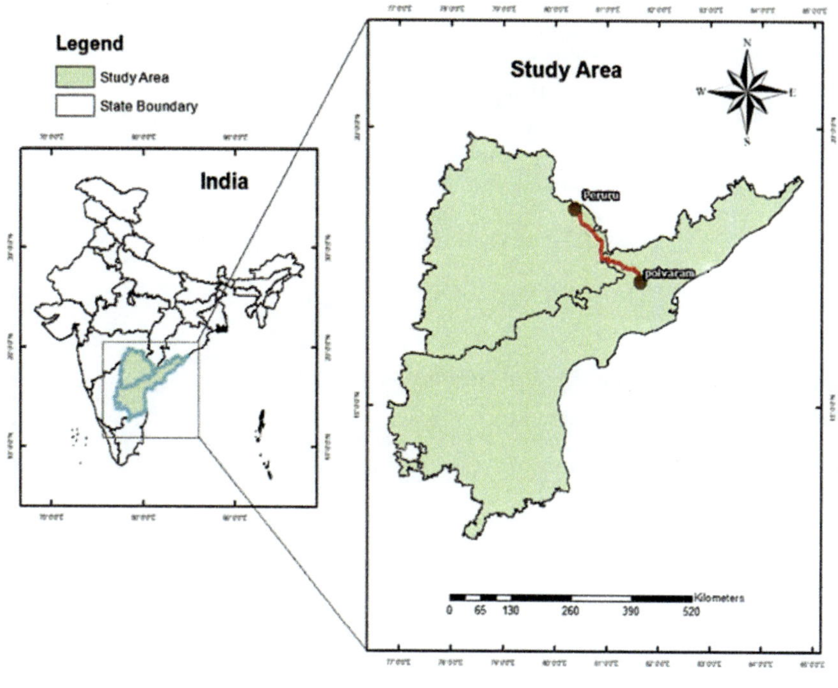

Fig. 1 Location of study area

Table 1 Location of upstream and downstream boundary stations

Station	Latitude	Longitude	Boundary
Perur	18° 33′ 00″	80° 22′ 00″	Upstream
Polavaram	17° 14′ 45″	81° 39′ 35″	Downstream

between the cross-sectional lines is proportional to bankfull surface width of the channel. The inclusion of additional cross sections may not necessarily increase the model accuracy once the optimal spacing is attained [7]. The river reaches in this study has been divided into 105 cross sections with an average distance of 2.5 km between each cross section as shown in Fig. 2. HEC-GeoRAS extension in ArcGIS is used to create the geometry file and export it into HEC-RAS where bank stations at each cross section are adjusted to bankfull depth manually.

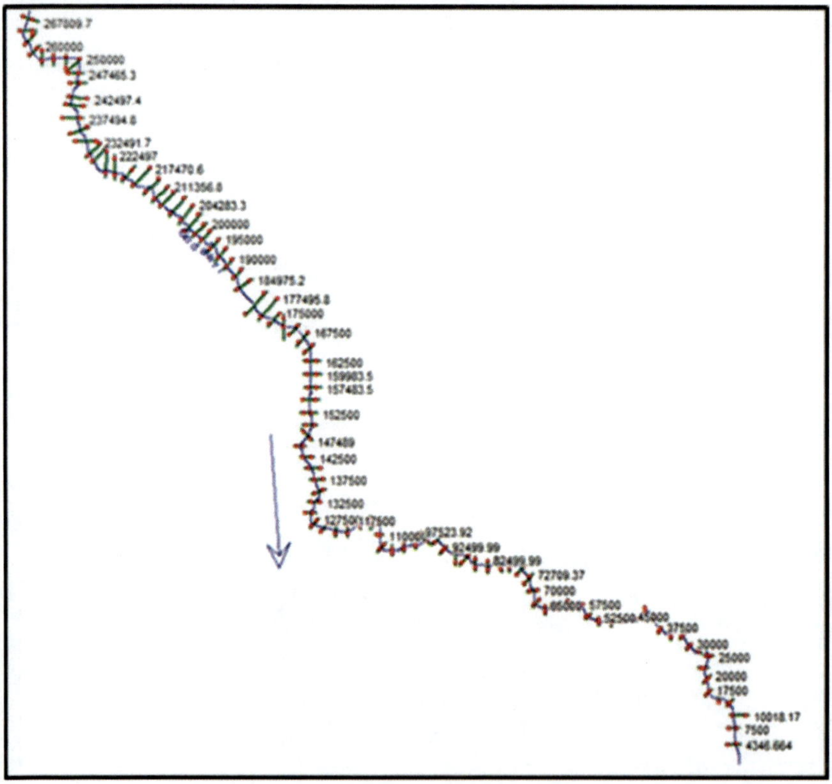

Fig. 2 Study reach of Godavari River between Perur and Polavaram

2.2 One-Dimensional Unsteady Flow Model

The Manning's roughness coefficient is calibrated using the one-dimensional unsteady flow model. The governing equation for one-dimensional unsteady flow in HEC-RAS is the Saint Venant equation which comprises the continuity equation (Eq. 1) and momentum equation (Eq. 2) solved using the four-point implicit scheme. The model computes the hydraulic properties to provide simultaneous solutions for discharge and stage at each computational time step for all cross sections.

$$\frac{\partial A}{\partial t} + \frac{\partial Q}{\partial x} - q = 0 \tag{1}$$

$$\frac{\partial Q}{\partial t} + \frac{\partial (QV)}{\partial x} + gA\left(\frac{\partial z}{\partial x} + S_f\right) = 0 \tag{2}$$

where A is the cross-sectional flow area, Q is the flow discharge, q is the lateral inflow per unit length, V is the velocity of flow, z is the water surface elevation and S_f is friction slope.

Stability of the unsteady flow model in HEC-RAS depends upon the computational intervals chosen. At large time steps, certain peak flows in the inflow hydrograph might be missed at some cross sections. Continuous monitoring of inflow hydrograph, to identify the change in flow rate from one time step to another, improves the stability of the unsteady flow model.

2.3 Sediment Transport Model

In HEC-RAS the Exner's equation (Eq. 3) is used to route sediment continuity wherein it computes the difference between the inflowing and outflowing sediment load in a control volume.

$$(1 - \lambda_p)B\frac{\partial \eta}{\partial t} = -\frac{\partial Q_s}{\partial x} \tag{3}$$

where, λ_p is the porosity of bed surface layer, B is the channel width, η bed surface elevation and Q_s is the transported sediment load.

If the transport capacity of the control volume is lesser than the inflowing sediment supply, the surplus sediment load is stored in the bed surface layer as a multiphase sediment–water mixture, causing sediment deposition. The deficit is removed from the control volume if the transport capacity exceeds the inflowing sediment supply, resulting in sediment erosion. The change in the elevation of the bed surface layer is indicated by the porosity of the multiphase mixture [8]. In HEC-RAS, the sediment transport potential of the control volume is computed independently for each grain class using empirical sediment transport algorithms that translate the hydrodynamic conditions at each cross section into transport. The total transport capacity is computed by assessing the proportion of all grain classes involved in the transport [9].

The boundary condition at upstream cross section is the quasi-unsteady inflow hydrograph. In a quasi-unsteady condition, the continuous inflow hydrograph is transformed into a series of discrete intervals consisting of steady flow profiles over the flow duration. Sediment transport computations in HEC-RAS assume no change occurs in the elevation of the bed surface layer over a computational time step. The 24-h flow duration is further subdivided into variable computational intervals to reduce model instability as higher flows tend to increase the change in bed surface elevation. The boundary condition at the downstream cross section is the normal depth which requires the channel slope to be given as input. The slope of the river reach between Perur and Polavaram is calculated from the profile of the geometry in HEC-RAS. The mean diameters of the bed sediment particles are obtained from samples collected along various points in the river bed. The bed sediment gradations are first defined in a database and then assigned to the upstream and downstream cross sections respectively. For intermediate cross sections, the bed gradations are interpolated from the samples. The mean diameters of the bed material at Perur and Polavaram are 1.31 mm and 1.09 mm respectively. The sediment flow characteristics are defined using a rating curve consisting of five flow-load points encompassing the entire range of flow. The erodible limits are set within the bank extents. Unlike the equilibrium load condition where sediment discharge is equated to its transport capacity in a control volume, non-equilibrium transport model computes the boundary sediment load based on inflow hydrograph and sample load points.

3 Results and Discussion

3.1 Calibration of Manning's Roughness Coefficient (N)

The inflow hydrograph, from 1st September 2017 to 31st October 2017, defined at the upstream boundary is continuously monitored for large changes inflows. The computational intervals are adjusted when the difference in flow rate between time steps exceeds the critical value. The Manning's roughness coefficient (n) is calibrated by simulating the unsteady flow model for different values of n along the cross section. To evaluate the performance of the hydraulic model, simulated discharge values are compared with observed measurements at Polavaram station (refer Fig. 3). Weighted coefficient of determination $\left(\omega r^2\right)$, Nash–Sutcliffe efficiency (E), modified Nash–Sutcliffe efficiency (E_1) and Modified index of agreement (d_1) are considered to provide an objective assessment of how well a simulated model fits the recorded observations for different values of Manning's coefficient. HydroGOF function in R

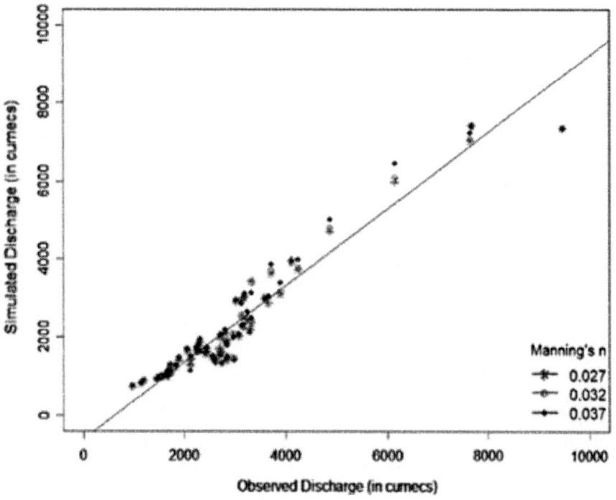

Fig. 3 Observed and simulated discharge for different Manning's roughness coefficient (n) values at Polavaram station

Table 2 Efficiency criteria for different values of manning's roughness coefficient (n)

Manning's roughness coefficient (n)	ωr^2	E	E_1	d_1
0.027	0.749	0.723	0.278	0.705
0.032	0.753	0.727	0.295	0.714
0.037	0.752	0.728	0.298	0.715

is used in the estimation of efficiency measures. The most appropriate value of n is selected based on these efficiency measures.

From the results presented Table 2 and Fig. 2, it can be observed that Manning's roughness coefficient of 0.037 has the best values for E, E_1 and d_1. Hence, 0.037 is chosen as the final calibrated value of n for sediment analysis.

3.2 Sediment Transport Function

To compute the total transport capacity, the model is simulated for the entire flow duration combining various sediment transport functions with armouring techniques and fall velocities. It involves routing of sediment at cross sections considering the sediment dynamics. The simulated sediment discharge at Polavaram station is compared with the recorded observations to select the most suitable transport function. The performance of various sediment transport models is summarized in Table 3.

It is crucial to identify transport functions that define sediment transport accurately. For evaluation of model performance based on ωr^2, information about the gradient integrated into its calculation is also considered. Gradient values closer to one indicate good agreement. The Wilcock-Crowe transport function had a gradient

Table 3 Efficiency criteria indicating model performance with different sediment transport functions

Transport function	Sorting method	ωr^2	E	E_1	d_1
Acker's White	Thomas (Ex 5)	0.264	0.237	−0.004	0.533
Engelund-Hansen	Thomas (Ex 5)	0.476	0.576	0.168	0.620
	Active Layer	0.466	0.561	0.161	0.615
Laursen (Copeland)	Thomas (Ex 5)	0.326	0.341	0.138	0.576
Tofaleti	Thomas (Ex 5)	0.173	−0.021	−0.147	0.476
Meyer Peter Muller	Thomas (Ex 5)	0.252	0.200	0.007	0.532
Wilcock-Crowe	Active Layer	0.585	0.736	0.365	0.699
MPM- Tofaleti	Thomas (Ex 5)	0.227	0.112	−0.060	0.507
Yang	Active Layer	0.358	0.412	0.153	0.587

of 0.675 which was higher than the other gradients and also produced the best result of 0.585 for ωr^2.

E values closer to one indicate good correlation and for lower values E_1 the model performance is interpreted as poor. Efficiency criteria lesser than zero indicates the mean of the observed time series would produce better predictions than the model. From Table 3, it is observed that there is poor agreement between the modelled and observed hydraulic behaviour when Tofaleti, MPM-Tofaleti and Acker's White transport functions are considered. The values of E and E_1 for Tofaleti,E_1 for MPM-Tofaleti and Acker's White are all less than zero indicating poor model performance. The Wilcock-Crowe function gave the best values for $E(0.736)$ and $E_1(0.365)$ amongst the functions considered in this study. It also has the best value of 0.699 for d_1 (Value of 1 implies perfect fit). The sediment discharge at Polavaram, computed using the Wilcock-Crowe transport function, is compared with the recorded observations at the station (refer Fig. 4).

The efficiency measures produced more accurate and consistent results for the Wilcock-Crowe transport function. It is therefore used in computing the erosion and aggradation at each cross section along the river reach.

3.3 *Predication of Mean Effective Invert Change*

The surplus or deficit sediment load at a cross section is transformed into equivalent values of depth, indicating aggradation or erosion at that section. The mean effective invert change provides the average change in bed elevation at a cross section after the flow duration. In sedimentation analysis, the mean effective channel invert provides a more realistic measure of erosion and deposition at station over the invert change which only considers the lowest point of elevation in a cross section at the end of simulation.

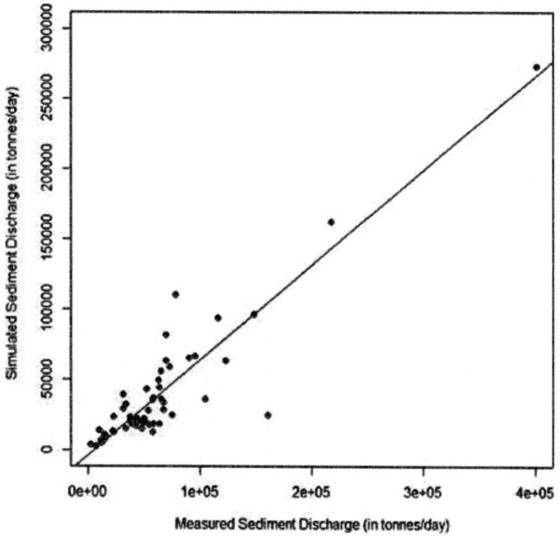

Fig. 4 Measured and simulated sediment discharge using Wilcock-Crowe transport function at Polavaram station

The bed elevation changes across 105 river stations, computed using the Wilcock-Crowe transport function, are shown in Fig. 5. The river stations are denoted from upstream to downstream. It is observed, at certain stations there is an alternating pattern of high erosion followed by deposition. These patterns could be consistently associated with abrupt changes in the relative elevation of the river's profile between successive cross sections. Significant erosion and deposition are observed in the river

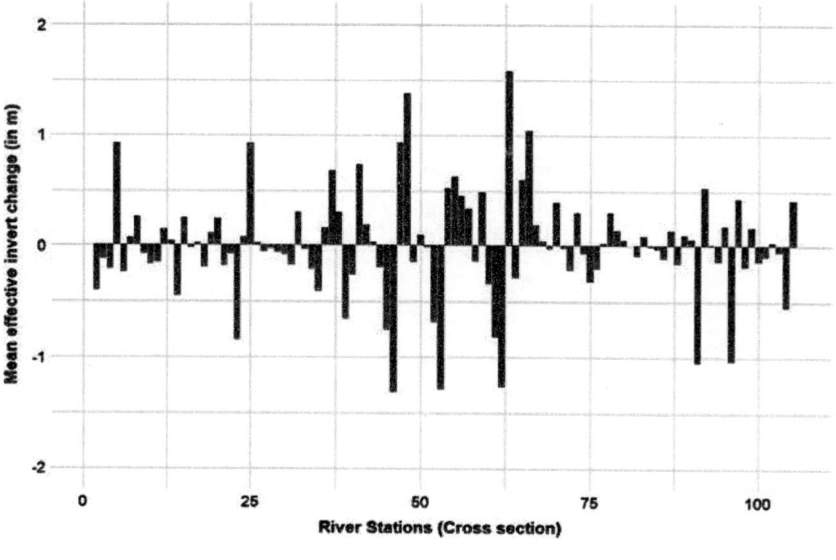

Fig. 5 Mean effective invert change across different cross sections

reach between stations 44 and 67 where the river reach undergoes a sharp change in its direction of flow. A gradual rise in erosion and deposition behaviour is also noted towards the end, between stations 90 and 97, where the river again changes its direction of flow. Maximum depth of erosion of 1.316 m is observed at river station 46. The deposition is maximum at the 63rd river station with a depth of 1.583 m.

4 Conclusion

In this study, we have considered the reach of Godavari River between Perur and Polavaram stations. Unsteady flow conditions were chosen over the conventional steady flow approach to determine Manning's roughness coefficient. To reproduce the natural hydraulic behaviour of the river reach, the model was calibrated by adjusting n values. Manning's roughness coefficient of 0.037 was selected based on the efficiency criteria.

Sedimentation along the river reach was computed using one-dimensional non-equilibrium sediment transport model. The most appropriate transport function was decided by calibrating the sediment discharge at downstream boundary. Values of ωr^2, E, E_1 and d_1 were comparatively higher for the Wilcock- Crowe transport function which provided a better estimation on sediment discharge in river reach between Perur and Polavaram. It should be noted that not all criteria will accurately quantify the model performance based on flow dynamics. Hence, it is imperative to choose criterion's that are positively correlated and provide a consistent assessment. The average change in bed elevation, depicted using the mean effective invert change, revealed that erosion and deposition in the river reach are influenced by both abrupt variations in the riverbed geometry and the change in direction of flow.

The maximum erosion and deposition were observed in these zones. It is noted that the accuracy of the model depends primarily on the quality of topographic data, hydraulic conditions in the river reach and the sediment transport function chosen. The characteristics of these empirical functions are to be compared with that of the flow scenario before incorporating it into the analysis. It is essential to understand and identify the limitations in each sediment transport function especially when they are associated with the modelling of sediment dynamics in natural flows.

References

1. Bikshamaiah G, Subramanian G (1980) Chemical and sediment mass transfer in the Godavari. J Hydrol 46:331–342
2. Kadhim Hameed L, Tawfeek Ali S (2013) Estimating of manning's roughness coefficient for Hilla river through calibration using HEC-RAS model. Jordan J Civ Eng 7(1):44–53
3. Hummel R et al (2012) Comparison of unsteady and quasi-unsteady flow models in simulating sediment transport in an ephemeral Arizona stream. J Am Water Resour Assoc 48(5):987–998. https://doi.org/10.1111/j.1752-1688.2012.00663.x

4. Das B, Sil BS (2017) Assessment of sedimentation in Barak river reach using HEC-RAS. In: Garg V et al (eds) Water science and technology library. Springer International Publishing, Cham, pp 95–102. https://doi.org/10.1007/978-3-319-55125-8_8
5. Krause P et al (2005) Comparison of different efficiency criteria for hydrological model assessment. Adv Geosci 5:89–97. https://doi.org/10.5194/adgeo-5-89-2005
6. USACE: HEC-RAS river analysis system hydraulic reference manual version 5.0. Hydrol. Eng Cent February, 547 (2016)
7. Castellarin A et al (2009) Optimal cross-sectional spacing in preissmann scheme 1D hydrodynamic models. J Hydraul Eng 135(2):96–105. https://doi.org/10.1061/(asce)0733-9429(2009)135:2(96)
8. Brunner GW, Gibson S (2005) Sediment transport modeling in HEC RAS. In: Impacts of Global Climate Change. American Society of Civil Engineers, Reston, VA, pp 1–12. https://doi.org/10.1061/40792(173)442
9. Brunner GW (2016) HEC-RAS river analysis system User's manual. US army corps of engineers–hydrologic engineering center

Decision Support Tool for Blast Mitigation

C. Murali Krishna and Tezeswi P. Tadepalli

Abstract In the current geopolitical scenario, it has become essential for urban planners to consider terrorism threats in the built environment. For emergency responders and law enforcement agencies, blast damage prediction is a critical requirement. A standalone and simple MATLAB-based Geographic Information System (GIS) tool for blast damage prediction has been developed, which assists planners to predict blast damage and primary blast mitigation efforts such as access control, standoff, and hardening of critical infrastructure. Various blast scenarios such as man-portable packages and automobiles are considered, and air blast effects modified for interaction with buildings are superimposed over an urban environment.

Keywords Blast · Mitigation · Emergency responders · Terrorism · Law enforcement agencies · MATLAB® · GIS

1 Introduction

In the current geopolitical scenario, terrorism threat has become essential for urban planners to consider in the built environment (Table 1). Improvised explosive devices (IEDs) can cause catastrophic damage to buildings, both externally and internally, leading to causalities. Preparedness for such threats and mitigating their effects is the most critical challenge for administrations and security agencies. Figure 1 shows the number of casualties in India due to various bomb sizes [1]. The data shows that the most significant number of deaths (fatalities and injuries) is due to car bombs.

This paper presents a simple tool for predicting the effects of air blast loads superimposed over urban terrain and environment, providing approximate estimates of the damage due to air blast in an urban environment while implementing public domain information.

C. Murali Krishna (✉) · T. P. Tadepalli
National Institute of Technology Warangal, Warangal, Telangana, India

T. P. Tadepalli
e-mail: tezeswi@nitw.ac.in

C. Ghosh and S. Kolathayar (eds.), *A System Engineering Approach to Disaster Resilience*, Lecture Notes in Civil Engineering 205, https://doi.org/10.1007/978-981-16-7397-9_12

Table 1 Terrorist blasts in India state-wise incidents: 1998–2004 [1]

State	Number of fatalities	% of total fatalities	Number of incidents	% of total incidents
Andhra Pradesh	90	2.99	48	6.12
Arunachal Pradesh	1	0.03	1	0.13
Assam	376	12.5	85	10.84
Bihar	156	5.2	26	3.32
Chandigarh	0	0	1	0.13
Chhattisgarh	21	0.7	2	0.26
Delhi	25	0.83	14	1.79
Goa	0	0	1	0.13
Gujarat	2	0.07	8	1.02
Himachal Pradesh	46	1.53	4	0.51
Jammu and Kashmir	1658	55.11	480	61.22
Jharkhand	86	2.89	11	1.4
Karnataka	0	0	2	0.26
Kerala	0	0	3	0.38
Madhya Pradesh	22	0.74	1	0.13
Maharashtra	93	3.09	14	1.79
Manipur	94	3.12	17	2.17
Meghalaya	12	0.4	1	0.13
Mizoram	8	0.27	1	0.13
Nagaland	12	0.4	1	0.13
Orissa	7	0.23	3	0.38
Punjab	10	0.33	4	0.51
Tamil Nadu	72	2.39	18	2.3
Tripura	179	9.95	25	3.19
Unknown	2	0.07	3	0.38
Uttar Pradesh	23	0.76	4	0.51
Uttaranchal	2	0.07	1	0.13
West Bengal	11	0.37	5	0.64

2 Blast Effect Phenomena

The blast effects analysis was started in the twentieth century circa World War-II, which provided a plethora of blast data. An explosion with a high-pressure blast wave results in a rapid exothermic chemical reaction; as the reaction progresses, the explosive material either in solid or liquid form is converted into a hot, dense, high-pressure gas [3]. A high explosion causes shock waves at very high velocities to reach

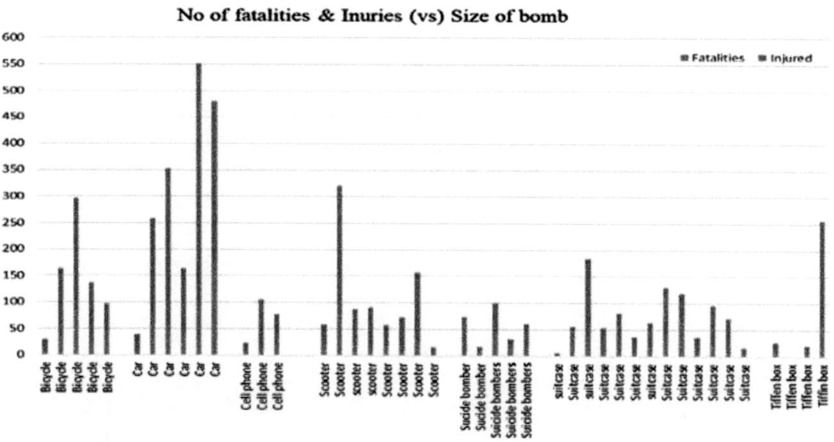

Fig. 1 Number of casualties versus size of the bomb [2]

equilibrium within the compressed air, traveling radially outward from the source at supersonic velocities. This initiates the process of blast shock wave propagation in the urban environment [4].

As the shock wavefront expands, pressure decays back to ambient pressure, a negative pressure phase, as shown in Fig. 2. The negative phase is usually neglected in design.

The blast pressures versus standoff distance graphs are typically available for free-field. However, the urban terrain offers multiple opportunities for the blast wave to be reflected, refracted, and focused. In this paper, the wavefront parameters produced by spherical explosives reported by Kinney and Graham [6] are modified based on street pressures and impulses enhanced by blast focusing [7]:

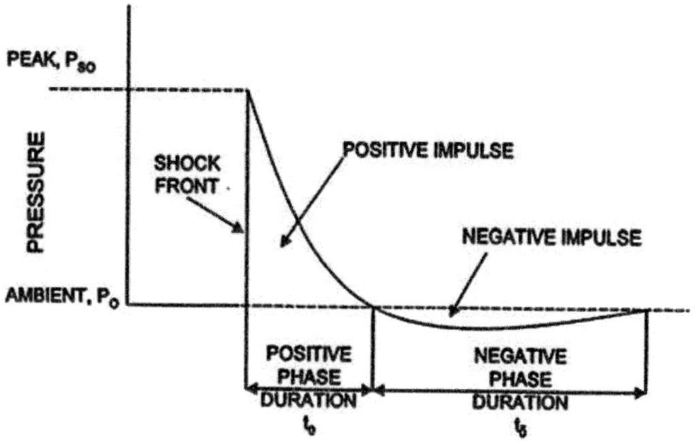

Fig. 2 Typical pressure–time history [5]

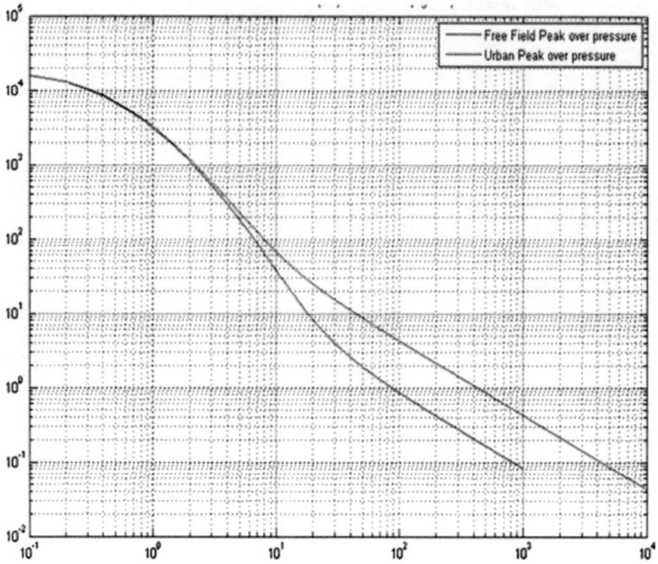

Fig. 3 Comparison of peak overpressure versus standoff [6, 7]

Peak pressure:

$$\frac{P_S}{P_O} = \frac{1200 \times 1 + \left(\frac{Z}{2}\right)^2}{\left\{\left[1 + \left(\frac{Z}{0.05}\right)^2\right] \times \left[1 + \left(\frac{Z}{0.315}\right)^2\right] \times \left[1 + \left(\frac{Z}{1.35}\right)^2\right]\right\}^{\frac{1}{2}}}$$

Time duration:

$$\frac{t_S}{W^{\frac{1}{3}}} = \frac{980 \times \left[1 + \left(\frac{Z}{0.54}\right)^{10}\right]}{\left\{\left[1 + \left(\frac{Z}{0.02}\right)^3\right] \times \left[1 + \left(\frac{Z}{0.75}\right)^6\right] \times \left[1 + \left(\frac{Z}{6.9}\right)^2\right]\right\}^{\frac{1}{2}}}$$

Impulse per unit area $= \frac{1}{2} \times P_s \times t_s$.

Figures 3 and 4 show the effect of urban terrain on the peak blast pressure and impulse.

3 Building Damage/Injury Criteria

The level of damage, i.e., the extent and severity due to an explosion, is uncertain and depends on several factors such as building geometry, construction type, etc., which may modify the blast effects. Past studies show that the unique specifics of a

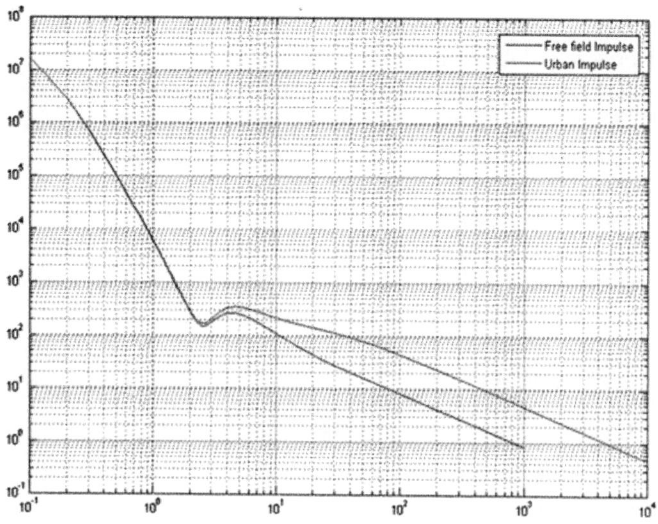

Fig. 4 Comparison of impulse versus standoff [6, 7]

building's failure sequence significantly affect the damage level. Even though there are uncertainties in predicting explosive damage level, it is possible to indicate the overall level of wear and injuries based on the TNT yield, standoff distance, and assumptions about the structure's construction [7].

Damage to the structure can be divided into two types based on the air blast shock wave, i.e., direct air blast effects and progressive collapse. With the association of peak values and impulses of both hydrostatic and dynamic pressure, a specific level of damage or injury can be defined. The degree of harm or injury will be related to the pressures' peak values, and the peak value duration or impulses defined as the time integrals of the pressures during the peak value positive phases. A longer positive phase duration for a massive explosion will have higher peak pressure causing specific damage or injury to the buildings and people [8].

4 Blast Mitigation Tool

In the GUI of the blast mitigation tool, the first and foremost step is loading a geocoded Google map/ user-defined shapefile. For uploading the map, a shapefile has to create a shapefile database, and a path is defined for loading within the defined boundaries of the axes. To enable loading a shapefile, the type or style of objects used are static text and push button. The static text area and push button components are added to the UI, and the components are aligned. After aligning the components, the push button is labeled in the property inspector by modifying the static text in the property inspector. After saving the layout to load shapefile code, the push button's behavior

save the UI layout [9]. The input to latitude and longitude is through; the components used are static text and the edit text from the menu control panel. The components are placed in the location panel. The static text and edit text in the property inspectors are labeled and modified before saving the UI layout. The behavior of the edit text is coded by using the callback function of the latitude and longitude.

The map (shapefile) gets the (X Y) coordinates from the cursor and outputs the X-coordinate as latitude and Y-coordinate as longitude. The latitude and longitude are the source centers, i.e., the charge of explosives in kg TNT (Trinitrotoluene). The charge of explosives in kg TNT is given as an input to calculate the peak overpressure, and the time duration of the blast wave and contours are developed (Fig. 5).

The peak overpressure (vs.) distance graph as an input gives the required pressure in kPa units (kilopascal) such as 6.89 kPa (1 psi), 13.79 kPa (2 psi), 20.68 kPa (3 psi), and so on. The data is sorted to get the radius. From the radius, contour with latitude and longitude as the center is developed. The blast peak overpressure contours are converted to a shapefile and placed as a layer over the shapefile of the map. The pressures within the contours correspond to various levels of expected damage to buildings and occupants. Appropriate mitigation measures can be taken according to the damage level predicted within the contour.

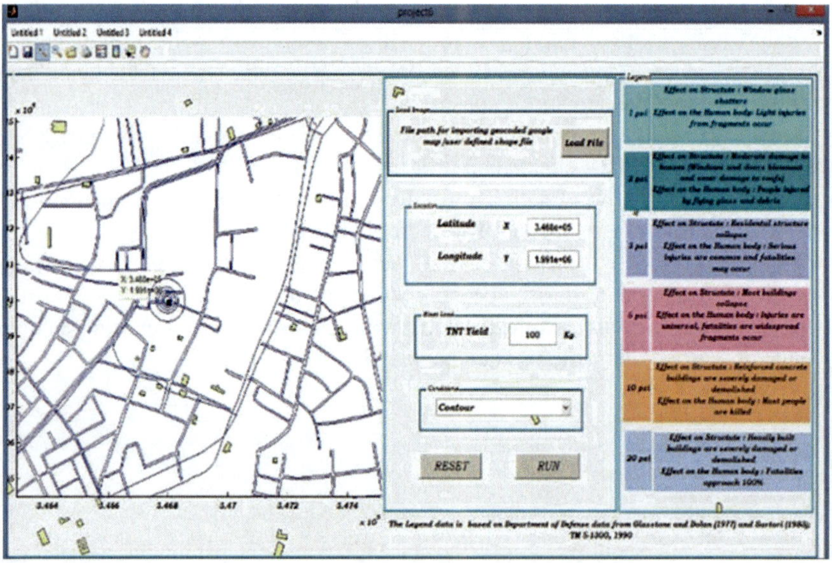

Fig. 5 MATLAB GUI (Decision Support Tool)

5 Results and Discussion

- This tool helps to mitigate the blast effect over people and buildings by finding the range of the blast effect contours from the center of the charge and enables urban planners and security agencies to plan for minimum effect due to the blast.
- Contours of 6.89, 13.79, 20.68, 34.47, 68.95, and 137.9 kPa peak overpressure corresponding to various critical levels of blast damage within the radius of these peak overpressures are plotted in a user-defined GUI environment.
  - Within the 6.89 kPa peak overpressure contour, there will not much effect on structures and humans. The structure's effect is just window glass shatters, and light injuries from fragments will occur to people.
  - If the structure is within the 13.79 kPa peak overpressure, the blast causes the effect of moderate damage to houses like windows and doors blown out and severe damage to roofs. For people in this region will have injuries by flying glass and debris.
  - The 20.68 kPa peak overpressure causes the collapse of residential structures. Most people will have serious injuries, and fatalities may occur.
  - For 34.47 kPa peak overpressure, most of the buildings or structures will collapse, and the effect on the people will have universal injuries, and the fatalities are widespread.
  - For the 68.95 kPa peak overpressure, most of the reinforced concrete buildings are severely damaged or demolished, and most of the people are killed because of enormous heat and fire.
  - For the 137.90 kPa peak overpressure, almost all structures in the contour, such as heavily built concrete buildings, are severely damaged or demolished, and the fatalities approach 100%.

6 Scope and Limitations of Work

The presented work focuses on the estimation of blast damage in an urban environment. In the study, some simplifying assumptions are considered to reduce the complexity of implementing the code. The following are the limitations of the study:

- Only explosions caused by high explosives (chemical reactions) are considered within the study. High explosives are solid in form and are commonly termed condensed explosives. TNT (trinitrotoluene) is the most widely known example.
- The shock wave and thus peak overpressures are considered to be modified by interaction with buildings in this article. Within a specified contour region, the peak overpressure and corresponding building damage levels and casualties are constant.
- In this tool, the effect of the negative phase of a blast wave is neglected. The impact of this on actual response and damage is negligible.

7 Conclusion

A self-contained and simple MATLAB® -GUI-based GIS tool has been developed to predict blast damage to buildings and human beings. The conclusions from the study are as follows:

- This tool fills the gap of a self-contained blast mitigation tool that is not publicly available.
- It will enable planners, administrators, and security agencies to predict the amount of damage occurring to the buildings and people based on distance from the center of charge and plan mitigation measures.
- It will help locate the casualties over a wide range in the blast region, and this data will help emergency agencies and first responders prioritize their routes, which can have a tremendous effect on response times and save many lives.

8 Future Study

Within the limited scope of the present work, this work's broad conclusion has been reported. However, further development of the software tool can be undertaken.

- This study can be further to be extended to ground shock also.
- Blast shadow regions and complex reflections and refractions in dense urban areas need to be included to enable more accurate blast pressures.
- The inclusion of the P-I curve-based structural response to blast loading will enable the determination of building-specific damage.

References

1. Borooah VK (2009) Terrorist incidents in India, 1998–2004: a quantitative analysis of fatality rates. Terror Polit Violence 21(3):476–498. https://doi.org/10.1080/09546550902970165
2. List of terrorist incidents in India - Wikipedia. Accessed: Mar. 07, 2021. [Online]. Available: https://en.wikipedia.org/wiki/List_of_terrorist_incidents_in_India
3. Smith PD, Rose TA (2006) Blastwave propagation in city streets—an overview. Prog Struct Eng Mater 8(1):16–28. https://doi.org/10.1002/pse.209
4. B. of Indian Standards, IS 4991 (1968): Criteria for blast resistant design of structures for explosions above ground
5. FEMA 427 Primer for Design of Commercial Buildings to Mitigate Terrorist Attacks |WBDG-Whole Building Design Guide. https://www.wbdg.org/ffc/dhs/criteria/fema-427. Accessed 07 March 2021
6. Kinney GF, Graham KJ, Kinney GF, Graham KJ (1985) Explosions. In: Explosive shocks in air. Springer Berlin Heidelberg, pp 1–17
7. Remennikov AM, Rose TA (2005) Modelling blast loads on buildings in complex city geometries. Comput Struct 83(27):2197–2205. https://doi.org/10.1016/j.compstruc.2005.04.003

8. Unified Facilities Criteria (UFC) Minimum Antiterrorism Standards For Buildings Appendix 1 E 2012. Accessed: Mar. 07, 2021. [Online]. Available: http://dod.wbdg.org/
9. MATLAB® Creating Graphical User Interfaces R2015b. 2000. Accessed: 07 March 2021. [Online]. Available: www.mathworks.com

Pavement Design Considering Changing Climate Temperature

Swapan Kumar Bagui, Atasi Das, Renu Sharma, and Yash Pandey

Abstract Global air temperature is progressively increasing. Presently, conventional flexible pavement is generally designed for a design period of 20 years, and perpetual pavement is designed for a design period of 30–50 years. Therefore, pavement temperature should be designed considering this increasing pavement temperature. Presently, average annual pavement temperature is considered as 35 °C. Based on various research reports, it is presumed that air temperature will rise by 1.5 °C (approximately) in the next 20 years. Thus, the average annual pavement temperature in the coming years should be minimum 37 °C and may go up to 40 °C for conventional pavement and perpetual pavement, respectively. Softening point of bitumen will be increased, and the conventional viscosity grades of bitumen like VG 30 and VG 40 will not be suitable for usage in the bituminous layers of the pavement. Performance grade (PG) or polymer modified bitumen (PMB) with higher softening point may be used to cater for the thermal changes. Air temperature and pavement temperature models have been considered for pavement design. E values of mix at different average annual pavement temperatures (AAPT) are considered, and a correlation has been developed between pavement temperature and E value of mix for VG 40 bitumen and presented graphically. A linear correlation equation has been derived as $E = 10{,}000 - 200 \times \text{AAPT}$. The E values at different temperature will be taken from this equation, and same will be used in pavement design. Two case studies are adopted, i.e., conventional pavement design and perpetual pavement design and presented in this paper. Pavement thicknesses are compared; cost variation and life cycle cost analyses are conducted and presented in this paper.

Keywords Pavement design · Temperature · Resilient modulus

S. K. Bagui · R. Sharma
Intercontinental Consultants and Technocrats Pvt. Ltd, Delhi 110016, India
e-mail: renu.sharma@ictonline.com

A. Das (✉) · Y. Pandey
G.R. Infraprojects Limited, Gurugram 122015, India

C. Ghosh and S. Kolathayar (eds.), *A System Engineering Approach to Disaster Resilience*, Lecture Notes in Civil Engineering 205, https://doi.org/10.1007/978-981-16-7397-9_13

1 Introduction

Bituminous pavements are environmental sensitive infrastructure. When there is adverse change in environment conditions, pavement deterioration may occur faster; thus, incurring additional costs to the road authorities. If no action is undertaken, the burden will fall on the users in light of loss in safety, time, and fuel consumption. On a national level, this means the total amounting cost incurred because of change in the climate perhaps become significant, and extra financial resources will be required for adaptation of climate and also to mitigate future requirements.

There has been incessant increment of 0.85 °C in surface temperature between 1880 and 2012 round the globe, and the variation in the rate has become swifter in the present decades. Meanwhile, rising in the sea level and drastic changes in weather events, such as hurricanes, floods, and heat waves, have become more common in several areas. In near future, there likely be the change in climatic conditions [1]. So, it is vital requirement to take in account the climatic resilience in pavement design and management; moreover, it is necessary to find (1) How do the interaction between climate and pavements takes place (2) Ongoing researches for evaluating effects of climate behavior on bituminous pavements? (3) Impact of climatic behavior change on bituminous pavement systems (including repair/rehabilitation cycle, performance and financials) in a pavement life cycle perspective? (4) Present gaps in research areas for climate adaptation and mitigation for bituminous pavements.

Generally, environmental conditions can directly be affected by change in climatic conditions and result in variation in pavement performance. The climate stressors could disturb the balance of moisture and energy of pavement and as a result the pavement performance would also be affected directly. From the literature, the mostly used climate stressors are precipitation, groundwater, temperature, wind speed & cloud cover [2]. Typically, pavement performance is most influenced by temperature and moisture, and the long-term impacts from the climate stressors can be significant [3, 4].

2 Future Increase of Pavement Temperature

Presently, conventional flexible pavement is generally designed for the next 20 years, and perpetual pavement is designed for the design period of 30–50 years. Therefore, pavement temperature should be designed considering this increasing pavement temperature. Presently, average annual pavement temperature is considered 35 °C. Based on various research reports, it is presumed that air temperature will rise by 1.5 °C (approximately) in the next 20 years. Thus, the average annual pavement temperature in the coming years should be minimum 37 °C and may go up to 40 °C for conventional pavement and perpetual pavement, respectively. Softening point of bitumen will be increased, and the conventional viscosity grades of bitumen like VG 30 and VG 40 will not be suitable for usage in the bituminous layers of the pavement.

Performance grade (PG) or polymer modified bitumen (PMB) with higher softening point may be used to cater for the thermal changes. Air temperature and pavement temperature models have been considered for pavement design. E values of mix at different average annual pavement temperatures (AAPT) are considered.

2.1 IRC: 37-2018 Provision

The prevalent codal provision for flexible pavement design in India is the IRC: 37-2018 [5], and according to it, VG 40 bitumen is adopted for pavement design. E values of mix using VG 40 bitumen at different temperatures are presented in Table 9.2 of IRC: 37-2018, and relevant values are presented in Table 1.

These results are plotted graphically and presented in Fig. 1. A good co-relation is found, and regression equation is developed and presented in Fig. 1 i.e.,

$$E = -200 \times \text{AAPT} +, 10000 \tag{1}$$

This equation will be useful to determine E values of mix at different pavement temperatures.

Presently, we determine pavement thickness considering AAPT as 35 °C for the next 20 to 30/50 years. It is apparent that this temperature will be increased and exceed 35 °C. It is also apparent that with the consideration of AAPT as 35 °C, we are using a conservative value of *E* in pavement design. It is presumed that

Table 1 Relation among pavement temperature and *E* value of mix

Pavement temperature (°C)	20	25	30	35	40
E value of BC/DBM (MPa)	6000	5000	4000	3000	2000

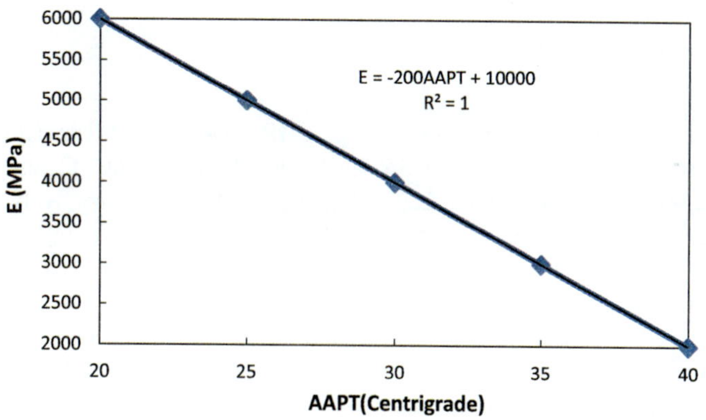

Fig. 1 Correlation between average annual pavement temperature and *E* value of mix

design pavement temperature will be 37 °C, 39 °C, and 40 °C in 2040, 2060, and 2070. Hence, values of E in mix should be considered as 2600 MPa, 2200 MPa, and 2000 MPa, respectively.

Rainfall, solar radiation, latitude, wind speed, and air temperatures are some of the deciding parameters for pavement temperature [6]. Furthermore, among said factors, latitude and air temperature are considered as the important one. In order to frame, regression co-relation, taking into account effect of latitude and air temperature for pavement temperature, linear regression equation with two variables is assumed [7].

The coefficients of the equation are determined by the in-built linear regression function in MATLAB and given as follows [7]:

$$P_t = 0.7147 + 1.3023A_t + 0.1103L \tag{2}$$

where P_t = pavement temperature (°C), A_t = air temperature (°C), and L = Latitude of the selected location.

This equation may be revised as:

$$P_t = 0.7147 + 1.3023A_t + 0.1103L + x \tag{3}$$

where x varies from 1 to 5 depending on future design years which may be 10, 20, 30, 40, and 50 years.

2.2 Case Studies

Two case studies are considered. One conventional pavement for the design period of 20 years and perpetual pavement for design period of 50 years are considered for analysis.

2.3 Conventional Pavement

Assume design life of 100 MSA and design CBR 10%. Average annual pavement temperature (AAPT) is assumed as 35 °C, 37 °C, 39 °C, and 40 °C, and E values of mix are 3000 MPa, 2600 MPa, 2200 MPa, and 2000 MPa, respectively. IIT Pave software is used to determine pavement thickness and presented in Table 2.

Typical rates are taken for the determination of initial cost of pavement and presented in Table 3.

A typical cross section has been considered for the length of 10 km of road. Unit rates of different construction items are taken based on basic rates of 2018, and initial costs for different pavement temperatures are presented in Table 4 for the year 2020.

Table 2 Pavement compositions

AAPT (°C)	E value of mix (MPa)	Pavement compositions (mm)			
		BC	DBM	WMM	GSB
35	3000	50	110	250	200
37	2600	50	120	250	200
39	2200	50	130	250	200
40	2000	50	135	250	200

Table 3 Typical rates of construction items

Description	Unit	Rates (INR)
BC	Cum	13,000
DBM	Cum	12,000
Tack coat	Cum	15
Prime coat	Cum	30
WMM	Cum	4000
GSB	Cum	3300

Table 4 Initial construction costs

AAPT (°C)	*E* value of mix (MPa)	Total pavement construction cost (Rs Million)[a]
35	3000	81.8
37	2600	84.1
39	2200	86.4
40	2000	87.6

[a]Cost excludes cost of structures, road furniture cost, and miscellaneous item

3 Perpetual Pavement

A case study is considered for perpetual pavement for design CBR of 10%. Average annual pavement temperature (AAPT) is assumed 35 °C, 37 °C, 39 °C, and 40 °C, and E values of mix will be 3000 MPa, 2600 MPa, 2200 MPa, and 2000 MPa, respectively. IIT Pave software is used to determine pavement thickness and presented in Table 5. Pavement compositions have been finalized based on fatigue strain and subgrade strain limits of 80 micron and 200 microns, respectively.

A typical cross section has been considered for the length of 10 km road. Unit rates of different construction items are taken, and initial costs for different pavement temperatures are presented in Table 3. Initial pavement cost has been determined and use for life cycle cost analysis.

Table 5 Pavement compositions

AAPT (°C)	*E* value of mix (MPa)	Pavement compositions(mm)			
		BC	DBM	WMM	GSB
35	3000	50	260	150	200
37	2600	50	280	150	200
39	2200	50	305	150	200
40	2000	50	320	150	200

4 Analysis for Life Cycle Cost (LCCA)

In order to check the feasibility of the design alternatives, LCCA is performed, in particular, to find the most cost-effective alternative to build and maintain. The major costs that are taken in account for LCCA are initial construction cost, rehabilitation cost, maintenance cost, salvage value, user delay (during upcoming maintenance or resurfacing), and vehicle operational cost. The starting four are agency costs that have the most influence on approach selection. While, when considered, the last two user costs may have major effect on selection of approach that is most cost-effective overall [8]. LCCA program uses actual cost to determine the most economic design.

Design life of long-life pavement is considered as 50 years and 20 years for conventional pavement. Routine maintenance, periodic surfacing of pavement is considered at every seventh year for the simplification of analysis. Climatic variation in India varies widely, and overloading vehicles are plying on roads which are not fully controlled. No periodic maintenance data is available in India. Hence, there is a chance of damage of top 50 mm layer due to rut and top-down cracking, and a periodic maintenance is required at every seventh year. Damaging effect during application of load through these seven years is negligible. Based on this assumption, a case study has been considered for new four lanes divided carriageway with pavement compositions as mentioned in Tables 2 and 5 for conventional pavement and perpetual pavement.

Life cycle cost analysis has been carried out for conventional pavement for design periods of 20 years and 50 years for perpetual pavement. Initial cost and life cycle cost are presented in Figs. 2 and 3 for conventional pavement and perpetual pavement.

Initial pavement cost and life cycle cost are determined taking E value of mix from 3000 to 2000 MPa and presented graphically as shown in Fig. 3.

5 Discussion

Due to rapid climate change, pavement temperature is increasing, and presently pavement design temperature is considered 35 °C in major parts of India, but it should be increased considering global warming. Variation of average annual pavement temperature (AAPT) may be increased in the range of 37–40 °C next 50 years. Therefore,

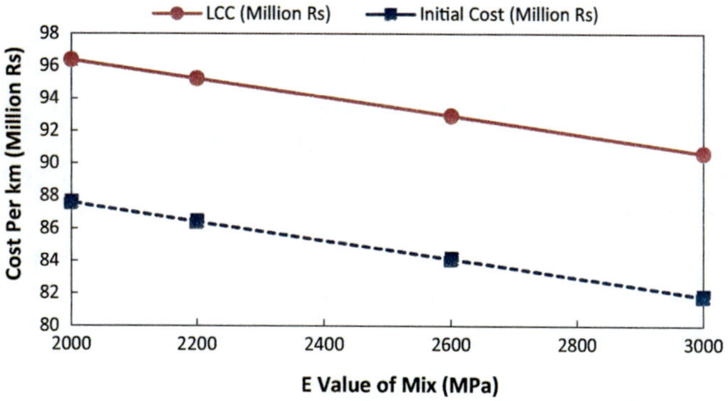

Fig. 2 Initial pavement construction cost and life cycle cost for design traffic 100 MSA

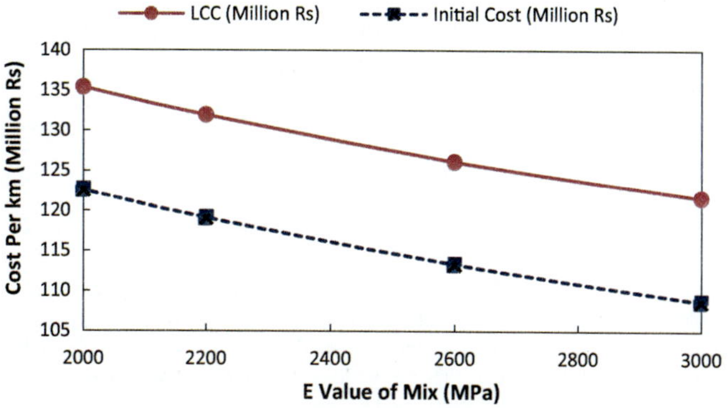

Fig. 3 Initial pavement construction cost and life cycle cost for perpetual pavement. *Note* User delay and vehicle operating cost are excluded in the analysis

this should be incorporated in the pavement design. Therefore, pavement design is adopted varying AAPT from 35 to 40 °C, and two case studies are considered. One of the important inputs for pavement design is *E* value of mix. It is found from Fig. 1 that *E* value of mix decreases linearly with negative slope with increasing temperature, and this demands more asphalt thickness and same is given in Tables 2 and 5 for conventional pavement and perpetual pavement. Initial pavement cost has been determined, and it is found that initial pavement cost increases with increasing pavement temperature for conventional and perpetual pavement. Life cycle cost (LCC) and initial construction cost of pavement are calculated and presented in Figs. 2 and 3 for conventional pavement and perpetual pavement. From these two figures, it is observed that LCC increases with decreasing E Value of mix, i.e., increasing pavement temperature. Therefore, climate change increases initial pavement construction cost and LCC of pavement. Climate aspect may be considered for pavement design.

6 Conclusions

Based on this present study, it is found that climate change aspect should be included in the pavement design. IRC: 37–2018 may be revised/ relooked considering this aspect. Special circular may be issued from Ministry of Transport, Government of India. Based on present study, following conclusions may be drawn:

- Presently pavement design temperature is considered as 35 °C. This may be increased in the range of 35–40 °C in major parts of India.
- Increasing pavement temperature in pavement design increases pavement thickness;
- Initial pavement cost will be increased due to global warming.
- Life cycle cost (LCC) will also be increased.
- Initial pavement cost and LCC vary linearly with negative slope with increasing E value of mix.
- Pavement temperature as mentioned in Eq. 2 may be used for the determination of design pavement temperature considering average value of 12 months.

References

1. IPCC (2014) Climate Change 2014: Synthesis Report. Contribution of Working Groups I, II and III to the Fifth Assessment Report of the Intergovernmental Panel on Climate Change [Core Writing Team, R.K. Pachauri and L.A. Meyer (eds.)], IPCC, Geneva, Switzerland, 151 pp
2. Mechanistic-Empirical Pavement Design Guide (MEPDG) (2009) Version 1.1, NCHRP, American Association of State Highway and Transportation Officials (AASHTO), USA
3. Thom NH, Brown SF (1987) Effect of moisture on the structural performance of a crushed-limestone road base. Transp Res Rec 1121:50–56
4. Dawson A (2014) Anticipating and responding to pavement performance as climate changes. In: Gopalakrishnan K, Steyn W, Harvey J (eds) Climate change, energy, sustainability and pavements. Green Energy Technol 127–157
5. Guidelines for the Design of Flexible Pavements (2018) 4th Revision, IRC 37, Indian Roads Congress New Delhi
6. Nivitha MR, Krishnan JM (2014) Development of Pavement Temperature Contours for India. J Inst Eng (India): Series A 95:83–90
7. Al-Abdul Wahhab HI, Al-Dubabe IA, Asi IM, Ali MF (1998) Performance based characterization of arab asphalt. Build Environ 33(6):375–383
8. Walls J, Smith MR (1998) Life cycle cost analysis in pavement design, FHWA-SA-98–079, Federal Highway Administration, Washington, USA

Application of GIS and AHP-Based Integrated Methodology for Mapping and Characterizing Socioeconomic Vulnerability to Natural Hazards: A Case Study of Southwestern Coastal Bangladesh

Nur Mohammad Ha-Mim and Md. Zakir Hossain

Abstract Southwestern Coastal Bangladesh is well-known for its vulnerability to natural hazards and climate-induced disasters. However, a little initiative is taken by the national and international organizations to analyze the vulnerability condition of this coastal region with consistently undervaluing the importance of socioeconomic factors. Consequently, no detailed vulnerability map is provided, and the ability to plan for effective disaster management is hindered. Additionally, over the past decade, socioeconomic vulnerability assessment has been recognized as an effective and leading tool to analyze the nature and extent of human vulnerability to climate-induced stress and natural hazards. Thus, this study analyzes and characterizes the vulnerability of the southwestern coastal communities considering the major socioeconomic factors that influence spatial vulnerability's differentiated nature. We have selected 20 indicators to construct the socioeconomic vulnerability index under three major components: physical and infrastructural, socio-demographic, and economic components. We have considered census data for all the twenty indicators published by the Bangladesh Bureau of Statistics. Spatial data analysis has been completed by following three major steps: Firstly, the major component-specific index value is generated using "indexing method" and "analytical hierarchy process"; secondly, all the major components value is converted into maps at the local level using geospatial techniques; and thirdly, the overall vulnerability map is produced through integrating all the major components. The results demonstrate the extent of socioeconomic vulnerability as very high (17.8%), high (46.6%), moderate (21.7%), low (11.5%), and very low (2.4%). In general, eastern, central, and southern regions exhibited a higher vulnerability than the northwest part of the study area. This study is crucial for policymakers to make decisions regarding development strategies and to plan for disaster risk reduction by exploring the level and extent of vulnerability at the local level.

Keywords Socioeconomic vulnerability · Natural hazard · Indexing · Geographic information system (GIS) · Analytical hierarchy process (AHP) · Bangladesh

---

N. M. Ha-Mim (✉) · Md. Z. Hossain
Urban and Rural Planning Discipline, Khulna University, Khulna 9208, Bangladesh

C. Ghosh and S. Kolathayar (eds.), *A System Engineering Approach to Disaster Resilience*, Lecture Notes in Civil Engineering 205, https://doi.org/10.1007/978-981-16-7397-9_14

1 Introduction

Bangladesh is marked as one of the most natural disaster-prone countries in the world [1, 2], which is ascribed to the geographical setting of the country that makes it most vulnerable to natural hazards (i.e., cyclone, tidal surge, drought, flood, earthquake, salinity intrusion, tornado, river erosion). The flat topography, heavy monsoon rainfall, discharge of sediments, drainage congestion, active fault line, low river gradients, and shallow funnel-shaped Bay of Bengal are the major factors behind the frequent landfall of different natural hazards in Bangladesh [1]. These natural occurrences frequently disrupt local inhabitants' existence by injuring/damaging the population, economy, property, infrastructure, lifelines, and agricultural land [3, 4]. Thus, it is important to develop and deploy an advanced integrated methodology to assess and map the associated socioeconomic vulnerability to natural hazards to inform better disaster management framework, policy planning, and decision-making. Therefore, this study concentrates on applying GIS and AHP-based integrated methodology for analyzing spatial extents and levels of associated socioeconomic vulnerability to natural hazards in the southwestern region of Bangladesh.

Vulnerability is conceptualized in various ways by different research communities as most of the vulnerability research is highly interdisciplinary in nature, which provides numerous approaches to theorize and analyze different components of vulnerability [5, 6]. In 1992, Dow [7] defined vulnerability as the degree to which a system, sub-system, individual, group, or community is likely to be affected by exposure to natural hazards based on the condition of differential physical and social attributes. Similarly, Adger [8] defined vulnerability as the negative consequence of external stressors or hazards on the life and livelihood of individuals, groups, or communities. Again, social vulnerability refers to an individual or group's inability to respond to and recover from the impacts of any external shock placed on their livelihood and well-being [5]. The prime difference between the traditional view of vulnerability and social vulnerability is the separation of biophysical parameters from the human dimension of vulnerability. The assessment of social vulnerability covers various attributes, such as density, education, well-being, race, age, social class, employment, ethnicity, elderly population, quality of the built environment, which provide much-needed insights into the sensitivity and susceptibility of a system for hazard time planning and response.

Over the past decade, mapping and characterizing vulnerability to natural hazards have emerged as an important technique to support risk management, preparedness plan, emergency response plan, and evaluation plan across the Global South [9, 10]. However, most of the studies on coastal communities' vulnerability are concentrated on physical factors, ignoring the local level social, economic, and cultural attributes, which provide a more realistic assessment of potential hazard impact. Thus, a vulnerability assessment exclusively concentrated on socioeconomic components will be imperative for understanding disaster impact and formulating appropriate management strategies. On this basis, this study intends to address the last critique of vulnerability assessment and aims for a cerebral discussion of socioeconomic vulnerability using a pragmatic approach.

Many tools and techniques are available in global literature to assess vulnerability to natural hazards at different spatial scales. Sahana et al. [11] followed an indexed-based geospatial approach to assess the socioeconomic vulnerability of 38 villages to climate-induced disasters in the Sundarbans Biosphere Reserve, India. Alam and Haque [12] integrated technique for order preference by similarity to ideal solution method (TOPSIS) and analytical hierarchy process (AHP) with spatial analysis tools for the assessment of vulnerability to the earthquake in the residential area of Mymensingh City, Bangladesh. Choudhary et al. [13] used a spatial modeling approach to understand natural and environmental vulnerability based on remote sensing and geophysical data in Astrakhan, Russia. In this study, we applied a multi-criteria analysis technique to assess socioeconomic vulnerability to natural hazards that integrate the indexing method and analytical hierarchy process (AHP) using geospatial techniques to quantify, characterize, and map the degree of vulnerability for the southwestern coastal region of Bangladesh.

The relationship between hazard and vulnerability has been considered in many studies, yet mapping and characterization of vulnerability considering the coastal communities' socioeconomic profile have not been done in Bangladesh. Moreover, there are no individual vulnerability scales to identify the probable impact of a particular hazard. To make the information readily available for the stakeholders, it is necessary to prepare a vulnerability map to identify the vulnerable zones easily. This study will help planners, policymakers, and disaster managers to make decisions regarding risk-sensitive land use planning, layout planning, land use management, building improvements, formulation of development strategies, adaptation planning, sustainable livelihood planning, etc., for different locations considering the different aspects of respective socioeconomic vulnerability to natural hazards.

2 Materials and Methods

This study aims to analyze, characterize, and map the socioeconomic vulnerability of coastal communities to natural hazards via integration of the analytical hierarchy process (AHP) and index method using geospatial techniques. To achieve this goal, the following steps are considered.

2.1 Study Area

Bagerhat, Khulna, and Satkhira districts in Bangladesh are selected as the case study site (cf. Figure 1) for this study because of their dynamic nature of physical and

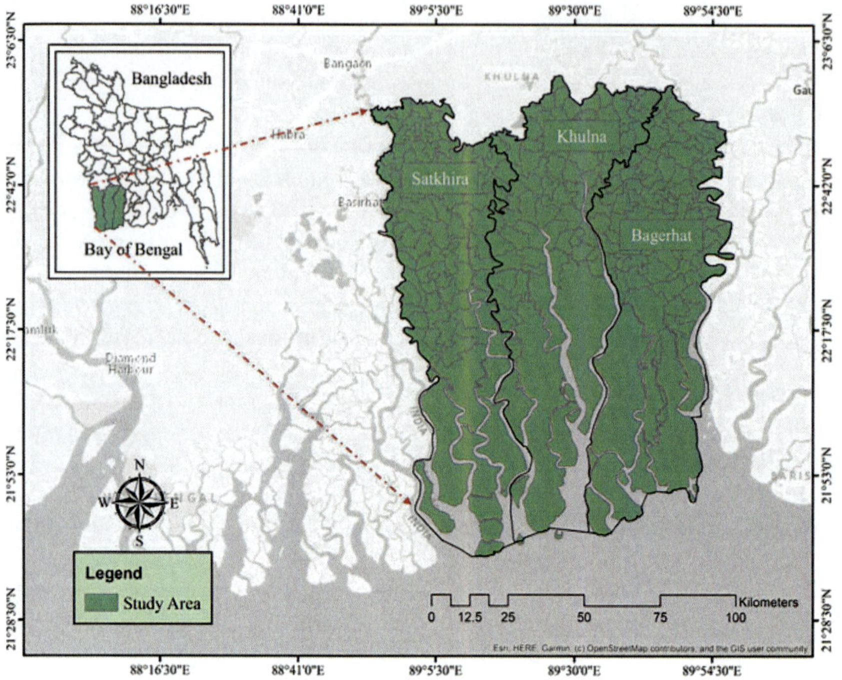

Fig. 1 Map of the study area. *Source* Generated by authors using the data provided by the Local Government Engineering Department (LGED)

geological factors. These three districts approximately occupy 12,211 km^2. of land area with an average population density of 474 per km^2 [14]. The area lies between 21°40′ and 22°58′ north latitudes and between 88°53′ and 89°59′ east longitudes. The Bay of Bengal is situated in the southern part of the study area, including the world's largest mangrove forest with a dynamic ecosystem, important biodiversity, and aquatic resource. The main source of livelihoods of the rural inhabitants living in these areas is farming, fisheries activity, animal husbandry, and the Sundarbans' resources. These three districts are susceptible to many natural hazards, ranging from frequent, regularly occurring hazards (e.g., tidal surge, flood) to less frequent but higher magnitude hazards such as cyclone and tornado. Floods, for example, occur regularly during heavy precipitation events and the annual monsoon season, whereas large-scale cyclones or tornados occur periodically.

2.2 Data Collection and Analysis

This study is performed based on the secondary data source. The geo-referenced vector map of the smallest administrative unit (also known as Union) is collected

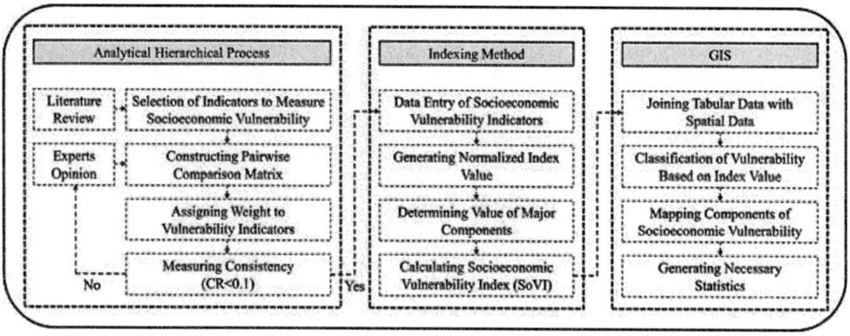

Fig. 2 Methodological framework of the study

from the Local Government Engineering Department (LGED) of Bangladesh [15], and the socioeconomic data for each of the administrative units (Unions) is extracted from the Population and Housing Census of Bangladesh, 2011 [14].

The methodological framework that is followed for the fulfillment of this study is presented in Fig. 2. Based on the literature review, we included three major components (that comprise a total of 20 indicators) to measure socioeconomic vulnerability index (SeVI) (cf. Appendix 1). Appendix 1 includes an explanation of how each indicator is quantified and its functional relationship with vulnerability. Additionally, for each of the major components and indicators, weight is assigned based on the analytical hierarchy process (cf. Appendix 2).

2.3 *Analytical Hierarchy Process (AHP)*

Analytical hierarchy process (AHP) is a powerful mathematical method developed by Saaty [16] for estimating the weight of variables based on experts' opinions. This study used five experts' responses with thorough experience of vulnerability analysis and mapping to generate the weights. The AHP-derived weights are further used for the calculation of socioeconomic vulnerability indices based on multiple criteria. The AHP method follows three steps to generate weights for a set of variables or criteria. In Step 1, a comparison matrix is generated on a scale of 1–9 based on the experts' response in which 1 refers to equally important factors and 9 indicates the extreme importance of a factor over another. The scale of importance, developed by Saaty [16], required to fill up the AHP questionnaire is shown in Table 1.

In Step 2, a normalized matrix is generated by totaling the value of each column of the comparison matrix and then dividing each entry of a column by the sum of that column. After normalization of each column following the same procedure, the sum of each column of the matrix must be 1.

In Step 3, the consistency ratio (CR) is measured using Eqs. 1 and 2 to evaluate the consistency of experts' judgments. A CR value above 0.10 indicates that the

Table 1 Magnitude of importance for pairwise comparison

Intensity of importance	Definition
1	Equal importance
2	Weak or sight
3	Moderate importance
4	Moderate plus
5	Strong importance
6	Strong plus
7	Very strong or demonstrated importance
8	Very, very strong
9	Extreme importance

Table 2 RI values for the corresponding number of variables [16]

N	1	2	3	4	5	6	7	8	9	10	11	12
RI	0	0	0.58	0.9	1.12	1.24	1.32	1.41	1.45	1.49	1.52	1.54

comparison matrix has inconsistency that is unacceptable. Thus, it needs to be iterated or revised until it shows acceptable consistency (CR < 0.1).

$$\text{Consistency Index, CI} = \frac{\lambda_{\text{max}} - n}{n - 1} \tag{1}$$

$$\text{Consistency Ratio, CR} = \frac{\text{CI}}{\text{RI}} \tag{2}$$

Here, λ_{max} = maximum eigenvalue of the matrix, n = dimension of the matrix, and RI = random index. The variation of the RI value depends on the number of variables, which is shown in Table 2.

The weights assigned for each of the major components and sub-components of socioeconomic vulnerability following the AHP method are listed in Appendix 2. The consistency ratio of all the AHP model satisfied the criteria of CR value less than 0.1, which indicates the consistency of all the matrix.

2.4 Construction of Composite Socioeconomic Vulnerability Index (SeVI)

The indexing approach is based on a total of 20 indicators or sub-components under three dimensions or major components for developing "socioeconomic vulnerability index (SeVI)" (cf. Appendix 1). The methodology used for indexing in this research follows the calculation procedure of the "livelihood vulnerability index (LVI)" [17], "climate vulnerability index (CVI)" [18], and "household livelihood vulnerability index (HLVI)" [19, 20]. The indexing method comprises three steps to generate SeVI for each Union (local-level administrative unit). In Step 1, all the sub-components are normalized to make them comparable (as sub-components are in different unit or scale) using Eqs. 3 and 4. Equation 3 is used to normalize the sub-components with a positive functional relationship, and Eq. 4 is used to normalize the sub-components with a negative functional relationship.

$$\text{Index}_{N_s} = \frac{X_s - X_{\text{min}}}{X_{\text{max}} - X_{\text{min}}} \quad (3)$$

$$\text{Index}_{N_S} = \frac{X_{\text{max}} - X_s}{X_{\text{max}} - X_{\text{min}}} \quad (4)$$

Here, Index_{N_S} is the normalized index value of a sub-component for Union *S*, and X_s is the actual value of the sub-component for Union *S*. X_{max} and X_{min} refer to the maximum and minimum values of the sub-component among all the Union. After normalization, in Step 2, the value of major components for each of the Union is calculated using Eq. 5.

$$M_s = \sum_{i=1}^{n} \text{Index}_{N_S^i} \times W_{SC^i} \quad (5)$$

Here, M_s refers to the value of one of the major components (socio-demographic component (SDC), economic component (EC), physical and infrastructural component (PIC)) for Union *S*, $\text{Index}_{N_S^i}$ is the normalized index value of the *i*-th sub-component for Union *S*, W_{SC^i} is the weight of the *i*-th sub-component that is derived from the AHP, and *n* is the total number of sub-components under the corresponding major component. Once the value of major components for all the Unions are calculated following the same procedure, Eq. 6 is used to obtain the socioeconomic vulnerability index (SeVI) value for each of the Unions.

$$\text{SeVI}_s = (\text{SDC}_s \times W_{\text{SDC}}) + (\text{EC}_s \times W_{\text{EC}}) + (\text{PIC}_s \times W_{\text{PIC}}) \quad (6)$$

Here, SeVI_s = value of socioeconomic vulnerability index for Union *S*, SDC_s = value of socio-demographic component for Union *S*, EC_s = value of economic component for Union *S*, and PIC_s = value of physical and infrastructural component for Union *S*. W_{SDC}, W_{EC}, and W_{PIC} are the AHP-derived weights of socio-demographic component (SDC), economic component (EC), and physical and infrastructural component, respectively.

3 Results and Discussions

To illustrate the findings, this section is summarized into two main parts as (i) spatial pattern and spatial variation of vulnerability under different major components are mapped and analyzed; and (ii) socioeconomic vulnerability is presented through investigating and mapping the index score of the Unions.

3.1 Individual Assessment of Vulnerability Components

This study has developed the socio-demographic, economic, and physical and infrastructural indices by integrating the corresponding indicators/sub-components' value and weight. Afterward, we have produced a comprehensive vulnerability map for each of the components and quantified the degree of vulnerability to natural hazards by categorizing the index score into five levels (i.e., very low, low, moderate, high, and very high). The index score ranges between 0 and 1, where a higher value represents high vulnerability and vice versa. Following Mudasser et al. [20], the categorization is done by dividing the range between the highest and lowest index score of a component into five equal distance intervals.

The study area comprises Satkhira, Khulna, and Bagerhat districts with 3858.36 km^2, 4394.45 km^2, and 3959.11 km^2. However, due to the Sundarbans and enormous rivers across the district, the actual human habitable area of Satkhira, Khulna, and Bagerhat is, respectively, 2243.24 km^2, 2054.99 km^2, and 2011.29 km^2. Moreover, the Satkhira, Khulna, and Bagerhat districts include 79, 97, and 77 Unions (smallest administrative unit in Bangladesh), respectively, which together (253 Unions) represents the entire Southwestern Coastal Bangladesh. In this study, analysis and statistics are performed only for the habitable areas and registered Unions. The component-specific map of vulnerability will help decision-makers, disaster managers, and responsible stakeholders better understand the complex vulnerability scenario at the Union level. It will help to make effective and efficient spatially targeted policies to increase the resilience of coastal communities.

Socio-demographic Component The vulnerability map of the socio-demographic component (cf. Figure 3) portrays the greatest vulnerable areas as the northeast region along Khulna and Bagerhat districts and the southern region along the coast of Satkhira. The central part of the study area is classified as a low or moderate vulnerability zone. The variation in the degree of vulnerability based on the socio-demographic component for a total of 253 Unions of Satkhira, Khulna, and Bagerhat districts is presented in Table 3. Most of the Unions are registered in moderate vulnerability class for all the regions and only a few in very high vulnerability class. Interestingly, high and low vulnerability persist almost equally across the study area, and very low vulnerability is completely absent in the Satkhira district.

Economic Component The variation in the degree of economic vulnerability (cf. Table 4) across the study area represents that most Unions are in a highly vulnerable

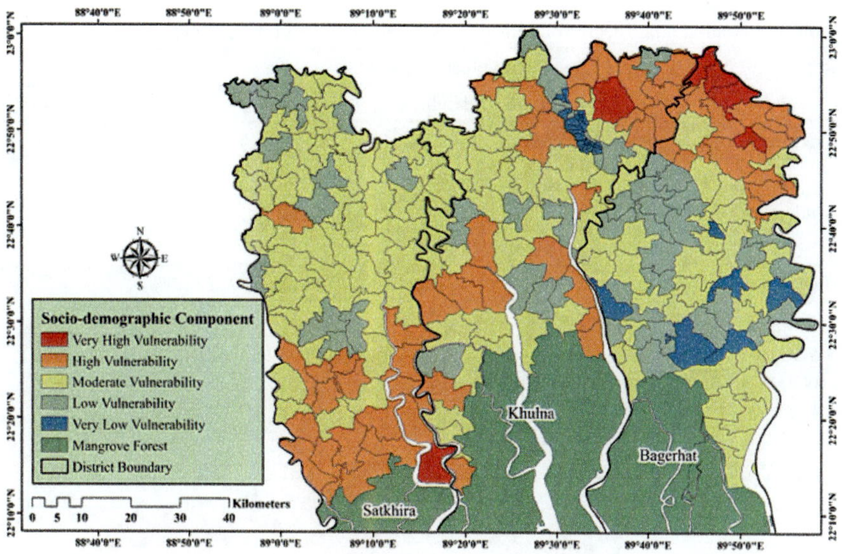

Fig. 3 Degree of vulnerability based on the socio-demographic component at Union level

Table 3 Variation in the degree of vulnerability based on the socio-demographic component

Region		Degree of vulnerability (SDC)				
		Very high	High	Moderate	Low	Very low
Satkhira	Union (count)	1 (1.3%)	17 (21.5%)	47 (59.5%)	14 (17.7%)	0 (0%)
	Area (km^2)	33.73	545.11	1351.96	312.44	0
Khulna	Union (count)	1 (1%)	22 (22.7%)	32 (33%)	16 (16.5%)	26 (26.8%)
	Area (km^2)	49.92	690.45	947.27	331.47	35.88
Bagerhat	Union (count)	4 (5.2%)	12 (15.6%)	32 (41.6%)	23 (29.9%)	6 (7.8%)
	Area (km^2)	89.72	315.80	912.02	538.12	155.63
SW BD (Total)	Union (count)	6 (2.4%)	51 (20.2%)	111 (43.9%)	53 (20.9%)	32 (12.6%)
	Area (km^2)	173.38	1551.35	3211.24	1182.02	191.51

condition. The very high, high, and moderate vulnerability classes account for 91.3% of 253 Unions. This is due to the acute unemployment, economic, and agricultural dependency over the southwestern belt, which is often exacerbated by catastrophic natural hazards. Furthermore, this area is susceptible to climate change and climate-induced disaster, which continuously imprints a negative impact on the life and livelihood of coastal communities. The vulnerability map of the economic component (cf. Figure 4) clearly shows the dominance of very high, high, and moderate vulnerability over the study area.

Physical and Infrastructural Component The vulnerability map of the physical and infrastructural component (cf. Figure 5) portrays a semi-circular concentric zone

Table 4 Variation in the degree of vulnerability based on the economic component

Region		Degree of vulnerability (EC)				
		Very high	High	Moderate	Low	Very low
Satkhira	Union (count)	7 (8.9%)	59 (74.7%)	13 (16.5%)	0 (0%)	0 (0%)
	Area (km^2)	223.06	1712.34	307.85	0	0
Khulna	Union (count)	9 (9.3%)	47 (48.5%)	21 (21.6%)	19 (19.6%)	1 (1%)
	Area (km^2)	333.70	1465.42	208.15	44.78	2.93
Bagerhat	Union (count)	23 (29.9%)	45 (58.4%)	7 (9.1%)	2 (2.6%)	0 (0%)
	Area (km^2)	694.35	1103.57	190.81	22.55	0
SW BD (Total)	Union (count)	39 (15.4%)	151 (59.7%)	41 (16.2%)	21 (8.3%)	1 (0.4%)
	Area (km^2)	1251.10	4281.33	706.81	67.33	2.93

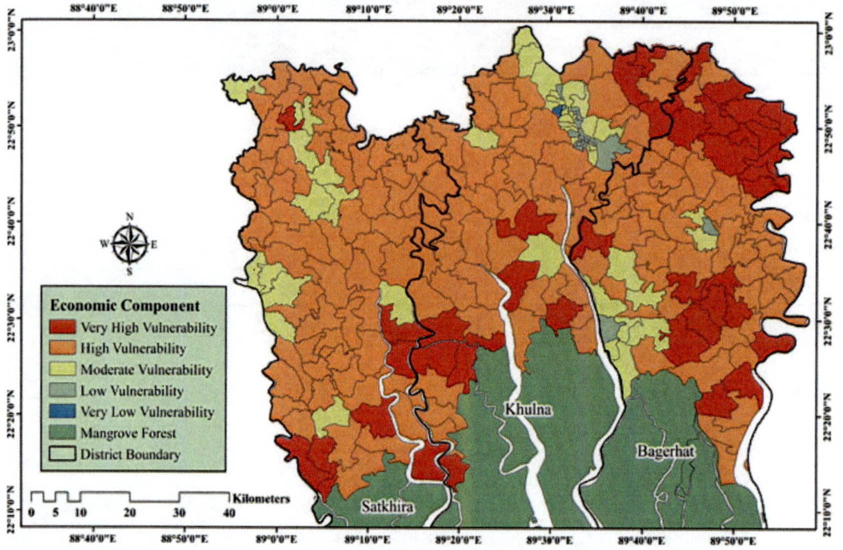

Fig. 4 Degree of vulnerability based on the economic component at Union level

pattern across the study area. The first zone closest to the Sundarbans and the coast is the very high or high vulnerability zone. The second and middle zone is a moderate vulnerability zone. Finally, the third or peripheral zone is classified as a low or very low vulnerability zone. This map represents that the communities living across the coastal belt of Southwestern Bangladesh have a high physical and infrastructural vulnerability, although they are most sensitive to the effect of natural hazards due to their relative distance from the coast. The variation in the degree of physical and infrastructural vulnerability for a total of 253 Unions of Satkhira, Khulna, and Bagerhat districts is presented in Table 5.

4.2 Crash Phase

Most non-motorized drivers, pedestrians, and two-wheeler drivers suffer severe injuries or fatalities during the crash phase. Open area and residential areas influence most fatalities during this phase. Open area allows drivers to accelerate the vehicles at maximum speed which may cause an error in the driver's perspective or mechanical failure of the vehicle.

4.3 Post-crash Phase

The quick first aid responses to the victims are a must to save a victim's life. The absence of trauma centers near an accident blackspot increases the chances of a victim's death. Often the ambulance and other quick response vehicles are delayed due to heavy city traffic conditions. Delay of emergency vehicles is often neglected while forming policies for road safety. Additionally, citizens have very little knowledge of road safety practices which causes uncertain situations around crash spots during the post-crash phase.

5 The Haddon Matrix Analysis with Crash Prevention Strategies

The effective use of the Haddon matrix as the accident analysis tool has been used since 1970. The matrix provided with the subdivision of crash phases as Pre-crash, Crash, and Post-crash; facilitating factors involved within each of the stages [7, 8]. But, still, the evaluation of crash severity often does not rely on the Haddon matrix. The following analysis is covering the evaluation of accident data based on the crash influencing factors suggested by William Haddon [7].

A particular study provides a direct insight into the factor influencing the road hazards within every crash phase, provided with the prevention strategies. Table 4 provides the Haddon matrix for the state of Gujarat with systemic approaches to reduce road accident hazards. The most influenced determinants which influence the road crashes most are only presented within the matrix.

The Haddon matrix indicates the most affecting crash determinants for the state of Gujarat. A well-planned strategic approach for policymaking with technological modification is a must for the state to reduce accident hazards. The policymakers of the state must imply an educational program related to road safety practices. The program must be included as part of the school curriculum and for technical studies too. The law enforcing the cancellation of driving license for rash driving develop safe driving practices within the drivers. Added use of public transportation will reduce the urban traffic of major cities of the state with the overall reduction

Table 4 The Haddon matrix of road crash hazard determinants with crash reduction and prevention strategies

	Human factors	Vehicular factors	Road factors	Environmental factors
Pre-crash Phase	– Victim's age – Victim's gender – No registered license	– Non-motorized vehicles – Vehicle's age	– Open area – Uncontrolled traffic points – Staggered sections	– Visibility conditions clear sky/sunny day – Month of May
Crash Phase	– Hitting from back – Use of Helmet and Seat belt	– Vehicle's crashworthiness	– Strait roads – City area	– Morning rush hours and Lunch hours
Post-crash Phase	– Injury severity of driver and passenger	– Vehicle's crash condition	– Proximity to trauma centers – Delay timing in the arrival of emergency vehicles	– Weather conditions like heavy rain, hail, storms
Crash reduction and prevention strategies	– Implementation of road safety awareness programs at every desired educational level – Strict legal actions against the guilty driver with the provision to suspend the license and impoundment of the vehicle [9]	– Strengthening the policies related to the use of Public transportation over private vehicles – Maximizing safety standards of vehicles – Introduction of the automatic emergency brake system [10]	– Development of road network connecting trauma facilities [8] – Designing the roundabouts to reduce the road crash [11] – Application of skid resistance coating for the wet condition [12] – Lane separation for motorized and non-motorized vehicles [13]	– Critical analysis of accident hotspots under adverse weather conditions – Strengthening the traffic controls during pick hours

in the use of private vehicles. The particular strategy has the potential to reduce traffic congestion, which directly reduces the probability of a road crash occurring. The vehicles must be enabled with the emergency braking systems to reduce the reaction time of drivers with the reduction of braking distance as well [10]. Proper road network planning becomes more essential to handle heavy urban traffic. To handle heterogeneous traffic, lane separation rises the safety advantages for non-motorized vehicles [13]. The introduction of skid resistive coating on the pavements helps motorized vehicles to grip vehicles well in adverse climate conditions [12].

6 Conclusion

The uncontrolled growth in private vehicles with a rising population rings the bells for India to reduce road crash hazards. A well-integrated multidisciplinary collaborated works having the potential to come out with newly developed crash safety practices become more important. The simple yet effective approach of the Haddon matrix analysis provides a clear idea about influencing crash determinants of the study area. The Haddon matrix analysis for the state of Gujarat highlights the area to be considered most while developing road safety policies of the state. The analysis states that the majority of road crashes are directly or indirectly influenced by human factors, so further analysis becomes essential. The present analysis supports the importance of road safety awareness education among citizens. Intrinsically, existing road safety practices according to crash phases have to reconsider for further improvement with interdisciplinary crash hazard reduction strategies.

References

1. Vos T, Barber RM, Bell B, Bertozzi-Villa A, Biryukov S, Bolliger I, Charlson F, Davis A, Degenhardt L, Dicker D, Duan L (2013) Global, regional, and national incidence, prevalence, and years lived with disability for 301 acute and chronic diseases and injuries in 188 countries, 1990–2013: a systematic analysis for the global burden of disease study 2013. The Lecent 386(9995)2015
2. Singh SK (2016) Road traffic accidents in India: issues and challenges. Elsevier, Sanghai
3. Bucsuházy K, Matuchová E, Zůvala R, Moravcová P, Kostíková M, Mikulec R (2020) Human factors contributing to the road traffic accident occurrence, vol 45, pp 555–561. Elsevier, Rome
4. Georgiev N, Velyova V, Dimitrova M (2014) Road infrastructure and traffic parameters—main factors affecting traffic safety. In: Intenational scientific technical conference
5. Huvarinen Y, Svatkova E, Oleshchenko E, Pushchina S (2017) Road safety audit, vol 20, pp 236–241. Elsevier
6. Government of India (2019) Ministry of road transport and highways. Road accidents in India-2019. New Delhi
7. Haddon W (1980) Advances in the epidemiology of injuries as a basis for public policy. Publ Health Rep 95:411–412
8. Rustagi N, Kumar A, Norbu L, Vyas D (2017) Applying Haddon Matrix for Evaluation of road crash victims in Delhi, India. Indian J Surg 80
9. Brubacher JR, Chan H, Brasher P, Erdelyi S, Desapriya E, Asbridge M (2014) Reduction in fatalities, ambulance calls, and hospital admissions for road trauma after implementation of new traffic laws. Am J Publ Health 104
10. Edwards M, Nathanson A, Wisch M (2014) Estimate of potential benefit for Europe of fitting autonomous emergency braking [AEB] systems for pedestrian protection to passenger cars, vol 15, pp S173–S182. Tylor & Francis Online
11. Al-Maraf MN, Somasundaraswaran K, Ayers R (2020) Developing crash modification factors for roundabouts using a cross-sectional method, vol 7. Elsevier
12. Mayora JM, Piña RJ (2009) An assessment of the skid resistance effect on traffic safety underwet-pavement conditions, vol 41. Elsevier
13. Aldred R, Elliott B, Woodcock J, Goodman A (2017) Cycling provision separated from motor traffic: a systematic review exploring whether stated preferences vary by gender and age. Transp Rev 37

No Fine Concrete Pavement—A Sustainable Solution for Flood Disaster Mitigation

R. Jeya Prakash, B. Soundara, and Christian Johnson

Abstract No Fine concrete (NFC) pavement is an ecologically sensible and sustainable substitute for conventional impervious concrete or asphalt pavement structures. Due to the omission of fine aggregates, the concrete can exhibit a porous structure called Pervious or No Fine concrete (NFC). The key design of the NFC system is to introduce acceptable void content so that excess runoff water does freely infiltrate being a self-resilient infrastructure. This can be achieved by controlling or totally removing the proportion of fine aggregates from the mixture design. In this current research, the mechanical properties including compressive strength, split tensile strength, and the hydraulic conductivity (i.e., permeability) of Fibre Reinforced No Fine Concrete (FRNFC) were discussed. Fibres with an effective length of 36 mm, and dosage rates of 0.15, 0.30 and 0.45% are taken for this present investigation. The volume fraction of the water to binder ratio is kept constant at 0.28. The addition of fibre doesn't have substantial effects on strength parameters and diminish the permeability of NFC to an insignificant degree. However, this polypropylene fibre reinforcement is done, to ensure the durability parameters such as abrasion and freeze–thaw resistance which are the perennial concern for implementation.

Keywords No fine concrete · Fibre reinforcement · Permeability · Porosity · Flood mitigation · Sustainable concrete

R. Jeya Prakash (✉)
Nandha Engineering College, Erode, Tamilnadu, India
e-mail: jprakashraja@nandhaengg.org

B. Soundara
Bannari Amman Institute of Technology, Sathyamangalam, India

C. Johnson
Erode Sengunthar Engineering College, Erode, Tamilnadu, India

C. Ghosh and S. Kolathayar (eds.), *A System Engineering Approach to Disaster Resilience*, Lecture Notes in Civil Engineering 205, https://doi.org/10.1007/978-981-16-7397-9_19

1 Introduction

1.1 Problem Statement

No Fines Concrete (NFC) is an extremely sustainable, environmentally friendly material that creates an open cell structure due to the absence of fine aggregates which allows permeability in it. The storm water runoff loss estimated in the rural areas and villages was about 14–19% with above 80% of infiltration rates. Besides, the same measured in urban areas reach up to 94% of runoff losses allowing only 6% of volume for infiltration [1]. This is an effect of increased volume of impervious layer over the surface of the earth in urban areas, causing high environmental impacts [2]. This is also considered to be a source of pollution, in which various pollutants over the surface are washed and mixed into the water bodies at the time of runoff [3]. To reduce this adverse effect of storm water runoff, there should be a proper drainage facility and rainwater harvesting at the source level should be encouraged among the residents. The government has taken many steps to spread awareness about rainwater harvesting and its benefits, but still, this method is not suitable for cities like Chennai with densely populated. This can also be avoided by installing pervious or NFC pavements, besides these environmental benefits some of the drawbacks like less strength, durability, and high chance of clogging restrict its application in real-time [4].

1.2 Research Significance

The Literature study inferred that the durability parameters such as the resistance offered against abrasion and freeze–thaw durability of NFC have been enhanced significantly due to the addition of fibre, but still, there is no technical guidance about the dosage and fibre length [5, 6]. Further, literature shows a variety of compressive strength values ranging from 3.5 to 25 N/mm^2 [7]. If the strength is of primary concern, NFC can be produced by several practices such as increasing the compaction energy, confinement to the sample, etc., with low permeability [8]. The main objective of this study is to produce an optimal mixture proportion for FRNFC with higher performance in strength parameters without compromising their permeability value and to investigate the effects of aggregate size, aggregate to binder ratio, and the fibre proportion on their mechanical and hydraulic properties.

2 Methodology

Methodology of this research includes the selection of aggregates as in Fig. 1 and the selection of fibre as in Fig. 2.

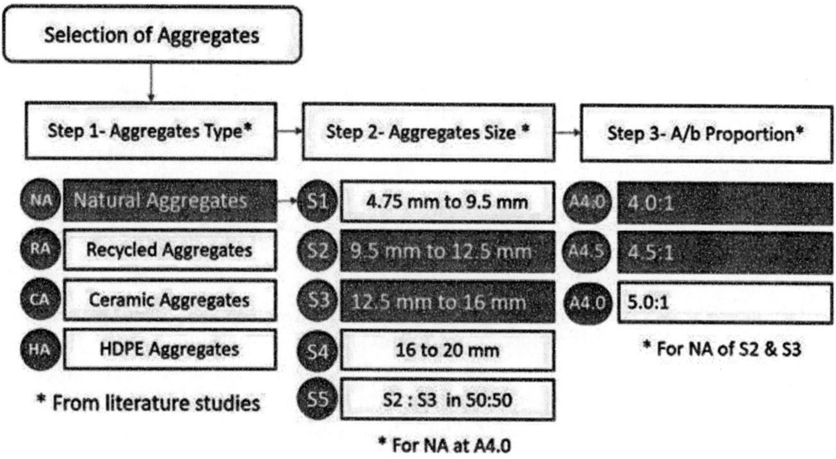

Fig. 1 Selection of aggregates

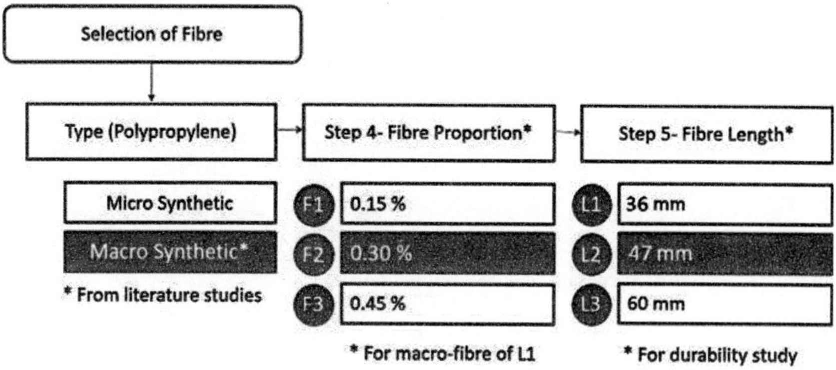

Fig. 2 Selection of fibre

Among the various type of aggregates and fibre: natural aggregates and macro synthetic fibres are taken for this study based on the literature study conducted [9, 10]. This paper presents the test values of structural and hydraulic properties of fibre reinforced no fine concrete. The additional characteristics such as effects of fibre length on the resistance against abrasion and freeze and thaw, the pore size distribution of FRNFC can be studied using imaging technology [11].

3 Material Properties and Testing

This section presents the test results of the materials used in this study. Among the various grades of cement available in the market, Ordinary Portland cement of 53

Table 1 Properties of OPC 53 grade based on test results

Specific gravity	Fineness (%)	Standard consistency (%)	Initial setting time (min)	Final setting time (min)	Bulk density (kg/m^3)
3.15	8	30	33	570	1411

grade—Zuari Cement (Commercial name) opts for this study [12]. The various test results of cement are given in Table 1.

The aggregates are categorized into S1, S2, S3 and S4 [13, 14] (S1—passing through 9.5 mm sieve and retained on 4.75 mm sieve, S2—passing through 12.5 mm sieve and retain on 9.5 mm sieve, S3—passing through 16 mm sieve and retained on 12.5 mm sieve and S4—passing through 20 mm sieve and retained on 16 mm sieve) and their test results are given in Table 2. The aggregates of the same size range produce high values of permeability. Whereas aggregates of the different sizes are used in the same mixture, the lower size aggregate fill the pore space between the large aggregate resulting in high strength but comparatively very less permeability. The aggregate to binder ratios of 4.0:1, 4.5:1, and 5.0:1 are taken and their effects on mechanical and hydraulic properties of NFC have been examined. For NFC, the optimum water cement ratio can be taken between 0.26 and 0.30 [2] and in this study, it is kept constant as 0.28.

The macro synthetic polypropylene fibre of 0.15, 0.30, and 0.45% in the volume of cement is added to NFC to study their effects and their properties are listed in Table 3.

Table 2 Aggregate properties based on test results

Aggregate size	Specific gravity	Water absorption (%)	Bulk density (kg/m^3)
S1—4.75–9.5 mm	2.86	0.98	1595
S2—9.5–12.5 mm	2.68	1	1513
S3—12.5–16 mm	2.94	1	1542
S4—16–20 mm	2.91	1.15	1660

Table 3 Properties of macro synthetic polypropylene fibre

Specific gravity	Effective length (mm)	Aspect ratio	Young's modulus (kN/mm^2)	Tensile strength (kN/mm^2)	Bulk density (kg/m^3)
0.91	36	46	4.0	0.55	910

3.1 Casting and Curing of Test Samples

The concrete was batched and mixed using a rotating-drum mixer for appropriate mixing, and the fibres were added at last by sprinkling to ensure uniform mixing [15]. Then the prepared mixture was placed in cube molds of 150 mm × 150 mm × 150 mm size and cylindrical molds of 150 mm diameter and 300 mm height for the estimation of compressive and split tensile strength respectively. For permeability check using constant head permeameter, the samples are prepared by placing the mixtures in PVC cylindrical molds of 100 mm diameter and 200 mm height. The casted specimens are demolded after 24 h and subjected to curing for 28 days. All the test for strength parameters was conducted according to IS:516–1959.

3.2 Test Procedures

Flowtable Test. The Flowtable test is conducted to calculate the consistency in flow percentage and can be used to determine the workability of a freshly prepared concrete mix. It consists of a circular table, fixed with a rotating wheel and a mold is firmly placed over the center of table in which the concrete is filled in two layers. After leveling the surface, the mold is removed steadily upward without disturbing the sample. The flow table is raised and dropped from a height of 12.5 mm, 15 times in about 15 s. The average diameter of spread in six symmetrical directions in the table is used to measure the flow.

$$\text{Flow}\,\% = \frac{\text{Spread diameter(in cm)} - 25}{25} \times 100$$

Compressive Strength. Compressive strength is generally calculated for concrete cube specimen to evaluate their quality and performance. The values tabulated in Tables 4, 5, and 8 were reported based on the average values obtained from the compressive strength test of three cube specimens on 7 and 28 days of curing.

Split Tensile Strength. Cylindrical specimens of standard dimensions were tested against a split tensile strength test, after curing for 28 days. All the values tabulated were based on the average values obtained from three test samples. Since the application of this type of concrete is restricted to pavements applications, testing of beams (Flexural strength test) is neglected.

Hydraulic Conductivity. Hydraulic conductivity or Permeability is a property of any porous material which permits the flow of fluids through their interconnecting voids [16] and is measured using a constant head permeameter for cylindrical samples with 100 mm diameter and 200 mm height. The samples are subjected to vacuum wash, to get more accurate results.

Table 4 Trial mix design (for varying aggregate size, w/b ratio of 0.3 and A/b ratio of 4.0:1)

Mix ID	Mix name	Cement (kg/m^3)	Aggregate (kg/m^3)	Water (l/m^3)	Compressive Strength (N/mm^2) 7 days	28 days	Split Tensile strength (N/mm^2)	Flexural strength (N/mm^2)	Permeability (cm/s)
M1	A4.0S1	267	1208	53.0	11.12	15.86	1.53	2.87	0.89
M2	A4.0S2	267	1146	53.0	8.57	12.32	1.47	2.42	1.26
M3	A4.0S3	267	1168	53.0	5.36	8.65	1.32	2.34	1.40
M4	A4.0S4	267	1258	53.0	4.67	6.07	1.15	1.86	1.53
M5	A4.0S5	267	1157	53.0	10.28	14.87	1.40	2.15	0.97

Table 5 Trial mix design (for varying A/b ratio, aggregate size—S2 and S3, w/b ratio of 0.3)

Mix ID	Mix name	Cement (kg/m^3)	Aggregate (kg/m^3)	Water (l/m^3)	flow %	Compressive strength (N/mm^2) 7 days	28 days	Split Tensile strength (N/mm^2)	Flexural strength (N/mm^2)	Permeability (cm/s)
M2	A4.0S2	267	1146	53.0	110	8.57	12.32	1.47	2.42	1.26
M3	A4.0S3	267	1168	53.0	104	5.36	8.65	1.32	2.34	1.40
M6	A4.5S2	244	1178	48.4	98	10.45	14.50	2.06	2.12	1.37
M7	A4.5S3	244	1201	48.4	90	9.96	13.09	1.97	2.03	1.58
M8	A5.0S2	225	1205	44.6	84	7.81	8.49	1.34	1.98	1.06
M9	A5.0S3	225	1228	44.6	52	4.94	7.14	1.23	1.56	1.14

4 Mix Design

The effects of aggregate size and proportion on No Fine Concrete (NFC) are studied, based on the test results the best performing mixes [17] were taken to investigate the effects of fibre reinforcement.

The compressive, split tensile strength, and permeability values are based on the average value of three samples [18–20]. It is observed that the mixture containing S1, S2, and S3 produces a high value of compressive strength compared to the mixture containing S4. This is because the thin film of cement pastes forms better bonding with smaller-sized aggregates. While considering the coefficient of permeability, the mixture containing S3 and S2 performs well compared to that of the mixture containing S1.

This may be caused because of the decrease in pore size with a decrease in the nominal size of the aggregates. A new mixture ID, M5 is prepared with the aggregates of sizes S2 and S3 in equal proportion (i.e., 50:50). In which about 40% of pores in S3 type aggregates are filled with S2, and thereby increasing the strength parameters and decreasing the overall porosity. From the results obtained, further testing is restricted to the aggregate size of S2 and S3. Thus, the effects of aggregate proportion on NFC are studied for S2 and S3 with an aggregate to binder ratio of 4.0:1 (A4.0), 4.5:1 (A4.5), 5.0:1 (A5.0). Change in aggregate to binder ratio affects the workability of the mixture to a significant extent [21]. The increase in aggregate proportion decreases the flow value index and has produced a significant increase in strength parameters up to an extent but holds comparatively low permeability.

The further increase in aggregate proportion (i.e., >5.0:1) reduces the strength parameters, which may be due to the insufficient binder paste around the aggregates. And it is also very hard to work with mixtures containing high aggregate contents. Similarly, for mixtures with less aggregate content (i.e., <4.0:1) the flow value index increases, and segregation takes place. From the above trial mixes in Table 5, it is highly recommended to choose M2, M3, M6, and M7 for finding the effects of varying fibre proportions (Table 6).

Fibre reinforcement may reduce some specific performance, to stabilize and enhance the desired mechanical characteristics of Fibre Reinforced No Fine Concrete (FRNFC) such as bond strength between aggregates and cement paste, workability of the mixtures, additional admixtures such as viscosity modifying agent, VMA (Eucoplacant-721) and water-reducing agent, WRA (Auramix-400) confirming to the requirement of IS: 9103–1979, are added in optimal dosage as given in Table 7.

Along with these two admixtures, 12 mixture designs were prepared for three dosages of varying fibre proportions 0.15% (F1), 0.30% (F2) and 0.45% (F3) as shown in Table 8.

Table 6 Workability of mixture with respect to flow percentage

Flow percentage	0–20%	20–60%	60–100%	100–120%	120–150%
Consistency	Dry	Stiff	Plastic	Wet	Sloppy

Table 7 Admixtures composition

Admixture	VMA	WRA
Dosage (%)	0.30	0.25

5 Result and Discussion

This section presents the test results for FRNFC specimens containing various fibre proportions in Table 8. It includes the effects of change in aggregate size and proportion, the effects of change in fibre proportion in their mechanical and hydraulic characters of various mixture proportions. The volume fraction of water to binder ratio is kept constant at 0.28 for all mixtures.

5.1 Effect of Change in Aggregate Size

The aggregate size determines the pore structure of concrete, say for smaller aggregates the pores present were also small, and for larger aggregates, the pore structure was comparably large. The above conditions changed vice-versa considering the strength parameters. The line chart in Fig. 3, stretches the effects of aggregates size on permeability and strength parameters. From this, we can evidently notice that with the increase in aggregate size, strength decreases, and permeability increases.

For A4.0S5 (M5), the sudden increase in compressive strength is due to the usage of different size aggregates. Here the pore space between the larger size aggregates was filled by the lower size aggregates resulting in high strength but comparatively very less permeability. Thus, the mixture proportions A4.0S2 and A4.0S3 (i.e., M2 and M3) are taken for further studies to examine the effects of aggregate to binder proportions.

5.2 Effect of Change in Aggregate Proportion

The change in aggregate proportion readily affects the workability of mixtures. The mixtures with high aggregate contents are hard to work and the mixtures with less aggregate content are easy to work, have high value of flow index. The effect of change in aggregate to binder ratio in permeability and flow index is given by Fig. 4, and this variance observed was most likely due to an increase in surface tension of the aggregates. From these observations, mixtures with compromising permeability and flow index A4.0S2, A4.0S3, A4.5S2, and A4.5S3 (i.e., M2, M3, M6 and M7) are taken to study the effects of change in fibre proportions.

The mixture proportions are prepared in such a manner by controlling the void content and fresh unit weight to produce less difference in harden unit weight of the samples and to study the exact effect caused by the fibers [22]. The observations

Table 8 Mix designs (with varying fiber proportion for selected trial mixes)

Mix ID	Mix name	Cement (kg/m^3)	Aggregate (kg/m^3)	Water (l/m^3)	Fibre (g/m^3)	Chemical admixtures		Flow (%)	Unit weight (kg/m^3)		Compressive Strength (N/mm^2)		Split tensile strength (N/mm^2)	Flexural strength (N/mm^2)	Permeability (cm/s)
						WRA (g/m^3)	VMA (g/m^3)		Wet	Dry	7 days	28 days			
M10	A4.0S2F1	267	1146	50.6	401	668	802	108	1960	1850	8.63	13.11	1.82	2.91	1.21
M11	A4.0S2F2	267	1146	50.6	802	668	802	103	1975	1860	8.92	13.66	2.01	3.32	1.18
M12	A4.0S2F3	267	1146	50.6	1203	668	802	96	1985	1860	9.06	13.72	2.43	3.45	1.11
M13	A4.0S3F1	267	1168	50.6	401	668	802	104	1980	1855	5.54	8.99	1.6	2.83	1.36
M14	A4.0S3F2	267	1168	50.6	802	668	802	99	1995	1860	6.02	9.87	1.98	3.21	1.2
M15	A4.0S3F3	267	1168	50.6	1203	668	802	93	2010	1870	6.95	9.94	2.62	3.33	1.07
M16	A4.5S2F1	244	1146	46.4	366	610	732	98	1990	1865	11.04	15.11	2.71	2.86	1.34
M17	A4.5S2F2	244	1146	46.4	732	610	732	90	2015	1875	11.61	15.63	3.13	3.24	1.26
M18	A4.5S2F3	244	1146	46.4	1099	610	732	82	2020	1885	12.15	15.98	3.61	3.35	1.19
M19	A4.5S3F1	244	1168	46.4	366	610	732	90	1995	1870	9.96	13.21	2.19	2.79	1.55
M20	A4.5S3F2	244	1168	46.4	732	610	732	81	2005	1875	9.99	13.57	2.45	3.2	1.41
M21	A4.5S3F3	244	1168	46.4	1099	610	732	73	2015	1880	10.13	13.72	2.64	3.35	1.26

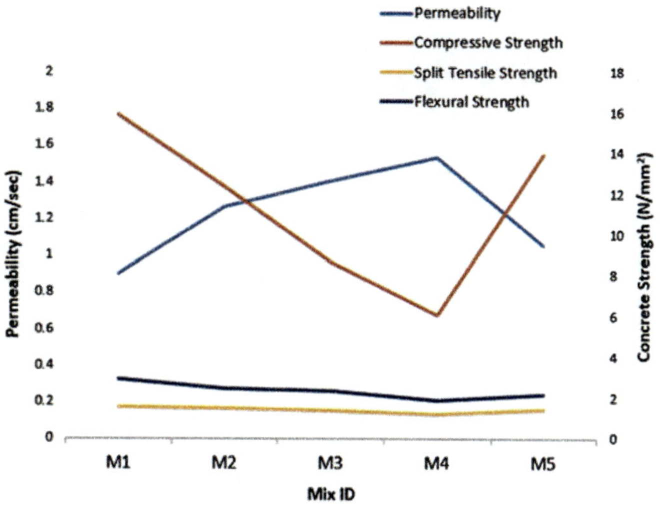

Fig. 3 Effect of change in aggregate size

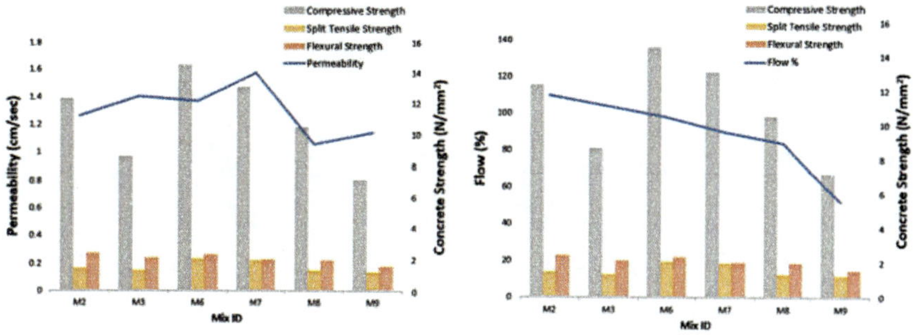

Fig. 4 Effect of change in aggregate proportion

made show that there is an appropriate relationship between the hardened (or) dry unit weight [23, 24] and compressive strength/split tensile strength as shown in Fig. 5a, b.

5.3 *Effect of Change in Fibre Proportion*

Mechanical Effects. Based on the reported preliminary test results (Table 5), the four mixtures M2, M3, M6, and M7 were taken for finding the effects of varying fiber proportion F1(0.15%), F2(0.30%) and F3(0.45%). There was no significant change observed in compressive strength values after adding fibre in Fig. 6a, but

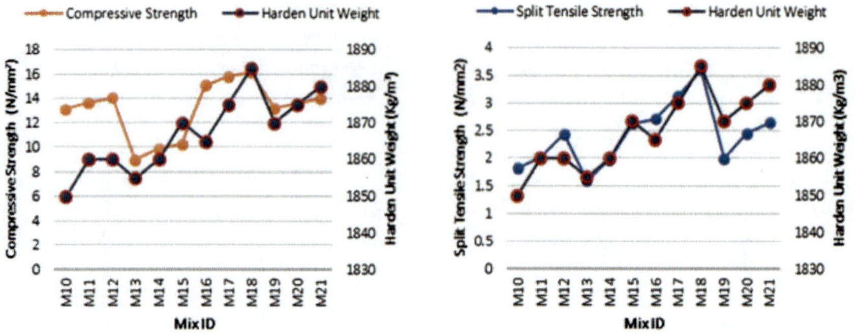

(a) Compressive Strength at 28 days (b) Split Tensile Strength at 28 days

Fig. 5 Relationship between harden unit weight and Strength parameters

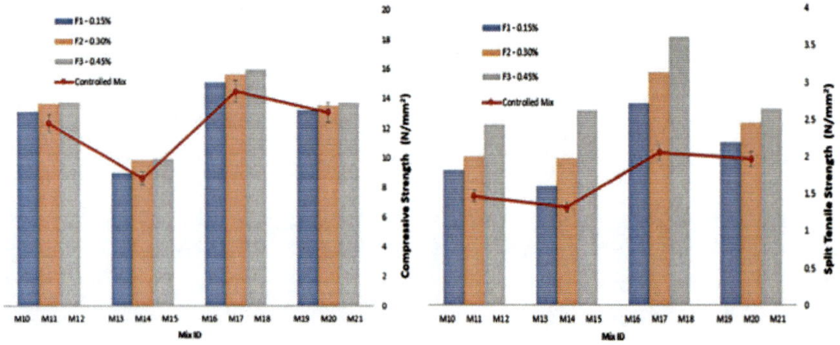

(a) Compressive Strength at 28 days (b) Split Tensile Strength at 28 days

Fig. 6 Effect of fibre reinforcement in NFC

still, the fibre reinforcement has enhanced the strength gradually to the mixture up to a minimum extent. While considering the split tensile strength, the fibre adds an additional tensile property to the controlled mix (i.e., mix without fibre) Fig. 6b.

Hydraulic Effect. Permeability is the most desirable factor for NFC, fibre reinforcement has a diminishing effect on it. Permeability decreases with fibre content and increases slightly with aggregate size and proportion as shown in Fig. 7 and has a linear relation with hardened unit weight.

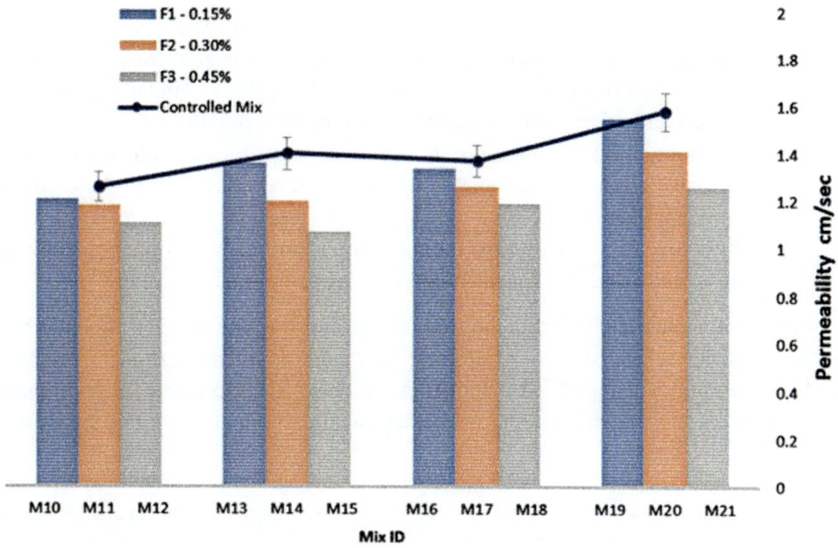

Fig. 7 Effect of fibre reinforcement in permeability of NFC

6 Conclusion

This experimental investigation presents the effects produced on mechanical and hydraulic properties of FRNFC with various experiments such as flow table test, compressive strength test, split tensile test, constant head permeability test.

About 21 mixture proportions (M1-M21) were prepared and studied in detail. The effects of aggregate size and proportions were examined for M1-M9. In addition, the effects of fibre with constant effective length 36 mm and three dosages of proportion (0.15, 0.30 and 0.45%) were tested on the sample mixtures M2, M3, M6, M7, and the following conclusions are drawn.

(1) The average values for compressive strength range from 8.99 to 16.18 N/mm^2 and the average values for split tensile strength ranges from 1.60 to 3.61 N/mm^2. Which is found to be, within the limit as reported in various literature.
(2) The permeability values of FRNFC range from 1.07 cm/s to 1.55 cm/s with respect to the mixture design. Through which, the concrete exhibits pervious behavior, and the values are within the acceptable limit as stated in literature.
(3) This result clearly indicates that both the compressive strength and permeability of FRNFC linearly depend on the dry unit weight of the samples.
(4) The aggregates' size has a significant effect on both structural and hydraulic properties of NFC. The increase in aggregate size increases the pore size and thus the coefficient of permeability, due to the lack of bonding the strength decreases.
(5) The change in aggregate to binder ratio mainly affects the workability of mixtures i.e., the mixtures with high aggregate proportion are hard to work

and for the mixtures with less aggregate content the flow value index increases, and segregation takes place. The variances observed were most likely due to surface tension of the aggregates. However, the water to binder ratio has an inverse effect to that of the aggregate to binder ratio in NFC.

(6) The accumulation of fibre doesn't produce any considerable changes in compressive strength and reduces the hydraulic conductivity of NFC to an insignificant degree.

(7) From the overall observations, the mixture proportion with fibre content had shown a gradual performance compared to conventional concrete.

Finally, it was concluded from the study that polypropylene macro synthetic fibre of 30% and aggregate to binder ratio 4.5:1 for both aggregate size 9.5–12.5 mm and 12.5–16 mm, (i.e., A4.5S2F2 and A4.5S3F2) was the most promising mixture proportion among the various mixtures tested against both strength and hydraulic parameters.

Acknowledgements I wish to express my deep sense of gratitude and sincere thanks to my research supervisors Dr.B.Soundara and Dr. S.Christian Johnson for their inspiring guidance, constant encouragement. And I am thankful to the Management of Nandha Engineering College, Perundurai and Excel Engineering College, Namakkal (former workplace) for the facilities provided and general support during the entire work.

References

1. Jing Y, Jiang G (2003) Experimental study on properties of pervious concrete pavement. Mater Cement Conc Res 33(3):381–386
2. Jeya Prakash R, Soundara B (2019) Hydraulic properties of fibre reinforced no fine concrete. In: Proceedings of international conference on recent advancement in concrete materials and engineering structures, organized by school of civil engineering, held during (18th to 20th September 2019) at Vellore Institute of Technology, Vellore
3. Dong X, Gao J (2011) Effects of fiber type and fiber volume content on frost resistance of fiber-reinforced concrete in airport pavement. In: Proceedings of 3rd international conferences on transportation engineering (ICTE), ASCE, Reston, VA, pp 1524–1529
4. McCain GN, Dewoolkar MM (2009) Strength and permeability characteristics of porous concrete pavements. Transportation research board annual meeting. Washington DC
5. FORTA Corporation (2013) Technical report on FRP—fiber reinforced pervious. Grove City, PA, USA
6. Kevern T, Biddle D (2014) Effects of macrosynthetic fibers on pervious concrete properties. American Society of Civil Engineers. ISSN 0899–1561/06014031(6)
7. Obla K (2007) Pervious concrete for sustainable development. In: Proceedings of 1st international conference on recent advances in concrete technology, Washington
8. Jeya Prakash R, Soundara B (2019) Study on structural properties of fibre reinforced no fine concrete. In: Proceedings of 1st national conference on recent trends in architecture and civil engineering towards energy efficient and sustainable development, pp 509–514
9. ACI Committee 522 (2006) Pervious concrete, 522R-06. American Concrete Institute, Farmington Hills
10. Suozzo M, Dewoolkar MM (2014) Evaluation of strength and hydraulic testing methods of pervious concrete. ACI Mater J 23–34

11. Dufour J, Trottier J, Forgeron D (2006) Behaviour and performance of monofilament macro-synthetic fibres in dry-mix shotcrete. In: Proceedings of 10th international conference on Shotcrete for underground support, ASCE, Reston, VA, pp 194–205
12. Indian standards method of physical test for hydraulic cement, IS 4031 (Part 2) of Indian standard New Delhi
13. ASTM C-33 (2003c) Standard specification for concrete aggregates. In: Annual book ASTM stand, vol 4, no 2. PA
14. Indian standards methods of tests for aggregates for concrete, IS 2386 (Part 2), Bureau of Indian standards New Delhi
15. Tighe SL, Rizvi R, Henderson V, Norris J (2009) Laboratory sample preparation techniques for pervious concrete. Transportation research board annual meeting. Washington
16. Kevern JT, Schaefer VR, Wang K (2009) Predicting performance of pervious concrete using unit weight. In: Proceedings of NRMCA concrete technology forum—focus on performance prediction, National Ready Mixed Concrete Association, Silver Springs, MD
17. Indian standards on recommended guidelines for concrete mix design, IS10262:2009, Bureau of Indian standards New Delhi
18. Indian standard code for plain and reinforced concrete, IS 456:2000, Bureau of Indian standards New Delhi
19. Indian standards methods of tests for strength of concrete, IS:516–1959, Bureau of Indian standards New Delhi
20. Indian standards methods of sampling and analysis of concrete. IS:1199–1959, Bureau of Indian standards New Delhi
21. Cosic K, Korat L, Ducman V (2015) Influence of aggregate type and size on properties of pervious concrete. Constr Build Mater 78:69–76
22. Kevern JT, Schaefer VR, Wang K (2011) Mixture proportion development and performance evaluation for pervious concrete for overlay applications. ACI Mater J 108(4):439–448
23. ASTM C-1688 (2008a) Standard test method for density and void content of freshly mixed pervious concrete. In: Annual book of ASTM standards, vol 4, no 2. PA
24. ASTM C-1754 (2012b) Standard test method for density and void content of hardened pervious concrete. In: Annual book of ASTM standards, vol 4, no 2. PA. PA
25. ACI Committee 522 (2010) Report on pervious concrete, 522. American Concrete Institute, Farmington Hills
26. ACI Committee 522 (2013) Specification for pervious concrete pavement, 522 American Concrete Institute, Farmington Hills
27. ASTM C-192 (2003b) Standard practice for making and curing concrete test specimens in the laboratory. In: Annual book of ASTM standards, vol 4, no 2. PA

Disaster Resilience and Rehabilitation in Kerala: A Critical Review of CARe-Kerala's Housing Scheme

Amrita Vinod and Manoj Kumar Kini

Abstract Global warming and climatic changes have an enormous impact all over the world. Kerala has witnessed disasters such as tsunamis, flash floods, landslides, rising temperatures, multi-intensity rainfalls, and heavy downpours in the past few decades. Recurring floods in the past three consecutive years added to the catastrophes amidst the rapid urbanization experienced across the state. This crisis necessitated the government to respond with immediate mass housing solutions for the affected population. However, general methods were not possible in Kerala, across different flood-prone regions with diverse challenges. The traditional approaches cause delays and involve financial losses in the process, also causing challenges in directing funds on behalf of the beneficiaries. Consequently, the Kerala government initiated a novel approach, the CARe-Kerala, CARe-Home housing scheme, which completed 2000 houses by July 2020 (Praveen in *The Hindu*, Thiruvananthapuram, 2020 [1]), across Kerala's flood-prone regions and is continuing at present. CARe-Kerala housing projects, handled by Author[2] and his team, experimented with alternative solutions that can be successfully implemented in specific geographic areas. This paper critically reviews these CARe-Kerala housing projects, which provided disaster-resilient rehabilitation housing solutions during the 2018 Kerala floods. After evaluating the review variables of the assessment criteria relevant to the projects based on its crucial factors and outcomes, the critical review utilizes these factors and the potential success criteria variables to understand various key aspects of the CARe-Kerala housing projects. In essence, this research is an elucidative assessment with a critical examination of the prominent features of CARe-Kerala housing projects.

Keywords Disaster resilience · Alternative solutions · Amphibian houses

A. Vinod (✉)
Kerala State Institute of Design, Chandanathope, Kerala, India

M. K. Kini
Department of Architecture, College of Engineering, Trivandrum, India

C. Ghosh and S. Kolathayar (eds.), *A System Engineering Approach to Disaster Resilience*, Lecture Notes in Civil Engineering 205, https://doi.org/10.1007/978-981-16-7397-9_20

1 Introduction

Climatic changes exceedingly affect nature, and they inflict severe damages on lives around the globe by threatening the vital integrants of health. According to the World Health Organisation, approximately 250,000 additional deaths per year may occur due to climate change between 2030 and 2050 [2]. Because of the same, the environment of Kerala is also altering, leaving the region hazard susceptible and vulnerable to many severe disasters. Kerala's State Disaster Management Plan assesses 39 types of known and reported hazard types in the state that may turn disastrous in the event of lack of proper preparedness and risk reduction planning [3]. Given its location along the sea coast and steep gradient along the slopes of the Western Ghats, the region is prone to hazards such as cyclone, monsoon storm surge, coastal erosion, sea-level rise, tsunami, flood, drought, lightning, landslide (debris flows), land subsidence (due to tunnel erosion or soil piping) and earthquake [4]. Kerala experienced an abnormally high rainfall from 1 June 2018 to 19 August 2018 resulted in severe floods of 2018, and it also reoccurred the next two consecutive years [5]. The vulnerable floodplain settlements face flood water throughout the years affecting the physical and mental health of the population during the ruckus. Realizing adaptation as the solution to the recrudesce situation when the general rehabilitation mass housing techniques fail to serve, the alternate adaptive techniques emerged.

In response to the devastating floods and landslides in 2018, the Government of Kerala took out a large-scale rehabilitation program, CARe-Kerala, in which CARe-Home housing projects worked with no prior models in co-operation with the community. These projects took up alternative and amphibious construction techniques to achieve adequate services and practical solutions. Accounting for the wide acceptance and satisfaction among the public, a critical review of these rehabilitation housing units will exhibit the critical factors, characteristics, and methods implemented to evaluate this novel approach for mass housing projects in Kerala. In the present wavering circumstances of environmental, social, and economic behaviors, adapting to the transformation process using accessible technologies through possible remedies becomes the way to move forward in the rapidly urbanizing Kerala. Moreover, this review intends to scrutinize the unconventional and new approach and its features to pace towards better disaster resilience, rebuilding, and housing in Kerala.

1.1 Aim

To critically review the CARe-Kerala housing projects, CARe-Home, using potential success criteria variables and thorough assessment of the projects' key components.

1.2 Objectives

- To critically examine various elements of the CARe-Kerala housing projects.
- Review the disaster-resilient solutions of the Housing scheme using potential success criteria variables.
- To evolve an evaluation criteria relevant to the projects based on several outputs and evaluation factors critical to the examination.
- To bring out a clear understanding of the novel approach's different aspects to mass housing solutions for Kerala's disaster rehabilitation.

1.3 Research Question

How successful was the novel approach of CARe-Kerala housing projects in disaster rehabilitation, and what factors made the projects widely accepted and appreciated among the communities?

1.4 Methodology

A critical review of CARe-Kerala housing projects, a new approach in the public housing sector, carries out the process in two main sections. The first section intends to review variables of evaluation criteria relevant to the projects based on several key factors, context, and outcomes—these review variables are further set to review the housing projects and understand their features. The second section focuses on evaluating the projects with Potential Success Criteria Variables and inferences from both concludes to the final review outputs.

1.5 Need for the Study

Deciphering Kerala's urbanization profile and disaster vulnerability maps, the presence of high population sprawl in the most susceptible lands alerts the urgent need for alternative and novel interventions to adapt to changing situations and serve the population's needs. Moreover, the general methods opted for mass housing face challenges, such as mismanagement of resources leading to wastage, delay in work, lack of stakeholder participation, and clarity in the process, widening the gap with beneficiaries resulting in lack of satisfaction in the projects. CARe-Kerla housing projects are an attempt to address these shortcomings through a unique approach in this domain. The review of the same to understand its characteristics and evaluate though different potential variables of criticism is a step towards further advancements in disaster resilience and mass rehabilitation housing in Kerala.

2 Background Studies

2.1 Kerala Disaster Vulnerability and Floods

Kerala has a humid tropical climate, with both the South-West (June to September) and North-East (October to December) monsoons being the prevailing climatic phenomena [4]. The steep slopes and rough terrain of the state, broadly classified as highlands, lowlands, and midlands, are hugely susceptible to disasters like landslides, floods. The monsoon storms of high intensity lead to heavy discharges into the rivers and lead to extreme flooding, making floods the most common natural hazard that impacts the state. For some districts, flood-prone areas even cover about 50% of their total area [4], and among them, low lands with high populations have a significantly higher disaster risk.

The Western Ghats is a global biodiversity hotspot with an abundant natural heritage that serves as the backbone of the state's ecology and economy [6], rising on average to 1500 m (4900 ft) above sea level to around 2500 m (8200 ft) [7]. With the monsoon's onset, approximately 1500 km^2 in the Western Ghats are susceptible to landslides and pose a significant threat [3]. Climate change impacts compounds by the state's absence of the adaptive ability to floods, droughts, and mudflows, which increase the disaster frequency and severity. Kerala experienced abnormally high rainfall, 42% above the normal, in 2018, causing severe flooding in Kerala. The state witnessed 482 deaths and 14 lakh displacements of people, and a total of 54 Lakh people were reportedly affected by the floods [8]. Floods reoccurred in the following two consecutive years, crippling people's lives and livelihoods. Unsustainable and weak management of natural resources and low awareness of the changing climatic condition and disaster risks, an absence of risk-informed urban planning, and poorly enforced land-use patterns and practices constitute the main reasons for rapid and unforeseen changes [4].

A large population inhabited the lowlands, and these flood-prone areas of the region frequently face recurring floods in Kerala. Relocation of the people from the flood-prone areas will damage the people's livelihoods, which persuade them to encounter disasters and fall further into physical, mental, and financial distress. These circumstances pose challenges, and adapting and building resilience becomes the need. Thus, the relevance of bringing out alternative solutions using novel methods and techniques arises as an unabated response.

2.2 CARe-Kerala Housing Scheme, CARe-Home Projects

The Rebuild Kerala initiative by the state government, which respond to the 2018 floods, included CARe-Kerala projects to rehabilitate the flood-affected population. The CARe-Kerala Scheme consists of three projects: CARe-Home, CARe-Loan,

CARe-Grace, in which CARe-Home envisages 1500 first phase houses and 2500-s phase houses with a cumulative outlay of 200 crore rupees, entirely funded by contributions from the Member Relief Fund of the co-operative sector [9]. The projects emphasized resilient modules utilizing alternative methods and construction techniques. With the Rebuild Kerala initiative's co-operative alliance, the projects employed Kerala's co-operative department's extensive networks of 15,624 co-operative societies across the state for the projects. Eighteen proposed designs were encouraged to address the problems raised across the state's 131 blocks and benefitted 61.17% [10] of the below poverty line population.

3 Overview of the Review

The critical re-evaluation of CARe-Kerala housing projects is divided into two main sections. The paper, "Approaches to evaluation of affordable housing initiatives in Australia" [11], refers to significant elements of housing evaluation which can be broadly summarised to—the context, including the general issues, site conditions, and major stakeholders; design and methodology; process and participation, impacts and benefits evaluation and the financial viability and effectiveness. Moreover, the case-study analysis of the National Housing Corporation of Kenya low-income housing projects [12] also refers to social response or the ontological depths of housing and their outcomes. The projects are scrutinized based on execution, technologies, materials used, financial transparency, user satisfaction, participatory process, and practices to tackle challenges in the first part, considering the features of the CARe-Home projects and the evaluation factors. The second examines the projects using 13 Potential Success Criteria Variables employed in "Evaluation of Critical Success Criteria for public housing projects in Nigeria". [13] to evaluate public housing projects.

Definition of Potential Criteria Variables [13]:

- **PSC 1, Overall Project Cost**—Final cost of the overall project.
- **PSC 2, Cost of Individual house units**—Final cost for individual housing units.
- **PSC 3, Overall project duration**—Time taken to complete the project.
- **PSC 4, Rate of delivery of Individual housing units**—Time taken to deliver individual house units.
- **PSC 5, Overall project and individual house quality**—Quality of project, including associated infrastructure.
- **PSC 6, Overall Client satisfaction**—Satisfaction of client with overall project outcomes of individual house unit.
- **PSC 7, Extent of admission of natural ventilation/lighting on individual housing units**—The extent to which natural ventilation and lighting are incorporated into the design.
- **PSC 8, Overall risk containment**—The extent to which risks can be contained, minimized, or managed on the project.

- **PSC 9, Overall/ individual house unit environmental impact**—Impact of construction waste, environmental degradation, pollution, and waste from individual house units on the general public.
- **PSC 10, Health and safety measures with individual house units**—Health and safety hazards posed by the living environment, materials, and construction practices.
- **PSC 11, Technology transfer/Innovation**—The extent to which new technology significantly improves the design and construction of living space by decreasing installation cost, increasing performance, improving the construction process applied, and integrating local artisans.
- **PSC 12, Higher use of Local Materials**—The extent to which local materials are used to reduce cost/ make it affordable.
- **PSC 13, Easy and Cheaper to Maintain**—The ease and cheapness to carry out maintenance over time.

3.1 Features of CARe-Kerala Housing Projects

Method of Execution. CARe-Kerala housing projects opted for a co-operative practical approach, a novel step. Kerala's co-operative department, a web of primary co-operative societies, indulged in the flood rehabilitation and mass housing project in 2018. The state-level project implementation Unit (PIU) was formed to implement the projects, which constitute the Kerala co-operative department secretary, local government departments, revenue department, and primary co-operative societies [10]. Further, under the district collector, each district exercised an implementation committee for the project operation. However, the execution is carried out through co-operative institutions, as authorized by the PIU. A committee chaired by the chairman of the Uralunkal Labour Contract Society—a reputed co-operative agency with experience in undertaking large-scale public projects—constitutes the technical advisory unit for the project operation with the director of the Co-operative Academy of Professional Education (CAPE) as the convener of the team (Fig. 1).

The District nodal officer is responsible for the project implementation, and the resource group formed for the projects provides inputs for supporting the project. At the Implementation Agency level, the beneficiary committees were established with the chairman and other concerned members of the Governing Board of the selected co-operative society, the secretary of the society, the beneficiary, and the representatives of the District Collector and Grama Panchayat [10]. This committee works with an institutional system, exercised from the central body, reaching the grassroots level, bringing out the most beneficial solutions through co-operation and discussions. Methodical and meticulous planning ensured quality services on time with reduced misuse of resources achieved through efficient progress strategies, systematic arrangements, and activity dispositions according to resource availability and time constraints for completing the project.

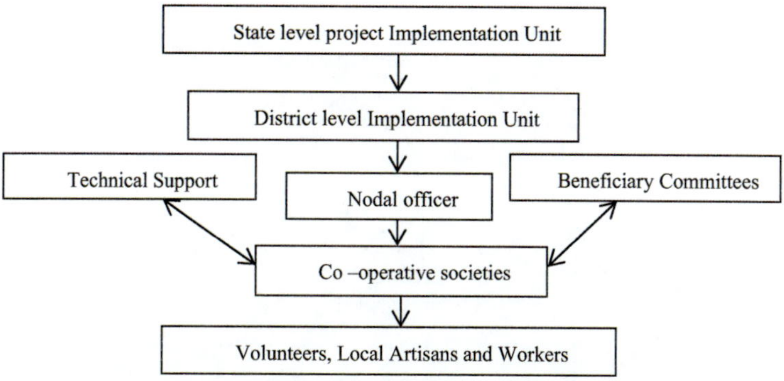

Fig. 1 Method of execution, CARe-Kerala housing projects. *Source* Author

Fig. 2 Residence at Karthikappalli, Alappuzha, Kerala. *Source* Author[2]

Technologies and Materials. The committee for technical support and advisory provided appropriate interventions on the diverse terrains of construction to ensure maximum efficacy and safety with optimum resource consumption. For instance, enabling modifications that created pillar-built light-structured houses, well-based pillar structures to combat the instability of loose clayey soil, and two-story valley-side houses on exceedingly small plots [10].

The modular units employed in the design (Fig. 2) achieve faster and more efficient construction without compromising the quality. The aluminum fabricated window

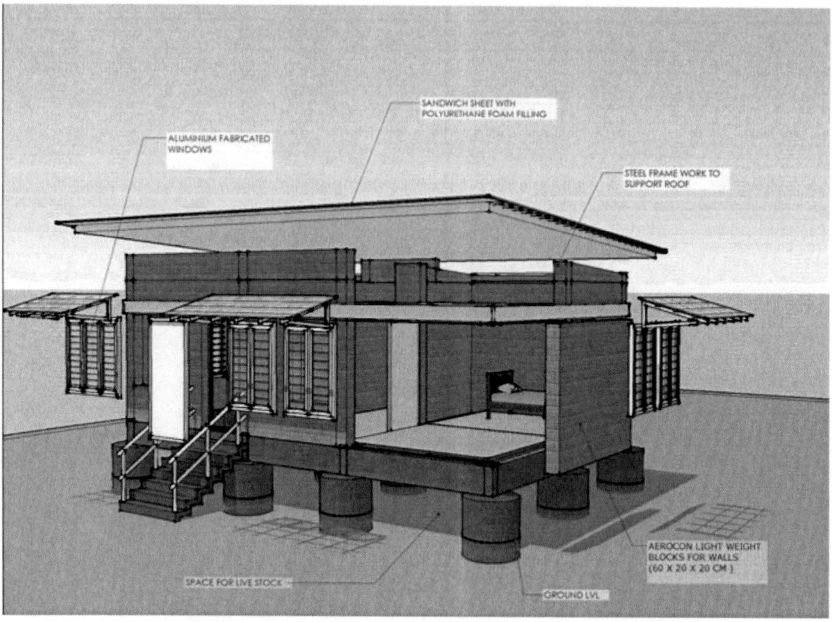

Fig. 3 Residence at Karthikappalli, Alappuzha, Kerala. *Source* Author[2]

(Fig. 3) is one of such elements employed to accomplish this goal. Moreover, modular construction techniques support modified uses in the future, which can also be easily dismantled, transported, and re-assembled on a different site. The project used lightweight components such as AEROCON blocks to construct walls and partitions, sandwiched sheets, and polyurethane form filling used for roofing with steel-frames supporting the structure deviates from the conventional construction materials.

Practices to tackle challenges. CARe-Kerala projects focused on on-site responsive solutions that are adaptable and stable on the landscapes, ranging from flood-prone low lands to high range valleys with restricted land area and location choices. The plasticity and freedom of designs broke the uniformity and facilitated appropriate design innovations and interventions according to the site conditions. The concrete rings (Fig. 4) used to adjust the foundation height of the housing unit in the flood-prone site is such a flexible design intervention.

Financial Transparency. Structured mechanism of financial management supported the project to ensure proper accounting and transparency. Initially, the project was built with an allocation of five lakhs rupees per house, constituting four lakhs from the mobilized fund by Co-operative Department through donations from banks and societies. The State Disaster Response Fund allocated a sum of 1, 01, 900–95,100 rupees per house, and a few projects gained additional local fund mobilization at various construction stages [10]. Beneficiary committees discuss and utilize the fund allocated through clear accounting strategies with periodical monitoring. Moreover,

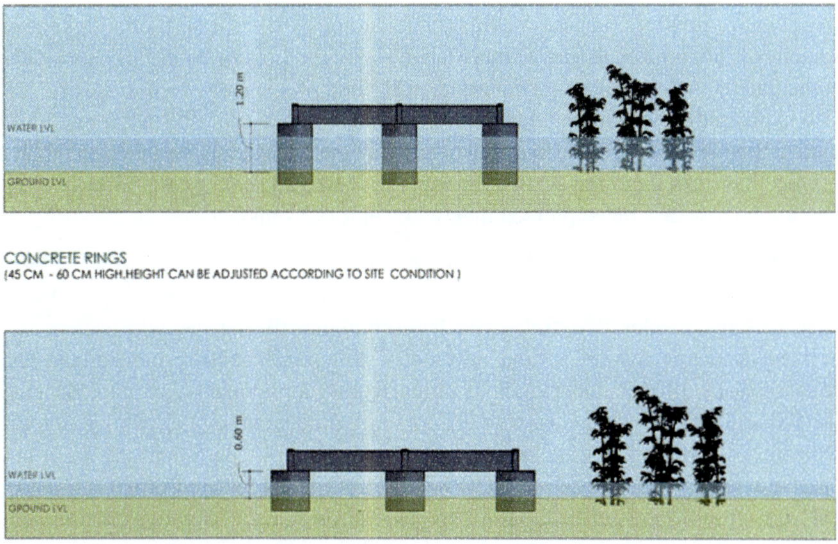

Fig. 4 Concrete rings (foundation) in flood-prone areas. *Source* Author[2]

the local support groups (mainly from schools, religious institutions, political parties, local governments, community development societies, relatives and family support, NGOs, and business enterprises) raised additional funds. Work progress and funds are checked periodically and are audited by the co-operative bank auditors. The co-operative framework of fund management facilitated voluntary contributions with transparent operations and eliminated misuse of funds (Fig. 5).

User Satisfaction. CARe-Kerala housing projects succeeded in incorporating the flood victims' needs regardless of their age and circumstances. Three-quarters of the total projects varied between 600 and 400 ft^2 of plinth area [10]. 80% of the beneficiary families have a new house with a greater plinth area than their previous one, improved resilience and safety factors, and a sense of protection and ownership [10]. Gopalakrishnan from Alappuzha reported that he is satisfied and no longer fears floods as he procured a flood-resilient house [1] under the CARe-Home project. In 90% of the cases, the initiative provided beneficiaries with new homes in the areas of their original homes [10]. Due to this strategy, no disturbance to livelihoods occurred and created adaptable and safe solutions for resilience in future catastrophes. Efforts

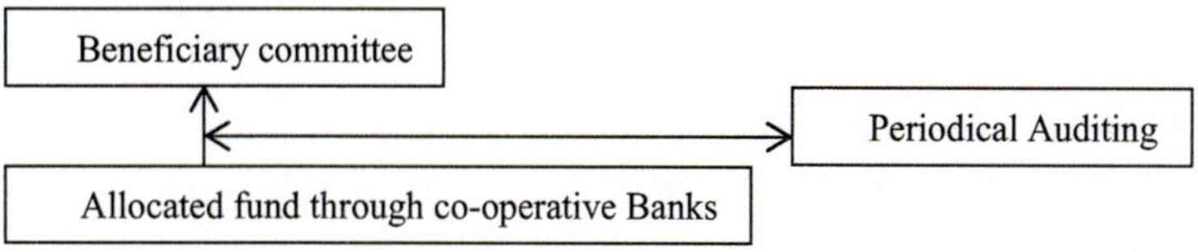

Fig. 5 Financial flow, CARe-Kerala projects. *Source* Author

for inclusive progress focused on vulnerable sections [10]. The staff of co-operative societies, Kudumbashree (the Kerala State Poverty Eradication Mission), and NGOs appreciated CARe-Kerala housing projects. Several officials involved in the projects also expressed satisfaction and happiness in their work as it has been the first of its kind in their service life. The merging of the project with existing schemes, including the localities in collaborative works, earned trust within the community for delivering quality work within the stipulated time with complete satisfaction.

Participatory Process. The exemplary participatory process devised in CARe-Kerala included volunteers, students, and teachers from State Engineering Colleges, local artisans. Besides, two students each got continuously engaged with each house, utilized academic resources, and developed skills and social responsibility. The convergence with Mahatma Gandhi National Rural Employment Guarantee Scheme (MGNREGS) assured on-site workers for 90 working days [14]. Under officers with the construction responsibility in the co-operative department and local co-operative society, the participation of local governments, elected officials, NGOs, religious groups, and political parties created a favorable co-operative environment throughout the implementation process [10]. The additional resources mobilized, including cash and voluntary work, raised the average overall cost (more than 100,000 rupees/house). Unlike other mass housing projects, the co-operative societies were involved with high enthusiasm. These projects with proper division of responsibilities among the stakeholders were widely accepted among people. The teamwork and unity procured with active social interaction developed an emotion of togetherness, safety, and ownership within the community. Thus, the work quality and satisfaction at the completion stage get invigorated substantially.

3.2 Evaluation Using Potential Success Criteria Variables for CARe-Kerala Housing Projects

PSC 1, Overall Project Cost—The completion of 2000 houses in the first phase across the state by July 2020 [1] has the total sum spent to about 118.82 crores with multiple outlets resulted in additional fund mobilization; own donations and those contributed to the kitty by individuals and agencies [10].

PSC 2, Cost of Individual house units—On average, this lifts to about 619,842 rupees per house, compared to the initially expected expenditure of about 500,000 rupees per house, which included mobilized funds of four lakhs from the Co-operative Department and around one lakh by the State Disaster Response Fund.

PSC 3, Overall project duration—CARe-Kerala housing projects were initiated soon after the floods of 2018 and completed 231 new houses [15] under CARe-Home project by February 2019. By July 2020, CARe-Kerala housing scheme, CARe-Home, achieved its first phase of 2000 houses.

PSC 4, Rate of delivery of Individual housing units—For the beneficiary families identified from the list of flood victims prepared by the District Collectors and Disaster Management Department, 2000 houses were delivered across the state by July 2020—CARe-Kerala housing scheme.

PSC 5, Overall project and individual house quality—Climate and site-responsive resilient housing of CARe-Kerala ensured user satisfaction and essential services. Usage of lightweight materials, innovative technologies, and local resources with user participation checked the desired quality.

PSC 6, Overall Client satisfaction—User satisfaction at all phases of projects is one of the primary focuses of the collaborative approach through the beneficiary committee, including the client as one of the major participants. Change of paradigm from relocation to adaptation in CARe-Kerala housing scheme eliminated the challenges such as unemployment and disruption of livelihood source.

PSC 7, Extent of Admission of natural ventilation/lighting on individual housing units—Every housing module ensured adequate natural ventilation and lighting, maximum utilization of available area, and experimented with better—resilient housing solutions tackling the sites' challenges.

PSC 8, Overall risk containment—Floods are the most recurring disaster that affects construction in the past three years. CARe-Kerala addresses this challenge without relocation through adaptive and resilient construction techniques. Thus, the risk factor decreases, making the living environment resilient to future catastrophes.

PSC 9, Overall/ individual house unit environmental impact—Modular components enable easy maintenance and dismantling for re-construction elsewhere. Environmental impact is considerably low compared to conventional housing methods.

PSC 10, Health and safety measures with individual house units—CARe-Kerala housing projects put the users' safety and health as a vital consideration of the rehabilitation process. Design elements such as the concrete rings used to increase foundation height in flood-prone areas exemplar this aspect.

PSC 11, Technology transfer/Innovation—The technical advisory and support from students and teachers of State Engineering Colleges collaborated in the projects. The liberty to deviate from the conventional methods substantially increased its efficiency and functionality through innovative approaches.

PSC 12, Higher use of Local Materials—Compared with the former housing initiatives, CARe-Kerala housing projects consider local materials and resources suitable for site-responsive solutions. However, resilient housing in future catastrophes held the primary focus of the resilient public housing initiative.

PSC 13, Easy and Cheaper to Maintain—Adaptable constructions that can be cheaply maintained were significant for the projects. Modular building units such as aluminum fabricated windows, and AEROCON blocks enabled easy construction, transportation, re-construction, and maintenance over time.

3.3 Inferences

With defined and distinct implementation strategies on an institutional structure, CARe-Kerala housing projects exhibited collaborative nature by gaining broad stakeholder engagement, technical advisory, support from local communities and organizations, local resource mobilization, and successful and satisfactory completion time. Co-operation within and between the responsible groups, the beneficiary committees at different management levels, encourage sufficient voluntary efforts, including NGOs, students, and teachers from the State Engineering Colleges. Top-to-bottom development structure decreases the total expenditure by approximately 25–35% and uses cost-effective methods, systematic inspections, and appropriate changes, assuring a better quality of work. CARe-Kerala housing projects solved many challenges faced by the general mass-housing methods, such as the gap between the designers, workers, public, beneficiaries leading to unsatisfactory and incomplete projects, non-systematic management and loss of time and resources, compromised design due to various influences, and the non-context responsive design affecting the overall output quality. However, by devising a collective approach through extensive co-operative society networks, the projects created a platform ensuring beneficiary participation and arriving at the best possible solutions with the present circumstances and available resources. These participatory operation methods revealed every stage of construction, leveling out financial transactions, resources, and work completion, making them transparent and effective throughout the project. Two–way benefits of collaborations such as the academic co-operations utilized the academic resources and built skills, social awareness for future professionals; local support and participation create a sense of ownership and responsibility, improve satisfaction, and gain wide acceptance among the public. The co-operative society networks proved to be a successful medium of operation for CARe-Kerala housing projects, a novel approach of alternative solutions, with its extensive networks and communication all over the state.

4 Conclusion

Review on CARe-Kerala housing projects unfolded a collaborative and inclusive approach through co-operative societies, a novel model, towards mass rehabilitation housing in Kerala. Notable features of these projects have substantially elevated housing quality and increased stakeholders' satisfaction after the project completion. The distinct methods of execution, technologies, and materials used, financial transparency provided through the co-operative bank networks across the state, and the overall user satisfaction, participatory process, and practices mark the novel approach as an effective, practical, and successful rehabilitation housing project in Kerala. Examining CARe-Kerala features, using the evaluation variables and potential success criteria variables, also reveals the projects' distinct and vital initiations. The characteristics and the widely accepted outputs set CARe-Kerala housing projects, CARe-Home, among the most successful and appreciated housing projects across the state. This initiative is evidence of evolving dynamic co-operative responses in the state and is a remarkable model that can be emulated elsewhere in the future.

References

1. Praveen SR (2020) 2000 houses built under Care Home in Kerala, *The Hindu*, Thiruvananthapuram, 21 June 2020
2. Climate change, *World Health Organization*. https://www.who.int/westernpacific/health-topics/climate-change. Accessed 21 Dec 2020
3. Kerala State Disaster Management Plan, Kerala State Disaster Management Authority Department of Revenue and Disaster Management Government of Kerala, 2016. (Online). Available: https://sdma.kerala.gov.in/wp-content/uploads/2018/11/Kerala%20State%20Disaster%20Management%20Plan%202016.pdf
4. Initiative RK. Rebuild Kerala Development Programme, A resilient recovery policy framework and action plan for shaping Kerala's Resilient, risk-informed development and recovery from 2018 floods. (Online). Available: https://rebuild.kerala.gov.in/reports/RKDP_Master%2021May2019.pdf
5. Study Report, Kerala Floods of August 2018, Government of India Central Water Commission Hydrological Studies Organisation Hydrology (S) Directorate, 2018. (Online). Available: https://reliefweb.int/sites/reliefweb.int/files/resources/Rev-0.pdf
6. Report of the Western Ghats Ecology Expert Panel Part I, Submitted to The Ministry of Environment and Forests, Government of India, Aug 2011. (Online). Available: https://www.cppr.in/wp-content/uploads/2013/03/Gadgil-report.pdf
7. Kerala topographic map, elevation, relief. topographic-map.com. https://en-gb.topographic-map.com/maps/lpvo/Kerala/. Accessed 25 Dec 2020
8. Assistance to CARe KERALA (New Scheme)—Department of Cooperation, Government of Kerala. https://cooperation.kerala.gov.in/2019/05/24/assistance-to-care-keralanew-scheme-2/. Accessed 17 Dec 2020
9. Sreelu NS. Evaluation report on CARe-Home Project, Aluva, Evaluation Report. (Online). Available: https://cooperation.kerala.gov.in/wp-content/uploads/2020/07/Evaluation-Report-on-CARe-Home-Project-16.03.2020.pdf
10. Milligan V and Australian Housing and Urban Research Institute, Approaches to evaluation of affordable housing initiatives in Australia: National Research Venture 3 : housing affordability for lower income Australians. Melbourne: Australian Housing and Urban Research Institute 2007
11. Makachia Leuven PA (1995) Starter Unit concept, a case study analysis of national Housing Corporation of Kenya low income housing projects. A Dissertation presented in part fulfilment of the requirements for the Master of Architecture in Human Settlements Degree
12. Mohammed IY (2015) Evaluation of critical success criteria for public housing projects in Nigeria. J Environ Sci Resour Manage 7(2)

13. CareHome, Construction of houses—guidelines. Department of Co-Operation Office of the Registrar of Co-operative Societies Jawahar Sahakarana Bhavan DPI Junction, Thycaud P.O Thiruvananthapuram -695014 Kerala, India, 12 December, 2018. (Online). Available: https://drive.google.com/file/d/1INMzpX4YIlLBaA08aqznwaqXF6lm_mOP/view?usp=embed_facebook. Accessed: 24 Dec 2020
14. Kerala: 31 families get new houses under Care Home project, *Times of India*, 27 February, 2019

Community Resilience Measures

Measuring Disaster Resilience at Community Level and Exploring the Prospects of Revitalizing Communities Coalescing Disaster Risk

C. A. Bindu and Subha Vishnudas

Abstract Increasing the efficiency of disaster response, discouraging development in vulnerable areas and increasing the resiliency of community towards disasters are the three major ways of dealing with disaster risk reduction and mitigation. The paper focuses on the third method of enhancing disaster resilience at community level where community in the broader sense includes family, neighborhoods, panchayats, towns and cities. Though this is the most difficult one as the factors contributing to the increased or diminished capacity of a community to resist, absorb or restore the pre-disaster state has to be measured, evaluated, benchmarked and also assessed and compared across space and time. Several international organizations have put enormous effort and have devoted abundant resources in building resilient communities. Investing in Disaster Risk Reduction is one of the main thrust among the four of Sendai Framework for Disaster Risk Reduction (SFDRR). The application of resilience can lead to transformation of communities as the concept of resilience can encompass different disciplines with same purpose. A resilient community can be built by revitalizing its pillars (Social, Economic, Environmental and institutional), likewise revitalization projects also helps in building up a resilient community, which has well been exemplified in various cases where different strategies of revitalization has led to disaster resilience of communities. Enhancing the disaster resilience of a community or revitalizing a community, both requires political will, strong leadership and institutional capacity. The paper concludes by establishing that coalescing disaster risk into development activities contributes to long term endurance, resurgence, resilience and revitalization of the community.

Keywords Community resilience · Revitalization · Disaster risk reduction

C. A. Bindu (✉)
Faculty of Architecture and Planning, Government Engineering, College Thrissur, Thrissur, Kerala, India
e-mail: binduca@gectcr.ac.in

S. Vishnudas
Faculty of Civil Engineering, Cochin University of Science and Technology, Kochi, India
e-mail: v.subha@cusat.ac.in

C. Ghosh and S. Kolathayar (eds.), *A System Engineering Approach to Disaster Resilience*, Lecture Notes in Civil Engineering 205, https://doi.org/10.1007/978-981-16-7397-9_21

1 Introduction

Increasing the resilience of the community became recognized as one of the major ways of dealing with disaster risk reduction along with increasing the efficiency of disaster response and bringing development control measures in vulnerable areas. Therefore, in order to explore the possibilities of coalescing disaster risk in revitalizing communities, it is highly important that we understand the concept, definitions and meanings of Urban Resilience and Urban Revitalization, their dimensions, interdependencies and inter linkages. Though both concepts intervene in blighted areas (reasons may vary) and have the common goal of betterment of the society, little work has been done integrating these concepts. Hence, the paper seeks to answer two questions-How can resilience be measured in a society? And how does enhancing the resilience of a community contribute to the revitalization of an area? The paper explores the concept of resilience and analyses the available methods to measure community disaster resilience and establishes how methods to enhance resilience can lead to revitalization of the place. Along with the concept and dimensions, the strategies used for revitalization is also studied and the analogies and variances of both the concepts is explored. The purpose of this study is to explore the possibilities of interlinking the concepts so that any revitalization project will help to enhance the resilience of the community and any attempt to enhance the resilience and mitigate disaster will have an added benefit of revitalizing the place itself.

2 Resilience and Measuring Disaster Resilience

There is no universally agreed definition on community resilience [1–4]. The malleability of the concept is depicted as its strength as well as weakness. The multiple meanings and interpretations of resilience portray the popularity of the term and the range of fields it is used [5]. The definition of resilience has evolved over the years and is still evolving and is constantly redefined [2]. After the adoption of Hyogo Framework for Action (HFA) 2005–15, there was a shift in vulnerability assessment method and the 'resilience-based approach' became more popular [6]. Subsequently, there was a proliferation of definitions on resilience by various authors and organizations globally and several international organizations devoted abundant resources in building resilient communities.

Among the many popular definitions of resilience, the one given by Walker et al. (2004) and cited by most authors is, 'the capacity of a system to absorb disturbance and reorganize while undergoing change so as to still retain essentially the same function structure identity and feedback' is often designated as resilience [7, 8]. Being resilient also means the ability to grow and improve in the face of hazards [9] and it is only in a resilient system there is opportunity for growth and development, renewal and revitalization.

The literature study reveals that a consensus has not been reached regarding the measurement of resilience and the volume and complexity of issues related to disaster reveals that a reliable measurement of resilience is not possible until a community has experienced a disaster and has recovered from it [10]. Though post disaster recoveries are too often addressed, planning for future disasters or measures to be taken by the community to face future disasters are seldom communicated. The assessment of resilience should also take care of the asymmetries within it, among different groups and individuals of the community. This denotes that the social capital and the vulnerability along various cross sections of the community need to be focused.

Though the method for assessing community resilience is not fully developed [11] and remains a challenge [12], the factors contributing to the increased or diminished capacity of a community to resist, absorb or restore the pre-disaster state has to be measured, [8, 11, 13] evaluated. Therefore, a framework that is capable of addressing these is needed rather than a technical apolitical framework. These frameworks can either be standardized or tailor made to the context in which it is used or it can be a combination of both the methods. The former method can be used in any country as those works on generalized assumptions whereas the latter takes care of the local conditions. When framing the resilience frameworks, all the mutually reinforcing dimensions of resilience fail to get included. The technical and political interpretations get highlighted while ecological and social aspects often take a backseat. A typical example has been found in the post disaster interventions in New Orleans following hurricane Kathrina [14].

2.1 Scales of Measurement

Scale is important in expressions of resilience [15]. The geographical scale varies from global level to individual level. Global level is the highest level of measurement. National level or country level is the common high level of measurement. Examples are Hyogo framework for action, Global focus model, prevalent vulnerability index, etc. Sub national or community level measurements are taken in three forms. It can be using political boundaries (District, Panchayats), distinguishing rural and urban (Cities, Towns) or defining a geographical area. Examples being Resilience Capacity Index, Baseline Resilience Indicators for Communities (BRIC), ResilUS, etc. Household or individual level is the smallest level or smallest unit of analysis. Example, Community-Based Resilience Analysis (CoBRA) [4].

2.2 Characteristics of Measurement

Disaster resilience can be measured in different ways. The approach adopted for measuring depends on the elements included in measurement, levels of measurement, the dimensions of resilience included and the smallest unit of analysis taken. The appropriateness of measurement in a context depends on the elements of disaster resilience included [4]. The measurements of resilience capacity tracks inputs (Govt inputs, inputs from community, sector or firms, household themselves), Outputs (reduction of exposure to disasters, vulnerabilities, resilience capacities and actions), Outcomes (actual losses or modeled losses base on probabilities) and impact (degree of well being maintained despite disasters) [4].

Resilience measurements can either use standard metrics, context specific metrics or a combination of both. Standard metrics are not flexible and fail to capture local conditions and circumstances. Context specific metrics are tailored to countries, communities, households or individuals. Example, National Response Coordination Center (NRCC) in Nepal andCommunity Disaster Resilience Index (CDRI) for coastal communities of US. A combination of both contains set of standard indicators with additional locally tailored measurements. Example, Community Based Disaster Resilience (CoBRA), Rural Resilience Index (RRI). Tailored measurements can be deduced using participatory processes.

2.3 *Dimensions/Capitals*

The major dimensions included in measurement of resilience of a community are Social, Economic, Human, Physical and Natural. These dimensions have been described as Community Capital [6]. These capitals portray the relationship that exists between individuals and their larger neighborhood. The most common capitals discussed in all literature include capitals namely Social, Economic and Natural, though Physical, Institutional, Political, Human capitals are also widely discussed capitals.

Economic capital indicates financial resources of the community. A stable or growing economy implies enhanced resilience whereas a community with declining and unbalanced economy implies increasing vulnerability or decreasing resilience. Economic capital can be measured through income, savings, investments, property, value, employment, etc., [6]. All the various earth systems comprising of atmosphere, water systems, soil and land, biologic and climatic are included in environmental capital, which is also referred to as natural capital. A healthy environment capital will contribute to other forms of capital. It refers to an eco system that has unpolluted air, water and soil. It is measured through air quality, water quality, soil quality wetland, forest, bio diversity, parks, etc., [6]. The four basic functions of environmental capital are regulation (that keeps our ecosystem in balance. Example, ozone layer), carrier (which provides space for human habitation, agriculture, production and recreation activities), production (what environment gives beyond basic subsistence Example, materials for building and manufacturing, fuel and energy) and information (includes varied perspectives of aesthetics, heritage, culture and science) [16]. Physical capital majorly refers to public structures which are always under the threat of destruction due to exploitation. The quality and location of the Physical capital is very important and it includes all physical and social infrastructures including residential buildings, public buildings, bridges, dams, canals, etc., [13]. Physical capital gains strength when the community has a strong human, social and cultural capital [17]. Human capital which is both innate and accumulated is one that enhances human labor productivity as it denotes skilled and trained working age population [6]. Additional to education and skills human capital also includes physical and mental health, emotional stability, etc. Enhancing human capital can be accomplished through institutions like schools, churches, recreation centers, community gathering spaces, etc., that will also support in building community cohesion [17]. Human capital is measured through educational status, health, dependence ratio, housing quality, etc., of the community which is also a prerequisite for capacity building and economic development.

The literature study reveals that the Social, Economic and Environmental capitals are critical to resilience of a place. The resilience of a community depends on the balance of its different capitals. The energy of one capital definitely affects the other forms of capital as all these are inter related, some deep and some subtle. Example, depletion of fishes can cause serious concern to social and economic capital of fishermen community [17].

The researcher has come across more than one hundred resilient assessment works in the literature study of which 25 popular assessment efforts were selected for detailed study based on the agency supporting the program, the year in which the effort was started, the context in which the framework was developed and the assessment method used, the location of study area and the scale of the study. The study revealed that the context of the study was majorly hazards to climate change, floods, hurricanes and cyclones followed by draught and earthquake. The majority of toolkits and indexes are to measure resilience at community level, though national and city level is not uncommon. It was also observed that the majority of tools were developed and applied in United States. Indonesia, Philippines, Thailand and India are other countries were assessment tools have been applied at city level and community level.

The majority of frameworks were developed using participatory method in which an initial set of indicators were developed, which was then modified by reaching a consensus with the stakeholders and expert group opinions. After the indicators are finalized, weights are assigned to each to assess the resilience of the community, except 'BRIC' and CCR-2, which solely depended on literature study. Very few frameworks were developed using public opinion and hence local needs and aspirations are not reflected in any of them. Currently there is no overarching method to develop a framework integrating literature framework and stakeholders and experts perceptions. Thus developing a new framework using a participatory approach has become the need of the hour.

3 Resilience and Sustainability

The concept of sustainability has shifted over the years. From 1960s to 70s the environment, society and economy was studied as separate disciplines, from 1970s to 1990s the emphasis was given to the interdependency of environment, society and economy and from 1990s to 2000s a dynamic model was evolved from a more static model. The concept of resilience, which is fundamentally the socio-ecological capacity to resist, cope and adapt to changes was incorporated into the linkages and dependencies of the three pillars of sustainability- Environment, Society and Economy to make it a more ideal scientific model. Resilience was first discussed associated with sustainability at 1st world summit on sustainable Development at Johannesburg in 2012, where the focus was on managing current resources assuring the welfare of future generations. Later resilience studies was considered as a necessary approach in building sustainability and started emerging in various sustainability debates and different policy domains as well [18]. According to Bene et al. 2014 the concept of resilience became the central criterion for many disciplines replacing sustainability as the ultimate objective of development. It is argued that in SDG goal 11, the concept of 'resilience' was poorly and too narrowly defined [19].

Resilience and sustainability are two distinct concepts positively correlated, though sometimes used interchangeably [19]. They are not mutually exclusive but are interwoven to transform the future towns and cities [20]. The world summit on sustainable Development at Johannesburg in 2002 asserted that both the concepts sustainability and resilience have certain common principles like precaution against overuse of resources, restraint from vulnerability and fostering ecological integrity [18]. Many authors have presented resilience as an important and crucial component of sustainability [21, 22] that works in the context of long term sustainability objectives [20]. Sustainability is increased resource efficiency and a sustainable community is one which strives to maintain a high quality of life, absorbs and adapts to internal and external stresses and persists through time with a healthy and thriving society, environment and economy [23]. Chellari et al., quotes Holling and Walker, 2003 that a region that is economically, ecologically and socially sustainable is also a resilient region.

4 Concept, Definition and Strategies Used for Revitalization

Every city grows through changes and development. Planning interference becomes inevitable as city grows, matures, becomes old, undergoes physical decay, gets struck with disasters (both natural and manmade) and becomes unfit for residential or business use as time passes. As time passes the existing land use may become incompatible with the surrounding land use. For example, the commercial area may expand into residential area, factories and prison built long ago can now be in the middle of the city, schools may be now situated in busy streets, there may exist outdated water supply lines and sewage and drainage line becoming detrimental to the modern society. These are common phenomenon that happens in a city. Hence to bring back the old vitality, improve or maintain the quality of life revitalization, regeneration, renewal, etc., becomes inevitable.

The meaning of revitalization according to Oxford dictionary is to impart new life or vigor. It also means 'Bringing again into activity and prominence'. It is the process of infusing vitality into areas that are judged to be in some way substandard. Revitalization means the physical development of blighted areas by improving the local infrastructure, creating additional jobs and may also involve elimination of undesirable business and groups [24]. According to Ujwala and Priya [25], urban revitalization is the process of rebuilding thriving economically, environmentally and socially sustainable urban areas and population, in areas that have been in decline. The goal of revitalization of degraded areas is not only to stop the deterioration of urban areas but also to rebuild the city, strengthen and enhance social cohesion, improve economic activities, provide good quality environment, provide adequate recreational facilities, regenerate historic centers and urban services and improve the quality of life [26, 27].

Though various strategies are used for revitalization of towns and cities, the most popular one is the 'cultural development strategy' that played a major role in the development of towns and cities, despite its size and demographic profile. The cultural activities and events facilitate to bolster a city's or town's image, attract tourism and foster economic development, and thereby museums, performing centers, conventional centers, galleries, etc., are built as a part of wider urban-regional development and revitalization strategy. The Cultural development can be achieved in multiple ways and hence can be grouped into three based on strategy goal, focus and target audience. They are entrepreneurial strategies, creative class strategies and progressive strategies. In entrepreneurial strategies, the brand identity of the city is reinforced and a proactive market driven approach is pursued, guided by solely economic objectives. Creative class strategies seek economic development through the provision of quality of life and providing recreational amenities to attract the creative class which includes software engineers, artists, architects, writers, etc. Progressive strategies follow a more grass root and neighborhood-based approach where local community needs and their cultural aspects are addressed ensuring equitable access to cultural resources [16].

Human investment strategies aim to improve the peoples capacities especially of youth and children by investments in human capital, job training, education enhancement, mentoring and internship, career counseling, etc., targeted to the unemployed and underemployed in order to give those individuals the necessary skill in the increasingly service oriented economy. The key process is to build human capital in deteriorated cities and create an infrastructure of support for disadvantaged. Example, Baltimore and New Orleans in US had made this strategy the foundation of all its revitalization efforts [28].

Downtown revitalization encompasses a wide range of individuals and activities. Therefore, it requires cooperation and funding from a multitude of sources like local government, chamber of commerce, private sectors, civic organizations and other key institutions. Downtown revitalization should include new housing and commercial businesses, after school programs, anti crime initiatives, youth development and employment services, arts, recreational opportunities and public transit and many more.

5 Interdependencies and Inter-Linkages of Concept of Resilience and Revitalization

According to a study conducted by Schreurs and Miranda in 2021, the city also needs informed people and trained specialists apart from the support of a strong government in order to achieve a sustainable resilient revitalization plan. A framework called Sustainable Resilient Urban Revitalization (SRUR) framework was developed to renovate the existing residential buildings in a historic district wherein the respondents' awareness of sustainability and resilience, prioritization of dimensions and promotion strategies were evaluated through Delphi method.

Tables 1 and 2 depicts the analogies and divergences of the concept of resilience and revitalization respectively. Table 1 discusses the similitude of the concepts, dimension, intervention areas, scale of the projects, approach followed, major strategies used, time scale of action, acceptance level of the concept, dependency and the final goal and outcome. Table 2 distinguishes resilience and revitalization conceptually even though the end goal and outcome are one and the same.

Table 1 Analogies in resilience and revitalization concepts

Characteristics	Similitude
The concept	Both the concept implies imparting new life, strength and vitality to an area or neighborhood
Dimensions	Both concepts are multi dimensional. The common dimensions of resilience and revitalization are social, economic, environmental, physical, institutional and human
Intervention area	Both concepts are applied in blighted areas and work on regaining the functionality
Scale of the project	Varies widely spatially
Approach	Bottom up interventions required as each community is unique having its own history, geography, culture, etc.
Major strategy	Public and private partnership, especially for physical development or infrastructure improvement
Time scale of action	Long term process, yet involves short term goals
Acceptance level of the concept	Both concepts are portrayed as positive desirable process
Dependency	Social capital/ neighborhood networks
Goal and outcome	Positive livelihood outcome –building a cohesive inclusive community

Table 2 Divergences in the concept of resilience and revitalization

Resilience	Revitalization
Emerged in 1973, but became popular only after 2000	Emerged in 1970s
Varies widely conceptually and spatially. Disaster resilience is the most popular one though other narrow forms of resilience also exist	No wide variations. It is the process of infusing vitality into sub standard areas, though emphasis is given on conserving identity, culture, etc.
Ability to bounce back after a stressful event	Bringing back again into activity and prominence
Speed of recovery or transformation is important	The temporal scale of revitalization is not so important
Arguments on the limitations of resilience are that the concept is complex and difficult to operationalize	Though revitalization is a broad concept with wide implications on all sectors, mostly practiced in a smaller area (core areas or along a stretch)

The application of both resilience and revitalization requires thorough analysis of economic, social, environmental and human aspects. The economic analysis includes the financial resources, livelihood pattern, employment and unemployment status, economic vitality of the community, education and health. The social analysis includes social capacity, social wellbeing, social cohesion, community facilities, affordable housing status and literacy level, extend of participatory planning, etc. The environmental analysis includes the natural resources, biodiversity, integrated solid waste management, etc. The human capital looks into the physical and mental health and the emotional stability of the dwellers. These inputs when combined with external drivers of change like policies, risk reduction strategies, progressive revitalization strategies, etc., along with internal drivers of change like availability of resources, inherent resilience capacity of the community leads to the desired outputs like economic development, physical improvement, social upliftment, environmental protection and cultural enhancement that reinforces the fact that disaster risk reduction and mitigation strategies and enhancement of community disaster resilience can lead to resurgence and revitalization of the area (refer Fig. 1).

6 Revitalizing Communities Coalescing Disaster Resilience

Increasing disaster resilience can lead to a new path in which the responsibilities as well as the merits of resilience are distributed within the community. This calls for incorporating resilience in our public policies. Only when a disaster strikes a community or country, these policies with broader goals and visions, surface to forefront that too only with a strong political will and leadership [10]. Example, in Fukushima, Japan the160,000 evacuees in 2012 had reduced to 43,000 in 2018, when

Fig. 1 Schematic diagram showing the interdependencies and interlinkages of Sustainability, resilience and revitalization concepts. *Source* Author

Fukushima prefecture issued a vision for revitalization which stressed on safe and secure sustainable society free of nuclear energy. Subsequently, the share of nuclear energy in its electricity mix reduced from 30% in 2011 to 6% in 2020 added by a dramatic shift and development in alternate energy sources. Today Japan has the largest installed photovoltaic capacity in the world [29].

7 Conclusion

Efforts to build back better with stronger infrastructure and technology, enhancing resilience and environmental quality will lead to a double bonus of reducing risks and revitalizing the villages, towns and cities [29]. A sustainable reconstruction approach that can conserve our resources for future generations is what is needed after a disaster. An immediate reconstruction after a disaster generally leads to a recreation of existing vulnerabilities and similar losses in future. Hence, long term policies for enhancing sustainability and resilience need to be incorporated in post disaster planning. To cite examples- In Nepal after 2015 earthquake, previous crops were replaced with a mix of Cardamom and Alder that helped to stabilize soil, increase biodiversity and reduce the risk of landslides. After 2009 earthquake, Italy decided to construct eco villages [30]. Hence the aim should be to create resilient cities and towns actively participating in promoting urban resilience policies. A resilient city is one that is dynamic, adaptive, transforming, always interacting with nature and addressing quality of life through better and greener urban planning [20]. Therefore, resilience is a process of maintaining an acceptable equilibrium in spite of continuously changing environment which needs continuous improvement and effort.

References

1. Nilding N (2011) Exploring community resilience in times of rapid change. Firey Spirits supported by Carnegie U K Trust, UK
2. *Review Article: Resilience, Poverty & Development.* Bene, Christopher, et al. 2014, Journal of International Development, 26, pp. 598–623.
3. Sharifi A, Yamagata Y (2014) Resilient urban planning: major principes and criteria. Energy Proceedia 61:1491–1495
4. Winderl T (2014) Disaster resilience measurements-stocktaking of ongoing efforts in developing systems for measuring resilience. United Nations Development Program
5. Aksha SK, Emrich CT (2020) Benchmarking community disaster resilience in Nepal. Int J Environ Res Publ Health 17(1985):1–22
6. Mayunga JS (2007) Understanding and applying the concept of community disaster resilience: a capital based approach. Munich. Draft working paper for Summer Academy for Social Vulnerability and Resilience building, Germany
7. Kunath A (2012) Exploring the resilience of urban systems; impact of social change on disaster risk management in shrinking cities. [book auth.] Lorenzo C, Marta O. Multidisciplinary perspectives on urban resilience. BC3 Basque Centre for Climate Change, Spain, Bilbao
8. Meerow S, Newell JP, Stults M (2016) Defining urban resilience: a review. Landscape and Urban planning 147, pp 38–49
9. Atreya A, Kunreuther H (2016) Measuring community resilience: the role of the community rating system (CRS). Pennsylvania: working paper 2016–17, Wharton risk management center, University of Pennsylvania
10. National Research Council (2012) Disaster resilience: a national imperative. The National Academies Press, Washington DC
11. Akamani K (2012) A community resilience model for understanding and assessing the sustainability of forest dependent communities. Hum Ecol Rev 19(2):99–109

12. Cutter SL et al (2008) A place based model for understanding community resilience to natural disasters. Glob Environ Change 18:598–606
13. Kaluarachchi Y (2018) Building community resilience in the resettlement of displaced communities. Proceedia Eng 212:443–450
14. Scoppetta C (2016) Natural disasters as (Non-Liberal) opportunity? Discussing post hurricane Kathrina urban regeneration in New Orleans. TeMA J Landuse Mob Environ 9(1):26–41
15. Robinson GM, Carson DA (2015) Resilient communities: transitions, pathways and resourcefulness. Geograph J 1–9
16. Grodach C, Loukaitou-Sideris A (2007) Cultural development strategies and urban revitalization. Int J Cult Policy 13(4)
17. Callagham EG, Colton J (2008) Building sustainability and resilience: a balancing of community capital. Environ Sustain 931–942
18. Chellari L, Olazabal M (2012) Multidisciplinary perspectives on urban resilience. BC3, Basque Centre for Climate Change, Bilbao, Spain
19. Elmqvist T et al (2019) Sustainability and resilience for transformation in the urban century. Nat Sustain 2:267–273
20. Tabibian M, Mohaved S (2016) Towards resilient and sustainable cities: a conceptual framework. Scientia Iranica 23(5):2081–2093
21. Meerow S, Newell JP (2016) Urban resilience for whom, what, when, where and why? Urban Geography
22. Adger WN (2000) Social and ecological resilience: are they related? Progress Hum Geograp 24(3):347–364
23. Mackendrick NA, Parkins JR (2004) Frameworks for assessing community sustainability: a synthesis of current research in British Columbia. Edmonton: Information report NOR-X-392, Canadian Forestry Service
24. Sean Z (2000) The art of Revitalization-improving conditions in distressed inner city neighbourhoods. Garland Publishing Inc., New York
25. Ujwala C, Priya C (2009) Revitalizing Chitar Oli, a street with a tradition. ITPI Journal 6(1):59–68
26. Alpopi C, Manole C (2013) Integrated urban regeneration- solution for cities revitalize. Proceedia Econ Fin 6:178–185
27. Ramlee M et al (2015) Revitalization of urban public spaces: an overview. Proceedia Soc Behav Sci 360–367
28. Wagner FW, Joder TE, Mumphrey AJ (2003) Human capital investment for central city revitalization. Routlege Publications, US
29. Schreurs MA (2021) Reconstruction and Revitalizationin Fukushima a decade after the 'triple disaster' struck: striving for sustainability and a new future vision. Int J Risk Reduction 53
30. Davidson A (2020) Disasters as an opportunity for improved environmetal condition. Int J Disaster Risk Reduction 48

Safeguard and Preventive Measures of Natural Disasters Using Early Warning Systems—A Comprehensive Review

S. Arvindan and D. S. Vijayan

Abstract A natural disaster is a progression of connected or unconnected events in nature that generates collapse, eradication, and losses of livelihood, life, property, and many more with extreme destruction, which is not caused or controlled by humans. Natural disasters affect natural resources and human-made property; therefore, to minimize the losses caused by natural disasters to save property, resources, and life. Addressing these problems becomes essential; hence, disaster management decides to adopt early warning system (EWS) to anticipate disaster to evacuating, safeguarding, and preventing humans as soon as possible. This paper presents the role of early warning systems in major natural disasters such as earthquakes, tsunamis, landslides, volcanos, wildfires, and epidemics. EWS attempts to reduce the risk of disasters by providing adequate and timely information by adopting numerous processes and tools to produce warning data through technical monitoring. Consequently, it generates awareness among the public for forecasting and predicting disaster, together with it has potentiality and reliability to operate 24 h a day. In the present day, many countries remarkably minimize the number of deaths by adopting EWS, but preventing infrastructure is still questionable for sudden disaster; however, moderate outbreak disasters can contribute considerable time to build up barriers and retrofitting buildings. EWS does not deliver satisfactory outcomes unless early action and communication are performed flawlessly; furthermore, warnings are still not efficiently communicated in developing countries and some developed countries due to not being technically vital in understanding the nature, locations, and frequencies. This proposed article provides detailed insight into the natural disasters using EWS for all major disasters and its evolution. Progress on the various aspects of EWS and its operation is reviewed in detail along with future scope and recommendations.

Keywords Early warning system · Natural disaster · Earthquakes · Volcano · Landslides · Epidemic

S. Arvindan (✉) · D. S. Vijayan
Civil Engineering, Aarupadai Veedu Institute of Technology (AVIT), Vinayaka Missions Research Foundation (VMRF), Paiyanoor, Chennai 603104, India

D. S. Vijayan
Anand School of Architecture, Chennai 603103, India

C. Ghosh and S. Kolathayar (eds.), *A System Engineering Approach to Disaster Resilience*, Lecture Notes in Civil Engineering 205, https://doi.org/10.1007/978-981-16-7397-9_22

1 Introduction

In order to avoid disasters and alert the early warning system (EWS), it is very critical before taking appropriate precautions. Improving EWS would boost the ability of all related national entities to provide prompt and successful early warnings. These projects are designed to help minimize risks, strengthen protection, and raise consciousness in regions that are vulnerable to disasters and climate change. Providing and improving monitoring equipment, building capacity, and training in the way weather stations are maintained and data collected would enable communities to become more resilient. Mao et al. demonstrated an iBMW, integrated biosensor system with mobile health and wasted water-based epidemiology to monitor the feasibility of the widespread COVID-19 worldwide. This system also helps prevent the rapid intervention and diagnosis concerning the other technologies with point-of-care biosensors' help. The POC biosensors respond to the information everywhere so quickly. Mainly, to minimize the pandemic's effect and prevent, monitor, and intervene in disaster management, the iBMW was proposed as an ideal framework [1]. Hammood et al. studied the successful utilization of flood early warning and response system (FEWRS) to prevent flood disaster's hazardous impact. The information system (IS) was conducted in FEWRS for the factors of educational quality, confirmation, perceived risks, complexity, relative advantage, user experience, compatibility, perceived ease of use, net benefits, intention to use, perceived usefulness, service quality, user satisfaction, information, and service quality in this whole study. Based on Regan and Wymer's standards, these factors were analyzed in disaster management to improve the performance of FEWRS and the utilization of the correct information technology system [2].

Zhao et al. analyzed the characteristics of different earthquake antecedents and the advantages of satellite remote sensing mechanisms for earthquake prediction. The data collected from the diversity of earthquake antecedent signals, the hypocenter's unobservability, and the features of the complexity were discussed. Four kinds of remote sensing technologies were adopted for these bottleneck processes, such as; gravity remote sensing, earth deformation remote sensing, electromagnetic remote sensing, and thermal infrared remote sensing to resolve them by reducing the risk of earthquakes in advance [3]. Li et al. presented that the initiate asperity theory from seismology enhances the embodiment level of landslide injury. The injury management interface is evenly spaced between four pore water pressure sensors and four soil pressure sensors. The results of the screening show that the sliding interface has asperity competency, and the landslide error is a movement process nonlinear. In order to do this, we are building the corresponding monitoring sensors on the surface area. An early warning method of terrestrial disasters was used for asperity theory. In future, this would boost incarnation and monitoring [4].

Fakhruddin et al. presented that the work discusses the value of danger communication as a critical component of early alerting and explores the same challenges that vulnerable communities face. The too sophisticated forecasting models and emerging early alerting methods that can be rendered in impactive is not communicated clearly. These challenges are used to fast onset dangers such as tsunamis and cyclones and slow down onset dangers such as the present COVID-19 pandemic [5]. Nury Morales-Simfors et al. studied that the critical reviews stride in random-based operations from the year 2000 onward and index anomalous random variations found in groundwater and soils. Many precursors have been remarked before the temblor or volcanic incident. Thus, no precursor can be applied for forecasting, yet retrace due to netting various complex overlapping and interacting chemical and physical methods. A dense network would require potentially viable quick and precise measurements of random over huge regions, resulting in underline valuable and episodic statistical data [6].

2 Floods

The most common form of natural disaster is the flooding, occurring when an overflow of water is overwhelmingly dry. Heavy rainfall, quick snowmelt, or a tropical cyclone or tsunami in coastal areas also cause flooding. Perera et al. studied the flood early warning system (FEWS) involving warning community and communication response capabilities. With these public collaborations, the financial and technical restraints were discussed under disaster risk reduction (DRR) policies at all levels of FEWS. Moreover, civil society organizations (CSOs) were adopted to respond positively to provide the solution for community concerns at local level challenges and to boost resilience to disaster, campaigns were held for DRR awareness at local areas [7]. Almoradie et al. explained the advantages of flood risk management (FRM) at Ghana in West Africa and found the recent gaps in developing resilience. For this opportunity of development based on the response of 53 commodities, an online investigation was conducted as the FRM in Ghana includes various pressures, drivers, and actors and multifaceted. The main focus of FEWS is to improve public awareness and the willingness of civilians and stakeholders to co-operate with FRM. From the above observation, it is concluded that the FRM is reactive rather than preventive, and the researched actors perceive FRM, interviewed stakeholders were different in contrasting approach of the success of Ghana's FRM [8].

Eibl et al. demonstrated the advanced early warning system in Iceland's subglacial flood area. The seismic ground vibration (SGV) data, GPS data, and unusual multidisciplinary hydrological data were analyzed to tracing the subglacial flood front. Before entering the river, the flood's size and time were achieved for small and large floods. For the small flood, the accretion time is 1.3 years and peak discharge = 210 ~ 380 m^3/s, and for the large flood, the time is 5.25 years, and peak discharge is more fabulous than 3000 m^3/s approximately [9]. Hussain et al. narrated a statement on the farmers' livelihoods during the natural disaster. Due to a lack of accurate information, the extreme weather changes affected farmers economically and financially as they adopted coping techniques in Multan, Punjab. By diversification of

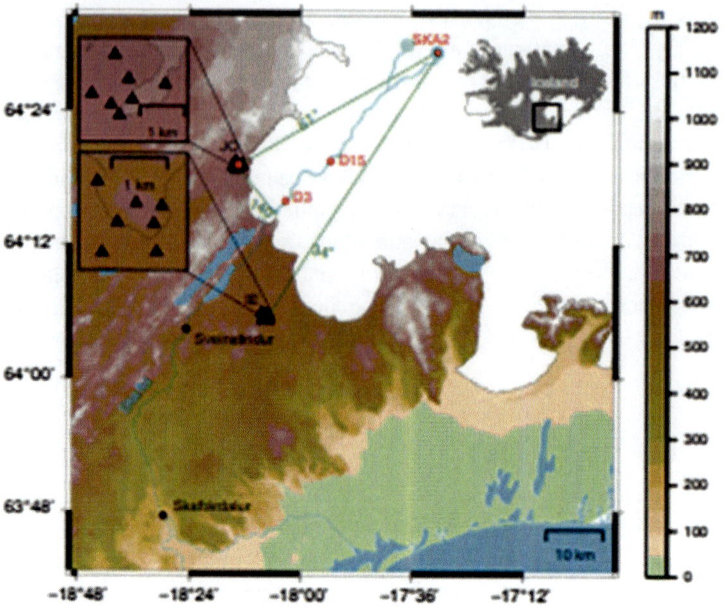

Fig. 1 Multidisciplinary flood monitoring [11]

their income and adopting sustainable natural resource conservation and management programs, the risk of daily living can be reduced. To make the farmers more capable of coping with the weather shock, some skill improvement events need to be made, and advanced early warning systems with lower access technology and information to spread public awareness. Also, some cash support like small exchangeable loans and money transfers can help them so far [10]. Figure 1 depicts monitoring of flood by adopting multidisciplinary techniques.

Chang et al. developed an advanced self-organized map that can trace typhoons up to two days earlier in Taiwan for flood prognosticates. In this study, the machine learning procedure may develop the flood early warning system (FEWS) for reservoir and risk management. This method was used to track typhoons by using flood hydrographs and the used modeling-induced predicting flood hydrographs, clustering vectors, and identifying typhoon track vectors [12].

3 Earthquake

Earthquake can be described as earthquake, induced by waves moving down and down the surface of the earth that cause: vibration of the region, vibration of tremors, license, slides, post-shocks, and/or tsunamis. The time and severity of the aftershocks are aggravating factors. Tomofumi et al. revealed the effectiveness of various kinds of succeeding generation downward forced gradiometers to detect the earthquake earlier through simulations. Based on seismic waves, both the small (*Mw* 7) and large (*Mw* > *8*) earthquakes were estimated according to their magnitude, and the small earthquake was proposed as more effective in induced gravity signals of earthquake early warning systems (EEWSs). With the help of signal-to-noise ratio (SNR) value and earthquake detector and focal mechanism, the occurrence of earthquake epicenter about 140 km in the distance can be detected within 10 s [13]. Julia et al. investigated Aotearoa New Zealand citizens' survey to find out the public response to the utilization of the earthquake early warning (EEW) system. The EEW system was considered positively through people's anticipated actions during the earthquake. The public acceptance of EEW will help the future better by the more comfortable and quicker action taken within a short period (<10 s) to prevent an earthquake [14].

Francesco et al. estimated an uncertain kernel-based density calculator to evaluate the location density with given time individually with smartphone applications. The maximum high spatio-temporal intention location data collected from the advanced phones with GPS were estimated for worldwide early warning systems in time. The ungenerous is more acceptable to model location data collected by using social networks [11]. Masaru et al. insisted on the tsunami scenarios of megathrust earthquakes. Based on slip probability density function (SPDF), the framework of earthquakes for anticipated future *Mw* 8.2 Tonankai earthquake in Japan was estimated. The predicted and peak tsunami entrant time and amplitude were computed for both uniform and heterogeneous slip distribution in tsunami disaster assuagement from the estimation [15]. Figure 2 shows initial prediction of Tsunami using advanced technologies.

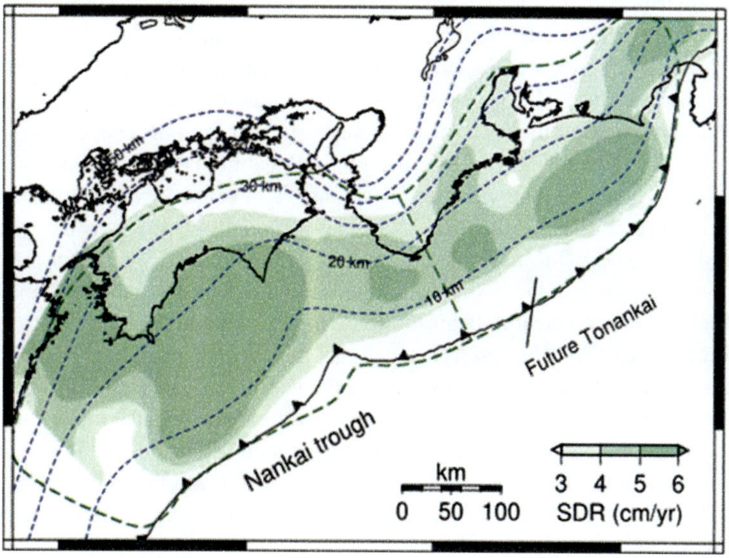

Fig. 2 Prediction of Tsunami occurs due to earthquake [16]

Yuan et al. reported an estimation about the entrance of the evolutionary enormousness for EEWS in the Sichuan-Yunnan zone in China. In this analysis, 273 programs have estimated the magnitude with τcand Pd (early warning parameters) along with P-wave time windows (PTW), where the combination of Pd and τc was considered to confirm the exact estimation for low-magnitude programs with vigorous magnitudes estimated for large earthquakes. Moreover, from the Ms 8.0 Wenchuan earthquake, the collected data's effectiveness during 2016–2017 enhanced the upcoming execution of the EEWS in the seismically vulnerable zones in China [17].

4 Landslides

Landslides can be triggered in pistes already on the rim of runoff, snowmelt, water level changes, water erosion, ground water changes, earthquakes, volcanic activity, or some combination thereof. Roberto studied a new methodology for defining the rainfall threshold for perfunctory landslides. A physically rooted transient rainfall infiltration and grid-based regional slope-stability (TRIGRS) model was applied for multiple computations of safety factors using various rainfall events. This technique could increase the effectiveness of the present LEWS, which could allow the analyses of specific areas of interest due to high susceptibility to shallow early warnings [18]. In the hilly area of the Sichuan Diocese, Zhihen et al. conveyed the data from the thorough discovery of landslides and plumes. The research analyzed the impacts on the occurrence of landslides of both rainfall and environmental factors. A landslide susceptibility index was measured using a multi-component perceptron model to express environmental factors in order to return the local landslide sensitivity. There is a probability model that combines the vulnerability and rainfall index for landslides. A logistic regression dissection was used to quantify the terrestrial threat. The conclusions indicate that it is necessary to incorporate the susceptibility index and precipitation system to improve the timeliness and precision of local early warning slides [19]. The movement of the soil using InSAR technology in landslides in Fig. 3.

Luca et al. presented the work that designates a new user-friendly tool to apply the EDuMaP process. For the "SMART" alarm model operating in the Piemonte region of Italy, the EDuMaP tool was applied. There are also significant problems and optimistic issues in the juxtaposition between the outputs of shallow landslides movement announced in rainfall thresholds (SMART) with other models that are used in different Te-LEWS. The results showed that the above approach could lead to an inaccurate and unprofessional assessment of the warning model [16]. Johannes et al. (2020) suggested the analysis of the upcoming big miscarriage of the rock slope at the Hochvogel summit. A measurement tape extensometer indicates a 35 cm opening of a central seam, with mean campaign speeds of 9.6 mm/month between 2014 and 2020. A high-resolution crack-opening and rain data automated geotechnical operating process is in operation from 2018 [20].

Chun et al. reported that the united multi-temporal landslide inventories in logistic return patterns could be seen as the embodiment of rainfall that triggered landslide

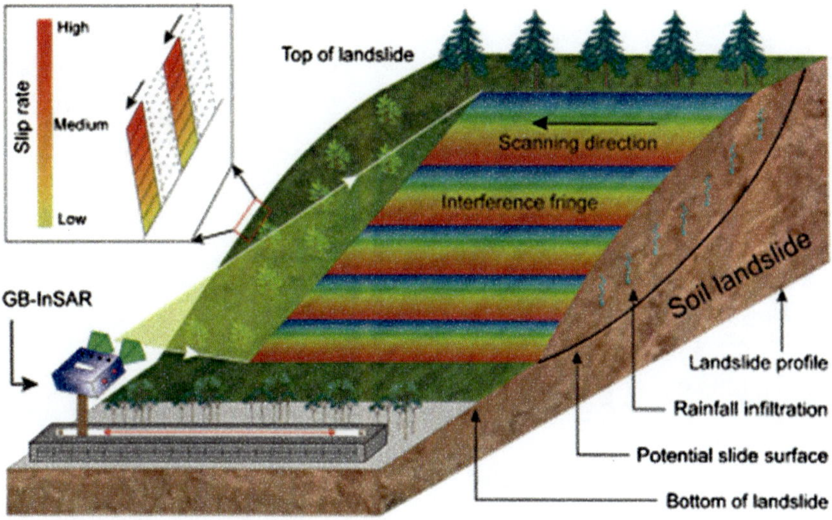

Fig. 3 Anticipation of soil movement using ground-based InSAR [4]

danger beneath weather change. A technology called quantitative precipitation estimation and segregation using multiple sensors (QPESUMS) was adopted to gain a spatio-temporal rainfall model and help prevent hill slope disasters beneath weather change. The overall outcomes show that the calibrated model 2005 is elevated in the general period with the precision of 78%; for highly rainfall typhoons, the calibrated pattern of 2009 would perform excellently (72%) [21].

5 Tsunami

A tsunami is a massive wave of devastation that is possible due to any disruption that quickly displaces a large mass of water triggered by an earthquake, volcanic eruption, or the impact of a meteorite. However, an undersea earthquake is the most common cause. Alexa et al. said that the study showed that there is a significant shift in convictions when it comes to an immediate evacuation and tsunami. It is over-sized for those in the flooded region in contrast to those outside the hazardous zone, despite the sense of tension associated with potential evacuations. These findings increase anxiety, given the importance for those confronted with difficulties for personal and evacuation intentions. Our findings show how different perceptions from the same perception of danger impact: urgencies and future plans for evacuation in different ways [22]. The magnitude Mw 7.8 Palu, Indonesia temblor occurred on September 28, 2018 at 10:02 UTC, Jann-Yenq et al. There, the tsunami moving ionospheric disturbances are observed by records of the five terrestrial worldwide satellite navigation systems (GNSS) reception systems (TTIDS). A total of 15 TTIDS

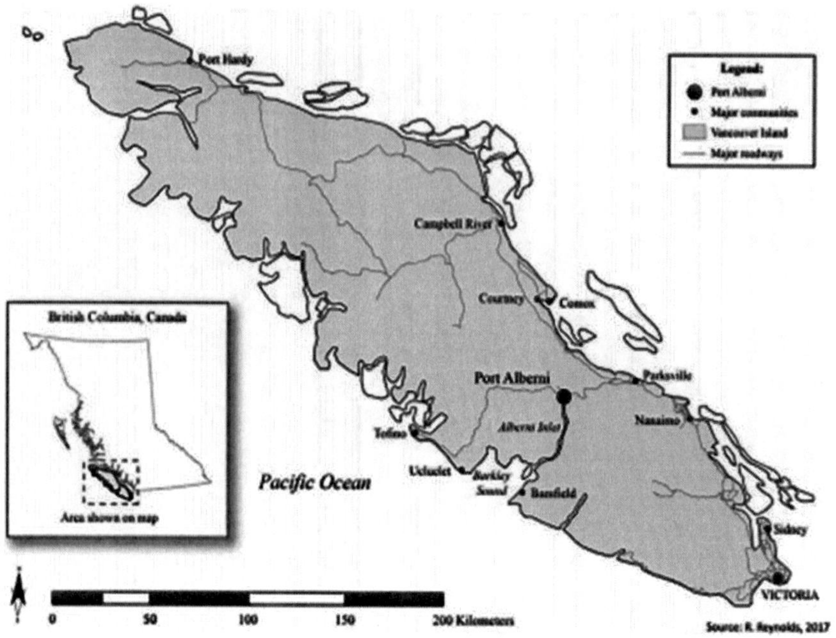

Fig. 4 Tsunami prediction in Vancouver Island [25]

were found. The tsunami source place, rooted in the results of both techniques, also includes a bootstrap method. They have also used the method of monitoring the tsunamis in order to assess the possible sites in Palu Bay. They identify coastal landslides through video study, field survey, and satellite images [23].

Sofyan et al. presented that the researchers examined how Acens disaster management and preparedness have developed since the 2004 center point of its early warning system (EWS), and especially, how the timely united EWS approach has been incorporated into its evolution and monitoring. Much research is made where the findings recommend that a multi-hazard EWS is not well-evolved, and a linear EWS pattern is imminent. The adequate instructions are made to review policy and practice for Aceh governments at territorial and district levels and other stakeholders to enhance the present EWS [24]. Figure 4 depicts map of Vancouver Island to predict Tsunami.

6 Volcano

Volcanic eruptions are general exits of hot magma (lava) or earthen materials, which form high pressure and temperature flight from the mantle through various crustacean defaults or vents. Often the magma gets its way out of the mantle due to intense pressure and heat. The tectonic movement or movement of the different layers of the crust can also cause the volcanic eruption. Aloisi et al. proposed a combining systematic and FEM modeling of all achievable continuous deformation data, centering on signals over 24–25 December when continuous distortion networks recorded clean variations straightly related to the dyke ascent. There is also a high-price GPS enabled soon and reliable source model. There are borehole types of equipment starting one hour before those recorded by GPS and mainly made it able to enhance the dyke ascent modeling [26]. Asyik et al. presented the application operating for active volcanoes applying wireless sensor network (WSN) and Internet Of Things (IoT). Our primary purpose was to generate low-energy consumption resilient, integrated, dolly to deploy, and power saving. Indonesia hosts 127 active monitorable for the activity around the clock. It shows that the higher the number of monitoring points, the more costly it will be to earn the equipment needed for the volcano monitoring. Thus, it needs monitoring devices that are dominant and efficient [27].

Chu et al. have expressed the evolution of the latest volcanic hot spots automated detection algorithm (FYVOLC) using new-generation Chinese satellite FY-4A data. By adding a regular brightness temperature difference index (NbIDI), FYVOLC improves the sensing capability of the volcanic anomaly program (VAST) algorithm to lower the impact of cold cloud. The FYVOLC algorithm is stable with more accurate detection and less inaccurate or false detection betide. The FYVOLC overall wrong rate was 12%; the 11% misstate the right rate was 89–97%. The variations of thermal anomaly can also be introduced by FYVOLC during time [25]. The entire volcanic eruption phase in Mount Etna is shown in Fig. 5.

Giudicepietro et al. submitted the main volcanic crisis in Stromboli in the last decades and its implications for hazards and injuries during the eruptive stage of

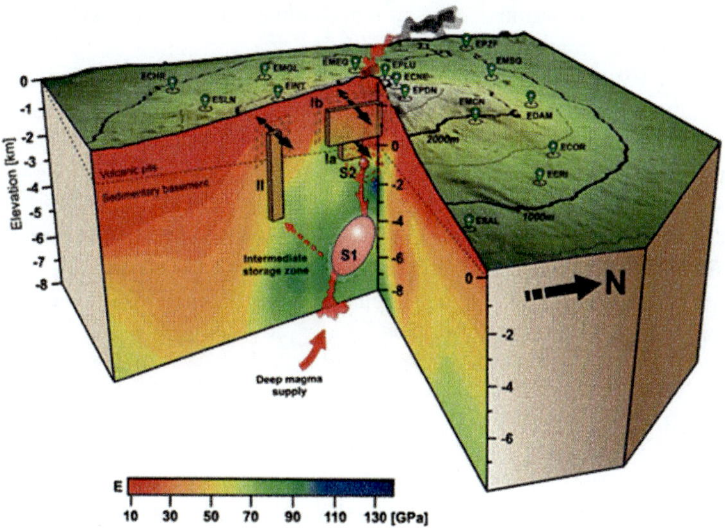

Fig. 5 Process of volcanic eruption in mount etna [28]

July–August 2019. More precisely, before the start of the eruptive crisis in July–August 2019 there were no remarkable changes in seismic amplitude. However, the VLP (several long period) and VLP amplitudes increased sharply between about a month before the height of July 3. These changes suggest higher gas content in the explosive activity of Stromboli. Our study recommended that gas be a big part of the eruptive dynamics of Stromboli and that two kinds of magmas, LP, and HP magma co-exist. These parameters could mitigate the effects on the island of potential violent explosion [29].

Mereu et al. studied the relevance for the competence of paroxysmal operation in Etna of the combined use of the TIR camera, the polarimetric X-band, and the Doppler L-band radars. In 2013 and 2015, current dissection 5 Etna eruptions took place. We implemented a retrieval algorithm for the Jet Areas (JR3A) rooted in a verdict tree combining the observable polarimetric X-band with the impaction of 1band radar, aiming at exantheme IJR height detection. In an early warning system, it offers information of all climatique conditions and the advantage of using a polarimetric X-band climate radar. We also show that JR3A can also be collected in unclean environments if data cannot be processed by the thermal infrared (TIR) camera [30].

7 Future Scope and Recommendation

Future scope and recommendation of the EWS will improve the broad research areas and efficiency in this system very effectively. Some of the predicted progress and recommendations are given below.

- EWS can be used as a monitoring system continuously from the beginning till the end for both short and long-term
- Future of EWS requires a greater understanding of technical gadgets used for applications like signal processing, instrumentation, and mathematical techniques to predict natural disasters or any unusual events
- The future approach toward EWS should consider cost consumptions to apply this technique even in remote areas
- EWS systems should be designed to favorable for all environmental conditions to predict the event more accurately
- Advanced technology should be adopted to predict natural disasters with higher efficiency and lower cost

8 Conclusion

The current paper has presented a critical review of methodologies applied to enhance the early warning systems for natural disasters to alert people before the event. Best practices strategies were discussed to improve the early warning systems provided by crucial guideline refine from the literature. Key findings from this review article are outlined below.

- The most comprehensive studies provided in this analysis with detailed operational evaluation and monitoring systems all-inclusive before and after disasters events
- The review has focused on a wide range of approaches being applied in the literature when undertaking operational evaluation
- The approaches applied in each case study were influenced by the pivotal performance of early warning systems for major natural disasters such as earthquake, volcano, landslides, tsunami, epidemic, and extreme flooding
- The early warning system is based on the decision-making process with monitoring data and previous experience.
- Discussion on various advanced early warning systems to predict natural disasters as early as possible to take precautions

Application of early warning systems has been discussed in detail with the help of previous works reported.

References

1. Mao K, Zhang H, Yang Z (2020) An integrated biosensor system with mobile health and wastewater-based epidemiology (iBMW) for COVID-19 pandemic. Biosens Bioelectron 169. https://doi.org/10.1016/j.bios.2020.112617
2. Hammood WA, @Asmara SM, Arshah RA, Hammood OA, Al Halbusi H, Al-Sharafi MA (2020) Factors influencing the success of information systems in flood early warning and response systems context. Telkomnika (Telecommunication Comput Electron Control 18(6):2956–2961. https://doi.org/10.12928/TELKOMNIKA.v18i6.14666
3. Zhao X, Pan S, Sun Z, Guo H, Zhang L, Feng K (2021) Advances of satellite remote sensing technology in earthquake prediction. Nat Hazards Rev 22(1):03120001. https://doi.org/10.1061/(asce)nh.1527-6996.0000419
4. Li S, Li C, Yao D, Liu C (2020) Interdisciplinary asperity theory to analyze nonlinear motion of loess landslides with weak sliding interface. Landslides 17(12):2957–2965. https://doi.org/10.1007/s10346-020-01479-3
5. Fakhruddin B, Clark H, Robinson L, Hieber-Girardet L (2020) Should I stay or should I go now? why risk communication is the critical component in disaster risk reduction. Prog Disaster Sci 8:100139.https://doi.org/10.1016/j.pdisas.2020.100139
6. Morales-Simfors N, Wyss RA, Bundschuh J (2020) Recent progress in radon-based monitoring as seismic and volcanic precursor: a critical review. Crit Rev Environ Sci Technol 50(10):979–1012. https://doi.org/10.1080/10643389.2019.1642833
7. Perera D, Agnihotri J, Seidou O, Djalante R (2020) Identifying societal challenges in flood early warning systems. Int J Disaster Risk Reduct 51:101794. https://doi.org/10.1016/j.ijdrr.2020.101794
8. Almoradie A et al. (2020) Current flood risk management practices in Ghana: gaps and opportunities for improving resilience. J Flood Risk Manag 13(4). https://doi.org/10.1111/jfr3.12664
9. Eibl EPS, Bean CJ, Einarsson B, Pàlsson F, Vogfjörd KS (2020) Seismic ground vibrations give advanced early-warning of subglacial floods. Nat Commun 11(1). https://doi.org/10.1038/s41467-020-15744-5

10. Hussain A, Memon JA, Hanif S (2020) Weather shocks, coping strategies and farmers' income: a case of rural areas of district Multan, Punjab. Weather Clim Extrem 30:100288. https://doi.org/10.1016/j.wace.2020.100288
11. Nakano M, Murphy S, Agata R, Igarashi Y, Okada M, Hori T (2020) Self-similar stochastic slip distributions on a non-planar fault for tsunami scenarios for megathrust earthquakes. Prog Earth Planet Sci 7(1). https://doi.org/10.1186/s40645-020-00360-0
12. Chang LC, Chang FJ, Yang SN, Tsai FH, Chang TH, Herricks EE (2020) Self-organizing maps of typhoon tracks allow for flood forecasts up to two days in advance. Nat Commun 11(1):1–13. https://doi.org/10.1038/s41467-020-15734-7
13. Shimoda T, Ampuero J, Montagner J (2020) Early earthquake detection capabilities of different types of future-generation gravity gradiometers
14. Becker JS, Potter SH, Vinnell LJ, Nakayachi K, McBride SK, Johnston DM (2020) Earthquake early warning in Aotearoa New Zealand: a survey of public perspectives to guide warning system development. Humanit Soc Sci Commun 7(1):1–3. https://doi.org/10.1057/s41599-020-00613-9
15. Finazzi F, Paci L (2020) Kernel-based estimation of individual location densities from smartphone data. Stat Model 20(6):617–633. https://doi.org/10.1177/1471082X19870331
16. Piciullo L, Tiranti D, Pecoraro G, Cepeda JM, Calvello M (2020) Standards for the performance assessment of territorial landslide early warning systems. Landslides 17(11):2533–2546. https://doi.org/10.1007/s10346-020-01486-4
17. Wang Y, Li S, Song J (2020) Threshold-based evolutionary magnitude estimation for an earthquake early warning system in the Sichuan-Yunnan region, China. Sci Rep 10(1):1–12. https://doi.org/10.1038/s41598-020-78046-2
18. Marin RJ (2020) Physically based and distributed rainfall intensity and duration thresholds for shallow landslides. Landslides 17(12):2907–2917. https://doi.org/10.1007/s10346-020-01481-9
19. Wang Z, Wang D, Guo Q, Wang D (2020) Regional landslide hazard assessment through integrating susceptibility index and rainfall process. Nat Hazards 104(3):2153–2173. https://doi.org/10.1007/s11069-020-04265-5
20. Leinauer J, Jacobs B, Krautblatter M (2020) Anticipating an imminent large rock slope failure at the Hochvogel (Allgäu Alps). Geomech Tunn 13(6):597–603. https://doi.org/10.1002/geot.202000027
21. Tseng C-W et al (2020) Application of high-resolution radar rain data to the predictive analysis of landslide susceptibility under climate change in the Laonong watershed, Taiwan. Remote Sens 12(23):3855. https://doi.org/10.3390/rs12233855
22. Tanner A, Reynolds R (2020) The near-miss of a tsunami and an emergency evacuation: the post-exposure effects on future emergency preparedness and evacuation intentions. Nat Hazards 104(2):1679–1693. https://doi.org/10.1007/s11069-020-04239-7
23. Liu JY et al. (2020) The source detection of 28 September 2018 Sulawesi tsunami by using ionospheric GNSS total electron content disturbance. Geosci Lett 7(1). https://doi.org/10.1186/s40562-020-00160-w
24. Sufri S, Dwirahmadi F, Phung D, Rutherford S (2020) Progress in the early warning system in Aceh province, Indonesia since the 2004 earthquake-tsunami. Environ Hazards 19(5):463–487. https://doi.org/10.1080/17477891.2019.1653816
25. Chu SS et al (2020) Automated volcanic hot-spot detection based on FY-4A/AGRI infrared data. Int J Remote Sens 41(6):2410–2438. https://doi.org/10.1080/01431161.2019.1688887
26. Aloisi M, Bonaccorso A, Cannavò F, Currenti G, Gambino S (2020) The 24 December 2018 eruptive intrusion at Etna volcano as revealed by multidisciplinary continuous deformation networks (CGPS, Borehole Strainmeters and Tiltmeters), vol 125(8)
27. Hidayatullah NA et al (2020) Volcano multiparameter monitoring system based on internet of things (IoT). Aust J Electr Electron Eng 17(3):228–238. https://doi.org/10.1080/1448837X.2020.1817250
28. Aloisi M, Bonaccorso A, Cannavò F, Currenti G, Gambino S (2020) The 24 december 2018 eruptive intrusion at Etna volcano as revealed by multidisciplinary continuous deformation networks (CGPS, borehole strainmeters and tiltmeters). 125(8)

29. Giudicepietro F et al (2020) Geophysical precursors of the July-August 2019 paroxysmal eruptive phase and their implications for Stromboli volcano (Italy) monitoring. Sci Rep 10(1):1–16. https://doi.org/10.1038/s41598-020-67220-1
30. Mereu L, Scollo S, Bonadonna C, Freret-Lorgeril V, Marzano FS (2020) Multisensor characterization of the incandescent jet region of lava fountain-fed tephra plumes. Remote Sens 12(21):1–18. https://doi.org/10.3390/rs12213629

Potentiality Assessment of Community Open Space for Disaster Management Purpose: A Participatory Approach to Reduce Disaster Vulnerability on a Community

Sharmin Akter, Most. Asma Khatun, Tanmoy Dev, Nazia Hossain, and Dulal Sarker

Abstract Urban open spaces can be defined as one of the most critical component of city design that provides recreational, social, and other facilities to the city dwellers. Besides, these places have a great influence on repairing climate change impact and solving other environmental issues. Nevertheless, the concept of integrating the planning and management strategies of urban open spaces with disaster management strategy development remains unanticipated in the context of urban planning. In this study, the concept of the community participated disaster vulnerability reduction has been applied to identify associated risk, capacity, and potentiality of using open spaces for disaster management purposes. At every step, various types of participatory planning tools were used to identify the best reliable options. In the first step, the community assessed and identified associated risks regarding existing open space and waterbody preservation and use. Community people identified rapid urbanization as the major cause of open space and waterbody reduction. In the second phase, community capacity in terms of institutional organization and community resources was identified. At the final stage, opinion from community people, interview of the key informant, and expert opinion survey helped a lot to identify the potentiality of open spaces and water bodies for disaster management purposes. Community developed strategies and different types of proposals from community peoples and experts have also proposed to identify the ultimate potentiality. Although this study was conducted only for a specific community, the method can be applied to identify all of the aspects of disaster management for other communities as well.

Keywords Community open space · Water bodies · Community participation · Disaster management · Participatory vulnerability reduction (PVR)

S. Akter (✉) · Most. Asma Khatun · T. Dev · N. Hossain · D. Sarker
Department of Urban and Regional Planning, RUET, Rajshahi, Bangladesh

C. Ghosh and S. Kolathayar (eds.), *A System Engineering Approach to Disaster Resilience*, Lecture Notes in Civil Engineering 205, https://doi.org/10.1007/978-981-16-7397-9_23

1 Background of the study

Social spaces are the mirror of society [17]. Open space in urban areas is an urban space that is open and accessible in nature. Accessibility system is open for people of all ages, gender, classes, ethics or socio-economic level. As like, Parks and Open Green grounds are open and accessible in nature. And these open spaces are successful only when these places become able to meet the recreational, social and psychological needs of the space users as well as the city dwellers [3, 5]. Apart from fulfilling social, recreational and psychological needs of the city dwellers, spatial planning and modelling of open spaces also aims of maintaining the environmental quality of the city. But, decreasing number of open spaces at urban areas creates a threat towards maintaining the environmental and social quality of the city [1]. According to the updated master plan of Rajshahi city at 2008 by Rajshahi Development Authority (RDA), the identified number of open spaces were 95 with the area of 125.37 acres. But in recent time, through ground-truthing of the identified places, presence of only 65 open spaces were confirmed with the area of 89.73 acres [15]. Not only the reduction but also less use and not used at all is one of the major problems in most of the urban open spaces. But in case of making cities more resilient and sustainable, increasing recognition, use and development of urban open spaces is must require [7]. Beyond the use of the open spaces for recreational purpose, effective management and implication of these open places can also have a great impact to make the city more resilient [10]. But, lack of proper and planned consideration such an important resource of our city is losing its significance day by day. Plans regarding using urban open spaces as a strategy for disaster resilient city development will be more effective if the community people can be incorporated in the planning process. So, this study aims to analyze existing using scenarios of the open spaces and to provide some community-based solutions for effective management of existing open spaces as well as using these places at the time of natural disaster (fire hazard, waterlogging).

2 Literature Review

2.1 Concept of Community Open Spaces and Their Importance

A smart urban management can fulfill the goal of making city more resilient that can also be termed as qualitative urban planning. Effective and sufficient number of open spaces at the city area provides the benefits of improving urban performance in case of normal situation or at the eve of any disaster situation [9]. Community open spaces provide space for community gathering, for relaxation and for different types of cultural and physical activities. Mostly, it plays vital role in social interaction and influences people's behavior [9, 16]. Green open spaces play vital role for physical activities of city dwellers and are potential to reduce stress as well as mental health improvement of them [4]. In most of the cases, open spaces at city area act as a space to celebrate diversified activities, a place to meet strangers, to spend a quality time at natural environment [21]. Recreational use of public open spaces added huge economic benefit to city's development. Presence of natural, architectural, cultural and recreational elements at public places increase property value as well as revenue of municipalities [8]. Small food carts, street hops are common in urban open spaces and parks which adds an economic value to these spaces.

2.2 *Using Open Spaces as a Tool for Disaster Management*

Potentiality of using open spaces can be integrated at three main aspects of disaster management. These are emergency response phase, recovery phase, and mitigation strategy development. At present, planning and designing consideration of open spaces mainly focuses on social issues. After that economic and environmental issue comes. All of three items are mainly the pillars of sustainability. And sustainable development always includes the issues of disaster resilience at the city design and development manual. so, at the time of planning and design consideration of open spaces these issues must be considered [14]. Due to rapid growth, urbanization, encroachment of open lands, green coverage of the city reduced and impermeable surface increases. Thus, water holding capacity of ground surface has decreased much [11]. In different case studies of flood occurrences in US, concluded that maintaining the wetlands was far cheaper option to reduce flood occurrences than building any kind of Dam or dykes. The case study of San Francisco earthquake (1906) was examined through morphological analysis and found a relationship between city's-built form and open spaces at the time of earthquake and subsequent fire. Open spaces during that time were transformed into shelter for survivors [2]. In order to mitigate disaster such as, fire hazards, earthquake, major role played by the open space network is to rescue the victims to safer place. Regulations of National Disaster Management Agency No 11/2008 states that high accessibility at the households and adequate number of open spaces are most important for post disaster recovery activities. Network of open space also identified as a most effective tool for rescuing in a short time and also evacuation of victims [18].

2.3 *Community-Based Approaches for Disaster Management*

Community-based disaster management (CBDM) approach for disaster management mainly helps to increase the community capacity for assessing the community vulnerability against any natural and human-made disaster. In this process, community peoples are always encouraged to work together accepting the ownership to reduce the disaster vulnerability and also develops strategies to reduce the risks at multiple levels [13]. CBDM aims to reduce vulnerabilities, increasing capacities, prevent or minimizing the loss and damage of life, environment, minimizing human suffering, and hasten recovery [6, 13] Apart from these, in case of disaster management from prevention, mitigation, response, relief, and recovery, community is the first level responder [19]. So, active community participation and CBDM is the most needed to achieve sustainability in dealing with the risks of any disasters [12]. In recent times, studies have been carried out to integrate public participation to reduce the disaster vulnerability and to increase the community capacity. Among all of the relevant studies the concept of Participatory Vulnerability Reduction (PVR) incorporating the concept of CBDM was introduced by some researchers. The main concept of PVR stands to assess community vulnerability, capacity, and strategies developed by the community that considers community capacity and resources. The framework of PVR includes 3 basic things. These are vulnerability assessment, capacity assessment and community Action [20]. According to them, PVR more specifically includes the following things,

1. *Vulnerability assessment:* Identifying vulnerable groups, location and root causes of vulnerability.
2. *Capacity assessment:* Identifying community resource, organizational structure, and institutional context.
3. *Community Action:* Developing community-based plan to overcome root causes and developing community leading organizational setup for coordinated actions.

3 Methodology

3.1 Study Area Profile

Among 30 wards of Rajshahi City Corporation, Ward-25 has been selected for conducting the study. The study area has a close proximity at the north bank of the mighty river "the Padma" with two localities named Talaimari and Raninagar. Previously a high volume of open spaces was present at the RCC area. According to the master plan of 2008, total area of open spaces were 125.37 acres. But recently, the area decreases at 89.73 acres [15]. According to the study Ward-25, ward-26, ward-28 have been identified as most vulnerable for open space reduction. After selecting these places, a systematic field reconnaissance survey along with consulting with ward councilor has been conducted where Ward-25 has been identified according to the study potentiality (Fig. 1).

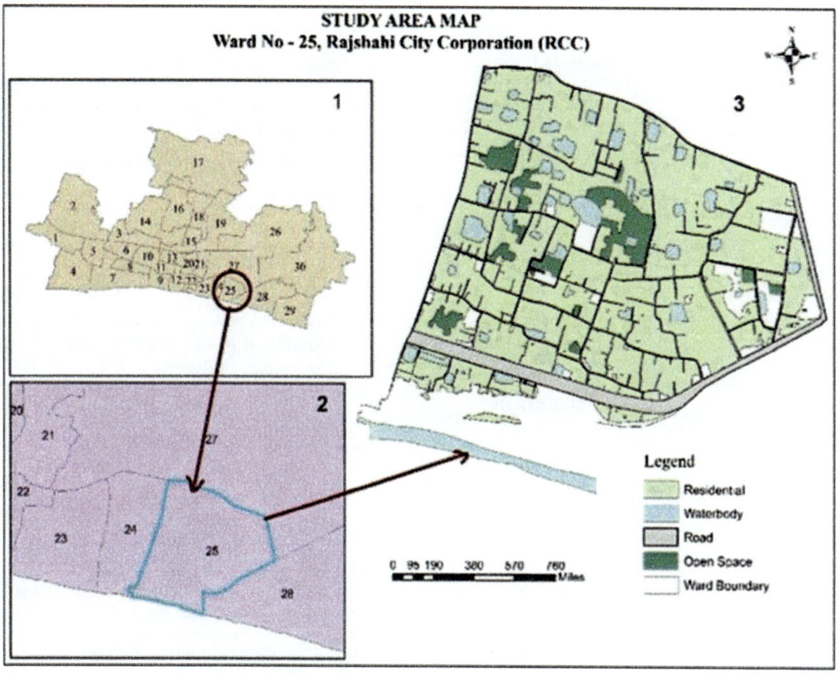

Fig. 1 Location and Land use of the study area

3.2 Implication of PVR Technique

The method of participatory vulnerability reduction (PVR) was used in this study through using different types of tools of Participatory Urban Appraisal (PUR). As the study is about disaster management strategy development so the whole study has been divided into three aspects. The 3 aspects are 1. Disaster risk assessment 2. Capacity assessment 3. Potentiality assessment. In each step of the study, different types of participatory tools were implied. Different types of tools used and expected outcome of the tools has given below (Table 1).

4 Results and Discussion

This section mainly describes the tools used at different phases of the study and explains the results generated from the study integrating with the current situation of the study area.

Table 1 Implication of participatory tools

Aspects	Tool used	Expected outcome
Disaster risk assessment	Social map	Existing socio-physical condition of the selected area
	Timeline analysis	Historical background of open space and waterbody reduction
	Cause effect diagram	Analyzing major problems, causes and the consequences towards the open space and waterbody reduction in the study area
	Pairwise ranking	Ranking of problems and identifying root causes of the risk
Capacity assessment	Resource map	Identifying resource availability at the community
	Mobility map	Extent of influence area, transport use, visits in group or singly, etc
	Venn diagram	Understanding organizational structure and collaboration
	Key informant	Existing management system of open space and water bodies
	Focus group discussion (FGD)	Analyzing community human resource availability,
Potentiality assessment	SWOT analysis	Identifying community strength and opportunities considering weakness and threats
	Focus group discussion (FGD)	Community willingness regarding open space use and developing community-based organizational setup for further actions
	Key informant interview	Potentiality of using community open spaces at local context
	Expert opinion	Existing plan for the space, potentiality towards using area for disaster management

4.1 Vulnerability Assessment

To assess the existing disaster vulnerability associated with the study location, 4 different participatory tools were used. These are historical timeline analysis, social map, cause-effect diagram, and pair-wise ranking matrix. Each of the tools helped to identify different types of vulnerability in the study area.

Historical Trend of Open Space and Waterbody Reduction. A comprehensive historical background of any area provides to access historical trends and patterns of any development of any area. Through analyzing the trend major problems towards any development can also be identified. The historical trend of the area of the study area has been shown in this study through a timeline series. Data for the timeline series was collected from a focus group discussion. At the time of historical trend analysis, a number of resource persons were suggested to know more about the historical trend of the area.

At the time of historical data collection through focus group discussion, questions were asked to the participants creating a landmark on historical events. Different types of problems specific questions were also asked to know the source and root time of the problem started (Table 2).

Historical trend of the community shows that after the establishment of city administrative authorities, more focus was given on the development of the community. The establishment of a water treatment plant, deep tube-well, and drainage system shows a planned development procedure of the study area. But the problems started after 2000. In between 1987–2011, the city corporation authority focused on developing accessibility at the whole city corporation area. And improved accessibility

Table 2 Historical trend of physical change in the community

Year	Events	Remarks
1825	Establishment of district head quarter	–
1876	Municipality establishment	–
1987	Establishment of city corporation	–
1977	Water supply connection at ward 25	–
1980	Establishment of Baitul Hamed mosque	–
1984	Water treatment plant	Developed water quality
1992	Construction of deep tube-well	Availability of drinking water
1994	Construction open drain	Drainage was developed to minimize water logging issue. But due to mismanagement and unstructured drainage outfall the problem was not completely solved
2000	High building density	Open space reduction
2002	Decrease water body	Ecological imbalance
1987-2011	Construct of road network	Increase connectivity and accessibility
2013	Gas connection and drainage facilities	Another attempt to solve the problem with water logging issue
2014	Prohibit outlet of septic tanks in open drain	–
2016	Filling the pond and construction of high-rise building	Waterbody reduction and ecological imbalance
2018	Filling the pond and construction of high-rise building in open spaces	Pond filling and open space reduction
2019	Continued construction of building	Open space reduction

Source Field survey, 2020

advanced the development to rapid infrastructural development in the study area. Rapid infrastructural development caused open space and waterbody reduction of this area. After that in 2016, trends of high-rise building development started again for the development of different types of building developer groups and the trend is still ongoing. As a result, the rapid reduction of open space and waterbody is seen in the study area. And still the process is ongoing. According to development history, the area has not experienced massive fire hazard incidents, but the community is the worst sufferer of waterlogging issues. Community peoples always face the problem of waterlogging whenever a little rainfall occurs. When the matter is about heavy rainfall the situation is as much as worse that is beyond expression. Besides, low cluster housing area and riverside slum area is more vulnerable to fire hazard due to housing conditions with narrow alloys and no wide road facilities.

Existing Social and Physical Vulnerability of the Area. Raninagar and Talaimari of the study area are mostly close to the CBD area of the Rajshahi city with greater connectivity and other facilities. All of these facilities lead to the rapid development of the study area. As almost all of the open spaces are private property, so the owners of the lands prefer to construct buildings on their own land for economic and financial benefit. A social map (Fig. 1) has been prepared to show the existing infrastructural, transportation, educational, recreational, and other facilities.

In broader classification, the area can be divided into three—1. Cluster housing area with limited or no open spaces contributing fewer potential scopes for disaster management; 2. Low-density housing area with a number of water bodies, open spaces, and potential scopes for disaster management, and 3. Riverside slum area which is more vulnerable to disaster.

Cluster Housing Area. With limited or no open spaces contributing fewer potential scopes for disaster management: houses are closely built up providing 1'-2' gap or no space (shared wall) in between. At these locations, open spaces, water bodies, and greeneries are hardly visible in google images as well as in the field. People cannot visit open spaces for regular refreshment and children (below 10 years old) hardly access to playground or open spaces. Again, in case of heavy rain, the area is fully dependent on drainage infrastructure for storm water management resulting in water logging at many spaces (Fig. 2).

Low-density Housing Area. With a number of water bodies, open spaces, and potential scopes for disaster management: houses are closely built up with a nearby central open space (mostly private land) or water body and greeneries. The open spaces are used by children of surrounding households as playgrounds and groups of women are also found to gossip. Some spaces are restricted for the playing of children by members of surrounding households. Some spaces and low lands are used as dumping sites.

River Side Slum Area. Which is more vulnerable to disaster in river side slum areas, poor class housing builds up with much fewer spaces or no spaces in between. Open spaces are found on the riverbank side and at some locations, water bodies are also found in poor condition. From the top, a large flat structure (a no. of households and hundreds of populations) is viewed. Peoples living in the riverside slum area and Raninagar area are highly vulnerable to any fire hazard incident as the area is one of

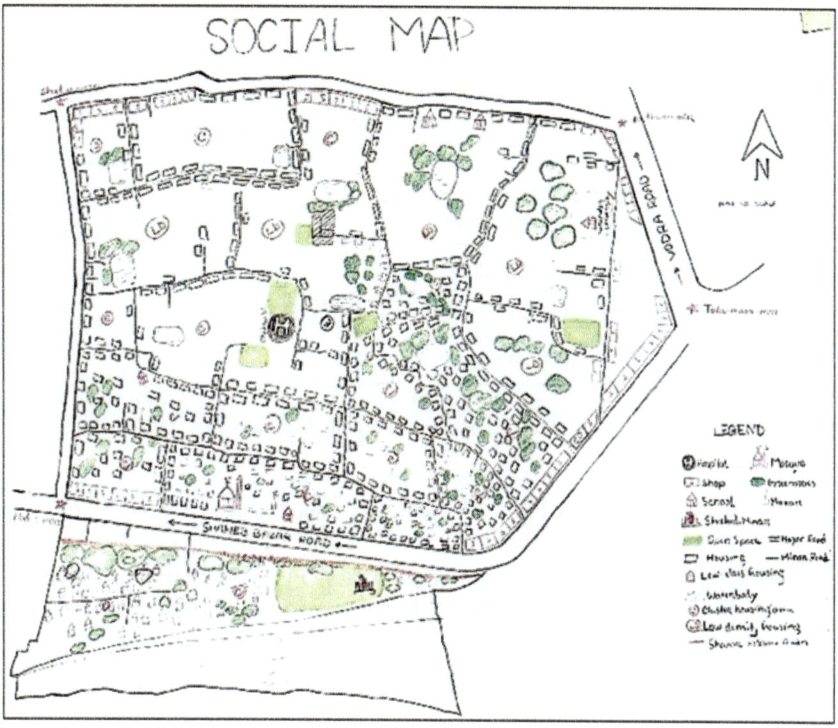

Fig. 2 Existing social condition of the study area *Source* Field Survey, 2020

the densest areas. People of these area uses a narrow alloy to reach their home. And there has no emergency lane where emergency transport can get access whenever necessary. The buildings are so close that, if any fire accident occurs it will not take much time to spread over the whole community.

Major Problems Related to the Use of Open Space and Water bodies. At present days, due to population growth and rapid urbanization, extra pressure is being created on community open spaces and water resources. As a result, the rapid reduction of open space and pond filling is a common phenomenon to meet extra infrastructural and other utility demand. In that sense, 2 most important problems related to the open space and waterbody have been identified by the community people. These are,

1. Reduction of open space and waterbody
2. Un-use and underuse of open space.
3. After identification of these two problems, the inherent causes and their effect on the community people have also been identified.

Major Causes Behind Reduction of Open Space and Waterbody and Its Effect. There is a number of causes of reduction of open spaces and water bodies of which some are more vibrant than others (Fig. 3).

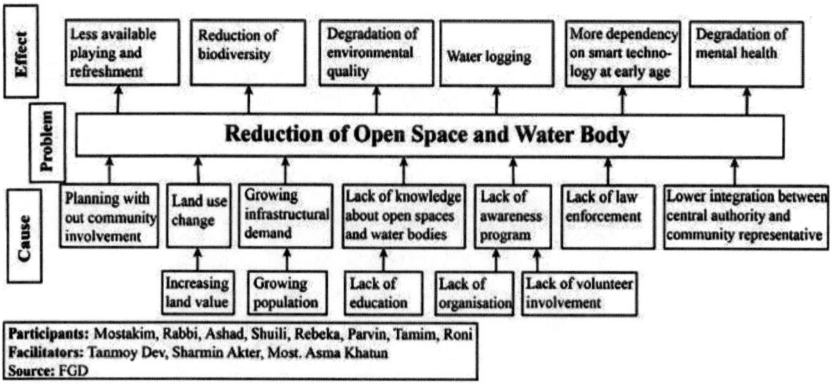

Fig. 3 Cause-effect diagram of reduction of open space and water body. *Source* Field Survey, 2020

The pair-wise ranking method is utilized to rank the causes or sub-problems and finding the most vibrant issues. In the pair-wise ranking method two problems are compared at a time and the frequency of each item preferred the comparison is ascertained which gives the idea of preference of people. Thus, the method is utilized in the study, and the 1st, 2nd, and 3rd ranked causes are extracted. These are:

1. Lower integration between central and local authorities
2. Planning without community
3. Growing demand for infrastructure

Lower integration of RCC, RDA with community representatives and local organizations (exempt Ward commissioner) plays a vital role in the reduction of open spaces and water bodies. Weak planning structure and lack of awareness of the community people regarding the benefits of open spaces and water bodies and the consequences of their reduction contributing to the problem of lower integration between central and local authorities. This in turn contributes to not taking any initiative regarding the preservation of open spaces and water bodies.

With the increase in population, the demand for infrastructure is constantly rising and it is highest in urban areas. An increase in population and an increase in land value are contributing to the increase in infrastructure demand which causes rapid infrastructural development. And it ended up filling ponds and constructing at a handful of open spaces.

"Planning without incorporating the community people" often causes great trouble. For example, there are some open spaces left with no concern, and ended up utilizing it as a dumping site. If the planning was made with community people with due concern to this issue, the scenario would be different now. Lower Providence of responsible authorities and Lack of initiative regarding long-term planning are the causes behind planning without community.

Major Causes Behind Un-use and Underuse of Open Space and Waterbody and Its Effect. Being unused and underused has been identified as the second problem regarding problems related to open space by the community people. A significant number of causes have also been identified that are responsible for this problem.

After that pair-wise ranking matrix has been created through community involvement for prioritizing the causes and to find out the most influential causes. In this respect mostly influential causes regarding open space being unused and underused are,

1. Poor management system of existing open spaces
2. Surrounding the built environment
3. Lack of proper knowledge regarding open space utilization

After that most influential causes have been identified as problems and further causes and effects have been revealed. Management issue is found one of the most important things for any site development or to determine the quality of any space. Community people argues that, poor management of the existing spaces encourage water dumping and makes places less attractive to everyday users. Besides placing construction materials for a longer time period makes places less user friendly. All of these problems lead to make places less accessible as well as less available open spaces. The major causes behind this kind of problem are a lack of awareness and cooperation among the landowner and related stakeholders (Fig. 4).

Surrounding the built environment has been identified as the second most prioritized problem for being an unused or underused condition of any space. Different types of building structures and building materials used (e.g.: glass at the window) make places more vulnerable in view of playing children around the building. So, the owners usually restrict children from playing in these areas.

In the study, a huge number of unused open spaces has been identified through field survey, but the guardians of the children are not aware of this, and they do not have any headache regarding them. Rather they allow their children to use smart

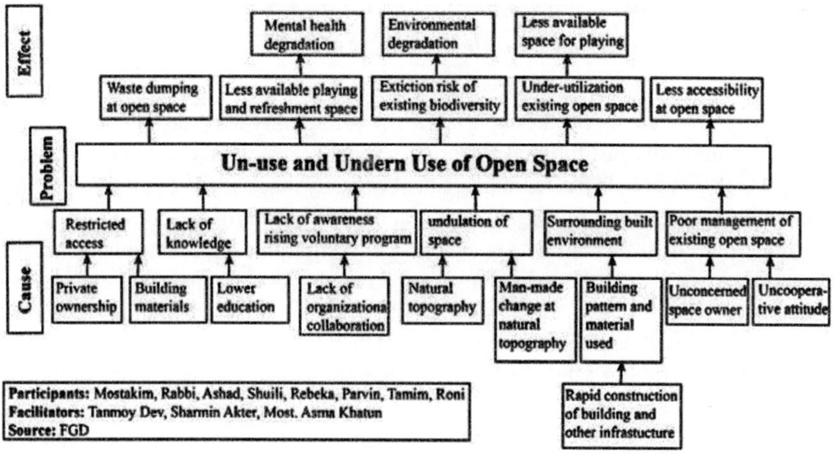

Fig. 4 Cause effect diagram of un-use and under use of open spaces. *Source* Field Survey, 2020

technology. That happens because of lack of knowledge and awareness among the community peoples.

5 Capacity of Community to Reduce the Risk on Open Space and Waterbody

5.1 Resource Availability in the Study Area

The resource map shows the existing available open spaces and the demolished open spaces as well. It also shows the open spaces that are in under demolition. The results of this mapping show the higher demolition rates of the open spaces and lower number of open spaces according to the community requirement. As the number of community open spaces is declining day by day people use small social spaces as a place of social interaction in the study area and these areas have also been identified. Although the pond filling scenario is severe in the Rajshahi city corporation area, this study area is also in a vulnerable condition. In some parts of the area, building has been constructed by filling the waterbody. This results in waterlogging, and other problems in the study area.

In the study area Hadir mor to city hospital road, Raninagar pro-poor residential area and Hadir mor to Shadhur mor road have been identified as the most vulnerable to waterlogging. But till now, the existing amount of waterbody shows higher potentiality regarding the management of waterlogging situation through incorporating the use of existing open spaces at different policy issues (Fig. 5).

5.2 Institutional Arrangement and Dependency of the Community People

Whenever we want to assess the capacity of any community for disaster management purposes community institutional and organizational capacity assessment is as much as important as national disaster management capacity assessment. So, it is important to understand the community organizations and active groups of any community. And how the groups interact with others and outsider institutions must be studied as well. This approach will help the policymakers and the plan development, executive, and management committee to identify the existing institutional gaps among different institutions and will be helpful to make the relationship stronger (Fig. 6).

Institutions Having High Influence. Ward council of the area is located near the "Talaimari Katchabazar" area. A Ward council is an organization where a group of community representatives is included along with the ward councilor. And the ward council has a great influence regarding open space management and waterbody preservation. In the study area, almost 1 acre of the land area of the ward councilor

Fig. 5 Existing community resource of the study area *Source* Field Survey, 2020

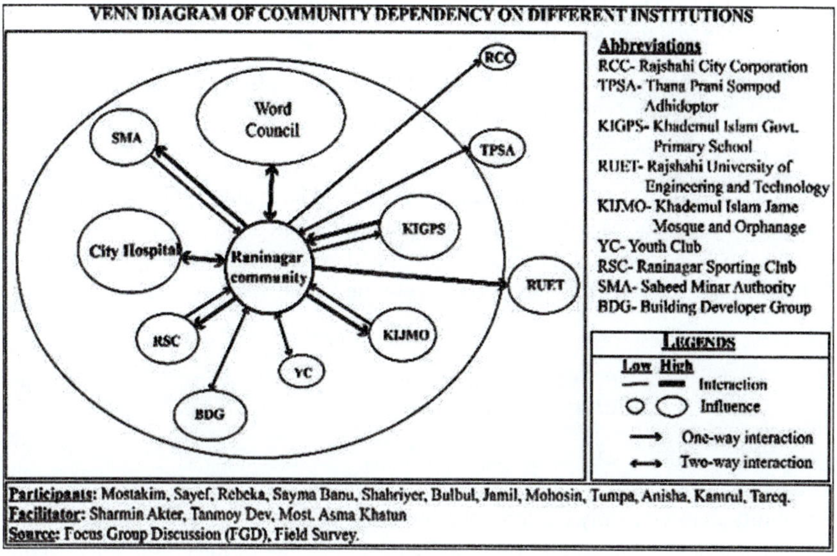

Fig. 6 Institutional dependency related to open space use. *Source* Field Survey, 2020

has been declared as open space and the waqf initiative has been taken for further preservation of the spaces. A small part of the area is using as a settlement for rootless people in a condition of not hampering any existing features of the area. In this regard, the ward councilor of the area said that,

> The designated land is our inheritance property and obviously private property. As this area is a large open area so my grandfather allowed some rootless people for living here. But some restrictions have been given on them not to hamper any trees or other features of the area. And the peoples are also living there happily.
>
> —(Key informant interview__1)

In this respect, a resident of this area named Rebeka said that,

> "I am living here since my childhood. Ward councilor has given us all types of utility facilities regarding electricity, water facilities. So, we do not have any other wanting from him and we always try to respect his words."
>
> —(Focus group discussion__1)

Apart from this RUET playground and City hospital playground is most attractive to the children group. They usually go weekly to the RUET playground and the other time they prefer City hospital or shaheed Minar playground.

Institutions having lower influence Among all the institutions Raninagar sports club, Khademul Islam govt. primary school, Khademul Islam Jame Mosque, and Orphanage have significantly lower influence. Among them Khademul Islam govt. primary school has potentiality for space use but the entry is restricted. In this respect, a student named kalam said that,

> "Khademul school is very close to my house. But I am not a student of this school and none of my friends can go there to play."
>
> —(Focus group discussion__2)

Besides Khademul mosque and orphanage do not have any significant space and Raninagar sports club uses the city hospital playground for annual sports competition. Beyond this, the orphan children and club members use the city hospital field and shaheed Minar for daily playing or other activities.

5.3 Mobility Pattern of Community People Regarding Open Space Use

A mobility map generally explores the mobility pattern of the community people. It shows the movement pattern of an individual, a group, or the community. Major focus is given on where, how and for what people go to the significant places. It reflects the people's perception of movement patterns and the reasons thereof.

From the study, it is found that only children below 18, women visit open spaces for the purpose of playing and refreshment. A mobility map is used here to explore their movement pattern to the open spaces. Children regularly visit there nearby

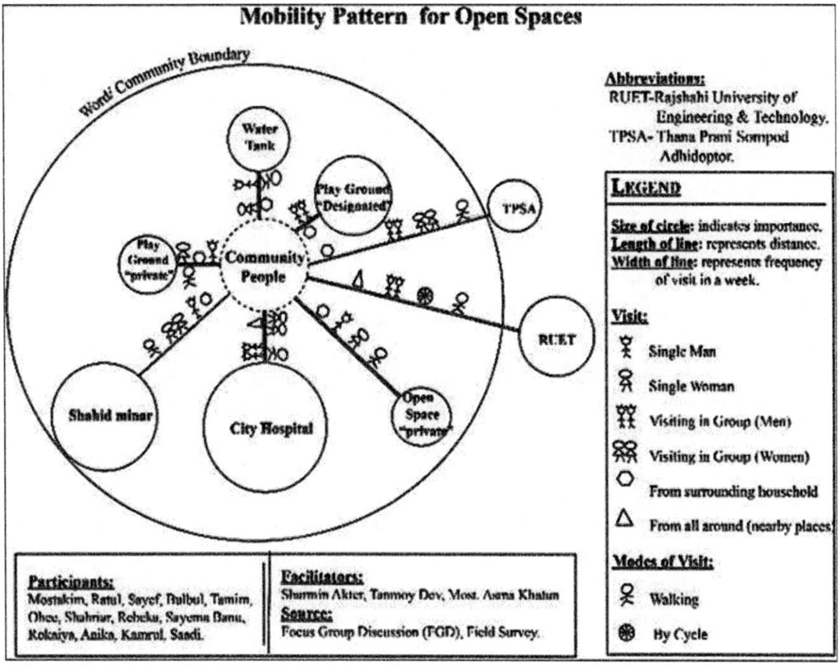

Fig. 7 Community mobility pattern regarding open space use. *Source* Field Survey, 2020

small open spaces (mostly private lands, not designated playground) in a group or singly for playing. There is socially designated two playgrounds (Shahid Minar-field, playground of city hospital) fall within the ward boundary and one (RUET playground) outside the boundary. More specifically, the playground of city hospital being in the central zone serves the whole ward. On weekends, children used to visit in groups either RUET playground or Shahid Minar-field (Fig. 7).

6 Potentiality of the Open Spaces and Water Bodies Towards Disaster Management Strategy Development

6.1 Insight of Community People Regarding Using the Open Spaces for Disaster Management

In the case of community-based disaster management strategy development, the insight of the community people is the most important thing. To find out the potentiality of community open space and water bodies for disaster management purpose, both positive and negative response were assembled. One of the residents of that area named Aminul Huq said that,

> We are suffering from waterlogging area for a long time, the whole golley (narrow pathway) of this area sink with water whenever it rains. Sometimes if heavy rainfall occurs water level raise so high that it comes up at our front yard. And the wastes of drainage always mix with the rainwater that is very much irritating. If the problem can be solved with proper management of open space and water bodies, it will be really good for us. We all will cooperate with the authority and we all will help according to our capacity.
>
> —(Focus group discussion__3)

But the problem occurred with some of the owners of the vacant land. According to one of the owners,

> This vacant land is my private property. As I have my own house now, the area is vacant and the children always play there. But in the future, my children's will make their house for themselves in this land. And the disaster problem is the problem of the whole community. So, everyone should contribute to their land.
>
> —(Focus group discussion__3)

After taking the insights and the problems of community people in consideration, these issues were discussed with Mr. Tariqul Islam Paltu, who is the honorable councilor of Ward-25. He is also a key informant of this study. After hearing the insights and comments from the community people he shared his insight regarding the potentiality of open space and waterbody use for disaster management purposes.

Key Informant Name: Md. Tarikul Islam Paltu
Designation: Councilor, Ward No-25, Rajshahi City Corporation (RCC)
In case of space potentiality, he says, "*Our ward area is blessed with a large number of water bodies and greeneries. But after 2016, the amount suddenly started to decrease at a rapid rate. These two factors work that is rapid urbanization and lack of awareness. We cannot stop the urbanization, but we can increase the awareness level easily. We all know the general importance of open space and water bodies, but addressing the potentiality of these issues for disaster management purposes is really new for us. I think if we can form a committee in this respect that will be much effective. But unfortunately, we do not have any committee in this regard. Besides, if we can involve school college-going children's, that can carry a good fortune. In that case, school-level committee formation can be more effective.*"

6.2 *Insights of Experts Regarding the Use and Potentiality of Open Spaces and Water Bodies*

Experts have shared their views regarding the use and potentiality of community open spaces and water bodies. Their insights regarding this issue addressed core problems lies within organizations and human behavior and also opened up so many scopes and potentialities of the area. Experts have presented their valuable insights according to their area of expertise. Their opinions are presented below:

Debasis Chacrabarty emphasized more on the bottom-up planning approach in order to the successfulness of plans and proposals regarding the conservation of open spaces and water bodies as well as to address community problems and proper utilization of the spaces.

Expert Name: Debasis Chacrabarty,
Designation: Land use expert, Rajshahi Development Authority (RDA), Rajshahi
"All of the community open spaces are private property, but, while the issue is about planning, these places are considered as open spaces. Being private property government cannot rule over the community spaces. Moreover, mismatching in existing land-use and land-use at mouza, less consideration towards community open spaces, no control over pond filling cause decrease in open spaces & pond filling".
He also discussed about the presented project that RDA and RCC going through. He says,
"At recent times, according to the ongoing master plan, a strong barrier will be created on the case of pond filling and will also re-excavate clogged water bodies. In this case, unused and clogged waterbody (locally known as Doba) will give equal importance. If at any purpose, pond filling is must be needed, they have to submit a particular fee to RDA. In this way, waterlogging issues will be reduced to some extent".
"The problem of waterlogging is mainly due to the dead-end drainage structure and no existence of outfall of drainage. Drainage outfall has to be well structured and some of the water bodies can be these outfalls".

Another expert of his study, Md. Fakrul Alam has emphasized on community organization who will address community need to higher authority through maintaining a proper channel and also focused on the transparency and accountability within the organization. She also accuses the poor drainage condition of massive waterlogging issues.

Expert Name: Md. Fakhrul Alam
Designation: Planner, Urban Development Directorate (UDD)
"To use open space for a particular use, especially, for disaster management, it requires to know the size of the space available. The case is the same for water bodies. Here, whether the available water bodies and open spaces can address disaster management issues or not is the prime question".
He emphasized community organizations for the successfulness of plans, proposals and also presented the lack between different organizations. On this aspect, she says, *"About the successfulness of plan, it depends on organogram of organization and maintaining of a chain of command. Failure of most plans, proposals is due to not following the chain of command. Moreover, community organizations should be taken under definite organogram to address their problems from time to time as well as for directing the community in a proper channel and compelling them to follow policies, rules, and regulations (waterbody and wetland conservation act, open space act, etc.)".*

6.3 SWOT Analysis

The greater problem at the urban scale is the result of problems faced at the community scale. The problems laying within the community, their weak points, opportunities, and threats regarding the use and potentiality of open spaces and water bodies have been found out in order to get to the root of problems at the urban scale. Thus, the study focused on the community and the key findings from this study have been summarized below:

Strength. Community institutional arrangement, locational accessibility, effective ward council, active participation and eagerness of community people for using open spaces for disaster management are the major strengths of the community. These are the qualitative and potential factors of the community to reverse the present poor situation of community open spaces and water bodies.

Weakness. Lack of local level policies and acts, lower integration with central authority, high infrastructural development and lack of proper knowledge are the main weakness of the study area. Although the week points are clear, it will be hard to address when these are taken to practical field.

Opportunity. Positive influence of individual and other responsibilities for development and effective use of water bodies and open spaces, the willingness of local authority for open space preservation and development open the door of opportunities for the development of open spaces.

Threat. Poor management and rapid reduction of open, lack of intra and inter sectorial coordination, Lack of information and capacity building programs, no rules over private community open spaces, Rapid activities of development by the building developer group are the major threats.

7 Recommendations and Conclusion

7.1 Recommendations by Key Personnel and from the Community

Analyzing the study and recommendations by different key personnel's, experts, and community people some proposals have been presented below:

1. At first, clear documentation of the potential open space and water bodies is must require. A specific plan integrating disaster management strategy should also be developed.
2. The main problem of waterlogging is dead end drainage structure and no outfall of existing drainage. So, first of all, drainage outfall should be well structured. In that case drainage foe, rainwater flow outfall can be at water bodies.

3. Immediate actions must be taken to stop ongoing open space reduction and pond filling activities. And unused open spaces must be made usable. Same as for water bodies.
4. Rehabilitation can be ensured during fire emergencies in community open spaces.
5. Much greeneries at community open space can increase groundwater infiltration.
6. Reserved waters from water bodies can be helpful to manage emergency water needed for any fire incidents.
7. A bottom-up planning approach must be encouraged for the best practice of community open spaces.
8. Community organizations (private) should be linked with the higher organization (government) through an intermediate organization, so that help, when requires can reach the needy people. In that case, each and every organization should strictly follow the chain of command. NGOs can also cooperate with community organizations. It is very possible if community organizations are taken under a specific organogram.
9. In the case of community organizations, Ward Disaster Management Committee (WDMC) can be formed that will perform different types of awareness programs and help the community when a disaster occurs. Besides, School Disaster Management Committee (SDMC) can be formed where students will learn pre-disaster, during disaster, and post-disaster activities.
10. There should be transparency, accountability within organizations so that the case of corruption can be minimized and acts, laws, and policies can be established in practices. In this way, people will be compelled to take actions according to the waterbody and wetland conservation act, open space acts, and all other relevant acts as well.
11. Community organizations often suffer from lack of funding, though it depends on the community people's participation, here requires the intervention of the government.
12. Water bodies can be used as natural outfall of drainage following the topography.
13. Providing a water-reservoir tank at a specific height (so that it is out of reach of children) in open spaces can be used for the collection of rainwater that may be useful for any fire incidents. Govt. provided fire hydrant can be placed at community open spaces for ensuring easy accessibility and access.

7.2 Conclusion

Development of planning policies introducing disaster management strategies for any area development is giving priorities in recent years. In that case, the community-based disaster management plan policy development can be one of the most effective planning tools. While the traditional disaster management approach requires much time and has a high potentiality of failure of the plan, the community-based approach helps to find the root cause of the problems and also helps to find out the most reliable solution to the problems. The participatory approach helps to empower the community and helps to make them believe that they are also a part of the comprehensive planning procedure [6]. This process helps to create self-respect, ownership, accountability, and awareness among the community people [3]. It also finds out the importance of community institutions in disaster management plan policy development and execution [2].

Having huge scope of the study, there have some limitations also. Although most of the community people agreed to use the open space for disaster management purposes, some of the people opposed the proposal. They do not think that the places have so much potentiality. Sometimes lack of knowledge and awareness becomes a great challenge towards participatory plan development. Some the recommendations were given on the basis of community capacity, risk assessment, taking expert opinion survey, key informant survey, and community opinion to prevent waterlogging and fire hazard issues open spaces and water bodies. So, this well structured study methodology may be applicable to other areas as well to minimize the disaster risk and also to take necessary steps at disaster time emergency situation and post-disaster activities as well.

References

1. Agarwal R (2019) Environmental impacts of urban green space. 6:37–40
2. Allan P, Bryant M (2010, March) The critical role of open space in earthquake recovery: a case study. In EN: Proceedings of the 2010 NZSEE Conference (2010, Nueva Zelandia) pp 1–10
3. Askari AH (2014) Assessment of Urban public spaces: cases of Kuala Lumpur City Center. University of Malaya, Malaysia
4. Bhuiyan MSA (2008) Reduction of open space in urban planning: a case of Osmani Odyan
5. Billie G, Melissa HB, Knuiman M, Collins C, Douglas K, Ng K, Lange A, Donovan RJ (2005) Increasing walking: how important is distance to, attractiveness, and size of public open space?. 28(2-supp-S2):0–176. https://doi.org/10.1016/j.amepre.2004.10.018
6. Brown D, Howes M, Hussein K, Longley C, Swindell K (2002) Participatory methodologies and participatory practices: assessing PRA use in the Gambia. Network Paper No. 124, Agricultural Research and Extension Network
7. Carmona M (2010) Contemporary public space: critique and classification, part one: critique. J Urban Des 15:123–148
8. Chiesura A (2004) The role of urban parks for the sustainable city. Landscape Urban Planning 68(1):129–138
9. David K, Katarina R (2019) The potential of open space for enhancing urban seismic resilience: a literature review. Sustain Rev
10. Gill SE, Handley JF, Ennos AR, Pauleit S (2007) Adapting cities for climate change: the role of the green infrastructure. Built Environ 33(1):115–133
11. Gupta AK, Nair SS (2010) Flood risk and context of land-uses: Chennai city case. J Geogr Reg Plan 3(12):365–372
12. Huq SMS (2016) Community based disaster management strategy in Bangladesh: present status, future prospects and challenges. Eur J Res Soc Sci 4(2):22–35

13. Islam K (2013) Community-Based Disaster Management in Bangladesh. https://www.researchgate.net/publication/333972153_Community_Based_Disaster_Management_in_Bangladesh
14. Jayakody PRJC, Amarathunga D, Haigh R (2018) Integration of disaster management strategies with planning and designing public open spaces. Procedia Eng 212:954–961
15. Kafy AA, Faisal AA, Ferdous L (2018) A participatory assessment to identify the causes and impacts of open space reduction in Rajshahi City Corporation (RCC) Area, Bangladesh. Int J Environ Plann Dev 4(2):16–28
16. Khan M (2014) Study of open spaces in the context of dhaka city for sustainable use: a syntactic approach. IACSIT Int J Eng Technol 6(3)
17. Kumar R (2017) Overview: social spaces in urban areas. Int Res J Eng Technol 04(04):1032–1039
18. Mirza F (2015) Disaster mitigation approach of urban green structure concept in coastal settlement dimension. J Architect Built Environ 42(2):51–58
19. Pariyar RK (2019) Community based disaster risk management: a case study of Mahakali River Basin Kanchanpur. Geogr Base 677–686. https://doi.org/10.3126/tgb.v6i0.26169
20. Rahman MM, Barua U, Khatun F, Islam I, Rafiq R (2018) Participatory Vulnerability Reduction (PVR): an urban community-based approach for earthquake management. Nat Hazards 93(3):1479–1505. https://doi.org/10.1007/s11069-018-3364-2
21. Thompson CW (2002) Urban open space in the 21st century. Landsc Urban Plan 60(2):59–72

Approach to Simulate the Rainwater Runoff at Site Level Using Rhino Grasshopper

Naga Venkata Sai Kumar Manapragada and P. C. Icy

Abstract The world community is presently facing the early impacts of Climate change. The floods have today become the new normal, natural hazard which has been most expensive and devastating. The Intergovernmental Panel on Climate Change (IPCC) has projected the gradual increase in global precipitation exceeding 0.05 and 0.15 mm day^{-1} for Representative Concentration Pathways (RCP) 2.6 and RCP8.5 scenarios, respectively. The major threat from the projected future phenomena is for megacities. The increase in the built environment with impervious surfaces in urban areas have been choking the naturally formed stormwater channels that usually lead water to surface water and aquifers. Flooding thus becomes more pervasive and hazardous in urban areas in comparison to rural areas. The Landsat and Radarsat data are commonly used to determine the spatial and temporal distribution of floods at the urban level. However, the cause for the blockade in runoff conveyance networks at the site level or street level becomes challenging. The simulation of site surface stormwater runoff for possible rainfall scenarios could aid the architects and urban designers to account for water inundation due to terrain and other site objects. Measures to avoid the conveyance networks blockade could be achieved by geospatial visualization of simulation results. Therefore, this study presents an approach to model and simulate the rainwater runoff using Rhino Grasshopper (Rhino-Gh) and Rainwater + tools. Detailing the approach in the tool facilitates the architects and urban designers to inculcate the assessment as a part of the early design analysis.

Keywords Climate change · Floods · Simulation · Rhino grasshopper · Rainwater +

N. V. Sai Kumar Manapragada (✉)
Assistant Professor, Manipal School of Architecture and Planning, Manipal Academy of Higher Education (MAHE), Karnataka, India
e-mail: nagavsk.m@manipal.edu

P. C. Icy
Nitte Institute of Architecture, Mangalore, India
e-mail: icy@nitte.edu.in

C. Ghosh and S. Kolathayar (eds.), *A System Engineering Approach to Disaster Resilience*, Lecture Notes in Civil Engineering 205, https://doi.org/10.1007/978-981-16-7397-9_24

1 Introduction

Climate change (CC) concerns have heightened in the world community after its early impacts experiences. Every social, cultural, traditional, economic and technological system on earth is either directly or indirectly connected to climate. Thus, predicting the impacts, risks and vulnerabilities become necessary to recognize the mitigation and adaptation measures. The urban regions of today are considered a complex socio-technical system, which is densifying rapidly. The fifth assessment report [1] published by Intergovernmental Panel on Climate Change (IPCC) infers that the CC would broadly impact a broad spectrum of infrastructure systems, services, ecosystem services and the built environment in cities. The two majorly known global threat with the CC is the increase in ambient temperatures and precipitation. The IPCC [2] has projected the gradual increase in global precipitation exceeding 0.05 mm day^{-1} and 0.15 mm day^{-1} for the Representative Concentration Pathways (RCP) 2.6 and RCP8.5 scenarios, respectively.

India being a tropical nation and the peninsular region, floods are usually experienced during monsoons. Several studies conducted in recent times [3 , 4] have observed the increase in the frequency of floods in India. The studies have also been inferred [5 , 6] that the frequency of flooding has been increasing in India with the increase in air temperature. The increase in mortality and morbidity along with economic losses is associated with extreme precipitation events [7]. Major cities in India are located in coastal belts and seashores and face urban floods [8]. The increase in the impervious surfaces in urban areas [9] interrupt the stormwater runoff networks causing the inundation. The stormwater runoff, drainage pipes and catch basins for building and site level projects are usually calculated and designed by the hydrology engineers. The participation of hydrology engineers is mostly nil or passive for small-scale projects that account for the significant stake in urban fabric configuration. There is a need to integrate stormwater management during the conceptual design phase for a low impact design (LID) development.

The geospatial distribution of floods assessment is performed using Landsat and Radarsat data [10]. The Geographic Information System (GIS) is a standard tool used to capture and analyze geospatial data. The Landsat and Radarsat data in GIS aids in mapping the flood extent and depth for a chosen location. However, the GIS-based approach would not be applicable to.

- Assess the site-specific stormwater runoff directions
- Predict the deviations in the stormwater runoff directions for the changes proposed
- Recognize and evaluate the key locations to integrate the LID practices

The simulation of urban rainwater runoff and assessment of potential LID practices with respect to the context and climate of a location serves the architects, Landscape and urban designers to mitigate flooding at the micro and meso levels. Such dynamic processing and representation of the geospatial data are termed geospatial analytics. Geospatial data science requires knowledge in programming languages, database management, cloud computation, Artificial intelligence and

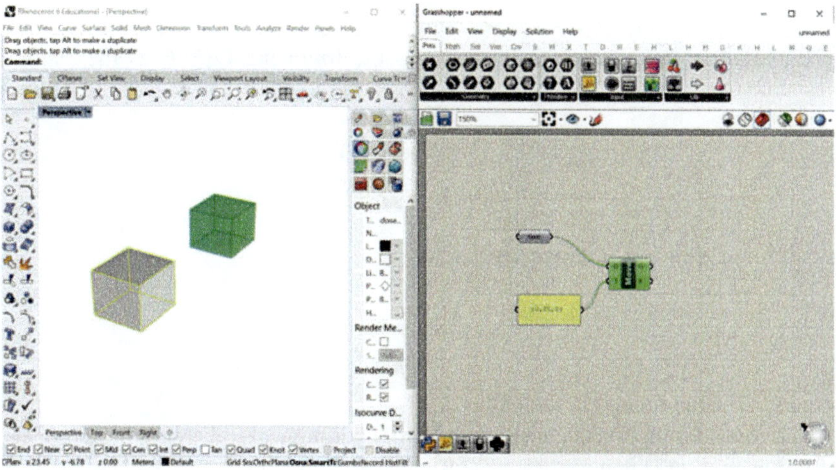

Fig. 1 Rhino interface (on the left) illustrating one cube modelled manually and another cube generated from Recipe created in Gh (on the right)

Machine Learning [11]. Stakeholders from different disciplines can avail the above mentioned five skills with available e-learning resources. However, the visual scripting tools such as Rhinocerous Grasshopper (Rhino-Gh) with its geospatial plugins enable the enthusiasts to perform geospatial analytics without the five skills.

The Rhinocerous (Rhino) [12] is the non-object-oriented modelling tool where designers from different domains can digitally model their conceptualized objects. The Grasshopper (Gh) is a plugin of Rhino that enables algorithmic modelling in Rhino through its visual programming interface (Fig. 1). The computational logic created with components available in the Gh is usually termed as Recipe.

The experts from remote sensing and GIS disciplines with programming interests are developing their plugins to compute, automate, simulate, analyze and visualize the information. The Rainwater + [13] is a recipe that has been designed to assess the stormwater runoff for a given site level or urban level geographical inputs. The Rainwater + allows the users to perform terrain analysis, runoff volume calculation, sizing and assess LID practices' performance. The tool uses Curve Number (CN) method [14–16] developed by the United States Department of Agriculture. The following Eqs. (1), (2) and (3) describe the CN method.

$$P_e = \frac{(P - I_a)^2}{(P - I_a) + S} \tag{1}$$

where

P_e = Depth of effective precipitation.
P = Total rainfall depth in storm event.
I_a = Equivalent depth of initial abstractions.

S = Maximum possible water retention

Equation (1) has been transformed into the following Eq. (2) as the Natural Resource Conservation Service data analysis inferred that on average, $I_a = 0.2S$.

$$P_e = \frac{(P - 0.2S)^2}{(P + 0.8S)} \tag{2}$$

where

$$S = \frac{1000}{CN} - 10 \tag{3}$$

and *CN* is the runoff curve number

The cover description of curve numbers for hydrological soil groups have been by Cronshey et al. [14] in his article. The Rainwater + tool refers to that curve number table based on the user inputs related to the land cover condition and soil type of the surface. Although the tool can assess the LID systems such as Bioretention, Subsurface infiltration system, Permeable pavement, Green roof and Rain harvest with capacity limitations [13], the major constrain is the precipitation input. The Rainwater + tool available only comprises percentile data and recurrence interval data inputs of 13 major cities in the United States of America. The users from outside of these 13 major cities of the USA cannot use the tool unless they possess the historically extreme years' hourly precipitation data. Thus, the present study aims to discuss an approach to model and simulate the rainwater runoff using the Rainwater + tool in Rhino-Gh. The objectives of this study are to analyze.

- The deviation in the stormwater runoff for a natural terrain versus the modified terrain scenario
- The inundation due to proposed changes in the site in the modified terrain scenario

2 Methodology

2.1 Site Selection

As shown in Fig. 2, an institutional site located in the outskirts of Mangalore has been chosen to demonstrate the simulation approach. Mangalore is a west coast city of India vulnerable to disasters such as Floods and Tsunami. The site chosen for this study is less vulnerable to Tsunami compared to floods due to its distance from the high tide line zone. According to the National Building Code of India [17], Mangalore belongs to a Warm-Humid climate. Precipitation in the form of rainfall can be observed in Mangalore for four to six months a year. The site chosen is characterized by the slope declining from the Northeast to the Southwest in direction.

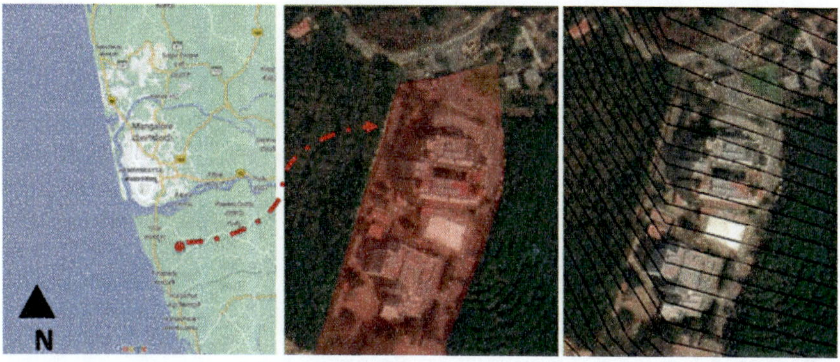

Fig. 2 Selected site location and its contours

The interval between the two successive contours shown in Fig. 2. is 0.5 m. The total site area is 5.54 acres.

2.2 *Precipitation Data*

The hourly rainfall data has been obtained from the Global Precipitation Measurement (GPM) Mission of NASA (National Aeronautics and Space Administration) for the chosen site. The GPM [18] mission is the successor of the Tropical Rainfall Measuring Mission (TRMM) that provides the next generation of global observations of rain and snow sourced from the international network of satellites. There are nine websites and tools available to download the GPM and TRMM data. The five years (2015 to 2019) of historical weather data [19] with 0.5° × 0.5° spatial resolution and sub-hourly temporal resolution has been downloaded from NASA Goddard Earth Sciences (GES) Data and Information Services Center (DISC) [20]. The five-year sub-hourly precipitation data was available in 80,440 NetCDF4 file formats. Thus, a python script has been generated to compile and export the rainfall data into Comma Separated Variable (CSV) file format.

Boxplots have been generated to recognize the year having the maximum outliers from the precipitation dataset. As shown in Fig. 3. the year 2018 possessed maximum outliers in comparison to other years. Further analysis of precipitation data for the year 2018 has shown (Fig. 4) extreme precipitation even in May, which is three times higher than in previous years. The day-wise assessment (Fig. 5) of precipitation data for May in 2018 has inferred extreme events between 25 and 30th.

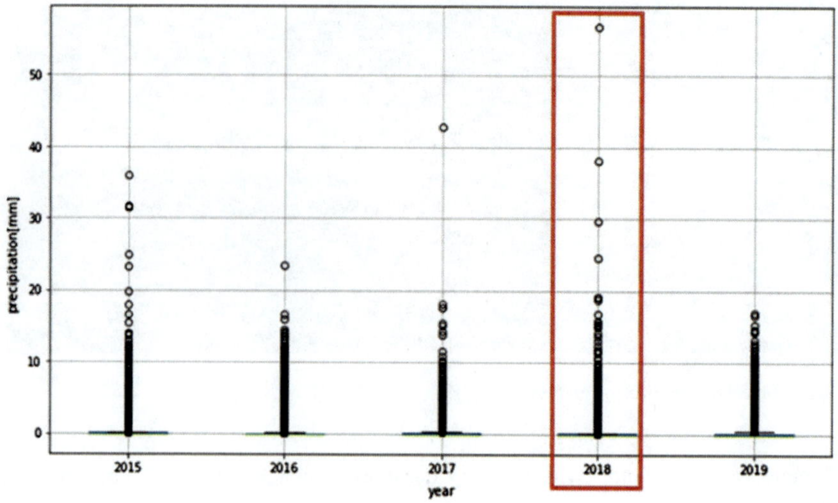

Fig. 3 Showing year-wise boxplots for precipitation data

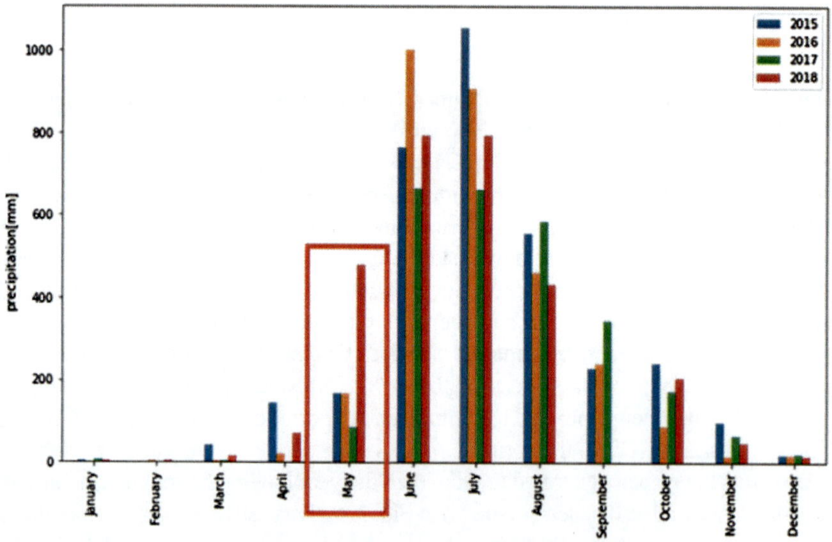

Fig. 4 Showing month-wise cumulative precipitation from 2015 to 2018

2.3 Validation

Although the GES DISC data has shown the extreme event between 25th May and 30th May of 2018, there was a need to validate using historical evidence. The study has discovered few media reports [21–23] that confirmed the extreme event in the

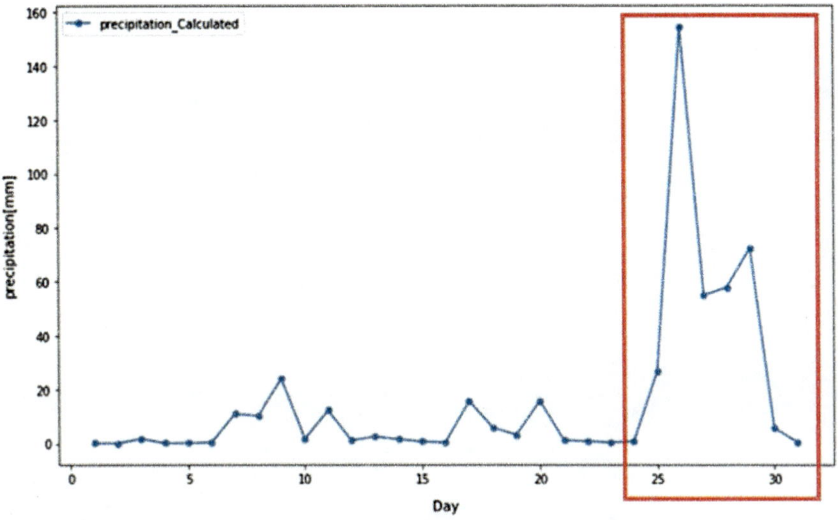

Fig. 5 Showing day-wise precipitation for May 2018

same timeframe. This paper assumes the extreme event occurred to be assumed as a typical event of future climate.

2.4 *Model Inputs*

The study considered two scenarios for the site. The first scenario considers the site's natural terrain topography, while the second scenario assumes built forms and other hypothetical changes to the site's topography, as shown in Fig. 6. Thus the first scenario will be referred to as a natural site and the second scenario as the proposed site. The Rainwater + interface requires the annual hourly precipitation data, 3D

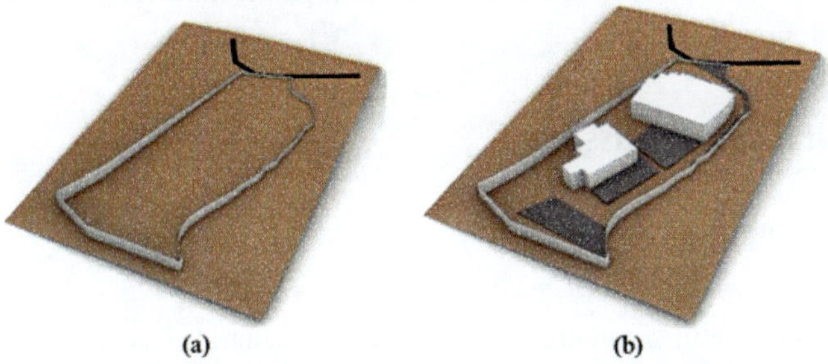

Fig. 6 **a** DTM representing natural site; **b** DTM representing the proposed site with impervious pavements and buildings

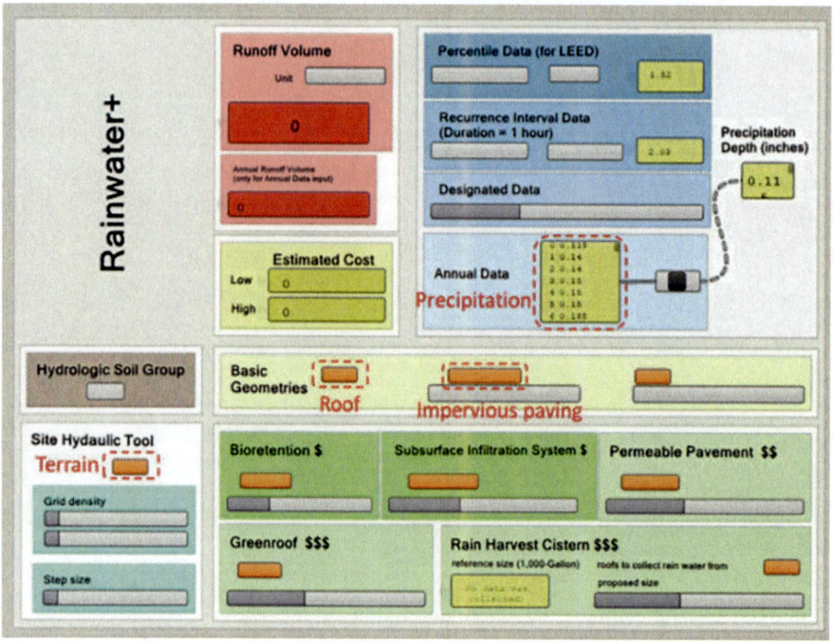

Fig. 7 Highlights the Grasshopper components available to provide numeric, 3D and 2D model inputs for simulation

digital terrain model (DTM) and 2D surfaces of roads, pavements, roofs and other site features as highlighted in Fig. 7.

The method to obtain the annual hourly precipitation data for an extreme year has already been outlined in sub-Sect. 2.2. The 3D DTM for the site scale spatial resolution can be modelled in Rhino with contour maps or by directly importing from the 'Location' plugin of the SketchUp tool [24]. The urban level spatial analysis, the 3D DTM could also be imported from the Shuttle Radar Topography Mission (SRTM) of NASA using Digital Terrain Mesh (DiTeMe) [25] plugin in Rhino-Gh. The rest of the 2D surfaces could be modelled in Rhino through the modelling tools available.

3 Results and Discussion

3.1 Runoff Direction

The stormwater runoff simulation for both the site scenarios has been performed to recognize the critical flow direction. As shown in Fig. 8a, the flow's critical cardinal direction is the Southwest direction for the natural site scenario. The boundary wall

Fig. 8 Shows runoff direction for both the site scenarios

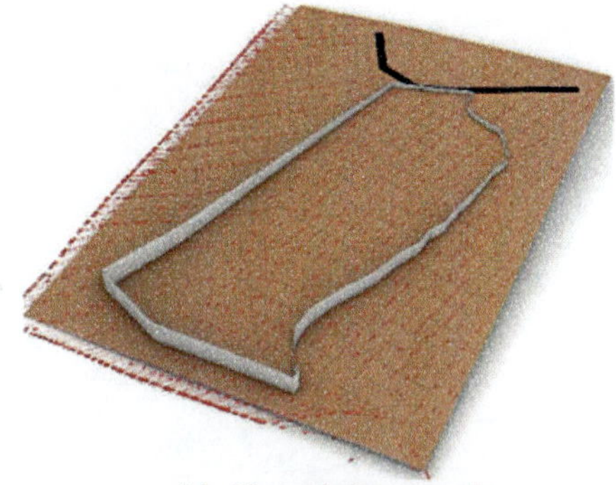

(a) Natural site scenario

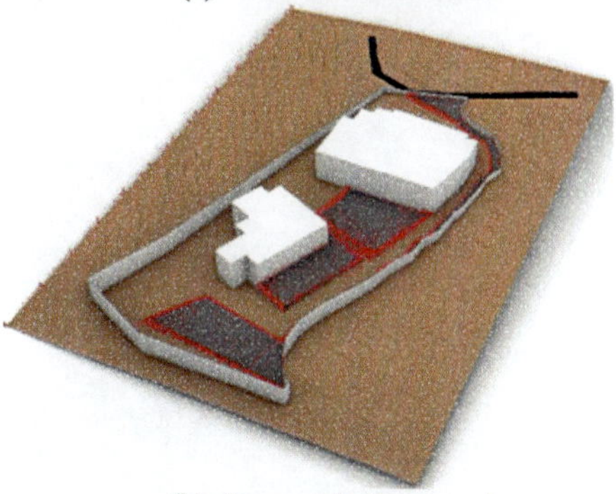

(b) Proposed site scenario

has not been considered by the tool. Else, the inundation could have been presented by the tool in the form of clustered arrows.

The clustering, however, can be observed in the proposed site scenario. Considering the buildings, roads and pavements as part of morphed terrain, we can see the inundation in the form of red coloured arrows cluttering at the edges in Fig. 8b. The need for stormwater runoff channels around the impervious built forms can be observed. The suitable location for rainwater harvesting could also be recognized from the stormwater runoff direction presented in Fig. 8b.

3.2 Rainwater Inundation

The site possesses the B group type of soil as per the United States Department of Agriculture classification. The study observed nearly 1.0 to 1.23 inches of precipitation depth on site for the precipitation intensity considered in the natural site scenario. However, the site approach road is predicted to have more than 3.9 inches depth of precipitation, as shown in Fig. 9a. The internal road and building frontages are also predicted to have more than 3.9 inches of precipitation depth (Fig. 9b) due to their

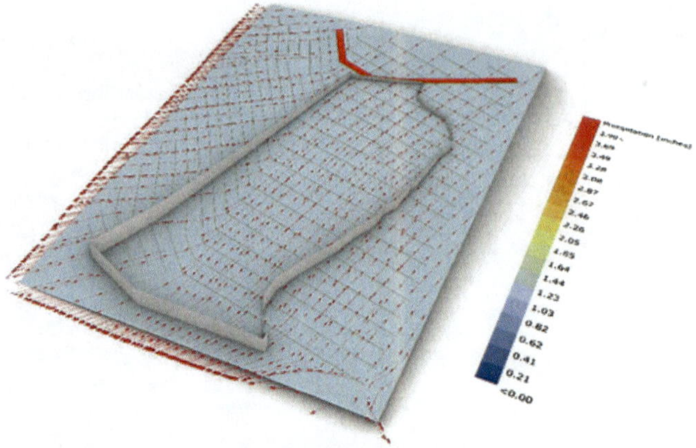

(a) Natural site scenario

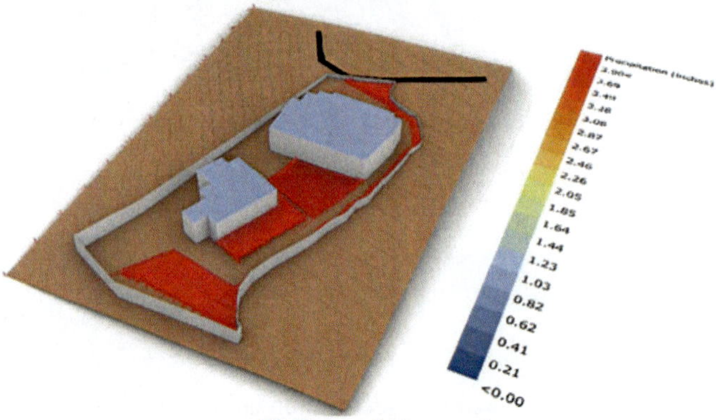

(b) Proposed site scenario

Fig. 9 showing the rainwater inundation on the previous and impervious surfaces on site in both scenarios

imperviousness. The rooftop, however, was observed to have less precipitation depth similar to that of an open site. The higher precipitation depth noticed in roads, pavements and frontages of buildings need to be addressed by the site designers. The friction loss between the vehicle tire surfaces and the road is very much possible with such high precipitation depth. Similarly, the chances of pavement users being carried away are also possible with such high rainwater inundation on pavements. The permeable pavements and roads could be a resourceful measure to avoid accidents with rainwater inundation on roads and pavements.

4 Conclusion

The CC is evident and the increasing weather extremities pose a significant threat to the natural and human-made ecosystems. Along with global warming, the increase in flood disasters has become a serious concern. The vulnerability of floods is higher in urban centres due to the increased footprint of non-pervious surfaces. The stormwater runoff assessment for site level and urban level is essential to reduce the disturbance to the natural stormwater runoff conveyance networks. The state-of-art 3D modelling tools such as Rhino-Gh and Rainwater + recipes enable the architects, Landscape and Urban designers to simulate the precipitation depth and stormwater runoff direction specific to the given site conditions. The significant gap identified is the unavailability of default extreme year precipitation data for every location. Thus, the present study demonstrated an approach to avail the extreme year precipitation data and simulated the DTM for the chosen location and its scenarios. Dissemination of this approach could help the landscape and urban designers integrate LID practices in the pre-design phase. Following this approach at the pre-design stage of site design and development can ensure reduced site stormwater inundation risks and urban flood disasters.

5 Limitation and Future Scope

Usually, the CN method forecasts runoff volume but not the peak runoff. However, as mentioned in the Validation sub-section, the study assumes the present extreme rainfall scenario as a future business-as-usual scenario. The study observed the need for scripting expertise to extract the location-specific extreme year precipitation data. Additionally, the study observed the use of the old Gh components in the Rainwater + recipe. Thus the authors of this paper are in the process to.

- Develop extreme year precipitation database for the Indian locations
- Script the Rainwater + logic as Gh components to reduce the need for more computation power for simulation.

References

1. Revi A, Sattwethwaite D E, Argon-Durand F, Corfee-Morlot J, Kiunsi R B R, Pelling M, Roberts DC, Solecki W (2014) Climate change 2014: impacts, adaptation, and vulnerability. In: Part A: global and sectoral aspects. contribution of working group II to the fifth assessment report of the intergovernmental panel on climate change. Cambridge University Press, Cambridge, United Kingdom and New York, NY, USA, pp 535–612
2. Collins M, Knutti R, Arblaster J, Dufresne JL, Fichefet T, Friedlingstein P, Gao X, Gutowski WJ, Johns T, Krinner G, Shongwe M, Tebaldi C, Weaver A J, Wehner M (2013) Long-term climate change: projections, commitments and irreversibility. In: Climate change 2013: the

physical science basis. Contribution of working group I to the fifth assessment report of the Intergovernmental panel on climate change
3. Anil KG, Sreeja SN (2016) Urban floods in Bangalore and Chennai: risk management challenges and lessons for sustainable urban ecology. pp 1638–1645
4. Gosain AK, Sandhya R, Debajit B (2006) Climate change impact assessment on hydrology of Indian river basins. pp 346–353
5. Haider A, Parth M, Vimal M (2019) Increased flood risk in Indian sub-continent under the warming climate
6. Menon A, Levermann A, Schewe J, Lehmann J, Frieler K (2013) Consistent increase in Indian monsoon rainfall and its variability across CMIP-5 models
7. Pascaline W, Guha-Sapir D, McClean D (2015) CRED, UNISDR, The human cost of natural disasters—a global perspective. Center for Research on the epidemiology of Disasters
8. Farhat R, Sirajuddin A, Shamshad A, Amir AK (2016) Urban floods in India. Int J Scientif Eng Res
9. Zbigniew WK, Yukiko H, Shinjiro K (2010) River floods in the changing climate—observations and projections. Water Resources Manage 2633–2646
10. Dewan AM (2013) In: Floods in a megacity: geospatial techniques in assessing hazards, risk and vulnerability, Springer, Dordrecht Heidelberg, New York, London
11. Abdishakur H (2018) The Top 5 must-have skills for geospatial data science. [Online] Available https://medium.com/spatial-data-science/the-top-5-must-have-skills-for-geospatial-data-science-64fe687a0a6
12. McNeel R (2020) Associates. rhino3d," 22 12 2020. [Online] Available https://www.rhino3d.com/mcneel/about/
13. Chen Y, Samuelson HW, Tong Z (2016) Integrated design workflow and a new tool for urban rainwater management. J Environ Manage 180:45–51
14. Cronshey R (1986) In: Urban hydrology for small watershed. US Dept. of Agriculture, Soil Conservation Service
15. Durrans SR, Dietrich K (2003) In: *Stormwater conveyance modeling and design*
16. USDA S (1985) Hydrology, national engineering handbook, Section 4. US Department of Agriculture, Washington, DC
17. Bureau of Indian Standards (2005) National Building Code of India, New Delhi
18. NASA (2020) Global Precipitation Measurement. [Online]. Available https://gpm.nasa.gov/missions/GPM. Accessed 24 Dec 2020
19. Huffman GJ, Stocker EF, Blovin DT, Nelkin EJ, Jackson T (2020) GPM IMERG Final Precipitation L3 Half Hourly 0.1 degree x 0.1 degree V06. Greenbelt, MD, Goddard Earth Sciences Data and Information Services Center (GES DISC), [Online]. Available https://disc.gsfc.nasa.gov/datasets/GPM_3IMERGHH_06/summary. Accessed 17 Dec 2020
20. NASA (2020) GES DISC. [Online]. Available https://disc.sci.gsfc.nasa.gov/. Accessed 24 Dec 2020
21. Press Trust of India, Magaluru (2018) Floods in Mangaluru as heavy rains lash Karnataka's coastal districts. The Hindustan Times, 29th May 2018. [Online]. Available https://www.hindustantimes.com/india-news/floods-in-mangaluru-as-heavy-rains-lash-karnataka-s-coastal-districts/story-TInSFQinzGAIkBsqh1g0VN.html. Accessed 21 December 2020
22. Davies R (2020) India—3 Dead, Hundreds Rescued After Record Rainfall in Karnataka. FloodList, 30th May 2018. [Online]. Available http://floodlist.com/asia/india-record-rainfall-floods-karnataka-may-2018. Accessed 20th December 2020
23. FE Online (2020) Mangalore Rain: PM Modi prays for safety of public in Karnataka as several cities submerge under water. Financial Express, 29th May 2018. [Online]. Available https://www.financialexpress.com/india-news/mangalore-rain-live-pre-monsoon-rains-hit-life-rescue-operations-on/1185717/. Accessed 20 Dec 2020
24. Schreyer A (2012) In: Architectural design with sketchUp. Hoboken, NJ, Wiley
25. Saldarriaga JF (2019) Importing topography in grasshopper using DTM. Columbia

Applications of AI in Health Monitoring of Structures in Potential Seismic Areas—A Review

C. P. Ginan and B. R. Jayalekshmi

Abstract Artificial Intelligence (AI) can be used to solve complex problems in civil engineering which involve time-consuming and arduous tasks, such that, the hurdles that appear when these works are completed using mere human labour can be completely overcome, by employing various techniques of AI. Furthermore, where testing fails or is hardly possible, AI can suffice the required design. AI can be of its best use when applied to the field of Structural Health Monitoring (SHM), which serves to identify and detect the current state and behaviour of structures. This article outlines the applications of AI in SHM in potential seismic zones. SHM functions in seismically prone areas by evaluating on field, the resistive power of a building against earthquakes and simultaneously it's potent to carry forth the services. The paper studies certain observations from research conducted during past few decades on development of artificial intelligence in SHM technologies in seismically intensive areas, in case of multistorey buildings, bridges, special structures and lifeline structures. The article begins with a brief introduction to artificial intelligence, further, detailing applications of AI in SHM in seismically prone areas. Subsequently, the contemporary applications of AI in the field are reviewed, alongside, the adaptability, sufficiency and potentiality of those methods to overcome the barriers of the conventional methods are discussed.

Keywords Artificial intelligence · Structural health monitoring · ANN · Potential monitoring · Damage prediction · Bridges

---

C. P. Ginan
NITK, Surathkal, Karnataka 575025, India
e-mail: ginan.181cv213@nitk.edu.in

B. R. Jayalekshmi (✉)
Department of Civil Engineering, NITK, Surathkal, Karnataka 575025, India
e-mail: brjaya@nitk.edu.in

C. Ghosh and S. Kolathayar (eds.), *A System Engineering Approach to Disaster Resilience*, Lecture Notes in Civil Engineering 205, https://doi.org/10.1007/978-981-16-7397-9_25

1 Introduction

Civil structures are very important to be monitored for damage prevention as it houses people and facilitate the activities of mankind. The strength of engineering structures depletes with age and by natural disasters. Each structure must be monitored and its current state and behaviour need to be predicted. Prediction allows us to find the damage zones of the structure so that we can concentrate on such zones. Post-earthquake monitoring shall also be performed to know whether the structure is safe to take loads further or if the damage is propagating in the structure.

The application of AI in monitoring the response of structures in seismically potential zones is the focus of this article. Civil engineering can be an ideal field where AI can be applied. This is because, by feeding into a machine, the same level and amount of data that any experienced, talented and expert civil engineer possesses, AI can exhibit an accurate and precise outcome, as expected from the said human expertise with lesser human effort. AI is being used in all fields, from design to the monitoring of structures. Mathematical methods are used for structural monitoring such as EDMS (Earthquake Disaster Management System) had been in use for a long period of time, but AI provides a better method with the development of technologies such as pattern matching, which is very complex for human brains. Prototype models are created and placed on a testing plate upon which artificial seismic load is applied. Then, artificial data are recorded for training AI for future earthquake responses. Notably, this technology can be employed to detect earthquakes of the kind that we have never witnessed to date.

This paper reviews the prediction and health monitoring of structures, multistory buildings, bridges, underground structures and liquid storage tanks. The AI methods discussed in this article are Artificial Neural Network (ANN), pattern recognition, machine learning and genetic algorithm, in which ANN is predominantly used. Further, ANN with different architecture giving different precision are discussed. The use of wireless sensors and automated AI software has made permanent monitoring a reality. The damage effects of both static and dynamic load on the structure and monitoring based on dynamic behaviour are also discussed.

2 Artificial Intelligence

Artificial Intelligence (AI), a modern technology that started its development in the 1950s, attributes to machines, human intelligence and behaviour, seeking to solve problems without complex human interventions. It can be described as a set of various technologies that enable machines to act and comprehend with intelligence in a human-like manner. AI ascribes to almost all the components of human intelligence, focusing on reasoning, perception, problem-solving, learning, etc. From Alan Turing's test to determine if a machine really is intelligent, to its official emergence in 1956 that introduced applications of AI which contributed to proving mathematical theorems and later to the programming language and finally to the development of a Project Debater that helps people argue with proper evidence and with little bias or ambiguity—Artificial Intelligence has emerged to be a very promising field of study. AI, when considered as a set of various technologies, the subset of this wide pool of study includes Machine Learning (machine learns and reprograms itself) and Deep learning (a subset of machine learning that uses neural networks with multiple layers). With these subsets and various other classifications like strong AI and Weak AI, Artificial Intelligence, in general, engage itself in speech recognition, Neural language processing (NLP), image recognition, real-time recommendations, etc. Image recognition is a major application of AI that identify and distinguish images, texts, object, or people (moving or non-moving). Pattern recognition is another sign in the field of artificial intelligence, that makes use of machine learning data to segregate data by performing special algorithms.

2.1 Machine Learning

Machine Learning, being a branch of Artificial Intelligence, seeks to build applications that can improve its accuracy of prediction or decision-making over time, that is derived from learned data, independent of programming to do so. Here, features and patterns are found out by equipping with trained algorithms, such that predictions and decisions are made with respect to new data. Machine Learning works basically in four steps. Once a training data set is chosen and prepared for, then an algorithm would be chosen for the training data set. The choice of an algorithm depends on the data type, whether it is labelled or unlabeled.

2.2 Artificial Neural Network

A major tool employed in machine learning, Artificial Neural Network (ANN) systems that intend to mimic human learning. These are structures that replicate the organizational principles seen in the brain. Pattern recognition, function approximation and classification are the areas in which ANN is applied to its best. In ANN, human brain-like structure is achieved as neuron nodes are interconnected like a web, each neuron, being made up of a cell body that is accountable for information processing while they carry information through inputs and outputs. First, the ANN undergoes training to learn pattern recognition. ANNs are of two different topologies, namely, Feed Forward and Feedback, in which, the former is used in pattern recognition, generation, or classification, with fixed inputs and outputs. Various strategies, classified as supervised learning, unsupervised learning and reinforcement learning, are employed for ANNs to be trained. A training or learning algorithm called the Backpropagation (BP) Algorithm, which learns with example is employed and is ideal for pattern recognition. ANN constitutes layers that are categorized into three—An Input layer, Hidden Layers and Output layer. ANN is a typical case of weighted graphs; the inputs and outputs are calculated based on the artificially assigned weights of the data. The input signals are received as patterns and images as vectors by ANN and these inputs are mathematically represented as notations. Each of these inputs is multiplied by their weights to solve the problem to obtain output signals, as each weight represents the relation between the input and the process.

Wavelets Transformation, Nonlinear Time history analysis (NTH) and Principal Compound Analysis (PCA) are applied with AI for better results. PCA is used along with AI, so that huge data is compressed. The compressed data can be then, easily processed by AI. The best performance of the AI method is evaluated based on Mean Scale Error (MSE), Regression and CPU time. When the data recorded contains noise in it, PCA helps to remove the noise, which in turn, helps to improve prediction.

3 AI in Structural Health Monitoring

Generally, all the references related to AI use similar methods other than articles that mention pattern recognition and genetic algorithm. This paper, therefore, mainly focuses on the applications of AI that employ methods that stand out from the rest, for example, those applications that combine AI with many other technologies such as PCA, NTH, wavelet transformation, etc. Differential factors that come with the data used for training, testing and validation are the next distinguishing feature that this article tends to look upon. When some articles used real recorded data, the other articles derived data from prototypes. Most of the references in this article use ANN but with differences in its architecture such as changes in the number of layers in the input, hidden and output layers and the number of neurons used.

4 Prediction of Damage

Prediction of the damage induced by earthquakes was a hard job for engineers. Two methods were mainly used for it, Seismic vulnerability curves and nonlinear Finite Element Method (FEM). In that FEM can only be used to assess a single important structure in any analysis process and as the number of structures increases the method becomes ineffective and time-consuming. Seismic vulnerability curves are better than FEM and can be applied to a class of similar structures but this method only takes a limited number of structural properties and ground motion is described using only one single parameter. If dissimilar structures want to be evaluated such as structures with a different number of stories or bays, this method cannot be applied. These shortcomings motivated the researchers to find a method that is more efficient and can be used on different classes of structures and use a broader number of parameters to label ground motion. As a solution for this ANN was used, to represent both the ground motion and structure using a greater number of structural properties and ground motion parameters. ANN was trained for various time periods of an earthquake and it was used to predict maximum response in a single-story structure directly to the matching time period [1]. Simulation was done using feedforward and Error Backpropagation Training algorithm with one hidden layer with varying nodes, consisting of one input layer and one output layer, it was understood that the response was good. If the network is trained for different time periods of an earthquake, then this model can be used to predict the response of the corresponding time period of an earthquake whose data were not been used for training the network. The analysis [2] was made on two-dimensional (2D) RC frames with different damping, stiffness, topology and strength and were subjected to different magnitudes of ground motions and the response data was used for predicting the seismic damage. The performance of ANN was tested using many examples and ANN was almost successful inaccurate prediction. The above articles were published before 2009 and it was at the early stage of AI application in seismic damage prediction. The author also explains that the ANN cannot be used in a place where we lack data such as previously unseen earthquake is a challenging task, as ANN studies from the data input and it interpolates between these data and gives the result but any extension would require additional data for training. After this article has been published, many scientists have worked in this field and made many discoveries using models and the data acquired within this period.

Method for prediction of nonlinear structural behaviour when earthquake load was applied using an adaptive scheme was reported in [3]. The prediction of damage using ANN can be applied in the performance based design framework, aiming at reducing computational cost when dynamic analyses were performed. The training of the ANN with different sets of data helps in the better performance of ANN. For the training purpose, artificial records were used, which were better than natural records as it produces more cycles of data and it produces nonexistent data which was helpful in training ANN for a future seismic event. Prediction by adaptive and non-adaptive schemes are examined by this article: (i) Non-adaptive scheme, is a method where ANN was trained once over the accelerogram data and the prediction of structural seismic response for all time steps was based on it. (ii) Adaptive scheme is where the ANN is trained once but the prediction was rectified by performing conventional NDA in certain predefined time steps. The performance prediction of the non-adaptive scheme was good in the case of structures with linear to slightly nonlinear but it produce unacceptable results when it was used for highly nonlinear structures. Small errors were accumulated and the result deviated from its real value but this accumulation was not present for linear structure. An adaptive scheme accurately predicts the behaviour of the nonlinear structure as it corrects the accumulated errors periodically. Resulting in highly accurate values as compared to the non-adaptive scheme.

4.1 Multistorey Buildings

The prediction of damage in multistory buildings is also calculated by ANN. Suryanita et al. [4] has investigated the use of ANN for the prediction of earthquake-induced damage state of buildings. For this, a 10-story building model was tested with earthquake loads based on the past time history record. The prediction of damage states was done using a backpropagation multilayer ANN in MATLAB toolbox. This ANN was trained using the time history of earthquake data load and the response of the model structure. There were 4 ANN architecture models tested with displacement, velocity and acceleration as input. Model 1 had all the above, model 2 had displacement, model 3 had the velocity and model 4 had acceleration respectively as input. Damage levels of the structure were the output of NN. The damage levels are categorized as Safe, Immediate Occupancy, Life Safety, or in a condition of Collapse Prevention. Among these models, the first model gives maximum accuracy of 95% and model 4 gives the least accuracy of 80%. All the models have an average accuracy of 85%. There was a total of nine sets of data in which eight sets were used to train ANN and the ninth set was used to check the accuracy of the trained ANN.

The basic 3-layer architecture of ANN was used to predict the damage, an input layer, hidden layer and an output layer were employed in [5]. Ground motion parameters of an earthquake were selected from 34 provinces as input parameters. Multistory building structures of RCC with shear walls were made as models for testing, three different building heights were used, 10 stories, 15 stories and 20 stories. Model response spectrum analysis was carried out to get the responses of the model structures. Thus 6345 data sets were obtained. This data was used to train, validate and test the ANN. The BP ANN architecture was used to predict the damage in which 3-layer architecture with 8 (only eight) neurons in the input layer, 2(only two) neurons in the hidden layer and 6 (only six) neurons in the output layer. The main output parameters of ANN are velocity, story acceleration and story displacement. For training ANN, a total of 6345 data sets were used in which, 72% of data sets were used to train ANN, 14% for validation and 14% for testing. The trained ANN performance was evaluated and a 96% rate of prediction was achieved.

Damage prediction of the multistory building was reported in [6] as a task for Multilayer Neural Network and was time-consuming. Hence Functional Link Neural Network was used for better prediction of seismic response of tall shear buildings. "A Functional Link Neural Network (FLNN) is a single-layer neural network where the hidden layer is replaced by a functional expansion block for enhancement of the input vectors. FLNNs are highly effectual, computationally more efficient and faster learning than multilayer neural networks (MNNs)" [6]. FLNN consists mainly of two parts, one was a learning part and the other was a functional expansion part. FLNN uses ground acceleration data as input and response of each story of a multistory structure as output. The structural response of the multistory building was predicted using FLNN and the polynomial used in the expansion block of input vectors for the enhancement are Legendre and Chebyshev polynomials. When results were compared, FLNN is faster than MNN as FLNN does not have a hidden layer.

In FLNN, to minimize a given cost function, the weights were updated. The weights were updated using Error backpropagation algorithm. A feedforward and error back-propagation algorithm was used for learning. the MNN uses 3-layer architecture input, hidden and output layer. An error BP algorithm was used to train MNN. The conventional method of MNN takes more time to execute complex earthquake data and FLNN was developed for the main purpose of executing such complex data with a minimal amount of time. In testing, FLNN proves to be a better method as it is more accurate in predicting the response. Prediction was then developed by Convolution Neural Network [7] making it more precise.

5 Damage Identification

The position of damage on the structure by seismic load can be identified by using image processing of AI. The damage of reinforced concrete column was automatically identified using Region-based Convolution Neural Network (RCNN) image processing. An interactive labelling process was done automatically by MATLAB. For learning, 400 images of post-earthquake damaged images taken by consumer-grade cameras were used. [8] reported that the trained RCNN can automatically detect the multitype seismic damage up to a precision of 80%. Convolution base along with region proposal network (RPN) and an RCNN Module makes the RCNN faster. The faster RCNN thus produced detects and identifies the damage in the image and it produces the rectangular bounding boxes around the damaged part. When an image is inputted, the output is of the image with rectangular bounding boxes showing the damaged part of the structure. The fast RCNN predicts whether the input image presents any damage which is among the four types of damage, rebar buckling, rebar exposure, concrete spalling and concrete cracking based on training data.

5.1 Buildings

The structural damage identification was carried out by Ni et al. [9] using measured Neural Network (NN) and Frequency Response Function (FRF). In this article, a 38-story reinforced concrete building with 1:20 scale was used as the model. It was tested on a 5 m*5 m shaking table by exerting earthquake loads. It was tested level wise with low to high damage, till the model was completely damaged. FRFs were generated from the above vibration for seismic damage detection. The FRFs obtained from the Polyvinylidene Fluoride (PVDF) film sensors were usually used to train the NN for prediction but as this FRF data was huge in size, computation of this data using NN causes the problem and reduces efficiency. And half use of this data would result in loss of valuable information, so this data was compressed using Principal Component Analysis (PCA). PCA filters the noise and reduces dimensionality. The compressed FRF data provides accurate identification. When damage identification is compared, PCA methods provides much higher accuracy than FRF method.

Using modal parameters and artificial neural network, seismic damage identification method was developed for steel moment-frame structures with regular geometry both in plan and elevation. It was a 2-stage process in which, the first stage was to calibrate the structure data such as mass and stiffness before seismic action or at the initial stage. The second stage was the evaluation of the final mass and stiffness of the structure after the seismic load was applied. A typical office structure, a 5-story building with 16 m*18 m dimension and a height of 4 m for the first story and rest with 3 m was used for simulation through a basic Finite Element Method (FEM) data the NNs were trained. The multilayer perceptron (MLP) and radial basis functions were used for damage detection by NNs. A 2-layer feed forward MLP was applied in this work. In this method, mass was considered an important parameter. The effect of modal data error was studied using Gaussian noise, as Gaussian noise was added to the modal parameters and the result was compared with the previous one, it is shown that the variation due to modal error should be less than 1% for a damage prediction of 95% [10]. The damage caused by seismic load in the braces of a steel structure is identified using Deep Neural Network [11]. The E-simulator data generation was used to train the AI.

Damage to the shear wall was detected using artificial neural network in [12]. The concrete shear wall helps in resisting the building against lateral loads. Pushover analysis which is also known as Nonlinear static analysis was the approach used in this method. Pushover analysis is a method that applies the lateral force of monotonically increasing nature on the structure till it fails or reaches a target displacement. A FEM model (nonlinear) of a 5-story building with shear wall was created and pushover analysis was applied to get plastic hinges and inter-story drifts. For inputs and outputs to the neural network, the inter-story drifts and plastic hinges were used. NN with single hidden layer and multilayer feed forward network was used. By trial and error method, the number of neurons in hidden layer was obtained. From these results, the MLP neural network predicts the damage of the shear wall when it was compared with nonlinear time history analysis values.

Vafaei et al. [13] demonstrates the damage identification of cantilever structure was done by using Wavelet Transformation (WT) and Artificial Neural Network. "WT is a time–frequency analysis based on a windowing technique, which employs variable-sized regions to decompose signals" [13]. There is a sharp transition in the dynamic response of a structure when the stiffness of the structure varies due to damage. There would be spikes in the decomposed signals which reflect discontinuity in signal when WT was used to check the damage. For damage identification, the seismic acceleration data was taken from a strategically selected location. PCA was used to compress the decomposed data by WT which was used by ANN to predict the damage. The method was applied to a tall tower located at Kuala Lumpur Airport. This article employed multilayer feed forward NN also for damage identification. The result predicted by the method is reported as accurate and because of the use of PCA, there was very negligible effect of noise.

The Fuzzy Neural Network was used to predict the damage caused by the seismic action [14]. The acceleration data of earthquakes recorded were having errors, due to human or instrumental error, so this data was called Fuzzy and when this data was used to predict using NN it becomes Fuzzy Neural Network (FNN). A probabilistic approach to such data is limited as it requires a huge amount of data that may not be available in all parameters. The FNN cannot be used for negative data, which means bipolar data cannot be used in FNN. The bipolar data was converted to α-cut form and that data was used for training, later it was retransformed from unipolar to bipolar. Using this data FNN architecture was trained and the prediction was done. Once FNN was trained, it can be used to predict the damage due to real earthquake data.

5.2 Bridges

Permanent and automated health monitoring can improve information about long-term behaviour and the current state of the bridge. The permanently applied sensors continuously recording the measurement of the bridge help in permanent monitoring. ANN has been used to predict the health monitoring of bridges caused by earthquake acceleration [15]. Low intensity loads of ground acceleration were used to simulate numerical data. Feed forward and backpropagation algorithm was used in which acceleration data from sensors was used as an input and the output was the damage level of bridge. The damage level range from low to high; they are: (i) Immediate Occupancy (IO), (ii) Life Safety (LS), (iii) Collapse Prevention (CP). Usually, the analysis would be done after monitoring, that is the results obtained in the monitoring process and expertise engineers were required to do the analysis but the intelligent system created in this article monitors and analyses the bridge using ANN. There is no need to know how the monitoring works or input–output relationship, linear or nonlinear data, the ANN with an adequate number of hidden layer neurons can learn and approximate the damage. Using Visual Basic Programming Seer Monalisa-ANN was created which conducts the prediction process. ANN was trained using 835 acceleration data and it was tested with 234 data. For seismic health monitoring of bridges, ANN can be used successfully.

Peak Ground Acceleration (PGA) is a key parameter to check the damage of the bridges. ANN was used to estimate PGA at the site of 21 bridges with almost 500 m length [16]. The input for the ANN was local magnitude, focal length and epicentre distance. For better performance of ANN in the prediction of PGA, hybrid approaches like NN and a genetic algorithm can be used. The architecture of the ANN was, one neuron in the output layer and the hidden layer with three neurons was used to train and predict the seismic estimation analysis. 70% of data was used to train ANN and 30% was used to adapt and check the method. This ANN can only use the seismic data of Richter scale magnitude above 5.0 otherwise there would be unwanted noise. There are two methods to estimate PGA at the bridge location from the recorded seismic data. NN1 (model 1) was a simple method that takes the data from nearby station of the bridge and use weighting factors to obtain PGA at the bridge. NN2 (model 2) was a method where it finds the epicentre from the recorded seismic data and this new parameter was inputted to a weight based NN and the PGA was predicted.

This paper [17], aims to compare the performance of ANN with displacement and acceleration as the data domain, to identify which data domain predicts the damage more accurately. The ANN architecture uses 1-layer input, 1 and 2 hidden layers and an output layer. The output is of the bridge condition, values from 0–3, in which 0 stands for safe and 3 stands for high risk. The output bridge condition was predicted using a finite element analysis program. The study considered three spans of box girders on which earthquake load was applied. Displacement, velocity and acceleration were used as input. The linear behaviour of the piers was considered during the health monitoring of bridges due to the earthquake. The acceleration and displacement data domain were evaluated based on different parameters such as MSE (Mean Square Error), Regression (R mean), CPU time (running time). For a better method, the value of MSE should be less as it is the error in calculation, R means should be more; favourably value to be close to one which is 100% accurate prediction and the CPU time should be short. The best performance was achieved by displacement data domain with one hidden layer which gives an 80% regression. The monitoring of bridges using ANN was recommended to use the displacement data domain with one hidden layer.

This article [18] introduces the Nero-Genetic hybrid method to estimate the damage of bridges. It is a fusion of Artificial Neural Networks and Genetic Algorithm, for numerical modelling techniques. Genetic algorithm was used to optimize the acceptance of NN weight in Neuro-Genetic hybrid. In the hybrid, Back Propagation NN uses Genetic Algorithm to estimate the weights. For prediction by NN, it is not essential to have the input–output relation, it can be used for a nonlinear relationship between the input and output. Whereas the genetic algorithm uses selection, mutation and crossover operations. 70% of the data was used to train the Neuro-Genetic Hybrid, 15% for validation and the remaining for testing. The activation function, network architecture model and initial weight were the parameters on which the performance of the neuro-Genetic method depends. The best method for the prediction of damage due to earthquake load was the neuro-Genetic method with a sensor recording data system, which predicts 97% accuracy to the actual damage.

5.3 Underground Structures

The damage to underground structures due to seismic load is very dangerous. It is hard to evaluate the damage propagation in underground structures as it cannot take successive seismic loads. Ubiquitous Sensor Network (USN) are the sensors used to identify changes and for communication in the underground. Many such sensors form a network and detect the damage. The finite element model of Ulchiro- 3ga station was used to train and test the ANN. From acceleration data, the history of damage and damage pattern was obtained. The article [19] employs unsupervised learning recognition for statistical pattern identification. The change in the structure or the damage propagation is recognized on a timely basis so that the current state and behaviour of the structure can be predicted. When there was a high difference in acceleration amplitude between good and damaged conditions, the increase of stiffness degrading ratio was observed. The stiffness degrading ratio was increasing whereas the value of reliability interval was decreasing. When the stiffness degrading ratio is 40%, the methodology used in this study is useful.

5.4 Liquid Storage Tanks

ANN was used to predict the damage of liquid storage tanks in the seismic area [20]. For training ANN, response of strong earthquake experienced liquid tanks were used, a total of 240 sample data were taken in which 190 data were used to train the ANN and 50 for testing. Six parameters were used as input for the ANN, they were, PGA, tank height, tank diameter, liquid height during an earthquake, percentage fill and the output was the damage state of the storage tank. There are many input parameters, it was very hard to obtain a mathematical relation of this nonlinear and uncertain input data, which makes ANN a powerful tool in predicting the damage as it does not require any mathematical representation. The ANN model was constructed and trained using the back propagation (BP) algorithm. The supervised network was constructed and trained using MATLAB NN toolbox. It was concluded from this study that ANN can be used to predict the damage of the storage tank.

6 Conclusion

AI has improved the damage prediction from the Seismic vulnerability curves and nonlinear Finite Element Method (FEM), in which all the structural parameters were hard to be used in analysis and it was hard to apply for dissimilar structures. AI has been a breakthrough in health monitoring of structures under earthquake zones. Prediction is the main focus area in which AI is used in SHM in the seismically potential zones. The damages induced by the earthquake and whether the structure can withstand the seismic load or is it safe to carry a live load are all predicted with the application of AI. ANN is a favourite area of study under AI and its applications in SHM for researchers today. ANN makes the distinction between linear and nonlinear functions insignificant because of the process of self-learning that ANN conducts from the input and output data. ANN applied with other operations such as wavelet transformation, PCA, NTH, etc. helps in predicting a much higher precise damage state and deal with noise and complex data hazards. Data from previous records of earthquakes or from the new data obtained from the models created are used to train the AI. Around 70–75% of such data is used for the training purpose, 10–15% for testing and 10–15% for the validation process. Other than ANN, pattern recognition and genetic algorithm is used for damage identification.

Other methods of AI such as machine learning, deep learning, etc. are yet to be developed in SHM of seismic zones. It is still in the developing phase as it requires precise data. The present recorded data are not precise and accurate as it has errors due to human mistakes and equipment malfunctioning. The maximum accuracy to date obtained for a normal structure damage identification is 97%. However, it can be improved to much higher accuracy. The applications of AI in liquid storage tanks and underground structures are yet to be improved. The damage caused by earthquakes with higher magnitudes is still hardly possible to be predicted. The use of advanced sensors and much more advanced AI methods can jointly improve SHM in severe seismic zones and thus, automated seismic SHM can be achieved, which makes the structures safer and enduring.

References

1. Chakraverty S, Marwala T, Gupta P, Tettey T (2007) Response prediction of structural system subject to earthquake motions using artificial neural network. Asian J Civ Eng 7(3):301–308
2. de Lautour OR, Omenzetter P (2009) Prediction of seismic-induced structural damage using artificial neural networks. Eng Struct 31
3. Lagaros ND, Papadrakakis M (2012) Neural network based prediction schemes of the non-linear seismic response of 3D buildings. Adv Eng Softw 44:92–115
4. Suryanita R, Maizir H, Yuniarto E, Zulfakar M, Jingga H (2017) Damage level prediction of reinforced concrete building based on earthquake time history using artificial neural network. MATEC Web Conf 138:02024
5. Suryanita R, Maizir H, Jingga H (2016) Prediction of structural response due to earthquake load using artificial neural networks. In: International conference on "engineering and technology, computer, basic and applied sciences ECBA
6. Sahoo DM, Chakraverty S (2018) Functional link neural network learning for response prediction of tall shear buildings with respect to earthquake data. IEEE Trans Syst. Man Cybernet Syst 48
7. BK Oh, Park Y, Park HS (2020) Seismic response prediction method for building structures using convolutional neural network. Struct Control Health Monit 27(5):e2519
8. Xu Y, Wei S, Bao Y, Li H (2019) Automatic seismic damage identification of reinforced concrete columns from images by a region—based deep convolutional neural network. Struct Control Health Monit 26
9. Ni YQ, Zhou XT, Ko JM (2006) Experimental investigation of seismic damage identification using PCA-compressed frequency response functions and neural networks. J Sound Vib 290:242–263
10. Gonza´lez a MP, Zapico JL (2008) Seismic damage identification in buildings using neural networks and modal data. Comput Struct 86:416–426
11. Yamashita T, Kohiyama M, Watanabe K (2020) Deep neural network for detecting earthquake damage to brace members installed in a steel frame. Jpn Archit Rev. https://doi.org/10.1002/2475-8876.12188,(2020)
12. Vafaei MR, Adnan AB, abd. Rahman AB (2013) Real-time seismic damage detection of concrete shear walls using artificial neural networks. J Earthquake Eng 17:137–154
13. Vafaei M, Adnan AB, Abd. Rahman AB (2014) A neuro-wavelet technique for seismic damage identification of cantilever structures. Struct Infrastruct Eng Maintenance Manage Life-Cycle Design Performance 10

14. Chakraverty S, Sahoo DM (2017) Fuzzy neural network based response of uncertain system subject to earthquake motions. In: Papadrakakis M et al. (eds) Computational methods in earthquake engineering, computational methods in applied sciences, vol 44. https://doi.org/10.1007/978-3-319-47798-5_13
15. Suryanita R, Adnan A (2010) Application of artificial neural network in bridges seismic monitoring system. In: 3rd International graduate conference on engineering, science and humanities (IGCESH) school of graduate studies Universiti Teknologi Malaysia
16. Kerh T, Huang C, Gunaratnam D (2011) Neural network approach for analyzing seismic data to identify potentially hazardous bridges. In: Hindawi Publishing corporation mathematical problems in engineering, vol 464353
17. Suryanita R, Adnan A (2013) Application of neural networks in bridge health prediction based on acceleration and displacement data domain. In: Proceedings of the international multi conference of engineers and computer scientists Vol I, IMECS 2013, March 13–15, Hong Kong
18. Suryanita R, Azlan Adnan M (2017) Intelligent bridge seismic monitoring system based on neuro genetic hybrid. TELKOMNIKA 15(4):1830–1840
19. Kim JH, Kim NE (2014) Earthquake damage monitoring for underground structures based damage detection techniques. IJR Int J Railway 7(4):94–99
20. Razzaghi MS, Mohebbi A (2011) Predicting the seismic performance of cylindrical steel tanks using artificial neural networks (ANN). Acta Polytechnica Hungarica 8(2)
21. Molas Gl, Yamazaki F (1995) Neural networks for quick earthquake damage estimation. Earthquake Eng Struct Dynam 24:505–516
22. Ramhormozian S, Omenzetter P, Orense R (2013) Artificial neural networks approach to predict principal ground motion parameters for quick post-earthquake damage assessment of bridges. In: 2013 NZSEE conference
23. Bitarafan M, Zolfani SH, Arefi SL, Zavadskas EK, Mahmoudzadeh A (2014) Evaluation of real-time intelligent sensors for structural health monitoring of bridges based on Swara Waspas; a case In Iran. vol 9(4), pp 333–340, ISSN 1822–427X / eISSN 1822–4288

State-Funded Macro-Insurance Policy for Disaster Resilience: A Study on National Disaster Insurance Policy in Sri Lanka

K. L. A. K. T. Liyanage, G. Wedawatta, P. A. Vijekumara, and U. Kulatunga

Abstract Natural hazard-induced disasters are a common occurrence in many parts of the world. Though preventive steps are taken to lessen the effects of disasters, disasters still have an impact on the country's social, economic and environmental aspects. Over the last decade, Sri Lanka has been affected by a variety of natural disasters. As a result of the catastrophic consequences of these incidents, more attention is being paid to disaster resilience. In 2016, 'National Natural Disaster Insurance Policy (NNDIP)' was established to cover for damages and compensate the victims of natural hazard-induced disasters. Although the policy was established, there are issues and challenges in the implementation and administration of the policy. To identify the issues and challenges, initially, literature was reviewed. To achieve the aim of the study which is to identify the issues and challenges in the NNDIP, a qualitative approach was followed with ten (10) expert interviewees. Content analysis was used to analyse the collected data. From the study, key challenges and issues were identified as loss adjustment and claim management, delay in processing claims, insufficient staff and lack of clear guidance on the claim process.

Keywords Disaster resilience · Insurance claims · Insurance policy · Loss adjustment · Macro-insurance · Post-disaster recovery

1 Introduction

Over the past decade, throughout the globe, disasters have increased enormously and it has affected the communities on a large scale [1]. The key reason for the increase of natural disasters is identified as climatic change [2]. Disasters such as earthquakes,

K. L. A. K. T. Liyanage (✉) · U. Kulatunga
Department of Building Economics, University of Moratuwa, Moratuwa, Sri Lanka
e-mail: kushanil@uom.lk

G. Wedawatta
Department of Civil Engineering, Aston University, Birmingham, UK

P. A. Vijekumara
National Building Research Organization, Colombo, Sri Lanka

C. Ghosh and S. Kolathayar (eds.), *A System Engineering Approach to Disaster Resilience*, Lecture Notes in Civil Engineering 205, https://doi.org/10.1007/978-981-16-7397-9_26

Tsunamis, floods, droughts, storms, landslides create significant impacts on the lives of affected people in both social and economic aspects. Further, the government holds the responsibility to replace and repair infrastructure and allocation provisions for the least able victims of the disaster and it is considered to be the post-disaster role of the government [3].

Over the past years, a number of such disasters took place in Sri Lanka [4]. After the 2004 tsunami disaster in Sri Lanka, the need for a proper institutional structure for disaster management increased and, as a result, the National Disaster Management Centre was formed under the Ministry of Highways, Social and Health [5]. As per the authors [2], institutes related to disaster management in Sri Lanka has undergone several changes since 1995 and only after 2004 Tsunami disaster and these institutions and the overall disaster management process in Sri Lanka have received the most comprehensive reforms. Further, for the disaster reliefs, National Disaster Relief Services Centre (NDRSC) released the funding for relevant government authorities for reconstruction and rehabilitation until the introduction of National Natural Disaster Insurance (NNDI) policy in 2016 which was a major milestone in Disaster Risk Reduction (DRR) in Sri Lanka [6]. NNDI policy was introduced to Sri Lanka with the aim of compensating the victims of natural disasters. Though the policy was introduced to compensate the victims, there are issues and challenges in implementing the NNDI policy. Therefore, the study aims to identify the issues and challenges in the NNDI policy.

2 Literature Review

2.1 Disaster and Disaster Management

The number of disasters occurring worldwide has almost increased over the last three decades. Disaster can be defined as an event that is natural or manmade with a progressive or sudden occurrence that creates severe impacts on the affected community [7]. Moreover, authors [8] has stated natural catastrophe occurs when a significant geological, meteorological or hydrological phenomenon exceeds a community's capacity to respond to that occurrence. In addition to that, Jha [9] has categorised natural disasters under four categories, geophysical, hydrological, meteorological and climatological. Furthermore, through natural disasters, physical, social and cultural and environmental impacts take place [8, 10, 11]. Thus, systematic disaster management needs to be available in every country. Disaster management can be defined as the management of disasters and their post consequences through appropriate and immediate actions [12].

When considering the global context, Sendai Framework has been identified as the globally accepted framework for disaster risk reduction [13]. In the Sendai Framework for disaster risk reduction, four priorities for action, seven targets and 13 guiding principles can be identified [14]. Moreover, Sustainable Development Goals also look into disaster risk reduction [15]. Furthermore, USA's Federal Emergency Management Agency (FEMA) guidelines can also be shown as a guideline which helps for disaster management work where there are 14 emergency support functions to be followed after a disaster [16]. In addition to that, the Australian Institute for Disaster Resilience guideline (AIDR) provides a priority sequence of events in disaster management [17].

The government plays a major role in post-disaster management in countries. That is, by serving as the "last resort insurers" to reinstall the infrastructure and cover for private sector losses [3]. As per Petrucci [10], the government is "the most effective insurance instrument of the system". Further, the author has stated that the reason for this is the ability of the government to spread and diversify the risk over a large population. Moreover, [18] have highlighted that the objectives of international efforts to avoid or respond to extreme weather events are followed in order to protect human health and safety, the climate and the economic stability of nations.

2.2 Disaster Management in Developed and Developing Countries

2.2.1 Developed Countries

This role of the government is considered significant in developed countries. Around a third of the USD, 6.2 billion direct damages from the US midwest floods in 1993 were repaid by federal and state government assistance, according to reports [19]. Further, authors have stated after the devastating flooding of the Upper Tisza River in Hungary in 2001, approximately 1000 houses were completely rebuilt by the government. Additionally, Varangis et al. [20] have detailed the kind of taxpayer solidarity with flood victims is common for many mostly developed European countries. Kerjan and Kunreuther [1] also have highlighted the impact of insurance and government in the aftermath of catastrophes in developed counties mentioning they are playing major roles in ensuring economic and social resilience.

According to Linneroth-Bayer and Mechler [21], the involvement of government in assisting in post-disaster management varies even among developed countries. As per them [21], around 48% of the direct losses from 1997 floods were borne by the Polish government and only 4% of affected Kobe earthquake households in Japan from 1995 were covered despite having a national public–private seismic insurance scheme. Authors have stated that in both these cases government had to fund private victims despite having to reinstate damaged infrastructure. Whereas in the USA private sector insurance providers covered 30% of all private and public direct damages from the 1994 Northridge earthquake, while the federal government covered just 20% of total losses by helping state governments rebuild damaged infrastructure [21].

Most developed countries provide monetary compensation and post-disaster assistance to the victims often in state and private sector partnerships of insurers [21]. Further to them [21], official public–private insurance schemes for natural disasters such as flooding, earthquakes and all hazards have been enacted by many developed countries such as Japan, France, the United States and New Zealand. Authors have said that the National Flood Insurance Program (NFIP) implemented in the USA is a good example of this. This was done to expand the insurance industry's position in developing flood insurance policies whereas flood peril had been considered as uninsurable while taking all the risks to the government in the objective of passing the eventual risk to the industry and persons living in risky areas.

2.2.2 Developing Countries

Usually, low-income countries depend on government and foreign assistance to deal with severe floods [1]. Nevertheless, Linnerooth-Bayer and Mechler [21] accentuated the fact that the minimal support from the government in such counties. According to them [21], in developed countries, the scheme of government insurance and public–private partnerships is insufficient to fund low- and middle-income countries. Further, authors have highlighted the fact of the inability of residents of those countries to cover their risks through commercial insurance even though they are being backed by the government should be noted. Moreover, as mentioned earlier, the government is also unable to confront the liquidity deficit. As per Gurenko [22], in such situations, governments turn into international donors and development banks. Linnerooth-Bayer and Mechler [21] stated that still with international donors, governments of developing countries would struggle to confront the liquidity deficit apart from a few exceptions such as the Indian Ocean Tsunami disaster in 2004. This has resulted in half-complete projects and half-complete houses even many years after the reconstruction process in some instances [23].

Cohen and Sebstad [24] have stated the willingness of disadvantaged and oppressed people to participate in such processes must be considered in any discussion of how to facilitate risk pooling and transfer in developing countries. Reciprocal exchange, such as kinship links and group self-help, are the alternatives available. As per authors these arrangements may not be enough for major disasters and losses but work to a satisfactory level for less severe events. Micro-insurance is considered to be a credible alternative. As per Mechler et al. [25] disaster micro-insurance has been implemented in developing countries with the aim of facilitating affordable life and health insurances and also covering the loss of small scale assets from natural disasters. Authors stated that the micro-insurance is seen by the disaster risk management community as part of a wider, integrated disaster risk management system including risk prevention, preparedness and risk transfer. However, according to authors [25], there is a limited number of micro-insurance cover against disaster risks in developing countries.

2.3 Insurance for Disaster

Deductibles can be considered as a well-established and effective means to encourage private loss migratory measures which mean the insurer has to bear a part of the damage as per this principle [26]. Further authors have stated that deductibles shall be linked to the risk of the insured. Hence, high-risk prone households or other insured objects shall have the strongest incentives for migratory actions. As per the authors [25], insurance only indemnifies any loss through pooling the risks in exchange for a premium and does not reduce the immediate impact of the disaster which means affected people get compensated from the contributions of the number of unaffected. Thus, receiving larger compensation than the premium. Authors [25] have also explained micro-insurance by accentuating the difference of micro-insurance from other types of insurance through the affordability of such insurances by low-income people. Furthermore, micro-insurance provides timely financial assistance following extreme-event shocks, it reduces the long-term consequences of disasters.

Thieken et al. [26] have proposed insurance companies encourage their insured in private mitigation activities. They have proposed to educate the policyholders on disaster mitigation activities and any reward system for them for adhering to rules and regulations which has been imposed to minimise the effect of natural disasters. According to Kreimer et al. [27], the concentration is now being shifted to preventing losses and providing safety nets, that is from the earlier emphasis of emergency relief and rehabilitation. Gurenko [22] has also accentuated the fact of international financial institutions and the disaster management community are now placing great emphasis on pre-disaster, proactive disaster planning to reduce and transfer risks.

2.4 Sri Lankan Disaster Management and Insurance Policy

Sri Lanka has undergone many major natural hazard-induced disasters in the recent past, such as drought cycles, floods and landslides, with the government facing a pattern of rising relief payments [2]. Thus, the government and streamlined non-government organisations provided relief for the causalities of such disasters [6]. The author [6] has highlighted that through financial assistance and rehabilitation programmes these institutes have succeeded to some extent in overcoming the situation. Nevertheless, the Disaster Management Act was enacted in 2005 to include appropriate immediate legal guidelines in order to efficiently handle all stages of a disaster and to strengthen the community's resilience and was subsequently updated into a national framework [2]. In addition, the authors claimed that the Disaster Management Centre (DMC) was also set up and currently DMC, which works under the Ministry of Disaster Management, set up a disaster management program in 2014 and intended to incorporate the Sendai System into disaster management in Sri Lanka.

In the past, National Disaster Relief Services Centre (NDRSC) released disaster relief directly to the appropriate government agencies for recovery and restoration activities [6]. As per the regulations, families to be eligible for relief on any widespread disaster even though being a causality must have a monthly income of less than LKR. 3000.00 for the whole family. Divisional Secretaries shall decide on the relief eligible families and collect provisions relevant to their relevant divisional secretariat. The NNDI policy was proposed as a Budget plan in 2016 to boost the country's economy and growth. This is to be done under the joint oversight of the Ministry of Disaster Management and the National Trust Fund for Insurance under the Ministry of Finance.

3 Research Method

A study of prior literature is important to recognize the gaps in current knowledge [28]. Hence, literature was collected from books, journal articles, industry reports, conference proceedings and from documents related to disaster, disaster management, disaster management in developed and developing countries, disaster management in Sri Lanka and insurance policy. Further, Kumar [29] stated that to achieve the desired objectives of a research study, it is necessary to identify the most appropriate research approach, strategy and techniques. The research approach can be discussed under three categories as a qualitative, quantitative and mixed approach [30]. As the study focuses on the issues in the existing NNDI policy, limited literature is available as the policy was introduced in 2016. When research requires the experience and different perspectives of the people, the ideal approach is the qualitative approach [31]. Further, through a qualitative approach, in-depth opinions and attitudes of the participants, experiences and behaviours can be observed while conducting the interviews with the participants [32]. Thus, to identify the current status of the NNDI policy, a qualitative approach was used. As the study followed the qualitative approach, ten (10) semi-structured interviews were conducted with the experts who have sound knowledge in disaster management and NNDI policy. Data gathered from semi-structured interviews were analysed using content analysis manually. Table 1 shows the profile of the respondents.

4 Analysis

4.1 Disasters in Sri Lanka

Sri Lanka, being situated in a path of two monsoons has resulted in adverse weather conditions which leads to several natural hazard-induced disasters. In the recent past decade, Sri Lanka faced several tragedies like landslides, floods, tsunami,

Table 1 Profile of the Respondent

Profession	Code	Years of experience
Assistant Manager in Insurance Regulatory Commission of Sri Lanka	E1	18
Kegalle District Secretary	E2	15
Scientists in the National Building Research Organisation (NBRO)	E3	7
Assistant Director in Disaster Management Centre (DMC)	E4	20
Engineer in National Housing Development Authority (NHDA)	E5	16
Chief Executive Officer (CEO) in the National Insurance Trust Fund (NITF)	E6	28
Senior Lecturer in Disaster Management	E7	13
Assistant Professor in Disaster Management	E8	18
Assistant General Manager in NITF	E9	12
Director in NDRSC	E10	21

storms, droughts and forest fires. Furthermore, respondent E4 said, "*when a natural phenomenon takes place continuously by creating damages to property and community, it leads to disasters. As an example, if we take the flood that took place in the Kolonnawa Divisional Secretariat in 2016, it created huge damages to the properties. Those property damages were categorised into five criteria depending on the extent of damage as, less than 10,000, 10,000–25,000, 25,000–250,000, 25,000–2,500,000 and above 2,500,000. Number of property damages in each criterion is, 56(2%), 112(4%), 2484(85%) and 279 (10%) respectively*".

Almost all the respondents highlighted that human activities in the environment have resulted in changes in the environment which has led to long-term disastrous situations. Moreover, respondents highlighted that as Sri Lanka is facing more landslides and floods frequently, the most common reasons for these disasters are continuous heavy rainfalls, lowland reclamation, forest clearance in hilly areas, sand mining in the river valleys, changes and blocks in waterways, use of mountain areas for construction activities in an improper way and water storing in highlands. Similarly, respondent E4 stressed, "*Aranayake landslide which took place in the Sri Lanka was basically due to the mismanagement of the land use by the humans has lead for the landslide in the long run*". When a disaster hits the country, it impacts the economy, social life and also the environment in an adverse manner. Impacts of disasters are mainly, destruction of harvest, food scarcity, the spread of epidemic diseases, destruction in biodiversity, loss of property and life, damages caused for infrastructure. Therefore, to bring back the daily lifestyle of the people after a disaster, it is necessary to have a proper system to compensate the needful victims. Thus, NNDI policy is considered as one of the ideal solutions to build back the lifestyle of the victims of a disaster.

4.2 Process of Disaster Evaluation and Compensation in Sri Lanka

Before compensating the victims of a disaster, it is necessary to evaluate the losses caused due to the disaster. Thus, interviewees were asked to explain the loss evaluation process in case of a disaster. Hence, respondent E2 said, "*When a disaster hits the country, several parties like National Council on Disaster Management (NCDM), Disaster Management Centre (DMC), National Building Research Organisation (NBRO), National Disaster Relief Centre (NDRC) which operated under the Ministry of Disaster Management (MDM) get together to compensate the victims of the disaster*". Before the introduction of NNDI policy in 2016, MDM used funds from the Treasury to compensate the victims of the natural disaster. Furthermore, respondent E9 said, "*Before 2016, in case of a natural disaster, victims whose income limit is up to Rs. 5,000.00 were eligible to receive compensation in a natural disaster. That means almost all the Samurdi beneficiaries were considered to receive the compensation*".

In a natural disaster, for a full house damage maximum payment, was up to Rs. 100,000.00 while for the partially damaged houses up to Rs. 50,000.00 were paid before the implementation of the NNDI policy. After 2016, NNDI policy is executed with the joint collaboration of MDM and National Insurance Trust Fund (NITF) and it is operated under the supervision of the Finance Ministry. Respondents E1, E4 and E8 highlighted that policy covers all the disasters except droughts and fire. Therefore, when a tragic disaster takes place in the country, in order to compensate the victims, the first damage assessment is being carried out by the district secretaries and Grama Niladari (government officials liaising with communities at a village level). Further, responded E7 stated, "*In the disaster situation, disaster management employees, stakeholders, divisional and district secretaries, Grama Niladari and ministries get together*".

To compensate the victims, LKR 250,000 is being paid in death and for property damage LKR 2,500,000 is being paid. Further, respondent E9 stated, "*Until the victims come back to their normal life style, weekly dry rations are being provided*". After quantifying the damage that needs to be paid for the victim, compensation is directly credited to their bank account. Before providing the claim to the victim, details of the victim is verified through the Identification of National Identity Card (NIC) number, claim form and through the ownership of the property. Once the details are verified, compensation is being paid for the victims as shown in Fig. 1. Furthermore, respondent E10 highlighted, "*Though compensation is provided for the victims, betterment is not covered through the NNDI policy*".

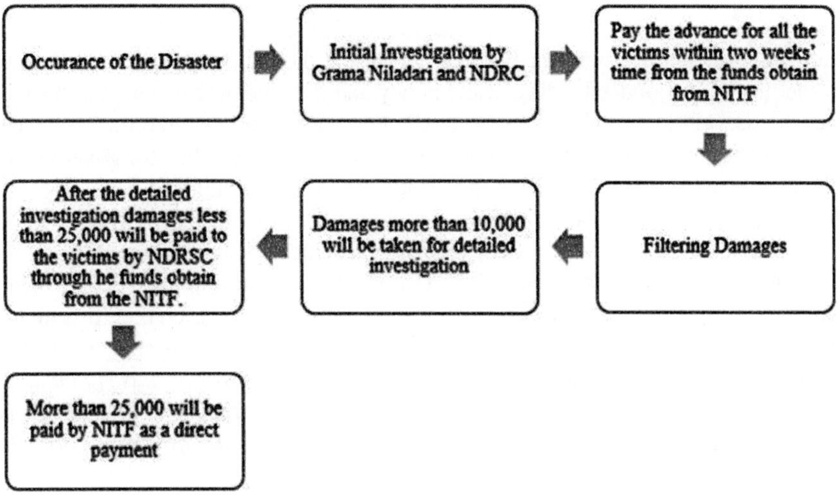

Fig. 1 Process of disaster evaluation and compensation in Sri Lanka

4.3 Issues and Challenges in the NNDI Policy

Though the NNDI policy was introduced in 2016 to compensate the victims of the disaster, there are drawbacks to the policy. Thus, interviewees were queried on "What are the issues and challenges in the NNDI policy?".

Although NNDI policy helps the victims of a disaster, respondents stated that there are issues and challenges that need to be addressed. One of the key challenges highlighted by the respondents is loss adjustment and claims. Respondent E5 said, "*Misguidance of the stakeholders in the process of loss adjustment and claims has resulted in issues in compensating the victims*". Furthermore, respondents stated that if the NITF do any changes in the claims by reducing the claim size, there is no way to communicate the change for the beneficiaries. Moreover, respondents also highlighted the issue of delay in processing the claim. Before the victims claim for their losses, it is required to carry out the damage assessment. When the assessment gets delayed, it ultimately results in a delay in the processing of the claims. In addition to that, respondents also highlighted the issue of insufficient staff. In a disaster, on behalf of the insurance, district secretaries take responsibility for assessing the damages. Along with the district secretaries, technical officers also get involved to assess the damage. Respondent E2 highlighted, "*due to the availability of limited number of technical officers, real assessment of the disaster faces difficulties and this has resulted in the delay in the claim process also*". When a claim is to be paid, the path is so long and people cannot wait. It is one of the major challenges. People cannot wait for a long period till the reconstruction take place and the greater value of insurance policy and the scheme is diminished by the delays of the operations of government structure.

Lack of guidelines on the claim process has also resulted in delays in claiming the compensation. Respondent E3 highlighted that the main reason for this is due to the insufficient understanding of the policy and the guideline is not clear for the stakeholders. Furthermore, respondents E2, E4 and E9 said that exposure towards the policy is also needed to be improved in the stakeholders. Further, the government has announced a system to resettle the identified families in high-risk areas through a Cabinet decision. Although the process takes some time, the real difficulty is in finding suitable land to resettle. To resettle people, land should be in a safer location and it needs to be certified by NBRO. But the major problem is to find suitable land. Since the people in these areas, nearly 15,000 families, they started their dwellings from very past. They have been living in these areas for two to three generations. That is their outright property. Similarly, respondent E2 added, "*because of climate changes we are receiving these unusual weather changes which we have not seen previously. Until government give a solution we have to look after the people in high-risk areas*".

In Kegalle area, lands that are identified as the high-risk areas are their cultivated land. There is vegetation like tea, cardamom and cloves in these areas. If those lands are acquired, then the people living in those areas will be facing a lot of problems with their livelihood. Therefore, as a policy, the acquisition of their lands will not take place. But with the help of NBRO, the government is trying not to settle anybody in a risky area which is identified by NBRO. But this process will take some time. In addition to that, NBRO has introduced a very sophisticated system with the community which Ministry of Disaster Management and other technical agencies were not being able to introduce. Further, NBRO has community-based early warning system. This early warning system has helped to reduce the damages to life. But this early warning system is available only for landslides and early warnings for floods are issued by the Irrigation Department. Respondent E7 stressed that it is important to introduce an early warning system for floods and other disasters also.

Moreover, the lack of knowledge on indemnity base assessment of DS staff is also identified as a challenge faced in compensating the victims through the NNDI policy. Due to the lack of knowledge in the DS staff, has resulted in issues like over-estimation and under-estimation of the claims. Similarly, respondents highlighted that due to the issues in record-keeping, wrong information about the damage is considered in compensating the victims and also victims try to maximise the benefits than covering the damage. Furthermore, omission of Built back better concept from the policy was also identified as an issue through the study. Respondent E6 said, "*if a house had been affected by a high wind situation, repairing should be done with some resilient features to withstand for any possible disaster. If you do not repair with resilient features and if another disaster take place in the same location again, then another claim can be recorded in next time. Thus, if the government objective is to make country's housing stock a resilient housing stock, then build better concept to this insurance policy is a must*". Further, having a proper valuation method for all the properties in high-risk areas will help to reduce the gap after a disaster. Respondent E3 highlighted, "*people try to maximise the insurance because those who are not affected by the flood submit and demand that they have a claimant.*

They continuously wrote to the president and prime minister and even asked for the 0.5 million compensation. In 2016 and 2017, there were issues like that".

People tried to maximise benefits rather than doing the compensation for the actual damage. Therefore, collecting the proper data is the challenging part. Creation of a database with proper details is the challenge. If a proper database can be created, then the estimation of resilience and costing part will be easy. An additional burden for the government is also another challenge highlighted by the respondents. In a disaster situation, the allocated amount for compensation is 2.5 billion. Though the amount is allocated as 2.5 billion if the requirements are higher than the allocated amount, then payments are carried up to 4.5 billion. Further, respondent E4 said that in the process of processing the claims, cost of officers, fuel and admin costs are considered as an additional burden which the government has to bear. Respondent E-6 stated, "*We have to have some sort of matching with the gap between the resettlement and the reconstruction*".

Reconstruction is the easiest and fastest way to reconstruct houses. Resettlement takes a lot of time and resettlement decisions are taken based on the risk associated with the location. Respondent E1 highlighted, "*There are houses without a single crack, but the location is highly vulnerable for a landslide. In such instance, it is proposed to resettle those houses*". Although the reconstruction part is addressed in the policy, the extent of focus on the reconstruction is lesser than resettlement. When the resettlement of the people take place, it is necessary to look into Built back better concept and resilient houses. The key part is that resilient features need to be added. Adding resilient features is betterment. So resilient features have to be covered from some financial resources but not from the policy since betterment is not covered from the policy. Insurance policy is based on exact indemnity value. If the risk factor is reduced, then the policy can be improved and solutions and compensations can be increased in future. Further, structural damages can be reduced by construction with resilient features.

Moreover, unavailability of monitoring mechanism to monitor the use of insurance claims is identified as another issue in the NNDI policy. In any insurance scheme, there is a monitoring part. Respondent E1 said, "*If our vehicle gets into an accident and when we are going to claim the insurance, then we need to show that we have properly repaired the vehicle with approved claims. But when it comes to NNDI policy, nobody knows how people used their claims. Whether they have actually repaired their house damages or not*". Therefore, such situation may lead to misuse of insurance programmes and some people can reclaim the damage in another disaster also. Thus, there should be a proper monitoring mechanism to monitor the use of insurance claims. Hence, issues and challenges in the NNDI policy can be summarised as shown in Table 2.

Table 2 Issues and challenges in NNDI policy

Issue and challenges	E1	E2	E3	E4	E5	E6	E7	E8	E9	E10
Loss adjustment and claim management	√	√	√	√	√	√	√	√	√	√
Delays in processing claims	√	√	√	√	√	√	√	√	√	√
Insufficient staff	√	√	√	√	√	√	√	√	√	√
Omission of built back better concept from the scheme	√		√	√		√	√	√		√
Lack of clear guidance on the claim process	√	√	√	√	√				√	√
Lack of knowledge on indemnity base assessment of DS staff			√	√	√	√		√	√	√
Inadequate record-keeping	√	√	√	√	√		√	√	√	
An additional burden for the government		√	√	√		√	√		√	√
Unavailability of monitoring mechanism	√		√		√		√		√	√

4.4 Conclusion

When a disaster hits a country, harmful impacts are affected by the people in the society. Therefore, to overcome the adverse consequences of disasters, migratory actions are being followed. As an initial step, compensation is being provided for the victims of the disasters to cover up their losses. When considering Sri Lanka, over the recent past years the country was affected by several natural hazard-induced disasters like Tsunami, landslides, floods and cyclones. Thus, the government took the initiation in introducing the NNDI policy with the aim of, improving the development and economy of the country. Through the policy, compensation is being provided to the victims—over and above the relief previously available to affected households. Being one of the first of its kind as a national-level macro-insurance policy providing coverage for all the properties in a country against natural hazard-induced disasters, the case of NNDIP in Sri Lanka can be considered as a good opportunity to explore the potential for such an approach. It can be seen that many of the households affected by a disaster event during the time the scheme was in operation have benefitted from the policy. Though compensation is provided, there are issues and challenges such as loss adjustment and claim management, delay in processing claim, insufficient staff, omission of Built back better concept from the scheme, lack of clear guidance on the claim process and unavailability of monitoring mechanism to monitor the use of insurance claims. Hence, for the successful implementation of the policy, these issues need to be addressed.

References

1. Kerjan E, Kunreuther H (2011) Redesigning flood insurance. Disaster Manag 408–409
2. Siriwardana C, Jayasiri G, Hettiarachchi S (2017) Investigation of efficiency and effectiveness of the existing disaster management frameworks in Sri Lanka and practice in disaster risk reduction, ICBR2017. Procedia Eng 1091–1098
3. Linnerooth-Bayer J, Quijano-Evans S, Lofstedt R, Elahi S (2001) The uninsured elements of natural catastophic losses: seven case studies of earthquake and flood disasters. IIASA, Laxenburg, Austria
4. Disaster Management Centre (2017) Situation report
5. Ministry of Disaster Management (2014) Annual Performance Report
6. Kumarasiri W (2016) Insurance as a risk transfer method to disaster management in Sri Lanka. In: Risk awareness and future challenges, pp 209–212
7. Carter W (2008) Disaster management. Asian Development Bank, Philippines
8. Lindell MK, Prater CS (2003) Assessing community impacts of natural disasters. Nat Hazard Rev 4(4):176–185
9. Jha AK (2010) Safer homes, stronger communities: a handbook for reconstructing after natural disasters. WORLD BANK, Washington
10. Petrucci O (2012) The impact of natural disasters: simplified procedures and open problems. In: Approaches to managing disaster—assessing hazards, emergencies and disaster impacts, pp 109–132. https://doi.org/10.5772/29147
11. Tripathi S (2013) Disaster and its socio-cultural implicaion: a study with culture and personality approach of anthropology. Soc Sci Humanit 1(16):58–64
12. Manesh AK (2017) Handbook of disaster and emergency management
13. Maini R, Clarke L, Blanchard K, Murray V (2017) The Sendai framework for disaster risk reduction and its indicators—where does health fit in? Int J Disaster Risk Sci 150–155
14. UNISDR UN (2017) Sendai framework for disaster risk reduction 2015–2030. Retrieved from http://www.wcdrr.org/uploads/Sendai_Framework_for_Disaster_Risk_Reduction_2015-2030.pdf
15. Shaw R, Scheyvens H, Prabhakar S, Endo I (2016) Disaster risk reduction for sustainable development. Institute for Global Environmental Strategies
16. US Department of Homeland Security (2016) Response federal interagency operational plan, 2nd edn.
17. Australian Institute for Disaster Resilience (2018) Australian disaster resilience handbook collection. Available at: https://knowledge.aidr.org.au/collections/handbook-collection/
18. Shaw R, Team I (2009) Climate disaster resilience: focus on coastal urban cities in Asia. Asian J Environ Disaster Manage 101–116
19. Freeman P, Martin L, Linnerooth-Bayer J, Mechler R, Pflug G, Warner K (2003) Disaster risk management: national systems for the comprehensive management of disaster risk and financial strategies for natural disaster reconstruction. InterAmerican Development Bank, Washington
20. Varangis P, Skees J, Barnett R (2005) Weather indexes for developing countries. In: Climate risk and the weather market. Risk Books, London
21. Linnerooth-Bayer J, Mechler R (2007) Disaster safety nets for developing countries extending public-private partnerships. Environ Hazards 1–14
22. Gurenko E (2004) Catastrophe risk and reinsurance: a country risk management perspective. London
23. Wedawatta G, Ingirige B, Sugathapala K (2018) Long-term sustainability and performance of post-disaster housing projects. In: CIOB Bowen Jenkins Legacy Research Fund Research Report
24. Cohen M, Sebstad J (2003) Reducing vulnerability: the demand for microinsurance. MicroSave-Africa, Nairobi, Kenya
25. Mechler R, Linnerooth-Bayer J, Peppiatt D (2006) A review of microinsurance for natural disaster risks in developing countries. Provention Consortium

26. Thieken A, Petrow T, Kreibich H, Merz B (2006) Insurability and mitigation of flood losses in private households in Germany. Risk Anal 26(2)
27. Kreimer A, Arnold M, Freeman P (1999) Managing disaster risk in Mexico: market incentives for mitigation investment. World Bank, Washington
28. Webster J, Watson R (2002) Analyzing the past to prepare for the future: writing a literature review. MIS Q 26(2):xiii–xxiii
29. Kumar R (2011) Research methodology, 3rd edn. SAGE, London
30. Creswell J (2014) Research design; qualitative, quantitative, and mixed method approaches. SAGE Publications Ltd., London, United Kingdom
31. Bricki N, Green J (2007) A guide to using qualitative research methodology 1–37
32. Dawson C (2002) Practical research methods. How to Books, United Kingdom

Hydrological Analysis for Flood Forecasting at Sg Golok River Basin Malaysia

Lariyah Mohd Sidek, Hidayah Basri, Mohd Ruzaimie Yalit, Mohamad Hafiz bin Hassan, Siti Azura binti Mat Daud, and Thayalam A/L. Sekaran

Abstract Large areas of Malaysia repeatedly suffer from prolonged, significant floods and in past, several flood-related disasters happened due to heavy rainfall in the Golok River Basin at the Kelantan state of Malaysia. Therefore, in this research, the hydrological analysis is being conducted in that area and five extreme flood disasters are chosen for validating the analysis. The preliminary event-based and gauge-based analysis is shown in this research for validation. The results showed that during the disasters in 2008, 2009, 2014, 2016, and 2017 shows that this hydrological analysis will be a significant element for the National Flood Forecasting and Warning System (NaFFWS) program for Malaysia.

Keywords NaFFWS · Flood forecasting · Hydrological analysis · Sg Golok

1 Introduction

Floods are chronic natural disasters with potentially very serious consequences. Weather events that caused many fatalities over the past decade have perpetuated the notion that, whether due to global warming or not, floods are becoming worse, more widespread, and more frequent [1–3]. Therefore, flood warning became a key research area in flood management. This means that previous methods of detailed interpretation of predictions from standardized sites will no longer be sufficient [4–6]. Although "the heart of any flow forecast system is a hydrological model", water modeling is one of the most important factors on which the effectiveness and efficiency of a flooded alignment and warning system be contingent [7].

L. M. Sidek (✉) · H. Basri
Institute of Energy and Infrastructure, Universiti Tenaga Nasional, Kajang, Selangor, Malaysia
e-mail: Lariyah@uniten.edu.my

M. R. Yalit
Asset Management Department, Tenaga Nasional Berhad, Kuala Lumpur, Malaysia

M. H. bin Hassan · S. A. binti Mat Daud · T. A/L. Sekaran
Department of Irrigation and Drainage, Kuala Lumpur, Malaysia

C. Ghosh and S. Kolathayar (eds.), *A System Engineering Approach to Disaster Resilience*, Lecture Notes in Civil Engineering 205, https://doi.org/10.1007/978-981-16-7397-9_27

A flood forecasting system will ultimately help on improving the effectiveness of the flood mitigation system. This adds to the importance of flood modeling so that flood forecasts provide a warning in stormy conditions to reduce human losses and property damage. However, rainfall data with good temporal and spatial resolution and accuracy are required for a better hydrological model [8, 9]. Besides the rain details must also be available in real-time. A flood warning is a non-structural method that is effective and cost-effective to reduce the negative effects of flooding [10, 11]. A national agency such as the Department of Irrigation and Drainage (DID) of Malaysia provides flood forecasting services and warnings. DID introduces a system based on the phased implementation of the system, which brings together the new National Flood Forecasting and Warning System (NaFFWS) for its key river basins [12].

The "NaFFWS Phase 1" plan was finalized in 2017. The phase was developed by using a very popular integrated catchment modeling (ICM) software named InfoWorks ICM for hydrological and hydrodynamic models and ICMLive shell for flood forecasting. The main river reaches the main streams as a 1-D boundary, and the floodplain associated with these rivers must be used with a 2-D mesh. With appropriate rainfall details, the ICM model can determine river flow including water level, water depth, and velocity in the upper layer. However, an additional tool that can upload the real-time weather data or active alerts automatically by analyzing the weather forecasts. Therefore, the ICMLive system is required.

The main objective of this research is to boost the NaFFWS performance by introducing ICMLive support. In this way, flood forecasting can be done using the national network data, the telemetry and radar data, and most importantly the rainfall forecast data. This paper will describe the pilot case that covers the key river basins on the east coast of Malaysia named as Sungai Golok River Basin of the Kelantan state. The study area is important as it was directly affected by the northeast monsoon.

2 Methodology

Figure 1 illustrates the map of DID rainfall, water level, and streamflow station that are owned by DID in which the data extracted from these stations will be used for hydrological analysis in this study.

The steps of doing the hydrological analysis are shown in Fig. 2.

The first step was by identifying the rainfall stations in the Golok River Basin. There are 12 rainfall stations operated by DID, which are in good condition and have been selected for hydrological analysis in Golok River Basin. The average total annual basin rainfall/areal rainfall in Golok River Basin is illustrated in Fig. 3. It is observed that Golok River Basin receives about 3200 mm of rainfall annually.

The 2nd step of this research is analyzing the rainfall characteristics using the rainfall double mass curve analysis process. It is noticed from the plot of each station (as shown in Fig. 4) in Golok River Basin that the selected stations are portraying good consistency and quality as most of the plots are having a slope value of close to one. In this research, the Intensity–Duration–Frequency (IDF) curves are used which

Fig. 1 DID rainfall, streamflow, and water level station in Golok River Basin

Fig. 2 Hydrological analysis steps for Golok River Basin

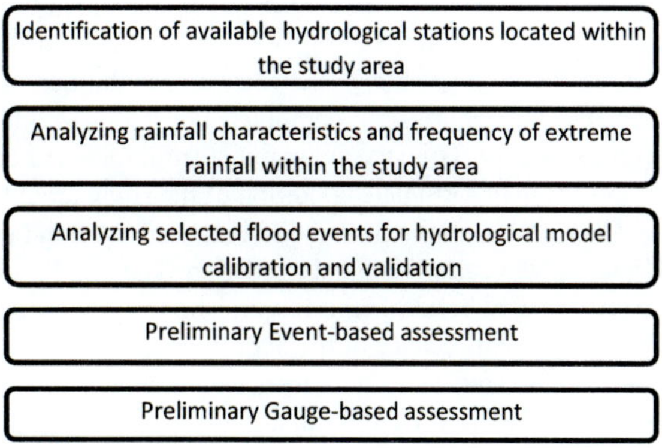

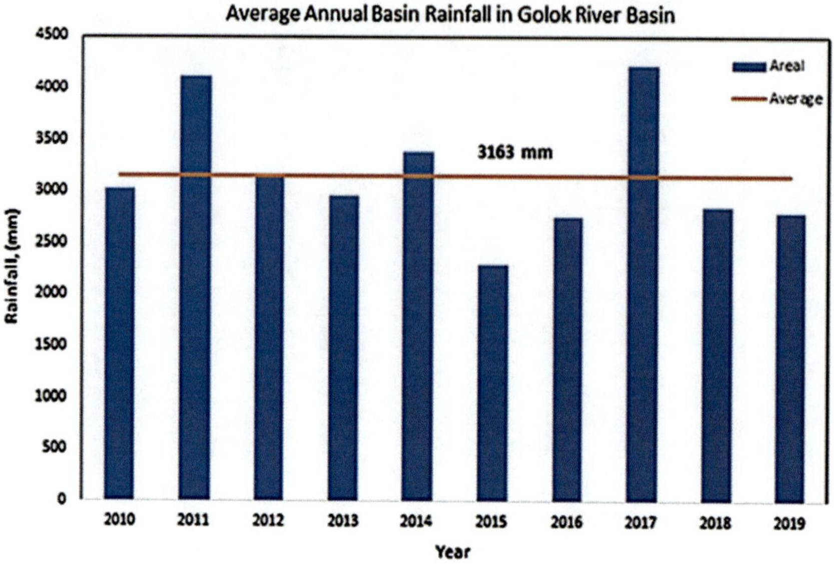

Fig. 3 Average total annual basin rainfall in Golok River Basin

describe the relationship between rainfall intensity/magnitude, rainfall duration, and return period (or its inverse, probability of exceedance). IDF curves are commonly used in the design of hydrologic, hydraulic, and water resources systems. Apart from that, it is also used as a reference to identify the magnitude of rainfall amount that induced floods. IDF curves are obtained through frequency analysis of rainfall data collected in the rainfall stations of different rainfall intervals.

The rainfall frequency in this study was conducted by extracting the annual maximum rainfall amounts of different rainfall intervals from the stations located within the study area. These observed annual maximum rainfall amounts were fitted to theoretical Extreme Value (EV) Type 1 distribution (Gumbel distribution) for estimating the corresponding exceedance probabilities of particular rainfall amounts. The IDF curves are only computed for stations with long and consistent rainfall records as only IDF curves computed from long and consistent rainfall records can reflect the actual climatic condition of the study area.

Then in this research, five different extreme flood events are selected for hydrological model calibration and validation. The flood events are the 2008, 2009, 2014, 2016, and 2017 floods. In this research flood events in Kelantan state is being selected to show the significance of the hydrological analysis of the Golok River Basin. The flood events and their consequences are shown in Table 1. There are quite a few floods are reported by DID that due to heavy rainfall in Golok River Basin. The latest disastrous flood happened on 31 December 2016 and it has caused the water level in Sungai Golok at Kampung Jenob to exceed the designated danger level. Continuous rainfall warning code had been issued by MMD for the flood on 31 December 2016. The consequences of the flood in 2017 are summarized in Table 1

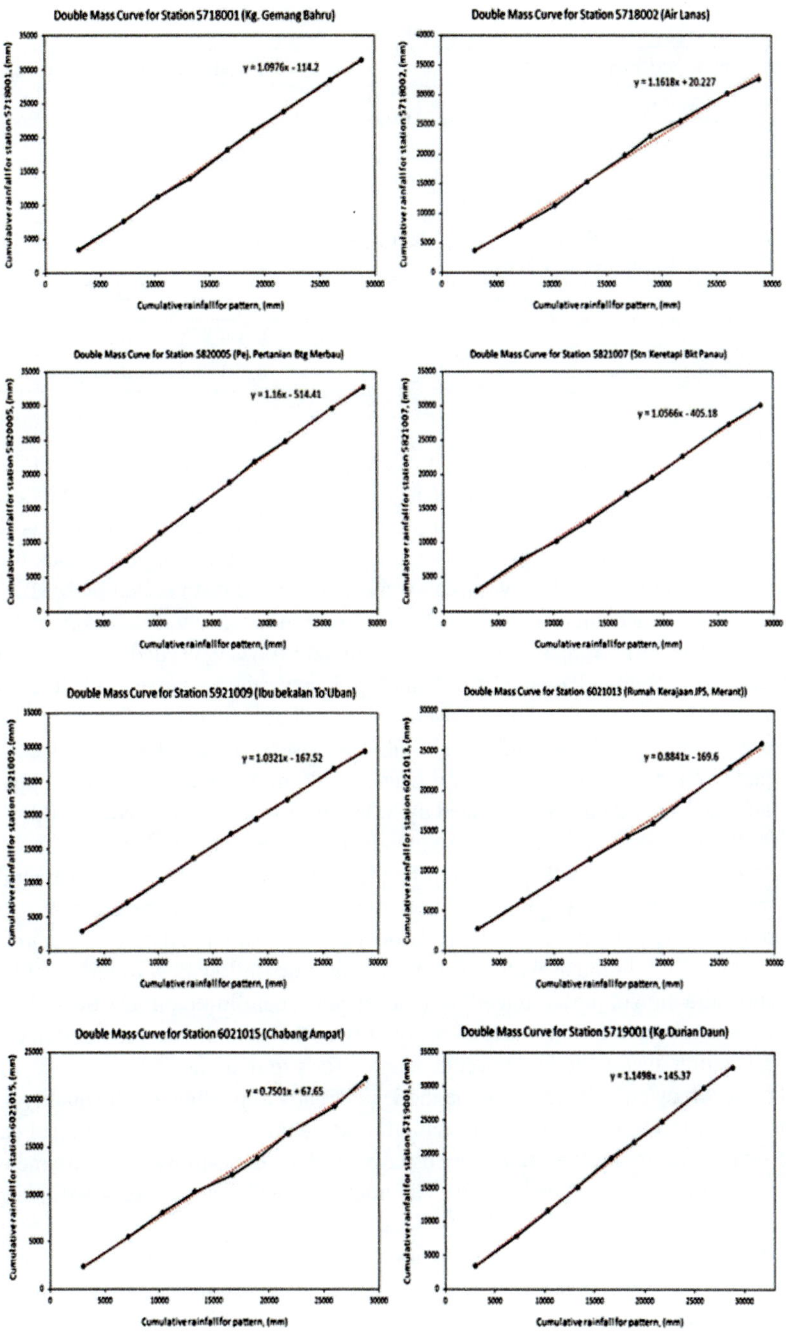

Fig. 4 Double mass curve computed for selected stations in Golok River Basin

Table 1 Consequences of flood in 2017 at Golok River Basin

Year	Inundated area	Flood depth	Evacuation (ppl)
2017	Kg. Muring	0.3–0.9	–
	Kg. Padang Kijang	0.3–1.8	27
2016	Kg. Siram, Kg. Pade Pak Atap, Bukit Lata, Kg Tokdeh, Kg Lachang and Tersang	0.1–0.3	
2014	Kota Bahru, Kuala Krai, Machang, Pasir Mas, Pasir Puteh, Tanah Merah, Tumpat	0.5–7.0 m	19,445 (4 death)
2009	Pasir Mas	1–1.5 m	2940
	Tumpat	0.6–1.8 m	1088
2008	Pasir Mas	0.5–1.5 m	405

and it is being shown that flood depth reaches up to 1.8 m. Another flood in 2016 has caused the water level in Golok River at Rantau Panjang to exceed the designated danger level. Thunderstorm and heavy raining warning code had been issued by MMD for the flood on 20 December 2016. In 2014 the most disastrous flood happened and the orange heavy rainfall warning code had been issued by MMD for the flood on 15 December 2014. In 2009 the continuous heavy downpours had led to the water level in Sungai Golok rose rapidly and it has exceeded the designated danger level in Rantau Panjang by 0.78 m. Red heavy rainfall danger code had been issued by MMD for the flood on 6 November 2009. The heaviest rainfall events were observed on 28 and 29 November in 2008. The observed water level exceeded the designated danger level in Rantau Panjang by 1.26 m that year. The orange heavy rainfall warning code had been issued by MMD for the flood on 30 Nov. 2008.

Finally, the event and gauged-based analysis is conducted in this research. The selected flood events will be used for calibration and validation of the model constructed in this study for flood forecasting purposes. Thus, the efficiency and functionality of the model depend greatly on the quality of input data such as rainfall data used for simulation as well as water level and streamflow flow used for calibration and validation of the simulated water level and streamflow data. The event-based assessment was carried out to assess the quality of the rainfall data recorded in each rainfall station during the flood events selected for simulation.

The accuracy and efficiency of the model is greatly depending on the quality and errors in the input data. Apart from rainfall data as input data, the water level data recorded in the streamflow station are usually used for the estimation of parameters and calibrating the simulated results. The hourly water level data recorded in each streamflow station during the selected flood events are assessed. It will be checked whether the water level data during the flood events are abnormal or missing. On top of that, the observed water level data is also assessed against the designated warning level and danger level.

3 Results and Discussion

Figures 5 and 6 illustrate the IDF curves derived for station Air Lanas (5,718,002) and station Kg Durian Daun (5,719,001) in the Golok River Basin for rainfall intervals from 1-h to 120-h (5 days).

The research also generates the rainfall time series of flood events in 2017, 2008, and 2009. The magnitude and ARI of the maximum 1-day, 2-day, and 3-day for 2017 floods are depicted in Figure 7 and the rainfall spatial distribution map for 1-day, 2-day, and 3-day maximum rainfall during those flood events is illustrated in Fig. 8.

The Preliminary Event-Based Assessment is done in this research. The hourly rainfall data recorded in the respective rainfall station during the selected flood event was compared to the 99% confidence interval of the rainfall data recorded in neighboring rainfall stations at an identical time frame. The 99% confidence interval of the

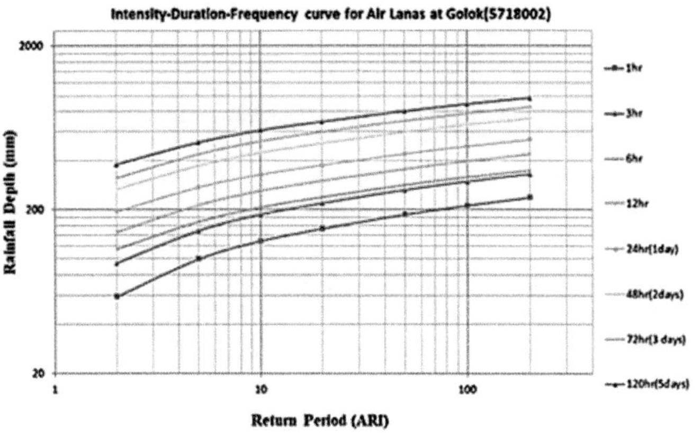

Fig. 5 IDF for station Air Lanas (5,718,002)

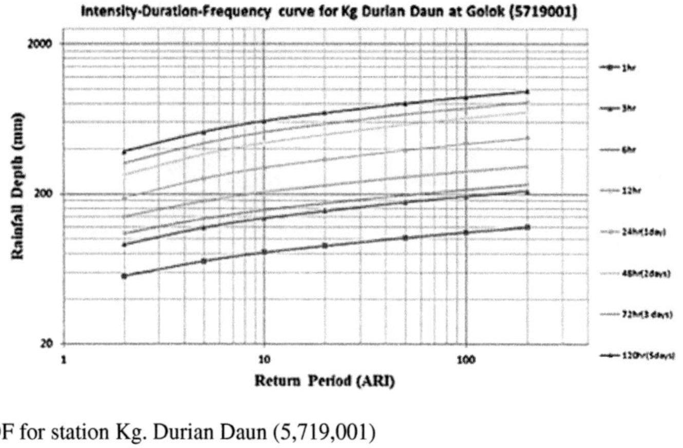

Fig. 6 IDF for station Kg. Durian Daun (5,719,001)

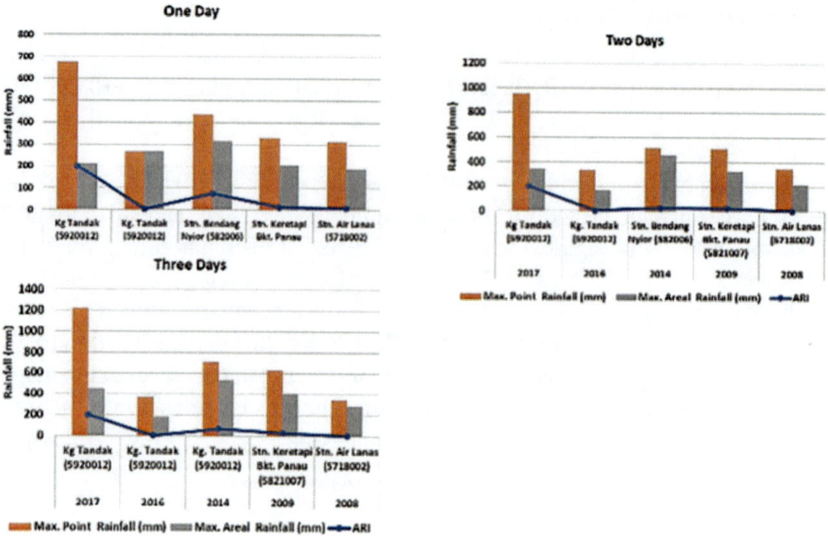

Fig. 7 ARI and maximum point rainfall for floods in Golok River Basin

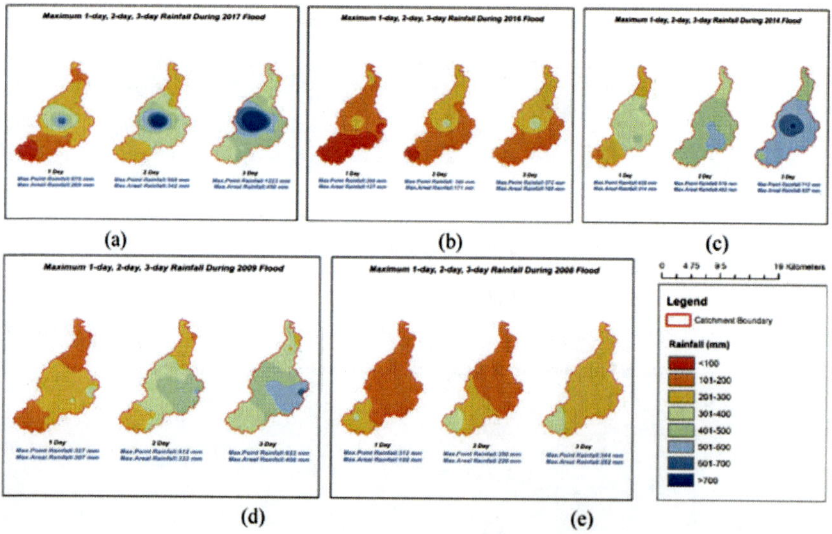

Fig. 8 Rainfall spatial distribution map for 1-day, 2-day, 3-day maximum rainfall during flood events in the Golok River Basin

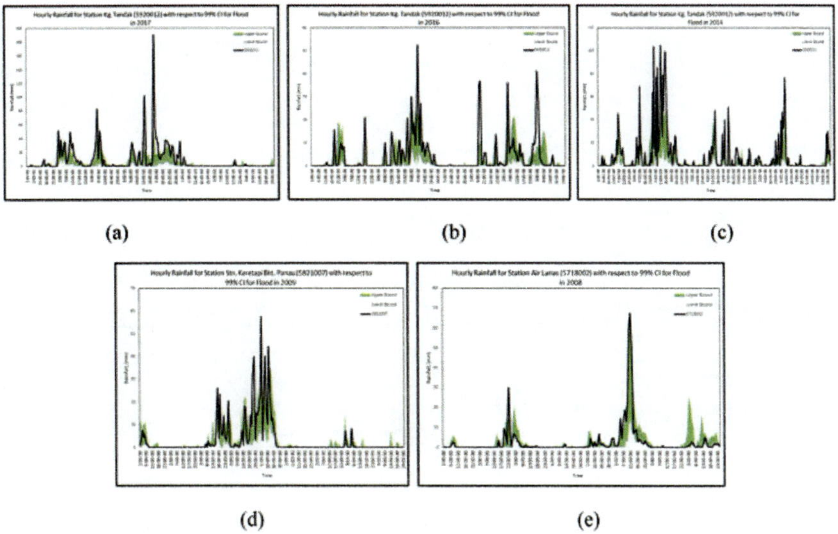

Fig. 9 Results of event-based assessment for hourly rainfall recorded at different stations of the Golok River Basin

rainfall data from neighboring rainfall stations represents the rainfall trend/pattern of the study area at a particular duration. If the rainfall data recorded in a station violates the rainfall pattern observed from a neighboring rainfall station, in which the observed rainfall data locate beyond the range of 99% confidence interval, then it is suspected that there may be errors for the observed rainfall data in that particular station and correction may be required for that observed rainfall data. The modeler may use the data of this event-based assessment to help them to correct the rainfall input data if it is necessary. According to Fig. 9, it is being shown that mostly the rainfall data recorded in each rainfall station during the floods in 2008, 2009, 2014, 2016, and 2017 is in good condition and no large variation is observed for any rainfall station when compared to the rainfall pattern of neighboring stations. However, the modeler may correct the rainfall amount (as long as it follows the rainfall pattern of neighboring stations) according to the requirements of the constructed model if it is necessary.

The preliminary Gauge-based Assessment was also accomplished in this research to validate the rainfall analysis. Figure 10 illustrates the results of gauge-based assessment for hourly water level data recorded at different stations during the flood events occurrences. It is being shown that the station Jenob (5,818,401) and the station Rantau Panjang (6,019,411) from 31 December 2016 to 8 January 2017 during a flood event in 2017 exceeded the designated warning level and danger level, which is validating to the selected flood event in 2017. Also, in the Figure, the station Jenob (5,818,401) and station Rantau Panjang (6,019,411) from 17 to 25 December 2016 during a flood event in 2016 shows the exceedance of water level, whereas the station Jenob (5,818,401) and station Rantau Panjang (6,019,411) from 16 to 29

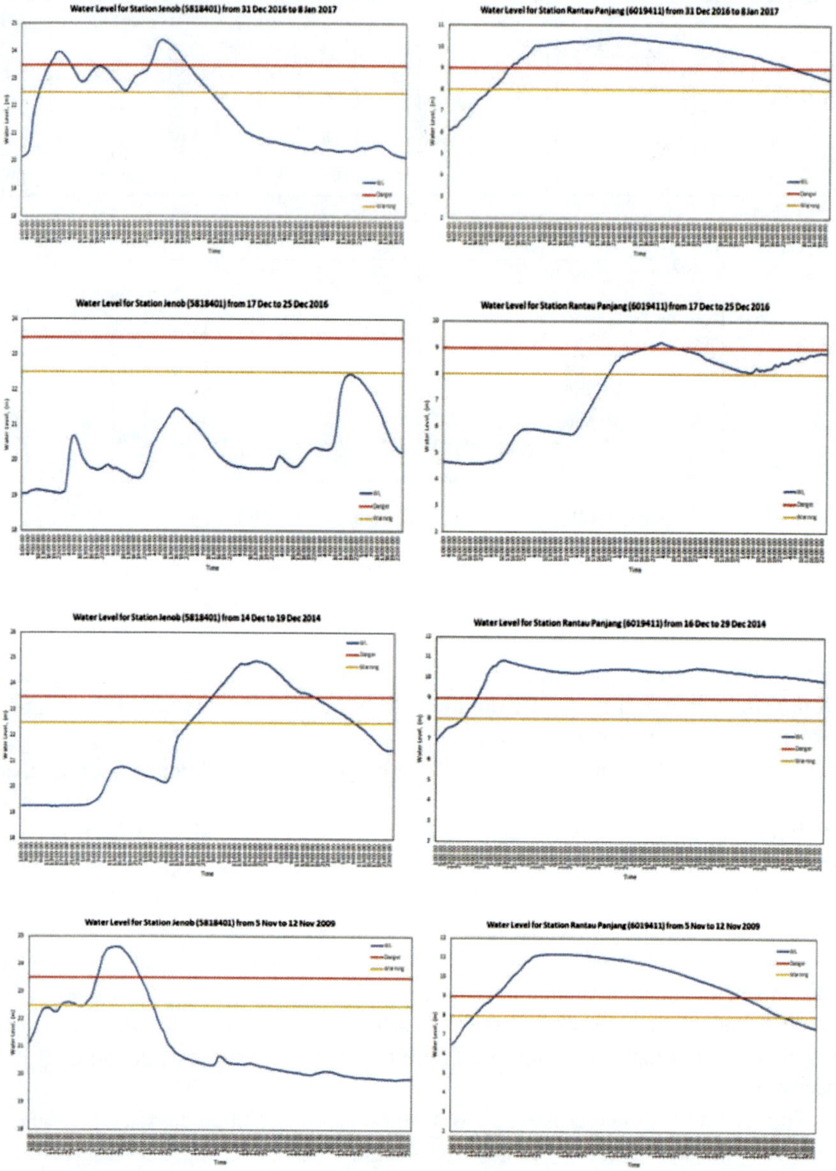

Fig. 10 Results of gauge-based assessment for hourly water level recorded during flood events in the Golok River Basin

December during a flood event in 2014 proves the water level is exceeded. In the 2008 and 2009 flood event the stations that show dangerous water levels are station Jenob (5,818,401) and station Rantau Panjang (6,019,411) from 27 November to 5 December during a flood event in 2008 and station Jenob (5,818,401) and station Rantau Panjang (6,019,411) from 5 November to 12 December during a flood event in 2009 respectively.

4 Conclusion

An innovative and new approach to provide a flood forecasting and warning service to the public by the Malaysian Government's Department of Irrigation and Drainage is launched as National Flood Forecasting and Warning System (NaFFWS) program. In this research, the hydrological analysis for the NaFWWS program is described to prevent one of the deadly disasters in Malaysia, floods. The research shows the steps related to the hydrological analysis and compared the results with the most five devastating floods that occurred due to the Golok River Basin in Malaysia. In 2008, 2009, 2014, 2016, and 2017 there are severe floods occurred and the hydrological analysis is validated using the data related to those disasters. The gauge-based assessment for hourly water level recorded during flood events in the Golok River Basin proved that few stations are overtopped during the flood and the event-based assessments, as well as the spatial rainfall distribution, are shown in this research. The research will be an important guideline to build the NaFFWS system in the future.

References

1. Osman S et al (2018) Application of stochastic flood forecasting model using regression method for Kelantan catchment. MATEC Web Conf 203
2. Basri H et al (2019) Investigation of multimodel ensemble performance using machine learning method for operational dam safety. In: International conference on dam safety management and engineering. Springer, Singapore
3. WMO (2017) Multi-hazard early warning systems (MHEWS). Available at: https://www.wmo.int/pages/prog/drr/projects/Thematic/MHEWS/MHEWS_en.html
4. Moore RJ et al (2006) Issues in flood forecasting: ungauged basins, extreme floods and uncertainty. In: IAHS publications-series of proceedings and reports, vol 305, pp 103–122
5. Sammen SS et al (2017) An evaluation of existent methods for estimation of embankment dam breach parameters. Nat Hazards 87(1):545–566
6. Sidek LM et al (2019) Flood hydrograph generation for Kenyir dam using hydrological modeling system. In: International conference on dam safety management and engineering. Springer, Singapore
7. Serban P, Askew AJ (1991) Hydrological forecasting and updating procedures. IAHS Publ 201:357–369
8. Pathirana A, Gersonius B, Radhakrishnan M (2012) Web 2.0 collaboration tool to support student research in hydrology-an opinion. Hydrol Earth Syst Sci 16(8):2499–2509

9. Razad AZA et al (2018) Reservoir inflow simulation using MIKE NAM rainfall-runoff model: case study of cameron highlands. J Eng Sci Technol 13(12):4206–4225
10. Ventimiglia U, Candela A, Aronica GT (2020) A cost efficiency analysis of flood proofing measures for hydraulic risk mitigation in an urbanized riverine area. Water 12(9):2395
11. Pappenberger F et al (2015) The monetary benefit of early flood warnings in Europe. Environ Sci Policy 51:278–291
12. Azad WH et al (2019) National flood forecasting and warning system of Malaysia: an overview. In: International conference on dam safety management and engineering. Springer, Singapore

Developing the Flood Risk Matrix for Impact-Based Forecasting in Kelantan River Basin, Malaysia

Lariyah Mohd Sidek, Mohammed Haziq Mohammed, Siti Noratiqah Mohamad Deros, Norashidah Md Din, Nor Azura Ishak, Aminah Shakirah Jaafar, Sazali bin Osman, Bibi Zarina binti Che Omar, Fariza Yunus, and Sabri Abdul Mulok

Abstract Impact-based forecasting (IBF) is a relatively new concept to implement in Malaysia. The catastrophic effects of natural disasters such as floods can be minimized if an early forecasting system is being developed. Also, by using the IBF concept, people can forecast the devastating impact of natural disasters such as flood, which is very prone to happen in Malaysia. In this research, one of the most dangerous flood events in 2014 at Kelantan state in Malaysia is chosen as a case study area and the developed flood risk matrix (FRM) is validated. The FRM was developed by determining the scoring value by integrating receptors' impact with 16 flood scenarios and the flood depth as weightage. The results showed that using the IBF concept and the impact threshold values, the ArcGIS based FRM map can predict the impact in the nearby area of the Kelantan river basin. This FRM matrix will be generated in other areas and help produce the flood guidance statements for Malaysia.

Keywords IBF · Flood forecasting · Kelantan river basin · Flood risk matrix

1 Introduction

Many floods are happening in Malaysia and floods due to potential adverse consequences in the crisis scenario. This is understood in compliance with Article 3 of the Crisis Management Act of 26 April 2007 as "a situation which adversely affects the level of safety of people, the property of significant size or the atmosphere, resulting

L. M. Sidek (✉) · M. H. Mohammed · S. N. M. Deros · N. M. Din · N. A. Ishak · A. S. Jaafar
Institute of Energy Infrastructure, Universiti Tenaga Nasional, Kajang, Selangor, Malaysia
e-mail: Lariyah@uniten.edu.my

S. Osman · B. Z. C. Omar
Jabatan Pengairan Dan Saliran Malaysia, Kuala Lumpur, Malaysia

F. Yunus
Jabatan Meteorologi Malaysia, Petaling Jaya, Malaysia

S. A. Mulok
National Disaster Management Agency, Putrajaya, Malaysia

C. Ghosh and S. Kolathayar (eds.), *A System Engineering Approach to Disaster Resilience*, Lecture Notes in Civil Engineering 205, https://doi.org/10.1007/978-981-16-7397-9_28

in significant restrictions on the functioning of the related public administration bodies due to the inadequacy of the forces and possessed means" [1]. According to a famous newspaper in Malaysia named Bernama Dec 2019, continuous rain-triggered 18 temporary flood evacuation centres in Kelantan accommodate 456 evacuees from 119 families. 149 evacuees from 40 families were registered in Tanah Merah, while 68 evacuees from 20 families were registered in Pasir Mas and both districts currently have two evacuation centres available to respond to flood victims. In Kusial, Tanah Merah, the water level of Sungai Kelantan also showed rising waters with a 14.94 m reading above the 14 m warning level. Four sites, meanwhile, were at the alert stage, namely Sungai Galas in Dabong, Kuala Krai as well as Limau Kasturi, Gua Musang, with readings of 32.75 m and 57.23 m respectively, while Sungai Pergau registered a water level of 72.13 m in Air Bol, Jeli and in Air Bol, Jeli. The water level of rivers in seven locations in Kelantan has been slowly rising, with two heading beyond the risk level [2].

The early warning of any natural hazard and disaster reduce the impact significantly. Likewise, flood-related disasters can be forecasted and the adverse impact can be calculated early [3–6]. Therefore, The World Meteorological Organization (WMO), conveying the outcomes of the Third UN World Conference held in Sendai [7], has highlighted the need for impact-based forecasting and warnings (IBFW) services to bridge the gaps hindering effective EWSs [6]. Impact-Based-Forecasting (IBF) is a method that gathers and incorporates information to estimate the impact of impending disasters on disadvantaged people living in areas subject to such disasters [8]. The IBF concept has already been introduced in a very recent article by Sidek et al. [9]. When communities can adapt proactively to a catastrophe through early warning and early intervention, injury, distress and the cost of emergency assistance can decrease. There are three crucial components, i.e. understanding risk, identifying impact and forecasting trigger value. It is essential to carry out a preliminary flood risk assessment for the production of flood risk maps, considering the process of estimating the value of possible flood damages in individual land-use groups. The paper proposes using matrix methods for the analysis and assessment of flood risk under the applicable legislation. The flood risk matrix will eventually support the IBF concept and the results will be validated using the flood disaster that happened at Kelantan in 2014.

2 Study Area and Data Collection

Sungai Kelantan river basin is located on the Northeast coast of Peninsular Malaysia. The catchment is 11,900 km^2, with the length of its catchment being approximately 248 km and the maximum width reaches 140 km. Sungai Kelantan is the main and largest river in Kelantan state and divided into several rivers; Sungai Galas, Lebir, Neggiri and Pergau. Sungai Kelantan flows northward, from upstream to downstream area and passing through Kuala Krai, Tanah Merah, Pasir Mas and Kota Bharu before blending with the South China sea. Sub basins in the Kelantan river basin are shown in

Fig. 1 Kelantan river basin

Fig. 1. Nearly each Northeast monsoon season that occurs annually results in flooding on the Sungai Kelantan catchment area. This is due to the Northeast monsoon that also known as the wet season, carrying heavy rainfall. This monsoon season contributes to the high annual rainfall (2500 mm) of the Sungai Kelantan catchment, usually from mid-October to mid-January each year.

The data required in this study was supplied by several government agencies that collaborate in this study. The data used in this study involved the Digital Elevation Model (DEM), Flood Hazard Map, soil, land use and road and railway data supplied by the Malaysian Department of Irrigation Drainage. The Malaysian Department of Statistics supplied other data such as population data. In contrast, other data such as evacuation centres, utilities, agricultural area and transportation infrastructure were provided by National Disaster Management Agency (NADMA), Ministry of Energy and Natural Resources, Malaysian Department of Agriculture and Ministry of Transport, respectively. This study involved seven (7) receptors; agriculture, housing and properties, population, public facilities, road and railway, transportation infrastructure and utilities. The component of each receptor is shown in Table 1.

As a data preparation, these data are overlaid with each other among their mutual receptors for further process. Then they will be used for further analysis that will be explained further in the next section.

Table 1 Receptors and their elements for impact-based forecasting study

Receptors	Element
Agriculture	Paddy fields Rubber estates Oil Palms Coconut plantation areas Other plantation
Housing and properties	Houses Villages Industry buildings
Population	People/residents
Public facilities	Hospitals and clinics Schools Fire and rescue station Police station Halls Government office, Etc
Road and railway	Road Railways Expressway
Transportation infrastructure	Railway station Bridges Airports Jetties
Utilities	Electricity infrastructure Dam Petrol station Telco towers and infrastructure

3 Research Methodology

Flood Risk Matric (FRM) is the final product of an impact-based forecasting study. This FRM is in a 1 km × 1 km grid. Collected data are grouped in a respective grid and the total number of each receptor in each grid was calculated. The main objective is to estimate the level of impact of receptors in each grid. Figure 2 summarizes the Flood Risk Matrix (FRM) process to forecast the impact of the flood. As mentioned in the previous section, data preparation grouped all elements into their main receptor category. Then, the grid was overlaid into each receptor and intersected spatially for statistical analysis. Grid-based statistical analysis was applied to each receptor to count each receptor's total number in an individual grid.

Each receptor's total count number was then inferred to the impact threshold developed to score the impact into four levels; minimal, minor, significant and severe. Table 2 shows the impact threshold developed by the discussion with related agencies and departments according to previous flood events.

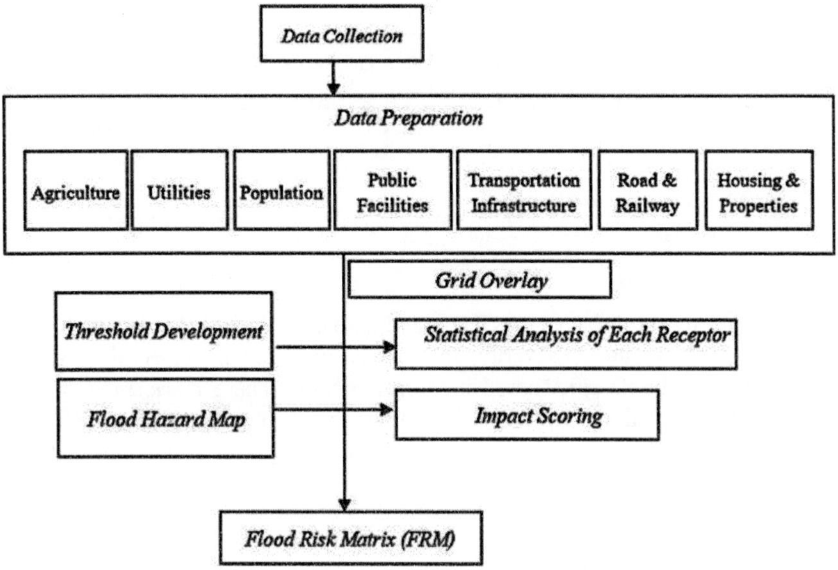

Fig. 2 Flood risk matrix development framework

Table 2 1 km × 1 km grid impact threshold

1 km^2 grid impact threshold				
Receptors	Impact level			
	Minimal	Minor	Significant	Severe
Agriculture (area percentage)	<20	20–50	50–80	>80
Housing and properties (number)	<10	20	50	>100
Population (number)	0	1–10	11–100	>100
Public facilities (number)	0	1	2	>3
Road and railway (km)	0–0.2	0.2–0.5	0.5–2.0	>2
Transportation infrastructure (number)	0	1	2–3	≥4
Utilities (number)	0–2	3–6	7–8	>8

Table 2 shows how the impact score of each receptor was determined. The agricultural area was assigned in a grid and the percentage of area covered with agricultural was determined and the higher the percentage of the agricultural area in a grid contributes to a higher score for impact level. This is contrary to other receptors such as housing and properties, population, public facilities, transportation infrastructure and utilities that count the number of receptors in one grid to estimate the impact level. Road and railway impact, on the other hand, were estimated by their length in one grid.

Table 3 Scoring matrices of flood and rainfall likelihood

Final scoring	Rainfall likelihood	Likelihood percentage	Tier	Impact category	Impact colour
0–2	Very low	<20	0	Minimal	Green
3–5	Low	20–40	1	Minor	Yellow
6–8	Medium	40–60	2	Significant	Orange
9–21	High	>60	3	Severe	Red

Then, each receptor's score was integrated spatially using the flood depth to estimate each receptor's impact severity. This process produces the impact score in one grid that then will be classified based on scoring matrices. These matrices then will be integrated further with the rainfall forecast event and then produced the Flood Risk Matrix (FRM). Table 3 summarizes the scoring matrices developed in this study.

4 Results and Discussions

4.1 Receptor's Impact by Impact Threshold

An essential feature of effective flood warning dissemination, particularly to the general public, is the use of receptors itself where early warning systems are well understood and effective response actions based on the local communities' preparedness. Figure 3a–g presents the 1 km cell for the seven receptors after the event's refinement based on the impact threshold in Table 2, where the maximum of all criteria is also included.

Figure 3a shows the impact of agriculture and the coverage area is dominated by a mixture of agriculture and seems no severe impact on that particular area. Based on the impact threshold for housing and properties, the result shows that the Kota Bahru area is more highly affected because the area is more densely populated than other districts. However, the population's impact is the same as housing and properties as these two parameters are connected. Besides, Kota Bahru is the capital state of Kelantan and the population density of the town is highly dense as public facilities impact is more severe the downstream where a large number of populations will be affected during heavy rain and flood events. Road and railway receptors are some of the receptors that have a significant impact on the threshold. Previously, the length of road and railway is determined directly from the statistical analysis made in ArcGIS 10.0 software. The maximum length in one grid cell carries a summation of length; 16 km. However, the minimum of 2-m road length with at least 1.2-m flood depth had been considered as severely impacted. This is because the network that connects people for help and mobility of victims was affected and hindered the rescue process. As it depends and there is a chance of affecting people's lives, the numbers need to be reduced to allow emergency responders to react precisely in an appropriate manner.

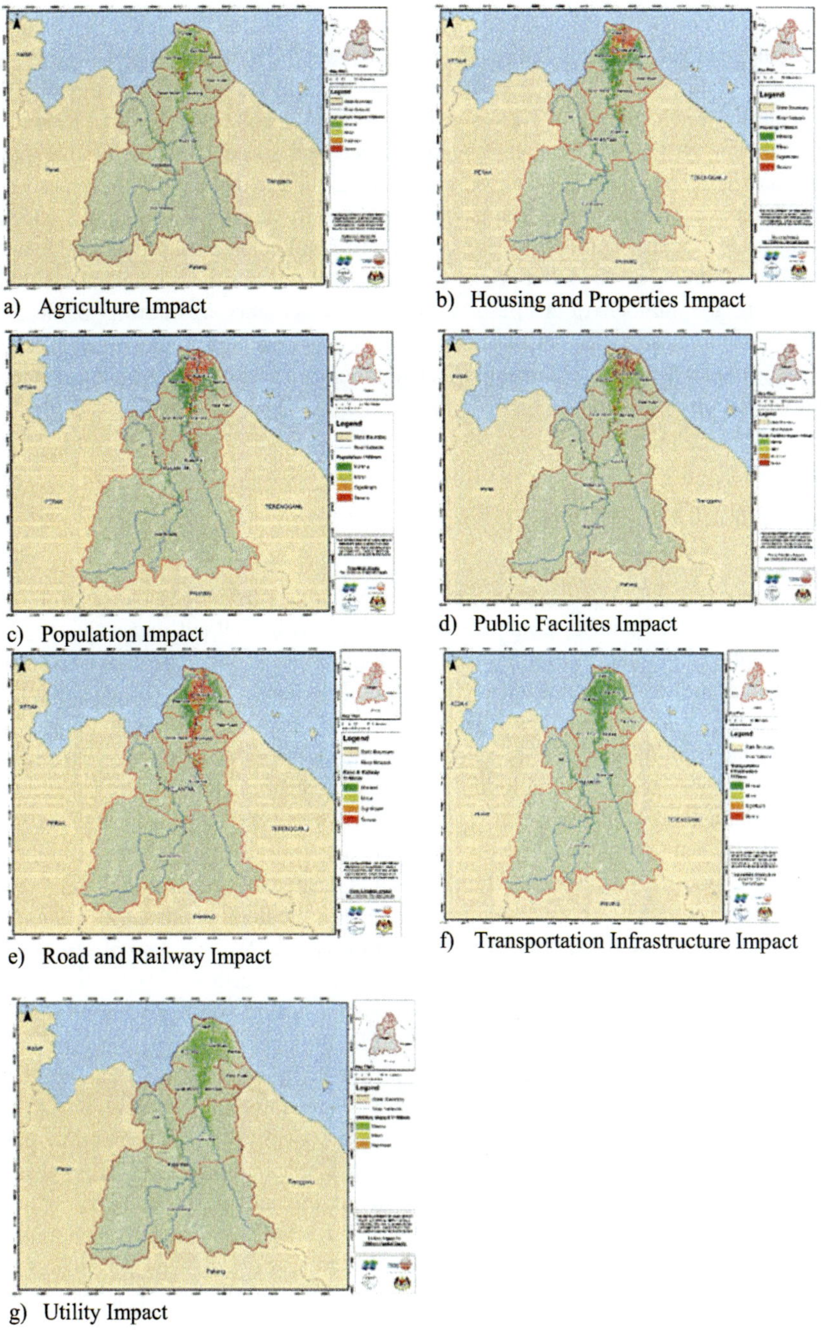

Fig. 3 **a–g** Receptors impact for Kelantan flood risk matrix

The red area colour is being broadened to Kota Bahru's side resulted in the change number of thresholds. Kota Bahru area is considered the most developed city among Kelantan states. Most of the development infrastructure, building, road, the railway is centralized in Kota Bahru. The extension of the green colour upstream of Kelantan can be seen as the threshold had been reduced and space is given for the short length to be seen in the map. Transportation Infrastructure threshold impact has been identified as a critical point, whereas it includes jetty, terminal bus, airport, etc. It contributes to a vast number of people who will be affected during the flood event. The development of Kelantan is not as fast as the state in the Klang Valley area. Therefore, the numbers of utilities are not as many as others. Most utility points are far from people except for petrol stations. Due to that reason, there are no significant changes made to the impact threshold. The numbers are based on the literature review and workshop discussion.

4.2 *Flood Risk Matrix for Sungai Kelantan*

The Flood Risk Matrix (FRM) in Sungai Kelantan was developed by determining the scoring value by integrating receptors' impact with 16 flood scenarios and the flood depth as weightage. Figure 4 shows the Flood Risk Matrix (FRM) of Sungai Kelantan at the worst flood event; 1100 mm rainfall depth. Figure 4 shows that the severe impact will occur mainly in the downstream area involved Kota Bharu district at 1100 mm rainfall depth. This reflects that all receptors' total scoring was more than 9, with flood depths from Flood Hazard Map being more than 2 m. It can also be observed that there were also severe impacts in Machang, Kuala Krai and Jeli district area. Figure 5 shows the grid's details that produce 18 in its final score; the highest score for Flood Risk Matrix (FRM). This grid is located at Tumpat, Kelantan.

As we can see in Fig. 5, the height field indicates the flood depth shows 1.999 m. This may reflect the flood depth is either 2 m or more. We can also observe that the agricultural area's percentage impacted in the 1 km^2 grid is 87.7% and results in a high impact score, 3. The number of housing in this 1 km^2 grid is 304 units of the house per grid with 3. This is followed by the population where it estimates 1520 people per grid, giving an impact score for the population as 3. The number of public facilities in this grid is 38 and marks this receptor's impact level as 3. The road and railway length in this grid is 6.948 kms and gives an impact level score of 3. There was 2 transportation infrastructure in this grid that involved Taxi Terminal and Station. This gives the transportation infrastructure impact level is equal to 2, which classified as a significant impact. The final receptor is the utility receptor that marks 3 number of utilities involving transmission towers in the grid. This contributes to scoring 1, the minor impact on utility receptors. The total score sums up all receptors and final score scores integrate the height of flood depth by weightage. The final score is equal to 18, where it was categorized as *severe* impact.

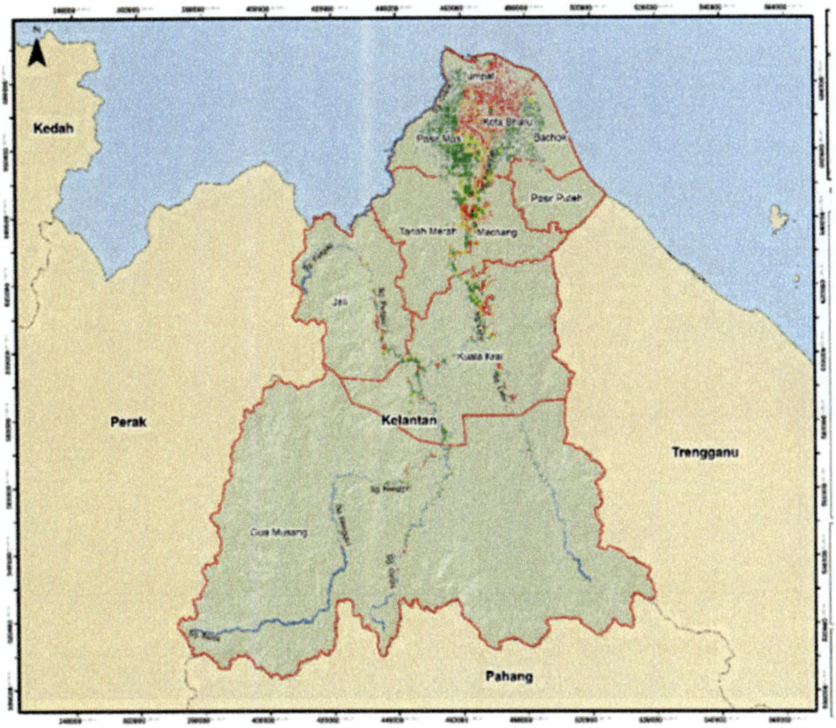

Fig. 4 Flood risk matrix (FRM) for 1100 mm rainfall depth

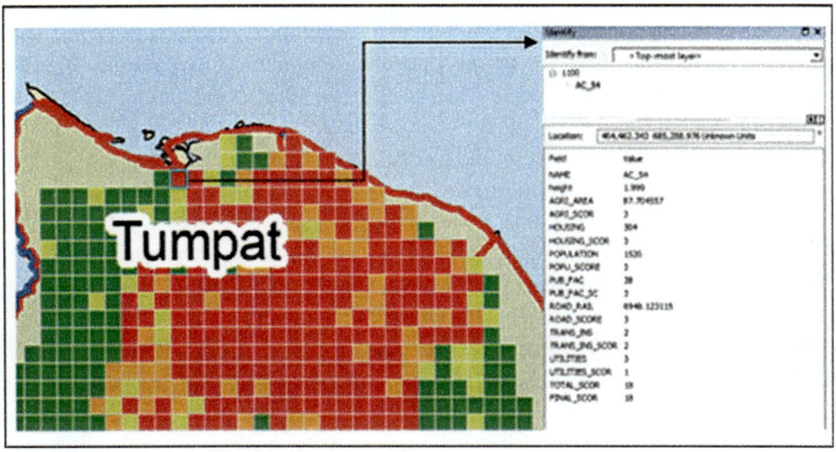

Fig. 5 Highest FRM score grid identity

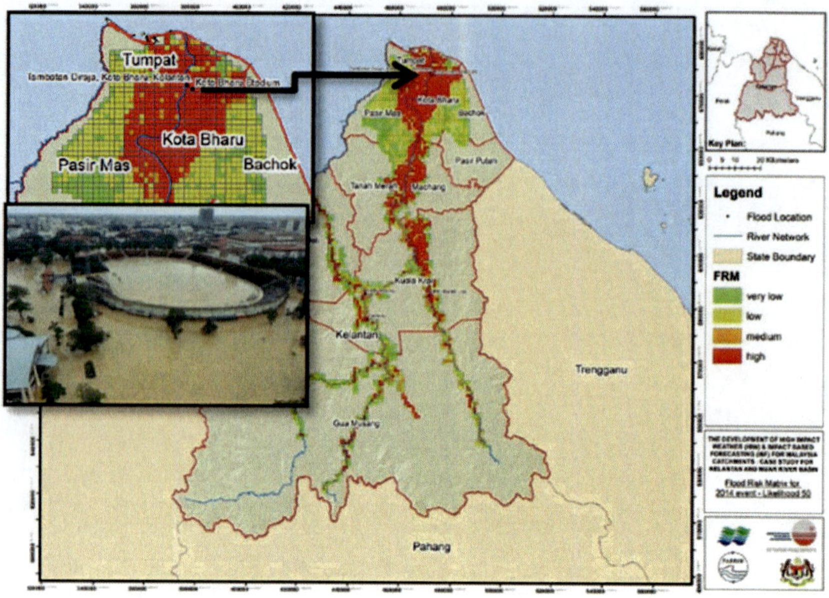

Fig. 6 Flood risk matrix based on 2014 event

4.3 Verification Flood Risk Matrix for Flood 2014

The flood management system's efficiency is essentially important because it influences two vital components: losses of human lives and property damage. It happens in Kelantan in the year 2004 was mainly due to the continuous heavy rainfall from 21 to 23 December 2014, whereby the water level in the river exceeded those recorded floods in Kelantan until 2014. Figure 6 shows the Flood Risk Matrix based on the revised version of the threshold impact. Kota Bahru stadium has been identified as the severe flood was filled with floodwaters.

This verification indicates that Kota Bahru stadium's particular location is in a red 1 km grid cell that shows high and severe impact based on the revised threshold. This event shows that the areas with an active and high concentration of development activities and densely populated regions with significant infrastructure investment are more vulnerable than other areas. Likewise, some areas are not highly prioritized for flood protection. This is because there is nothing valuable to protect or are not the most critical to flooding. Therefore, the most vulnerable areas in the Kelantan River basin are identified and flood risk matrix indices of each place in a 1 km grid cell were generated concerning flooding areas and threshold impact. It can be concluded that the threshold number has made a significant impact on to flood event 2014 and it can be considered an excellent parameter to predict the area.

5 Conclusion

The complete result of FRM shows that the impact of floods can be predicted early in the Kelantan area. The FRM is the summation of all receptors such as public facilities, agriculture, population, housing and properties, road network, infrastructure transportation and utilities. In this research, the analysis of FRM was made with the highest number of flood hazard maps, i.e. 1100 mm. Based on the result obtained with a comparison on the 2014 flood event, the results validate that the FRM produced is accurate and reflects the threshold and flood location. The impact threshold in Kelantan has been verified and agreed upon by government agencies with local expert authority. In the future, the range of impact thresholds can be tested with other states. This is to ensure that the threshold can be used in the whole of Malaysia.

References

1. Szczurek T, Szczurek M (2018) Protection of national and European critical infrastructure. Studia Bezpieczeństwa Narodowego 8
2. Bernama (2019). Available at: https://www.malaymail.com/news/malaysia/2020/12/19/kelantan-records-over-400-flood-evacuees-as-of-11pm-last-night/1933316
3. Sidek LM et al (2019) Flood hydrograph generation for Kenyir dam using hydrological modeling system. In: International conference on dam safety management and engineering. Springer, Singapore
4. Basri H et al (2019) Investigation of multimodel ensemble performance using machine learning method for operational dam safety. In: International conference on dam safety management and engineering. Springer, Singapore
5. Razad AZA et al (2018) Reservoir inflow simulation using MIKE NAM rainfall-runoff model: case study of cameron highlands. J Eng Sci Technol 13(12):4206–4225
6. Azad WH et al (2019) National flood forecasting and warning system of Malaysia: an overview. In: International conference on dam safety management and engineering. Springer, Singapore
7. UNISDR (2015) Sendai framework for disaster risk reduction 2015–2030. In: Third UN world conference in Sendai, Japan. Available at: http://www.unisdr.org/files/43291_sendaiframeworkfordrren.pdf
8. WMO (2015) WMO guidelines on multi-hazard impact-based forecast and warning services, World Meteorological Organization (WMO), Geneva, Switzerland. Available at: http://library.wmo.int/pmb_ged/wmo_1150_en.pdf
9. Sidek et al Towards impact-based flood forecasting and warning in Malaysia: a case study at Kelantan River. In: IOP Conference Series: Earth and Environment Science, (Accepted)

Dams and Slope Mitigation

Hydrodynamic Simulation and Dam-Break Analysis Using HEC-RAS 5

Darshan J. Mehta, Sanjaykumar M. Yadav, Nikunj K. Mangukiya, and Zalak Lukhi

Abstract The Ukai Dam is built on the Tapi River in Gujarat, mainly for agricultural activities, power generation, and flood control. However, large potential energy from the Ukai Reservoir would impose a risk of sudden breach of containment leading to loss of life and property at Surat city in the downstream area. This paper is deemed to provide a dam-break analysis of the Ukai Dam to generate a breach hydrograph and flood map as a result of the dam-break event under piping and overtopping failure. The process of collecting and preparing data, estimating breach parameters, developing a one-dimensional and two-dimensional unsteady flow model in HEC-RAS 5 software, performing dam-break analysis, and mapping of flood propagation are outlined in this paper. The result shows that the peak discharge of the dam-breaking flood hydrograph is 237759 $m^3 s^{-1}$ with a maximum velocity of 9.18 $m s^{-1}$, and a maximum water surface elevation is 35.68 m. The computed hydraulic parameters through simulation can be useful for preparing flood hazard risk maps and emergency action plans.

Keywords Dam-break · Flood · HEC-RAS 5 · Hydrodynamic model

1 Introduction

The dam brings many benefits to society, but some of the most destructive events of the last two centuries have also been triggered by floods arising from the failure of constructed dams [1]. Dam-break event is of special interest, though it occurs rarely its occurrence can be very devastating, causing more casualties and damages than any other man-made structure failure [2]. This is because of the flood wave's intrinsic disruptive force that will be unleashed as a consequence of a sudden failure [1]. The dam can be vulnerable to failure due to various reasons, depending on the

D. J. Mehta (✉) · Z. Lukhi
Department of Civil Engineering, Dr. S. & S. S. Ghandhy Government Engineering College, Surat, Gujarat 395001, India

S. M. Yadav · N. K. Mangukiya (✉)
Department of Civil Engineering, Sardar Vallabhbhai National Institute of Technology, Surat, Gujarat 395007, India

C. Ghosh and S. Kolathayar (eds.), *A System Engineering Approach to Disaster Resilience*, Lecture Notes in Civil Engineering 205, https://doi.org/10.1007/978-981-16-7397-9_29

type of dam and site-specific locations. Some of the reasons include overtopping, piping or seepage, structural overstressing of dam components, surface erosion due to high velocity and wave action, internal erosion, earthquake, and seismic failure [3]. Dam breach can be summarized as a partial or catastrophic dam failure leading to an unregulated release of water. Such an event could have a significant impact on the population and the property downstream of the failed structure [4]. If warning and evacuation are not possible, the destructive force of dam-break water waves can be devastating and cause an inevitable loss of life [5]. The transport of significant amounts of sediment or debris as well as the potential for spreading contaminants from sources such as chemical or mine operations in flood-risk areas are additional characteristics of such extreme floods.

The construction of dikes and dams gives people the impression that the floods are fully controlled and that therefore urban and industrial growth takes place in floodplain areas. If these structures fail, then, the damages caused by the flooding would be much higher than it would have been without existence of the structure [6]. Considering the historical failures of the structures, one might ask what can be done to reduce the risk posed by a dam or dike failure event. Analyses of dam-break inundation are used to quantify the possible risks associated with failure of dam, including estimation of the parameter of dam breach, estimation of the hydrograph of dam-break outflow, routing of the dam-break hydrograph, and estimation of the flood inundation extent and severity in downstream area [7]. Several dam-break simulation models are used to forecast the geometry and duration of the dam-break [1, 2, 4, 8–11]. In general, dam-break simulation models are based on empirical data obtained from several case studies of the earth and rockfill dam failures. The empirical equations available relate the parameters of dam-break to the properties of the dam and reservoir, such as the shape of reservoir, the volume impounded, size of dam structure, and its erodibility [7]. The one-dimensional (1D) and two-dimensional (2D) hydrodynamic models are used for routing the dam-break outflow hydrograph. In general, 2D hydrodynamic models are used where higher levels of precision are needed or where the flow situations are non-channelized. From these simulated results, flood maps are prepared using geographic information systems (GIS) and on the basis of that high potential impact areas can be identified for the preparation of mitigation measures [10].

In the present study, a dam-break analysis of the Ukai Dam has been carried out to develop dam-break outflow hydrograph and inundation map as a result of the dame-break event under overtopping and piping failure. The required data were collected from dam authorities, municipal corporations, state agencies, and national agencies. These data were used to develop the 1D and 2D unsteady flow model using HEC-RAS v5 software. The calibrated and validated model was used to estimate peak flood discharge, maximum wave velocity, and depth of flood inundation at various locations in the downstream area. The computed hydraulic parameters through simulation can be useful for preparing flood hazard risk maps and emergency action plans.

2 Study Area and Data Collection

The Tapi River is the second-largest west-flowing river in India, which initiates in Madhya Pradesh from the Multai forest in Betul district. The elevation at the beginning is approximately 752 m to the mean sea level. The total length of the Tapi River from the source to the ocean's meeting point is 724 km. It flows 282 km through Madhya Pradesh, 228 km through Maharashtra, and 214 km through Gujarat to merge into the Arabian Sea at Dumas, approximately 19.2 km west of Surat city. As shown in Fig. 1, the Tapi River basin is divided into three sub-basins, among which lower Tapi basin was considered as the study area. The estimated length of lower Tapi River is 122 km. The Ukai Dam is a large reservoir located at the beginning of lower Tapi River, supplying almost half of its drainage to hydropower generation, agriculture, and other facilities. The Ukai Dam is located approximately 29 km upstream of Kakrapar Weir. The catchment area up to the dam site is 62,225 km^2. The live storage capacity of the Ukai Reservoir is 7369 MCM with a water spread of approximately 600 km^2 at its Full Reservoir Level (FRL) of 105.156 m. The maximum water level (MWL) of 106.99 m is expected to be attained by the reservoir when passing the probable maximum flood (PMF) of 59,920 $m^3\ s^{-1}$. Figure 2 shows the picture of the Ukai Dam. The Ukai Dam is a combination of concrete and embankment dam with a maximum height of 80.77 m from its lowest foundation. The overall length of the dam is 4927 m, of which the zoned fill type of earth dam is 4058 m and the remaining length is occupied by a masonry gravity dam. The 425.2 m long spillway is provided with a total of 22 radial crest gates of size 15.55 m × 14.78 m. The maximum discharge capacity of spillway is 46,270 $m^3\ s^{-1}$ at MWL and 37,860 $m^3\ s^{-1}$ at FRL. The water released from the powerhouse of the Ukai Dam is stored in the Kakrapar

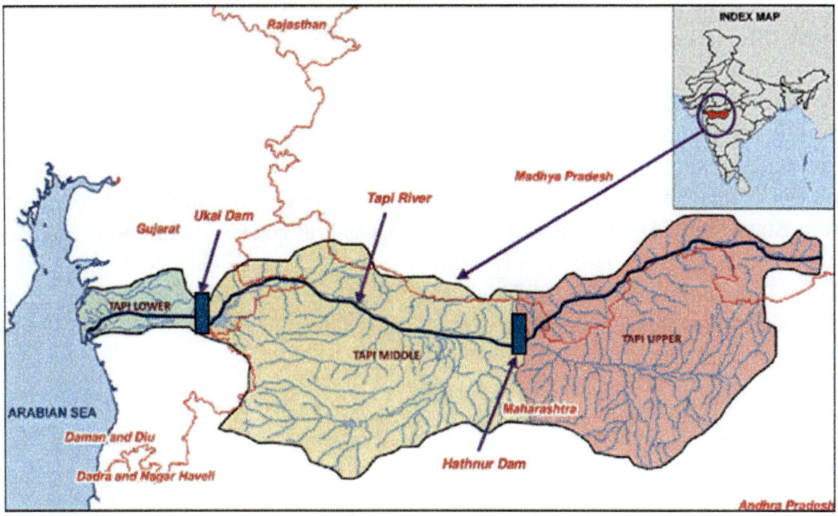

Fig. 1 Sub-division of Tapi basin. *Source* iomenvis.nic.in

Fig. 2 Picture of Ukai dam. *Source* guj-nwrws.gujarat.gov.in

Weir in order to improve irrigation of the Kakrapar scheme. The Kakrapar Weir and Singanpor Weir are the two inline structures on lower Tapi River. Total four river gauging stations are located on lower Tapi River, which are Hope Bridge, Singanpor Weir, Ghala, and Kakrapar Weir.

The details about 313 river cross-sections for one-dimensional modeling are collected from the Surat Municipal Corporation (SMC) and the Surat Irrigation Circle (SIC). The hourly and daily discharge data of the Tapi River at the Ukai Dam, elevation-storage data, the cross-section of the dam, and gate opening data of the dam are collected from the Ukai Dam Authorities. The cross-sectional details of Kakrapar Weir and Singanpor Weir are collected from SIC and SMC respectively. The tidal level data of the Arabian Sea at Dumas are collected from Gujarat Maritime Board (GMB), Surat. The stage hydrograph of intermediate gauging stations is collected from State Water Data Centre (SWDC) and Central Water Commission (CWC), Surat. For the bathymetry data of two-dimensional hydrodynamic modeling, Shuttle Radar Topography Mission (SRTM) Digital Elevation Model (DEM) of 30 m grid interval are downloaded from the United States Geological Survey (USGS) Earth explorer portal.

3 Methodology

The methodology includes data collection, development of the one-dimensional and two-dimensional hydrodynamic model, estimation of dam-break parameters, and dam-break analysis. Figure 3 shows the flowchart of methodology.

The one-dimensional hydrodynamic model for 122 km of river length has been developed using the U.S. Army Corps of Engineers Hydrologic Engineering Center's River Analysis System (HEC-RAS v5) software. The geometry data of the Tapi River and the Ukai Dam are generated from SRTM DEM using ArcGIS v10.5 and given as input to HEC-RAS. The cross-sectional data and structural data collected from SMC, SIC, and the Ukai Dam Authorities have been entered in geometry files. The water level of the reservoir was given as the initial condition, and the flow hydrograph and gate openings of inline structures were given as boundary conditions for the simulation. The one-dimensional hydrodynamic model has been calibrated for the Tapi River flood event of 2006. The range of the channel roughness coefficient for calibration was taken from the literature [12] based on the original geographic condition of the channel bed. For the performance assessment of the model, Root Mean Square Error (RMSE) has been calculated. The calibrated model

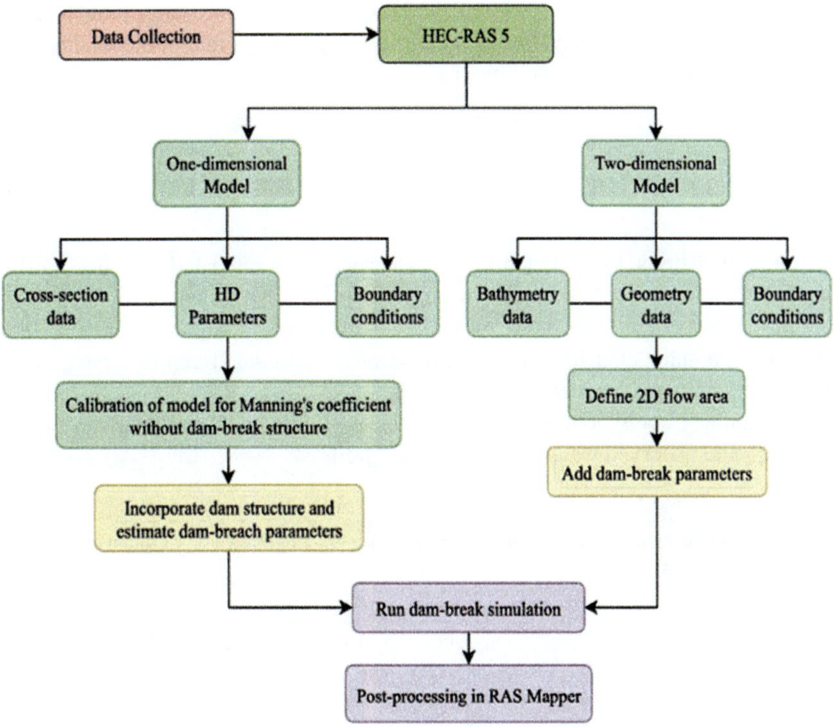

Fig. 3 Flowchart of methodology

is then validated by comparing simulated and observed levels of water at intermediate gauging stations.

The two-dimensional hydrodynamic model for dam-break simulation has been developed using HEC-RAS and RAS Mapper. The pre-processed DEM was given as input to RAS Mapper for the preparation of the bathymetry. The elevation-storage data of the Ukai Reservoir was given as an upstream boundary condition. The embankment station-elevation and spillway gate data of the Ukai Dam, Kakrapar Weir, and Singanpor Weir were also incorporated into the model as boundary conditions. For simulation, a computational mesh with a 100 m spacing in X and Y directions was generated. The dam-breach parameters for the Ukai Dam were calculated using the regression analysis method as specified by Froehlich (1995) [13]. Froehlich's regression equation for breach width and failure is given in Eqs. 1 and 2. Post-processing of the simulated model was performed using RAS Mapper to generate a flood map, breach hydrograph, and hydraulic parameters.

$$B_{\text{avg}} = 0.1803 K_0 V_w^{0.32} h_b^{0.19} \tag{1}$$

$$t_f = 0.00254 V_w^{0.53} h_b^{-0.9} \tag{2}$$

where, B_{avg} is average breach width (m), K_0 is constant (1.4 for overtopping failure), V_w is reservoir volume at the time of failure (m^3), h_b is the height of the final breach (m), and t_f is breach formation time (h).

4 Results and Discussion

The one-dimensional hydrodynamic model has been calibrated and validated for the Tapi River flood event of 2006. The range of Manning's coefficient of roughness for calibration was taken from 0.022 to 0.035 according to the literature [12]. RMSE (m) has been calculated for the comparison of the simulated and observed water levels. The simulated model shows a minimum RMSE at different gauge stations with Manning's coefficient of 0.03 as shown in Table 1. The comparison of the simulated and observed water levels is shown in Fig. 4.

Table 1 Comparison of simulated and observed stage hydrographs for different Manning's roughness coefficient

Manning's 'n'	Mandvi bridge	Ghala	Nehru bridge	Weighted RMSE
0.022	1.735	1.453	2.179	1.747
0.025	1.565	0.877	2.007	1.645
0.030	1.166	0.987	1.256	1.163
0.035	1.239	1.002	1.845	1.537

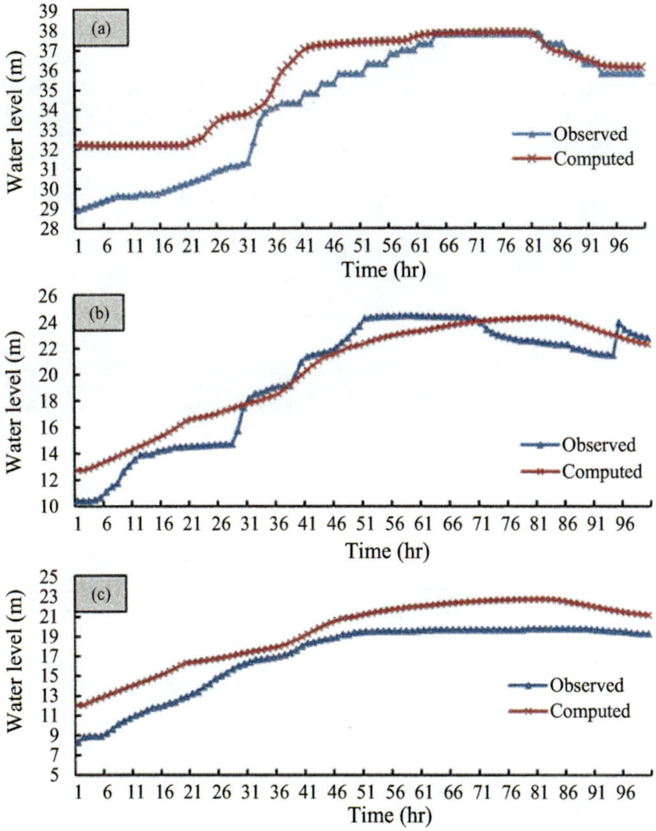

Fig. 4 Comparison of observed and simulated stage hydrograph corresponding to Manning's coefficient as 0.03 **a** at Mandvi bridge, **b** at Ghala, and **c** at Nehru bridge

The two-dimensional dam-break simulation has been performed incorporating the elevation-storage data of the Ukai Dam and Kakrapar Weir and Singanpor Weir inline structure as shown in Fig. 5. The dam-breach parameters for the Ukai Dam have been calculated using the Froehlich (1995) regression analysis method and shown in Table 2. The simulated results were mapped using RAS Mapper. The Tapi River flood event of 2006 is simulated for 16 h, i.e., 07/08/2006 09:00 h. to 08/08/2006 00:00 h. The result shows that the peak discharge of the dam-breaking flood hydrograph is 237,759 $m^3\ s^{-1}$ with a maximum velocity of 9.18 $m\ s^{-1}$ as shown in Fig. 6, and a maximum water surface elevation is 35.68 m. The inundation depth and velocity results for the entire area are shown in Fig. 7. The villages which are most affected by the dam-break flood are Baleshwar, Beddha, Bhatkhai, Bhurivel, Bori, Ghantoli, Jamapur, Khoj, Kikvad, Limbi, Pipalvada, Sedhav, Serulla, Silatvel, Surat, Umarsadi, Vada, Vadhva, Vaghecha, Vaghnera, and Valargadh. Surat city is located downstream; it is divided into seven different zones. The simulated results show that the water

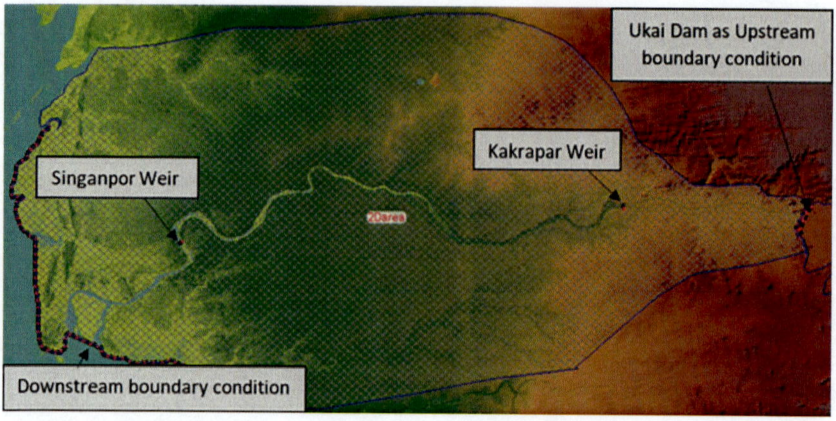

Fig. 5 2D mesh area and inline structure

Table 2 Estimated dam-breach parameters based on Froehlich (1995) for 2D

Breach parameter	Formulae	Calculated value for Ukai dam
Average width (m)	$B_{avg} = 0.1803 K_0 V_w^{0.32} h_b^{0.19}$	778
Side slope	1.4 for overtopping	1.4H:1 V
Formation time (h)	$t_f = 0.00254 V_w^{0.53} h_b^{-0.9}$	10.88

takes between 5 and 6 h to reach Surat city. The highest flood depth in the Surat city is 13.34 m in the West zone followed by 12.29 m in the North zone, 11.58 m in the South-East zone, 11.4 m in the South zone, 10.56 m in the East zone, 10.21 m in the South-West zone, and 8.32 m in the Central zone.

5 Summary and Conclusions

Dam-break event is a comprehensive and complicated process, and the mechanics of actual failure are still not well understood. In this paper, the attempt has been made to simulate a dam-break flood using the Froehlich (1995) regression equation for overtopping failure as suggested in the HEC-RAS software manual and training documents. The one-dimensional and two-dimensional hydrodynamic model for dam-break simulation has been developed for the inflow of the 2006 flood in the Ukai Dam.

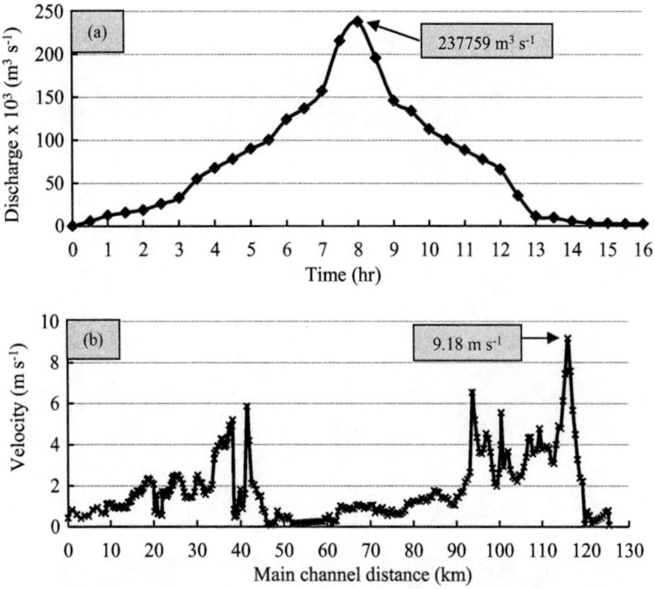

Fig. 6 **a** Dam-break flood hydrograph for the Ukai Dam, and **b** the profile velocity plot for dam-break flood simulation

The results of the one-dimensional hydrodynamic model show that Manning's roughness coefficient of 0.03 gives a minimum RMSE between observed and simulated water levels for the lower Tapi River. The results of the two-dimensional hydrodynamic model show that the peak discharge of the dam-break flood hydrograph would be 237,759 $m^3\ s^{-1}$, which is seven times higher than that of the 2006 flood in the Ukai Dam. The peak velocity of the dam-break flood hydrograph is 9.18 $m\ s^{-1}$. The maximum inundation depth is 35.68 m near Surat city. The flood inundation map shows that many villages including Surat city would be flooded by dam-breaking floods. The highest flood depth in the Surat city is 13.34 m in the West zone followed by 12.29 m in the North zone, 11.58 m in the South-East zone, 11.4 m in the South zone, 10.56 m in the East zone, 10.21 m in the South-West zone, and 8.32 m in the Central zone.

The hydraulic parameters computed through simulation will help to design flood protection measures and development of flood inundation maps for the downstream area of the dam. A proper analysis of the risks associated with dam failures can help to prepare land use and establish emergency plans in order to minimize the catastrophic loss to human life and property.

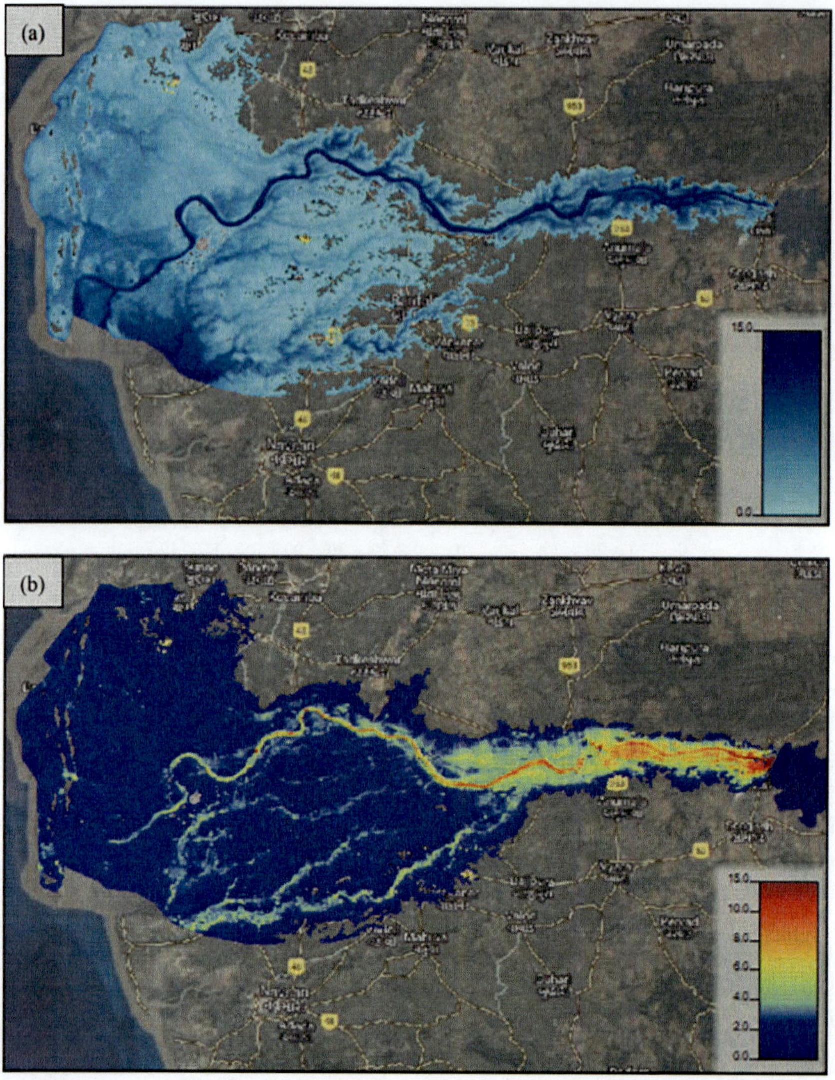

Fig. 7 **a** Inundation depth map, and **b** velocity magnitude plot

References

1. Xiong Y (2011) A dam break analysis using HEC-RAS. J Water Resour Prot 03:370–379. https://doi.org/10.4236/jwarp.2011.36047
2. Goodell CR (2005) Dam break modeling for tandem reservoirs—a case study using HEC-RAS and HEC-HMS. In: World water congress 2005: impacts of global climate change—proceedings of the 2005 world water and environmental resources congress
3. Zhang L, Xu Y, Jia JS (2009) Analysis of earth dam failures: a database approach. Georisk 3:184–189. https://doi.org/10.1080/17499510902831759

4. Brunner GW (2003) Dam and levee breaching with HEC-RAS. In: World water and environmental resources congress
5. Mehta DJ, Yadav SM (2020) Hydrodynamic simulation of river Ambica for riverbed assessment: a case study of Navsari Region. In: Lecture notes in civil engineering. pp 127–140
6. Yadav SM, Mangukiya NK (2021) Semi-arid river basin flood: causes, damages, and measure. In: Proceedings of the fifth international conference in ocean engineering (ICOE 2019). Lecture notes in civil engineering
7. Singh VP (1996) Dam breach modeling technology
8. Gallegos HA, Schubert JE, Sanders BF (2009) Two-dimensional, high-resolution modeling of urban dam-break flooding: a case study of Baldwin Hills, California. Adv Water Resour 32:1323–1335. https://doi.org/10.1016/j.advwatres.2009.05.008
9. Wang JS, Ni HG, He YS (2000) Finite-difference TVD scheme for computation of dam-break problems. J Hydraul Eng 126:253–262. https://doi.org/10.1061/(ASCE)0733-9429(2000)126:4(253)
10. Derdous O, Djemili L, Bouchehed H, Tachi SE (2015) A GIS based approach for the prediction of the dam break flood hazard—a case study of Zardezas reservoir "skikda, Algeria." J Water L Dev 27:15–20. https://doi.org/10.1515/jwld-2015-0020
11. Qi H, Altinakar MS (2012) GIS-based decision support system for dam break flood management under uncertainty with two-dimensional numerical simulations. J Water Resour Plan Manag. https://doi.org/10.1061/(ASCE)WR.1943-5452.0000192
12. Chow VT (1959) Open-channel hydraulics. McGraw-Hill, New York
13. Froehlich DC (1995) Embankment dam breach parameters revisited. In: International water resources engineering conference—proceedings

Dam Safety—Living with the Risk of Failure

David C. Froehlich and David Gonzalez Diaz

Abstract Dams provide numerous benefits, including flood protection, water supply, hydropower, irrigation and recreation. However, a dam also creates a potential hazard to people and property should a failure occur, leading to an uncontrolled release of impounded water. The effect of such an incident needs to be calculated to establish the risk of failure, particularly to the downstream inhabitants who would be affected. Key elements of this evaluation are maps that outline the area inundated by a dam-failure flood at a scale sufficient to identify the population at risk along with the critical infrastructure that would likely be damaged. Numerical models are used to assess the consequences of a potential failure and produce the essential flood inundation maps. The models are based on the solution of either one-dimensional cross-section-averaged (1D) or two-dimensional depth-averaged (2DH) unsteady open-channel flow equations. This analysis presents the results of both 1D and 2DH simulations of the flood caused by a potential breach of Hirakud Dam, a large dam in east-central India that impounds an enormous volume of water. Comparison of the generated inundation mapping shows mostly close agreement between the 1D and 2DH solutions. Although a 2DH model does have advantages where the 1D flow assumptions become unrealistic.

Keywords Dam safety · Dam breach · Flood · Emergency action plan · Flood risk · Flood mapping · Flood model

1 Introduction

India ranks third in the world after China and the United States in its number of large dams. These structures have been crucial in promoting rapid and sustained agricultural and rural growth and industrial development. However, they also present risks to those living downstream from them if they are not maintained and operated

D. C. Froehlich (✉)
Cary, NC, USA

D. G. Diaz
Egis Eau, R.K. Puram, Sector-1, New Delhi, India

C. Ghosh and S. Kolathayar (eds.), *A System Engineering Approach to Disaster Resilience*, Lecture Notes in Civil Engineering 205, https://doi.org/10.1007/978-981-16-7397-9_30

correctly. Although dam failures leading to uncontrolled releases of impounded water are infrequent, their impacts are usually catastrophic, with disastrous consequences that far exceed those from typical floods. An ever-increasing number of people live and work in areas that would be vulnerable to sudden flooding from India's dam failures.

Many people who live in areas inundated by an uncontrolled release of water from a dam are entirely unaware of the hazard looming upstream. Dam-failure floods are almost always more sudden and violent than regular river floods. However, even massive, controlled releases from a reservoir can be dangerous if sufficient warnings are not given to the downstream population. Adequate emergency preparedness and effective and sustainable dam safety programs can dramatically reduce the risk of failure.

Managing the contingencies caused by the failure of a dam and the uncontrolled release of water requires the coordinated efforts of both the dam owning/operating agencies and disaster management authorities. The beginning of such an undertaking is an Emergency Action Plan (EAP). An EAP for a dam is a written document that identifies potential emergency conditions and specifies preplanned actions to be followed in case of a potential emergency. A crucial element of an EAP is a mapping that outlines the area inundated by a dam-failure flood at a sufficient scale to identify the population at risk and dwellings, roads, low-water crossings and other critical structures likely to be directly affected. The travel time for floods to reach specific locations is one of the vital parameters to be evaluated. Others are the depth of flooding and velocity of flows, which indicate the flood severity.

Numerical models are used to assess the consequences of a potential failure and produce flood inundation maps. The models are based on the solution of either one-dimensional cross-section-averaged (1D) or two-dimensional depth-averaged (2DH) equations that describe the unsteady open-channel flow. In this analysis, the flood resulting from a breach of Hirakud Dam is simulated using both 1D and 2DH numerical models and the results are compared.

Both the 1D and 2DH models are shown to provide nearly the same estimates of the maximum water depth, the arrival time of the flood peak and the maximum water speeds at 32 index points located throughout the floodplain. However, the initial flood-wave arrival times differ slightly along the main river channel. Several advantages of the 2DH simulations are described.

2 Hirakud Dam

Hirakud Dam (Fig. 1) is a composite structure of earth, concrete and masonry. It spans the Mahanadi River, about 13 km upstream from Sambalpur in Odisha, India. It is the longest dam in India, measuring 25.8 km from end-to-end, including dikes, which fill low points between the adjacent hills. The main dam has an overall length of 4.8 km. The reservoir created by the dam is enormous, impounding nearly 6000 Mm^3 at the full-supply level (FSL).

Fig. 1 Hirakud Dam in Odisha, India

The vast floodplain immediately downstream from the dam (Fig. 2) is dotted with small hills and confluences with several tributary streams that drain urban districts. One of the urban areas is Sambalpur, the fifth largest city in Odisha. It is located on the banks of river Mahanadi, with a population of 335,761 (as per the 2011 census). Since the completion of Hirakud Dam in 1956, Sambalpur has undergone a significant transformation, supporting many agriculture-related businesses and metal-processing industries. Several educational institutes are about 5 km downstream from the dam at Burla, known as the education hub of Odisha.

3 Dam-Breach Model

In this analysis, breach development is considered to proceed in a presupposed way, growing in a trapezoid shape defined by its final dimensions and the time needed for the breach to form completely. Froehlich's [1] formulas were used to predict the parameters of a hypothetical failure of Hirakud Dam caused by overtopping. The average width of the final breach is calculated as follows:

$$B_{avg} = 0.28 \times k_M \times k_H \times \frac{V_w^{1/3}}{H_b} \times \left(\frac{W_{avg}}{H_b}\right)^{-1/6} \times H_b \tag{1}$$

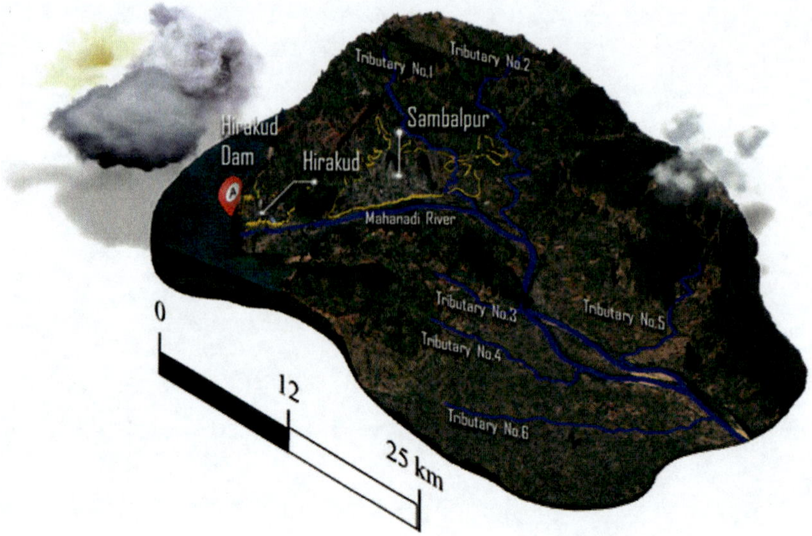

Fig. 2 Hirakud Dam and the downstream floodplain showing the Mahanadi River and the several tributaries that drain urban districts

where, V_w = the impounded volume of water above the final breach bottom elevation, W_{avg} = the average width of the embankment (from the upstream toe to the downstream toe) above the final breach bottom, H_b = the height of the final trapezoidal breach,

$$k_M = \begin{cases} 1.0, \text{ for internal erostion} \\ 1.5, \text{ for overtopping} \end{cases}, k_H = \begin{cases} \left(\frac{H_b}{H_s}\right)^{1/2}, \text{ for } H_b < H_s \\ 1.0, \quad\quad \text{ for } H_b \geq H_s \end{cases},$$

and $H_s = 6.1$ m (or 20 ft if U.S. Customary units are used). The average breach side-slope ratio m is given as

$$m = \begin{cases} 0.6, \text{ for internal erosion failures} \\ 1.0, \text{ for overtopping failures} \end{cases} \quad (2)$$

The breach formation time (in seconds) is found as

$$t_f = 50 \times \sqrt{\frac{V_w}{g H_b^2}} \times \left(\frac{W_{avg}}{H_b}\right)^{1/4}. \quad (3)$$

where g = gravitational acceleration.

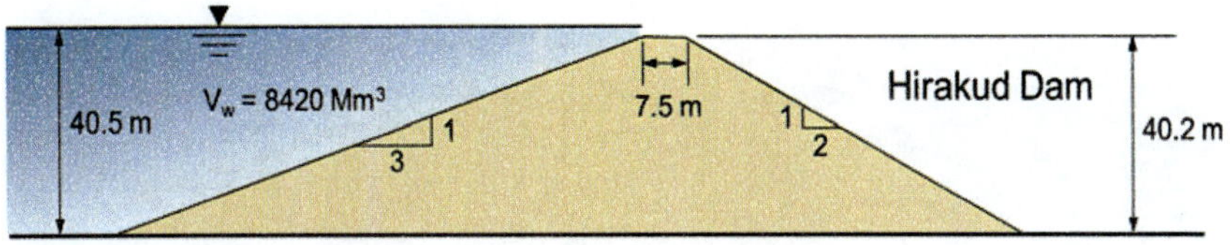

Fig. 3 Cross-section of Hirakud Dam earthen embankment where breaching occurs

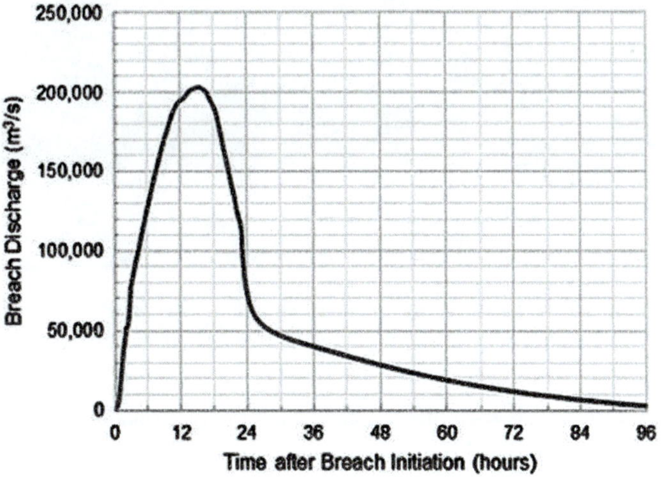

Fig. 4 Dam breach flood hydrograph

A cross-section of the earthen embankment section of Hirakud Dam where a breach is likely to form is shown in Fig. 3. For an overtopping failure of Hirakud Dam $V_w = 8{,}420$ Mm^3, $H_b = 40.2$ m and $W_{avg} = 108$ m. Then with $k_M = 1.5$ and $k_H = 1.0$, Eqs. (1), (2) and (3) give: $B_{avg} = 725$ m, $m = 1.0$ and $t_f = 46{,}650$ s = 12.96 h (rounded to 13.0 h). The dam-breach outflow flood hydrograph, which is input to both the 1D and 2DH models, is shown in Fig. 4.

4 Numerical Flood Models

The HEC-RAS (Hydrologic Engineering Center—River Analysis System) 1D and 2DH surface-water flow models [2] were used to simulate Hirakud Dam-failure floods caused by the breach in the main section of the earthen embankment. The 1D model is particularly applicable to long, well-defined river reaches. However, flood inundation studies that involve relatively flat terrain often have divided flows or require precise differentiation of flooding depths and durations (such as in high population areas) may require a 2DH model or a combined 1D-2DH model. Both

Fig. 5 The layout of the 1D model cross-sections along the Mahanadi River and six tributary streams. Tributaries 1 and 2 flow through the urban center of Sambalpur

the 1D and 2DH models solve the unsteady conservation equations for momentum and mass. However, different solution schemes are used. Details are given by Bruner [2].

The cross-section locations used to model the Mahanadi River and the six tributaries in the floodplain downstream from the dam are shown in Fig. 5. The two-dimensional computational mesh used to model depth-averaged flows downstream of the dam is shown in Fig. 6. Note that Sambalpur is covered by smaller cells than are used to model the remainder of the floodplain where 200 m × 200 m cells were used to construct the mesh. The refined mesh is needed to discretize adequately the two tributaries that flow through the urban district.

5 Comparison of 1D and 2DH Flood Simulation Results

Flood simulation results are compared at 32 index points, which are described in Table 1. The index points are located along the Mahanadi River and throughout the floodplain, as shown in Fig. 7. The comparison locations are ordered and numbered by their straight-line distances from the breach. The index point closest to the breach is Hirakud Bus Stand (No. 1) and the farthest point from the dam is Tababda (No. 32), which is located 39 km downstream from the dam measured along the Mahanadi. The flood-wave arrival times (the initial arrival time and the peak arrival time at which the maximum water depth was reached) at the index points are compared in

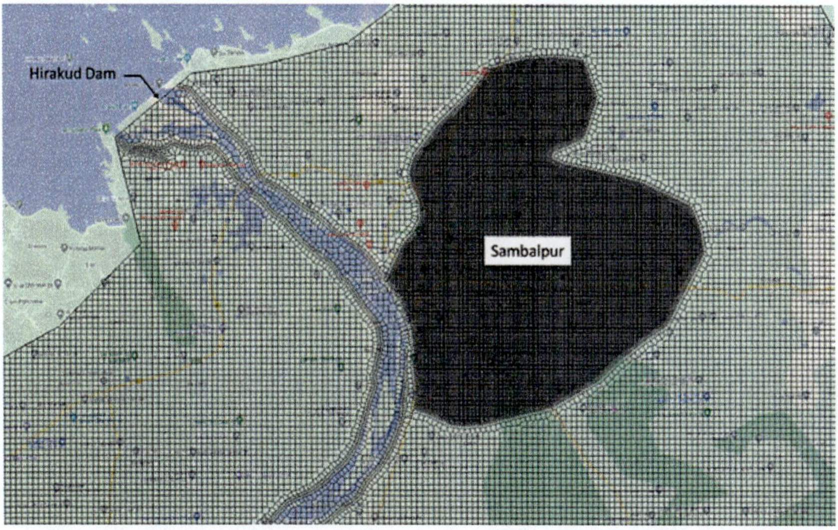

Fig. 6 Two-dimensional mesh of the Mahanadi River floodplain below Hirakud Dam. The urban center of Sambalpur is covered by smaller cells than in the surrounding floodplain

the bar graphs shown in Fig. 8. The maximum water depths are shown in Fig. 9. The maximum computed water speeds are compared in Fig. 10.

At five of the index points (Nos. 4, 6, 13, 15 and 18), located near the edge of the inundated floodplain, the 1D solution finds that the points are not flooded. This disagreement is caused by the interpolation between cross-sections that is needed to calculate values. Only at Nos. 4 and 5 (located close to the dam) were 2DH maximum water depths significant. The maximum water depths compared in Fig. 9 are remarkably close at all index points except those near the dam (Nos. 1 through 4). Similarly, the maximum water speeds are close at most index points except those near the dam (Nos. 1 through 5).

From Fig. 8, the most significant differences between the 1D and 2DH flood model results are the arrival times of the initial flood wave. The 1D flood-wave initial arrival time is shorter at most index points because flows at first are all confined to the main channel. In contrast, the 2DH solution allows water to spread across the floodplain immediately upon release through the breach. However, the peak flood-wave arrival times are nearly the same at all locations, resulting from the lengthy breach time (13 h) and flooding duration.

Table 1 Flood index point descriptions

No	Index Point Name	Distance[a] from the dam (km)	Location	
			Latitude	Longitude
1	Hirakud Bus Stand	2.538	21.52756	83.89874
2	Burla N.A.C. College	3.424	21.50590	83.88856
3	Burla	5.138	21.48864	83.88447
4	Sri Ram Vihar	6.882	21.47510	83.89570
5	Remed	8.204	21.49988	83.94542
6	Sikirdi	9.212	21.46687	83.92742
7	Nirankari Colony	9.440	21.48492	83.94958
8	Khetrapur	9.9460	21.48764	83.95732
9	Potapali	10.566	21.46735	83.94796
10	Modipada	11.817	21.47557	83.97051
11	Mundoghat	12.205	21.45892	83.96123
12	Sangsinghari	12.437	21.43396	83.92925
13	Budhajar	12.555	21.48042	83.98188
14	Barhakuni	12.868	21.45151	83.96243
15	Sambalpur	13.275	21.46683	83.98117
16	Jampali	14.489	21.43365	83.96462
17	Chaupur	14.587	21.43812	83.97147
18	Gengutipali	14.957	21.46577	83.99963
19	Jharapali	15.427	21.42699	83.97021
20	Gopal Bihar	15.894	21.44228	83.99297
21	Basantput	16.000	21.39497	83.91621
22	Naksapali	16.457	21.45988	84.01271
23	Brahmapura	16.855	21.41181	83.97180
24	Senhapali	18.210	21.39382	83.96658
25	Gunderpur	18.671	21.40668	83.99298
26	Bakbira	20.135	21.36293	83.94017
27	Jayghant	20.257	21.37641	83.97393
28	Chipilima	20.677	21.35016	83.90825
29	Mahanadi	21.839	21.34341	83.92810
30	Kardola	22.731	21.33055	83.90168
31	Marangola	23.362	21.32454	83.89903
32	Tababda	28.546	21.27908	83.91354

[a]The straight-line distance measured from the centre of the dam breach

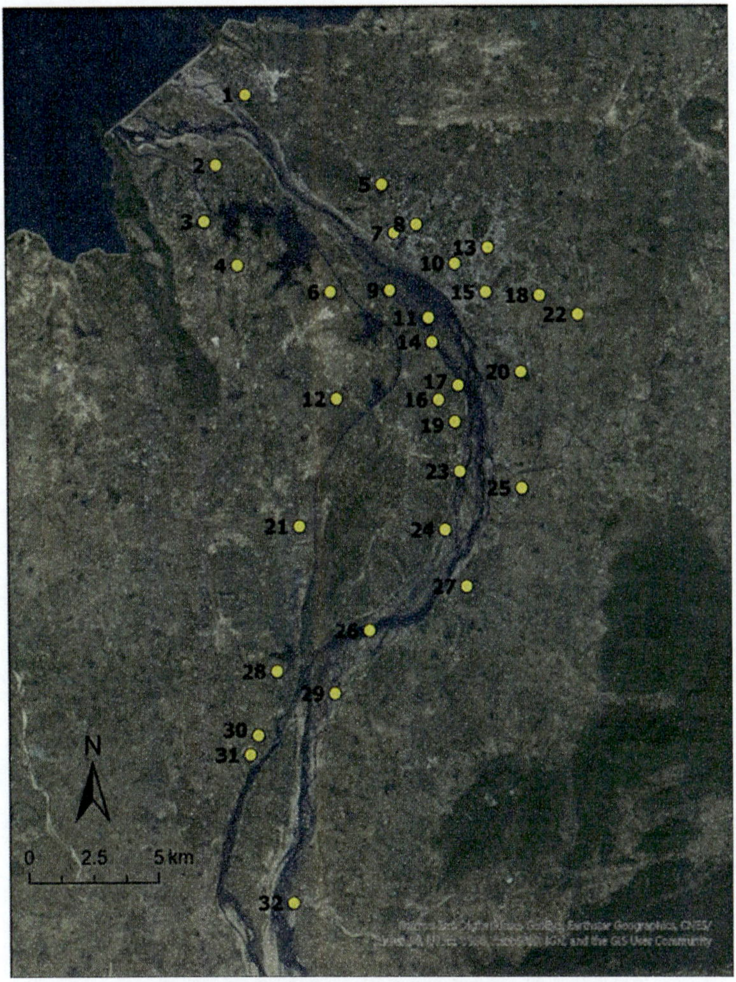

Fig. 7 Locations of the 32 flood index points downstream from Hirakud Dam

6 Summary and Conclusions

Both 1D and 2DH numerical models are used to assess the consequences of a dam breach and produce flood inundation maps. The type of model chosen is determined mainly by the physical characteristics of the river channel and floodplain. The comparison of dam-breach flood simulations by 1D and 2DH models in this study finds close agreement between the maximum water depths and flow speeds, except at several index points closest to the dam where the 2DH governing equations provide more accurate descriptions of the flow. The arrival time of the initial flood wave given by the 1D solution is consistently less than the 2DH calculation. Of course, good

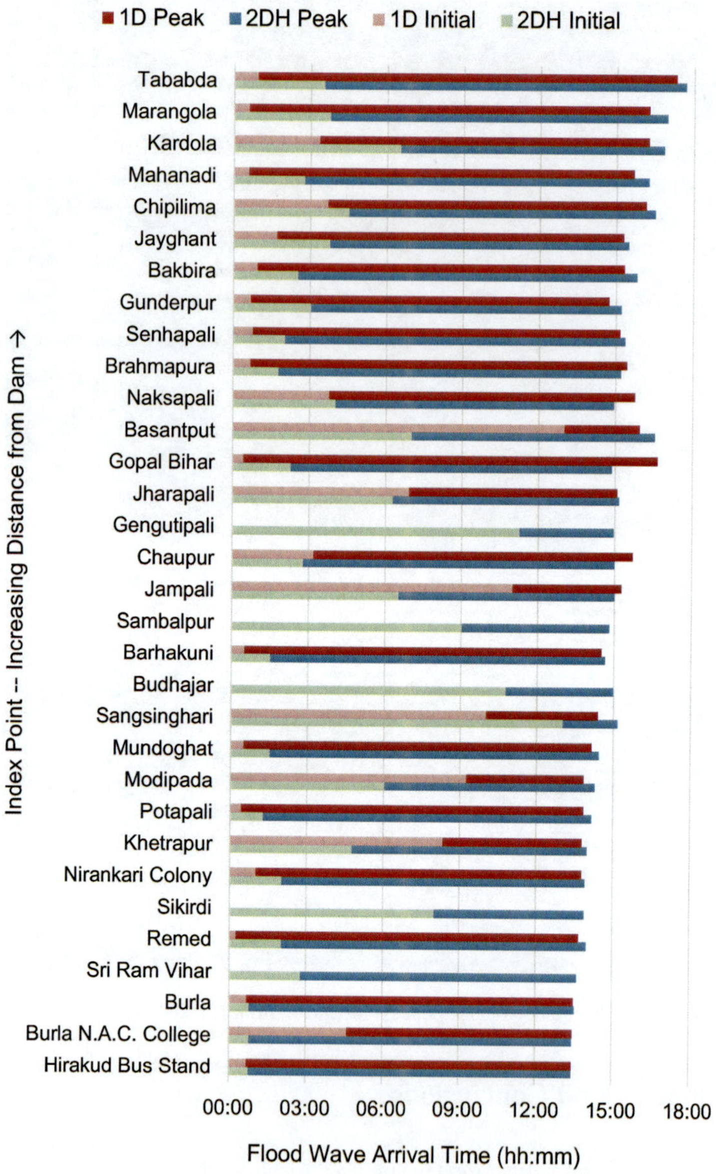

Fig. 8 The initial and peak flood-wave travel times to index points. Distance from the dam increases from the bottom to top

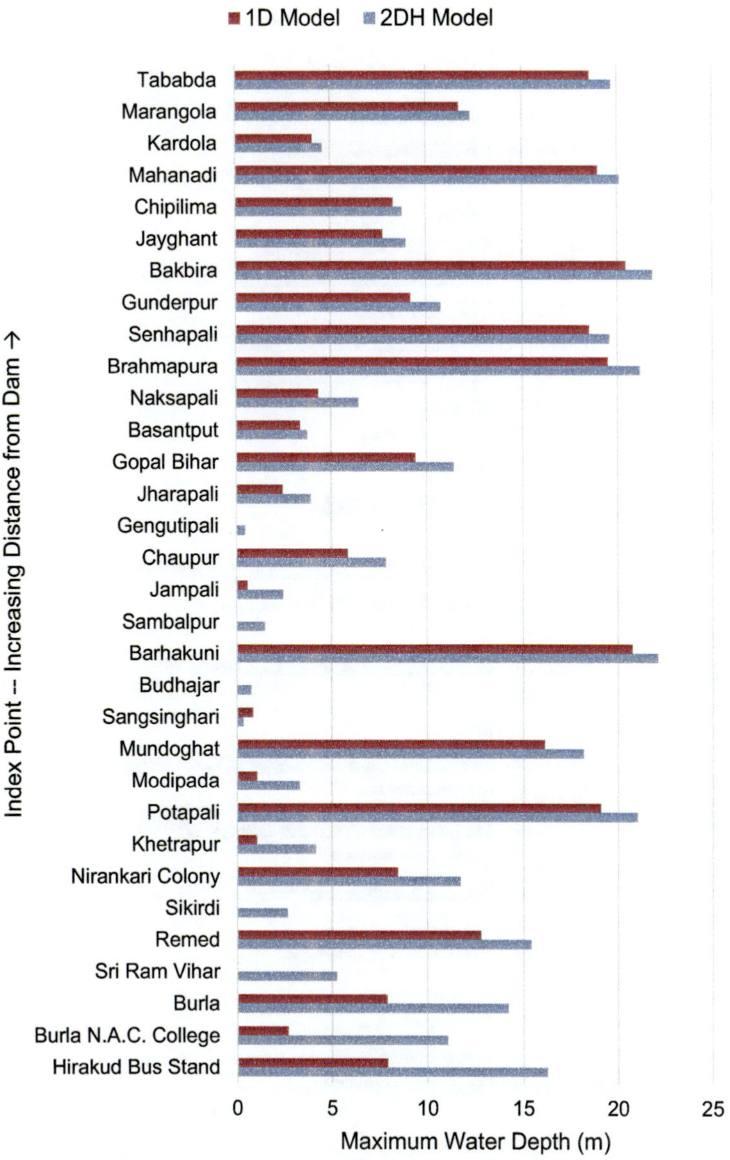

Fig. 9 The maximum water depth at index points from 1 and 2DH model simulations

agreement between the two modelling approaches depends on the skilful layout of cross-sections and construction of two-dimensional meshes.

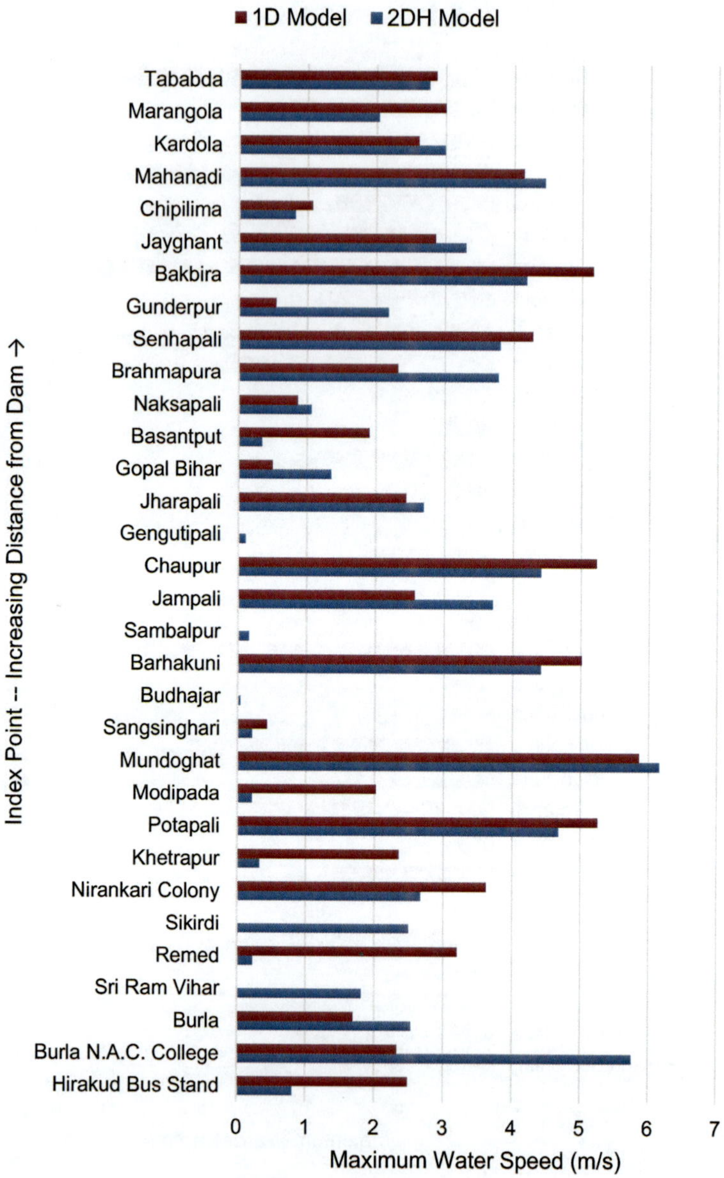

Fig. 10 The maximum water speed at index points from 1 and 2DH model simulations

References

1. Froehlich DC (2017) An empirical model of embankment dam breaching. In: Compendium of technical papers, third national dam safety conference, Doc. No. CDSO_NDSC3_COMP, New Delhi, India, Central Water Commission, Ministry of Water Resources, River Development & Ganga Rejuvenation, pp 532–539
2. Brunner GW (2020) HEC-RAS, river analysis system hydraulic reference manual, Version 6.0. Report Number CPD-69, Hydrologic Engineering Center, U.S. Army Corps of Engineers, Davis, California

Response of Hill-Slope Buildings Subjected to Near-Fault Ground Motion

Prabhat Kumar, Ashwani Kumar, and A. D. Pandey

Abstract The near-fault ground motion (NFGM) is composed of high frequencies, representing accelerations and one or more dominant long-period velocity pulses. This study is intended to analyze and interpret the response of hill-slope buildings under the effect of near-fault pulse-type ground motions in the Himalayan region. For this purpose dynamic analysis of two special moments resistant frame (SMRF) 3D configurations consisting of Step-Back (SB) and Step-Back-Set-Back (SBSB) models have been conducted. From a seismic safety point of view responses due to NFGMs are compared with the responses obtained from conventional types of seismic inputs. The Indian seismic codal spectra need modification to incorporate the effects of pulse-type ground motion due to moderate, large and great earthquakes for sites in the vicinity of fault regions, particularly for the Himalayas region. It has been further recognized that the large amplitude pulses, primarily related to directivity effect, control the response of medium- and long-period structures, whereas, the high-frequency part of the NFGM plays an important role especially for short-period structures.

Keywords NFGM · Long-Period · Velocity pulse · Directivity · Dynamic response · Hill-Slope buildings

---

P. Kumar (✉)
Department of Civil Engineering, College of Engineering Roorkee, Roorkee, UK 247667, India
e-mail: drpkpfce@coer.ac.in

A. Kumar · A. D. Pandey
Department of Earthquake Engineering, Indian Institute of Technology, Roorkee, UK 247667, India
e-mail: ashwnfeq@iitr.ac.in

A. D. Pandey
e-mail: adpanfeq@iitr.ac.in

C. Ghosh and S. Kolathayar (eds.), *A System Engineering Approach to Disaster Resilience*, Lecture Notes in Civil Engineering 205, https://doi.org/10.1007/978-981-16-7397-9_31

1 Introduction

Dominant source characteristics governing NFGM include: Rupture directivity, Fling-step, Hanging-wall and Vertical effects. Forward rupture directivity is responsible for increased low frequency content of ground motion at distances within 20 km-30 km from the hypocenter [1, 2] and sites close to fault experience large amplitude long-period pulse-motions [3]. NFGM, because of its complex nature, has been represented by equivalent pulse models, such as half-pulse, full-pulse and multiple-pulses models, with pulse-period (T_p). The fundamental controlling parameters of pulse models are: type of pulse, pulse-period and pulse-amplitude [4, 5]. However, it is to be emphasized that the use of equivalent pulse models is an approximation to represent NFGM which is very complex in nature. This aspect has been recognized by a large number of researchers all over the world. The pulse models have helped in quantifying seismic demands for structures in terms of controlling parameters of the NFGM namely, type of pulse, pulse-period (T_p), pulse-amplitude (V_p) and a number of predominant pulses (N) of the models. Near-fault effects have been incorporated in seismic design codes, namely, American UBC-1997, Chinese GB50011-2001 [6, 7] with a view to protecting the structures located in the near-fault regions. However, the Indian standard code of practice IS1893:2016 is silent about NFGM. Hall et al. (1995) examined the effects of NFGM on flexible buildings and emphasized that flexible-frame and base-isolated buildings, designed as per codal provisions, undergo severe non-linear deformations because of large rapid displacement pulses associated with the large long-period velocity pulses [8, 9]. Malhotra (1999) demonstrated that pulse-type ground motion leads to narrower velocity-sensitive regions shifted to longer periods [10]. This leads to an increase in base-shear and inter-story drift in high-rise buildings with an accompanying increase in ductility demand due to high PGV/PGA ratio. Studies have also demonstrated that spectral ordinates obtained from simplified pulse models are strongly related to the velocity spectral period and pulse waveforms [11].

2 Objectives of the Study

The main objective of the present study is to analyze and interpret the response of hill-slope buildings subjected to pulse-type ground motion in the Himalayan region and to compare the response of the buildings on hill-slope subjected to pulse-type ground motion with conventional seismic inputs (Indian seismic codal spectra and site-specific ground motion incorporating the near-fault factor) and make appropriate recommendations.

3 Pulse Characterization of Himalayan Earthquakes Adopting Wavelet Analysis

To allow measuring the SGM due to moderate and large earthquakes in the Himalayas, strong motion arrays were deployed by the Department of Earthquake Engineering, IIT Roorkee. The first strong motion array was installed in the Himachal Himalaya in 1983. SGM due to a moderate 1986 Dharamsala earthquake (Mw = 5.5) was recorded at **nine** stations. SGM of the 1991 Uttarkashi earthquake (Mw = 6.8) was recorded at **thirteen** stations and the 1999 Chamoli earthquake (Mw = 6.5) at **eleven** stations of the strong motion array installed in the Garhwal and Kumaun Himalaya [12]. These **33** strong motion recordings of three moderate sized Himalayan earthquakes have been analyzed for NFGM characterization by Kumar et al. [16].

Pulse characteristics of NFGM for these recordings are extracted adopting pulse detection methodology based on wavelet analysis given by Baker [13, 14]. Several mother wavelets, namely, Daubechies (db4 and db7), Haar (haar), Symlet (sym4), Coiflets (coif2), Reverse biorthogonal (rbio2.4) and Biorspline (bior1.3) have been used to extract the pulse from the velocity time history and predict the value of pulse-period, which is the most important characteristic associated with ground motion. Fault-normal components at three sites are computed using the procedure given by Somerville [15]. Out of the seven wavelets adapted for pulse detection, Daubechies wavelets (db4 and db7) provided the best results based on the pulse-indicators (PI), pulse-periods (Tp), spectral pulse-periods (Tv-p) and spectral shapes. However, the spectra of long-period pulses extracted using Daubechies mother wavelet of order seven (db7) are closer to the long-period spectral amplitudes of the FN components of ground motions at three sites. For the **Uttarkashi and Chamoli earthquakes**, recorded and computed fault-normal components at **Bhatwari and Gopeshwar stations** showed pulse-type ground motion in their velocity time histories. At **Bhatwari station** the pulse-periods of transverse, as well as fault-normal components, are 1.28 s and 1.30 s respectively. At **Gopeshwar station** the pulse periods of transverse and fault-normal components are 1.37 s and 1.39 s respectively. For the Dharamsala earthquake, **Shapur station**, transverse-component (also a fault-normal component) of the recorded velocity time history showed pulse-type ground motion with pulse-period (*Tp*) 0.52 s and pulse-indicator 0.94. Extracted pulse from Fault-Normal component of ground motion at Shapur, Bhatwari and Gopeshwar sites adopting db7 wavelet is shown in Fig. 1. Table 1 provides the details of the pulse-indicators (PI) and pulse-periods (*Tp*) obtained adopting different mother wavelets for fault-normal components at three sites. It is found that due to high **PGV/PGA** ratios, the acceleration-sensitive regions for the **Uttarkashi earthquake** at **Bhatwari station** and the **Chamoli earthquake** at **Gopeshwar station** extends up to 0.65 s and 0.53 s, respectively [16]. These values are higher than the codal value at hard soil (**0.40** s). Response spectra also show much higher spectral amplitudes in the velocity-sensitive region. Epicentres of three Himalayan earthquakes and locations of stations that contain near-fault pulses are shown in Fig. 2. As a consequence of widening of the acceleration-sensitive region, the structures designed according to IS 1893: 2016

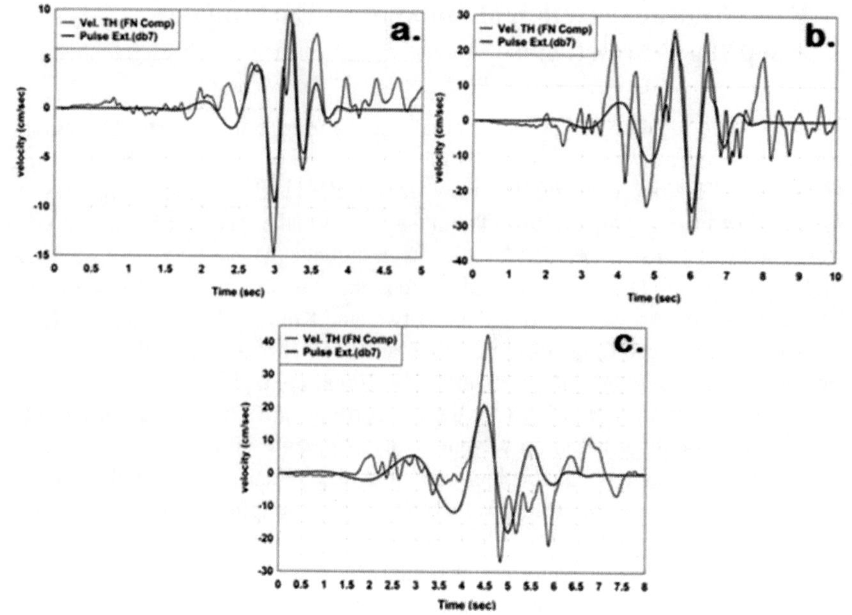

Fig. 1 Fault-Normal component ground motion at **Shapur (a), Bhatwari (b)** and **Gopeshwar (c)** sites along with extracted pulses from velocity time history using **db7 wavelet**

Table 1 Pulse-indicators and pulse-periods using different mother wavelets for Fault-normal components of SGM at Shapur, Bhatwari and Gopeshwar stations

Mother wavelet	Shapur site		Bhatwari site		Gopeshwar site	
	(PI)	Tp (s)	(PI)	Tp (s)	(PI)	Tp (s)
db4	0.9051	0.53	0.9112	1.09	0.9813	1.40
db7	0.9431	0.52	0.9300	1.30	0.9019	1.39
haar	0.7631	0.40	0.5111	0.78	0.9996	1.08
sym4	0.4241	0.59	0.5353	1.04	0.9886	1.37
coif2	0.5692	0.55	0.4941	1.02	0.9624	1.54
rbio2.4	0.6431	0.50	0.5307	1.15	0.9893	1.84
bior1.3	0.8223	0.47	0.3633	0.90	0.9990	1.22

as flexible structures shall behave as stiff structures in the near-fault region in the Himalaya. At Shapur station, the acceleration-sensitive region extends up to 0.35 s. This is slightly lesser than the codal value and also has lower spectral amplitudes compared to codal response spectral amplitudes (IS 1893: 2016). This is attributed to smaller magnitude of Dharamsala earthquake compared to Uttarkashi and Chamoli earthquakes.

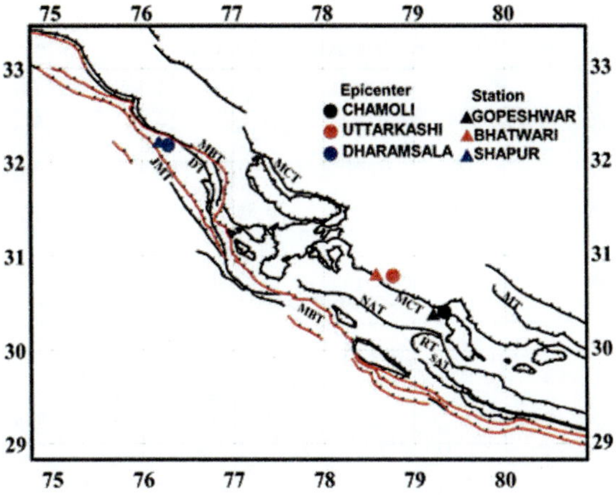

Fig. 2 Epicenters of three earthquakes and locations of stations that contain near-fault pulses

4 Estimation of Ground Motion Including Near-Fault Factor at Bhatwari, Gopeshwar and Shapur Sites

The peak horizontal ground accelerations (PHA), spectral accelerations (Sa) at 5% damping (between 0.01 s and 4.00 s periods) at three selected sites (Shapur, Bhatwari and Gopeshwar) located in the Lesser Himalaya incorporating the NFGM factor have been computed using the methodology given by Division of Engineering Services Geotechnical Services, Caltrans, 2012, for Developing Deterministic Acceleration Response Spectrum [17]. For this purpose NGA relationship given by Boore and Atkinson (2008) applicable for 'M_w' ranging between 5 and 8, $R_{JB} \leq 200$ km and $V_{S30} = 180$–1300 m/s were adopted [18]. For each site, the shortest distance between the site and the rupture surface, called Joyner-Boore distance *(R_{jb})*, for all seismic sources (faults) located within 30 km from the sites were computed using Arc Info GIS 7.2.1D [16]. The highest PHA is taken to represent maximum acceleration due to MCE at each site and corresponding spectral accelerations (Sa) at 5% damping between 0.01 s and 4.00 s with NFGM factor were estimated.

The maximum magnitude associated with each seismotectonic source is estimated from the surface rupture length adopting the general assumption that 1/3 to 1/2 of the total length of fault would rupture producing the maximum earthquake [19]. Using the relation, $Mw = 5.00 + 1.22\log(L)$, between the surface rupture length (L) and earthquake magnitude (Mw) for reverse fault; the Mw for each seismotectonic source is estimated and, the rupture width (RW) for each seismotectonic source is calculated from the relation, $\text{Log}(RW) = -1.01 + 0.32\,Mw$ [20]. In the calculation of R_{jb} distances, the dip-angle (α) is taken as 15° because most of the seismotectonic sources in the Himalayas are thrust types. The maximum value of PHA computed at three sites, along with seismotectonic sources/faults that have made maximum contribution are listed in Table 2. Six response spectra for the **Gopeshwar site** that falls in Zone V as per Indian seismic code, IS 1893: 2016 [21] are shown in Fig. 3.

Table 2 Computed peak horizontal accelerations (Ah (g)) at three selected sites along with location and source that has made maximum contribution

Site	Lat (°)	Long (°)	PGA (g)	Source, reverse fault type, $M_{w(max)}$
Shapur (SS1)	32.217	76.183	**0.50**	Jwala Mukhi Thrust (**JMT**),7.4
Bhatwari (SS2)	30.810	78.610	**0.58**	Main Central Thrust (**MCT**), 7.8
Gopeshwar (SS3)	30.667	79.550	**0.51**	Main Central Thrust (**MCT**), 7.8

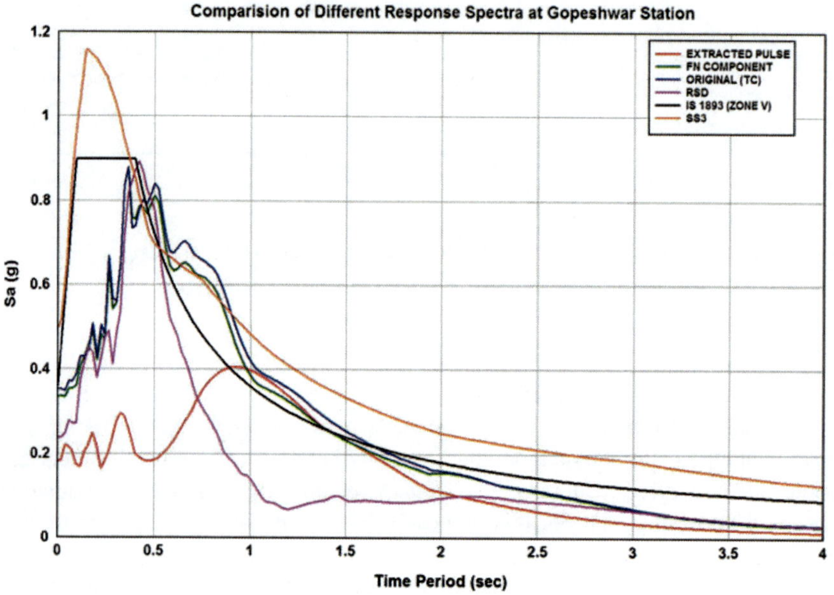

Fig. 3 Response spectra(s) of SSGM, original GM (TC), FN component, extracted pulse and residual (RSD) at Gopeshwar site and codal spectra (IS: 1893:2016)

The response spectra are: (i) Site-specific response spectra (**SS3**), (ii) Spectra due to recorded pulse-type ground motion (transverse-component (**TC**)), (iii) Spectra of fault-normal (**FN**) component, (iv) Spectra due to extracted pulse ground motion (**EXT**), (v) Spectra due to residual (**RSD**)/high-frequency part of fault-normal (**FN**) component and (vi) Codal spectra for Zone V as per Indian seismic code**.**

5 Dynamic Analysis of Hill-Slope Buildings

The buildings resting on sloping ground, generally existing in hilly areas, usually have a step-back (SB) configuration or a combination of step-back and set-back (SBSB) configuration as shown in Fig. 4. These models are selected because most of the residential buildings in the hilly regions are low-rise buildings with number of

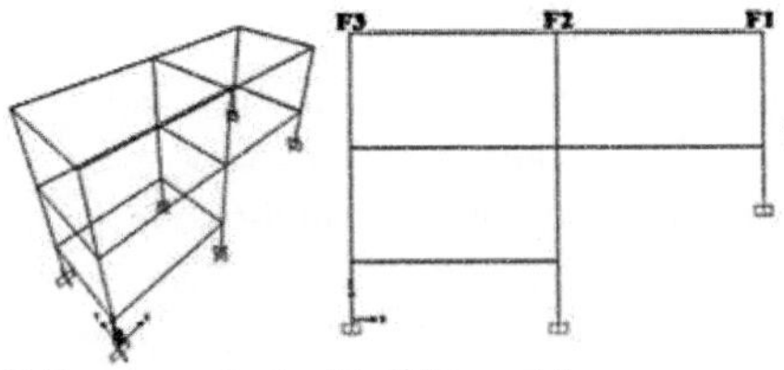

(a) Two storey step-back building model

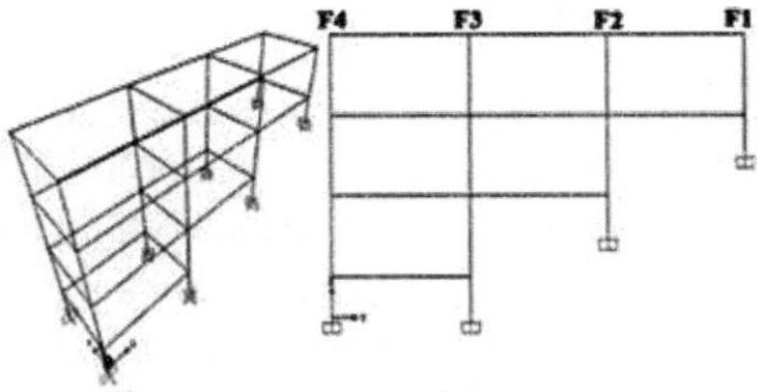

(b) Three storey step-back building model

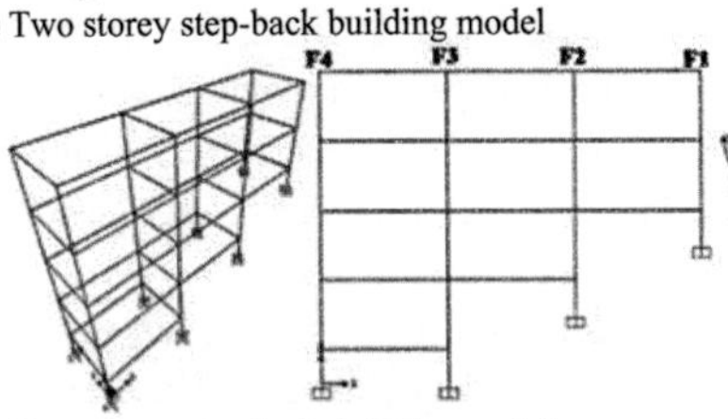

(c) Four storey step-back building model

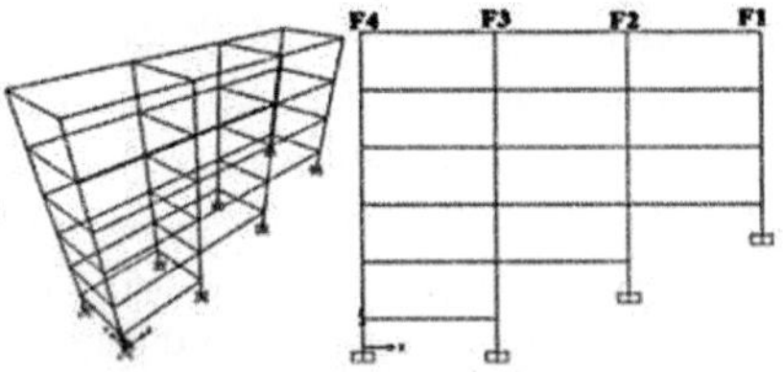

(d) Five storey step-back building model

(a) 212SB (b) 313SB (c) 413SB (d) 513SB Step-Back (SB) building models

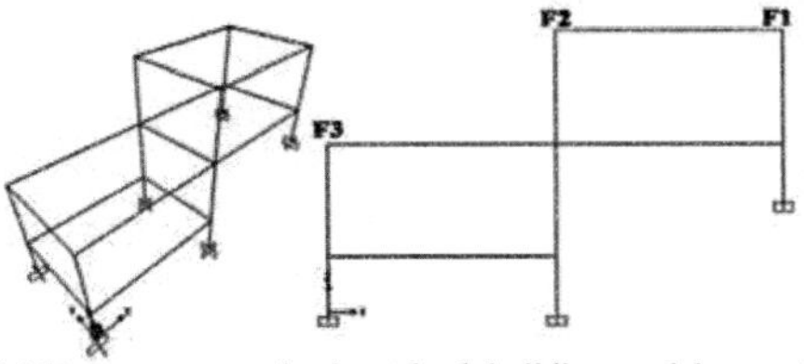

(a) Two storey step-back-set-back building model

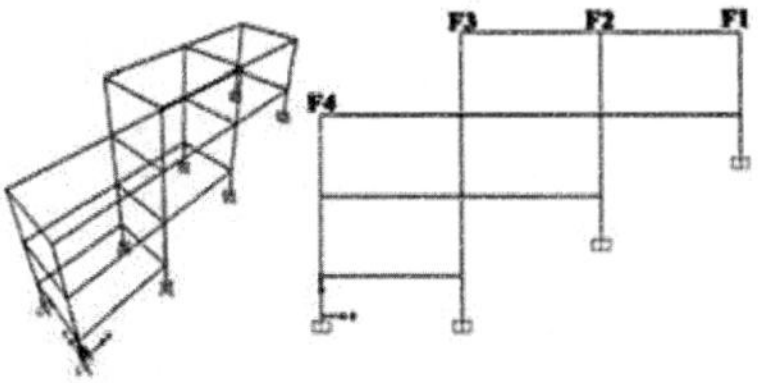

(b) Three storey step-back-set-back building model

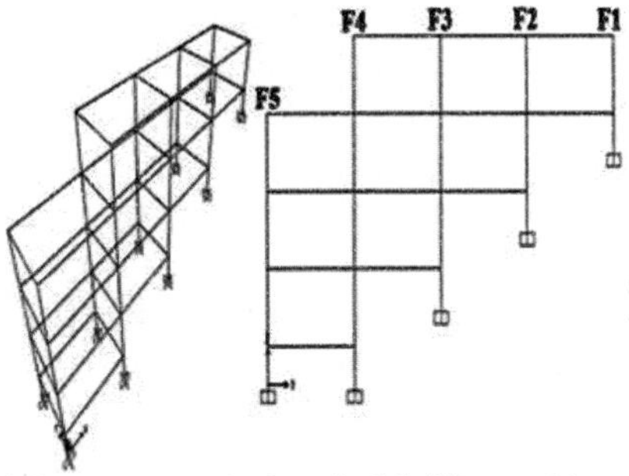

(c) Four storey step-back-set-back building model

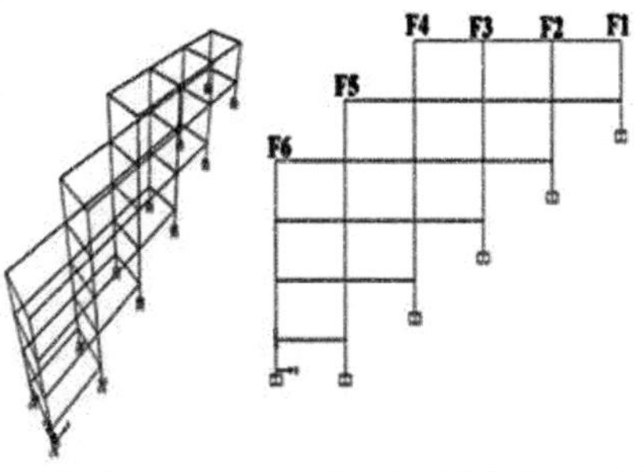

(d) Five storey step-back-set-back building model

(a) 212SBSB, (b) 313SBSB (c) 414SBSB (d) 515SBSB Step-Back-Set-Back (SBSB) building models

Fig. 4 Step-Back (SB) and Step-Back-Set-Back (SBSB) building models

storeys limited to five storeys in majority of cases. For both types of building models, the number of storeys has been varied from two to five.

Responses of R.C. framed buildings (Step-Back (**SB**) buildings and Step-Back-Set-Back (**SBSB**) buildings) on hill-slopes subjected to NFGMs are analyzed. From seismic safety point of view responses due to NFGMs are compared with the response obtained from conventional types of inputs. Earthquake response of buildings on hill-slope depends upon the distribution of mass and stiffness, both of which vary in the horizontal and vertical plane. For Step-Back (SB) buildings, various floor levels step back towards the hill slope keeping the top floor level same for all the bays. In case the building has set-back, then the building is called a Step-Back-Set-Back (SBSB) building [22]. Both types of buildings have columns of different heights at ground level, due to which the shorter columns attract more force as these are stiffer. The Indian seismic code recommends the dynamic analysis of such irregular structures. Eight special moments resistant frame (**SMRF**) building models, four SB and four SBSB (Fig. 4), models are analyzed in SAP2000. For both types of building models, the number of storeys varies from two to five.

The slope of the ground is taken as 27° with horizontal which is neither too steep nor too flat and also considered during many past studies [23–28]. The structural material is assumed to be isotropic and homogenous. Joint between the building elements (beams and columns) are modelled by using diaphragms as constraints. The dynamic analysis (Response Spectrum Analysis) of buildings is carried out for rigid base (fixed-base) laid on rock site conditions in longitudinal (along the slope, X) and transverse direction (across the slope, Y). The dynamic analyses of all the buildings were carried out adopting.

(i) Response Spectrum Method (according to **IS**: 1893 (Part 1)), (ii) Response Spectra obtained by NFGMs along with their extracted pulses (**EXT**) and residual components (**RSD**) and iii) Response Spectra obtained by site-specific ground motion (**SSGM**) at three sites (**SS1, SS2 and SS3**). Damping considered for all structural modes of vibration is five percent (5%). The computed results are expressed in terms of two parameters: floor displacements (horizontal) and shear forces in ground columns. Since the buildings are on the sloping ground, there should be short column-long column effect which could be major cause of structural failure. At Gopeshwar site, the results obtained on the dynamic structural response of two and five storey buildings (Fig. 5) are presented in Figs. 6, 7, 8 and 9. These results are discussed below on the trend basis considering various types of ground motions at the selected site. In the figures and texts, symbols XX, YX and YY stand for, seismic input in X, Y, Y directions and computed parameters in X, X, Y directions respectively.

Properties of considered building configurations and intensity of loads imposed on them are summarized as, Height of each floor: 3.5 m, Plan dimension of each storey block: 7 m × 5 m, Slab thickness: 0.15 m, Wall thickness: 230 mm, Parapet wall thickness: 230 mm, Density of concrete: 25 KN/m^3, Poisson's Ratio: 0.2, Damping: 0.05, Size of column: 230 mm x 500 mm, Size of beams: 230 mm x 500 mm, Material properties, M 25 & Fe 415, Slab dead—3.75 KN/m^2, Floor Live load—3 KN/m^2, Roof Live load—1.5 KN/m^2, Floor Finish—1 KN/m^2, Roof Finish—1.5 KN/m^2, Exterior Wall Load—16.15 KN/m, Interior Wall Load—10.5 KN/m, Parapet wall load—6.9 KN/m.

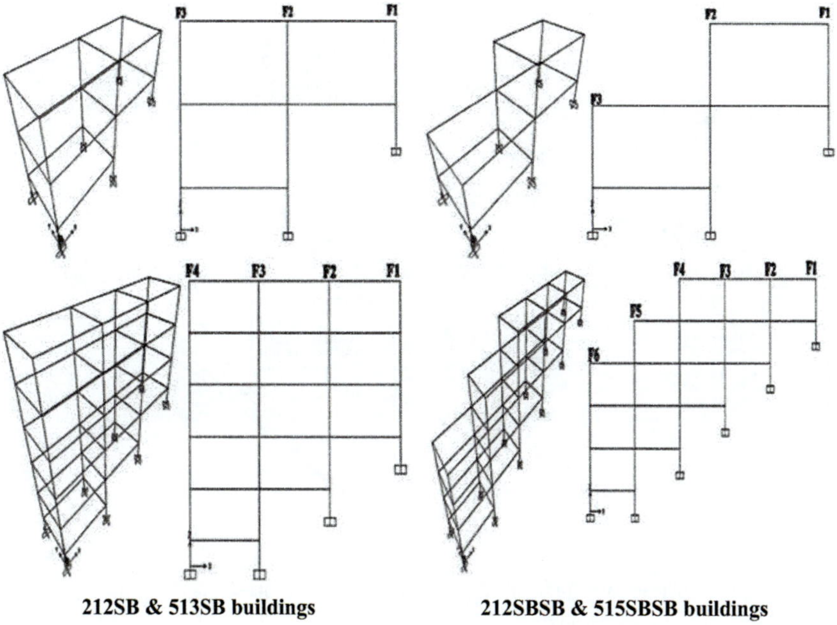

Fig. 5 Step-Back (**SB**) and Step-Back-Set-Back (**SBSB**) buildings (two and five storey buildings)

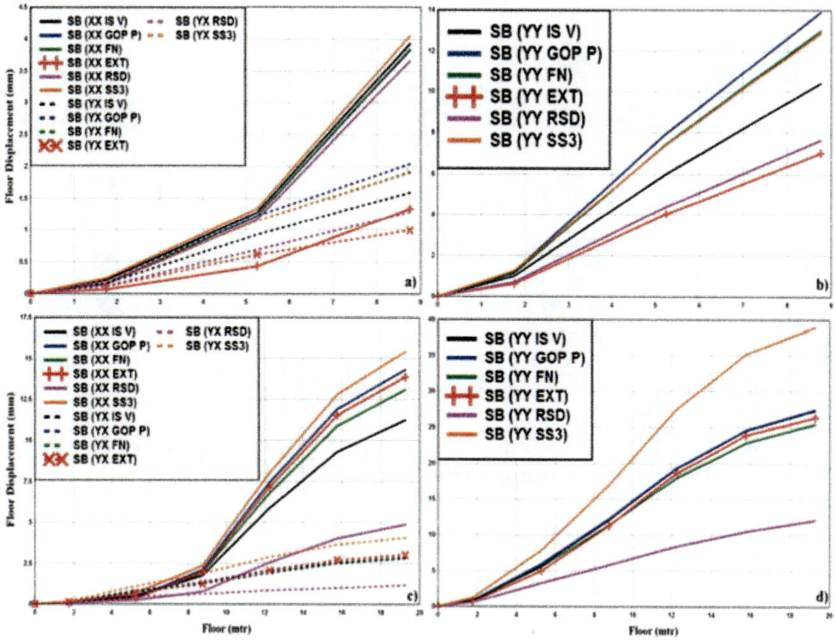

Fig. 6 Floor displacements (FD) of two (**a, b**) and five (**c, d**) storey Step-Back (212SB & 513SB) buildings

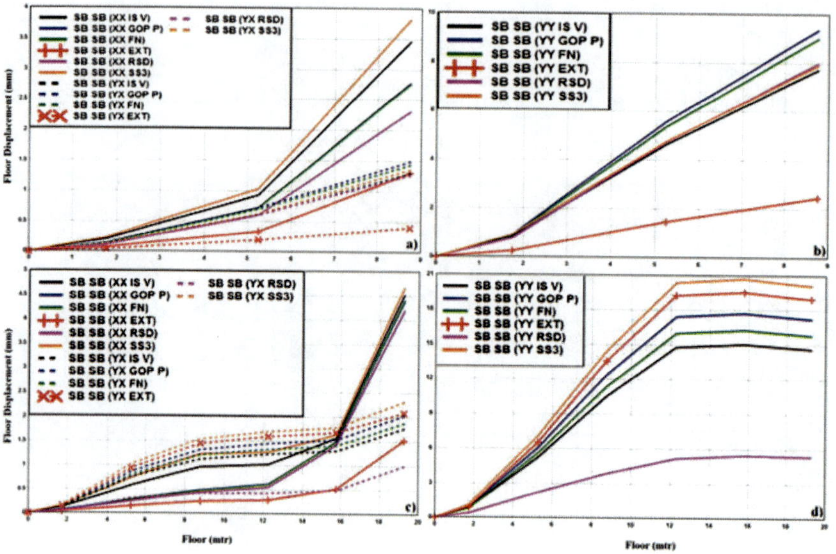

Fig. 7 Floor Displacements (FD) of two (**a, b**) and five (**c, d**) storey Step-Back-Set-Back (212SBSB & 515SBSB) buildings

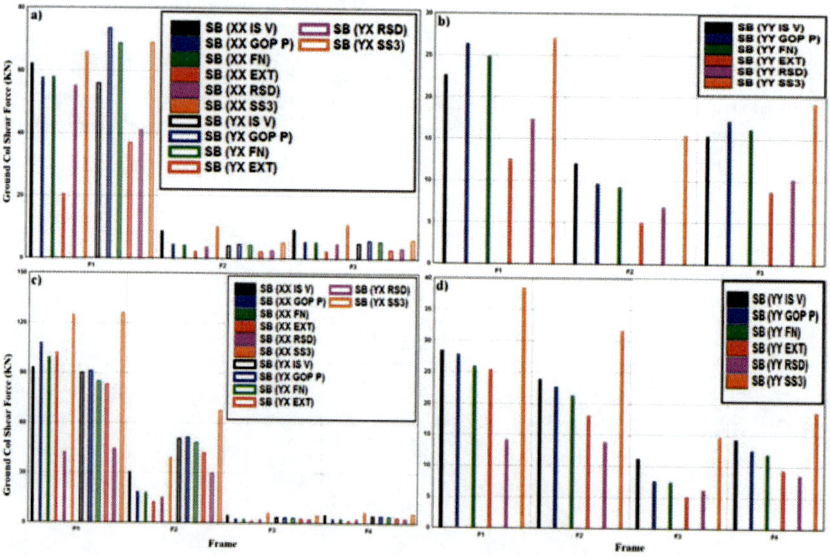

Fig. 8 Ground column shear force (GCSF) of two (**a, b**) and five (**c, d**) storey Step-Back (212SB & 513SB) buildings

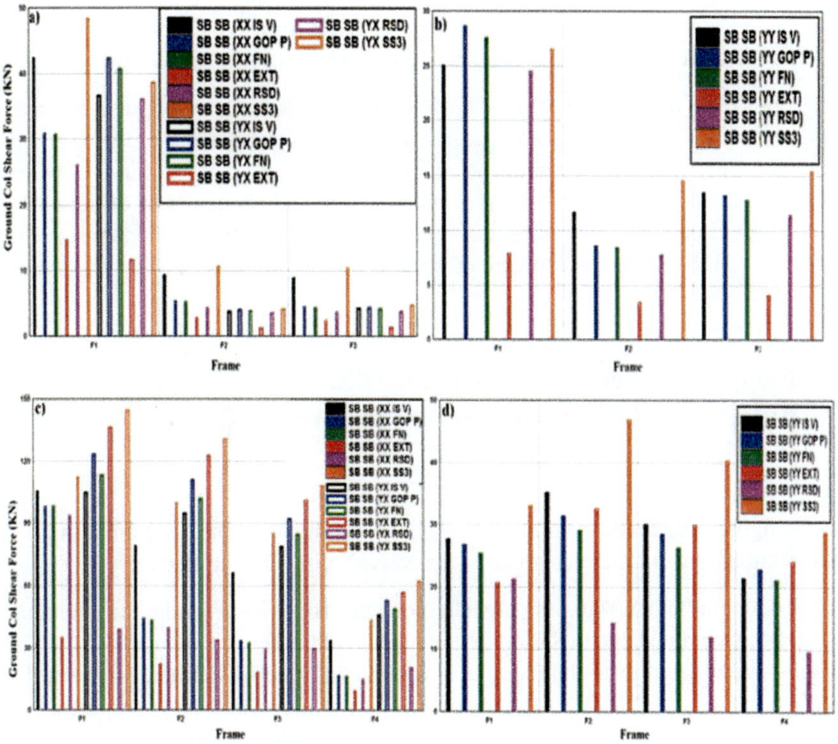

Fig. 9 Ground column shear force (GCSF) of two (**a**, **b**) and five (**c**, **d**) storey Step-Back-Set-Back (212SBSB & 515SBSB) buildings

6 Floor Displacement (FD) of 212SB & 513SB Building Models Along (X-Dir) and Across (Y-Dir) the Slope

In the figures and texts, symbols XX, YX and YY stand for, seismic input in X, Y, Y directions and computed parameters in X, X, Y directions respectively.

XX: Floor displacement in the X-direction (Fig. 6), for both types of building models subjected to SSGM (SS3), is higher than other seismic inputs. For 212SB, the FD due to residual part of the fault-normal (FN) component is much higher compared to FD due to extracted GM pulse. This is because the residual part of the GM is composed of high frequencies and natural time period of such a building is small. However, in case of 513SB, the FD due to extracted GM pulse shows significantly higher values compared to residual GM because of low frequency nature of extracted pulse and comparatively longer-period of structure.

YX: For 212SB model, Floor displacement (FD) in X-direction due to application of extracted GM pulse in the Y-direction has brought out comparatively higher values of FD at intermediate floors compared to "XX-EXT" shown in Fig. 6. However, for 513SB the effect of torsion (YX) is seen to be very less at all floor levels.

YY: For 513SB model, the FD in the Y-direction due to application of pulse-extracted GM in the Y-direction is almost comparable to that computed from the original recorded GM (transverse-component), FN component and codal spectrum. However, FD at all floor levels due to SSGM is much higher and residual part of the GM is much lower as compared to FD due to other seismic inputs (Fig. 6). For short-period structure (212SB) the effect of extracted pulse is found to be least.

7 Floor Displacement (FD) of 212SBSB & 515SBSB Building Models Along (X-Dir) and Across (Y-Dir) the Slope

In the figures and texts, symbols XX, YX and YY stand for, seismic input in X, Y, Y directions and computed parameters in X, X, Y directions respectively.

XX & YX: For both the building models, along the slope (X-direction) the maximum FD (XX) is obtained due to SSGM as compared to other seismic inputs (Fig. 7). This displacement is closer to that computed from codal spectra. Further, it is seen that for both models the FD (XX) due to residual part is higher than that computed from extracted GM pulse. This is because, in the X-direction, there is no significant change in the time period of the buildings. These displacements are in X-direction when the seismic inputs are applied in the X-direction. However, for 515SBSB model, floor displacements (FDs-YX) in the X-direction due to torsion effect (when the GM in Y-direction) is more significant at all intermediate floor levels for all types of GMs. The computed FDs (YX) due to extracted pulse GM is maximum at all floor levels and are comparable to SSGM, whereas the FD (YX) because of residual part of the GM is lowest at all floor levels.

YY: For 212SBSB model, floor displacements in the Y-direction due to residual part are seen to be much closer to displacement due to SSGM, codal spectra and much higher as compared to EXT pulse GM shown in Fig. 7. Whereas, in 515SBSB model, the FD due to the residual part of GM is much lower than all types of GMs. Further, the response due to EXT pulse GM and SSGM are comparable.

8 Ground Column Shear Force of 212SB & 513SB Building Models Along (X-Dir) and Across (Y-Dir) the Slope

In the figures and texts, symbols XX, YX and YY stand for, seismic input in X, Y, Y directions and computed parameters in X, X, Y directions respectively.

XX: For step-back building models (212SB & 513SB), because of short column effect, the shear force in columns at ground level in frame 'F1' attracts a much higher force in both directions as compared to other frames (Fig. 8). Comparison of responses between 212SB & 513SB has brought out that in 212SB the response due to residual part of FN component of GM is much higher (about three times) than the EXT pulse GM response. Because of the long-period, the response of 513SB due to original GM, FN component of GM and extracted pulse (EXT) GM exceeds the codal response. Response due to SSGM shows significantly higher values than all types of GMs for both the models because of high value of PGA.

YX: The application of seismic input in the Y-direction (across the slope) has shown that shear force in ground columns in X-direction (along the slope) due to torsional effect are equally important as they exceed non-torsional response for some GMs in 212SB. However, for 513SB the torsional and non-torsional responses are comparable. The torsional response due to extracted pulse GM in 513SB exceeds the residual response and is much closer to the response due to FN component of GM and original ground motion (OGM) in frames 'F1' and 'F2'. The shear force (SF) due to recorded ground motion (GOP P, transverse-component) and FN component of GM in 'F1' shows higher values compared to SSGM in 212SB (Fig. 8).

YY: The application of seismic input across the slope (Y-direction) has brought out that the shear force (Y-direction) due to SSGM is higher in ground columns of all frames for both 513SB and 212SB models. The response due to residual GM is more than the extracted pulse GM in all the frames (F1, F2 and F3) of 212SB building model but lower than the response due to extracted (EXT) pulse GM in 'F1' and 'F2' of 513SB (Fig. 8).

9 Ground Column Shear Force of 212SBSB & 515SBSB Building Models Along (X-Dir) and Across (Y-Dir) the Slope

In the figures and texts, symbols XX, YX and YY stand for, seismic input in X, Y, Y directions and computed parameters in X, X, Y directions respectively.

XX: For both Step-Back-Set-Back (SBSB) models 'XX' component of shear force shows higher response because of residual part of GM as compared to EXT pulse GM in building frames. Further, response due to residual GM is closer to response due to recorded transverse-component of GM and FN component of GM for both the models but lower than response due to IS codal spectra (**Fig. 9**). However, the response due to SSGM is highest.

YX: It is brought out that the effect of torsion is significant in 515SBSB model as torsional component (YX) due to all types of seismic inputs (GMs) exceeding respective 'XX' component (non-torsional response) in all building frames except

response due to residual GM. The response (YX) due to torsional effect of extracted pulse GM has exceeded significantly the response due to residual part of FN (GM) in all frames of 515SBSB model. This response also exceeds the codal, recorded, FN component response and is closer to SSGM (Fig. 9). Further, it is observed that torsion effect is significant in frame 'F1' as compared to other frames in 212SBSB model and response due to residual part of GM exceeds the response due to extracted pulse GM and is closer to response due to other GMs at the selected site (Gopeshwar).

YY: When the seismic inputs or excitations are in Y-direction, higher response (Y-direction) is observed due to residual part of FN-GM in 212SBSB model. This response is almost comparable with the response due to codal spectra, original GM, FN component and SSGM. Further, this response is significantly higher than the response due to extracted pulse GM in all the building frames (Fig. 9). However, in 515SBSB model, higher response is observed due to extracted pulse of FN ground motion compared to residual GM in all building frames.

10 Conclusions

Response of two types of building models (SB and SBSB) have brought out that as the number of storeys increases from 2 to 5, the extracted pulse response increases compared to response due to residual component GM; because as the height of the building increases the time period also increases resulting in decrease of high-frequency response. This is only true when the seismic inputs are across the slope (Y-direction) and direction of displacements is observed in the in-plane (X) and out-of-plane (Y) directions. However, for 2–4 storey "SBSB" buildings, the response due to the residual component is always higher than the EXT pulse response when the GM is applied in X-direction (along the slope) because there is no significant variation in the time periods of the models in X-direction. For similar types of earthquake loadings, the five story building (SBSB) the response due to EXT pulse GM is higher compared to RSD response.

With the increasing period of buildings, response due to extracted long-period pulse at three sites is in close agreement with responses due to recorded pulse-type ground motions & FN component of ground motions. This illustrates the adequacy of representation of NFGM with extracted long-period pulse. The Indian codal spectra need modification and the effects of pulse-type ground motion due to moderate, large, and great earthquakes should be incorporated for sites in the vicinity of near-fault regions particularly for the Himalayas region. However, for earthquakes with Mw ≤ 6, like the 1986 Dharamsala earthquake, the Indian seismic code is found to be adequate.

References

1. Rathje EM, Faraj F, Russell S, Bray JD (2004) Empirical relationships for frequency content parameters of earthquake ground motions. Earthq Spectra 20(1):119–144
2. Bray JD, Marek AR (2004) Characterization of forward-directivity ground motions in the near-fault region. Soil Dyn Earthq Eng 24:815–828
3. Mobinipour SA, Pourzeynali S (2019) Efficiency of near-fault ground motion pulses to evaluate seismic performance of the SMRF Systems. J Vibro Eng 21(1):170–186
4. Lili X, Longjun X, Marek AR (2005) Representation of near-fault pulse-type ground motions. Earthq Eng Eng Vib 4(2):193–199
5. Xia C, Liu C (2019) Identification and representation of multi-pulse near-fault strong ground motion using adaptive wavelet transform. Appl Sci 9(2)
6. Uniform Building Code (1997) International conference of building officials, Whittier, California
7. Ministry of Construction (2001) Code for seismic design of building GB50011–2001. Beijing, China Architecture and Building Press, pp 16–18
8. Hall JF (1995) Near-Source ground motion and its effects on flexible buildings. Earthq Spectra 11(4):569–605
9. Bhagat S, Wijeyewickrema AC, Subedi N (2018) Influence of near-fault ground motions with fling-step and forward-directivity characteristics on seismic response of base-isolated buildings. J Earthq Eng 25(3):455–474
10. Malhotra PK (1999) Response of building to near-field pulse-like ground motions. Earthq Eng Struct Dynam 28:1309–1326
11. Zhang C, Lu Jb, Jia Hy, Lai Z, Li Z, Wang P (2020) Influence of near-fault ground motion characteristics on the seismic response of cable-stayed bridges. Bull Earthq Eng 18:6375–6403
12. Chandrasekaran AR, Das JD (1995) Strong motion records from Uttarkashi earthquake. Mem Geol Soc India 30:133–147
13. Baker JW (2007) Quantitative classification of near-fault ground motions using wavelet analysis. Bull Seismol Soc Am 97(5):1486–1501
14. Tarbali K, Bradley BA, Baker JW (2019) Ground motion selection in the near-fault region considering directivity-induced pulse effects. Earthq Spectra 35(2):759–786
15. Somerville P, Smith N, Graves R, Abrahamson N (1997) Modification of empirical strong ground motion attenuation relations to include the amplitude and duration effects of rupture directivity. Seismol Res Lett 68(1):180–203
16. Kumar P, Kumar A, Pandey AD (2016) Spectral characterization of himalayan near-fault ground motion, Period Polytech Civil Eng 60(2):205–215
17. Caltrans (2012) Methodology for developing design response spectrum for use in seismic design recommendations. Div Eng Serv Geotech Serv
18. Boore D, Atkinson G (2008) Ground-motion prediction equations for the average horizontal component of PGA, PGV, and 5%-damped PSA at spectral periods between 0.01 s and 10.0 s. Earthq Spectra 24:99–138
19. Mark RK (1977) Application of linear statistical models of earthquake magnitude versus fault length in estimating maximum expectable earthquakes. Geology 5:464–466
20. Wells DL, Coppersmith KJ (1994) New empirical relationships among magnitude, rupture length, rupture area and surface displacement. Bull Seismol Soc Am 84(4):974–1002
21. IS 1893 (Part 1) (2016) Criteria for earthquake resistant design of structures—general provisions and buildings, Bureau of Indian Standards. New Delhi
22. Kumar S, Paul DK (1999) Hill building configuration from seismic consideration. J Struct Eng 26(3):179–185
23. Birajdar BG, Nalawade SS (2004) Seismic analysis of buildings resting on sloping ground. In: Proceedings of 13th world conference on earthquake engineering, vancouver, B.C., Canada, paper no. 1472, Aug 1–6
24. Kumar S (1996) Seismic analysis of step-back and set-back buildings. PhD Thesis, University of Roorkee, India

25. Kumar S, Paul DK (1994) Dynamic analysis of stepback and setback buildings. In: Tenth symposium on earthquake engineering, university of Roorkee, vol 1, pp 341–350
26. Kumar P, Kumar A, Pandey AD (2014) Comparison of seismic response of buildings on slopes. NCETEST-2014, Roorkee, India
27. Kumar P, Sharma S, Pandey AD (2012) Effect of soil-structure interaction on building response in hilly areas. IUP J Struct Eng 5(4):7–27
28. Kumar S, Paul DK (1997) A state of art: seismic safety of step back and set back buildings. Bull ISET 34(2):47–74

Microseismic Monitoring to Analyze Rock Mass Micro-Cracking in Underground Powerhouse to Mitigate Potential Disaster

Vikalp Kumar and V. R. Balasubramaniam

Abstract Rock mass equilibrium is disturbed when rocks undergo excavation through mechanical or blasting techniques. When the disturbance is rapid, it leads to unstable zones in the structure even after completion of structure in long term, and hence it becomes essential to monitor such underground excavated structure behavior continuously using microseismic monitoring. Microseismic Monitoring (MSM) is an effective technique to locate zones of micro-cracking in the rock mass and further for the demarcation of potentially unstable zones in underground excavation. This paper gives a brief account of the Microseismic Monitoring System that has been applied in the underground powerhouse of Tala Hydropower Plant (THP). Stability of the underground powerhouse was analyzed using various microseismic source parameters. Based on one-year of continuous monitoring, potential unstable zones were identified at the powerhouse of THP. Microseismic Monitoring System thus provides information ahead and helps audit the safety measures taken at any site. Therefore, this technique is an effective way to evaluate rock mass behavior before occurrence of any disaster and helps to diminish the potential damages.

Keywords Microseismic monitoring · Underground powerhouse · THP · Stability and disaster

1 Introduction

Keeping the underground excavated geo-structure safe and stable under different rockmass conditions is required for smoother operations of the intended activities. To maintain long-term stability and integrity of underground structures, such as powerhouse with valuable machinery and sustain the operations after the construction of the structure, is a challenge for any geotechnical professional. Such underground powerhouse structure has the risk of collapse, wall caving and rock burst. Due to the complex nature of rock mass, internal partial damage in rock mass may trigger

V. Kumar (✉) · V. R. Balasubramaniam
National Institute of Rock Mechanics, Bengaluru, Karnataka, India

C. Ghosh and S. Kolathayar (eds.), *A System Engineering Approach to Disaster Resilience*, Lecture Notes in Civil Engineering 205, https://doi.org/10.1007/978-981-16-7397-9_32

a series of chain damage, and which results in large-scale deformation and collapse of the structure fully or a portion there [1].

Rock masses are anisotropic and heterogenous material. Rock mass failure might be induced by the propagation of internal non-visible micro-cracks and further its coalescence. Propagation of these micro-cracks in underground excavated rockmass structure is a dynamic phenomenon. These micro-cracks may develop with time and space [2, 3] and finally the surface may collapse with large-scale rock mass deformation.

Traditional or conventional monitoring techniques that consist of equipments like convergence meter, surface subsidence monitoring, extensometer, load cell, Global Positioning System, etc. are effective to monitor the deformation of rock mass surface [4]. However, it is difficult for these equipments to effectively monitor the occurrences of micro-cracks inside the rock mass prior to the formation of a macroscopic rock fracture that may sometimes result in the detachment or loosening from the host medium, and eventually become unstable which may lead to a probable disaster.

The beginning, buildup and evolution of stress-induced micro-cracks release energy as seismic signals from the rock mass which are under stress in and around the opening of the underground excavations.

Occurrence of seismic signals releases energy that propagates in the form of P and S waves in the rockmass (Fig. 1) [5]. Longitudinal (P) and transverse (S) wave propagation patterns are demonstrated by the respective red/blue and green/yellow contours.

Microseismic monitoring system can transform the received seismic signal into electrical signals using geophones and/or accelerometers. Microseismic data processing and analysis techniques are used further to calculate the time (t), location (x, y and z) and local magnitude (m_L) of micro-cracking events in three-dimensional

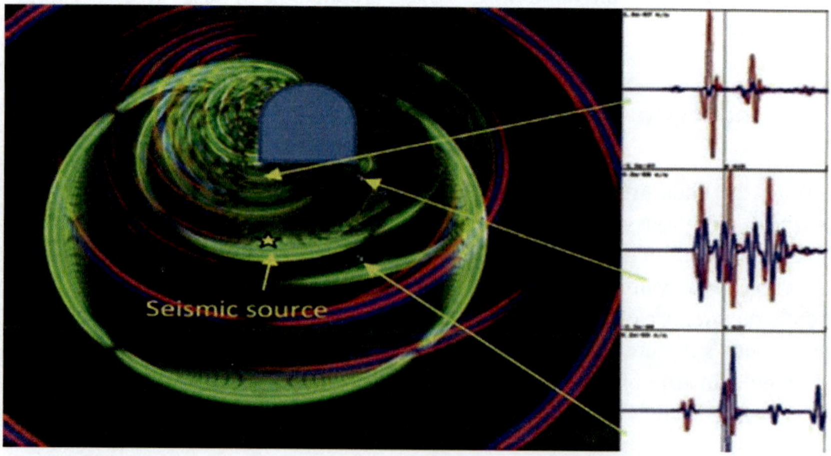

Fig. 1 Micro-cracking generates ground motion contours with synthetic wave forms for three sensors located below excavation

space, in addition to a host of seismic source parameters. Further the range (time, distance) of probable development of micro-cracks may be evaluated.

Microseismic signatures inside a rock mass are passive indicator of the progress of inelastic damage with time in a particular zone [6]. This method is viable and non-destructive to detect micro-cracks prior to a macroscopic rock mass failure. Incorporation of localized microseismic events with its seismic source parameter is used to visualize and provide status of a particular zone in three-dimensional space.

Microseismic Monitoring (MSM) technique is now a days being applied mainly in mining, underground powerhouse, dam, oil and gas storage cavern, hydraulic fracturing, etc. This method can also be used to prevent illegal mining by providing the three-dimensional spatial coordinates in real time in and around the government approved mining license areas to various stakeholders.

The site of investigation using MSM is THP underground powerhouse of Druk Green Power Corporation (DGPC) Ltd. (6*170 MW) located in Chukka, Bhutan. This underground powerhouse structure has an overburden rock mass of 500 m thickness on an average. It has encountered several rock engineering issues since construction, and which is continuing even during the power generation stage. Several incidences of rock mass failures occurred during its construction [7, 8]. There are reports of rock bolt failures in an irregular manner and risk to life of the working personnel and machine components at the site. The cavern's wall are also converging at a slow rate [9, 10]. Therefore, there is always an induced threat prevailing inherently in this structure and thus there is always a need to analyze the stress, displacements, etc. in various zones of this structure. National Institute of Rock Mechanics (NIRM) in collaboration with the Institute of Mines Seismology (IMS), Australia and DGPC ltd. has set up Microseismic Monitoring System at THP powerhouse to monitor and evaluate the powerhouse stability status.

2 Microseismic Monitoring System at Tala Hydropower Plant

THP powerhouse consists mainly of main access tunnel, powerhouse chamber (machine hall), transformer hall, bus ducts (3 numbers), connecting tunnel, escape tunnel and drainage gallery (Fig. 2) (Table 1).

Reconnaissance survey was conducted to identify sensor locations, energy attenuation characteristics, noise sources, longitudinal (P) and transverse (S) wave velocities [11]. Hammer tests were performed at a number of locations inside this underground rockmass cavern to find out the P and S wave velocities, signal attenuation from the recorded seismogram. P and S wave velocities obtained from the seismogram were 4500 m/s and 2600 m/s, respectively. At the same time, geological and modeling reports were studied which state that most of the failure in the rockmass

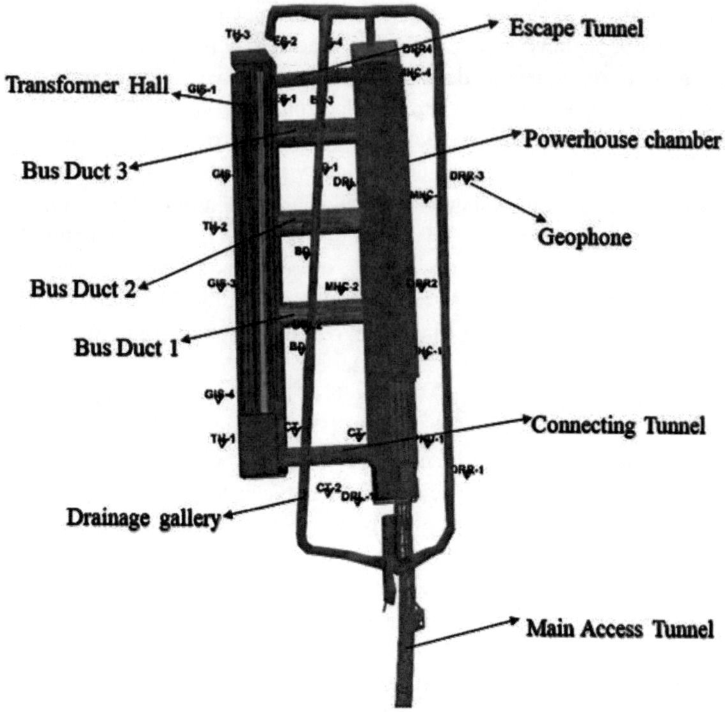

Fig. 2 Major tunnels of THP powerhouse with thirty installed geophones

Table 1 Major Tunnel dimension in the underground powerhouse of THP

S. No.	Name of the tunnel	Length (in m)	Width (in m)	Height (in m)
1	Main access tunnel	377	7.5	8
2	Powerhouse chamber	206	20.4	44.5
3	Transformer hall	191	16	26.5
4	Connecting tunnel	39.4	10	8.5
5	Escape tunnel	39.4	3	3
6	Bus ducts	39.4	10	8.5
7	Drainage gallery	590	3	4

occurred in machine hall during construction. Based on these data, an optimum three-dimensional microseismic monitoring network was installed to record, process and interpret waveforms generated in the underground powerhouse.

This network mainly consists of thirty geophones (installed at various locations inside the powerhouse), eight data acquisition units and underground laboratory (Fig. 3). Underground laboratory consists of central data recording server (CDRS) having duplex communication facility and central communication hub.

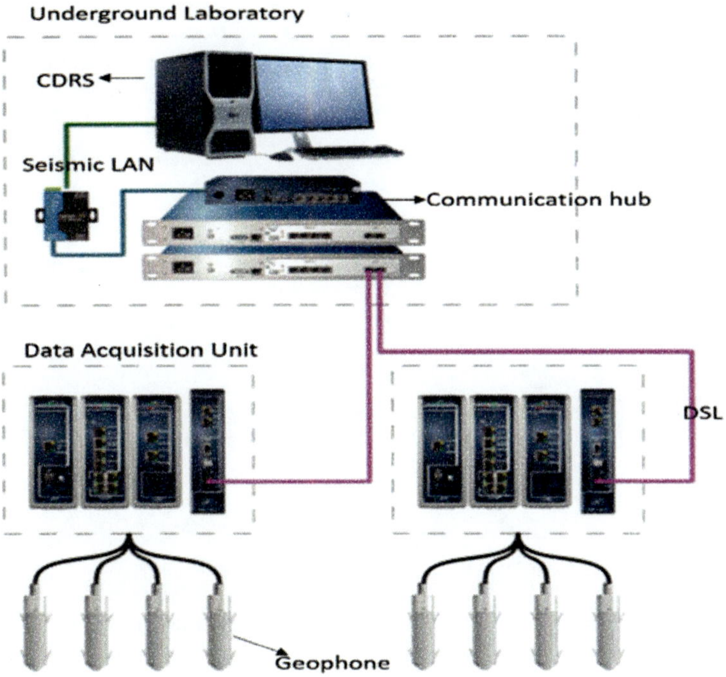

Fig. 3 Microseismic monitoring Network at THP

CDRS acquires and stores the waveforms in triggered mode. The signals from the sensors recorded are shown in Fig. 4. Source parameters of this microseismic signal, shown in Fig. 5, are of the event that occurred on 09 January 2018 at 15:26:11 h. and having local magnitude −2.3. The network consists of 30 sensors but signal was

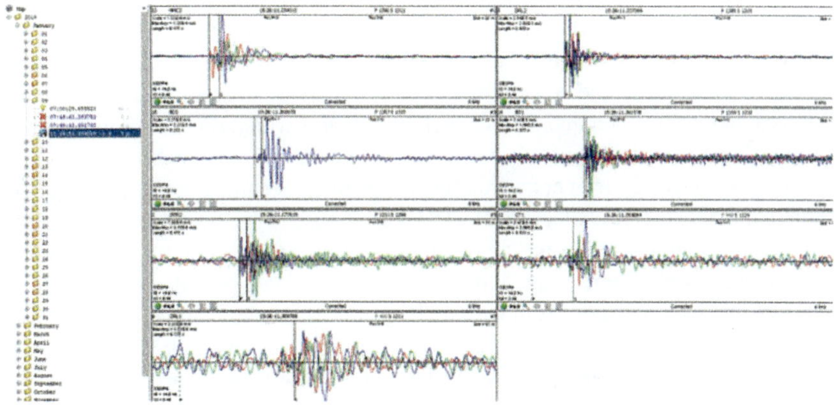

Fig. 4 Microseismic signal recorded by seven geophones

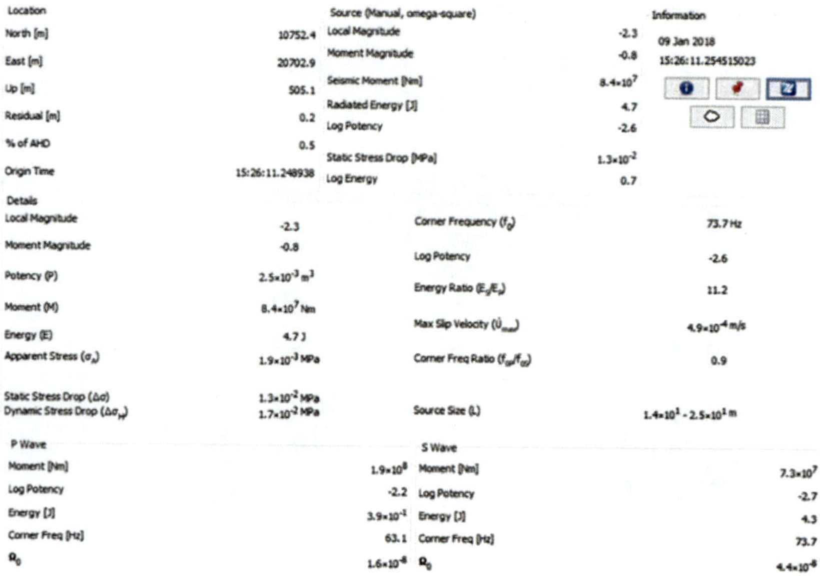

Fig. 5 Source parameters of the microseismic signal (09 January 2018, 15:26:11 h)

recorded by only seven sensors as only a low seismic energy of 4.7 J was liberated due to this microseismic event.

3 Microseismic Data Processing and Analysis

Various types of triggering waveforms at underground powerhouse cavern THP were recorded during one-year continuous monitoring from 01 January 2018 to 31 December 2018 which consist of microseismic events and noises. Major sources of noise are compressor signal, earthquake, electric circuit breaker and man-made activity at the underground powerhouse cavern (Fig. 6). The pattern of noise has been analyzed and established and further such waveforms which do not conform to the criteria of rockmass behavior related signals have been eliminated. After processing and analysis, only 130 triggers were accepted as microseismic events. These events were then mapped on 3D diagram of THP powerhouse (Fig. 7).

The average number of events amounted to 11 events per month. Local magnitude of the microseismic events ranged from −2.8 to 0. Radiated seismic energy of these microseismic events varied from 0.63 to 15,848 J. Maximum source location error was 3% having absolute error margin of 5 m. This microseismic monitoring network at THP enabled timely and periodic evaluation of rock mass status in and around this powerhouse. Given the geometry of the microseismic monitoring network in this

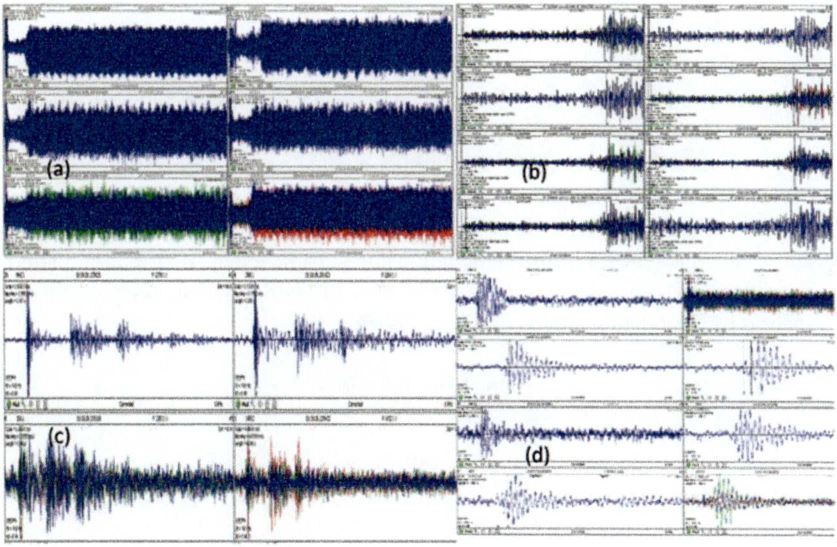

Fig. 6 Types of noises: **a** compressor signature, **b** micro-earthquake, **c** hammering noise and **d** electrical signature (50 Hz)

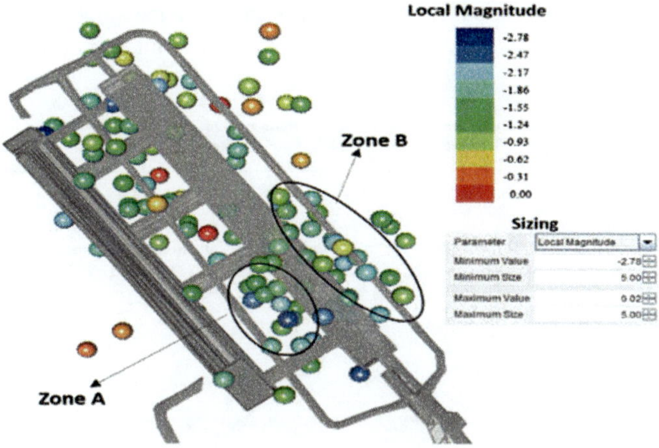

Fig. 7 Microseismic events on 3D layout of the powerhouse

underground powerhouse cavern, formation of cluster of microseismic events point out the micro-cracking zone inside the rockmass [12].

4 Stability Status of THP Powerhouse Cavern

Most of the events have occurred in and around the powerhouse chamber in comparison to the transformer hall (Fig. 7). Thus, machine hall seems to be seismically more active than the transformer hall. Further evaluation of microseismic events in the machine hall states that there are two major cluster of events namely zone A and B as follows: (a) between connecting tunnel and bus duct-1 and (b) from RD 20–100 m in the machine hall upstream wall. Microseismic events distribution pattern as per size in THP powerhouse during one year of continuous monitoring may be expressed by the relationship as follows [13] (Fig. 8):

$$\log_{10} N = a - b \qquad (1)$$

where N = cumulative number of microseismic events having local magnitude $\geq M$, a and b are constants that may be derived from the respective offset and gradient of the straight-line plot between $\log_{10} N$ and local magnitude M.

The parameter 'b-value' technically defines the relative number of large to small number of seismic events and 'a-value' describes productivity. Thus, the parameter b is a measurement of seismic environment in THP powerhouse and defines the probable pattern of seismicity in that region like stress build-up pattern. Standard value of parameter 'b' varies from 0.8 to 1.1 with a notional value of 1. Higher b-value signifies more occurrences of low energy microseismic events, whereas low

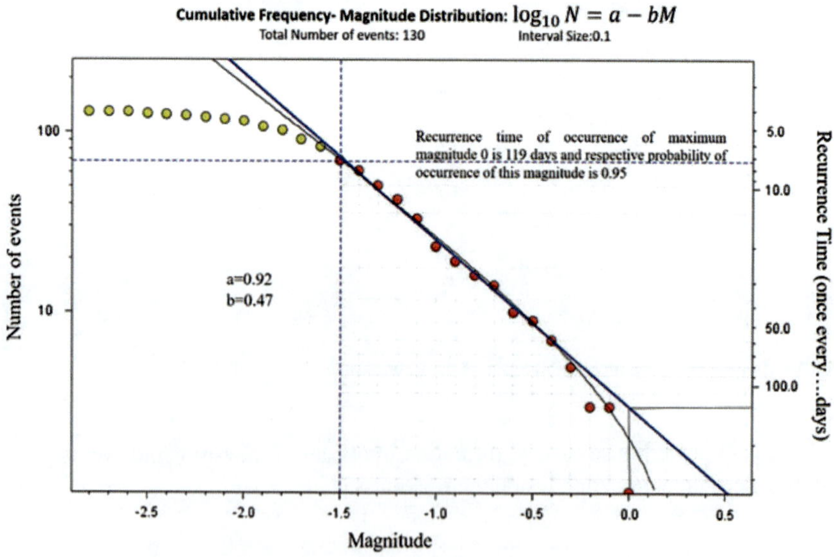

Fig. 8 Gutenberg Richter relationship for tala hydropower plant powerhouse cavern

value of the parameter 'b' may be implied as high magnitude microseismic events are dominant [14].

For this 130 microseismic events over one-year window at the powerhouse of THP, the respective obtained values of 'a' and 'b' are 0.92 and 0.47. As the b-value is toward higher side. So, it indicates that production of low energy (low magnitude) microseismic events are more at THP powerhouse. By using the same plot (Fig. 8), the recurrence of a particular value of local magnitude of seismic event can be computed by the following equation [15, 16]:

$$Tr \geq m = \Delta t / N(\geq m) \quad (2)$$

where Δt = monitoring period and
$N(\geq m)$ = number of seismic events.

At THP, maximum magnitude of microseismic event is 0. Using Eq. (2), for an event of this maximum magnitude 0 that occurred during this one year window, recurrence time is 119 days. Probability of this maximum local magnitude microseismic event occurrence in one year is 0.95 at this underground powerhouse.

Maximum log (apparent stress) is 3.58 (Fig. 9). As the figure depicts that maximum stress is coming from just outside the underground powerhouse cavern and it is more on the upstream wall of the powerhouse chamber compared to the other major tunnels of this powerhouse cavern. It might be the reason that machine hall is seismically more active than transformer hall and that results more micro-cracks in and around

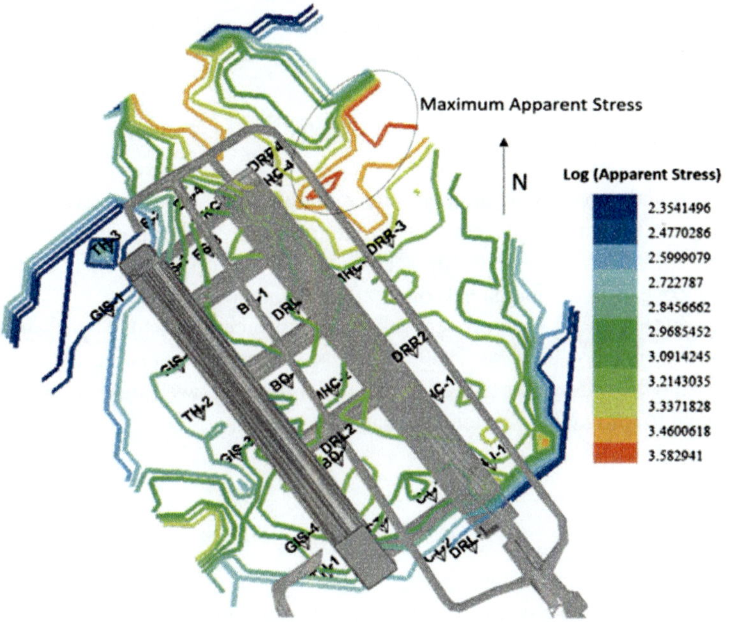

Fig. 9 Log (Apparent Stress) at THP powerhouse cavern

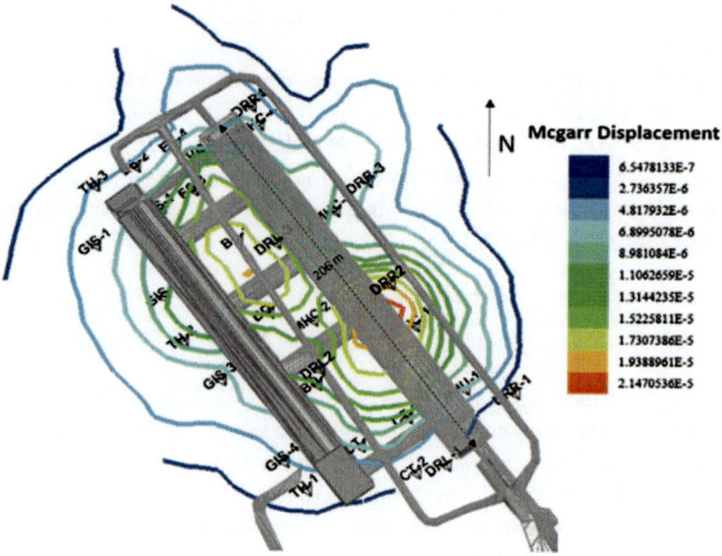

Fig. 10 Mcgarr Displacement at THP underground powerhouse cavern

the machine hall. It also depicts that if one compares both the walls of the machine hall, upstream wall is under more stress than downstream wall.

Mcgarr displacement is linked with seismic events that have average slip D over a smaller fault zone. Small scale seismic moment corresponding to the asperity failure is expressed by Mcgarr [17] (Fig. 10).

$$D = M/(\mu \pi r^2) \tag{3}$$

where M, μ and r are seismic moment, shear modulus and source radius respectively.

Maximum Mcgarr Displacement is in the upstream wall opposite to bus duct-1 (RD: 70–90 m). This is due to the occurrences of more number of microseismic events in Zone-B in comparison to other areas of the powerhouse.

Thus, Zone A and B need proper rock mass reinforcement and support system in THP underground powerhouse. Therefore, these various microseismic source parameters provide the timely assessment of this underground powerhouse stability status and prevent to mitigate any potential disaster.

5 Conclusions

Rock Engineering and Rock Mechanics problems are increasing in various infrastructure projects for the requirement of the mankind especially in the Himalayan region of Indian subcontinent. This study using the principle of microseismic monitoring provides stability status of one underground powerhouse rockmass cavern of THP hydropower project in Bhutan. As there is an occurrence of minor cracks inside the rockmass, it is evaluated to forewarn any disaster in terms of rockmass failure by using the microseismic system. This network at THP provides 3-D picture of micro-cracking propagation with time.

Out of all the recorded waveforms, only 130 waveforms are genuine microseismic events. There are two zones of microseismic events accumulation and both are in the machine hall but these have not been converted into any failure as the rate of events and number of microseismic events are significantly low but indicate for the required reinforcement/support measures to be taken timely. Rockmass strata of this powerhouse appears to be stable on the basis of microseismic source parameters evaluation but it required continuous monitoring to prevent any disaster at the site.

Acknowledgements This study is established on the Microseismic monitoring study done at THP, Bhutan. Thanks are also due to the Director, National Institute of Rock Mechanics for the support and consent to publish this work. Authors are also grateful to Mr. Sivakumar Cherukuri (Ex-Scientist, NIRM) and to the management of DGPC Ltd. Support of Mr. Karma (Head, I & MU, THP, DGPC ltd.) is also acknowledged during this study to arrange the required site literature, installation of microseismic monitoring equipment and other various support. The help of the colleagues of NIRM is also acknowledged. Dr. Iram Saba Amin is also thanked for proofreading and editing.

References

1. Hu G, Yang T, Zhou J, Yu Q, Xie L, Liu H, Zhao Y (2017) Mechanism of surrounding rock failure and crack evolution rules in branched pillar recovery. Minerals 7(6):1–19. https://doi.org/10.3390/min7060096
2. Cao RH, Cao P, Lin H, Fan X, Zhang C, Liu T (2019) Crack initiation, propagation, and failure characteristics of jointed rock or rock-like specimens: a review. Adv. Civil Eng. 31https://doi.org/10.1155/2019/6975751
3. Wang F, Wang M, Nezhad MM, Qiu H, Ying P, Niu C (2019) Rock dynamic crack propagation under different loading rates using improved single cleavage semi-circle specimen. Appl Sci 9(4944):20. https://doi.org/10.3390/APP9224944
4. Xu N, Tang C, Li H, Dai F, Ma K, Shao J, Wu J (2012) Excavation-induced microseismicity: microseismic monitoring and numerical simulation. J Zhejiang Univ Sci A 13(6):445–460. https://doi.org/10.1631/jzus.A1100131
5. Kaiser P, Cai M (2013) Critical review of design principles for rock support in burst-prone ground—time to rethink! In: Potvin Y, Brady B (eds), Seventh international symposium on ground support in mining and underground construction (p 37). Australian Centre for Geomechanics. https://doi.org/10.36487/acg_rep/1304_01_kaiser
6. Xu NW, Tang CN, Wu SH, Li GL, Yang JY (2011) Optimal design of microseismic monitoring networking and error analysis of seismic source location for rock slope. Open Civil Eng J 5:36–45. https://doi.org/10.4028/www.scientific.net/AMR.163-167.2991
7. Chowdhury AK (2007) Crown failure in the machine hall cavern of tala hydroelectric project, Bhutan Himalaya. In: S DR, Sthapak AK (eds), International workshop experiences gained in design and construction of tala hydroelectric project bhutan (pp 93–105). Institute of Rock Mechanics & Tunneling Technology,Tala Hydroelectric Project Authority and New Building Materials and Construction World

8. Tripathi SK, Yadava VS (2007) Some fundamental geotechnical aspects related to the behaviour of large caverns, tala hydroelectric project, bhutan. In: S DR, Sthapak AK (eds), International workshop experiences gained in design and construction of tala hydroelectric project bhutan (pp 86–92). Institute of Rock Mechanics & Tunneling Technology,Tala Hydroelectric Project Authority and New Building Materials and Construction World
9. Bhasin R, Pabst T (2014) Case study of a large underground cavern in the Himalayas. J Rock Mech Tunn Technol 20(1):5–20
10. Bhasin R, Pabst T (2015) Finite element and distinct element analysis of the stability of a large underground hydropower machine hall in the Himalayas. KSCE J Civ Eng 19(3):725–732. https://doi.org/10.1007/s12205-013-1351-4
11. Sivakumar C, Srinivasan C, N PC, L RA (2011) Stability monitoring of underground powerhouse cavern using microseismics. In: 45th U.S. rock mechanics/geomechanics symposium
12. Essrich F (2005) Mine seismology for rock engineers—an outline of required competencies. In: Potvin Y, Hudyma M (eds), Sixth international symposium on rockburst and seismicity in mines (pp. 359–364). Australian Centre for Geomechanics. https://doi.org/10.36487/ACG_repo/574_35
13. Gutenberg B, Richter CF (1956) Magnitude and energy of earthquakes. Ann Geofis 9(1):7–12. https://doi.org/10.4401/ag-4588
14. Dai F, Li B, Xu N, Zhu Y (2017) Microseismic early warning of surrounding rock mass deformation in the underground powerhouse of the Houziyan hydropower station, China. Tunn Undergr Space Technol 62:64–74. https://doi.org/10.1016/j.tust.2016.11.009
15. Mendecki AJ (2012) Size distribution of seismic events in mines. Aust Earthq Eng Soc 20
16. van Aswegen G, Mendecki AJ, Lachenicht R, Dzhafarov AH, Hofmann G, Radu S, Eneva M, M S, G K (1999) Mine layout, geological features and seismic hazard (Issue GAP 303)
17. Mcgarr A (1991) Observations constraining near-source ground motion estimated from locally recorded seismograms. J Geophys Res 96(16):495–508

Stability Analysis of a Debris Slope by Micropile Reinforcement Technique: A Case Study from the North-Western Himalayas

Koushik Pandit, Mahendra Singh, and Jagdish Prasad Sahoo

Abstract Debris slides take place when a mass of soil or debris slides down over a slip or failure surface. Mitigation or control of such sliding mass frequently poses an engineering challenge. Micropiles are many a times used to stabilize a slope under certain circumstances. To analyze the effect of micropiles on slope stability, one requires to determine the geo-mechanical properties of the strata, slope geometry, micropile diameter, lengths, and locations of such installations. Hence, it becomes a complex interaction problem. In the present study, an active landslide in Tehri Garhwal district of Uttarakhand state of India has been chosen for demonstration of micropile reinforcement technique. After characterization of the slope material, factor of safety of the untreated slope under different degree of saturation have been evaluated by utilizing different limit equilibrium methods for static and pseudo-static conditions. Since the failure surfaces for all the simulated scenarios have been obtained at deeper depths, it was fathomed that deep-seated slip movements need to be arrested partially or fully for which slope reinforcement with micropiles will be a good choice. A parametric analysis was conducted to assess stability of the slope with single rows of micropiles with different diameter, spacing, and aspect ratios. The results show that the slope stability improves satisfactorily for certain cases.

Keywords Landslides · Micropile reinforcement · Factor of safety · Pseudo-static analysis · Mitigation

1 Introduction

The construction process of micropiles involve drilling of a small diameter borehole (typically less than 300 mm) followed by insertion of a reinforcement element (steel section like an I-beam or H-section or a single rebar or a reinforcement cage)

K. Pandit (✉) · M. Singh
Indian Institute of Technology Roorkee, Roorkee 247667, India
e-mail: kpandit@ce.iitr.ac.in

J. P. Sahoo
Indian Institute of Technology Kanpur, Kanpur 208016, India

C. Ghosh and S. Kolathayar (eds.), *A System Engineering Approach to Disaster Resilience*, Lecture Notes in Civil Engineering 205, https://doi.org/10.1007/978-981-16-7397-9_33

and finally grouting of the borehole (illustrated in Fig. 1). A usual geotechnical drilling equipment is sufficient for drilling a borehole for micropiles since they are designed for a small diameter. This has many inherent advantages such as: (i) negligible disturbance to the nearby existing buildings and soil during construction, (ii) ease to install the micropiles in low headroom areas and in almost all typical ground conditions, (iii) flexibility to install the micropiles at a suitable desired angle for the intended use of the same, (iv) choice of using the same equipment for both installation and grouting. Micropiles have been found to be useful as supporting elements for building foundations in weak soils and as in-situ reinforcements to improve stability of slopes and excavations since micropiles can be designed to provide substantial axial load-carrying ability and modest lateral load bearing.

The North-Western Himalayas are home to several major landslides in the past. Landslides are natural hazards caused by natural or anthropogenic or both reasons. Usually, antecedent rainfall or earthquake motions cause catastrophic landslides in the form of debris slides or rock falls. Due to landslides, each year, many lives are lost, road connectivity is affected, and economy suffers. Hence, it is of utmost importance to develop not only landslide hazards maps through slope stability assessment, but also to prepare appropriate design of control measures. There are various control measures to mitigate the risk and effect of landslides, such as surface dressing and

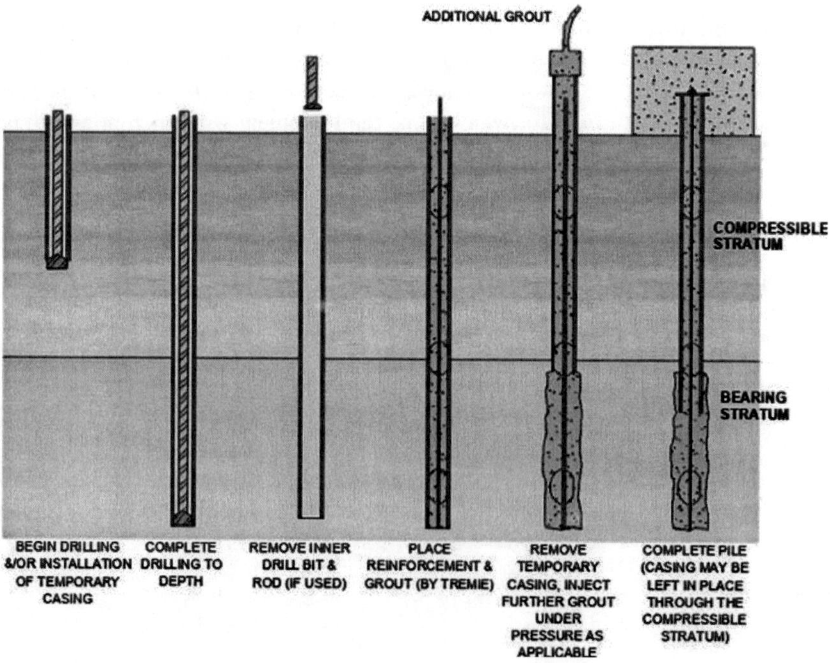

Fig. 1 Construction sequence of micropiles, after Sabatini et al. [1]

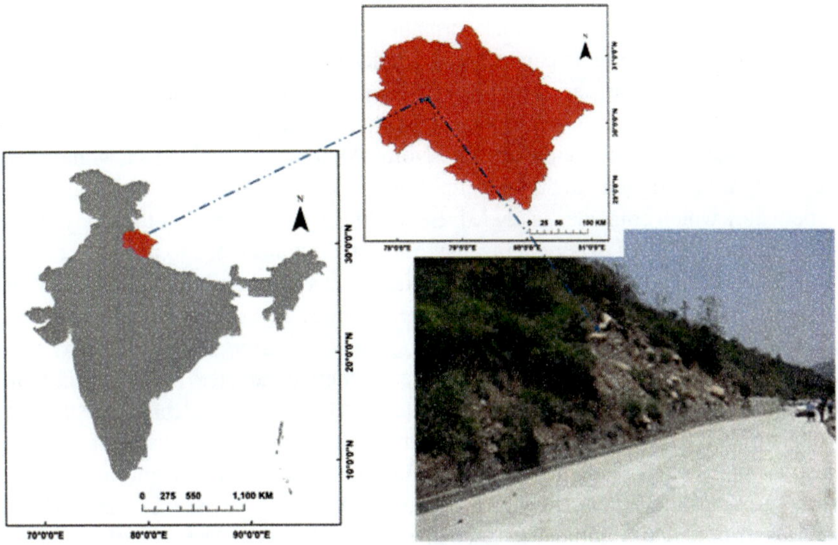

Fig. 2 Study location of the debris slope in the present work

reprofiling, geo-synthetic or soil nailing, rock-bolting, pile reinforcement, retaining walls, and bio-engineering measures or a combination of some of these methods.

In the present study, an active landslide in Tehri Garhwal district of Uttarakhand state of India (Fig. 2) has been chosen for demonstration of micropile reinforcement technique. After characterization of the slope material, factor of safety of the untreated slope under different degree of saturation have been evaluated by utilizing different limit equilibrium methods for static and pseudo-static conditions. Since the failure surfaces for all the simulated scenarios have been obtained at deeper depths, it was fathomed that deep-seated slip movements need to be arrested partially or fully for which slope reinforcement with micropiles will be a good choice. A parametric analysis was conducted to assess stability of the slope with single rows of micropiles with different diameter, spacing, and aspect ratios. The results show that the slope stability improves satisfactorily for certain cases.

2 Geotechnical and Geological Investigations

The study area is located at 30°16′00.00″N, 78°29′19.86″E coordinates, in the downstream of the Bhagirathi River and about 12.55 km away from the Tehri dam. Also, near the sliding zone, an old pump-house building is placed. Hence, safety of this building as well as the road crossing below is important. The study area has a highly undulating terrain. It has been observed from the exposed rocks in the study area that these rocks belong to the inner Lesser Himalayas, as well as to the outer Lesser

Himalayas. Details about these rock formation and sub-group classifications can be found in [2]. The underlain bedrock of the studied slope has mostly phyllites, a metamorphic rock, having experienced weathering in the range of moderate to high and possess well-developed foliation planes and discontinuities, thus making the slope extremely susceptible to landslide. The North Almora Thrust (NAT) is situated in the south of the study area. Also, a slip fault is existing parallel to the NAT in the same valley which coincides lastly [3]. Hence, it can be noticed that the study slope has high probability of experiencing a significant earthquake due to presence of this thrust line. The study area catchment experiences heavy rainfall throughout the year (1016 to 2630 mm/year) [4]. As part of the geotechnical investigations, sample debris and rock materials were collected from the site and laboratory tests were performed to characterize the slope materials. The shear strength parameters of the debris were determined through large size direct shear tests. Also, the equivalent shear strength properties of the rock mass have been determined by fitting the GSI value of the rock mass as obtained from field investigations into Rocdata, a software from Rocscience, which provides the equivalent Mohr–Coulomb parameters of the rock mass. These parameters hold high significance since they are key inputs to determine the stability a slope.

3 Limit Equilibrium Analysis

For slope stability analysis, limit equilibrium methods are widely utilized by the geotechnical research community because of their simplicity in obtaining the input parameters experimentally or through field observations. There are many limit equilibrium methods available; however, for the present study, to evaluate the global factor of safety of the slope under the influence of static i.e., gravity loading and pseudo-static loading conditions, the Bishop's method [5], Morgenstern and Price method [6], and Spencer's method [7] were used. For this, Slide2 program from Rocscience was used which incorporates various well-established and popular two-dimensional stability assessment. In the pseudo-static method, the basic principle is to apply a seismic load in terms of an equivalent static inertial force applied on the slope mass. The value of this equivalent static inertia is nothing but the product of a chosen seismic coefficient (k) according to the earthquake standard IS 1893:2016 and the weight of the potential sliding mass. The study slope is located in seismic zone IV. Also, the area receives ample amount of rainfall, especially during the monsoons. Hence, the slope is modeled and analyzed for different pore water pressure coefficient values with and without the inclusion of pseudo-static acceleration coefficient values. The soil is modeled by elastic perfectly plastic model with the Mohr–Coulomb failure criterion. However, an elastic pile was assumed for the analysis which means that the yielding of the pile itself cannot be identified, and it is a limitation of the present results.

The slope model section prepared is shown in Fig. 3. The slope material properties are also listed in the table provided with Fig. 3. The micropile location was finalized

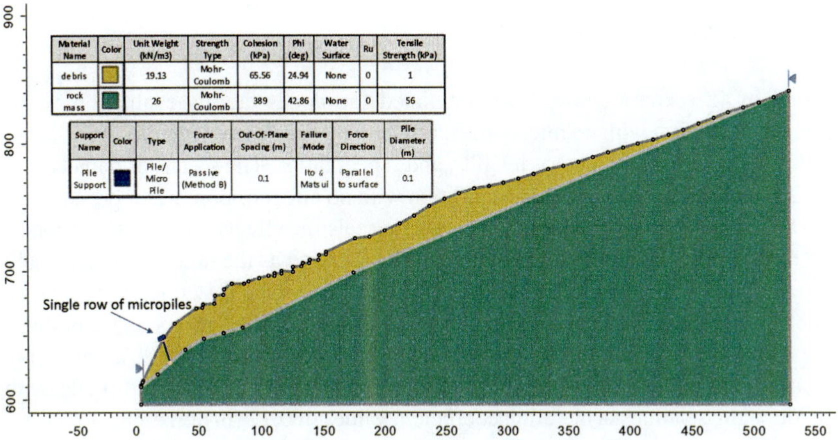

Fig. 3 Slope geometry showing proposed installation location of micropiles

after observing the most probable slip surface having the lowest global minimum safety factor for the untreated slope (Fig. 4). Once the location of micropiles was fixed, the next job was to carry out a parametric study on the design aspect of the micropiles, i.e., their diameters (d), in-plane spacings (s = 1-, 1.5- and 3-times diameter) and the aspect ratios (L/d). For this, two different diameters (d), e.g., 100 mm and 300 mm were considered with micropile lengths (L) of 19.43 m (the length from slope face to the interface between the debris and the underlying rock mass) and 25 m (assuming an almost 6 m socketed length inside the relatively stable rock mass).

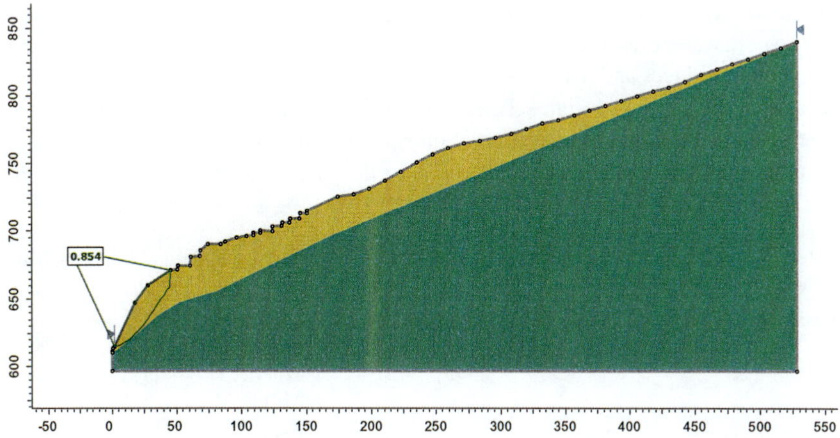

Fig. 4 Slope geometry showing the most probable slip surface having the lowest global minimum safety factor for the untreated slope

4 Results and Discussions

A total of 48 scenarios have been simulated for slope stability evaluation of the selected slope, first with no micropile reinforcements and then with micropile installations, with various diameters, lengths, and aspect ratios. The scenarios depict cases of slope stability from a dry slope condition with no effect of pore water pressure (as may be generated during a rainfall event) or any seismic effects, to a wet slope condition having pore water pressure coefficient (R_u, defined as the ratio of the generated pore pressure to the overburden pressure) value assumed as 0.1 (since as per Sassa, 1988 [8], around 90% saturation in debris material generally occurs at Skempton's pore water pressure parameter B = 0.1; in absence of any site data, 90% saturation is considered as the worst possible scenario for the present case study) and with pseudo-static seismic acceleration coefficient values of 0.12 (in horizontal direction) and 0.08 (in vertical direction). The global minimum safety factors (FoS) obtained from different limit equilibrium methods are listed in Table 1 for the untreated slope. As it can be seen that the slope is having FoS values less than the critical FoS of 1.0, hence, the slope is unstable inherently and need support measures to improve its stability. For this, micropile reinforcements have been proposed due to the obvious advantages associated with them. Also, the slip surface passes at greater depth, and hence, any surficial support installed on the slope face might not be that much useful, and may either add more overburden pressure on the slope, thus making the slope more unstable or, the installed support measure may get slide down along with the unstable slope mass beneath it due to the presence of a deeper slip surface. The FoS values as obtained for the different scenarios with micropile reinforced slope are provided in Table 2.

From the obtained results, it can be inferred that the stability of the slope increases sufficiently from below 1.0 value to 1.488 for scenario 1 which is dry slope condition with no pore water pressure and seismic effects. As the in-plane spacing increases, the safety factor reduces and reaches below 1.0 level for a few instances, which basically means that the support design schemes are inefficient in those cases and hence are to be discarded. Another vital observation was that since the slip surface is cutting the micropiles at a depth, hence socketing the piles inside the bedrock does not fetch

Table 1 Global minimum safety factors (FoS) as obtained from different limit equilibrium methods for the untreated slope

Scenario	Loading condition	Pore water pressure (R_u)	FoS from Bishop's LEM [5]	FoS from Morgenstern and Price's (MP) LEM [6]	FoS from Spencer's LEM [7]
1	Static	0	0.854	0.855	0.862
2	Pseudo-static	0	0.721	0.714	0.726
3	Static	0.1	0.752	0.747	0.749
4	Pseudo-static	0.1	0.635	0.624	0.625

Table 2 Global minimum safety factors (FoS) as obtained for the different scenarios with micropile reinforced slope

Sl	Loading	R_u	Diameter (m)	In-plane spacing (m)	Length (m)	FoS from Bishop's LEM [5]	FoS from MP's LEM [6]	FoS from Spencer's LEM [7]
1	Static (S)	0	0.1	0.10	19.43	1.464	1.461	1.488
2	S	0	0.1	0.10	25.00	1.464	1.461	1.488
3	S	0	0.1	0.15	19.43	1.466	1.463	1.486
4	S	0	0.1	0.15	25.00	1.461	1.459	1.488
5	S	0	0.1	0.30	19.43	1.293	1.230	1.249
6	S	0	0.1	0.30	25.00	1.298	1.235	1.243
7	S	0.1	0.1	0.10	19.43	1.345	1.346	1.367
8	S	0.1	0.1	0.10	25.00	1.345	1.346	1.367
9	S	0.1	0.1	0.15	19.43	1.344	1.342	1.367
10	S	0.1	0.1	0.15	25.00	1.342	1.344	1.369
11	S	0.1	0.1	0.30	19.43	1.182	1.113	1.121
12	S	0.1	0.1	0.30	25.00	1.182	1.110	1.117
13	Pseudo-Static (PS)	0	0.1	0.10	19.43	1.174	1.154	1.175
14	PS	0	0.1	0.10	25.00	1.173	1.153	1.174
15	PS	0	0.1	0.15	19.43	1.173	1.157	1.173
16	PS	0	0.1	0.15	25.00	1.177	1.158	1.173
17	PS	0	0.1	0.30	19.43	1.093	1.015	1.025
18	PS	0	0.1	0.30	25.00	1.086	1.022	1.028
19	PS	0.1	0.1	0.10	19.43	1.076	1.056	1.074
20	PS	0.1	0.1	0.10	25.00	1.074	1.056	1.075
21	PS	0.1	0.1	0.15	19.43	1.076	1.056	1.075
22	PS	0.1	0.1	0.15	25.00	1.076	1.058	1.076
23	PS	0.1	0.1	0.30	19.43	0.987	0.930	0.949
24	PS	0.1	0.1	0.30	25.00	0.991	0.918	0.948
25	S	0	0.3	0.30	19.43	1.464	1.461	1.488
26	S	0	0.3	0.30	25.00	1.464	1.461	1.488
27	S	0	0.3	0.45	19.43	1.464	1.459	1.490
28	S	0	0.3	0.45	25.00	1.465	1.460	1.488
29	S	0	0.3	0.90	19.43	1.290	1.228	1.242
30	S	0	0.3	0.90	25.00	1.301	1.232	1.242
31	S	0.1	0.3	0.30	19.43	1.345	1.346	1.367
32	S	0.1	0.3	0.30	25.00	1.345	1.346	1.367

(continued)

Table 2 (continued)

Sl	Loading	R_u	Diameter (m)	In-plane spacing (m)	Length (m)	FoS from Bishop's LEM [5]	FoS from MP's LEM [6]	FoS from Spencer's LEM [7]
33	S	0.1	0.3	0.45	19.43	1.346	1.342	1.368
34	S	0.1	0.3	0.45	25.00	1.344	1.343	1.367
35	S	0.1	0.3	0.90	19.43	1.180	1.108	1.117
36	S	0.1	0.3	0.90	25.00	1.175	1.114	1.122
37	PS	0	0.3	0.30	19.43	1.174	1.154	1.175
38	PS	0	0.3	0.30	25.00	1.173	1.153	1.174
39	PS	0	0.3	0.45	19.43	1.171	1.151	1.172
40	PS	0	0.3	0.45	25.00	1.168	1.152	1.173
41	PS	0	0.3	0.90	19.43	1.083	1.011	1.024
42	PS	0	0.3	0.90	25.00	1.094	1.018	1.022
43	PS	0.1	0.3	0.30	19.43	1.076	1.056	1.074
44	PS	0.1	0.3	0.30	25.00	1.074	1.056	1.075
45	PS	0.1	0.3	0.45	19.43	1.077	1.058	1.075
46	PS	0.1	0.3	0.45	25.00	1.079	1.062	1.078
47	PS	0.1	0.3	0.90	19.43	0.993	0.921	0.928
48	PS	0.1	0.3	0.90	25.00	0.981	0.938	0.946

much advantage in terms of the safety factor. Hence, cost saving can be achieved if the micropile length is restricted to 19.43 m. A design chart (Fig. 5) is prepared for the safety factor variation with respect to the in-plane spacing to diameter ratio. From the analysis of scenario 1 (Fig. 6), it can be observed that the shear strength has been increased and is larger than the shear stress generated along the most probable slip surface along which the global minimum safety factor is obtained. Figure 7 indicates that the micropile has significantly increased the shear strength.

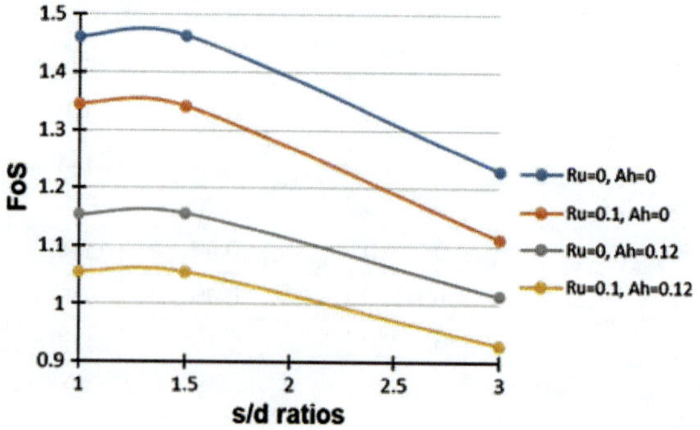

Fig. 5 Variation of the factor of safety values with respect to different spacing to micropile diameter ratios for 0.1 m diameter micropile

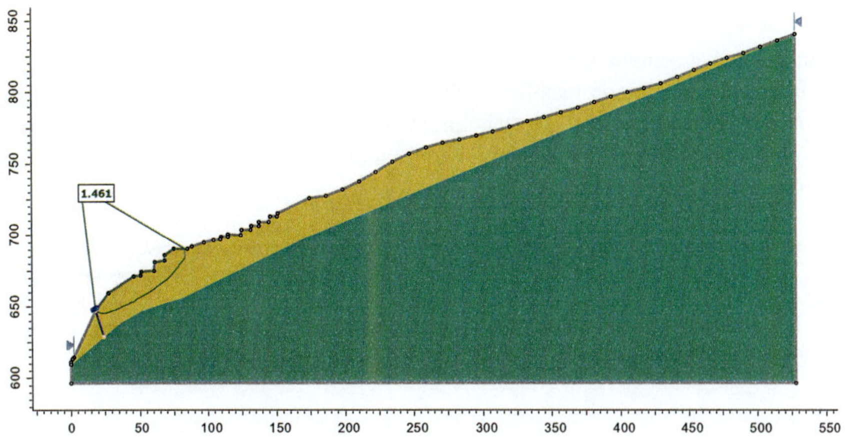

Fig. 6 Slope stability condition for scenario 1 with micropiles installed

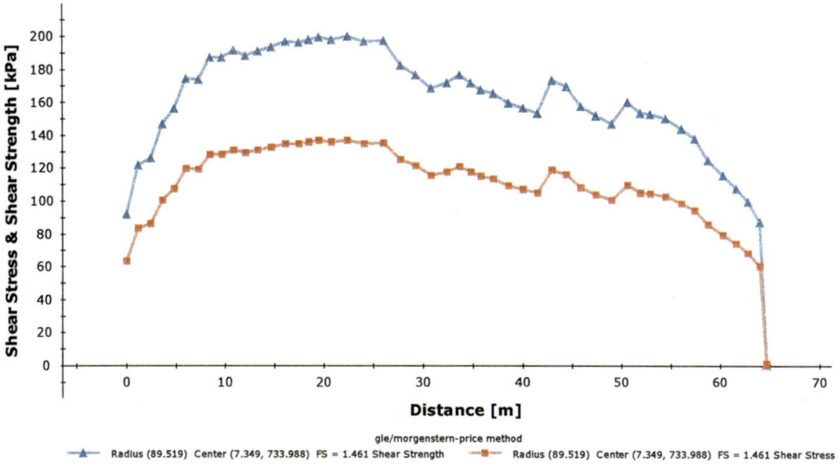

Fig. 7 Variation of the shear strength and shear stresses along the most probable slip surface (for FoS = 1.461) for scenario 1 of the slope with micropiles installed

5 Conclusions

The present study provides an overview of the stability assessment methods using the limit equilibrium methods, such as the Bishop's [5], Morgenstern and Price's [6], and Spencer's [7] methods. These methods are very popular and incorporate various assumptions and simplifications. Moreover, the deformation behavior of the slope strata cannot be obtained from the LEM, for which a finite element method can be adopted to perform the coupled analysis. The presented methodology can be adopted for a rapid stability analysis of the slopes which need micropile reinforcements to improve their stability. As it was found from the study that the micropiles even if installed in just a single row, can improve the overall slope stability significantly if the micropile installation location is chosen wisely and a parametric analysis such as that performed here can be very helpful in reducing cost of construction since the pile diameter, in-plane spacings and aspect ratios are optimized and chosen for the desired level of safety factor.

Acknowledgements A part of the financial support for the present study has been received from M/s. THDC India Limited, Rishikesh (Uttarakhand, India) under the project number: THD-1035-CED-16/17. The authors thank and acknowledge the financial support and technical help during the field investigation received from the M/s. THDC India Limited, Rishikesh (Uttarakhand, INDIA) in completion of this study.

References

1. Sabatini PJ Tanyu B, Armour T, Groneck P, Keeley J (2005) Micropile design and construction. U.S. Department of Transportation, Federal Highway Administration, Washington, DC, Report No. FHWA-NHI-05-039, 436p
2. Valdiya KS (1980) Geology of Kumaun lesser Himalaya. In: Interim report 291 of Wadia institute of Himalayan geology, Dehradun
3. Choudhury S, Gautam PK, Paul A (2013) Seismicity and reservoir induced crustal motion study around the tehri dam India. Acta Geophys 61:923–934. https://doi.org/10.2478/s11600-013-0125-1
4. Kumar R, Anbalagan R (2015) Landslide susceptibility zonation of tehri reservoir rim region using binary logistic regression model. Curr Sci 108(9):1662–1672
5. Bishop AW (1955) The use of the slip circle in the stability analysis of earth slopes. Geotechnique 5(1):7–17
6. Morgenstern NR, Price VE (1965) The analysis of the stability of general slip surfaces. Geotechnique 15(1):79–93. https://doi.org/10.1680/geot.1965.15.1.79
7. Spencer E (1967) A method of analysis of the stability of embankments assuming parallel inter-slice forces. Géotechnique 17:11–26. https://doi.org/10.1680/geot.1967.17.1.11
8. Sassa K (1988) Geotechnical model for the motion of landslides. In: Proceedings of 5th international symposium on landslides, "Landslides", Balkema, Rotterdam, vol 1, pp 37–56

Strengthening Measures

Optimal Design of True Negative Stiffness Damper as a Supplemental Damping Device for Base-Isolated Structure

Naqeeb Ul Islam and R. S. Jangid

Abstract An analytical study on a true negative stiffness damper (NSD) in the form of negative stiffness amplifying damper (NSAD) is presented. NSD proposed in this study for controlled base isolator displacement uses damping magnification effect that guarantees the efficient reduction in base displacement and inter-storey drift whilst utilising minimum damping coefficient of NSAD dashpot. Dynamic equations of motion are represented in the state-space form. A simple optimisation design for NSAD is proposed using complex eigenvalue analysis of the system matrix. Optimal parameters for NSAD are developed considering the stability of the system and effective fundamental mode damping. Optimal NSAD is supplemented to MDOF base-isolated shear structure as NSD. A suite of six ground motions consisting of three near-fault (NF) and three far-field (FF) motions are used in this study. For comparison purpose, viscous damper (VD) and visco-elastic damper (VED) are used as conventional supplemental dampers to the base-isolated shear structure. Base shear, top storey acceleration and inter-storey drift are three objective variables that are monitored for the effectiveness of supplemental dampers. Results of the time history analysis show that NSAD works as an efficient supplemental damping system for both NF and FF ground motions in contrast to conventional dampers.

Keywords Negative stiffness dampers · Passive structural control · Base isolation · Supplemental damping · Near fault motions

1 Introduction

Altering the dynamic response of a structure due to vibration input has been the most researched field in control dynamics over the past few years. Base isolation is considered a strong strategy in reducing the dynamic response of structures subjected

N. U. Islam (✉) · R. S. Jangid
Indian Institute of Technology Bombay, Powai, Mumbai 400076, India
e-mail: naqeebulislam@iitb.ac.in

R. S. Jangid
e-mail: rsjangid@civil.iitb.ac.in

C. Ghosh and S. Kolathayar (eds.), *A System Engineering Approach to Disaster Resilience*, Lecture Notes in Civil Engineering 205, https://doi.org/10.1007/978-981-16-7397-9_34

to strong ground motions or far-field (FF) motions. Although base-isolated structures have proven to be very protective against earthquakes, large isolator displacement is a big concern, especially under near-fault (NF) excitations. Forward site directivity produces near-fault motion (NF) having large velocity pulses and can bring seismic isolation devices to a critical working condition [1]. The near-fault zone is typically assumed restricted to within a distance of about 20 km from the ruptured fault [2]. Most of the service lines pass through the isolator slabs and can't withstand such large displacements. Standard practice to reduce base isolator displacement is to supplement the base isolator with conventional dampers. However, there is a problem associated with conventional dampers; when there is a higher demand for damping, it can result in higher mode participation. A high value of damping requirement for near-fault motions (to reduce isolator displacement) becomes exceptionally high for the case of moderate earthquakes or FF motions [1, 3]. Thus, the primary objective of base isolation (namely, reducing the superstructure drift and acceleration) is defeated. Hence, base-isolated structures subjected to near-fault motions benefit from high supplemental damping devices compared to those subjected to far-fault motions [4].

Over the past decade, negative stiffness dampers (NSD) have created a stir in structural control engineering. NSD is passive devices that utilise compressed spring (working on the principle of force assisting motion) and damper configuration. A combination of true negative stiffness (TNS) and a passive damper (PD) proposed by Nagarajaiah et al. [5], called 'adaptive negative stiffness device (ANSD), demonstrates shifting of yielding away from the main structure to ANSD. This device has shown promising results as a control device. Analytical modelling and experimental verification of ANSD are presented in the paper by Sarlis et al. [6], and it has been proven dynamic inertia can be neglected for the most practical cases. Experimental investigation for ANSD as a controlled device has shown that acceleration and base shear are reduced by more than 30% and displacement by more than 20% [7]. Shake table testing of an isolated three-storey building supplemented with ANSD has shown a substantial reduction in base displacement, base shear, floor acceleration and inter-storey drifts [8]. For optimal placement and number of TNS devices (based on the principle of ANSD) for efficient seismic control on the MDOF shear model, analytical studies have been carried out. It has been shown NSD is superior to the conventional damper in controlling the seismic response [9].

Another version of the true negative stiffness damper is negative stiffness amplifying damper (NSAD) [10] and is a modification of the negative stiffness mechanism proposed by Sarlis et al. [6]. NSAD consists of a parallel combination of viscous damper and negative stiffness, which is in turn series connected to a positive spring. This physical realisation of NSAD is shown in Fig. 1a. It has been shown that an SDOF system supplemented with NSAD (see NSAD model Fig. 1b) achieves a magnified damping effect and preserves negative stiffness as well [10]. The application of NSAD to MDOF system and modal optimisation has been investigated by Wang et al. [11].

In this study, the optimal design of the NSAD damper is investigated in a new direction, i.e. as a supplemental damper to a five DOF base-isolated structure. In view of viscous dampers (VD) shortcomings as a supplemental damper, NSAD has

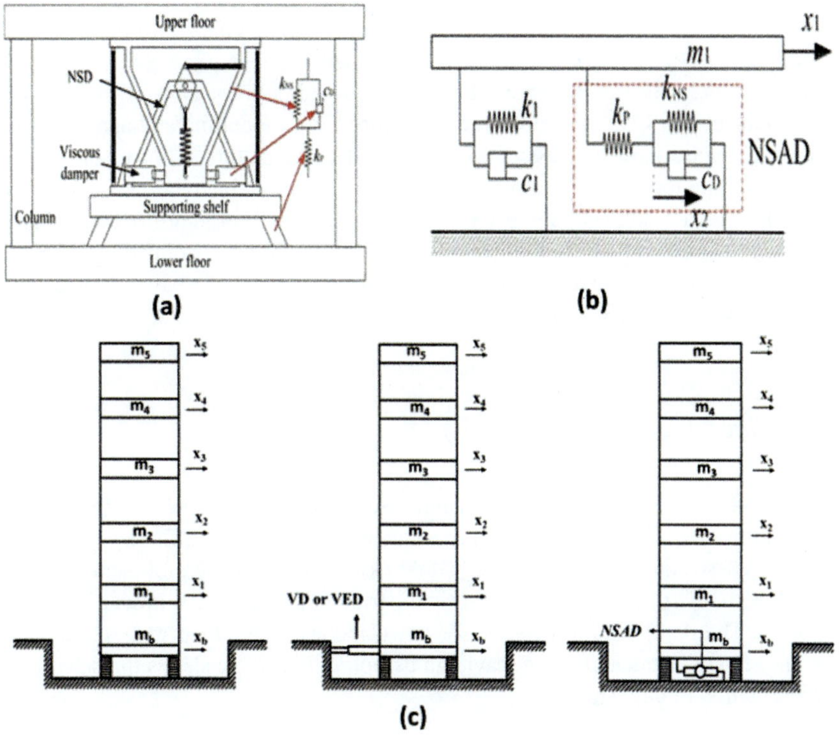

Fig. 1 **a** The physical realisation of NSAD [10] **b** An analytical model of SDOF supplemented with NSAD [10] **c** Schematic representation of four case studies

been proposed as a better supplemental damper alternative to VD. Using NSD as a supplemental damper to a base-isolated structure is the first of its kind.

2 Structural Model

Base isolation has been proved from time to time as a powerful seismic isolation technique. Examples of its implementation are many. Seismic isolation using rubber bearing is the main point of this study. From now onwards, base isolation will synonymously mean rubber base isolation. An analysis of displacement control of base isolators by supplemental damping devices is presented. The damping devices used in this study are viscous dampers (VDs), visco-elastic dampers (VEDs) and negative stiffness amplifying dampers (NSADs). Previously, it has been shown that supplemental dampers effectively reduce the base displacement of base-isolated structures [1]. However, using NSAD as a supplemental damper to a base-isolated structure is the first of its kind. In this study, a contrast between the effectiveness of VD, VED and NSAD as an additional damper for base displacement control (of base-isolated structure) has been shown.

A five-storey shear building has been isolated with a linear isolator to study the performance of NSAD as a supplemental damper. For modelling and analysing the structure, some simplifying assumptions are made: (i) structure is linear, and stories are rigid (ii) no torsional effect on stories (iii) soil-structure interaction is neglected. In total, five case studies have been made: (1) fixed base structure (FB) (2) base-isolated structure with no supplemented damping (BI) (3) base-isolated with NSAD (BINSAD) (4) base-isolated with viscous damper (BIVD) (5) base-isolated with visco-elastic damper (BIVED).

2.1 *Fixed Base Structure (FB)*

In this study, mass and stiffness are assumed to be uniformly distributed throughout the building, i.e. all lumped masses are equal, and each storey stiffness is the same. The mass associated with each DOF is 5000 kg, and the stiffness of each storey is 1.5228×10^7 N/m. The fundamental time period (T_n) for the FB model is chosen as 0.4 s. The damping ratio for the first two modes is assumed as 0.02, and the rest modes are calculated using Rayleigh damping. Figure 1c shows the schematic representation of case studies.

2.2 *Base Isolated Structure (BI)*

Properties of the base isolator (linear) are damping ratio $\zeta_b = 0.1$, isolating time period $T_b = 1.75$ secs and mass $m_b = 5000$kgs. Governing equation of motion for the base-isolated structure subjected to ground motion [12]:

$$\begin{bmatrix} m_t & \{r^T\}[m] \\ [m]\{r\} & [m] \end{bmatrix} \begin{Bmatrix} \ddot{x}_b \\ \ddot{x} \end{Bmatrix} + \begin{bmatrix} c_b & 0 \\ 0 & [c] \end{bmatrix} \begin{Bmatrix} \dot{x}_b \\ \dot{x} \end{Bmatrix} + \begin{bmatrix} k_b & 0 \\ 0 & [k] \end{bmatrix} \begin{Bmatrix} x_b \\ x \end{Bmatrix} = -\begin{Bmatrix} m_t \\ [m]\{r\} \end{Bmatrix} \ddot{x}_g \tag{1}$$

Here, m_t = total storey mass including base slab $[m]$, $[c]$ and $[k]$ are mass, damping and stiffness matrix of the 5-DOF fixed base structure, respectively; $\begin{Bmatrix} x_b \\ x \end{Bmatrix}$ is displacement vector with x_b base isolator displacement, and x is a vector of 5×1 dimension representing relative displacements with respect to base isolator of five storeys above base isolator; $\{r\}$ is the unit vector of 5×1 order.

2.3 Base Isolated with NSD (BINSAD)

The schematic representation of the NSAD has been shown in Fig. 2. NSAD can be practically introduced between the base slab foundation, just like isolator bearings. NSAD is defined by parameters named as alpha (α), beta (β) and gamma (γ). These parameters are defined as follows: α is the ratio of negative stiffness of NSAD (k_{ns}) and positive stiffness of NSAD (k_p); β is the ratio of positive stiffness of NSAD (k_p) and base isolator stiffness (k_b); γ is the ratio of NSAD damping (c_d) and base isolator damping (c_b).

Force equation for NSAD can be written as:

$$F_d = k_p(x_b - p) = c_d\dot{p} + k_{\text{ns}}p \tag{2}$$

Here, x_b is the total displacement of the base isolator, and p is the deformation of the NSAD dashpot, as shown in Fig. 2. In a modified form, this equation can be written as:

$$F_d + \frac{c_d}{k_p + k_{\text{ns}}}\dot{F}_d = \frac{c_d \times k_p}{k_p + k_{\text{ns}}}\dot{x}_b + \frac{k_p \times k_{\text{ns}}}{k_p + k_{\text{ns}}}x_b \tag{3}$$

$$or, \quad F_d + \tau\,\dot{F}_d = \pi\,\dot{x}_b + \sigma x_b \tag{4}$$

Matrix equation of motion of base-isolated structure with NSAD can then be written as:

$$\begin{bmatrix} m_t & \{r^T\}[m] \\ [m]\{r\} & [m] \end{bmatrix}\begin{Bmatrix} \ddot{x}_b \\ \ddot{x} \end{Bmatrix} + \begin{bmatrix} c_b & 0 \\ 0 & [c] \end{bmatrix}\begin{Bmatrix} \dot{x}_b \\ \dot{x} \end{Bmatrix} + \begin{bmatrix} k_b & 0 \\ 0 & [k] \end{bmatrix}\begin{Bmatrix} x_b \\ x \end{Bmatrix} + \{\lambda\}*F_d = -\begin{Bmatrix} m_t \\ [m]\{r\} \end{Bmatrix}\ddot{x}_g \tag{5}$$

or,

$$[M_{\text{NS}}][\ddot{X}] + [C_{\text{NS}}][\dot{X}] + [K_{\text{NS}}][X] + \{\lambda\}F_d = -[M_{\text{NS}}]\{rr\}\ddot{x}_g \tag{6}$$

Here, vector λ of 6 × 1 dimension is defined as:

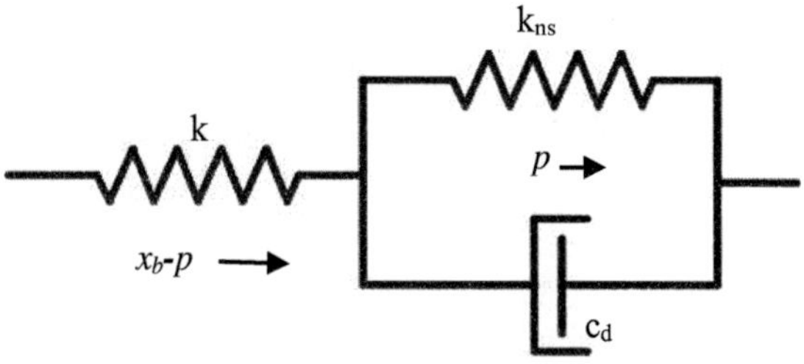

Fig. 2 Schematic representation of NSAD

$$\lambda = \begin{Bmatrix} 1 \\ 0 \\ 0 \\ 0 \\ 0 \\ 0 \end{Bmatrix} \tag{7}$$

Here, symbols have their usual meaning, as defined in the previous section. Force equation for NSAD is modified to a vector equation by using vector λ, X and $\dot{X}$. This equation is presented below:

$$F_d + \tau \dot{F}_d = \pi \lambda^T \dot{X} + \sigma \lambda^T X \tag{8}$$

Now, a state-space model is written for the base-isolated structure with NSAD as a supplemental damper. Three states are defined velocity, displacement and damping force. Thus, state variable z is defined as:

$$z = \begin{Bmatrix} \dot{X} \\ X \\ F_d \end{Bmatrix} = \begin{Bmatrix} \dot{x}_b \\ \dot{x} \\ x_b \\ x \\ F_d \end{Bmatrix} \tag{9}$$

The state-space representation matrices (*A, B, C* and *D*) are defined below. *A* is the state matrix, *B* is the input matrix, *C* is the output matrix, and *D* is the feedthrough vector.

$$A = \begin{bmatrix} -M_d^{-1}C_d & -M_d^{-1}K_d & -M_d^{-1}\lambda \\ 0_{6\times6} & I_{6\times6} & 0_{6\times1} \\ \left(\tau^{-1}\pi\lambda^T\right)_{1\times6} & \left(\tau^{-1}\sigma\lambda^T\right)_{1\times6} & -\tau_{1\times1}^{-1} \end{bmatrix}; B = \begin{bmatrix} rr_{6\times1} \\ 0_{6\times1} \\ 0_{1\times1} \end{bmatrix};$$

$$C = \begin{bmatrix} 0_{6\times6} & I_{6\times6} & 0_{6\times1} \\ -M_d^{-1}C_d & -M_d^{-1}K_d & -M_d^{-1}\lambda \\ 0_{1\times6} & 0_{1\times6} & I_{1\times1} \end{bmatrix}; D = \begin{bmatrix} 0_{6\times1} \\ rr_{6\times1} \\ 0_{1\times1} \end{bmatrix} \tag{10}$$

If *C* and *D* are used as defined above, then the output will be a 13 × 13 vector defined as:

$$y = \begin{Bmatrix} X \\ \ddot{X} \\ F_d \end{Bmatrix} = \begin{Bmatrix} x_b \\ x \\ \ddot{x}_b \\ \ddot{x} \\ F_d \end{Bmatrix} \tag{11}$$

Optimisation whilst introducing negative stiffness into the system, the stability of the system is the prime concern. NSAD parameters α, β and γ, are optimised to get the system's best possible response. Optimal values of NSAD parameters are calculated by taking into account the stability of the system. For static loading, NSAD becomes a series combination of positive stiffness (k_p) and negative stiffness (k_{ns}), and total stiffness of the system (K_{TE}) becomes:

$$K_{TE} = \frac{k_p k_{ns}}{k_p + k_{ns}} \tag{12}$$

Total stiffness K_{TE} can be written in the following form by using NSAD parameters:

$$K_{TE} = \frac{\alpha\beta}{1+\beta} k_b \tag{13}$$

For the stability of the system $K_{TE} + k_b > 0$. For this condition to be true, constrain on α for a chosen value of β can be written as:

$$\alpha > \frac{-1}{1+\beta} \tag{14}$$

The analytical analysis also shows that if α is less than the prescribed value, the system becomes unstable (diverging). To find the optimum value of γ for the other two NSAD parameters' chosen value, eigenvalue analysis of state matrix "A" is run for varied values of γ. Plots between modal damping ratios and γ are given in Fig. 3 for four values of α. Values of α are chosen for β = 2. From the plots following observations can be made: damping ratios for higher modes are very small and nearly constant for changing values of γ, which goes with basic tenants of base isolation. As the values of γ are increased, the first mode damping ratio increases to a maximum and then decreases. As the values of α are increased (magnitude), the peak value of first mode damping also increases. As the value of α increase (magnitude), peak values of first mode damping move towards the left, i.e. a lower value of γ attains peak. There is an upper limit to the maximum absolute value of α, so this value can't be increased beyond that limit (0.333 for β = 2). If the value of α is in the vicinity of its limit, the fundamental damping ratio peak increases to an overdamped one, i.e. greater than 1, which is desirable. However, it will result in instability of the system and hence, limit to the value of α is specified.

The magnitude of α in the study has been chosen 0.95/(1 + β), and this is the optimum value of α. Thus, for a given value of β, optimum value of α is fixed. This value is near to maximum limit on α so that the lower possible value of γ is required for a higher fundamental damping ratio. Thus,

$$\alpha_{optimum} = \frac{-0.95}{(1+\beta)} \tag{15}$$

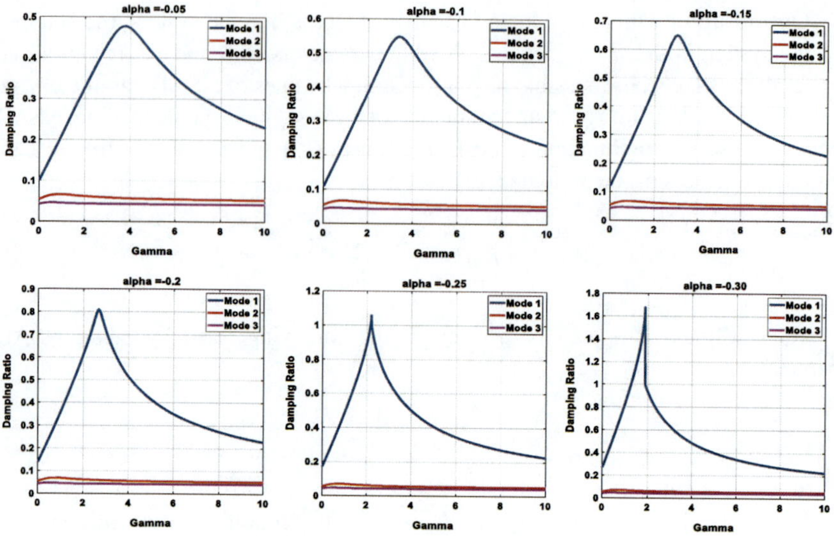

Fig. 3 Plots between damping ratio and gamma for various alpha

A three-dimensional optimisation plot between the first mode damping ratio, β and γ is plotted in Fig. 4. Each curve is plotted for $\alpha = \alpha_{\text{optimum}}$. These plots are utilised to choose the value of γ corresponding to the maximum first mode damping ratio. From the optimisation plots, for $\beta = 2$, the value of $\gamma = 1.85$ is selected for analysis.

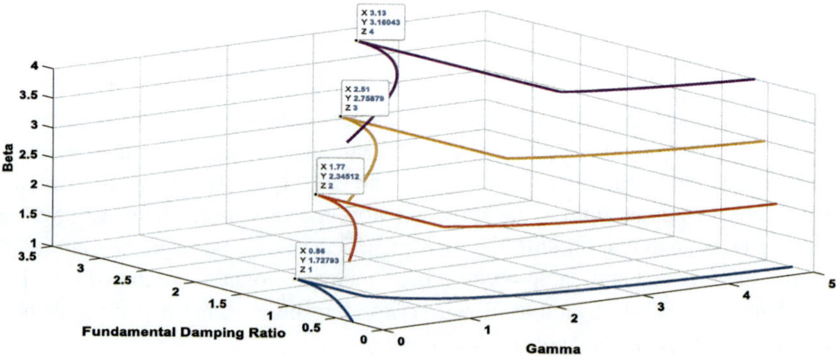

Fig. 4 Optimisation plots

2.4 Base Isolated with VD (BIVD)

A VD is used for comparison with NSAD. The damping ratio of VD (ζ_{VD}) used for the study is 0.185, which is the same as the NSAD damping ratio. Choosing the same value of damping will ensure proper comparative study.

2.5 Base Isolated with VED (BIVED)

The damping ratio of VED (ζ_{VED}) and positive stiffness of VED (K_{pVED}) are equal to the damping ratio of NSAD (ζ_{NSAD}) and magnitude of negative stiffness of NSAD (k_{ns}), respectively.

3 Numerical Study

In this study, six real earthquake records are selected to evaluate the effectiveness of NSAD as a supplemental damper to the base-isolated structures. Three far-field (FF) and three near-fault (NF) ground motions are described in Table 1. Base shear, top storey acceleration and inter-storey drift are three objective variables monitored for the effectiveness of supplemental dampers. Although conventional dampers reduce the base displacement to a certain level but at the cost of higher base shear, top storey acceleration and inter-storey. This section shows NSDs are more effective in comparison with conventional VD (Figs. 5, 6 and 7).

Base displacements for both FF and NF earthquakes are shown in Fig. 5. Note from the plot that NF motion base displacements are substantial for the BI case. However, after providing supplemental damping devices, there is a considerable decrease in base displacement. For instance, in Northridge (Sylmar Olive), ground motion residual displacements of 236 mm, 300 mm and 290 mm are reported for BINSAD, BIVD and BIVED, respectively. Whilst using supplemental dampers to control the base displacement, the acceleration of stories may increase substantially,

Table 1 A suite of ground motions in this study

S.No	Earthquake	Station	Magnitude	Rjb (km)	Type
1	Tabas Iran (1978)	Ferdows	7.35	89.76	FF
2	Loma Prieta (1989)	Richmond City Hall	6.93	87.78	FF
3	Imperial Valley-06 (1979)	Coachella Canal #4	6.53	49.1	FF
4	Northridge (1994)	Sylmar Olive	6.69	1.74	NF
5	Imperial Valley-06 (1979)	El Centro Array #6	6.53	0	NF
6	Northridge (1994)	Newhall Fire Station	6.69	3.16	NF

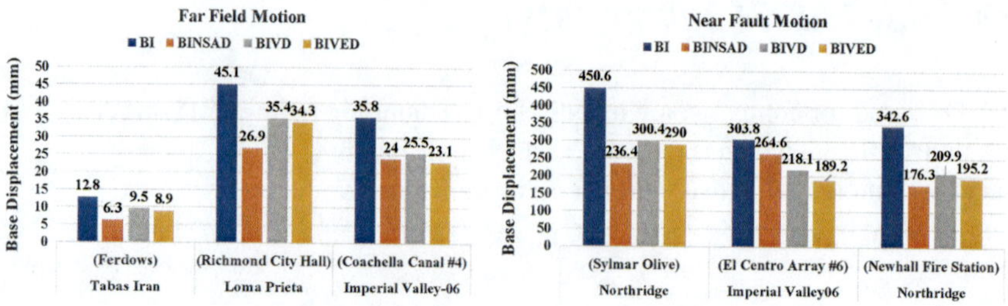

Fig. 5 Base displacement comparison plots

and this depends on the type of damper used. VED enhances the stiffness and hence increased accelerations. Variation of storey acceleration for various supplemental damping devices is shown in Fig. 7. Inter-storey shear and inter-storey drifts are related directly to each other. Variation of shear along storeys is given in Fig. 6. NSAD as a supplemental damper has proven to very effective in reducing the storey shear and base shear.

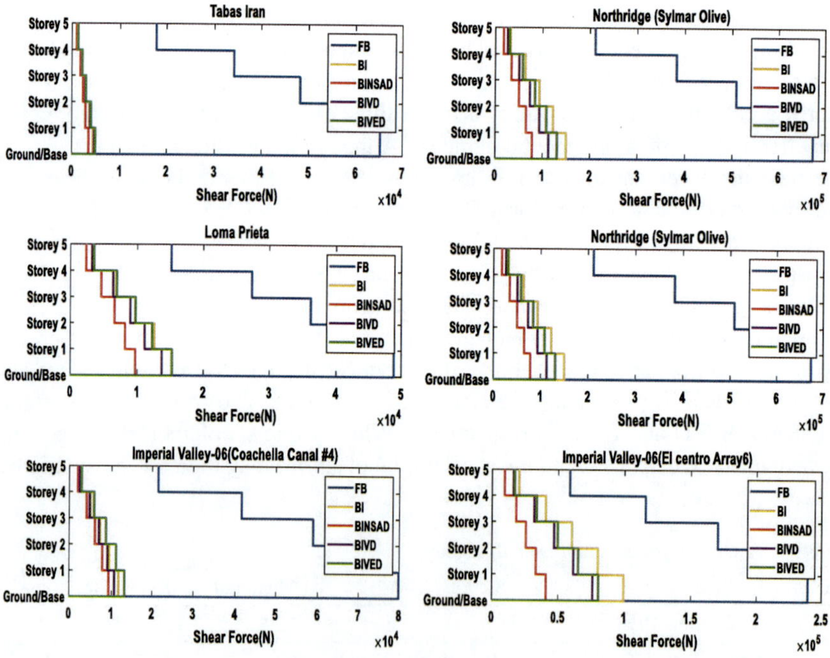

Fig. 6 Storey shear comparison **a** Far Field **b** Near Fault

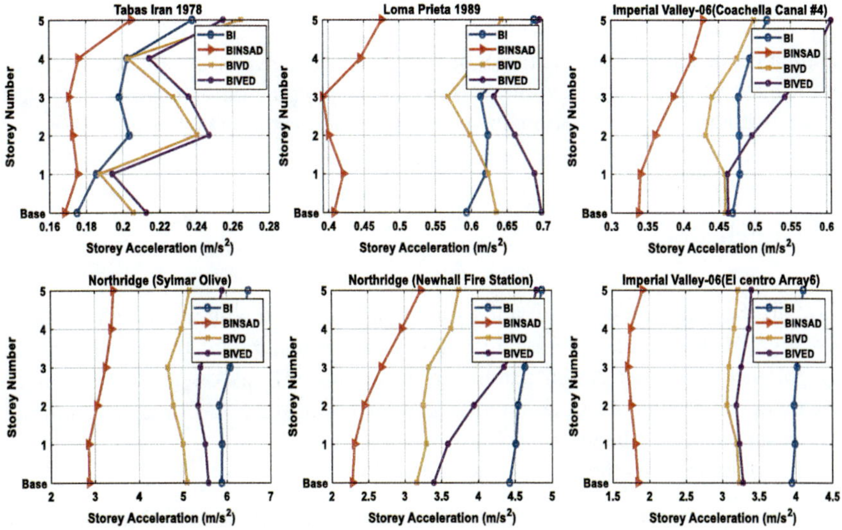

Fig. 7 Storey acceleration comparison. Top row for FF motion and bottom for NF motion

3.1 *Effectiveness of NSAD as a Supplemental Damper*

Standard practice whilst using a supplemental damper is to increase the damping ratio of the device. However, this tends to excite higher modes and result in higher storey accelerations. On the contrary, a small increase in the NSAD damping against the optimum required for FF motion decreases the base displacement and checks the storey accelerations. This has been shown in the FFT analysis results in Fig. 8.

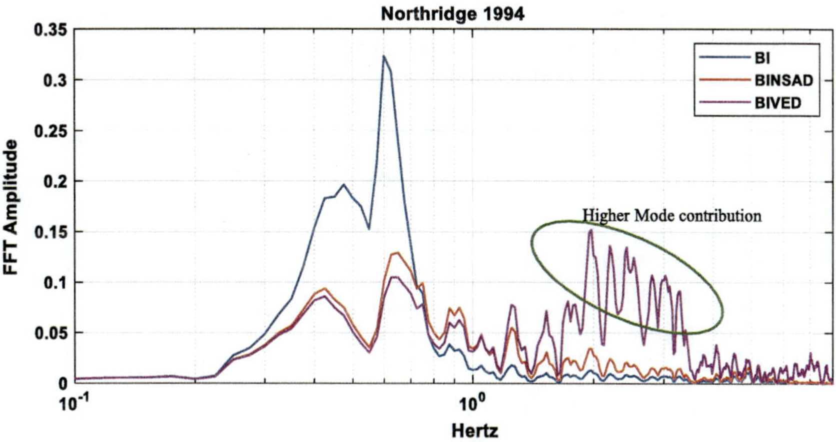

Fig. 8 FFT of top-storey acceleration for Northridge Newhall Fire Station (NF)

The viscous damping supplemented is 25 times base isolator damping, whilst NSAD damping is increased from the factor of 1.85 to 5. Thus, given a design displacement of the base isolator, one can't blindly increase the damping ratio of dampers. NSAD prevents higher mode excitation due to the dynamic magnification effect.

4 Conclusion

Base displacement reduction of a five-storey base-isolated building model has been investigated under 3-FF and 3-NF real earthquake ground motion by using NSAD as a supplemental damper. NSAD parameters are optimised based on stability and effective modal damping criteria. A contrast between optimised NSAD and conventional VD as supplemental dampers has been presented.

The following conclusions are drawn from this study:

1. Results of the dynamic analysis show effectiveness of the NSAD as a superior damper compared to VD and VED for NF and FF ground motions. In comparison with VD and VED, the reduction of base displacement is appreciable for the case of NSAD. Further on, NSAD checks storey accelerations, and values of top storey acceleration are within the vicinity of base-isolated (BI) case.
2. Optimal NSAD parameters are independent of the ground excitation. These parameters can be calculated based on stability analysis.
3. To prevent huge displacement demand corresponding to NF ground motions, introducing a higher value of damping results in higher mode excitation in the otherwise base isolation system. NSAD effectively prevents this violation of the fundamental vibration isolation principle.
4. NSAD removes the limitations of passive VD as supplemental dampers during NF event due to a higher stroke of dashpot for the same damping value.
5. Given a design displacement of the base isolator, one can't blindly increase the damping ratio of conventional passive dampers. The effectiveness of base isolation is upheld with NSAD as a supplemental damper compared to conventional passive dampers.

References

1. Providakis CP (2008) Effect of LRB isolators and supplemental viscous dampers on seismic isolated buildings under near-fault excitations. Eng Struct 30(5):1187–1198
2. Rong Q (2020) Optimum parameters of a five-story building supported by lead-rubber bearings under near-fault ground motions. J Low Freq Noise Vib Act Control 39(1):98–113
3. Lee JJ, Kelly JM (2019) The effect of damping in isolation system on the performance of base-isolated system. J Rubber Res 22(2):77–89
4. Zelleke DH, Elias S, Matsagar VA, Jain AK (2015) Supplemental dampers in base-isolated buildings to mitigate large isolator displacement under earthquake excitations. Bull New Zeal Soc Earthq Eng 48(2):100–117

5. Nagarajaiah S, Reinhorn AM, Constantinou MC, Taylor DP, Pasala DTR, Sarlis AA (2010) True adaptive negative stiffness: A new structural modification approach for seismic protection. In: Proceeding, 5th world conference structural control monitoring, Tokyo, pp 1–15
6. Sarlis AA, Pasala DTR, Constantinou MC, Reinhorn AM, Nagarajaiah S, Taylor DP (2013) Negative stiffness device for seismic protection of structures. J Struct Eng (US) 139(7):1124–1133
7. Pasala DTR, Sarlis AA, Reinhorn AM, Nagarajaiah S, Constantinou MC, Taylor D (2014) Simulated bilinear-elastic behavior in a SDOF elastic structure using negative stiffness device: experimental and analytical study. J Struct Eng (US) 140(2):1–13
8. Sarlis AA, Pasala DTR, Constantinou MC, Reinhorn AM, Nagarajaiah S, Taylor DP (2016) Negative stiffness device for seismic protection of structures: shake table testing of a seismically isolated structure. J Struct Eng (US) 142(5):1–13
9. Mathew GM, Jangid RS (2018) Seismic response control of a building by negative stiffness devices. Asian J Civ Eng 19(7):849–866
10. Wang M, Fei Sun F, Qi Yang J, Nagarajaiah S (2019) Seismic protection of SDOF systems with a negative stiffness amplifying damper. Eng Struct 190(7):128–141
11. Wang M, Fei Sun F, Nagarajaiah S (2019) Simplified optimal design of MDOF structures with negative stiffness amplifying dampers based on effective damping. Struct Des Tall Spec Build 28(15):1–26
12. Kelly JM (1993) Earthquake-resistant design with rubber. Springer, London

Material Uncertainty Based Seismic Robustness Assessment of Steel Moment-Resisting Frames

K. M. Shaijal, Muhamed Safeer Pandikkadavath, Sujith Mangalathu, and Robin Davis

Abstract The structural robustness, that characterizes the available margin of safety against the structural collapse subjected to material uncertainty, is significant in earthquake engineering. Robustness Index is defined as the ratio of mean annual frequency of exceeding a given limit state of interest neglecting structural uncertainties to the mean annual frequency of exceeding a given limit state of interest considering all the uncertainties is often used to quantify the structural robustness. The current study quantifies the Robustness Index of a four-storey steel moment-resisting frame. Incremental Dynamic Analysis is carried out to obtain the inter-storey drift and collapse fragilities. Finally, this study estimates the robustness index in terms of Uncertainty Robustness Index and corresponding modification factors for design strength reduction factors corresponding to different hazards levels.

Keywords Robustness index · Incremental dynamic analysis · Inter-storey drift ratio · Strength reduction factor

1 Introduction to the Investigation

The safety of structures against progressive failures or collapse (disproportionate between load and resistance) under the action of seismic events can be related to their degree of robustness. Robustness is characterized as the ability of a given system to minimize the progress of localized damage, so that there will not be extensive (global) damages that may lead to the collapse [1, 2]. Alternatively, robustness can be viewed as the available margin of safety against the progressive or disproportionate collapse of the structural systems. The seismic robustness of a system depends on the extent of seismic loading, the type of the structural system, and the material properties associated with the component members [2]. Several notable investigations have been

K. M. Shaijal · M. S. Pandikkadavath (✉) · R. Davis
National Institute of Technology Calicut, Kozhikode, India
e-mail: msafeerpk@nitc.ac.in

S. Mangalathu
Data Analytics Division, Equifax Inc, Atlanta, GA, USA

C. Ghosh and S. Kolathayar (eds.), *A System Engineering Approach to Disaster Resilience*, Lecture Notes in Civil Engineering 205, https://doi.org/10.1007/978-981-16-7397-9_35

carried out to quantity robustness based on typology of progressive collapse [1], considering stiffness, damage, and energy [3, 4] and incorporating direct risk, indirect risk, and total risk as per decision analysis theory [5]. Recently, these concepts have been extended to assess the seismic robustness of the building structures as well [4]; which includes the concepts relying on robustness index as a measure of mean annual frequency of exceeding a given limit state of interest [2] and based on the actually vulnerable intensities (hazard types) assimilating the potential extreme event classifications [6]. The present investigation aims to assess the robustness index of a four-storey moment-resisting frame as per the mean annual frequency exceedance of a given limit state of interest concept. A simplified expression that relates the robustness with the response dispersion (of the structure) due to uncertainty in structural modeling parameters and seismic record randomness suggested by [2] has been used for the evaluation. These relations further extended to obtain the modification factor for the strength reduction factor, R which can be utilized in building design provisions to account for the material uncertainty-related effects in the structures. For finding out the robustness-related parameters, incremental dynamic analysis under a selected suite of ground motion records is carried out. The overview of robustness index, analytical modeling details, and the methodology for structural performance assessment, analysis results, and discussions are presented below.

2 Overview of Robustness Index

Taking Robustness Index as the resistance (to progressive or disproportionate collapse) of the structural system resulted from uncertainty (aleatory or epistemic); uncertainty in Robustness Index, I_r can be expressed as the ratio of the two mean annual frequency of exceedance for the given limit state of interest.

$$I_r = \frac{\lambda_R}{\lambda_{RU}} \tag{1}$$

where λ_R and λ_{RU} are the mean annual frequency of exceedance of the given limit state of interest accounting aleatory (record to record associated) and both aleatory and epistemic (record to record and material associated) randomness respectively. Numerically I_r should be greater than zero with an upper limit of 1 (it is a theoretical case of no uncertainty in the structure). The inverse of uncertainty in robustness index, $1/I_r$ is a useful indicator of structural seismic safety that gives the increase of mean annual frequency of exceedance of the given limit state of interest due to the presence of all types of accounted uncertainties. For finding the expression for the mean annual frequency of exceedance, the probability of defying a certain performance level; that is, the demand exceeding the capacity depends on the seismic hazard at the selected location can be utilized. The corresponding hazard curve, $H(s)$ can be characterized by seismic intensity measure, s conforming to the first mode spectral acceleration period, S_a (T_1). Representing demand, D and capacity, C in terms of engineering demand parameter (EDP), the fragility (conditional failure probability) $P(C < D|s)$, the mean annual frequency of exceedance (for the given limit state), λ can be expressed as follows [7].

$$\lambda = \int_0^{+\infty} P(C < D|s)\,|dH(s)| \tag{2}$$

This expression can be simplified using an approximate (with suitable assumptions) closed-form equation as described below [8]. Using power-law fit and taking k_0 and k_1 as the corresponding intercept and slope of the hazard curve respectively (in logarithmic scale); the mean curve for hazard can be approximated as follows.

$$H(s) \approx k_0 s^{-k_1} = k_0 \exp(-k_1 \ln s) \tag{3}$$

Assuming lognormal distribution for the capacity, C engineering demand parameters at the given limit state with median $\hat{\theta}_c$ and dispersion $\beta_{\theta c}$; similarly, presuming lognormal distribution for demand, D engineering demand parameter (at a given value of intensity measure, s) with fixed dispersion of $\beta_{\theta d}$, the conditional median can be written as

$$\hat{\theta}(s) \approx a s^b \tag{4}$$

where a and b are positive real number constants. Further, if the capacity is expressed in terms of intensity measure, to exceed the given limit state and assuming lognormal variation with median $\hat{s}_c$ and dispersion β_{Sc}(aleatory related), mean annual frequency considering (only) record to record variation can be estimated as

$$\lambda_R = H(\hat{s}_c) \exp\left(\frac{k_1^2}{2}\beta_{Sc}^2\right) \tag{5}$$

Taking β_{USc} as the dispersion of material randomness in the structure (epistemic related) with lognormal variation; mean annual frequency of exceedance, considering both aleatory and epistemic randomness can be expressed as

$$\lambda_{RU} = H(\hat{s}_c) \exp\left(\frac{k_1^2}{2}(\beta_{Sc}^2 + \beta_{USc}^2)\right) \tag{6}$$

Substituting Eqs. (5) and (6) in Eq. (1); the expression for Uncertainty Robustness Index, I_r can be obtained as

$$I_r = \exp\left(-\frac{k_1^2}{2}\beta_{USc}^2\right) \tag{7}$$

where $\beta_{USc} = \sqrt{\beta_{RU}^2 - \beta_R^2}$; β_R is the dispersion considering record to record (aleatory) and β_{RU} is the dispersion considering both records to record and material uncertainty (aleatory and epistemic) randomness respectively.

The above-described expressions (Eq. 7) show that the Uncertainty Robustness Index, I_r is directly related to the slope (k_1) or severity of the hazard curve and the intensity measure dispersion due to model parameter uncertainties. Developing this information further, it can demonstrate that, the inverse of Uncertainty Robustness Index, $1/I_r$ gives the hike in mean annual frequency due to the presence of structural uncertainties and thus making it a realistic quantity with effects on the structural safety [2]. Another practical use of the Uncertainty Robustness Index is that it can be employed as a direct factor to correct the collapse mean annual frequency that is obtained without uncertainties. Hence these equations can be extended further as a correction/modification factor to strength reduction factor, *R* (used for seismic structural design) to account for the uncertainties [9]. To account for the robustness and the influence of structural uncertainties, a modification/correction factor R_r (for strength reduction) is sufficient (approximately), and thereby desired safety can be achieved (reduction of *R* value to account uncertainty) [2]. The relation between the modification factor for strength reduction factor and Uncertainty Robustness Index can be written as

$$R_r = I_r^{1/k_1} \tag{8}$$

where R_r is the correction for design strength reduction factor, I_r is Uncertainty Robustness Index and k_1 power-law fit constant.

3 Analytical Modeling Details

For the analytical investigation, a four-storey building consisting of four bays along the east–west direction and three bays along the north–south direction has been selected. The design details of the study frame can be found in the references [10]. The building has constant bay width of 9.1 m along with both horizontal directions (also in all the stories); the bottom storey has a height of 4.6 m and the top storey has equal heights of 3.7 m each. The two middle bays (only) that are moment-resisting type frames along the east–west direction have opted for the numerical investigation. A centerline model of the study frame with respective beam columns and relevant geometric details is shown in Fig. 1a, b. The columns at the bottom (most) of the storey are assumed to be fixed at the base and the beams are designed to meet the AISC [11] strong column-weak beam capacity-based design approach. The beams

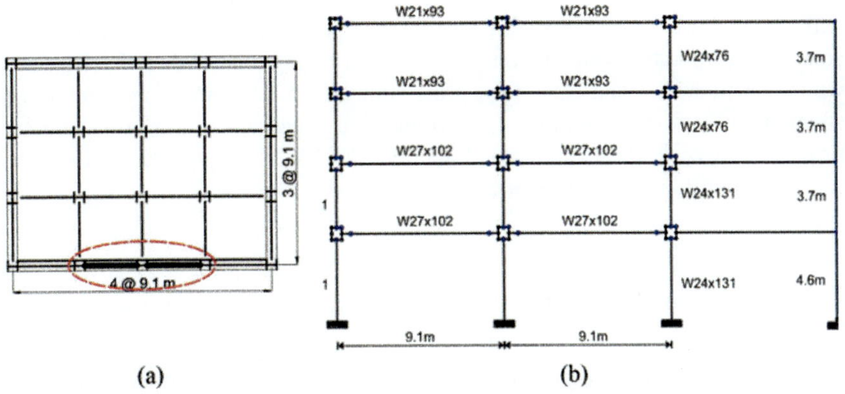

Fig. 1 **a** Plan view and, **b** structural model details of the study building frame

are incorporated with reduced beam sections near the fixity and detailed as per the FEMA recommendations to allow the plastic hinge formations [12].

The adopted 2D study frame is incorporated in the OpenSEES [13] modeling platform. The beams and columns are added as elastic elements with concentrated plasticity employing rotational springs at their respective ends. The zero-length rotational spring elements have a multi-linear hysteretic response as per the modified Ibarra-Medina-Krawinkler deterioration model (shown in Fig. 2) [14, 15]. To simulate first-order geometric nonlinearity, a P-Delta leaning column is provided at a distance of one bay width from the frame. The bottom of the leaning columns is pinned and at every other joint (with connecting axial link as well) it has moment release. This column is connected to the mainframe by an elastic axial link element

Fig. 2 Modified Ibarra-Medina-Krawinkler deterioration model for moment rotation relationship [14, 15]

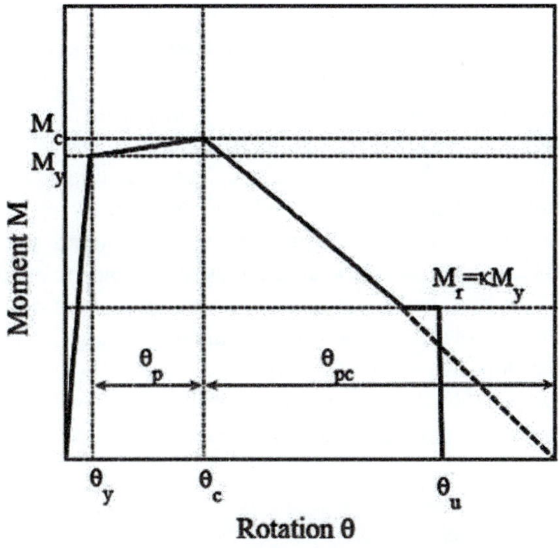

without any kind of stress transfer. The shear deformation due to connection panel zones is incorporated with a tri-linear force deformation relationship characterized with concentrated spring [16]. The spring simulated plastic hinge can capture the strength and stiffness variation of the connection panel zone during its nonlinear response range. A constant Rayleigh damping of 2% is considered for the first, second, and third modes of vibrations.

4 Methodology for Structural Performance Assessment

To assess the structural performance of the chosen four-storey moment-resisting frame Incremental Dynamic Analysis, IDA approach is opted [17]. It involves a series of nonlinear dynamic response analyses for a set of ground motion records scaled at increasing (respective) intensity levels. Based on the analysis IDA curves are developed considering intensity measure, IM as 5% damped first mode spectral acceleration, $S_a(T_1, 5\%)$ of the selected ground motion records and engineering demand parameter, EDP as peak inter-storey drift ratio, IDR. For the IDA, a suite of 30 far-field ground motion records on firm soil with Peak Ground Acceleration, PGA in the range of 0.20–1.40 g (g is the earth gravity acceleration); magnitude range 6.5–7.5 (in the standard scale) and distance range from faults 10–40 km has been selected. Similarly for establishing the IDA curve and the subsequent analysis, the IDR value corresponding to 10% is taken as the collapse of the study structure.

Initially, the uncertainty due to the aleatory parameter (record to record variability related) is accounted for in the response evaluation. The IDA curve for the selected frame with a record to record variability alone is developed and corresponding response value dispersions with respect to ground motions are obtained. In the next stage to account for the epistemic randomness (related material uncertainty); Latin Hypercube Sampling Technique obtained values are incorporated. The structural model uncertainties (with suitable variations) considered for the analysis (Latin Hypercube Sampling Technique generated) are the effective elastic stiffness, K_e; pre-peak plastic rotation, θ_p; post-peak plastic rotation, θ_{pc}; effective yield moment strength, M_y; post-yield moment strength ratio M_c/M_y and critical damping, ξ (refer Fig. 2.). Corresponding to these values 30 additional moment-resisting frame realizations are defined. Corresponding to that IDA is carried out and resulting IDA curves are developed. The obtained related dispersion has been used for further analysis. Based on the two dispersion values of the Uncertainty Robustness Index, the inverse of the same has been calculated to understand the structural performance indication in terms of seismic robustness of the frame. Additionally, seismic fragility curves are developed by taking fragility as the probability of the limit state capacity, C being exceeded by demand, D for a given intensity level, s. Once capacity and demand are expressed in terms of intensity level, the representation for fragility, $P_{LS}(s)$ can be as follows.

$$P_{LS}(s) = P(C < D|s) = P(s_c < s|s) = F(s_c|s) \tag{9}$$

where s_c is the intensity measure value of the capacity that when exceeds the record violation of the limit state. F [.] is the cumulative distribution function, CDF of the argument. That is the fragility curve is the CDF of s_c evaluated at the intensity level s. Taking lognormal distribution assumption for s_c

$$P_{LS}(s) = \varphi\left(\frac{\ln s - \ln s_c}{\beta_{sc}}\right) \tag{10}$$

where s_c is the median intensity measure value of the capacity and β_{sc} is the corresponding dispersion/standard deviation of the log data.

5 Analysis Results and Discussions

The influence of structural uncertainties over the considered capacity and demand are discussed below. As described earlier inter-storey drift ratio (maximum) is considered as the engineering demand parameter and the intensity measure is taken as the 5% damped first mode spectral acceleration S_a $(T_1, 5\%)$. Figure 3a, b shows the IDA curve for the cases with record to record variability (alone) and the case with record to record variability along with material uncertainty.

The median value of normalized (with respect to g) intensity measure, S_a $(T_1, 5\%)$ under the considered set of 30 ground motion generated IDA are obtained to be 2.1 and 1.9 respectively for record to record variability alone and record to record as well as material uncertainty cases. Similarly, the dispersion values corresponding to these cases are 0.38 (β_R) and 0.40 (β_{RU}) respectively. The fragility curves (as discussed in the previous sections) with respect to these two cases are plotted and

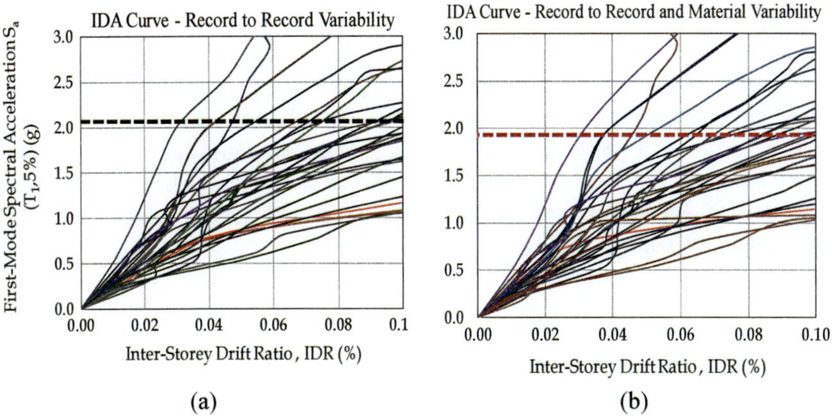

Fig. 3 IDA curves **a** Record to record variability only and **b** Record to record and material variability cases

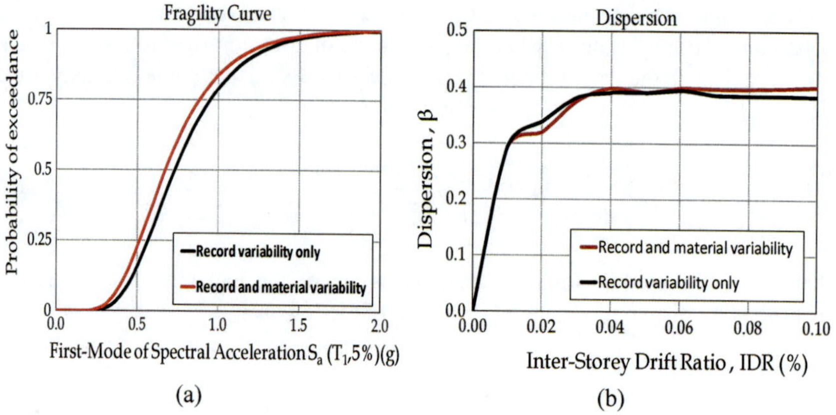

Fig. 4 **a** Fragility curves corresponding to record variability (only) and both record to record variability and material randomness and, **b** the corresponding dispersion values

shown in Fig. 4a. The collapse vulnerability corresponding to normalized intensity measure S_a (T_1, 5%) = 1.0 g is obtained as 79% for without material uncertainty (record to record variation alone) and the vulnerability corresponding to the second case is found to be 84% (with record to record as well as material uncertainty).

Figure 4b shows the variation of dispersion values from the IDA curves developed corresponding to the two cases considered. From the dispersion values of $\beta_R = 0.38$ (record to record variability only) and β_{UR} 0.40 (both record to record and material uncertainties) corresponding to collapse (IDR = 10%), the Uncertainty Robustness Index, I_r; the inverse of Uncertainty Robustness Index and modification factor, R_r for strength reduction factor, R can be obtained corresponding different values of k_I (different levels/severity of seismicity) [2]. The k_I values corresponding to 2, 3, and 4 (increasing levels of hazard severity) the values or I_r; $1/I_r$ and R_r values are given in Table 1.

More seismically active (severity) locations ($k_1 = 4$) the robustness index has a lower value compared to less seismically active (severity) locations. The I_r; $1/I_r$ and R_r values corresponding to $k_1 = 4$ are found to be 0.88, 1.14, and 0.96 respectively. That is, there is a 14% increase in the structural uncertainties due to the seismic hazard level at the chosen scenario. To account for this randomness, a modification factor of 0.96 needs to be incorporated for the strength reduction factor, *R* while designing the structure.

Table 1 I_r; $1/I_r$ and R_r parameters corresponding to different values of k_I

	$k_I = 2$	$k_I = 3$	$k_I = 4$
I_r	0.97	0.93	0.88
$1/I_r$	1.03	1.07	1.14
R_r	0.98	0.97	0.96

6 Concluding Remarks

A brief overview of past investigations on seismic robustness assessment has been carried out initially. Sequentially basic equations for finding out the Uncertainty Robustness Index have been reviewed and this information is extended to find the modification factor of strength reduction factor of the structural systems. A four-storey two-bay study frame is selected and modeled in the OpenSEES platform with applicable design provisions considering with and without suitable material variability. Additionally, 30 different study models are selected based on the Latin Hypercube Sampling method (structural model with material uncertainty). Afterward, a set of 30 far-field ground motion records are selected and nonlinear time historey dynamic analysis (incremental dynamic analysis) is carried out with and without material variability. Incremental Dynamic Analysis curves for both cases are developed and corresponding dispersions are also found. Using the respective medians and dispersions fragility curves for the two cases are also developed. Finally, the Uncertainty Robustness Index and its inverse and the correction factors for design strength reduction factor found for different hazard levels. It is concluded that when the hazard severity increases corresponding Uncertainty Robustness Index and modification factor for strength reduction factors decreases.

References

1. Starossek U (2007) Typology of progressive collapse. Eng Struct 29:2302–2307
2. Vamvatsikos D (2015) A view of robustness based on uncertainty. In: 12th international conference on applications of statistics and probability in civil engineering, ICASP12, Vancouver, Canada, July 12–15 2015
3. Starossek U, Haberland M (2011) Approaches to measure of structural robustness. Struct Infrastruct Eng 7(7–8):625–631
4. Mondal G, Tesfamariam S (2014) Effects of vertical irregularity and thickness of unreinforced masonry infill on the robustness assessment of RC framed buildings. Earthq Eng Struct Dynam 43(2):205–223
5. Baker JW, Schubert M, Faber MH (2008) On the assessment of robustness. Struct Saf 30:253–267
6. Asprone D, Risi RD, Manfredi G (2016) Defining robustness under seismic and simultaneous cations: an application to precast RC building. Bull Earthq Eng 14:485–499
7. Jalayer F (2003) Direct probabilistic seismic analysis: implementing nonlinear dynamic analysis. Ph.D. Thesis, Department of Civil and Environmental Engineering, Stanford University, Stanford, CA.
8. FEMA (2009) Quantification of building seismic performance factors—FEMA P695. Federal Emergency Management Agency, Washington DC
9. Cornell CA, Jalayer F, Hamburger RO, Foutch DA (2002) The probabilistic basis for the 2000 SAC/FEMA steel moment frame guidelines. J Struct Eng ASCE 128(4):526–533
10. Kazantzi AK, Vamvatsikos D, Lignose DG (2013) Seismic performance of a steel moment resisting frame subject to strength and ductility uncertainty. In: 11th international conference of structural safety and reliability (ICOSSAR 2013), New York
11. AISC (ANSI/AISC 341–16) (2016) Seismic provisions for structural steel buildings. American Institute of Steel Construction, Chicago, IL, USA

12. FEMA 350 (2000) Recommended seismic design criteria for new steel moment frame buildings. Federal Emergency Management Agency, Washington DC
13. McKenna F, Fenves G, Jeremic B, Scott M (2000) Open system for earthquake engineering simulations. <http://opensees.berkeley.edu>
14. Ibarra LF, Medina RA, Krawinkler H (2005) Hysteretic models that incorporates strength and stiffness deterioration. Earthquake Eng Struct Dynam 34(12):1489–1511
15. Lignos DG, Krawinkler H (2011) Deterioration modeling of steel components in support of collapse prediction of steel moment frames under earthquake loading. J Struct Eng ASCE 137(11):1291–1302
16. Gupta A, Krawinkler H (1999) Seismic demands for the performance evaluation of steel moment resisting frame structures. In: John A. Blume Earthquake Engineering Research Centre, Report No. 132, June, Stanford, CA
17. Vamvatsikos D, Cornell CA (2002) Incremental dynamic analysis. Earthq Eng Struct Dynam 31(3):491–514

Mitigation of Progressive Collapse of Multi-Storey Steel Building by Providing Chevron Bracings

Parthav P. Patel and Digesh D. Joshi

Abstract Progressive collapse of any structure causes disastrous failure of structure and significant loss of human lives as well as natural resources. Therefore, it is important to reduce the risk of progressive collapse of structure using various mitigation approaches to avoid disastrous consequences and economic & human losses. In the present study, the effectiveness of chevron bracing is evaluated for mitigation of progressive collapse of 9-storey regular steel moment resisting building. The bracings are provided in the alternate bays of the top storey. The progressive collapse potential of steel buildings is evaluated by following the Alternate Path Method (APM) as specified by U. S. General Services Administration (GSA 2016) guidelines. Linear static, nonlinear static and nonlinear dynamic analyses are performed using SAP2000 software under the middle column removal scenario from the ground floor of the perimeter frame in the longitudinal direction. The demand Capacity Ratio (DCR) of the beams and columns adjoining to the removed column are calculated by using linear static analysis. Nonlinear analyses are carried out to understand the failure mechanism of steel building and to obtain vertical displacement time history at the column removal location. From the results of linear static analysis, it is observed that the presence of bracing members significantly reduces the DCR of beams and columns and thus increases the progressive collapse resistance of the building structure. From nonlinear analyses, it is observed that the provision of bracings contributes to the redistribution of forces and effectively transfers the unbalanced vertical load developed due to the removed column to the adjoining structural members.

Keywords Progressive collapse mitigation · Steel chevron braced frame · Middle column removal

---

P. P. Patel (✉) · D. D. Joshi
Civil Engineering Department, School of Engineering, Institute of Technology, Nirma University, Ahmedabad, Gujarat 382481, India
e-mail: 19mclc13@nirmauni.ac.in

D. D. Joshi
e-mail: digesh.joshi@nirmauni.ac.in

C. Ghosh and S. Kolathayar (eds.), *A System Engineering Approach to Disaster Resilience*, Lecture Notes in Civil Engineering 205, https://doi.org/10.1007/978-981-16-7397-9_36

1 Introduction

Progressive collapse is one of the failure mechanisms, in which failure of a few critical structural elements leads to the collapse of large parts of a structure. It is a chain reaction failure of building members to an extent disproportionate to the original localized damage and also referred to as disproportionate collapse [1]. It is a dynamic failure mechanism that generally occurs under abnormal loading, which results in disastrous consequences and substantial loss of human lives and natural resources. Therefore, it is very important to mitigate the susceptibility of progressive collapse of a building, if it is having a high potential of progressive collapse. Since the collapse of Ronan Point Apartment, London in 1968 due to a gas explosion, many government authorities and local agencies have worked on developing some guidelines for designing progressive collapse-resistant structures. Among these guidelines, the U.S. General Service Administration [2, 3] and Unified Facilities Criteria (UFC) published by the Department of Defense (DoD), United States of America [4] describes detailed methodologies to resist the progressive collapse of RC and steel building structures.

The effectiveness of chevron bracings for the strengthening of 10-storey steel buildings against progressive collapse was studied by Chen et al. [5]. Bracings were provided in all the bays of top storey of building and from the study results, it was observed that provision of bracings significantly increased the potential of building against progressive collapse. Marjanishvili [6] discussed the four analysis procedures, i.e. linear static, nonlinear static, linear dynamic and nonlinear dynamic analyses for progressive collapse analysis of structures. Further, the progressive collapse potential of 9-storey steel moment resisting frame building was evaluated using different analysis procedures [7]. Khandewal et al. [8] analyzed the 10-storey steel braced frame building designed with concentric and eccentric bracings for progressive collapse and it was found that eccentrically braced frame has less vulnerability to progressive collapse as compared to the concentrically braced frame. Naji and Zadeh [9] evaluated the progressive collapse potential of 10-storey steel braced frame building having eccentric bracings and concentric bracings by performing incremental dynamic analysis. The effect of vierendeel action on progressive collapse resistance was examined by Qiao et al. [10] and based on study results, the author proposed a provision of bracings in the top story of building for effective utilization of the vierendeel action. Mahmoud et al. [11] carried out progressive collapse analysis of 5-storey steel moment resisting frame and braced frame building under seismic load using SAP2000 software. From the analysis results, it was observed that the fixity of beam-column connection played important role in the development of catenary action and thus reduce the vulnerability of building against progressive collapse. Mirjalali et al. [12] examined the influence of bracing type and topology on progressive collapse resistance of eccentrically braced frames. Authors have considered different types of bracings such as inverted V, diagonal, combination of V and inverted V, etc. and found that bracings effectively increase progressive collapse resistance. Parikh and Patel [13] presented three retrofitting strategies, i.e. increase in strength, increase in stiffness and increase in both strength and stiffness for mitigation of progressive collapse of 4-storey steel building. Linear and nonlinear analysis methods were adopted for progressive collapse analysis and found that an increase in strength of steel material effectively mitigates the progressive collapse.

In this paper, the effectiveness of chevron bracings is evaluated for mitigation of progressive collapse of 9-storey steel building. Chevron bracings are provided in alternate bays of the top story of the building. Linear static, nonlinear static and nonlinear dynamic analyses are carried out by following GSA 2016 guidelines under the middle column removal scenario from the ground floor of the perimeter frame in the longitudinal direction. The progressive collapse potential of moment resisting frame building is compared with that of braced frame building.

2 General Services Administration (GSA) Guidelines

The U. S. General Services Administration [2, 3] published the guidelines to reduce the progressive collapse potential of building structures. These guidelines are applicable to new and renovated federal buildings and buildings which are going under major modernization. It emphasizes the Alternate Path Method (APM) to ensure the structures' safety against progressive collapse. As per APM, the column should be removed from appropriate locations. The removal extent of the column includes the column removal from the middle of a long side, from the middle of the short side and from corner location. Also, the removal of a column should be considered from other critical locations as determined from engineering judgment. The effect of actions like axial force, shear force and bending moment on the beams and columns need to differentiate either in Force-Controlled Action (FCA) or Deformation-Controlled Action (DCA).

There are three analysis methods suggested in GSA guidelines, i.e. linear static analysis, nonlinear static analysis and nonlinear dynamic analysis. The load combination to be considered for progressive collapse analysis by a specified analysis method is shown in Table 1, where Ω_L and Ω_N is load increase factor and dynamic increase factor, respectively. These increased gravity loads need to be applied in the area adjacent to a removed column, while in the remaining area loads need to be applied as per the specified load combination without considering the load increase/dynamic increase factor.

Table 1 Load combination to be considered for progressive collapse analysis

Analysis method	Load combination	Load increase/Dynamic increase factor
Linear static	Ω_L (1.2DL + 0.5LL)	Ω_L depends on governing m-factor
Nonlinear static	Ω_N (1.2DL + 0.5LL)	Ω_N depends on yield and allowable plastic hinge rotation
Nonlinear dynamic	(1.2DL + 0.5LL)	–

3 Methodology

A 9-storey regular steel building is considered for the present study. The design of structural elements like beams, columns and bracings is carried out using Indian Standard IS 800: 2007 [14]. The progressive collapse potential of moment resisting frame and braced frame building is evaluated by following GSA 2016 guidelines under middle column removal from the ground floor of the perimeter frame in the long side. SAP2000 software is used to perform modelling, analysis and design of steel buildings considered for the study.

3.1 Description of Model

A 9-storey steel building considered for the study has 6-bays in longitudinal direction and 3-bays in the transverse direction. The centre-to-centre distance between columns in the longitudinal direction and transverse direction is 8.25 m and 9.75 m, respectively. The typical storey height of a building is 4.3 m. Chevron bracings are provided in alternate bays on the top storey. The typical floor plan and elevation of the braced frame building are shown in Figs. 1 and 2.

Connections between beams and columns are designed as fully restrained, considering Welded Unreinforced Flange-Welded Web (WUF-W) connections. The support condition of a column at the ground floor level is considered fixed. In braced frame building, chevron bracings are provided in alternate bays of the top storey of the building. The bracings are designed to carry the only axial force and its connection with beam and column is considered as pinned.

Loading on Building

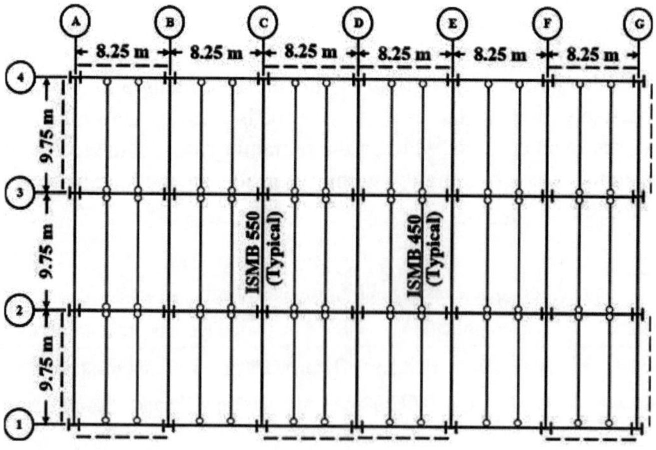

Fig. 1 Plan of braced frame building

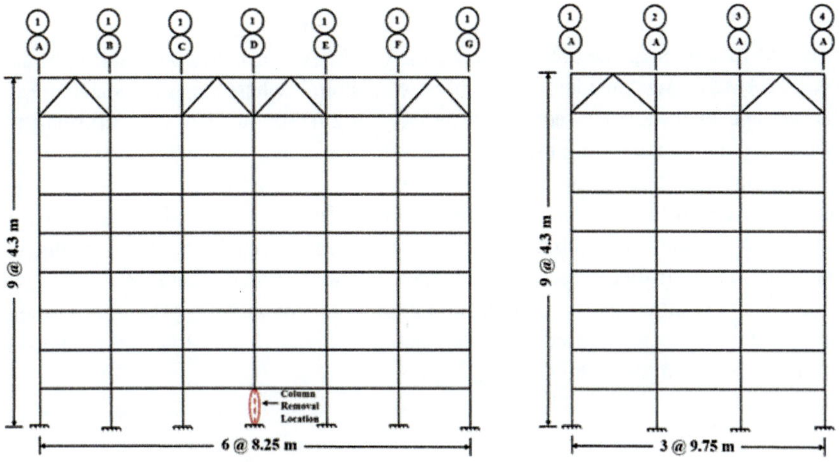

(a) Longitudinal Elevation (b) Transverse Elevation

Fig. 2 Elevation of braced frame building

There are two types of loadings, i.e. gravity loads and lateral loads are considered for designing moment resisting frame and braced frame building. Dead load and live load are applied as a part of gravity loading. The dead load includes the self-weight of beams, columns and bracings, the weight of the composite slab and wall load. The thickness of the concrete slab on the steel deck is 90 mm. A Wall load of 19.7 kN/m is considered on perimeter beams except on the roof. The live load of 3.5 kN/m^2 is considered on the floor and the live load on the roof is considered as 1 kN/m^2. The seismic load and wind load are applied automatically in SAP2000 software according to relevant Indian Standards IS 1893: 2016 (Part 1) [15] and IS 875: 2015 (Part 3) [16], respectively, considering that the building is located in Ahmedabad. The designed section of all beams is ISMB 550 on all floors and the designed section of all bracings is SHS 250 × 250 × 12, where, SHS indicates Square Hollow Section of 250 mm width, 250 mm height and 12 mm thickness. Columns are designed as a built-up section with a total depth of 550 mm, 400 mm flange width, 30 mm flange thickness and 25 mm web thickness. The density of steel and concrete is considered as 25 kN/m^3 and 78.6 kN/m^3, respectively. The yield strength of steel material is considered 310 N/mm^2.

4 Linear Static Analysis

The potential of building against progressive collapse is first evaluated through Linear Static Analysis (LSA), as results of the linear static analysis provide an indication about the vulnerability of the building against progressive collapse. Based on the results of linear static analysis, Demand Capacity Ratios (DCR) are calculated at selected locations for beams and columns. For LSA, the load combination of Ω_L (1.2DL + 0.5LL) is considered as mentioned in Table 1, where Ω_L is the load increase factor. The load increase factor is different for force-controlled and deformation-controlled action according to GSA 2016 guidelines.

The moment and shear in the beam are classified as deformation-controlled and force-controlled action, respectively. For columns, the axial force is classified as force-controlled action, but the moment can either be force-controlled or deformation-controlled which depends on the ratio of P/P_{CL}. For $P/P_{\mathrm{CL}} > 0.5$, the moment is classified as force-controlled action and for $P/P_{\mathrm{CL}} \leq 0.5$, the moment is classified as deformation-controlled action, where P_{CL} is lower bound axial compressive strength of the column.

4.1 *Determination of Load Increase Factor*

The load increase factor for force-controlled action (Ω_{LF}) is 2.00. Load increase factor for deformation-controlled action (Ω_{LD}) is determined from Eq. 1 given below.

$$\Omega_{\mathrm{LD}} = 0.9m_{\mathrm{LF}} + 1.1 \tag{1}$$

where m_{LF} is the smallest of 'm' for any primary beam or girder which is denoted as m-factor or demand modifier. m-factor for steel elements like beams & columns and m-factor for beam-column connections needs to be found out from Table 9–4 of ASCE 41–13 [17]. The m-factor for flexure in beam depends upon the ratio of the width of a flange to twice the thickness of flange and ratio of the depth of web of beam to twice thickness of web. These ratios need to be compared with limits as specified in Table 9–4 of ASCE 41–13 [17] for Collapse Prevention (CP) criteria and calculation of m-factor. The load combination for deformation-controlled action (G_{LD}) is given in Eq. 2.

$$G_{\mathrm{LD}} = 3.773(1.2\mathrm{DL} + 0.5\mathrm{LL}) \tag{2}$$

Calculation of Demand Capacity Ratio (DCR)

From a linear static analysis, the DCR of beams and columns located adjacent to removed columns are calculated. DCR is calculated for flexure for beams, while for column DCR is calculated by considering both axial force and bending moment. The equations to calculate DCR for beams and columns are as follows:

DCR for Beam—Flexure:

DCR in the beam for flexure is calculated as the ratio of the actual moment (M_{act}) to plastic moment capacity (M_P) of the beam section as shown in Eq. 3.

$$\mathrm{DCR\,(Beam - Flexure)} = \frac{M_{\mathrm{act}}}{M_P} \leq \mathrm{Governing}\ m - \mathrm{factor} \tag{3}$$

DCR for Column:

DCR for the column is calculated using various equations given in ASCE 41–13 [17] depending upon the ratio of P/P_{CL}. The DCR for the column is calculated using the following Eqs. 4–6.

$$\frac{P}{P_{\text{CL}}} > 0.5,\ \text{DCR} = \frac{P_{\text{UF}}}{P_{\text{CL}}} + \frac{M_x}{M_{\text{CL}x}} + \frac{M_y}{M_{\text{CL}y}} \leq 1.0 \tag{4}$$

$$0.2 \leq \frac{P}{P_{\text{CL}}} \leq 0.5,\ \text{DCR} = \frac{P_{\text{UF}}}{P_{\text{CL}}} + \frac{8}{9}\left[\frac{M_x}{m_x M_{\text{CE}x}} + \frac{M_y}{m_y M_{\text{CE}y}}\right] \leq 1.0 \tag{5}$$

$$\frac{P}{P_{\text{CL}}} \leq 0.2,\ \text{DCR} = \frac{P_{\text{UF}}}{2P_{\text{CL}}} + \frac{M_x}{m_x M_{\text{CE}x}} + \frac{M_y}{m_y M_{\text{CE}y}} \leq 1.0 \tag{6}$$

where,

$P_{\text{UF}} =$ Axial force in Column
$M_x =$ Bending moment in section about *x*-*x* axis
$M_y =$ Bending moment in section about *y*-*y* axis
$M_{CLx} =$ Lower bound flexural strength about *x*-*x* axis
$M_{\text{CL}y} =$ Lower bound flexural strength about *y*-*y* axis
$m_x =$ m-factor for column bending about *x*-*x* axis
$m_y =$ m-factor for column bending about *y*-*y* axis

The DCR is calculated for flexure in beams located between gridline C1 and E1 for all stories. DCR for calculated for columns located at gridline C1 and E1. Gridline C1 represents an intersection of gridline C and gridline 1. The comparative graphs of DCR calculated for Moment Resisting Frame (MRF) and chevron braced frame also referred to as Inverted V Braced Frame (IVBF) buildings for beam and column are shown in Figs. 3 and 4 respectively. The vertical line shown in the graph indicates the acceptance criteria for DCR calculated as per GSA 2016 guidelines.

From Fig. 3, it is evident that DCR for most of the beams at a beam-column junction in moment resisting frame building exceeds the acceptance criteria, while in braced frame building DCR at the same location is well within the permissible limit, which indicates that provision of bracings significantly increases progressive collapse resistance of steel building considered for the study. From Fig. 4, it is observed that DCR of a majority of the columns in braced frame building is lesser as compared to moment resisting frame building, which indicates the improved performance of braced frame building against progressive collapse. However, DCR for a column in lower stories exceeds the acceptance criteria because of increased axial force demand in column due to presence of bracings in top storey, which suggests the requirement of more bracing members to fully safeguard the steel building considered for the study against progressive collapse. The DCR for shear in beams and axial tension–compression in bracings satisfies the acceptance criteria for both the categories of building and hence their results are not presented here.

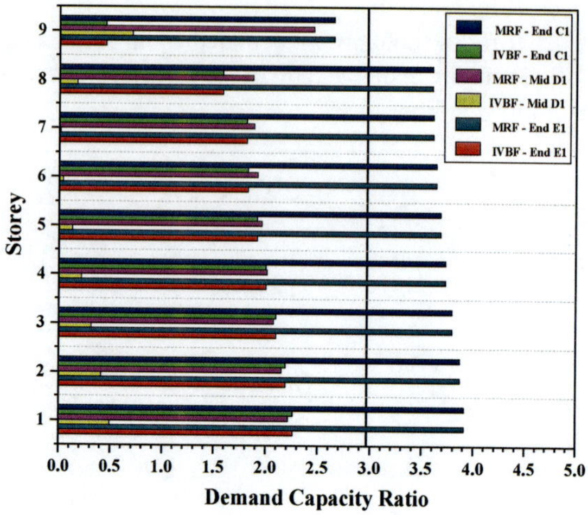

Fig. 3 DCR for Beam-Flexure

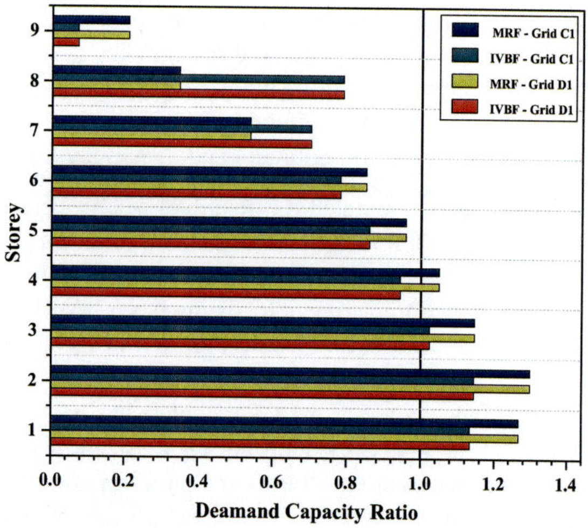

Fig. 4 DCR for Column

5 Nonlinear Static (Pushdown) Analysis

Nonlinear static analysis is carried out in order to find out the collapse load and failure mechanism of the building upon column removal. Generally in lateral load analysis nonlinear static analysis is termed as 'Pushover Analysis' but for progressive collapse, it can be termed as 'Vertical Pushover Analysis' or 'Pushdown Analysis'. The main advantage of this method is that it includes material and geometric nonlinearity. The load combination of Ω_N (1.2DL + 0.5LL) is considered for nonlinear static analysis as shown in Table 1. The important parameter in this load combination is to determine the dynamic increase factor (Ω_N), which depends on support yield rotation (θ_y) and allowable plastic rotation angle (θ_{pra}) for Collapse Prevention (CP) criteria. The dynamic increase factor is determined from Eq. 7.

$$\Omega_N = 1.08 + \frac{0.76}{\left(\frac{\theta_{\rm pra}}{\theta_{\rm y}} + 0.83\right)} \tag{7}$$

The ratio $\theta_{\rm pra}/\theta_{\rm y}$ is the smallest ratio for any primary element, component or connection in the model within or touching the area with increased gravity load. The load combination for nonlinear static analysis (G_N) with dynamic increase factor is given in Eq. 8.

$$G_N = 1.33(1.2\text{DL} + 0.5\text{LL}) \tag{8}$$

The geometric nonlinearity is included in the model by selecting the P-Δ option in SAP2000 software while defining the nonlinear static load case. The material nonlinearity is included in the model by assigning the M3 hinges to beams, P-M2-M3 hinges to columns and P (Axial) hinges to bracings. From the nonlinear static analysis, the graph of the percentage of total load versus vertical displacement is plotted at column removal location as presented in Fig. 5.

From Fig. 5, it is observed that both moments resisting frame and chevron braced frame building attain 100% of applied load without any significant failure. The moment resisting frame building enters into a nonlinear stage, which is evident from the formation of hinges in the beams, while chevron braced frame building remains within an elastic stage, as hinges are not formed in any of the elements. The deflected shape of the moment frame and braced frame building at the final load step is shown in Fig. 6.

From Fig. 6, it is evident that provision of bracings significantly reduces maximum vertical displacement at column removal location, which indicates that bracings

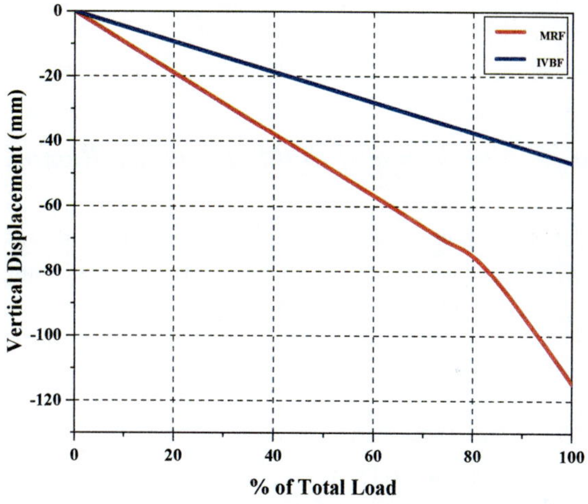

Fig. 5 Nonlinear static curve at column removal location

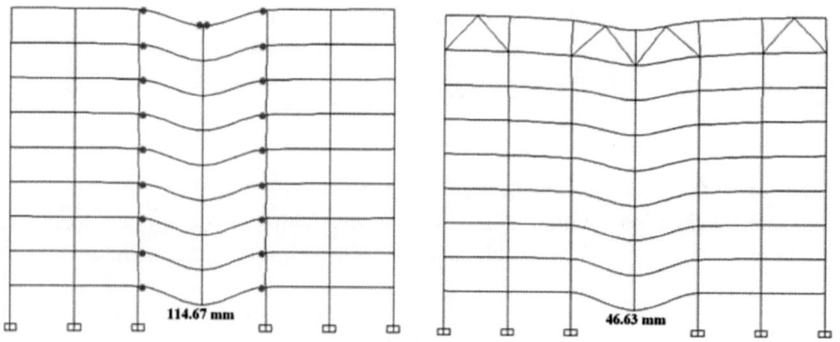

Fig. 6 Deflected shape of MRF and IVBF building—nonlinear static analysis

provide additional load paths to unbalanced load developed because of column removal and thus effectively contributing to progressive collapse mitigation.

6 Nonlinear Dynamic Analysis

Nonlinear dynamic analysis is a more accurate method for progressive collapse analysis because it simulates the actual condition of the building due to sudden column removal. It includes both dynamic effects as well as material and geometric nonlinearity. The load combination of 1.2DL + 0.5LL is considered for nonlinear dynamic analysis as given in Table 1. It does not require any dynamic increase factor because it includes both dynamic and nonlinear effects. The sudden removal of the column from the building results in large deformations, yielding of material, cracking and energy dissipation. For nonlinear analysis, simplified bilinear stress–strain material model is considered with structural steel behaviour of the 3% strain hardening slope of elastic slope.

6.1 Simulation of Sudden Column Removal

For simulating sudden column removal, first, the axial force is measured in the column that is to be removed. It is determined from equilibrium model considering the presence of column that is to be removed using linear static analysis. Subsequently, the column is removed from the model and equivalent axial load is applied as a joint load at the location of removed column. The gravity load including joint load is applied as an initial condition for nonlinear static analysis load case. This condition ensures that structure is stressed before removal of column. Then removal of column is replicated in model through ramp down function in which the axial force as per nonlinear dynamic load case is applied at column removal location. The duration of column removal is less than 1/10th of the time period associated with structural response model for element removal.

Defining the Damping to Nonlinear Dynamic Load Case

The damping plays an important role in the dynamic response of the building after sudden column removal. There is no external damping provided to the building, but the material is having its own damping properties. So, it is important to define the appropriate damping properties of a building while defining the nonlinear dynamic load case. In the present study, the Rayleigh Damping is used for analysis. For this type of damping Rayleigh Damping Coefficient α and β is calculated from Eqs. 9 and 10 respectively.

$$\alpha = \frac{2\omega_i \omega_j}{\omega_i + \omega_j}\xi \tag{9}$$

$$\beta = \frac{2\xi}{\omega_i + \omega_j} \tag{10}$$

Two different natural frequencies (ω_i and ω_j) and damping ratio (ξ) is determined for Eqs. 9 and 10. Modal analysis of the building with the removed column is carried out to find out ω_i and ω_j and the horizontal and vertical mode of vibration are identified. The damping ratio is considered as 2% which is generally used for steel material.

From a nonlinear dynamic analysis, comparative displacement time history is plotted at column removal location for MRF and IVBF building as shown in Fig. 7.

From Fig. 7, it is evident that the presence of bracing reduces the maximum dynamic displacement at column removal location to a great extent. Most of the beams in the MRF building adjacent to the removed column enter into the nonlinear stage but in the braced frame building, all the beams and bracings remain within an elastic stage. The deflected shape of the building for the moment frame and

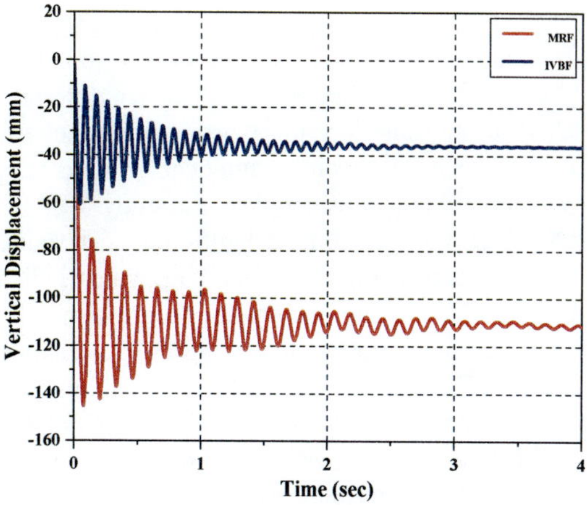

Fig. 7 Displacement time history at column removal location

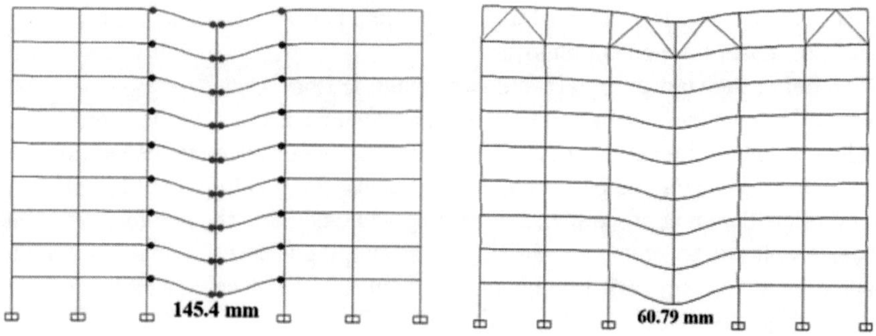

Fig. 8 Deflected shape of MRF and IVBF building—nonlinear dynamic analysis

braced frame building is shown in Fig. 8. The maximum axial force developed in the ground floor column at grid C1 (or E1) in moment resisting frame building (MRF) and chevron braced frame (IVBF) building after column removal is 5545 kN and 7069 kN, respectively.

7 Conclusions

In the present study, the progressive collapse potential of 9-storey regular steel Moment Resisting Frame (MRF) building and the Chevron Braced Frame building which is also referred to as Inverted V Braced Frame Building (IVBF) building is evaluated by following GSA 2016 guidelines. Linear static, nonlinear static and nonlinear dynamic analyses are carried out to evaluate the progressive collapse potential of buildings under the middle column removal scenario from the ground floor of the perimeter frame in a longitudinal direction. Based on the analysis results obtained for steel building considered for the present study, the following conclusions are derived:

- Demand Capacity Ratio (DCR) for flexure in beams for moment resisting frame (MRF) building exceeds the acceptance criteria, while in braced frame building DCR at the same location is well within the permissible limit, which indicates that provision of bracings significantly increases progressive collapse resistance of steel building considered for the study.
- DCR of a majority of the columns in braced frame building is lesser as compared to moment resisting frame building, which indicates the improved performance of braced frame building against progressive collapse.
- DCR for the column in lower stories exceeds the acceptance criteria because of increased axial force demand in the column due to the presence of bracings in the top storey, which suggests an arrangement of more bracing members with different configurations to fully safeguard the steel building considered for the study against progressive collapse.

- Nonlinear static analysis results revealed that both moments resisting frame building and braced frame building are able to resist 100% of the applied load. However, the formation of hinges indicates that beams in the MRF building near removed column enter into a nonlinear stage, while in braced frame building it remains in an elastic stage.
- From the results of nonlinear static analysis, it is observed that bracing configuration considered in the present study reduces maximum static vertical displacement at column removal location by 60% in braced frame building as compared to MRF building, which indicates that bracings are providing alternate load path to transfer unbalanced force developed due to column removal and thus effectively contributes to reducing risk of progressive collapse.
- The maximum dynamic displacement at column removal location from the nonlinear dynamic analysis is reduced by 58% in braced frame building as compared to MRF building.
- Axial force in the ground floor column at grid C1 in IVBF building increased by 28% as compared to axial force in MRF building after sudden column removal.
- The chevron bracing configuration in alternate bays at a top storey, considered in the present study is effective means to increase the progressive collapse resistance under the middle column removal scenario from the ground floor of the perimeter frame in a longitudinal direction.

References

1. Best practices for reducing the potential for progressive collapse in buildings. NISTIR 7396. National Institute of Standards and Technology, Department of Commerce, United States of America, Feb 2007
2. General services administration alternate path analysis & design guidelines for progressive collapse. The U. S. General Services Administration, Jan 2016
3. Progressive collapse analysis & design guidelines for New Federal Office buildings & major modernization projects. The U.S. General Services Administration, June 2003
4. Design of buildings to resist progressive collapse. Unified Facilities Criteria (UFC), Department of Defense, United States of America, June 2013
5. Chen J, Peng W, Renle M, Minjuan H (2012) Strengthening of horizontal bracing on progressive collapse resistance of multistorey steel moment frames. J Perform Constructed Facil ASCE 720–724
6. Marjanishvili S (2004) Progressive analysis procedures for progressive collapse analysis. J Perform Constructed Facil ASCE 79–85
7. Marjanishvili S, Agnew E (2006) Comparison of various procedures for progressive collapse analysis. J Perform Constructed Facil ASCE 365–374
8. Khandewal K, El-Tawil S, Sadek F (2009) Progressive collapse analysis of seismically designed frames. J Constr Steel Res Elsevier 699–708
9. Zadeh M, Naji A (2019) Progressive collapse analysis of steel braced frames. Pract Period Struct Des Constr ASCE.
10. Qiao H, Luo C, Wei J, Chen Y (2020) Progressive collapse analysis of steel braced frames considering Vierendeel action. J. Perform Constr Facil
11. Mahmoud M et al. (2018) Assessment of progressive collapse of steel structures under seismic loads. Alexandria Eng J 3825–3839

12. Mirjalali H, Ghasemi M, Labbafzadeh S (2019) Effect of bracing type and topology on progressive collapse resistance of eccentrically braced frames. Int J Steel Struct Springer 1497–1510
13. Parikh R, Patel PV (2011) Effects of retrofit strategies on mitigating progressive collapse of steel building, In: Nirma University international conference (NUiCONE)
14. IS 800: 2007, Code of practice for general construction in steel, Bureau of Indian Standards, New Delhi, India
15. IS 1893—2016 (Part 1), Code of practice for earthquake resistant design of structures, Bureau of Indian Standard, New Delhi, India.
16. IS 875—2015 (Part 3), Design loads for buildings and structures—code of practice wind load, Third Revision, Bureau of Indian Standards, New Delhi, India
17. ASCE/SEI 41–13, Seismic evaluation and retrofit of existing building, ASCE

Seismic Evaluation, Strengthening and Retrofitting of Schools in Shimla, Himachal Pradesh

Hemant Kumar Vinayak, Shailza Sharma, and Rishabh Singh

Abstract This paper presents strengthening and retrofitting of masonry and reinforced cement concrete buildings of schools in Shimla, Himachal Pradesh. The school buildings were either L-shape or building aggregate constructed with the combination of random rubble stone masonry, brick masonry or reinforced cement concrete. The integrated approach of qualitative assessment with visual inspection, non-destructive testing, masonry structure evaluation with analytical method for in-plane and out-of-plane safety and the method of capacity demand ratio based on elastic analysis and design was used for reinforced cement concrete structures. As per design requirements and fund availability, local retrofit techniques of jacketing stone masonry random rubble walls, splint bandage technique for brick masonry and jacketing of reinforced cement concrete beams and columns were carried out in phases to improve the lateral resistance and bring the structure to the original state. Bracing of trusses was proposed to increase the rigidity of existing flexible roof of masonry structure. The retrofitting and strengthening of building in seismic zone lead to the sensitization of the state disaster management authority about the necessity of developing building resilience of important buildings, thus reducing disaster causality and economic loss. This work highlights the need of seismic evaluation of schools to prioritize the retrofit activity across the network of institutions.

Keywords Seismic zone · Masonry building · Retrofit techniques · In-plane safety · Out-of-plane safety · Jacketing of wall

---

H. K. Vinayak (✉)
National Institute of Technical Teachers Training and Research, Chandigarh, India

S. Sharma
Indian Institute of Science, Bangalore, India

R. Singh
Larson and Toubro Infrastructure Development Private Limited, Ahmedabad, India

C. Ghosh and S. Kolathayar (eds.), *A System Engineering Approach to Disaster Resilience*, Lecture Notes in Civil Engineering 205, https://doi.org/10.1007/978-981-16-7397-9_37

1 Introduction

In today's scenario, elementary education is essential, and India has introduced many programs to increase the literacy rate. With the initiatives of Sarva Shiksha Abhiyan for universalization of elementary education, number of school infrastructure in Himachal Pradesh state, India has increased drastically during the last decades [1–4]. However, not much attention has been given to the seismic safety of schools, and unsafe buildings are continuously used for compulsory education [5–8]. The structure of school education system consisting of primary, middle and secondary school and the fund, space and infrastructural requirements varies. Further, the spaces are broadly categorized based on the function of spaces. It is the proper/improper organization and clustering of these built spaces developed by architect, which is further analyzed by civil engineers to make it habitable. Out of various assessments of any building in respect of dead, live, wind and snow load, the seismic load is one such type which needs special attention in the areas where probability of earthquake is high. This is the reason for disaster management authority to examine and improve the school safety policy [5]. There are immense examples of earthquake damaged school buildings in India. World Bank and Asian Development Bank reported in 2001 that Gujarat earthquake damaged more than 11,600 schools, institutes and universities [9]. This number can be less or much high in other earthquakes of India, but that is not the matter of concern. It is imperative that the safety of schools against the disastrous effects of earthquakes is addressed, especially in high risk zones.

The assessment of Sikkim earthquake of September 18, 2011 reported damages to 759 schools [10]. The study of behavior of old historical buildings during August 21, 1988 Bihar-Nepal earthquake revealed the failure of L-shape brick masonry building Madarsa Hamedia, Qila Ghat, Dharbhanga constructed in 1937 with 14 class rooms and verandah corridor consisting of brick masonry arches resting on brick pillars in the front portion of class rooms. The main reason of damage was the failure of verandah arch at one end due to lateral thrust and torsion of building which triggered a sequential failure of arches leading to loss of lives [11]. Janise Rodgers through her study on "Why schools are vulnerable to Earthquakes" showed that physical characteristics of school buildings such as large classroom windows, when combined with inadequate structural design and construction practices, create major vulnerabilities that result in earthquake damages [9]. Especially, buildings in *L*, *H*, *T* and *U* shape with re-entrant corners tend to suffer severe damages at the corners.

Poor construction techniques, implementation of common building design with seismic deficiencies and lack of professional knowledge on seismic resistant construction pose a biggest threat to existing structures in Himachal Pradesh [12–15]. Creating a safe earthquake resistant infrastructural environment is the only key to mitigate seismic hazards. As the codes have been upgraded in later years, many existing buildings in seismic zone turned out to be deficient, and thus, retrofitting becomes essential to reduce damages in existing life line and other important buildings [16–18]. Retrofitting is a prudent option to manage the economic aspects and immediate shelter problems rather than reconstruction. The present study deals with seismic evaluation and strengthening against seismic activities of L-shape school building in Seismic Zone IV. The cases discussed here are some specific examples of how retrofitting or strengthening is done when the data available with the concerned authorities are not up to the mark or are not enough for the calculations which are required for the analysis. In few cases discussed, the year of construction was confirmed from the serving staff members, and few calculations were done after the analysis was done during the site visit. In such situations, engineers and designers use their experience to analyze the condition of the structure and then recommend the required solutions, some innovative methods to make the structures seismically safe. Borri et al. [19] experimentally proved that masonry confinement can be done with the help of steel cords [19]. In the cases discussed here, we used different techniques and methods according to structures condition for making them seismically safe.

2 Structural Analysis of Masonry Buildings

The qualitative assessment and structural analysis of masonry structure were carried out to check the safety of structure against earthquake as per the codal provisions. The evaluation began with visual survey for reviewing the seismic performance of existing building in respect of material deterioration, deficiencies due to improper design and construction, non-implementation of upgradations desired due to revised byelaws. Non-destructive testing was carried out using half-cell for corrosion detection and strength test. After taking site measurements of outer and inner walls length, height and thickness, opening size and location, elevation and plan of the building are developed for the structural analysis and design calculations.

The analysis of masonry building can be either carried out with the kinematic model or equivalent static procedures. Valluzzi et al. [20] emphasized on the kinematic models involving the equilibrium of structural macro-elements for providing better seismic evaluation compared to standard hypotheses based assessment methods [20]. Asteris and Giannopoulos [21] developed a novel methodology for earthquake-resistant design of masonry structural systems, considering modeling a real structure to a robust quantitative (mathematical) representation to be very difficult and complicated task [21]. Parisi and Augenti [22] emphasized that engineering judgement should always be used when assessing whether and how uncertainty propagates from material properties to seismic capacity of an entire masonry structure [22].

The structural analysis of the masonry building compares the in-plane shear stress and out-of-plane bending capacity of the structural member due to applied loading. These evaluations depend on the length, height and thickness of wall and openings, location of openings and density of material used. Shear and bending forces applied to the structural member for design depend on member dimensions, material density and design horizontal seismic coefficient. Masonry buildings should be checked for extreme bending and shear, insufficient anchorage, poor shear transfer between diaphragms and countering walls, pounding caused by interference of adjoining roof levels, connection failure and failure of non-structural components.

2.1 In-Plane Safety Evaluation

The safety check is for extreme bending and shear where stiffness parameter plays an important role for calculating base shear and seismic forces in walls [23]. For stiffness calculation in walls, drawings of elevations of all the walls are prepared with opening locations. The wall is divided into three sections where upper section covers the top most wall pier, second section covers the door openings, window openings and piers, second and third covers the door openings and piers (Fig. 1). Spring model showing stiffness in different piers as per Eq. (1) for the wall pier without opening, Eq. (2) for sections with openings and Eq. (3) for calculating equivalent stiffness in the walls is shown in Fig. 2.

$$R_1 = \frac{\mathrm{Et}}{4\left(\frac{h}{L}\right)^3 + 3\left(\frac{h}{L}\right)} \quad (1)$$

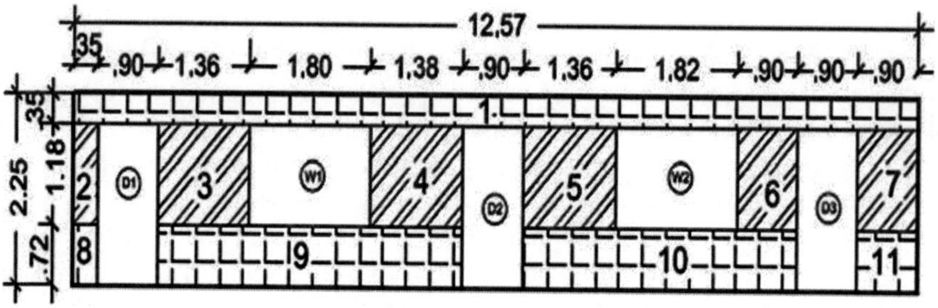

Fig. 1 Elevation of wall 1, first floor

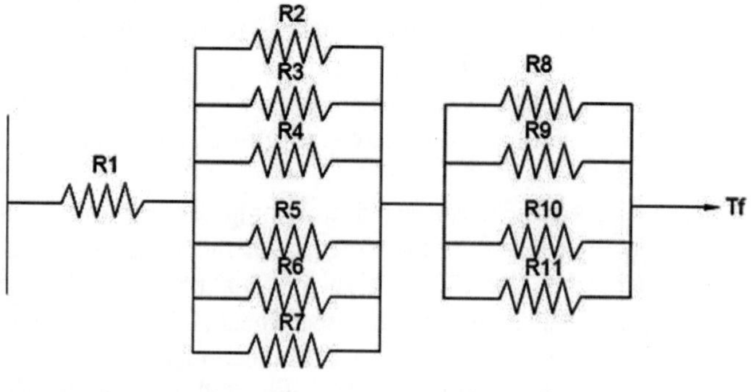

Fig. 2 Spring model of wall 1, first floor

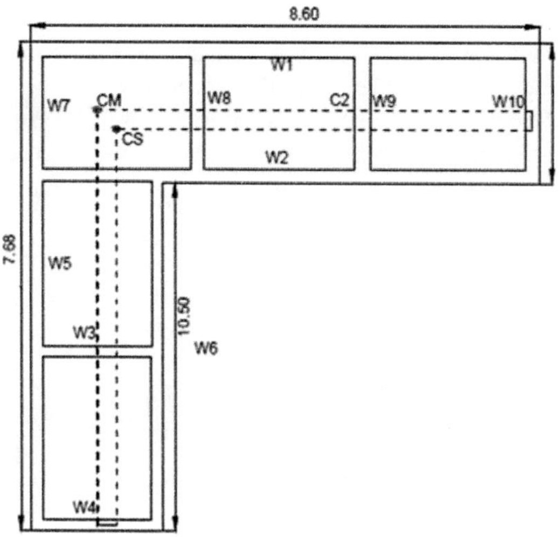

Fig. 3 Position of center of mass and center of stiffness

$$R_2 = \frac{Et}{\left(\frac{h}{L}\right)^3 + 3\left(\frac{h}{L}\right)} \tag{2}$$

$$\frac{1}{R_{Equ.}} = \frac{1}{R_1} + \frac{1}{R_2 + R_3 + R_4 + R_5 + R_6 + R_7} + \frac{1}{R_8 + R_9 + R_{10} + R_{11}} \tag{3}$$

where E, t, h and L are modulus of elasticity, thickness, height and length of wall. The equivalent stiffness is calculated by lateral stiffness of building in x- and y-directions. Torsional stiffness, center of stiffness and center of mass are calculated as per Eqs. (4) and (5), respectively (Fig. 3). Static eccentricity in Eq. (6) is calculated as the difference between center of mass and center of rigidity of floor. Design eccentricity is used for torsion calculations at floors. Eccentricity is calculated using static eccentricity values and rotational stiffness as per Eq. (7).

$$X_{CS} = \frac{\sum_{i=1}^{n} R_i X_i}{\sum_{i=1}^{n} R_i}, Y_{CS} = \frac{\sum_{i=1}^{n} R_i Y_i}{\sum_{i=1}^{n} R_i} \tag{4}$$

$$X_{CM} = \frac{\sum_{i=1}^{n} M_i X_i}{\sum_{i=1}^{n} M_i}, Y_{CM} = \frac{\sum_{i=1}^{n} M_i Y_i}{\sum_{i=1}^{n} M_i} \tag{5}$$

$$e_{SX} = X_{CM} - X_{CS}, \quad e_{SY} = Y_{CM} - Y_{CS} \tag{6}$$

$$e_{d1} = 1.5e_s + e_a, \quad e_{d2} = e_s - e_a \tag{7}$$

$$R_\theta = \sum_{i=1}^{n} R_{Xi} X_i^2 + \sum_{i=1}^{n} R_{Yi} Y_i^2 \tag{8}$$

where R_i, X_i, Y_i, M_i are equivalent stiffness of wall, distance of wall from assumed reference wall in x-direction, distance of wall from assumed reference wall in y-direction and mass of the wall, respectively.

To determine the total seismic forces in walls as per Eq. (9), calculation of base shear is done as per Eq. (10), seismic forces due to earthquake are calculated as per Eq. (11) and due to torsion as per Eq. (12). Distribution of wall forces to piers in the wall are done with spring model.

$$T_{fX} = F_{\mathrm{Xi}} + \Delta F_{\mathrm{Xi\,max}}, \quad T_{fY} = F_{Yi} + \Delta F_{Yi\,\mathrm{max}} \tag{9}$$

$$\mathrm{V}_b = \frac{Z}{2}\frac{I}{R}\frac{S_a}{g}B(\varepsilon)W \tag{10}$$

$$F_X = \frac{V_{\mathrm{bx}}}{\sum R_{\mathrm{Xi}}}R_{\mathrm{Xi}}, \quad F_X = \frac{V_E}{\sum R_{\mathrm{Xi}}}R_{\mathrm{Xi}} \tag{11}$$

$$\Delta F_X = \frac{V_{\mathrm{bx}}e_{\mathrm{dy1}}}{R_\theta}R_{\mathrm{Xi}}X_i, \quad \Delta F_Y = \frac{V_{\mathrm{by}}e_{\mathrm{dy2}}}{R_\theta}R_{\mathrm{Yi}}Y_i \tag{12}$$

where Z, I, R, Sa/g, R_{Xi}, R_{Yi}, e_{dy1} and e_{dy2} are zone factor, importance factor, response reduction factor, average response acceleration coefficient, equivalent stiffness in x- and y-directions, design eccentricity of walls, respectively.

The masonry building has many piers and it is not possible to check the retrofitting solution of all the components of the structural member. Hence, only the slender pier which is more prone to failure and masonry column are designed and checked for safety by calculating the self-weight of the wall, load from the slab, lateral load on the wall, total vertical load on the pier and wall, lateral load on the pier. Lateral load on the pier (F_i) is further used in calculating the moment on pier as per Eq. (13). Net tensile stress (F_t) is computed as per Eq. (14) to design retrofitting for in-plane action. Distribution of net tensile stress and combined compressive stress is checked for slender pier, and tensile force is further used to design the wire mesh as per Eq. (14) for that particular wall. Where F_i, h_i are lateral load on the pier and height of the pier, respectively. T and f_y are tensile force and characteristic strength of steel, respectively.

$$M = \frac{F_i h_i}{2} \tag{13}$$

$$A_{\mathrm{st}} = \frac{T}{1.33 \times 0.6 \times f_y} \tag{14}$$

2.2 Out-of-Plane Safety Evaluation

This failure occurs due to inadequate anchorage and limited tensile strength and leads to partial collapse of exterior, sometimes cracks at lintel and tops, masonry ejection. Evaluation for out-of-plane safety begins with moment calculations as per Eqs. (15)–(17).

$$A_h = \frac{Z}{2}\frac{I}{R}\frac{S_a}{g}B(\varepsilon) \tag{15}$$

$$P = A_h\,\gamma\,t \tag{16}$$

$$M = \frac{Ph^2}{8} \tag{17}$$

Where A_h, P, γ, t are horizontal seismic coefficient, horizontal force, density of material, thickness of wall.

To carry out stress analysis, self-weight of wall, vertical load from slab, total vertical load (W_t) for unit length are calculated. Compressive stress (f_c) as per Eq. (18) and bending stress (f_b) as per Eq. (19) are checked against permissible stress. In the present study, f_b–$f_c > f_t$ does not satisfy the criterion as per clause 5.4.2 IS 1905. Therefore, seismic band is required for safety against out-of-plane failure. Design of lintel band is done using total moment as per Eq. (20).

$$f_c = \frac{W_t}{t} \tag{18}$$

$$f_b = \frac{M}{Z} \tag{19}$$

$$M_t = \frac{P\left(h_1 + \frac{h_2}{2}\right)L^2}{8} \tag{20}$$

where $h1$ and $h2$ are height of lintel from floor and height of roof from the lintel. Design of band mesh requirement is done by evaluating tensile force, compressive force and moment developed in the band. Balance moment (M) is the difference between total moment and moment of band, which is further used in calculating area of steel.

3 Case Study 1

Himachal Pradesh, a part of NW Himalayas is very sensitive to seismicity, and most of the region falls in Zone IV and Zone V. Many earthquakes of slight, moderate and severe intensity have rocked the state in the past [24]. A comprehensive catalog on earthquake epicenters in Himachal Pradesh has been prepared by Chandel and Brar, and they have identified 533 earthquakes of varying intensities during the period 1800 to 2007 in the state [25]. Out of which, 520 earthquakes have occurred during the period 1964 to 2007, and Chamba district has experienced the maximum number of earthquakes, followed by 99 earthquakes in Lahaul and Spiti, 93 in Kinnaur, 53 in Mandi and 49 in Shimla. The most prominent Kangra earthquake of magnitude 7.8 in 1905 has killed around 20,000 people and destroyed 1,00,000 houses. These frequent earthquakes have affected the infrastructure made decades ago and lag behind in terms of safety parameters. Such old infrastructure requires upgradations with respect to the upgraded codes to meet the safety standards.

The school under study comprised of classrooms and administrative offices in combination of random rubble stone, brick masonry and reinforced cement concrete buildings along with other facilities of toilet, drinking water and assembly ground. The rapid visual survey revealed the necessity to analyze the seismic performance of these building and retrofit them to enhance their performance under seismic loadings. Among the various options available, the retrofit measure of jacketing masonry wall and column is proposed as per the design requirements to be implemented in phase-wise manner. Further, the proposed bracing of trusses would add to the rigidity of the existing flexible roof of masonry structure and resist collapse during earthquake. The necessary repair of non-structural elements and change at the site are also suggested to improve the structural behavior of the building. Although theoretical measures to strengthen every structural/non-structural element of the building can be suggested; however, it is practically not possible to implement all the suggested measures at site with the limited available resources and funds.

3.1 School Background (Government High School, Khalini)

The school that requires retrofitting is in Khalini area of Shimla city of Himachal Pradesh, India (Fig. 4a). Shimla, a hilly city, is in Zone IV and lies between $30^\circ 45' 48''$ and $30^\circ 43' 0''$ N latitude and $76^\circ 59' 22''$ and $78^\circ 18' 40''$ E longitude. The school building consists of two blocks:

(1) Two-story masonry structure with wooden roof truss was constructed around 1980 (Fig. 4b). The building is in L-shape with the single corridor for movement on the concave side and is supported on one-brick masonry column at regular intervals (Fig. 5). The ground floor outer and partition wall were constructed with the combination of dry (Fig. 6a) and wet rubble stone masonry (Fig. 6b). The measured thickness of ground floor walls was 0.5 m. The roof of the ground floor was of 125 mm RCC slab roof. The first floor outer and partition wall was constructed in half-brick masonry of 115 mm. The roof of first floor was a combination with rigid RCC slab over the corridor and flexible wooden roof truss on the classrooms/office. The staircase on one side of L-shape for

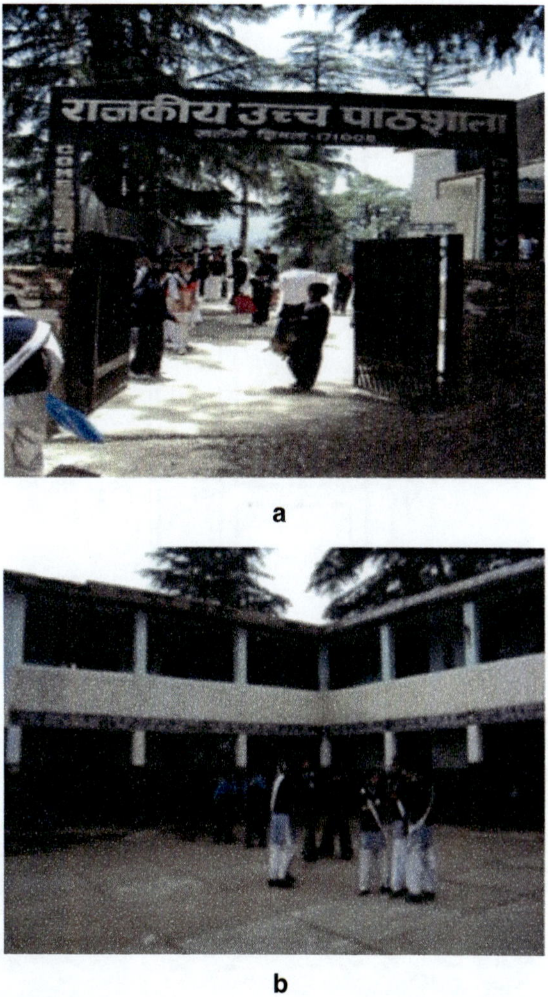

Fig. 4 **a** Govt. high school, Khalini, **b** Two-story masonry building with corridor

climbing to the first floor has water tank supported on the staircase landing roof (Fig. 7). The toilet was constructed adjacently at the back of the building (Fig. 8). The doors and windows were identical in ground and first floor from the front but were different at the back of the building.

(2) Three-story RCC frame building was constructed in around 1990 is another block (Fig. 9). The building has one story as basement which is used as store, ground floor as the faculty room and the first floor as classroom. The access to this RCC block in the first story is common with the masonry block. This three-story RCC-framed structure constructed adjacent to the random rubble masonry structure was measured, and the steel reinforcement used for construction was

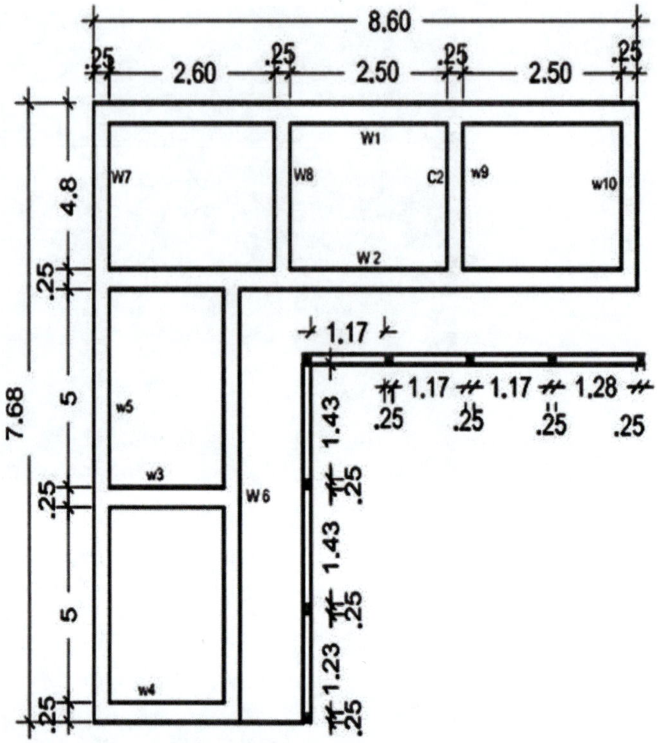

Fig. 5 Plan of first floor of L-shape Building on a scale of 1:200

a b

Fig. 6 **a** Dry rubble stone masonry, **b** Dry rubble stone masonry

Fig. 7 Staircase and water tank

Fig. 8 Toilet at the back of building

Fig. 9 Three-story RCC frame with basement

observed (Fig. 10). The infill walls in the building are constructed with half–brick masonry. Since in case of RCC building, the load is transferred from slab, beam, column to foundation, and the infill wall is non-structural member used to separate two spaces; hence, only the opening size is of importance to calculate the reduced loading of the infill wall not the opening location.

Fig. 10 Reinforcement detailing in column

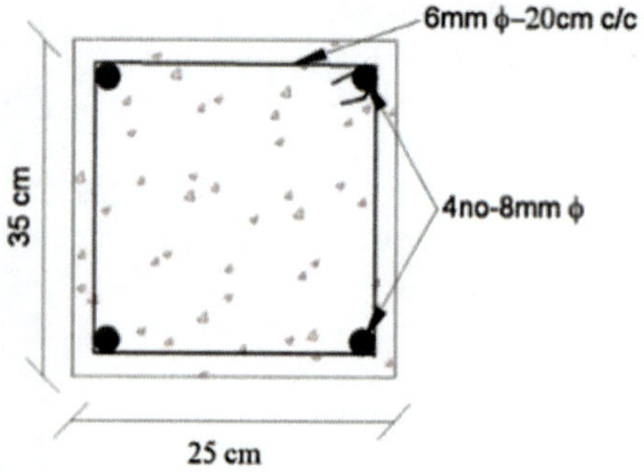

3.2 *Retrofitting Proposed for Masonry Part of School*

The proposed retrofitting solutions that are either cost-sensitive or time duration sensitive. Vicente et al. [26] worked out the efficiency of strengthening strategies in terms of deformation demands and cost–benefit analysis [26]. Bhattacharya et al. [27] gave the comparison of different methods of retrofitting for unreinforced masonry structures on the basis of economy, sustainability, feasibility and provided a useful insight [27]. Based on the qualitative analysis and structural assessment, proposed retrofitting solutions as per IS codes are:

(1) Random rubble masonry is always weak in shear whether dry or wet and dry random rubble are even weaker than wet random rubble masonry (Fig. 11a). For design purpose, such wall is considered as zero shear wall (Fig. 11b). So, to increase the shear strength of random rubble masonry wall, the inner and outer wall portions are tied together (Fig. 12), and reinforced cement concrete jacketing was carried out on both sides of the room. In the present case, the retrofitting solution of jacketing the ground floor wall both from inside and outside with 75 mm thick RCC wall and reinforcement of 8 mm @ 225 mm is proposed as shown in Fig. 13.

(2) The first floor of the building constructed with half-brick wall random rubble masonry is weak in shear. The solution in this case is jacketing of wall from

Fig. 11 Random rubble masonry wall **a** Shimla school **b** Damaged during Bhuj earthquake

Fig. 12 Through elements in wall [28]

Fig. 13 Jacketing of random rubble masonry

both sides with 75 mm thick RCC wall and reinforcement of 8 mm @ 225 mm is proposed as shown in Fig. 14. Alternative proposal was to demolish the first floor and reconstruct as per the codal norm. However, such procedure would have resulted in impaired functionality of the school building.

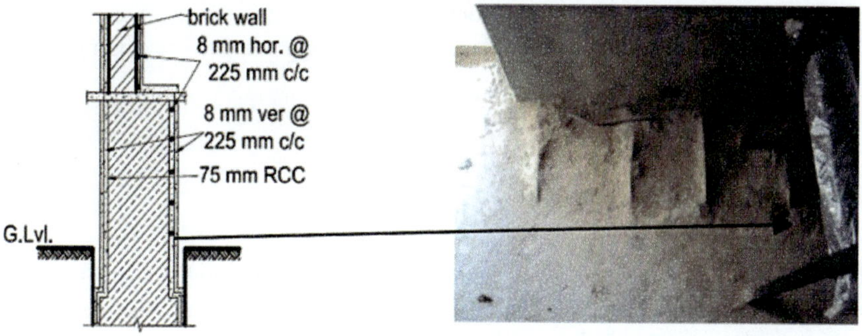

Fig. 14 Detail and GF wall jacketing reinforcement bent at floor level

Fig. 15 Cross-bracing in wooden roof truss

(3) The roof of the two-story random rubble masonry building is built with the wooden roof truss consisting of only rafters, purlins, intermediate tie member, thus making the roof a flexible part of the building. To convert the roof from flexible to rigid structure, proposed solution to install cross-bracing of size 38 mm × 38 mm × 3 mm between trusses is carried out as shown in Fig. 15.

3.3 Structural Analysis and Retrofitting of RC Part of Building

The structural analysis of RCC building consisted of idealizing the three dimensional building into beam, column and slab, applying appropriate live loading as per IS 875 (Part 2), i.e., 3 KN/m2, seismic loading as per IS 1893 ($Z = 0.36$, $I = 1.5$, $R = 5$, Sa/g = depending on modal calculations) [16, 29]. Based on the bending moment and shear force due to applied loading, required reinforcement has been proposed. The construction of RCC building was carried out in the year 1990, which was before the upgradation of IS 1893:2016 and IS 13920:2016 [16, 17]. The structure lacks strength against seismic forces, and analysis of RCC frame is carried out to determine the deficiency in the reinforcement of beam and column (Figs.16a, b and c).

The analysis of RCC frame and masonry building has been done independently to check the individual strength and behavior. It has been found necessary to isolate both the structures by breaking the continuity slab between the two buildings and seal the joint with flexible material like sealant and metal plate to prevent ingress of water.

4 Case Study 2

The school building (Fig. 17a) in which the retrofitting is proposed consists of three blocks. The analysis of the building is carried out to check if the structure is safe against earthquake as per the codal provision. In case the structure is unsafe, the analysis is again carried out with possible retrofitting solution.

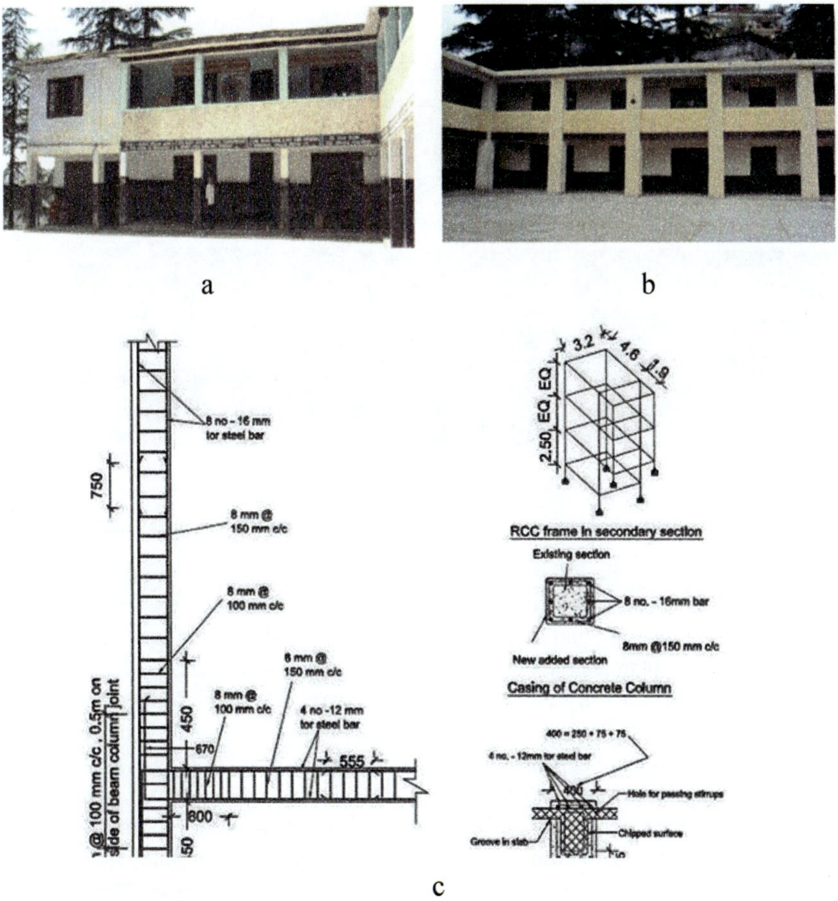

Fig. 16 Reinforced cement concrete frame details

4.1 School Background (Totu School)

Block A—One-story composite masonry structure is with wooden roof truss and MS sheet covering constructed around 1963 (Fig. 17b). The block consists of store, administrative office, principal office, physics laboratory, kitchen for mid-day meal, classroom and staff room. The building is rectangular with an additional room as store (Fig. 17c) in line with single corridor available for movement in the block. The corridor roof is supported on one and a half brick masonry columns at regular interval (Fig. 17d). The story is constructed with half-brick masonry. The outer and partition walls of the rectangular block were constructed with 0.5 m thick dressed stone masonry (Fig. 17d, Fig. 17e) and one-brick thick masonry wall, respectively. The door and windows in the front wall and the windows at the back wall are place almost at regular intervals (Fig. 17f). The site measurement consisting of outer and

Fig. 17 **a** GSSS Totu, **b** Aerial view, **c** Story in Block A, **d** Corridor, **e** 0.5 m outer wall, **f** Windows at regular interval

inner wall length, height and thickness, opening size and location was carried out. The elevation and plan are then generated as per site measurement.

(2) Block B—Two-story composite masonry structure with wooden roof truss is constructed with ground and first floor in around 1975 and 1977, respectively, (Fig. 18a, b). This block consisted of only classrooms. The building is rectangular with the ground floor outer and partition wall constructed as observed with 0.5 m wet random rubble stone masonry (Fig. 18c, d). The ground floor roof of reinforced cement concrete slab is 100 mm thick (Fig. 18e, f). The first floor outer wall is half-brick masonry, i.e., 115 mm (Fig. 18g). The roof is supported on wooden truss at regular interval of approximately 1.5 m (Fig. 18h). The staircase for climbing to the first floor is common and attached with Block C.

(3) Block C—Two-story composite masonry structure with wooden roof truss is constructed around 1990 (Fig. 19a, b). This block consisted of sport room, classroom and computer laboratory in the ground floor and classroom cum presentation room in the first floor. The building is rectangular with the ground floor outer and partition wall constructed as observed with 0.5 m dressed stone masonry as well as with half-brick wall (Fig. 19c, d). The roof of the ground floor is of about 100 mm thickness, constructed with reinforced cement concrete slab (Fig. 19e). The first floor outer wall is constructed in half-brick masonry, i.e., 115 mm with one-brick column at approximately 3.5 m interval (Fig. 19f). The roof is supported on wooden truss at regular interval of approximately 1.5 m (Fig. 19g). The landing in front of first floor entrance is common with Block B. (Fig. 19h).

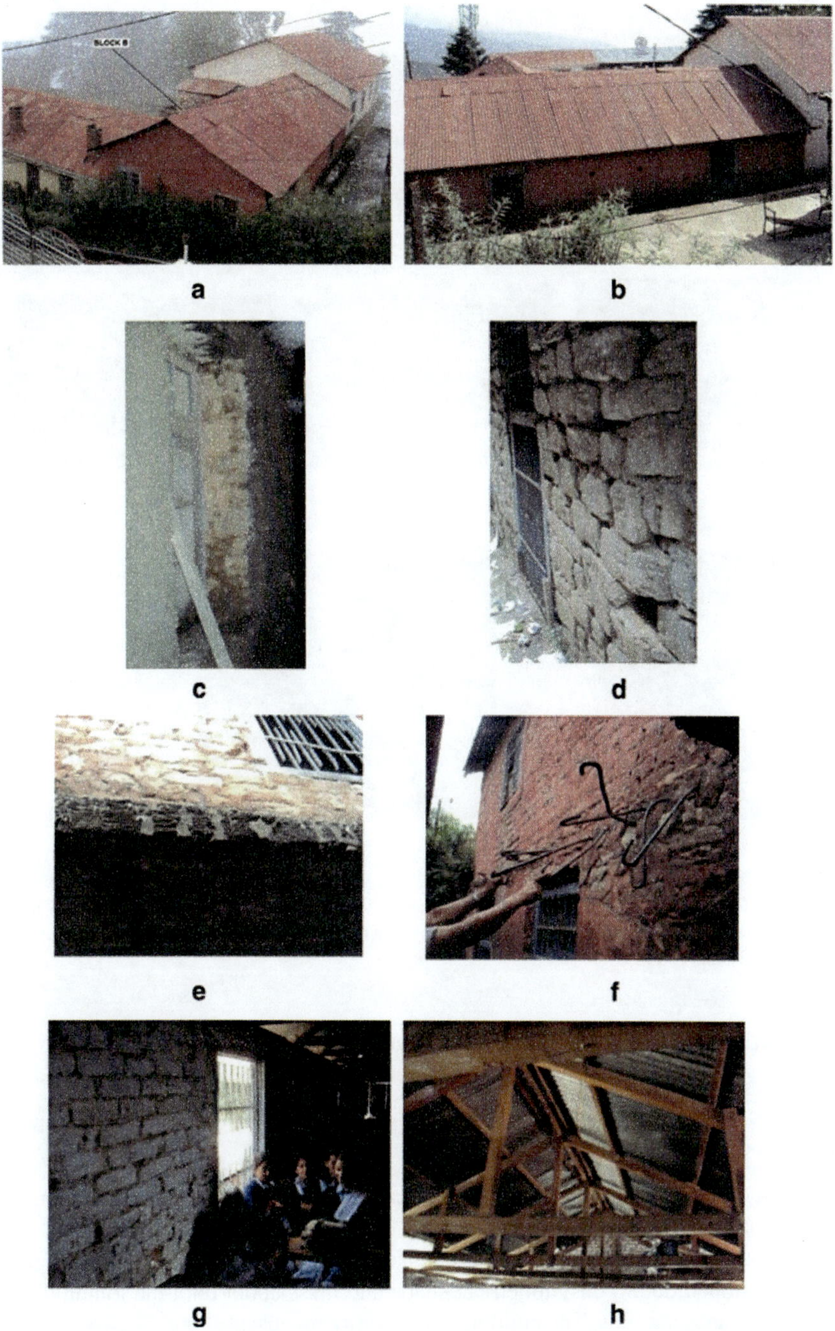

Fig. 18 **a** Block B—an aerial view, **b** Back side view, **c** Wet random rubble masonry, **d** Wall thickness 0.5 m, **e** Slab thickness 0.1 m, **f** Slab reinforcement, **g** First floor wall thickness 0.115 m, **h** Roof truss

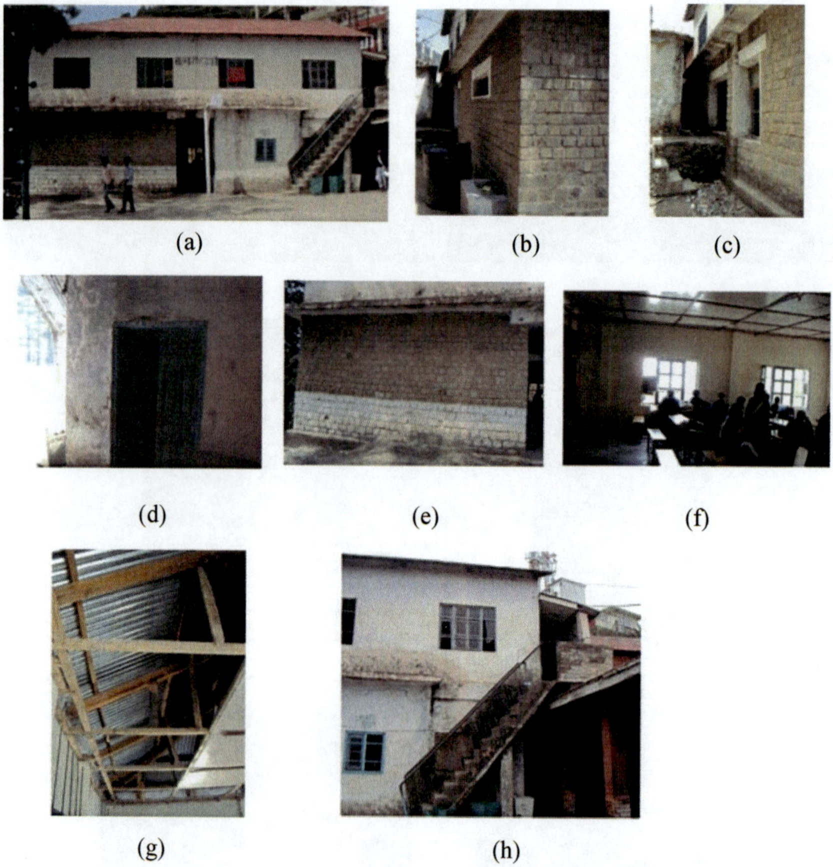

Fig. 19 **a** Block C—front view, **b** Back side view, **c** Wall thickness 0.5 m, **d** Wall—0.115 m, **e** Slab thickness 0.115 m, **f** First floor wall 0.115 m, **g** Wooden roof truss, **h** Common staircase and landing of Blocks B and C

4.2 Retrofitting Solutions Proposed and Carried Out

Deficiencies in the building and their retrofitting solutions if possible adhering to Indian codal provision are:

(a) Block A—This block is unsymmetrical due to high aspect ratio of approximately 5:1, and the storeroom is in line with corridor. Such buildings are always more susceptible to earthquake damage due to the torsion that gets developed due to unsymmetrical shape and mass about both the longitudinal and transverse axis. The building should be symmetrical about the two axes for reduced torsion effect. The removal of storeroom and creating separation joint in the block to reduce the aspect ratio are one solution. However, in the present case, such solution was not possible. Hence, the deficiency of unsymmetrical building plan will persist even after retrofitting. Since the wall was dressed stone masonry, hence, it is capable of taking the shear, tensile and compression stress. After calculation, it has been observed that all the walls are safe in out of plane bending and in-plane shear based on the permissible limit as specified in the Code 1905, expect for one wall in which the jacketing of the pier between windows have been proposed. The masonry corridor columns were acceptable based on the calculation; however, as a precautionary measure, the retrofitting of the masonry column with nominal reinforcement has proposed. During earthquake, the failure of column would be a hindrance for evacuation of the children. The replacement of two wall of storeroom constructed with half-brick masonry with one-brick masonry along with the removal of window, shifting of entry door of storeroom to the center of wall, was done (Figs. 20a, 20b). The wooden roof trusses are flexible diaphragms; hence, cross-bracings were introduced in between the two consecutive rafters (Fig. 20c). The chimneys projecting over the roof in vertical line with the fireplace have been in use, once the wood has been used to keep the room warm during winters (Fig. 20d). However, such chimneys are not in use now. Hence, remove the chimneys and

(a) (b) (c)

(d) (e)

Fig. 20 **a**, **b** Store room window to be removed, **c** Corridor roof, **d** Chimneys to be removed, **e** Corridor roof subjected to leakage

(a) (b) (c)

Fig. 21 **a**, **b** RCC wall both inside and outside **c** Roof truss with cross-bracings

plug from top. The end of the building adjacent to Block B is prone to leakage in the corridor at some places accordingly the sealing of roof to be carried out (Fig. 20e).

(b) Block B—This block has been constructed keeping one wall of Block A as common instead of independent entity, thus introducing the deficiency of non-separated building unit. The ground floor with random rubble masonry is a wall with zero shear resistance, and the first floor with half-brick masonry is deficient in respect of earthquake resistance. Hence, the jacketing is from ground to first floor with 75 mm thick reinforced cement concrete wall on both inside and outside the building with reinforcement of 8 mm @ 225 mm c/c. The walls of the building, which are inaccessible from outside, were retrofitted with 150 mm thick RCC wall with reinforcement 12 mm @ 300 mm c/c (Fig. 21a, b). The wooden trussed roof was cross-braced to reduce the flexibility of the diaphragms and, thus, reduces excessive displacement; however, the chimneys were not removed (Fig. 21).

(c) Block C—This composite block with the ground floor constructed having dressed stone and half-brick masonry and first floor with half-brick masonry was deficient in-plane shear and out-of-plane bending. The jacketing of deficient piers and replacement of half brick with full masonry were carried out. In case of first floor with half-brick masonry, jacketing from outside was not possible; hence, 150 mm thick RCC wall with reinforcement 12 mm @ 300 mm c/c was proposed and carried out. During earthquake, the RCC wall will resist the applied in-plane shear and out of plane bending; however, there is every possibility of half-brick wall collapsing; to prevent sudden failure, jacketing with wire mesh from outside was proposed and carried out.

5 Issues in Retrofitting

1. Though L-shape buildings are more prone to earthquake damages due to irregular configuration, they can be transformed into two independent rectangular blocks using separation joint. However, separation of existing L-shape building into simple blocks is not possible, and this deficiency will persist even after retrofitting.
2. Although chipping of walls is carried out before the jacketing of the wall; however, binding of new concrete with old plaster is an issue of concern.
3. Jacketing of RCC column and beam with reinforcement and concrete requires breaking and reconstruction of wall. Such activity leads to weakening of infill and apparently reduced stiffness.
4. To achieve absolute strengthening and retrofitting of the building structures, codal guidelines are always an issue due to lack of funds.

6 Conclusions

1. The deficiencies in the masonry buildings are due to inappropriate knowledge with the grass root construction workers.
2. The buildings with random rubble masonry can be retrofitted without hampering the functionality of the building.
3. The demolition of building can be avoided, and the structures can be upgraded keeping in sight that every department does not have excessive fund to create a new structure every time.
4. The imposed fund limitations limit the retrofitting to the extent required.
5. The hill state has their own constraints of material transport and availability of experienced workers for achieving efficient retrofitting work.

Acknowledgements The authors would like to thank Temasek Foundation Singapore for providing funds for carrying out retrofitting of schools, Prof. Yogendra Singh, Dept. of Earthquake Engineering, IIT Roorkee, for involving NIT Hamirpur and imparting the learning for strengthening and retrofitting of schools and SEED India for giving the consultancy work to NIT Hamirpur for providing design consultancy.

References

1. NDMA (2019) Earthquake disaster risk index report, National Disaster Management Authority Ministry of Home Affair, Govt .of India, New Delhi
2. Economic and Statistics Department (2014) Economic survey of Himachal Pradesh, Shimla. Govt. of Himachal Pradesh
3. Kapur A (2013) Sarva Shiksha Abhiyan, budget brief 8(1), accountability initiative, centre for policy research, New Delhi

4. Sikdar S, Singh B (2017) A study of financing public education in India. National Coalition for education
5. NDMA, National Disaster Management Authority School Safety Guidelines, National Disaster Management Authority, Ministry of Home Affair, Govt .of India, New Delhi (2016)
6. Arya AS, Padmanabhan G, Karanth A (2004) School safety, National Disaster Management Authority Ministry of Home Affair, Govt .of India, New Delhi
7. NDMA (2013) School safety projects (SSP), National Disaster Management Authority Ministry of Home Affair, Govt .of India, New Delhi
8. HPSDMA (2011) Himachal Pradesh State Policy on Disaster Management, Himachal Pradesh State Disaster Management Authority, Shimla
9. Rodgers JE (2012) Why schools are vulnerable to earthquakes, 15th WCEE Liboa, Portugal
10. Revenue L White paper on the high intensity earthquake, land revenue and Disaster Management Department, Gangtok
11. Thiruvengadam V, Wason JC (1992) Performance of buildings duiring Bihar Nepal earthquake. In: 10th world conference on earthquake engineering, pp 67–72
12. Vinayak HK (2012) Development of State specific guidelines for earthquake Safe construction. National Institute of Technology Hamirpur
13. Vinayak HK (2015) Development of State specific guidelines and model design for schools. National Institute of Technology Hamirpur
14. Vinayak HK (2017) Developing upgraded models of school structures in rural areas through existing innovative developed concepts. NIT Hamirpur
15. Vinayak HK (2019) Layout optimization of trusses using improved GA methodologies. NIT Hamirpur
16. IS: 1893 (2002), Criteria for earthquake resistant design 5th rev., Bureau of Indian Standard, New Delhi
17. IS 13920, Ductile detailing of reinforced concrete structures subjected to seismic forces—code of practice. Bureau of Indian Standards, New Delhi
18. IS 13828:1993, Improving earthquake resistance of low strength masonry buildings—guidelines. Bureau of Indian Standards, New Delhi (1993)
19. Borri A, Castori G, Corradi M (2013) Masonry confinement using steel cords. J Mater Civil Eng 25:1910–1919
20. Valluzzi MR, Cardani G, Binda L, Modena C (2004) Seismic vulnerability methods for masonry buildings in historical centres : validation and application for prediction analyses and intervention proposals, 13th WCEE, 2765
21. Asteris PG, Giannopoulos IP (2012) Vulnerability and restoration assessment of masonry structural systems. Electron J Struct Eng 12(1):82–94
22. Parisi F, Augenti N (2012) Uncertainty in seismic capacity of masonry buildings. Buildings 2(3):218–230
23. Agarwal P, Shrikhande M (2010) Earthquake resistant design of structures, PHI Learning Pvt. Ltd, New Delhi
24. HPSDMA (2019) Earthquake hazard profile of the state. Himachal Pradesh State Disaster Management Authority, Shimla
25. Chandel VBS, Brar KK (2010) Seismicity and vulnerability in Himalayas: the case of Himachal Pradesh, India, Geomatics. Nat Hazards Risk 1(1):69–84
26. Vicente R, Rodrigues H, Varum H, Mendes da Silva JAR (2011) Evaluation of strengthening techniques of traditional masonry buildings: case study of a four-building aggregate. J Perform Constr Facil 25(3):202–216
27. Bhattacharya S, Nayak S, Dutta SC (2014) A critical review of retrofitting methods for unreinforced masonry structures. Int J Disaster Risk Reduction 7:51–67
28. Murty CVR (2005) IITK-BMTPC earthquake tips—learning earthquake design and construction, NICEE, IIT Kanpur, India
29. IS. 875 Part 2, Code of practice for design loads (other than earthquake) for buildings and structures. Bureau of Indian Standards, New Delhi (2019)

Seismic Strengthening and Retrofitting Techniques and Solutions for an Existing RC Frame: An Overview

Praveen Anand and Ajay Kumar Sinha

Abstract Seismic performance of any existing reinforced concrete (RC) buildings is greatly influenced by the inadequacies associated with the design, stiffness, existing performance demands, degradation of materials due to aging, due to use over time and several other factors. It has been found that a large number of RC structures lacks the existing seismic demand and clearly reveals an urgent need to upgrade and strengthen this deficiency. A significant amount of investigations has been carried out to strengthen and retrofit the existing RC structures. The outcome of the researches was increased strength, stiffness, and ductility of the retrofitted structures. This article aims to present an overview of different techniques and practices available to strengthen the existing and damaged structures. The paper also presents the research gaps and identifies the scope of future research along with providing outlines for future direction of research in the establishing effective retrofitting solutions.

Keywords RC structures · Strengthening · Retrofitting jacketing · Bracing · FRP

1 Introduction

India is a country highly prone to earthquakes. Many devastating earthquakes had occurred here causing heavy losses of life and property. It is not the earthquakes which brings devastation, but it is the failure of faulty structures which does so. Ever since the devastating earthquakes which occurred in India whether it be the Bihar Nepal earthquake in 1934 or the Bhuj earthquake in Gujarat in 2001, there has been a constant revision and up gradation of seismic codes in India. Keeping in mind statistical records of their occurrence and the probabilities of their reoccurrence, there is a very urgent need of seismic evaluation of the existing RC framed buildings

P. Anand (✉)
Department of Civil Engineering, National Institute of Technology, Bihar, Patna 800005, India
e-mail: praveen.ce16@nitp.ac.in

A. K. Sinha
Department of Civil Engineering, National Institute of Technology, Bihar, Patna 800005, India
e-mail: aksinha@nitp.ac.in

C. Ghosh and S. Kolathayar (eds.), *A System Engineering Approach to Disaster Resilience*, Lecture Notes in Civil Engineering 205, https://doi.org/10.1007/978-981-16-7397-9_38

many of which has been designed for gravity loads and hence assess their seismic performance and accordingly retrofit them to increase their capability of withstanding severe earthquake forces.

Seismic retrofitting and up gradation of structures is an area over which various works and research has been done till now. Due to constant revision and upgradation of seismic design codes, it becomes very necessary in a country like India that there must be detailed assessment of the existing RC framed structures which has been mainly designed on the basis of gravity loads disregarding the effects of earthquake loads. Retrofitting of buildings shall comply with the design criteria and procedures of these standards for achieving the performance-based retrofitting. Retrofitting is one of the most suitable options to make an existing inadequate building safe against future probable earthquakes or other environmental factors.

In this paper, attempt has been made to present an overview and address the innovative, advantageous, and cost-effective retrofitting techniques for different types of existing reinforced concrete structures. The paper presents the researches and findings carried out across the globe on advanced retrofitting and strengthening techniques such as RC jacketing, steel jacketing, FRP jacketing, steel bracing system, and addition of shear walls.

2 Retrofitting Techniques

2.1 RC Jacketing

There are several techniques available for seismic retrofitting. One of the earliest and foremost method of retrofitting of structures is concrete jacketing. In this method, the cross section of column is increased with added reinforcement thus making the columns strong enough to withstand the forces. Concrete jacketing has been proved to be very effective method in seismic retrofitting which helps in the conversion of strong beam weak column into a strong column and weak beam thus inducing the formation of hinges in beams and not in columns during the formation of mechanism [1]. With this strong column weak beam principle, shear capacity of the column also gets enhanced. The fundamental advantage of this technique is that it increases the shear and flexural capacity and is easy to construct. Secondly, a substantial increase in ductility as well as stiffness of the section can be obtained depending upon the amount of reinforcement and type of concrete added in the jacket [2].

In general, it has been seen that column failures have caused significant damage to the RC structure. Studies done over the past earthquake damages, it was found that shear failures, shear cracks, and column shortening were observed in column members. The primary function of jacketing is to increase the load-carrying capacity of the structural elements against lateral loads. In the study conducted by Anand et al. [3], finite element analysis of a RC jacketed column model was carried out by providing 100 mm thick jacket, and a significant increase in the axial load-carrying capacity of the column was observed. Similarly, different researchers have used different thickness of jacket based on their suitability as enough research data is not available that can clearly validate the thickness to be used [4–8]. Another important factor influencing the performance of RC jacket is the interface treatment. Studying the bonding behavior between the existing column and the jacket layer is a critical phenomenon. Till date, enough research has been done to predict the influence of interface treatment, but a clear demonstration of the effect in yet not clearly depicted. The influence of surface preparations, the use of epoxy resins, as well as steel connectors was conducted [9–11]. Post analyzing the test results, they concluded by the use of bonding agents or steel connectors monolithic behavior of jacketed member can be established even without increasing the surface roughness. However, among the method adopted for surface preparation, sand blasting and notched surface were found to be the best treatment to achieve higher bond strength. Despite of the fact that sand blasting and notched surface were effective in achieving a good bond strength, a clear demonstration to predict the behavior is at the interface which is yet to be resolved. Based upon the results of previous studies, proper guidelines should be prepared for interface treatment (Fig. 1).

Fig. 1 RC jacketing of column [8]

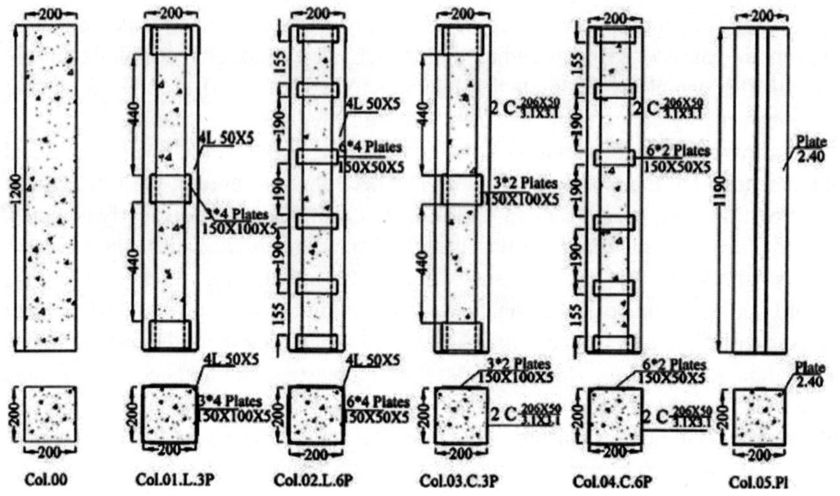

Fig. 2 Specimen configuration details [13]

2.2 *Steel Jacketing*

Steel jacketing refers to a method in which the column section is encased with the steel plates and the gap in between is filled with non-shrink grout. The encasing steel plates may be of full length or partial length of the encased column. Anchor bolts along with end stiffeners are also used to facilitate and simplify the connections. As compared to the other methods of jacketing, steel jacketing offers two most remarkable advantages (1) the amount of transverse reinforcement that can be provided can be increased significantly and (2) the spalling off of the shell concrete can be prevented which is considered to be the main reason for bond deterioration and buckling of longitudinal bars [12]. Behavior of RC columns strengthened with steel jackets was also studied by Belal et al. [13]. Main parameters that were studied included shape of the strengthening system, Size and shape of the batten plates. Seven specimens were constructed which was divided unstrengthened specimen with two units and strengthened specimen with five units as shown in figure. The experimental program was again verified with the finite element modeling in ANSYS which were in good agreement with each other. It was concluded that with the application of steel jacketing technique, load-carrying capacity increased up to 20% and the mode of column failure shifted from brittle to ductile (Figs. 2 and 3).

2.3 *Fiber Reinforced Polymer (FRP) Jacketing*

In the last two decades, due to extensive search for an alternative strengthening system, FRP composites have come out as a reliable material to be used for the

Fig. 3 Strengthened RC column with steel jackets with 3 battens, 6 battens, and complete steel plating [13]

retrofitting objectives. FRP jacketing is considered to be one of the most popular seismic retrofitting methods across the globe. This is because of the multiple advantages associated with it over the existing conventional method such as less labor work, ease and speed of installation, original geometry remains undisturbed, high strength-to-weight ratio, less curing time, significant fatigue strength, minimum disturbance to the occupants during installation. However, FRPs are relatively costly and its fire resistance properties must be addressed. Secondly, there exists an uncertainty regarding the durability of FRPs in their long-term performance. Strengthening of existing RC columns is one of the most common application of FRP as it increases the strength and ductility. While using FRP sheets for strengthening purposes, prime considerations include preparation of surface for existing concrete, anchorage of FRP sheets, numbers of FRP layers and their orientation. In order to apply FRP laminates, the surface should be made free from dust and oil, the resin should be applied uniformly to the prepared surface and entrapped air shall be removed before the resin sets (Fig. 4).

To analyze the effect of increasing the number of layers several researchers performed experimental analysis to study the behavior of axially loaded square and rectangular column confined by glass fiber reinforced polymer (GFRP) wrapping using different numbers of GFRP layers [15]. For increased number of layers of GFRP, better confinement was achieved which resulted in improvement of axial load-carrying capacity of the reinforced concrete column, and the ductility of columns was also improved. The increase in load-carrying capacity of a RC column with single layer of GFRP wrapping with rounded corners was studied by Anand et al. [16]. Finite element analysis was done using ABAQUS software where the ends of

(a) Preparation of surface (b) Putty application

(c) Layering of coated sheets (d) Removal of entrapped air

Fig. 4 Installation of FRP sheets procedure [14]

column to be retrofitted was rounded. It was concluded that rounded corner FRP jacket is able to provide better confinement to the concrete.

2.4 Steel Bracing

Steel bracing is highly efficient and economical method of retrofitting, and it has been seen that this method can resist the horizontal forces in a framed structure. The seismic performance of the building gets improved with the bracing as the lateral stiffness gets enhanced. This method of strengthening of existing structures is applicable for both steel as well as concrete structures. Similar to the other methods, bracing also has several advantages such as enhancing the strength, stiffness and ductility, low cost and time of installment, less increase in dead load as compared to other methods (Fig. 5).

Seismic retrofit of RC frames with steel bracings was first introduced by Sugano [18]. Several analytical and conceptual studies regarding bracing was done by Baduox et al. [17]. In their study, frames with short and weak column were studied, and it was found that bracing can be used to specifically target the strength and stiffness deficiencies, but inelastic buckling of braces should be avoided. Analytical study was carried out based upon the previous experimental research in which an RC frame was retrofitted with steel bracing system. The modeled frame shows how the axial load

Fig. 5 Steel braced building [17]

P coming from top on the column gets distributed among the two braces B1 and B2, thus reducing the tendency of column failure as shown in Fig. 1. P being the vertical load and H is the horizontal load. Effectiveness of seismic retrofitting comprising buckling restrained braces placed along the perimeter of the multistoried frame was studied by Sarno et al. [19]. Seismic performance of existing and retrofitted five-story RC structure was evaluated by Dwaik et al. [20] implementing two retrofitting techniques viz RC jacketing and eccentric steel bracing. Structural response was evaluated using static nonlinear and dynamic analysis in SAP2000. It was concluded that steel bracing turns out to be improved choice for retrofitting of medium height buildings (Fig. 6).

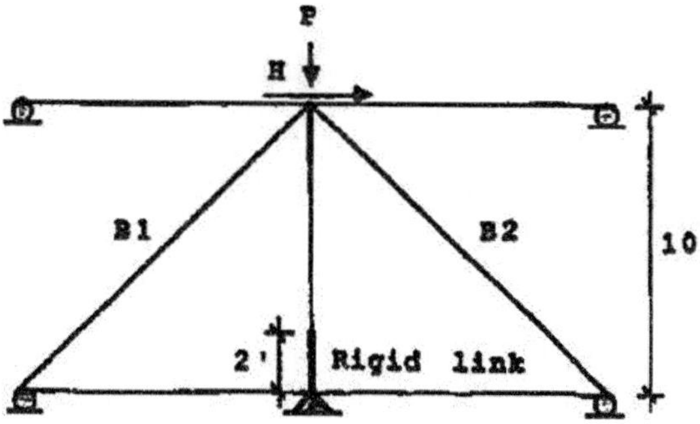

Fig. 6 Forces acting on a brace frame [17]

2.5 Addition of Shear Walls

In order to increase the stiffness and lateral strength requirement of building, shear walls can be provided which has proven to be quite effective in controlling the inter-story drift reducing the forces on columns, etc. Shear walls are generally placed between two columns, and they are rectangular in cross section. Columns on two sides of shear walls behave as two boundary elements which significantly increases the strength of wall in flexure and shear. Application of shear walls involves removal of existing partition walls and replaces with shear walls instead [21]. With such application, shear walls are able to withstand lateral loads along with reduction in building displacement as a result RC frames has to resist less amount of lateral loads. In order to examine the effectiveness of shear walls, finite element analysis was carried out by Ismael et al. [22] in which a three-story residential RC building was selected for response against earthquakes. SAP2000 was used for the analysis, and the building was subjected to wind load, seismic load along with gravity load. The building was reanalyzed for the aforementioned load combination with the addition of 5 mm, 7 mm, and 10 mm thick shear walls. It was observed that the moment in beams and columns were reduced considerably, thus reducing the seismic vulnerability of the building.

Wall section may fail in flexural tension or flexural compression. In order to prevent a brittle failure by sudden fracture of tension reinforcement the cracked flexural strength of the wall section shall be greater than its uncracked flexural strength. As the wall is subjected to gradual increase in moment, initially it behaves as an uncracked plane concrete section till the cracking moment is reached. On further increase in moment, the reinforcement alone resists all the tension. Walls not having boundary elements of increased thickness, vertical reinforcement shall be concentrated at the ends of the walls for better flexural strength.

3 Conclusion

The survey offered in this article focused on the different experimental as well as analytical programs with innovative seismic techniques available. Due to the updated design manuals and code of practice, urgency for retrofitting of seismically deficient structures has come out as a definite requirement. From the review presented in this paper, it can be clearly observed that each of the retrofitting techniques was able to enhance the strength of the existing structure. Similarly, each technique contributed in enhancing the stiffness and ductility. In addition to increasing the overall capacity of the existing buildings, these retrofitting techniques also contribute to sustainability. However, each method has its own advantages and disadvantages associated with it. Therefore, prior to application of any of these techniques, proper assessment of the current state of the existing structure is essential. All the techniques mentioned above relies on the experiments done by various researchers. Therefore, appropriate guidelines should be prepared in the form of codal provisions to apply these techniques reliably.

References

1. Rodriguez M, Park R (1994) Seismic load tests on reinforced concrete columns strengthened by jacketing. Struct. J. 91(2):150–159
2. Vaghani MV, Vasanwala SA, Desai AK (2014) Advanced retrofitting techniques for RC building: a state of an art review. Int. J. Curr. Eng. Technol. 4(2):579–584
3. Anand P, Sinha AK (2020) Effect of reinforced concrete jacketing on axial load capacity of reinforced concrete column. Civil Eng. J. 6(7):1266–1272
4. Alcocer SM (1993) RC frame connections rehabilitated by jacketing. J Struct Eng 119(5):1413–1431
5. Julio ES, Branco F, Silva VD (2003) Structural rehabilitation of columns with reinforced concrete jacketing. Prog Struct Mat Eng 5(1):29–37
6. Vandoros KG, Dritsos SE (2008) Concrete jacket construction detail effectiveness when strengthening RC columns. Constr Build Mater 22(3):264–276
7. Lampropoulos AP, Dritsos SE (2011) Modeling of RC columns strengthened with RC jackets. Earthq Eng Struct Dyn 40(15):1689
8. Kaliyaperumal G, Sengupta AK (2009) Seismic retrofit of columns in buildings for flexure using concrete jacket. ISET J Earthq Technol 46(2):77–107
9. Beushausen H, Alexander MG (2008) Bond strength development between concretes of different ages. Mag Concr Res 60(1):65–74
10. Clímaco JDS, Regan PE (2001) Evaluation of bond strength between old and new concrete in structural repairs. Mag Concr Res 53(6):377–390
11. Júlio ENBS, Branco FA (2008) Reinforced concrete jacketing-interface influence on cyclic loading response. ACI Struct J 105(4):471
12. Sakino K, Sun Y (2000) Steel jacketing for improvement of column strength and ductility. In: Proceeding of 12th WCEE conference Jan 2000
13. Belal MF, Mohamed HM, Morad SA (2015) Behavior of reinforced concrete columns strengthened by steel jacket. HBRC J 11(2):201–212
14. Handbook on Seismic Retrofit of Buildings (2007), Central Public Works Department & Indian Building Congress with IIT Madras
15. Kumutha R, Vaidyanathan R, Palanichamy MS (2007) Behaviour of reinforced concrete rectangular columns strengthened using GFRP. Cement Concr Compos 29(8):609–615
16. Anand P, Sinha AK (2020) Strengthening of reinforced concrete column by glass fiber reinforced polymer jacketing technique. Int. J. Adv. Res. Eng. Technol. 11(7):686–696
17. Badoux M, Jirsa JO (1990) Steel bracing of RC frames for seismic retrofitting. J Struct Eng 116(1):55–74
18. Sugano S (1981) Seismic strengthening of existing reinforced concrete buildings in Japan. Bull N Z Natl Soc Earthq Eng 14(4)
19. Di Sarno L, Manfredi G (2010) Seismic retrofitting with buckling restrained braces: application to an existing non-ductile RC framed building. Soil Dyn Earthq Eng 30(11):1279–1297
20. Al-Dwaik MM, Armouti NS (2013) Analytical case study of seismic performance of retrofit strategies for reinforced concrete frames: steel bracing with shear links versus column jacketing. Jordan J Civil Eng 159(701):1–18
21. Kaplan H, Yılmaz S (2012) Seismic strengthening of reinforced concrete buildings. In: Earthquake-resistant structures-design, assessment and rehabilitation, pp. 407–428
22. MA I, AE H (2013) Seismic retrofitting of a RC building by adding steel plate shear walls. IOSR J Mech Civil Eng (IOSR-JMCE) 7(2):49–62

Integrated Site Investigation Procedure (ISIP) for Managing Infrastructure Development

Rohayu Che Omar, Hairin Taha, Intan Nor Zuliana Baharuddin, Badariah Solemon, Rasyikin Roslan, Warishah Abdul Wahab, Mohd Muzad Fared, and Wan Nor Syazwani Wan Hashim

Abstract A new approach for landslide risk management and evaluation is presented in this paper as an Integrated Site Investigation Procedure (ISIP) and Landslide Maintenance Management by the application of the Geographic Information System (GIS). This latest technique would identify and generate land zoning for incorporation into the Malaysian Land Planning System for construction approval. ISIP can help develop cost-effective approaches for subsurface studies, site planning, sampling methods, data analysis, simulation prediction, and mitigation strategies for the particular areas. Non-technical decision-makers are often required to help determine the condition before taking necessary technological steps. The main objective of the research was to analyze, improve and evaluate desk studies and mapping methods that would allow fast and accurate landslide evaluations to be exercised from national to site-specific for the management of infrastructure planning. The suggested methods for risk identification and evaluation in this paper would promote risk determination by a potential empirical study of landslide hazards using a case study carried out in the district of Jeli, Kelantan, Malaysia. This latest approach is useful for the evaluation of landslide hazards for land suitability requirements, particularly in Malaysia.

Keywords Risk analysis · Landslide · Methodology · And System

1 Introduction

Environmental catastrophe is a common problem in many areas worldwide where citizens and the environment are in dispute. The susceptibility of the populated

R. C. Omar · H. Taha (✉) · I. N. Z. Baharuddin · B. Solemon · R. Roslan · W. A. Wahab
Institute of Energy Infrastructure, Universiti Tenaga Nasional, Kajang, Malaysia
e-mail: hairin@uniten.edu.my

R. C. Omar
e-mail: rohayu@uniten.edu.my

M. M. Fared · W. N. S. W. Hashim
Grid Maintenance Department, Grid Division, TNB, Kuala Lumpur, Malaysia

C. Ghosh and S. Kolathayar (eds.), *A System Engineering Approach to Disaster Resilience*, Lecture Notes in Civil Engineering 205, https://doi.org/10.1007/978-981-16-7397-9_39

regions to natural disasters is partly contributed by a series of decades of spatial planning policies that failed to consider adequate account of geo-risks in making decisions land of use planning and development. Therefore, it is important to establish more effective methodologies for integrating the reduction of natural disasters into spatial planning, particularly from national to site-specific. This paper discusses the strategies for tackling geohazard risk management in Malaysia by integrating the Strategy, Planning and Development Program by Integrated Site Investigation Procedure (ISIP) and Slope Management by incorporation of the Geographic Information System (GIS) and satellite imagery. Site Inspection Protocol (ISIP) and Slope Control through the application of the Geographic Information System (GIS) and the Virtual Reality (VR) Technology were used as a method procedure to collect all data and resources that include geohazard risk map. This will assist in the implementation of cost-effective approaches that can mitigate measures for the particular location.

1.1 Integrated Site Investigation Procedure (ISIP)

Integrated Site Investigation Procedure (ISIP) was developed in the context of the Basic Law for Physical Planning in Malaysia [1–10]. The development process was initiated by the Town and Country Planning Act 1976 (A172), which stipulates two approval phases, i.e., the Structure Plan (Sect. 7(3)) and the Local Plan (Sect. 12). Construction management and the consent process require consultancy and advice from multiple relevant bodies before land transfer authorization or the planning authorization [Act A172 Sects. 18 and 19(1)]. Development may occur only after Sect. 22 authorization or extension, following Sect. 24(3). The Town and Country Planning Department (TCPD), the Public Works Department (PWD), the Drainage and Irrigation Department (DID) and the Water Works Department (WWD) shall all coordinate local governments until approved. Legislation A133 was used to approve design during the management planning process. The reporting requirements, plan deposit, and construction and job inspection information was also included. Regulations require the local government to enact and enforce the Building Regulation. The primary objective of ordinance A133 is to ensure that people in or around buildings, buildings, or structures that may be affected have a reasonable level of health and safety. In terms of soil engineering, the central legislation governs the 1992 Earthworks By-Laws in which Erosion and Sedimentation are subject to Sect. 2(6)(a); Sect. 2(6)(e)(ix) slope stabilization; Sects. 2(8)(9), 2(12) and 2(11) provide the framework, and structural completeness set out in Sect. 85A of the A133 Act. By-Laws 1992 [3], Sects. 4(70(a)) & 4(70(b)) of Act A133 emphasize the need for inclusion of site and soil inspection as factors for geohazard risk assessment. No specific site inspections are, however, made, such as the type of investigation provided and the scope of the site research. Section 2(8) and Sect. 4 of Earthworks By-Laws 1992 currently only recommend detailed inspections of the site for piling status, end bearing load capacities; piling based on the unique surface characteristics. Some details are overlooked, including the vulnerability of each implementing partner to land erosion and landslide during development, and the level of detail required for earthworks to increase.

1.2 Integrated Site Investigation Procedure

In the course of the construction process, two modes of site investigation were incorporated which are the physical and resource planning site investigation (Fig. 1) and the construction site investigation (Fig. 2). The convergence mechanism of these two forms of site investigation would be a positive step to ensure that all information is handled and used accordingly to the legal framework and in the planning process of Malaysia integration. The process of integration is illustrated in Fig. 3. The integration process between the physical and resource planning development (Fig. 1) and the engineering construction site investigation (Fig. 2) provides a framework for the integrated site investigation. The Integrated Site Investigation Procedure (ISIP) comprised of accumulated general information and it becomes more detailed as shown in Fig. 4. Integrated site investigation procedures are divided into three different categories such as planning the site investigation, urban development investigation, and specialized investigation and mitigation. Each type of inquiry is unique, and the scope and detail of the proposed work are specified to minimize the possibility of misunderstanding between planners, engineers, geologists, developers, and decision-makers [11].

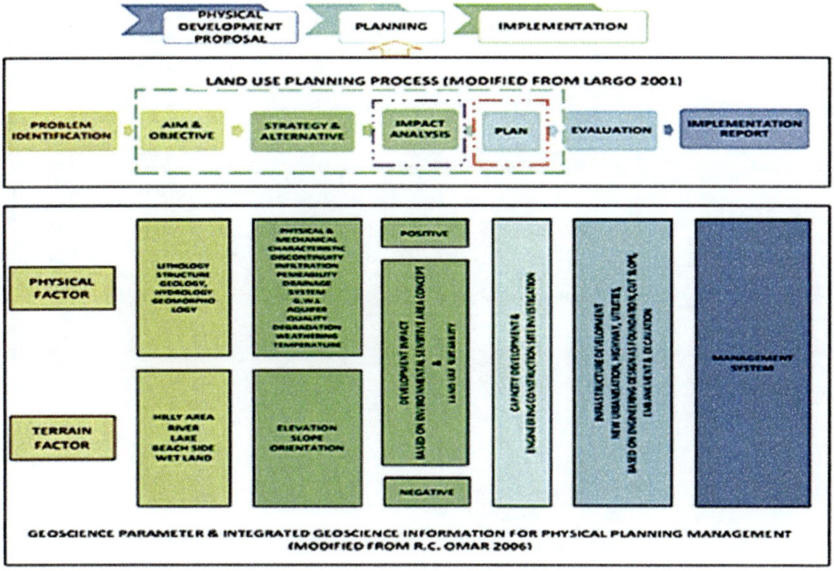

Fig.1 Site investigation for physical development planning [11]

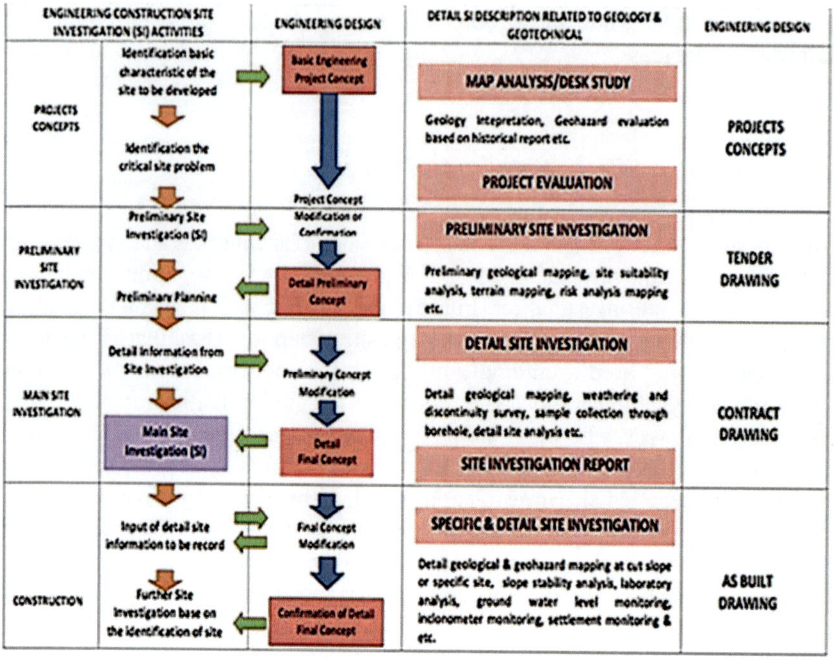

Fig.2 Engineering construction SI (Adapted from [11–14]

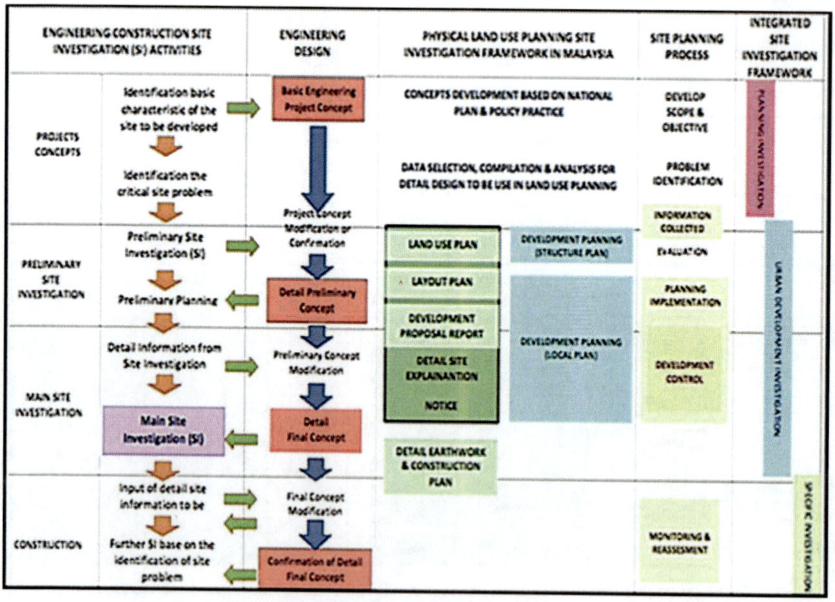

Fig. 3 Integration process from Figs. 1 and 2 [11–14]

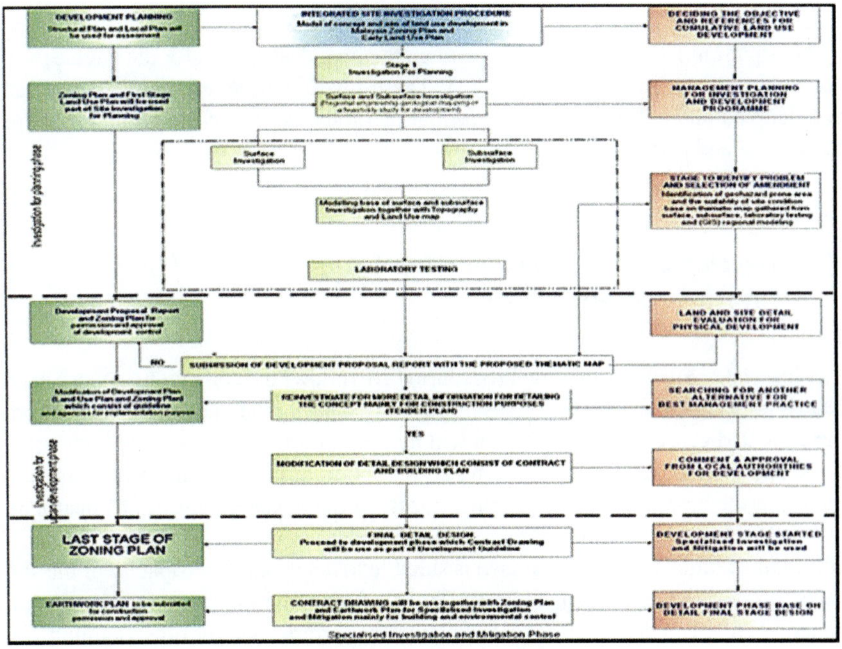

Fig. 4 Integrated Site Investigation Procedure [11–14]

The planning investigation provides comprehensive details on the geotechnical conditions of the site (Fig. 4). The planning investigation is the first stage in the assessment of a specific area for town planning purposes consisting of regional engineering geological mapping or feasibility study for the development of a particular site where information from local engineering geological mapping is not available [11–14]. This assessment is essential for the investigation of large areas specifically more than 1000 ha. The planning investigation consists of the planning of the future development of the urban regions, the assessment of the natural resources of areas intended for future growth, the conservation, and prevention of the natural resources, and the identification of geological problems at an early phase of the planned development for the environmental impact assessment of urban areas. Data from the first stage procedure are used to determine and formulate the objectives and references to cumulative land-use development [1, 11]. Investigation for urban development is required for an area of more than 10,000 ha in size. The evaluation of the planning investigation is used to assess the feasibility of using the site for urban development. The objective of this investigation is to identify and map the detailed engineering of the geological and geotechnical conditions of the terrain to define the regions of geotechnical constraint, as well as the implementation of development control and approval by local authorities [11–13]. The urban development investigation is further subdivided into two types, based on the size of the area considered, as the approach and execution of the geological and geotechnical engineering investigation of small regions differ significantly from that of larger areas. Specialized site investigation and mitigation (Fig. 4) generally depend on the final design plan for the engineering construction site investigation [11–14]. These investigations are more specialized and detailed and will provide full information on the design of the ground base for the zoning and earthwork plan.

1.3 Development of Thematic Map Using Integrated Site Investigation Procedure

The Integrated Site Investigation Procedure (ISIP) allows the collection of geoscience details to be considered at all stages of planning. During the planning investigation, the collected geoscience information will be used to formulate priorities and objectives, and also to define site issues based on optimum land use and environmental quality protection, which is the critical thrust in the development of physical land use in Malaysia [1]. At this stage, geoscience data is used to determine the suitability of the site. The map produced is suitable to determine the capacity of the site based on development needs [15–18]. Types of thematic maps produced by using general geological data such as rock, soil, weather profile, and rock discontinuity are tabulated in Table 1.

Overlaying various geoscience parameters can generate map varieties intended to assist developers in the determination of construction suitability and capacity that is incorporated into the zoning plan. The maps generated at this point are used as a criterion for planning guidance. Geoscience parameters such as rock type, topography, slope, elevation, and degradation can produce a detailed land classification map, as shown in Table 1. Geohazard potential risk map can be created from the integration of general geological information, topographic and geological profiles with physical and mechanical properties using a classification based on environmentally sensitive areas concepts as stated in Act 172. The geohazard potential risk map provides useful information in the development proposal report for obtaining development approval. The data acquired from the investigation of the urban development site (Planning Stage and the Specialized Investigation & Mitigation) for the redevelopment or development of new townships can be used as a guide for structural plans, local development plans, and reporting layouts.

1.4 Thematic Maps in Physical Development Plan

Integrating thematic maps into the planning process helps local governments develop and implement strategies in order to reduce the risks from multiple natural hazards [15–20]. Planning may also combine mitigation with development and growth management programs to establish integrated approaches that efficiently address

Table 1 Geoscience information parameter for thematic map using ISIS [11–13]

Geoscience parameter	Integrated site investigation		
	Investigation for planning	Investigation for urban development	Specialized investigation and mitigation
Rock type *Soil type* *Weathering* *Discontinuity data*	·Basic map ·Site suitability map ·Engineering geology map ·BH point map ·Site constraint map ·Construction material map ·Rock head map	·Bedrock thickness Map ·Weathering thickness Map ·Transported Soil Thickness Map ·Reclamation Map ·Site Map ·Foundation Map ·Slope Stability Map ·Site Contamination Map ·Erosion Potential Map ·Wetland Conservation and Constraint Planning Map ·Detail Geotechnical Classification Map ·Detail Site Constraint Map	
Geomorphology *Topography* *Slope* *Elevation*	·Topography map ·Isopach elevation map ·Terrain Classification Map ·Landform map	·Detail Terrain Classification Map ·Detail Engineering Geological Map	
Physical properties *Mechanical properties* *Degradation*	·Historical Geohazard Map	·Geohazard Potential Risk Map	

natural hazard mitigation and prevent competing outcomes, such as high-density urban development in a hazard-prone region. Planning can also target and mitigate the identified vulnerabilities as posing the highest risk to a proposed development area or redevelopment area. Integrating thematic maps into the land-use planning process is a step towards reducing risk by mitigating natural hazards. During initial land use, decision-making and construction are much simpler and more cost-effective than having to retrofit, change or upgrade existing infrastructure to withstand risks.

1.5 Example of Integrated Site Investigation Procedure

In this paper, a sample of geological information obtained from Jeli, Kelantan was analyzed to produce different types of thematic maps using the Integrated Site Investigation Procedure in the Geographic Information System (GIS) platform as tabulated in Table 2. Topography, slope, and geomorphology as shown in Figs. 5 and 6 were analyzed using investigation for planning to form Terrain Classification Maps as illustrated in Fig. 7. This example was used to provide information in an inquiry for planning (for large areas, typically greater than 10,000 ha), investigation for urban

Table 2 Thematic map from ISIS in physical development plan [11–14]

Malaysia physical planning process		
Current practice	Proposed implementation to include thematic maps from integrated site investigation	
National Physical Plan (Record Geohazard Event)	Geohazard ESA Site Identification	
State structure plan (Geohazard general risk map)	Geohazard that has occurred Overall Geohazard Area Determine Special Risk Area (areas identified as Special Area Plan for Risk Disaster	Basic Map DEM Map Engineering Geology Map Terrain Classification Maps Site Constraint Map Historical Geohazard Map
Local plan and special area plan (Geohazard strategic risk plan)	Geohazard Risk Area disasters follow specific risk levels Type of development that suitable for Geohazard Area Geohazard risk area that not suitable to develop	Slope Stability Map Erosion Potential Map Detail Geotechnical Classification Map Site Suitability Map Detail Terrain Classification Map Geohazard Potential Risk Map
Planning permission brief (Geohazard risk evaluation)	Identify methods to control specific Geo Hazard Identify activities that suitable in a particular area	Activities for control Geohazard based on Potential Risk Map

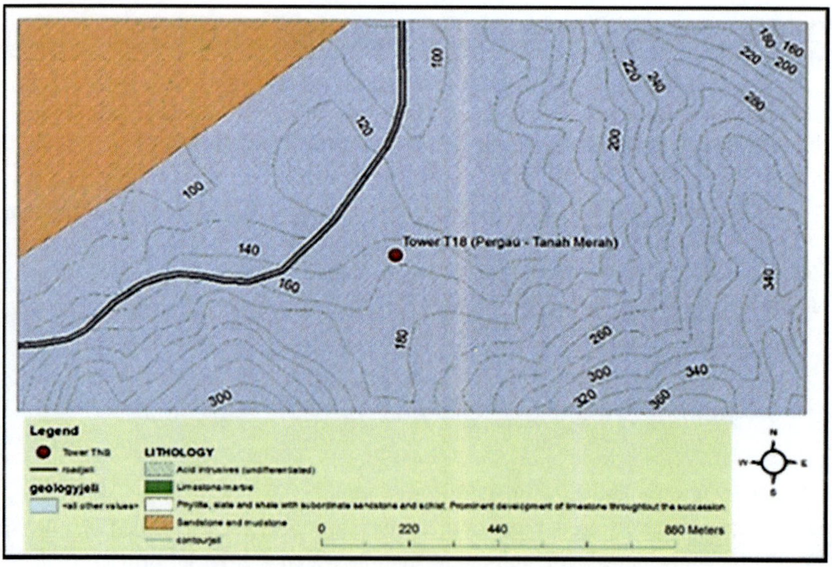

Fig. 5 Topographic map of Pergau, Tanah Merah, Jeli

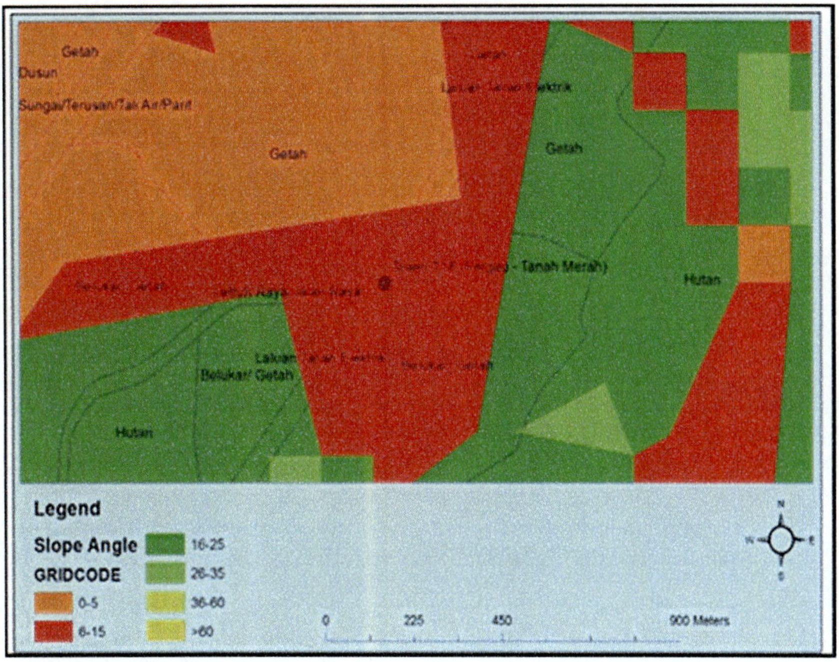

Fig. 6 Slope map for Jeli, Kelantan

development (an area more a less than 10,000 ha in size), and specialized investigation and mitigation (site-specific and more detail typically represent for less than 5000 ha).

Terrain Classification Map (Fig. 7) was used in the State Structural Plan for determining particular risk areas, geohazards that have occurred, and overall geohazard area. Terrain Classification Map consists of four criteria:

Zone 1 Very Low-Risk Level; Terrain in-situ hills slope angle from >15°

Zone 2 Low-Risk Level; Terrain in-situ—slope 15–35° with existing signs of erosion together with geological sensitive material or colluviums at the foot slope. The label (1lm1,2Hg2, 2E31, 3B31, 3D21) indicated that minor sheet erosions have occurred at these areas based on the slope gradient at foot slope or drainage slope.

Zone 3 Moderate Risk Level; Terrain in-situ slope from 25 to 35° without erosion sign and terrain in-situ-slope 15–25° with existing signs of erosion of sensitive geological material or colluviums. The classification is depicted as 4A21 in Fig. 7.

Zone 4 Terrain in-situ—slope > 35° with existing signs of erosion; terrain in-situ-slope 25–35° with existing signs of deterioration of sensitive geological material or colluviums.

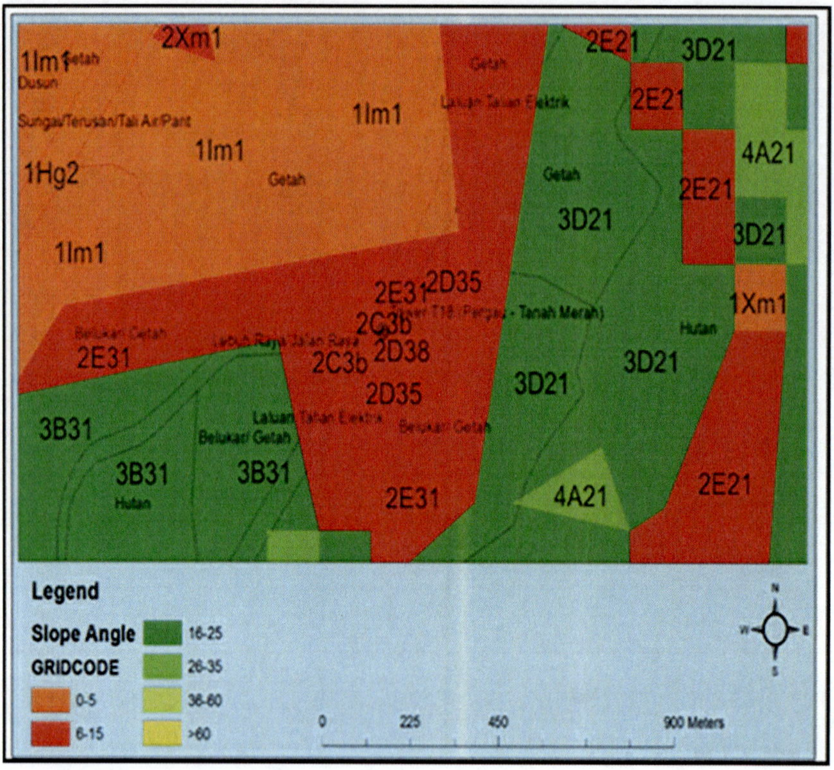

Fig. 7 Geological Terrain Classification Map of Jeli

Three zones were identified in the study site, marked as Zone 1, Zone 2, and Zone 3. Zone 2 was classified as 1lm1, 2Hg2, 2E31, 3B31, and 3D21, indicating that the site has a natural slope comprising of soil and rock material of which minor sheet erosion has occurred at foot slope or drainage slope. Zone 3, located mostly at hillcrest was covered by soil with little sheet erosion. Terrain classification map and topographic map overlay were translated to form the suitability maps using Investigation for Urban Planning which can be incorporated in the local plan. Zone 1 and Zone 2, less than 300 m in Jeli (Fig. 5) can be developed whereas Zone 1 and Zone 2 exceeding 300 m can be considered as tourism park areas. Zone 3 with the slope angle less than 20° and the site to be developed in this zone less than 20% can be constructed after the agreement with mountainous technical committee. However, 80% of the area in Zone 3 needs to be considered as the green zone. The suitability classification related to the development of a zoning plan based on criteria type of development that is suitable for geohazard area is compiled in Table 2.

Information gathered through Integrated Site Investigation Procedure such as landslide history (Fig. 8) overlaid with a topographical map, geological map, soil map, and terrain to produce Jeli Landslide Hazard Map is shown in Fig. 9. Jeli

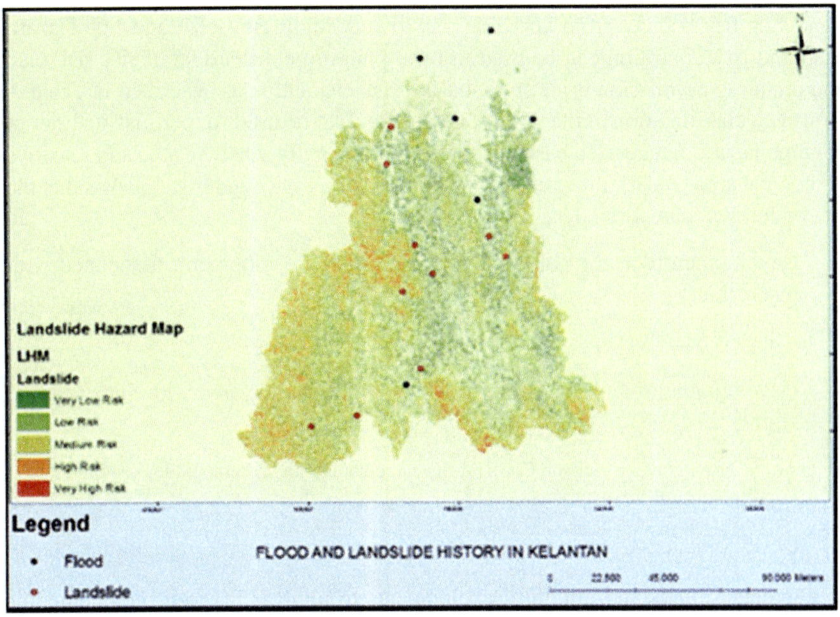

Fig.8 Landslide and flood historical map

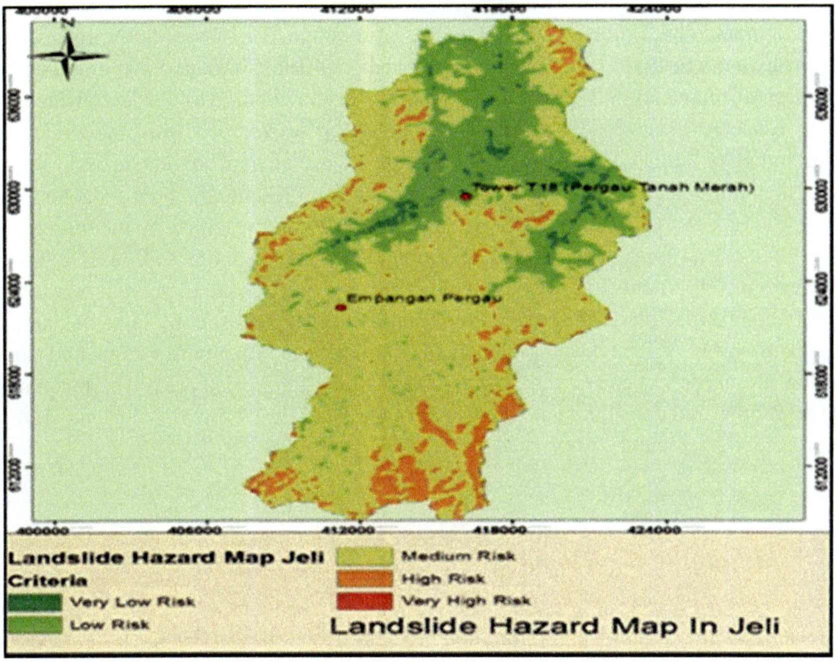

Fig.9 Jeli landslide potential risk map

Landslide Risk ranges from very low risk to very high risk. Jeli Landslide Hazard Map and risk condition can be used in local plan or geohazard strategies risk plan and planning permission brief or geohazard risk evaluation as described in Table 2. However, classification of the development criteria to be used for permission brief or zoning map are categorized based on the environmentally sensitive area and sensitive geological area [8–14]. Integrating information from Fig. 7 and Fig. 8 shows that the site of Jeli was categorized as:

a. Development category of Areas of Controlled Development: associated with Insensible

and Slightly Sensitive terrain or Class I and Class II terrain.

b. Development of Non-or Minimize development: associated with Sensitive and Highly

Sensitive terrain or Class III and Class IV. Special guidance and administration required for the development of these terrains.

c. Development can enhance socio-economic activities such as agriculture, quarry

aggregates, and sand mining. Developments to improve socio-economic conditions should be carried out and monitored once they are in operation

Development category was divided based on the zoning concepts described in Act 172 and Fig. 9. Jeli areas were categorized into three zones, namely restricted development zone, buffer zone, and conservation zone. The information translated from the thematic maps (Fig. 9) is briefly described in Table 3. Zone 1 is the area with an insensitive and slightly sensitive range from very low risk to low risk, considered as a restricted development zone. This zone can be developed from moderate to high intensity but needs to be regulated because these areas were considered as the area that can enhance the socio-economic. Zone 1 represents the area indicated as very low risk to low risk as shown in Fig. 9. Zone 2 is represented by medium risk area category as areas of controlled development (Fig. 9). Zone 2 is allowed to have intensity development from moderate to high with a buffer zone to prevent this zone from geohazard. Zone 3 is considered as moderate risk represent by high-risk area, as shown in Fig. 9. The development needs to minimize with a buffer zone, and part of the site needs to be reserved. Zone 4 is a restricted high-risk area, which cannot be developed and considered as a conservation area. Figure 9 shows a very high risk, represented by Zone 4.

1.6 Managing Development on Zone 2 and Zone 3

Specialized Investigation and mitigation procedure as shown in Fig. 4, was extended by integrating geoscience information in order to comply with guidelines of development as tabulated in Table 3. Specialized investigation and mitigation procedure as shown in Fig. 10, was formulated based on the integration of site investigation for

Table 3 Zoning based on Jeli landslide risk map [11, 13, 16]

Malaysia physical planning process			
Land suitability Restriction	Development Risk	Guideline of development	Development intensity
CLASS I *Insensitive* *Very low risk- Low risk*	Lower risk (low site investigation cost)	Areas of controlled development and development, which can enhance the socio-economic (Restricted development zone)	Intensity from moderate to high
CLASS II *Slightly sensitive medium Risk*	Slightly moderate risk (high site investigation cost)	Areas of controlled development (Restricted development zone and Buffer Zone)	Intensity from moderate to high
CLASS III *Sensitive* *High risk*	Moderate Risk (high site investigation cost)	Development of non-or minimize development (Buffer and conservation zone)	Intensity from moderate to high
CLASS IV *Highly sensitive* *Very high risk*	Highly Risk (extreme site investiga-tion costs)	Development of Non-or Minimize development (Conservation zone)	Intensity low (Green area, recreational area)

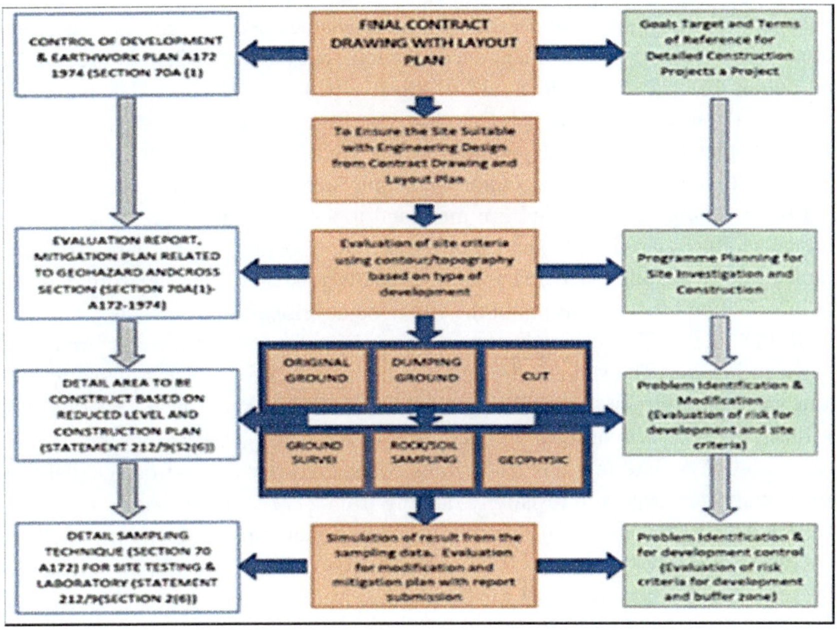

Fig. 10 Specialized investigation and mitigation procedure

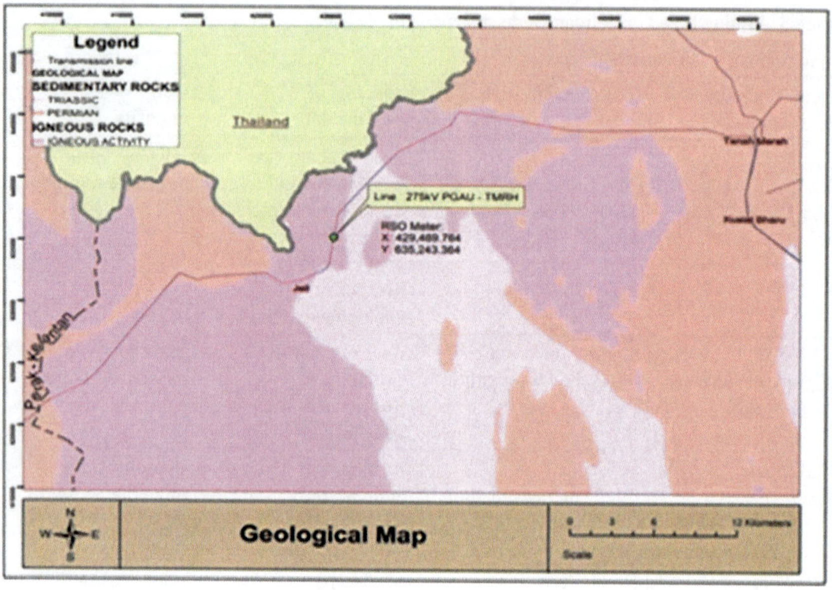

Fig.11 Study area and location of T18 [21]

construction and engineering design with policy named as, the control of development related to earthwork as mentioned in Sect. 70A (1) in A172 1974, Sect. 2(1) and details from a statement in 212/91 (Sect. 2(6)), 212/91 (Sect. 2(8)), 212/91 (Sect. 2(9)) and P.W.5178/85 [3]. Data analysis from satellite imagery and combination of spatial data from the geological map, land-use map, and topography map were used to interpret the best location for geophysics mapping [15–18]. Integration data from geological map, land-use map, and topography map were translated as surface geology map (Fig. 11) and geological cross-section (Fig. 12). Cross-section map is used as a guide to locate the non-destructive test and borehole drilling to get the information on the condition of the site to be developed.

At T18 site, a 200-m length of two lines resistivity survey was performed as shown in Fig. 13. The survey revealed that the subsurface consisted of sandy soil from weathered phyllite above the groundwater level, ranging from 251–260 Ω-m. From the resistivity test, the groundwater was located 10.0 m from the ground level. A 5.0 m × 10.0 m grade III boulders weathered phyllite was detected above the groundwater level with resistivity ranging from 2771 to 3390 Ω-m as shown in Fig. 13. This area consisted of entirely weathered rock with RQD values of 25 to 50%, and a quarter of the site has RQD values of 50 to 75%. A firm to very stiff sandy clay soil with SPT-N values from 7 to 29 was discovered below the groundwater level [21].

The discontinuity survey was conducted at T18 because the scars indicated that the area has a historic landslide [21]. To provide a back analysis of the slope stability prediction, a total of 100 discontinuity data was collected during the discontinuity

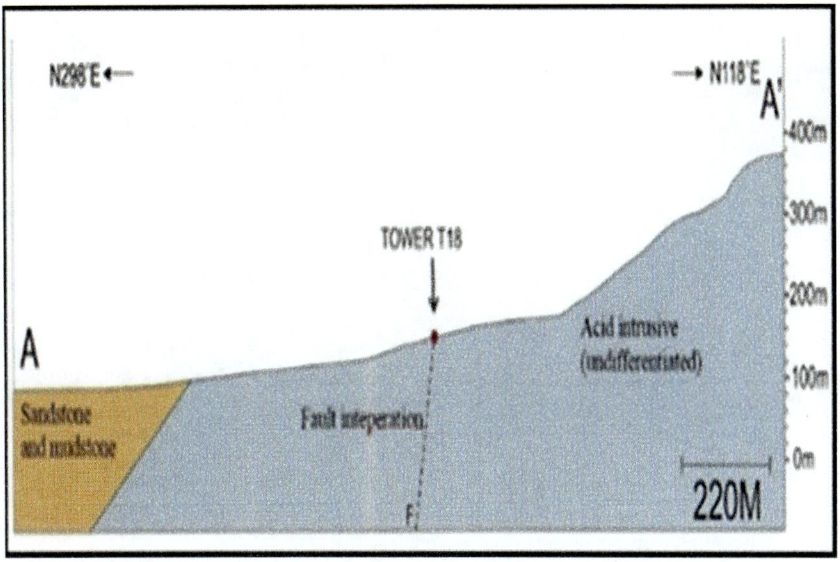

Fig. 12 Cross-section of T18 [21]

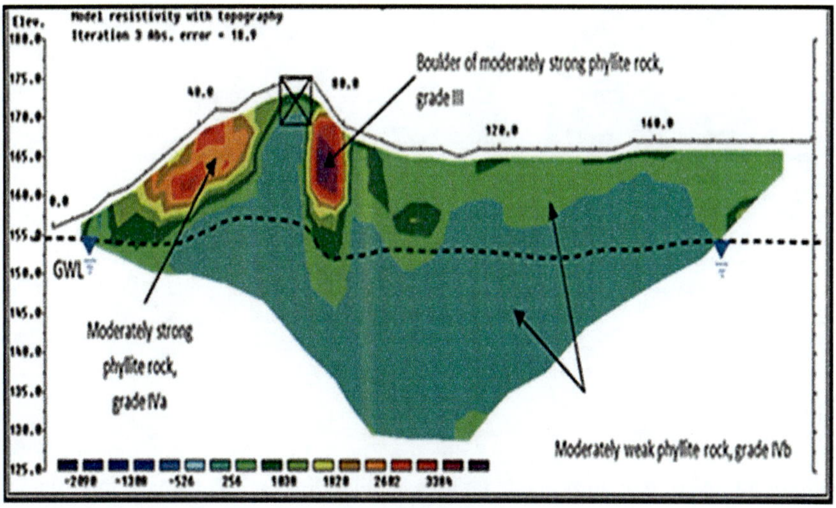

Fig.13 Resistivity profile at T18 Cross-section [21]

survey (Fig. 14) and kinematic analysis was carried out to predict the slope stability at T18 as shown in Fig. 15. The slope face has five-pole discontinuities marked as D1, D2, D3, D4, and D5, the highest concentration followed by others. The orientations of these poles are D1 = N312/E/47/E, D2 = N129/E/50/E, D3 = N162/E/21/E, D4 = N230/E/53/E and D5 = N236/E/29/E. Using 30° as an internal friction angle from

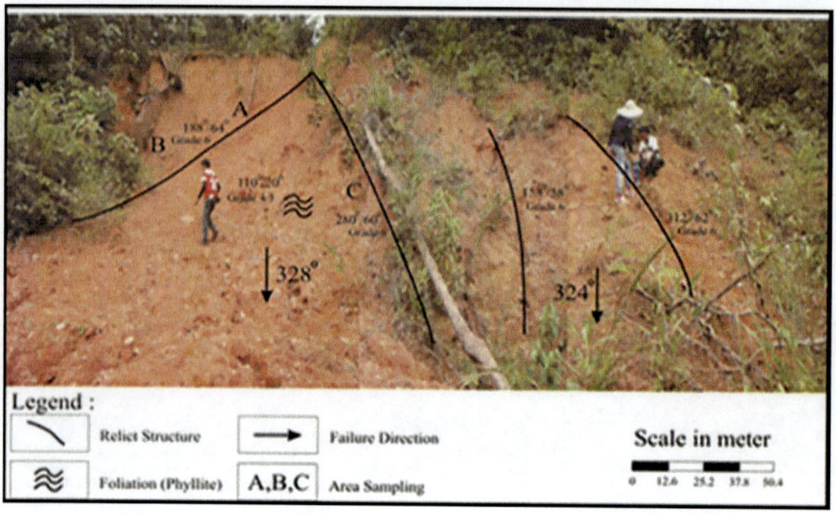

Fig.14 Discontinuity mapping and in-situ sampling at T18 [21]

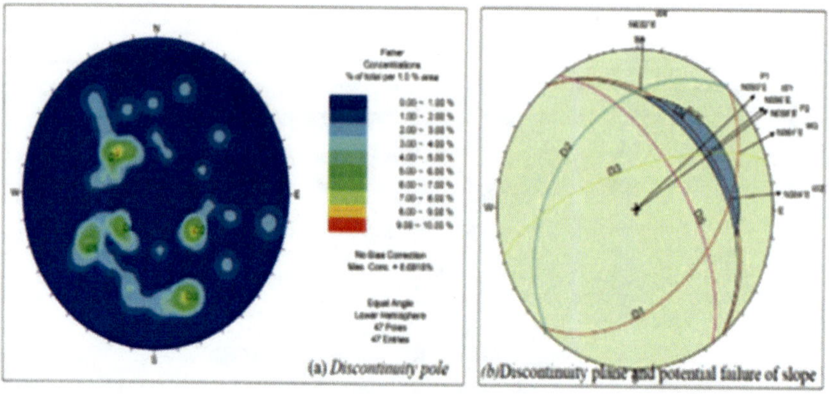

Fig.15 Kinematic analysis at T18 [21]

universal internal rock friction angle, this site's slope inclination strikes N320E with a dip of around 40o. Four possible failures are classified as P1, P2, W1, and W2, as shown in Fig. 15.

Thirty-six (36) in-situ samples from grade V and grade VI soils were obtained from T18 as shown in Fig. 14 for triaxial consolidated drained testing using the proposed technique shown in Fig. 16. The collection of sample-based on the direction of discontinuity data (Fig. 16) and results from the triaxial consolidated drained test were analyzed to predict the stability of the slope at the study area and to identify the cause of failure. Figure 17 shows the slope stability analysis by SLOPE/W, and the factor of safety value is 0.627, which is less than 1 (modification from [21]). Analysis

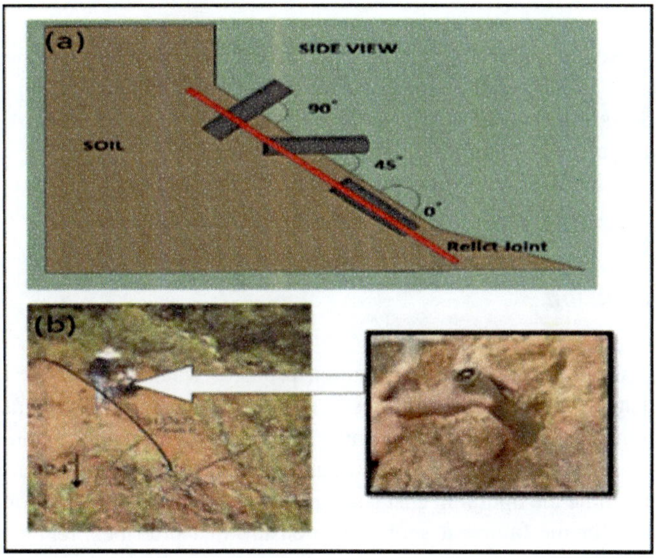

Fig. 16 Proposed sampling technique at T18 [21]

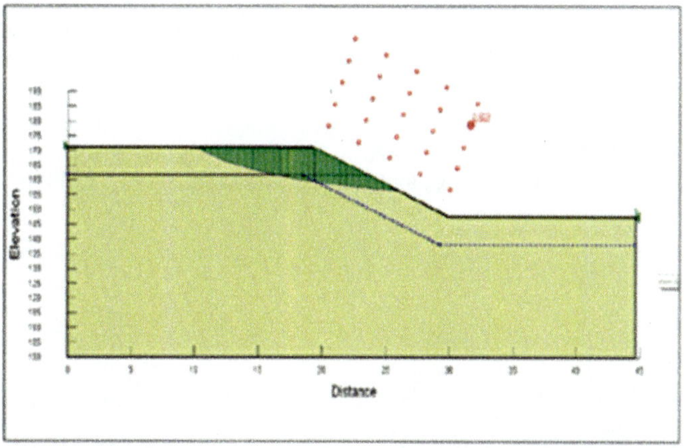

No.	Type of soil	Note	Unit weight	Cohesion	Friction angle
1.	Sandy SILT	Above ground water level	16.00 kN/m³	6.0 kN/m²	20°
2.	Saturated Sandy CLAY	Below ground water level	19.00 kN/m³	10.0 kN/m²	18°

Fig. 17 Results of slope stability analysis at T18 [21]

using kinematic technique and slope stability of the landslide zone sample revealed the presence region failure or weak zone caused by discontinuity and weathering cycle as tested earlier based on the geology cross-section, kinematic analysis, slope stability analysis, RQD values 50% to 75%, and SPT-N values from 7 to 29. It also can be shown clearly in a terrain map, indicated as 2C3b (Fig. 7) which was prone to erosion and landslide zone in between 10 to 50 m near the natural stream.

1.7 Conclusion

Developing an integrated site investigation protocol would be best for assessing landslide danger for land suitability restriction, particularly for Zone 2 and 3. The process requires an integrated approach in collecting geoscience information to make the optimal usage of resources while mitigating geohazards for construction risks in order to determine the optimum cost strategy for site analysis, not only for the short term but also for the future. It should also ensure that priorities, regulations, and management approaches regarding natural disaster reduction are integrated into the physical land-use plan. The structural plan with geohazard information encourages local land-use decisions to consider the risks posed by natural hazards. Additionally, by considering hazardous conditions in the land suitability analysis, the zoning plan can concentrate on the development and infrastructure expansion in those areas with lower risk.

Acknowledgements This research was funded by grant FRGS/1/2018/G08/UNITEN/02/1 (Landslide Hazard Safety Classification (LSC) for Community Insurance System—2018/0109FRGS).

References

1. Town and Country Planning Act 1976 (Act 172) (2010) Government of Malaysia, Kuala Lumpur. International Law Book Services
2. Road, Drainage and Building 1974 (ACT A133). Government of Malaysia, Kuala Lumpur. International Law Book Services
3. Uniform Building By-Laws 1984. Government of Malaysia, Kuala Lumpur. International Law Book Services
4. JPBD Semenanjung (1997) Physical planning guidelines for the MSC Volume 1–8
5. JPBD Semenanjung (1997) Physical development plan, multimedia super corridor, Cyberjaya
6. JPBD Semenanjung (2000) Manual Laporan Cadangan Pemajuan
7. Town and Country Planning (2010) Guideline development planning for Selangor hill site and mountainous area
8. Department of Town and Country Planning, Selangor (2005) Environmental sensitive area (ESA), Hilly and Highland Development, Department of Town and Country Planning, Selangor Darul Ehsan
9. Department of Town and Country Planning (2012) State of Penang, Penang Guideline for Hill site Development, Penang

10. Kuala Lumpur City Council (2010) Garis Panduan Perancangan Pembangunan Kawasan Bukit dan Cerun bagi Wilayah Persekutuan Kuala Lumpur, Kuala Lumpur
11. Omar RC (2016) Maklumat Geosains Terintegrasi Untuk Proses Perancangan Guna tanah Fizikal Pembangunan Lestari: Kajian Kes Cyberjaya. Unpublished, TesisPhd. UKM
12. Omar RC, Komoo I, Hashim HS (2001) Pembandaran mampan: Penggunaan pendekatan geosains dalam proses perancangan gunatanah di Malaysia
13. Omar RC, Roslan R, Baharuddin INZ (2013) Integrated site investigation procedure for environment protection toward sustainable development. In: IOP conference series: earth and environmental science, vol 16. no 1, pp 2131
14. BSI (1999) Code of practice for site investigation BS 5930. Her Majesty's Stationary Office, London
15. Mohamed Z (2015) Geotechnical risk and sustainable practices: lesson learned and a way forward. In: Proceeding in international seminar for Multihazard, Universiti Teknologi Malaysia, Kuala Lumpur
16. Abdullah CH (2013) Landslide risk management in Malaysia, disaster management and human health risk III, WIT transactions on the built environment, vol 133. www.witpress.com, ISSN 1743–3509 (online). https://doi.org/10.2495/DMAN
17. Lozano J, Aginako N, Quartulli M, Olaizola I, Zulueta E, Iriondo P (2015) Large scale thematic mapping by supervised machine learning on 'big data' distributed cluster computing frameworks. In: 2015 IEEE international geoscience and remote sensing symposium (IGARSS). https://doi.org/10.1109/IGARSS.2015.7326065
18. El-May M, Dlala M, Chenini I (2010) Urban geological mapping: geotechnical data analysis for rational development planning. Eng Geol Elsevier 116, 129–138. https://doi.org/10.1016/j.eng.geo
19. Downes NK, Storch H (2014) Current constraints and future directions for risk adapted land-use planning practices in the high-density Asian Setting of Ho ChiMinh City. Planning Practice & Research, Volume 29. Issue 3: AESOP Congress and PhD workshop, Delft-Utrecht. 220–237. https://doi.org/10.1080/02697459.2014.929835
20. Oliveira SC, Zêzere JL, Guillard-Gonçalves C, Garcia RAC, Pereira S (2017) Integration of landslide susceptibility maps for land use planning and civil protection emergency management. In: Sassa K et al. (eds) Advancing culture of living with landslides. https://doi.org/10.1007/978-3-319-59469-9_49
21. Baharuddin INZ, Omar RC, Roslan R, Khalid NHN, Hanifah MIM (2016) Determination of slope instability using spatially integrated mapping framework. In: International engineering research and innovation symposium (IRIS). IOP conference series: materials science and engineering 160:012080. https://doi.org/10.1088/1757-899X/160/1/01208